JOURNAL FOR THE STUDY OF THE NEW TESTAMENT SUPPLEMENT SERIES
192

ROEHAMPTON PAPERS
6

Sheffield Academic Press

Christian–Jewish Relations through the Centuries

edited by
**Stanley E. Porter and
Brook W.R. Pearson**

Journal for the Study of the New Testament
Supplement Series 192

Roehampton Papers 6

Copyright © 2000 Sheffield Academic Press

Published by
Sheffield Academic Press Ltd
Mansion House
19 Kingfield Road
Sheffield S11 9AS
England

Typeset by Sheffield Academic Press
and
Printed on acid-free paper in Great Britain
by Bookcraft Ltd
Midsomer Norton, Bath

British Library Cataloguing in Publication Data

A catalogue record for this book is available
from the British Library

ISBN 1-84127-090-3

CONTENTS

Part II
CHRISTIAN–JEWISH RELATIONS IN THE MODERN WORLD

ABBREVIATIONS

AA	*Auctores antiquissimi*
AB	Anchor Bible
ABD	David Noel Freedman (ed.), *The Anchor Bible Dictionary* (New York: Doubleday, 1992)
AGJU	Arbeiten zur Geschichte des antiken Judentums und des Urchristentums
ANF	Anti-Nicene Fathers
AOAT	Alter Orient und Altes Testament
BA	*Biblical Archaeologist*
BAGD	Walter Bauer, William F. Arndt, F. William Gingrich and Frederick W. Danker, *A Greek–English Lexicon of the New Testament and Other Early Christian Literature* (Chicago: University of Chicago Press, 2nd edn, 1958)
BASOR	*Bulletin of the American Schools of Oriental Research*
BDB	Francis Brown, S.R. Driver and Charles A. Briggs, *A Hebrew and English Lexicon of the Old Testament* (Oxford: Clarendon Press, 1907)
BETL	Bibliotheca ephemeridum theologicarum lovaniensium
Bib	*Biblica*
BibInt	*Biblical Interpretation: A Journal of Contemporary Approaches*
BJRL	*Bulletin of the John Rylands University Library of Manchester*
BJS	Brown Judaic Studies
BLG	Biblical Languages: Greek
BNTC	Black's New Testament Commentaries
BZAW	Beihefte zur *ZAW*
CBQ	*Catholic Biblical Quarterly*
CBQMS	*Catholic Biblical Quarterly*, Monograph Series
CII	*Corpus inscriptionum iudaicarum*
CRINT	Compendia rerum iudaicarum ad Novum Testamentum
CSCO	Corpus scriptorum christianorum orientalium
DJD	Discoveries in the Judaean Desert
DSD	*Dead Sea Discoveries*
EB	Etudes bibliques
EvT	*Evangelische Theologie*
ExpTim	*Expository Times*
HBT	*Horizons in Biblical Theology*
HDR	Harvard Dissertations in Religion

HNT	Handbuch zum Neuen Testament
HSS	Harvard Semitic Studies
HTR	*Harvard Theological Review*
HUCA	*Hebrew Union College Annual*
IB	*Interpreter's Bible*
IDB	George Arthur Buttrick (ed.), *The Interpreter's Dictionary of the Bible* (4 vols.; Nashville: Abingdon Press, 1962)
JAC	*Jahrbuch für Antike und Christentum*
JBL	*Journal of Biblical Literature*
JewEnc	*The Jewish Encyclopedia*
JJS	*Journal of Jewish Studies*
JPOS	*Journal of the Palestine Oriental Society*
JR	*Journal of Religion*
JRS	*Journal of Roman Studies*
JSJ	*Journal for the Study of Judaism in the Persian, Hellenistic and Roman Period*
JSJSup	*Journal for the Study of Judaism*, Supplements
JSNT	*Journal for the Study of the New Testament*
JSNTSup	*Journal for the Study of the New Testament*, Supplement Series
JSOT	*Journal for the Study of the Old Testament*
JSPSup	*Journal for the Study of the Pseudepigrapha*, Supplement Series
JSS	*Journal of Semitic Studies*
JTS	*Journal of Theological Studies*
Judaica	*Judaica: Beiträge zum Verständnis des jüdischen Schicksals in Vergangenheit und Gegenwart*
LCL	Loeb Classical Library
LEC	Library of Early Christianity
MGH	*Monumenta Germaniae Historica*
NCBC	New Century Bible Commentary
NIGTC	The New International Greek Testament Commentary
NovT	*Novum Testamentum*
NovTSup	*Novum Testamentum*, Supplements
NTOA	Novum Testamentum et orbis antiquus
NTS	*New Testament Studies*
NTTS	New Testament Tools and Studies
OPTAT	*Occasional Papers in Translation and Textlinguistics*
OTP	James Charlesworth (ed.), *Old Testament Pseudepigrapha*
PAAJR	*Proceedings of the American Academy of Jewish Research*
PAM	Palestinian Archaeological Museum
PG	J.-P. Migne (ed.), *Patrologia cursus completa… Series graeca* (166 vols.; Paris: Petit-Montrouge, 1857–83)
REJ	*Revue des études juives*
RevQ	*Revue de Qumran*
RHPR	*Revue d'histoire et de philosophie religieuses*
RILP	Roehampton Institute London Papers
RSR	*Recherches de science religieuse*
RSV	Revised Standard Version

SBLMS	Society of Biblical Literature Monograph Series
SBLPS	Society of Biblical Literature Pseudepigrapha Series
SBLTT	Society of Biblical Literature Texts and Translations
SC	Sources chrétiennes
SFSHJ	South Florida Studies in Historical Judaism
SJLA	Studies in Judaism in Late Antiquity
SJOT	*Scandinavian Journal of the Old Testament*
SNTG	Studies in New Testament Greek
SNTSMS	Society for New Testament Studies Monograph Series
SNTW	Studies of the New Testament and its World
SP	Sacra Pagina
SRM	*Scriptores rerum Merovingicarum*
StudPat	*Studia Patristica*
SR	*Studies in Religion/Sciences religieuses*
TDNT	Gerhard Kittel and Gerhard Friedrich (eds.), *Theological Dictionary of the New Testament* (trans. Geoffrey W. Bromiley; 10 vols.; Grand Rapids: Eerdmans, 1964–)
TOTC	Tyndale Old Testament Commentaries
TS	*Theological Studies*
TSAJ	Texts and Studies in Ancient Judaism
TU	Texte und Untersuchungen
TynBul	*Tyndale Bulletin*
TZ	*Theologische Zeitschrift*
UBSGNT	United Bible Societies' *Greek New Testament*
UTR	Utrechtse Theologische Reeks
VC	*Vigiliae christianae*
WBC	Word Biblical Commentary
WEC	Wycliffe Exegetical Commentary
WTJ	*Westminster Theological Journal*
WUNT	Wissenschaftliche Untersuchungen zum Neuen Testament
ZAW	*Zeitschrift für die alttestamentliche Wissenschaft*
ZNW	*Zeitschrift für die neutestamentliche Wissenschaft*
ZPE	*Zeitschrift für Papyrologie und Epigraphik*

LIST OF CONTRIBUTORS

Louis P. Blond, University of Surrey Roehampton, UK

Anne Clark, University of Surrey Roehampton, UK

Craig A. Evans, Trinity Western University, Langley, BC, Canada and University of Surrey Roehampton, UK

Crispin H.T. Fletcher-Louis, University of Durham, UK

Liam Gearon, University of Surrey Roehampton, UK

Arthur Gibson, University of Surrey Roehampton, UK

Felicity Harley, University of Adelaide, Australia

Mark Handley, University College London

Michael A. Hayes, University of Surrey Roehampton, UK

Pieter W. van der Horst, Utrecht University, The Netherlands

Sue Jackson, University of Surrey Roehampton, UK

Kevin McCarron, University of Surrey Roehampton, UK

Brook W.R. Pearson, University of Surrey Roehampton, UK

Pat Pinsent, University of Surrey Roehampton, UK

Stanley E. Porter, University of Surrey Roehampton, UK

Wendy J. Porter, University of Surrey Roehampton, UK

Jacqueline C.R. de Roo, University of Aberdeen, UK

Yvonne Sherwood, University of Glasgow, UK

Lawrence VanBeek, Trinity Western University, Langley, BC, Canada

Armida Veglio, Ursuline School, Wimbledon, UK

Cynthia Long Westfall, University of Surrey Roehampton, UK

Irene Wise, University of Surrey Roehampton, UK and London Guild-hall, UK

Melanie J. Wright, University of Cambridge, UK

INTRODUCTION:
CHRISTIAN–JEWISH RELATIONS INTO THE NEXT CENTURY

Stanley E. Porter and Brook W.R. Pearson

This sixth volume in the Roehampton Papers (formerly the Roehampton Institute London Papers) series represents the proceedings of a conference held at Digby Stuart College of what is now the University of Surrey Roehampton (formerly Roehampton Institute London) on 21 February 1999. The successful event was co-sponsored by the following Roehampton bodies: the Centre for Advanced Theological Research of the Department of Theology and Religious Studies, the Faculty of Arts and Humanities, and the Digby Stuart College Chaplaincy.

The topic for this conference—Christian–Jewish relations through the centuries—is one that is often discussed. There has been no dearth of studies dedicated to its various dimensions and sub-topics, some of which, during the latter half of the twentieth century, have been impossible to ignore. Since the Second World War, much of the work on anti-Semitism in general, or more specifically on the relationship between Christianity and Judaism, has been consciously undertaken in the light of the Holocaust. This event, its implications and its repercussions are by no means absent from the thought world to which the papers in this volume take us, but there is also a striking forward-looking thread woven through them. This is not just a volume about the past.

Neither is it a volume whose chief characteristic is homogeneity. The papers in this volume do not all necessarily take the same viewpoint, display the same approach, or even have the same concerns. The contributors come from both Jewish and non-Jewish, Christian and non-Christian backgrounds. Some consciously identify themselves with a particular faith tradition or ethnic background, others do not. What weaves these disparate contributors together is their common desire to understand the issue of Christian–Jewish relations from the standpoint of their particular areas of expertise, and to situate it within the cultures—ancient or modern—of which it is a part.

Consequently, we have chosen to present the papers in two main, roughly chronological sections. The first section consists of papers dedicated to the relation of Jews and Christians in the ancient world. The first two papers try to situate the initial split between Christians and Jews in terms of its cause (Craig Evans), and the way in which it was understood (Stanley Porter and Brook Pearson). Although these two papers take different perspectives, and present differing conclusions, each attempts to ground its analysis in evidence from the ancient world, and considers those directly involved in the split. The next two papers investigate various aspects of early Christian Christology in relation to their Jewish progenitors. Crispin Fletcher-Louis discusses the important role of Wisdom Christology in the separation between Christians and Jews. Brook Pearson and Felicity Harley, comparing the representation of resurrection in non-canonical gospels and in early Christian art, investigate the split between Jewish and non-Jewish Christians over Christology. The following four papers focus on issues connected with the New Testament and its Jewish background. Larry VanBeek looks at connections between the use of *1 Enoch* in Jewish and early Christian groups, appreciating the place of this enigmatic pseudepigraphal work. Jacqueline de Roo addresses one of the thorniest of recent issues in New Testament studies, when she compares and contrasts the idea of 'works of the law' in Jewish and Christian circles. Stanley Porter asks the question, 'Was Paul a good Jew?', and answers it in a way that raises questions for other dimensions of Pauline studies. Cindy Westfall illuminates the important role of the figure of Moses in the New Testament book of Hebrews. To round out this section, we have three papers dedicated to the investigation of this issue in late antiquity: Tracking 'Misguided Missals', Wendy Porter calls into question dogmatism on either side of the issue of whether early Christian music was Jewish or Graeco-Roman in origin; Pieter van der Horst contrasts two different Christian approaches to the relationship between Christianity and Judaism in Antioch at the end of the fourth century; Mark Handley demonstrates the role that epigraphy has to offer in re-constructing the place of Jews within early mediaeval Gaul. Lastly, Yvonne Sherwood's ' "Colonizing the Old Testament" or "Representing Christian Interests Abroad"' highlights the imperialistic identity of much Christian commentary on the Old Testament, and situates this within the rhetoric of colonization.

The second section of this book is dedicated to studies broadly concerned with Jewish–Christian relations in our own time; however, these are by no means without implications for our reading and interpretation of the relationships between Christians and Jews in the ancient world, especially since several of the essays treat biblically related topics. These essays are arranged somewhat thematically, with questions of Christian–Jewish relations in the arts beginning the section. Kevin McCarron analyses the postwar fiction of Philip Roth, Saul Bellow and Bernard Malamud, and argues that the idea of 'Jewishness' has become a literary trope for alienation within society. Liam Gearon examines the role of Christian–Jewish relations in the fiction of the Catholic novelist, Brian Moore, and Pat Pinsent excavates the role of Jewishness in children's literature of the nineteenth and twentieth centuries, while Irene Wise undertakes a similar analysis of the popular culture (largely German and British) of the past 200 years. The final paper in this vein, or perhaps the first in the next broad grouping dedicated to philosophical and theological perspectives on Jewish–Christian relations, is Arthur Gibson's analysis of the relationship between Richard Wagner's opera and writing, and the 'psychotic modernism' of Adolf Hitler.

The remaining papers in the volume all situate their concerns within the post-Holocaust era, and the vast rupture that this event has caused within the field of this volume's concern. Louis Blond's paper is a bold attempt to understand the Holocaust in metaphysical terms. Melanie Wright compares and contrasts the various responses of the 'Historic Peace Churches' (Quakers, Mennonites, and Hutterites) to the Holocaust, and finds a surprising variation between them. Michael Hayes chronicles and assesses the development of Catholic doctrine relating to Christian–Jewish relations since Vatican II, while Sue Jackson chronicles her own personal journey to Poland to reconnect with and attempt to understand the almost total destruction of Poland's Jewish community. Our final two papers illuminate the role that Christianity and Judaism have as partners, and where there is potential for further *rapprochement* as we contemplate a new century of Jewish–Christian relations. Armida Veglio argues that the role of 'mission' within both Judaism and Christianity compares favourably, and Anne Clark's discussion of and argument for the teaching of Judaism in schools emphasizes the historical relationship between Judaism and Christianity.

As is evident from the above brief summaries, there is much diversity in this volume, but without losing sight of its one overall aim. At the end of roughly 2000 years of Christian and Jewish relations, it is hoped that the papers in this volume not only contribute to the history of discussion of and between Christians and Jews, but that, as we approach a new millennium (on the Christian calendar), they accomplish an expansion of our understanding of 'Christian–Jewish relations'.

Part I

CHRISTIAN–JEWISH RELATIONS IN THE ANCIENT WORLD

ROOT CAUSES OF THE JEWISH–CHRISTIAN RIFT FROM JESUS TO JUSTIN

Craig A. Evans

In recent years the factors involved in the separation of Christianity from Judaism have stimulated much discussion and are themselves a by-product of a healthy Jewish–Christian dialogue that has been under way for some time. Review of these factors helps explain why Judaism and Christianity moved so far apart, even though both religions sprang from common roots, and helps in part explain the origin of anti-Semitism. Critical study of these religions' common roots and the causes of their separation is important and its continuation should be encouraged.

Christian and Jewish separation has often in recent years been referred to in terms of the 'partings of the ways'.[1] This more or less neutral language may, however, mask aspects of the bitterly opposed perspectives of early Jews and Christians themselves.[2] But my concern in this paper has to do with the root causes of the Jewish–Christian rift. There are several factors that could be reviewed. One that immediately comes to mind is Christianity's aggressive Gentile mission and lenient requirements for entry into the Church. Christian evangelization of Gentiles was out of step with Jewish proselytism. Jewish proselytes were to take on the yoke of the Torah (*m. Ab.* 3.5), which involved scrupulous observation of sabbath and food laws, and early Christian proselytism seemed, in the eyes of its Jewish critics, bent on removing

---

1. See especially J.D.G. Dunn (ed.), *Jews and Christians: The Partings of the Ways A.D. 70 to 135* (WUNT, 66; Tübingen: J.C.B. Mohr [Paul Siebeck], 1992); *idem, The Partings of the Ways between Christianity and Judaism and their Significance for the Character of Christianity* (London: SCM Press; Philadelphia: Trinity Press International, 1991).

2. On this point, see J. Lieu, '"The Parting of the Ways": Theological Construct or Historical Reality?', *JSNT* 56 (1994), pp. 101-19.

the yoke of the Torah. The Christian councils depicted in Acts 11 and 15 exemplify the nature of the problems brought on by early Christianity's aggressive Gentile mission. Pauline polemic against the 'Judaizers' (as seen especially in the Galatians epistle) offers first-hand evidence of how divisive this issue was.

Another serious point of disagreement between Christians and non-Christian Jews concerned the divinity of Jesus. The tendency of the Greco-Roman church to deify Jesus in the absolute sense, that is, to intensify Johannine and Pauline Christology in terms of Jesus as God (in contrast to Ebionite Christology, which accepted Jesus as Israel's Messiah and fulfillment of prophetic Scripture, but refused to ascribe divinity to him), only made Christianity all the more unacceptable to Jews. The divinization of Jesus stood in tension with strict Jewish monotheism; and in its extremest form of presentation appeared to be a direct violation of the first commandment (Exod. 20.3; Deut. 5.7).

Both of these factors—liberal inclusion of Gentiles and the deification of Jesus—only created a context for further estrangement. Failure to observe Jewish food laws, laws of purity, and sabbath observance forced complete separation between Gentile Christians and Jews, whether the latter were sympathetic to the Christian faith or not. Jewish membership in the early Church began to decline, while Gentile membership increased geometrically. The ethnic shift began to efface the Jewish character of the Church, which in turn discouraged entry of Jewish converts. The preference of the early Church, which within a generation of its founding was primarily Greek-speaking, was for the Septuagint (the Greek Old Testament), not for the Hebrew and its Aramaic interpretation in the Synagogue. Thus the choice of Bible version itself drove Gentile and Jewish believers further apart.

Jewish nationalist interests also played an important part in the growing rift between church and synagogue. A major catalyst that led to the partings of the ways was the destruction of Jerusalem and the Temple in 70 CE and the later Bar Kokhba defeat (135 CE), which resulted in the loss of Jerusalem as a Jewish city and the loss of Israel as a state. Prior to the destruction of Jerusalem, the Temple remained important to Christian Jews. We see this in the book of Acts especially (2.46; 3.1; 5.20, 42; 21.26; 22.17). The destruction of the Temple proved to be a significant loss of common ground shared by Gentile and Jewish Christians.

The Bar Kokhba war also intensified hostilities between Christian

Jews and non-Christian Jews. According to Patristic sources, Christians were persecuted by Simon ben Kosiba, who evidently had been dubbed 'bar kokhba' (Aramaic for 'son of the star'). Justin Martyr, a contemporary of Simon, relates that the Jews 'count us foes and enemies; and, like yourselves, they kill and punish us whenever they have the power, as you can well believe. For in the Jewish war which lately raged, Bar Kokhba, the leader of the revolt of the Jews, gave orders that Christians alone should be led away to cruel punishments, unless they should deny [that] Jesus [is] the Christ and blaspheme' (*1 Apol.* 31.5-6). Eusebius, possibly dependent on Justin, similarly states that 'Kokhba, prince of the Jewish sect, killed the Christians with all kinds of persecutions, when they refused to help him against the Roman troops' (*Hadrian Year 17*). Why did the Christians refuse to support Simon's bid for freedom? The most probable reason is that Simon was regarded as the Messiah, as both Jewish and Christian sources relate (Eusebius, *Hist. Eccl.* 4.6.1–4; *y. Ta'an.* 4.5; *b. Sanh.* 93b). Therefore, Christian allegiance to Jesus as the Messiah contradicted Simon's claims and undermined his authority. Christians 'alone' were dealt with severely, because among the Jews they alone regarded someone else as Israel's Messiah.

The Jewish hope of rebuilding the Temple created tensions of its own. William Horbury draws our attention to *Barn.* 16.1-4, a polemical passage which expresses criticism of the Jews for placing their confidence in the Temple and, after it had been destroyed, hoping to rebuild it.[3] Horbury thinks that the author of *Barnabas* was alluding to the Jewish hope to rebuild the Temple, perhaps at some time near the end of the Flavian dynasty. The author of *Barnabas*, as well as other Christians, may have feared a Jewish resurgence that would have undermined Christianity. In fact, such a resurgence was in some sense under way, and many Christian Jews were abandoning Christian teaching in order to remain loyal to the synagogue. Pressure to do so was greatly increased by the introduction of the *birkat ha-minim* (lit. 'the blessing [or cursing] of the heretics'). We may reasonably surmise that Jews willing to utter this 'benediction' tended to abandon Christianity, while Jews or proselytes unwilling to utter it were put out of the synagogue.

The Jewish wars for liberation from Roman control and the hopes for rebuilding the Temple tended to pit Gentile Christians against Jewish

---

3.   See W. Horbury, 'Jewish–Christian Relations in Barnabas and Justin Martyr', in Dunn (ed.), *Jews and Christians*, pp. 315-45.

Christians. For Jewish Christians this proved to be especially difficult, often forcing them to choose between their faith in Jesus on the one hand, and loyalty to their nation and people on the other.

All of the factors thus far surveyed are secondary to what I believe was the root-cause behind the Jewish–Christian rift. The fundamental sticking points for many Jewish people were the simple facts that Jesus had been put to death and the kingdom of God had failed to materialize. Both of these points apparently nullified any messianic claim, for the very definition of the messianic task, as it was understood in Judaism in late antiquity, envisioned the restoration of Israel and a long, prosperous reign of Israel's anointed king, the Messiah. Jesus' death, and with it the fading of hope for the appearance of the kingdom of God (which had been the essence of Jesus' proclamation), surely proved that he was not the Messiah after all. Even the proclamation of the resurrection, as marvelous as it was and as significant as it may have been for questions about the afterlife, could not overcome the simple facts that Jesus never began his reign over Israel and that Israel remained under Roman subjugation.

Jewish messianic expectation in late antiquity was diverse, to be sure, but it had important common ingredients. Among these was the anticipation of victory and tangible benefits. A heavenly reign of the Messiah, with no appreciable alteration of conditions on earth for Israel, did not correspond to a messianic expectation that, so far as I can determine, was ever held by anyone. Even among Jesus' own disciples there are indications of popular messianic expectation. Toward the end of his ministry, Jesus' talk of death, no matter how qualified in terms of scriptural fulfillment or atoning significance, led to the defection of even his closest followers. We should not be surprised that those who had not known Jesus and who had not had the opportunity to be impressed by his teaching and works of power would react with skepticism to assertions of Jesus' messiahship in the face of the facts surrounding his death.

The nature of Jewish messianic expectation is clarified in important ways by the actions of men who by all accounts attempted to fulfill this expectation in daring bids to win Israel's freedom and end Roman domination. Although scholars dispute the point,[4] I think it is probable that

---

4. Several of these men are regarded as messianic claimants by R.A. Horsley, 'Popular Messianic Movements around the Time of Jesus', *CBQ* 46 (1984), pp. 471-95; and by R.A. Horsley and J.S. Hanson, *Bandits, Prophets, and Messiahs:*

at least two or three of the following men regarded themselves as in some sense Israel's Messiah and deliverer. It will be useful to review their attempts, for they illustrate the point that is being made here, namely, the goal of the Jewish Messiah was the liberation of Israel, and this liberation necessitated the expulsion of the Romans.

Judas (of Sepphoris, Galilee) son of Hezekiah the 'brigand chief'. In the wake of Herod's death (4 BCE), Judas plundered the royal arsenals and attacked other kingly aspirants (*Ant.* 17.271-72; *War* 2.56). According to Josephus, this man 'became a terror to all men by plundering those he came across in his desire for great possessions and in his ambition for royal honor [ζηλώσει βασιλείου τιμῆς]'. Although Josephus is not explicit, Judas, as well as many of the other insurrectionists of this period of time, was presumably subdued by Varus, the Roman governor of Syria, who quelled rebellion in Galilee, Samaria, Judea, Jerusalem, and Idumea (cf. *Ant.* 17.286-98; *War* 2.66-79).[5]

Simon of Perea, a former royal servant. Evidently this Simon was another opportunist who arose after Herod's death. According to Josephus, he was a handsome man of great size and strength, who 'was bold enough to place the diadem on his head [διάδημά τε ἐτόλμησε περιθέσθαι], and having got together a body of men, he was himself also proclaimed king [αὐτὸς βασιλεὺς ἀναγγελθείς] by them in their madness, and he rated himself worthy of this beyond anyone else. After burning the royal palace in Jericho, he plundered and carried off the things seized there. He also set fire to many other royal residences...' (*Ant.* 17.273-76; *War* 2.57-59: 'he placed the diadem on himself [περιτίθησιν μὲν ἑαυτῷ διάδημα]'). His claim to kingship was even noted by Tacitus (*Hist.* 5.9: 'After the death of Herod...a certain Simon seized the title king [*regium nomen*]'). Simon was eventually slain by Gratus (4 BCE).[6]

Popular Movements at the Time of Jesus (San Francisco: Harper & Row, 1985), pp. 88-134. However, M. de Jonge (*Christology in Context: The Earliest Christian Response to Jesus* [Philadelphia: Westminster Press, 1988]) has his doubts. He comments: 'This is an attractive theory, but unfortunately difficult to substantiate from literary sources: we have only Josephus' very one-sided presentation of the facts' (p. 164).

5. For a summary of this man's activities and a study of his 'dynasty', see M. Hengel, *The Zealots: Investigations into the Jewish Freedom Movement in the Period from Herod I until 70 A.D.* (Edinburgh: T. & T. Clark, 1989), pp. 330-37.

6. See Hengel, *The Zealots*, pp. 327-28.

Athronges the shepherd of Judea. According to Josephus, one Athronges, 'remarkable for his great stature and feats of strength', though a mere shepherd of no special ancestry or character, 'dared to (gain) a kingdom [ἐτόλμησεν ἐπὶ βασιλείᾳ]'. 'Having put on the diadem [ὁ δὲ διάδημα περιθέμενος]', he began giving orders, exercising and retaining 'power for a long while [4–2 BCE], for he was called king [βασιλεῖ τε κεκλημένῳ]' (*Ant.* 17.278-84; *War* 2.60-65: 'He himself, like a king [αὐτὸς δὲ καθάπερ βασιλεύς], handled matters of graver importance. It was then that he placed the diadem on himself [ἑαυτῷ περιτίθησιν διάδημα]'). He and his brothers eventually surrendered to Archelaus.[7]

Judas (of Gamala) the Galilean.[8] I regard Judas the Galilean as one of the anointed kings, and not simply as a bandit, because of his 'bid for independence' (*Ant.* 18.4) and because of his mention in Acts 5.37, thus putting him in the company of Jesus and Theudas, both prophets and probably both messianic claimants. Furthermore, the fact that Judas's son Menahem claimed to be a messiah could suggest that he had inherited his kingly aspirations from his father (which may be hinted at by Josephus himself in *War* 2.433-34). Probably not the same person as Judas son of Hezekiah, this Judas called on his countrymen not to submit to the census administered by Quirinius, the Roman governor who had replaced the deposed Archelaus (*Ant.* 18.4-10; *War* 2.118). According to Acts, the Pharisee Gamaliel said that 'Judas the Galilean arose in the days of the census and drew away some of the people after him; he also perished, and all who followed him were scattered' (5.37). (This passage is problematic, especially if the 'Theudas' of Acts 5.36 is the Theudas of 45 CE.) It is significant that a parallel is drawn between Judas and Theudas (who will be considered below), at least in that both movements ended in the deaths of their leaders. (Josephus does not tell us what became of Judas.) Josephus describes Judas's movement as a 'rebellion' and as a 'a bid for (national) independence', as well as a 'fourth philosophy'. It is perhaps significant that, at the mention of Judas's call for civil disobedience, Josephus goes on to summarize the disturbances of the first century and to suggest that it was this sort of thinking that led to the violence and bloodshed which ultimately culminated in the catastrophe of 66–70 CE (*Ant.* 18.10: 'My reason for giving

7. See Hengel, *The Zealots*, p. 328.

8. Judas of Gamala may be Judas of Sepphoris; see Hengel, *The Zealots*, pp. 331-32.

this brief account of [the events that led up to the war] is chiefly that the zeal which Judas and Saddok inspired in the younger element meant the ruin of our cause'). Therefore, although Judas's personal role seems to have been principally that of a teacher, the effect of his teaching warrants regarding him as yet another founder of a movement that opposed foreign domination and, by implication, advocated the establishment of an independent kingdom of Israel. The crucifixion of his sons Jacob and Simon under Governor Tiberius Alexander (46–48 CE) may also have had something to do with rebellion (*Ant.* 20.102).

It is worth remarking that the context in which Judas and Saddok are described strongly suggests that the latter, a Pharisee, was a teacher. Following the description of Judas and Saddok, the principal figures who sowed the seeds of ruin, as Josephus viewed it, we are treated to the principal religious factions, or 'philosophies', of the Jewish people. Josephus tells his Roman readers of the Pharisees (*Ant.* 18.12-15), the Sadducees (*Ant.* 18.16-17), and the Essenes (*Ant.* 18.18-22). He then returns to Judas the Galilean, calling his faction the 'fourth philosophy', which he admits was Pharisaic (*Ant.* 18.23-25). I think this 'philosophy' was really an eschatological movement that was made up of Pharisees and non-Pharisees. They looked to the Deity (τὸ θεῖον) for assistance, they were filled with devotion (*Ant.* 18.5) and a passion for liberty, convinced that God alone was their sovereign (*Ant.* 18.23).[9] According to Josephus, this teaching infected the thinking of Jews and helped set the stage for the rebellion. Allowing for the obvious bias, I think Josephus is describing more than just a militant philosophy, but a worldview very much influenced by prophetic and apocalyptic scriptural traditions, such as the 'ambiguous oracle' discussed above. These traditions, in diverse forms, lay behind most, perhaps even all, of the freedom movements in the first century. The presence of an underlying theological-apocalyptic premise adds further justification for speaking of these would-be liberators as messianic figures.[10]

9. For further discussion, see M. Black, 'Judas of Galilee and Josephus' "Fourth Philosophy"', in O. Betz, L. Haacker and M. Hengel (eds.), *Josephus Studien* (Göttingen: Vandenhoeck & Ruprecht, 1974), pp. 45-54. In my view, Hengel rightly perceives the teaching of Judas and Saddok as having an 'eschatological perspective' (*The Zealots*, p. 123).

10. For discussion concerning the Pharisees' attitude toward and role in the first Jewish revolt, see C. Roth, 'The Pharisees of the Jewish Revolution of 66–73', *JSS* 7 (1962), pp. 63-80.

Menaḥem (grand)son of Judas the Galilean. Josephus tells us that Menaḥem (c. 66 BCE), either the son or the grandson of Judas the Galilean, plundered Herod's armory at Masada, arming his followers as well as other 'brigands', and then 'returned like a king [βασιλεύς] to Jerusalem, became the leader of the revolution, and directed the siege of the palace'. His followers occupied the Roman barracks and eventually caught and killed Ananias the high priest. As a result of his accomplishments, Josephus tells us, Menaḥem, believing himself unrivalled, became an 'insufferable tyrant [τύραννος]'. Finally, insurgents loyal to Eleazar son of Ananias the high priest rose up against him. Menaḥem, 'arrayed in royal [βασιλικῇ] apparel', was attacked while in the Temple. Although he initially managed to escape and hide, he was eventually caught, dragged out into the open, tortured and put to death (*War* 2.433-48).

John of Gischala son of Levi. Initially John of Gischala was commander of the rebel forces in Gischala (*War* 2.575). He later became part of the zealot coalition (*War* 4.121-46; 5.104-105; 5.250-51) which, having been forced to retreat into Jerusalem, gained control of most of the city and installed a high priest of its own choosing (*War* 4.147-50, 155-61). Although Josephus describes him as little more than a power-hungry brigand (*War* 2.585-89), apparently John did have kingly aspirations. Josephus tells us that he aspired to 'tyrannical power [τυραννιῶντι]', 'issued despotic [δεσποτικώτερον] orders', and began 'laying claim to absolute sovereignty [μοναρχίας]' (*War* 4.389-93). Fearing the possibility that John might achieve 'monarchical rule [μοναρχίας]', many of the zealots opposed him (*War* 4.393-94; see also 4.566, where the Idumeans turn against the 'tyrant'). When the city was finally overrun, John surrendered and was imprisoned for life (*War* 6.433). Later in his account of the Jewish war, Josephus evaluates John much in the same terms as he does Simon bar Giora (*War* 7.263-66; in 4.564-65 they are compared as the tyrants 'within' and 'without' Jerusalem; in 6.433-34 Josephus also compares their respective surrenders). One of John's worst crimes was his 'impiety towards God. For he had unlawful food served at his table and abandoned the established rules of purity of our forefathers' (*War* 7.264). What apparently was so reprehensible to Josephus the Pharisee, of priestly descent, was probably no more than different halakot, ones which were evidently more lenient and more popular. The disgust that Josephus shows is reminiscent of reactions that Jesus' table manners sometimes evoked (cf. Mk 2.15-17; 7.2; Lk. 15.1-2).[11]

Simon bar Giora of Gerasa. The most important leader of the rebellion was Simon bar Giora (Aramaic, גיורא בר = 'son of the proselyte'), a man from Gerasa (or Jerash).[12] Simon distinguished himself with military prowess and cunning (*War* 2.521; 4.353, 4.510, 514-20). He drew a large following by 'proclaiming liberty for slaves and rewards for the free' (*War* 4.508, 534 ['forty thousand followers']). His army was 'subservient to his command as to a king [βασιλέα]' (*War* 4.510). Josephus avers that early on in his career Simon had shown signs of being tyrannical (*War* 2.652 [τυραννεῖν]; 4.508 [ὁ δὲ τυραννιῶν]; 5.11; 7.32 [ἐτυράννησεν]; 7.265 [τύραννον]). Simon subjugated the whole of Idumea (*War* 4.521-28). The ruling priests, in consultation with the Idumeans and many of the inhabitants of the city, decided to invite Simon into Jerusalem to protect the city from John of Gischala (*War* 4.570-76). Simon entered the city and took command in the spring of 69 CE (*War* 4.577). Among the leaders of the rebellion, 'Simon in particular was regarded with reverence and awe...each was quite prepared to take his very own life had he given the order' (*War* 5.309). By his authority, coins were minted declaring the 'redemption of Zion'.[13] Finally defeated and for a time in hiding, Simon, dressed in white tunics and a purple mantle, made a dramatic appearance before the Romans on the very spot where the Temple had stood (*War* 7.29). He was placed in chains (*War* 7.36), sent to Italy (*War* 7.118), put on display as part of the victory celebration in Rome (*War* 7.154), and was finally executed (*War* 7.155).[14]

11. U. Rappaport, 'John of Gischala: From Galilee to Jerusalem', *JJS* 33 (1982), pp. 479-93; Hengel, *The Zealots*, pp. 371-76.

12. O. Michel, 'Studien zu Josephus: Simon bar Giora', *NTS* 14 (1968), pp. 402-408; Hengel, *The Zealots*, pp. 297-98, 372-76.

13. B. Kanael, 'The Historical Background of the Coins "Year Four...of the Redemption of Zion"', *BASOR* 129 (1953), pp. 18-20. Kanael argues that Simon bar Giora minted the copper coins whose legend reads: 'Year Four of the Redemption of Zion', in contrast to John of Gischala's silver coins, minted earlier, whose legend reads: 'Year Three of the Freedom of Zion'. He claims further that this difference 'throws light on the differences between Simon and John: John strove only for political freedom, while Bar Giora stood at the head of a Messianic movement; hence his coins bear the inscription "redemption of Zion"' (p. 20). I doubt that this difference in wording can support the weight of such an inference.

14. Still standing in Rome today, not far from the Forum, is the Arch of Titus in

Lukuas of Cyrene. During the reign of Trajan (98–117 CE),[15] the Jewish inhabitants of Judea, Egypt and Cyrene revolted. According to Eusebius, our most reliable source for this affair:

> In the course of the eighteenth year [115 CE] of the reign of the Emperor a rebellion of the Jews again broke out and destroyed a great multitude of them. For both in Alexandria and in the rest of Egypt and especially in Cyrene, as though they had been seized by some terrible spirit of rebellion, they rushed into sedition against their Greek fellow citizens, and increasing the scope of the rebellion in the following year started a great war while Lupus was governor of all Egypt. In the first engagement they happened to overcome the Greeks, who fled to Alexandria and captured and killed the Jews in the city, but though thus losing the help of the townsmen, the Jews of Cyrene continued to plunder the country of Egypt and to ravage the districts in it under their leader Lucuas. The Emperor sent against them Marcius Turbo with land and sea forces including cavalry. He waged war vigorously against them in many battles for a considerable time and killed many thousands of Jews, not only those of Cyrene but also those of Egypt who had rallied to Lucuas, their king [Λουκούᾳ τῷ βασιλεῖ αὐτῶν]. The Emperor suspected that the Jews in Mesopotamia would also attack the inhabitants and ordered Lusius Quietus to clean them out of the province. He organized a force and murdered a great multitude of the Jews there, and for this reform was appointed governor of Judaea by the Emperor. The Greek authors who chronicle the same period have related this narrative in these very words (*Hist. Eccl.* 4.2.1-5).[16]

Cassius Dio mentions this revolt, but calls the Jewish leader Andreas (*Hist. Rom.* 68.32; 69.12-13).[17] Although Dio's claim that hundreds of thousands perished is probably an exaggeration, the papyri and archaeological evidence confirm that the revolt was widespread and very

---

which this victory parade is depicted. On one side of the inside of the arch Titus and his chariot and horses are depicted; on the other side of the inside of the arch the Jewish captives, along with the menorah, golden trumpets, and other utensils from the Temple.

15. See K.H. Walters, 'The Reign of Trajan, and its Place in Contemporary Scholarship (1960–72)', *ANRW* 2.2, pp. 381-431.

16. Trans. K. Lake and J.E.L. Oulton, *Eusebius: Ecclesiastical History* (2 vols.; LCL, 153, 265; London: Heinemann; Cambridge, MA: Harvard University Press, 1926–32), I, pp. 305, 307.

17. It is conjectured that Lukuas and Andreas were one and the same person and that his full name may have been Λουκούας ὁ καὶ Ἀνδρέας; cf. P.M. Fraser, 'Hadrian and Cyrene', *JRS* 40 (1950), pp. 77-90, esp. pp. 83-84.

destructive.[18] Appian himself barely escaped Egypt, having witnessed the destruction of the temple of Nemesis by Jewish rebels (*Bell. Civ.* 2.90). Among other buildings destroyed were temples dedicated to Apollo and Hecate. In Cyrene the rebels destroyed temples dedicated to Apollo, Artemis, Hecate, Demeter, and possibly temples dedicated to Pluto, Isis, and others. Our scanty sources indicate that much of North Africa had to be rebuilt and repopulated following the end of the war.[19]

Several papyri provide us with disjointed but vivid details relating to the war and its aftermath.[20] *CPJ* 435 (115 CE), an edict from the Rutilius Lupus, Roman Prefect of Egypt, refers to a 'battle [μάχη] between

18. See E. Schürer, *The History of the Jewish People in the Age of Jesus Christ* (3 vols.; rev. and ed. G. Vermes, F. Millar and M. Black; Edinburgh: T. & T. Clark, 1973–87), I, pp. 530-33; A. Fuks, 'The Jewish Revolt in Egypt (A.D. 115–117) in the Light of the Papyri', *Aegyptus* 33 (1953), pp. 131-58; V.A. Tcherikover and A. Fuks (eds.), *Corpus Papyrorum Judaicarum* (2 vols.; Cambridge, MA: Harvard University Press, 1957–60), I, pp. 85-93; A. Fuks, 'Aspects of the Jewish Revolt in A.D. 115-117', *JRS* 15 (1961), pp. 98-104; Walters, 'The Reign of Trajan', pp. 426-27; E.M. Smallwood, *The Jews under Roman Rule: From Pompey to Diocletian. A Study in Political Relations* (SJLA, 20; Leiden: E.J. Brill, 1981 [1976]), pp. 389-427; M. Hengel, 'Messianische Hoffnung und politischer "Radikalismus" in der "jüdisch-hellenistischen Diaspora": Zur Frage der Voraussetzungen des jüdischen Aufstandes unter Trajan A.D. 115–117', in D. Hellholm (ed.), *Apocalypticism in the Mediterranean World and the Near East: Proceedings of the International Colloquium on Apocalypticism, Uppsala, August 12–17, 1979* (Tübingen: J.C.B. Mohr [Paul Siebeck], 1983), pp. 655-86; L.L. Grabbe, *Judaism from Cyrus to Hadrian* (2 vols.; Minneapolis: Fortress Press, 1992), II, pp. 565-69.

19. Tcherikover and Fuks (eds.), *Corpus Papyrorum Judaicarum*, I, p. 87 nn. 77-79, p. 90 n. 81; Fraser, 'Hadrian and Cyrene', pp. 77-90; S. Applebaum, 'The Jewish Revolt in Cyrene in 115–117, and the Subsequent Recolonisation', *JJS* 2 (1951), pp. 177-86. An inscription found at Cyrene records Hadrian's order to rebuild the public baths and other buildings: Imp(erator) Caesar divi Trajani | Parthici fil(ii) divi Nervae Neros | Trajanus-Hadrianus Aug(ustus) pontif(ex) max(imus) trib(unicius) potest(as) III co(n)s(ul) III balineum | cum porticibus et sphaeristeris ceteris | veadjacentibus ovae tumultu Judaico | dirvta et exusta erant civitati | Cyrenensium restititui jussit ('The Emperor Caesar, of deified Trajan the Parthian son of deified Nerva Nero, Trajan-Hadrian Augustus chief pontiff thrice (proclaimed, holder of) tribunician power, thrice consul, ordered the bath, with the porticos and the ball-courts and other adjacent enclosures, (which) were destroyed and burned in the Jewish rebellion [*tumultus Judaicus*], of the city of the Cyrenians to be restored'); cf. S. Perowne, *Hadrian* (London: Hodder & Stoughton, 1960), pl. 2.

20. All of these papyri can be found in Tcherikover and Fuks (eds.), *Corpus Papyrorum Judaicarum*, II, pp. 228-60.

the Romans and the Jews'. In *CPJ* 436 (115 CE) an anxious sister urges her brother not to go out without a guard (φυλακή). *CPJ* 438 (probably 116 CE) tells of a defeat at the hands of the Jewish insurgents: 'The one hope and expectation that was left was the push of the massed villagers from our district against the impious Jews; but now the opposite has happened. For on the 20th our forces fought and were beaten and many of them were killed [...] now, however, we have received news from men coming from [...] that another legion of Rutilius arrived at Memphis on the 22nd and is expected.' *CPJ* 439 (117 CE?) reports that a 'slave was coming from Memphis to bring the good news of his [i.e. Apollonius's] victory and success'. In *CPJ* 443 (117 CE) Apollonius requests a leave to tend to his damaged estates. *CPJ* 444 (late 117 CE or early 118 CE) refers to the recent 'Jewish disturbances', while *CPJ* 445 (perhaps early 118 CE) refers to the confiscation of Jewish property. Finally, *CPJ* 450 (late 199 CE or early 200 CE) expresses gratitude to the people of Oxyrhynchus for their 'friendship to the Romans which they exhibited in the war against the Jews [κατὰ τὸν πρὸς Εἰουδαίους πόλεμον συμμαχήσαντες], giving aid then and even now keeping the day of victory as a festival every year'.

Although we cannot be certain, given the fragmentary, biased and often unreliable sources, it is probable that Lukuas the Jewish 'king' was regarded in messianic terms. This is probable not only because 'Messiah' was understood to be a king, but the destruction of pagan temples and the resulting references to the Jews as 'impious' make it clear that a religious factor played an important role in the war, whatever the specific cause or causes of the war. Moreover, the intensity of the fighting, which led to exaggerated charges of savagery, testifies to the dedication and zeal of the Jewish insurgents. All of these factors suggest that Lukuas was regarded as the Messiah and that the war was a battle for the restoration of Israel.[21]

Simon ben Kosiba. Apparently Simon, either the son of a man named Kosiba or from a village (or valley) by that name, was the principal leader of the second Jewish rebellion against Rome (132–35 CE). (The rabbis often spell his name with the letter 'z' to make a word play with 'lie'.) According to rabbinic tradition, Rabbi Aqiba, contrary to other rabbis, regarded Simon as the Messiah (*y. Ta'an.* 4.5). Another tradition adds: 'Bar Koziba reigned two and a half years, and then said to the

---

21. So Tcherikover and Fuks (eds.), *Corpus Papyrorum Judaicarum*, I, p. 90: 'the only reason [for the revolt] was the Messianic character of the whole movement'.

rabbis, "I am the Messiah". They answered, "Of Messiah it is written that he smells [instead of sees] and judges: let us see if he [Bar Koziba] can do so"' (*b. Sanh.* 93b). Administering justice by smelling, instead of seeing, is an allusion to Isa. 11.3-5 ('He shall not judge by what his eyes see, or decide by what his ears hear; but with righteousness he shall judge the poor, and decide with equity for the meek of the earth...'). The talmudic passage goes on to say that Simon failed and so was slain. According to *y. Ta'an.* 4.5 (cf. *m. Ta'an.* 4.6; *b. Giṭ.* 57a-b; *Lam. R.* 2.2.4), Simon was defeated at Bether because of his arrogance against heaven ('Lord of the Universe, neither help us nor hinder us!') and his violence toward Rabbi Eleazar, one of Israel's revered teachers.

If some of these Jewish liberation movements of the first century had messianic overtones, and I believe that some of them did,[22] it is clear that there were Jews who hoped for a violent overthrow of Roman authority in Israel. Seen against these hopes, Jesus' crucifixion at the hands of the Romans, tinged with the mockery of the *titulus* that proclaimed him 'king of the Jews' (Mt. 27.37; Mk 15.26; Lk. 23.38; Jn 19.19-22), could hardly have been viewed by the synagogue in any other light than as evidence of Jesus' utter failure. The crucifixion of Jesus, from a Jewish perspective, would have been taken as political defeat and prophetic failure. For Jesus not only offered himself as Israel's anointed deliverer—by acting as a prophet; he proclaimed the advent of the kingdom of God, but the kingdom did not appear and its proclaimer was executed.

Jesus' apparent defeat at the hands of the Romans, along with his rejection by the religious authorities of Jerusalem, would have made Christian proclamation of Jesus' messiahship in the context of the synagogue ludicrous. An apologetic that would have any hope of persuading Jews that Jesus really was Israel's Messiah would have to explain both the religious rejection and the apparent political defeat. This apologetic, moreover, would have to be scripturally grounded, if it were to make any significant headway against the objections of the synagogue's teachers of Scripture. Although due allowance must be made for its obvious apologetic slant, the question with which Justin Martyr

---

22. So also Horsley and Hanson, *Bandits, Prophets, and Messiahs*, pp. 88-134. It is probable that both Menaḥem and Simon bar Giora (in the first war with Rome) made messianic claims of one sort or another, while it is virtually certain that Simon ben Kosiba (in the second war with Rome) claimed to be Israel's Messiah.

credits Trypho the Jew very likely approximates the misgivings many
Jews would have entertained when hearing Christian claims:

> Then Trypho remarked, 'Be assured that all our nation awaits the Mes-
> siah; and we admit that all the Scriptures which you have quoted refer to
> him. Moreover, I also admit that the name of Jesus by which the son of
> Nun was called, has inclined me very strongly to adopt this view. But we
> are in doubt about whether the Messiah should be so shamefully cruci-
> fied. For whoever is crucified is said in the Law to be accursed, so that I
> am very skeptical on this point. It is quite clear, to be sure, that *the Scrip-
> tures announce* that the Messiah had to suffer; but we wish to learn if
> you can prove it to us whether by suffering he was cursed' (*Dialogue*
> 89.1 [my emphasis]).

> 'Lead us on, then', [Trypho] said, '*by the Scriptures*, that we may also be
> persuaded by you; for we know that he should suffer and be led as a
> sheep. But prove to us whether he must also be crucified and die such a
> disgraceful and dishonorable death, cursed by the Law. For we cannot
> bring ourselves even to consider this' (*Dialogue* 90.1 [my emphasis]).

When Trypho says, 'the Scriptures announce that the Messiah had to
suffer', or 'we know that he should suffer and be led as a sheep', he is
alluding to Isa. 53.7: 'He was oppressed, and he was afflicted, yet he
opened not his mouth; like a lamb that is led to the slaughter, and like a
sheep that before its shearers is dumb, so he opened not his mouth'.
Trypho's admission that the Messiah was expected to suffer may very
well be genuine, for traditions of a period of woe preceding the coming
of the Messiah are attested in Jewish sources (such as in *m. Soṭ.* 9.15)
and are probably based on the general prophetic pattern of punishment
preceding restoration. One should also review Daniel 7, where a terrific
struggle is envisioned to take place before the people of God finally
prevail over the forces of evil.

The *Targum of Isaiah* attests messianic interpretation of the famous
song of the suffering Servant. However, discomfort with the idea of
suffering is also attested in the Targum. The suffering servant of Isaiah
53 is turned into a triumphant victor. His grave is not assigned with the
wicked (as in v. 9); on the contrary, he assigns the wicked to their grave!

However, suffering as prelude to victory did not envision death, and
certainly not a shameful death on a Roman cross. Even claims of resurrection would do little in a Jewish context to mitigate the evident failure
of Jesus' bid to be Israel's Messiah. Of course, Jews were not alone in
mocking the Christian proclamation that the crucified Galilean was
none other than Israel's King and God's Messiah. According to Origen,

Celsus regarded the notion as absurd, that someone betrayed, abandoned, captured, and executed could be regarded as God and Savior. The whole notion is preposterous (Origen, *Cels.* 2.9, 35, 68; 6.10, 34, 36).[23] To make any headway at all, especially in a Jewish context, a Christian apologetic would have to explain the circumstances of the passion and would have to show how the passion was in keeping with scriptural expectation.

Ultimately, however, Christian apologetic that was well grounded in Scripture failed to persuade a significant number of Jews. Despite rather sophisticated attempts by Paul and the Matthean and Johannine evangelists, Jewish misgivings arising from Jesus' apparent defeat and unmitigated shameful death (a death that may actually attest God's curse, cf. Deut. 21.23: 'a hanged man is accursed by God') were left unsatisfied. It is not for nothing that Paul tackles head on this very point in Galatians, a letter in which his teaching and authority have been undermined by 'Judaizers' (Gal. 3.10-14). The apostle must show that the curse endured by Christ hanging on the cross substitutes for the curse that attaches itself to any person who fails to observe all that is written in the Law (cf. Deut. 27.26). Paul's midrashic exegesis ultimately derives from the difficulty that the crucifixion posed for the Christian proclamation of Jesus as Israel's Messiah.

We may conclude that the primary objection to Christian claims that the crucified Jesus of Nazareth was in fact Israel's Messiah was the fact of his death, and a shameful one at that. From a Jewish perspective, this objection was fatal. The only possible way to answer was in terms a Jewish person would appreciate, and that was appeal to Jewish Scripture. If it could be shown in Scripture that the Messiah was to suffer, then perhaps Jesus could be accepted as Israel's Messiah after all. But this strategem ultimately persuaded very few Jews (though it did some, as attested by Ebionite Christianity[24]). It failed because the promised

---

23. See M. Hengel, *Crucifixion in the Ancient World and the Folly of the Message of the Cross* (Philadelphia: Fortress Press, 1977), pp. 1-10; *idem*, 'Christological Titles in Early Christianity', in J.H. Charlesworth (ed.), *The Messiah: Developments in Earliest Judaism and Christianity* (Minneapolis: Fortress Press, 1992), pp. 425-48, esp. pp. 425-30.

24. On Jewish Christianity and its relationship to the larger, predominantly Gentile Church, see R.A. Pritz, *Nazarene Jewish Christianity: From the End of the New Testament Period until its Disappearance in the Fourth Century* (SPB, 37; Jerusalem: Magnes Press; Leiden: E.J. Brill, 1988).

kingdom did not materialize, and Jesus did not return, as his followers expected.

As messianism faded in importance for Judaism (a fading probably resulting from the catastrophic wars against Rome[25]), the Christian message that Jesus was the Messiah became increasingly irrelevant. Early on, it mattered and was hotly disputed; later on, it mattered much less, and so was ignored. After Christianity swept the Roman Empire, the polemic between Christians and Jews took on a new complexion, becoming increasingly bitter and ugly. Christian polemic was open and explicit, while for obvious reasons Jewish polemic tended to be allusive, often buried in obscure talmudic and midrashic passages inaccessible to Christians. With the eventual extinction of Ebionite Christianity, the rift between Judaism and Christianity was complete.

25. Following the defeat of Simon in 135 CE, it would be three centuries before the reappearance of messianic fervor. Based on various calculations, it was believed that the Messiah would come either in 440 CE (cf. *b. Sanh.* 97b) or in 471 CE (cf. b. *'Abod. Zar.* 9b). Other dates were suggested. Answering this expectation, one 'Moses of Crete' (c. 448 CE) promised to lead the Jewish people through the sea, dry-shod, from Crete to Palestine. At his command many of his followers threw themselves into the Mediterranean. Some drowned, others were rescued. Moses himself disappeared (cf. Socrates Scholasticus, *Hist. Eccl.* 7.38; 12.33). Evidently, Moses typology had continued to play an important role in shaping restoration hopes. A variety of other pseudo-messiahs appeared in the Islamic period (especially in the eighth century), during the later crusades (especially in the twelfth and thirteenth centuries), and even as late as the sixteenth, seventeenth and eighteenth centuries (cf. *JewEnc*, X, pp. 252-55).

ANCIENT UNDERSTANDINGS OF THE CHRISTIAN–JEWISH SPLIT

Stanley E. Porter and Brook W.R. Pearson

1. The State of Affairs between Christians and Jews in the Fourth Century

At the beginning of the fourth century—the tail-end of the pre-Constantinian period—the relative position of Christians and Jews within the Roman empire was broadly comparable. Both groups were part of the larger body of Graeco-Roman religions,[1] neither was an official state religion, and both had undergone varying levels of persecution for a variety of different, but related, reasons.[2] Samuel Krauss describes the situation boldly: 'The long history of [the] polemic [between Christians and Jews] falls into two periods: that of the persecuted church, and that of the church in power'.[3] Krauss's formula is, however, rather one-sided, for the relationship between Judaism and Christianity extends further back than this brief defining moment between persecution and official state recognition for Christianity. Arguably, the *relationship* began with Jesus himself, when ethnic homogeneity characterized the first followers of Jesus as Jews.[4] The relationship, and with it the tension, became much more demonstrable when the new movement began to expand and spread under the leadership of such men as Peter, James

---

1. On personal religions in the Roman empire, see the survey of J. Ferguson, *The Religions of the Roman Empire* (Ithaca, NY: Cornell University Press, 1970), pp. 99-131, in which Christianity and Judaism are treated as two of many.

2. For a brief summary, see M. Cary, *A History of Rome down to the Reign of Constantine* (London: Macmillan, 1967), Chapter 43 *passim*.

3. S. Krauss, *The Jewish–Christian Controversy from the Earliest Times to 1789*. I. *History* (ed. and rev. W. Horbury; TSAJ, 56; Tübingen: Mohr Siebeck, 1995), p. 11.

4. See E.P. Sanders, *Jesus and Judaism* (London: SCM Press, 1985), for a study that attempts to come to terms with the Jewish dimension of Jesus.

and Paul.[5] By far one of the most noticeable elements of this expansion was the shift from early Christianity being a predominantly Jewish group to one with a large non-Jewish or Gentile contingent. As a result, the many interactions between 'the Jews' and various Christian leaders in the book of Acts would suggest that this relationship was already under question by the time that this book was written (opinion on which varies from the mid-first century to the mid-second),[6] and apparently even further back to the work of the apostle to the Gentiles himself, Paul, as seen especially in his letters. In the light of this, it would seem that the two-part scheme used by Krauss should extend back to these earlier days, and be divided into four parts: (1) the period of ethnic identification between Christians and Jews, because the earliest Christians were Jews; (2) the period of the Church/the early Christian movement being persecuted and/or threatened by other Jewish groups (whether actual or perceived); (3) the period of the Church's initial independence from 'Judaism', or as a sect in its own right (whatever date one assigns to this independence), when it was, to varying degrees, either persecuted or accepted by the Romans (see below, with regard to the various theories regarding the nature of the split between Judaism and Christianity—this is Krauss's first period); and (4) the period of the Church's legal and eventually dominant status (Krauss's second period). Even this scheme may be too facile, but it at least allows for a greater degree of development in the early stages of the relationship between Christianity and Judaism, and flags up the fact that the development of that relationship post-313 is actually only a solidification of the developments which had occurred at an earlier stage, when the relationship between the two groups was still (we would argue) somewhat in question.

There is, of course, some question regarding the *identity* of the polemic between Christianity and Judaism at this earlier time—the evidence we have at our disposal with regard to Christian anti-Jewish

---

5. Of these three, not much is known of Peter and James compared to Paul. Introductions to the life and thought of Paul abound (see below). On other figures in the early Church, see F.F. Bruce, *Peter, Stephen, James and John: Studies in Early Non-Pauline Christianity* (Grand Rapids: Eerdmans, 1979).

6. See the excellent discussion of issues of authorship of Acts in C.-J. Thornton, *Der Zeuge des Zeugen: Lukas als Historiker der Paulusreisen* (WUNT, 56; Tübingen: Mohr Siebeck, 1991), esp. pp. 8-68.

rhetoric is more plentiful than Jewish anti-Christian rhetoric.[7] As a result—as was also the case with the relationship between Christianity and Gnosticism prior to the Nag Hammadi finds—the exact content of Jewish anti-Christian rhetoric has always been somewhat difficult and tendentious to reconstruct by using Christian *adversus Iudaeos*-type writings.[8]

An interesting dimension of the extant Jewish rhetoric, as well as that which can be reconstructed from Christian writings, is that it seems to focus primarily upon Christian origins, specifically the life of Jesus. Mention of Paul is non-existent—unless one credits the talmudic story (*b. Šab.* 30b) of Gamaliel I's nameless renegade student as speaking of Paul.[9] The Church as an entity in its own right is not mentioned. Even if one does credit the story about Gamaliel's student as an attack upon Paul, the character of that story appears to be somewhat similar to the collected rabbinic stories about Jesus which together make up the *Toledoth Jesu*[10]—suggesting that one of the major lines of attack in Jewish anti-Christian rhetoric, like Christian anti-Jewish rhetoric, revolved around authority in the interpretation of the Scriptures. In the case of Jewish anti-Christian rhetoric, aspersions are cast on Jesus on both a moralistic level (for example alleging that he was the son of a prostitute by a Roman soldier [Origen, *Cels.* 1.28-32; cf. *b. Sanh.* 67a]) and, as in

---

7.   Summaries of this polemic, some of which is discussed in detail below, are found in L.M. McDonald, 'Anti-Judaism in the Early Church Fathers', in C.A. Evans and D.A. Hagner (eds.), *Anti-Semitism and Early Christianity: Issues of Polemic and Faith* (Minneapolis: Fortress Press, 1993), pp. 220-49; S.G. Wilson, *Related Strangers: Jews and Christians 7–170 C.E.* (Minneapolis: Fortress Press, 1995), pp. 169-94; and W. Horbury, *Jews and Christians in Contact and Controversy* (Edinburgh: T. & T. Clark, 1998), esp. pp. 14-25, and 127-99.

8.   Discussion of the reasons for the lack of similar anti-Christian literature among Jews is found in McDonald, 'Anti-Judaism in the Early Church Fathers', pp. 245-46. The term *adversus Iudaeos* comes from the anonymous Latin work probably from the third century, passed down by Cyprian of Carthage, and found in A.L. Williams (trans.), *Adversus Iudaeos* (Cambridge: Cambridge University Press, 1935). On this document, see Horbury, *Jews and Christians*, pp. 180-99.

9.   As does J. Klausner, *From Jesus to Paul* (trans. W.F. Stinespring; New York: Macmillan, 1943), p. 310. See also F.F. Bruce, *Paul: Apostle of the Free Spirit/ Heart Set Free* (Grand Rapids: Eerdmans; Exeter: Paternoster Press, 1978), p. 51.

10.   See C.A. Evans, *Life of Jesus Research: An Annotated Bibliography* (NTTS, 24; Leiden: E.J. Brill, 2nd edn, 1996), pp. 287-90 for a *précis* of the possibly more reliable passages, together with bibliography.

the strange 'putting up a brick' story (*b. Sanh.* 107b), with regard to Jesus' lack of authority, and rejection by his elders.[11]

Christian anti-Jewish rhetoric, at its most effective, mirrors this last element of Jewish anti-Christian rhetoric, in that disputes over interpretations of Scripture form the basis of most anti-Jewish or anti-Judaism rhetoric from the New Testament onwards (especially Justin Martyr). It even appears that the particularly Christian interpretations of many passages in the Septuagint may have formed the basis of the rejection of that translation by Jews in the first few centuries of the Common Era. The rabbinic passages which display this rejection include *Massakhet Sop.* 1.7-10 and the gaonic addition to the *Megillat Ta'anit*. The former compares the day that the translation was completed to that on which the nation of Israel made the golden calf, while the latter asserts that the world grew dark for three days when the Law was translated.[12]

Although the central controversy between the two groups may have begun over interpretative authority (and all of the related implications of this authority),[13] it seems that both groups also made liberal usage of current pagan criticisms of the other group, casting various aspersions of a less savoury character.[14] Other motivating factors for such antagonism may also have included rivalry for converts or the need to retain those already within the group, the need on both sides for self-definition, an underlying sense of insecurity that perhaps the other religious sect had something more to offer, and, for Christianity (at least in the earliest stages), the intimidation of being so greatly outnumbered by

---

11. Cf. E. Bammel, 'Christian Origins in Jewish Tradition', *NTS* 13 (1966–67), pp. 321-22, repr. in E. Bammel, *Judaica: Kleine Schriften I* (WUNT, 37; Tübingen: Mohr Siebeck, 1986), pp. 224-25.

12. See E. Tov, 'The Rabbinic Tradition Concerning the "Alterations" Inserted into the Greek Pentateuch and their Relation to the Original Text of the LXX', *JSJ* 15 (1984), pp. 65-89; and B.W.R. Pearson, 'Remainderless Translations: Implications for Modern Translational Theory of the Tradition Concerning the Translation of the LXX', in S.E. Porter and R.S. Hess (eds.), *Translating the Bible: Problems and Prospects* (JSNTSup, 173; Sheffield: Sheffield Academic Press, 1999), pp. 63-84.

13. Cf. also Horbury, *Jews and Christians*, pp. 200-25.

14. For a list of the various negative characterizations of Jewish practices, beliefs and character traits from pagan critics as found in their later Christian counterparts, see Krauss, *Jewish–Christian Controversy*, pp. 19-26; cf. McDonald, 'Anti-Judaism in the Early Church Fathers', pp. 220-25.

Jews.[15] In a sense, this rivalry simply highlights the continuing connection between these two religious groups—what may have begun as a parent–child controversy has, by the end of the pre-Constantinian period, become a sibling rivalry.

2. *Perspectives on the Split between Judaism and Christianity*

It is at this point that the question of the identity of the split between Christianity and Judaism takes on its full importance. Much recent work on this topic seems to rely very little on the ancient sources themselves, which we attempt to redress in this chapter by concentrating solely on the ancient models. The first, supersessionism, reflects the most prevalent Christian attitude toward and understanding of the split. The second, apostasy by Christians, reflects what seems to have been the most common Jewish view of the split, while the third, the Roman view, reflects the viewpoint of the government which would eventually legalize Christianity and elevate it over the head of Judaism. It is hoped that this brief survey will draw the focus of the modern debate over this issue back into the ancient sources.

a. *Supersessionism*
The supersessionist position, which has been the most prevalent in New Testament studies until the middle of this century, is also the oldest position held by Christians. It dates to some of the earliest times of the dispute and probably came early on to represent the position of the vast majority of Christians. This theory essentially holds to the view that whatever merits Judaism had, when Christianity came on the religious scene of the first century, it supplanted Judaism. This supersession meant that whatever typological or prophetic roles were played by such Jewish institutions as the Temple, circumcision or the Torah, they were all rendered no longer valid, replaced by Christian institutions and beliefs.

15. See McDonald, 'Anti-Judaism in the Early Church Fathers', pp. 237-45. These reasons all indicate that, contrary to some previous scholarly thought, Judaism continued to thrive in the second to fifth centuries CE. See M. Simon, *Verus Israel* (trans. H. McKeating; New York: Oxford University Press, 1986), whose position has now been adopted by a number of scholars, including J. Lieu, 'History and Theology in Christian Views of Judaism', in J. Lieu, J. North and T. Rajak (eds.), *The Jews among Pagans and Christians in the Roman Empire* (London: Routledge, 1992), pp. 79-96.

Jewish Christianity, as especially represented by the Jerusalem church, did not apparently hold to this position, however, which led to one of the first major conflicts within the Church, and probably hastened development of supersessionism. If Acts is to be believed, this problem was seen, at least from the Jewish–Christian perspective, to be largely the doing of Paul (Acts 15, 21), who had had noteworthy success in converting Gentiles on his missionary ventures (often after being expelled from the local synagogue). Scholars disagree about the factual basis of the Jerusalem Council in Acts 15,[16] but what is represented there certainly appears to represent a major conflict within the early Church and the kind of compromise solution that may have been suggested. The controversy revolved around whether those who converted to Christianity from outside of Judaism needed also to become Jews as well. For those who were already Jews, this posed no problem, but for Gentiles, who came from outside Judaism, this issue posed considerable difficulty. This conflict is reflected in a number of sources in the New Testament. These include, for example, Paul's conflict with the Judaizers in Galatia, as well as the conflict between James and Paul lurking in the background of Galatians 2, which comes more to the forefront in Acts 21 and James 2.[17] For Jewish Christians, the relation between Christianity and Judaism probably meant that Jesus as Messiah was a fulfilment by Christianity of the original purposes of Judaism, in which institutions such as circumcision and food laws could and should be maintained. For Gentile Christians, according to Paul, they did not need to become Jews to be Christians. This led to one of the first major splits within Christianity, and helped to draw the lines of demarcation between Christianity and Judaism. As Gentile Christianity grew in significance, soon outstripping Jewish Christianity, its supersessionist position also became prominent.

The supersessionist position is arguably represented in virtually every stratum of the New Testament writings, but the earliest evidence is

16. On these issues, see J.A. Fitzmyer, *The Acts of the Apostles* (AB, 31; New York: Doubleday, 1998), pp. 538-67.

17. Aspects of the F.C. Baur hypothesis, we believe, have much to offer in the reconstruction of the development of early Christianity. For a recent articulation of this hypothesis, with modifications, see M.D. Goulder, *A Tale of Two Missions* (London: SCM Press, 1994) On conflict between Paul and James, see S.E. Porter, *The Paul of Acts: Essays in Literary Criticism, Rhetoric, and Theology* (WUNT, 115; Tübingen: Mohr Siebeck, 1999), pp. 172-86.

probably to be found in Paul's writings. There has been much controversy over a number of passages in Paul's letters where he appears to state in strong terms his antagonism to Judaism (e.g. 1 Thess. 2.14-16).[18] Some have, as a result, accused him, and the New Testament along with it, of being anti-Semitic. Such passages, however, must be put in their proper context. There is a longstanding tradition within Judaism of offering a critique of its own institutions—a tradition within which Paul appears to be functioning when he uses such strong language.[19] There is the further question, however, of how Paul saw himself in relation to Judaism. It is indisputable that Paul was ethnically Jewish, and remained so for his entire life. In Gal. 1.13-14, however, he draws a contrast between his former life in Judaism and his current life in Christ, rejecting his former life of following the traditions of the fathers. In that sense, although remaining an ethnic Jew, Paul appears to have rejected Judaism. His acceptance of Jesus as Lord and Christ superseded the conventions of religious belief to be found in Judaism.[20] In Galatians, Paul roundly condemns those who appear to be abandoning the Christian faith to return to various Jewish practices; those who do works of the law he describes as being under a curse, with Christ having redeemed Christians from the curse of the law (ch. 3). In Rom. 10.4, Christ is said to be the end of the law. Whether this means the abolition or fulfilment of the law, the result is much the same. Regarding the dispute between the weak and the strong, Paul admonishes the strong in Romans to have concern for those who still pay attention to food laws and holy days. Similar sentiments are found in Philippians 3, where Paul labels those who practise circumcision as mutilators of the flesh. After he runs through his 'Jewish' qualifications (in response to opponents who, in all likelihood were *not* ethnic Jews themselves), Paul labels them as rubbish compared to his calling in Christ. Paul apparently believed that such practices that would have distinguished those

18. This passage has been highly debated regarding its anti-Judaistic or anti-Semitic features, as well as its authenticity. For discussion of this passage in the scholarly literature, see J.A.D. Weima and S.E. Porter, *An Annotated Bibliography of 1 and 2 Thessalonians* (NTTS, 26; Leiden: E.J. Brill, 1998), pp. 161-73.

19. See C.A. Evans, 'Faith and Polemic: The New Testament and First-Century Judaism', in Evans and Hagner (eds.), *Anti-Semitism and Early Christianity*, pp. 3-13.

20. See S.E. Porter, 'Was Paul a Good Jew? Fundamental Issues in a Current Debate', pp. 148-74 in this volume.

in Judaism had been nullified with the advent of Christianity (and hence should not be practised by or required of, *especially* those not born into Judaism). In Gal. 6.16, Paul speaks of the Israel of God, with apparent reference to the replacement of the Jewish people by the Church.

Scholars often do not differentiate other strata in the New Testament regarding views of Judaism.[21] However, at least three other strata with a similar position to Paul's are also worth noting. First is the Synoptic Gospel material. Mark 13, for example, depicts the Temple as being destroyed. Matthew—the most 'Jewish' of the Gospels—sees Jesus at odds with the Pharisees throughout (e.g. chs. 3, 23). Another stratum is that of the Johannine literature, especially the Gospel, where in chs. 9, 12 and 16, the issue of expulsion from the synagogue is raised as a serious threat (cf. ch. 8 also).[22] The third stratum to note here is that of the book of Hebrews, which some in the early Church apparently considered Pauline.[23] Wilson treats Hebrews under a chapter heading of 'supersessionism', finding in that book the clearest statement of a clear break with Judaism.[24] The book is apparently written from the standpoint of warning Christians about the dangers of reverting to Judaism (ch. 6). Whether one argues for early or later dates for many of the writings noted above, it is clear to the supersessionist that, by the end of the first century, virtually all of the New Testament writers considered a serious development to have taken place, in which Christianity was seen to have taken the place of Judaism.

21. One of the few to treat this material in a stratified way is W.A. Meeks, 'Breaking Away: Three New Testament Pictures of Christianity's Separation from the Jewish Communities', in J. Neusner and E.S. Frerichs (eds.), *'To See Ourselves as Others See Us': Christians, Jews, 'Others' in Late Antiquity* (Chico, CA: Scholars Press, 1985), pp. 93-115. Cf. S. Freyne, 'Vilifying the Other and Defining the Self: Matthew's and John's Anti-Jewish Polemic in Focus', in Neusner and Frerichs (eds.), *'To See Ourselves'*, pp. 117-43; D. Georgi, 'The Early Church: Internal Jewish Migration or New Religion?', *HTR* 88 (1995), pp. 35-68, esp. 37-56.

22. See H.J. de Jonge, 'Jewish Arguments against Jesus at the End of the First Century C.E. According to the Gospel of John', in P.W. van der Horst (ed.), *Aspects of Religious Contact and Conflict in the Ancient World* (UTR, 31; Utrecht: Faculteit der Godgeleerdheid, Universiteit Utrecht, 1995), pp. 45-55.

23. For discussion, see H.F.D. Sparks, *The Formation of the New Testament* (London: SCM Press, 1952), pp. 81-84.

24. Wilson, *Related Strangers*, pp. 110-27.

Similar ideas were picked up by a number of other writers in the early Church, writers whose anti-Judaistic comments have often been chronicled. We can see that such comments began early. In his letters, Ignatius condemns Judaizers, with their impositions of practices such as Sabbath worship (*Magn.* 8–10), and their teaching of such ideas (*Phld.* 5–6), which are incompatible with speaking Christ (*Magn.* 10.3).[25] Another example is the *Epistle of Barnabas*, where there is constant opposition between 'us' and 'them', representing Gentiles and Jews (chs. 2–5, 8, 10, 13, 14). Particular Jewish customs, such as fasting (ch. 3), are ridiculed, the law is reinterpreted and christologized (chs. 9, 10), as are the Temple and covenant (chs. 2, 4).[26] The *Epistle to Diognetus* condemns the fussiness of the Jews regarding various ritual practices, which Christians are not to follow (chs. 3, 4).[27] The later Church Fathers are notorious for saying similar things. Justin Martyr, in his *Dialogue with Trypho the Jew*, claims similarly that 'we [the Church] are the true Israelite race, the spiritual one, that of Judah and Jacob and Abraham' (11.5).[28] One of the best known comments is by Melito of Sardis, whose homily *On the Passover* states the supersessionist position clearly:

> The people was precious before the church arose and the law was marvellous before the Gospel was illuminated. But when the church arose and the Gospel came to the fore the model was made void giving its power to the truth and the law was fulfilled giving its power to the Gospel…so too the law was fulfilled when the Gospel was illuminated and the people made void when the church arose (42–43).[29]

25. See J. Lieu, *Image and Reality: The Jews in the World of the Christians in the Second Century* (Edinburgh: T. & T. Clark, 1996), pp. 26-39.

26. Wilson, *Related Strangers*, pp. 127-42.

27. For discussion of this at a somewhat later (although still relevant) date, see P.W. van der Horst, 'Jews and Christians in Antioch at the End of the Fourth Century', pp. 228-38 in this volume.

28. Cited in J. Lieu, '"The Parting of the Ways": Theological Construct or Historical Reality?', *JSNT* 56 (1994), pp. 101-119 (104). On Justin's dialogue, cf. *idem*, *Image and Reality*, pp. 103-53; G.N. Stanton, 'Justin Martyr's Dialogue with Trypho: Group Boundaries, "Proselytes" and "God-Fearers"', in G.N. Stanton and G.G. Strousma (eds.), *Tolerance and Intolerance in Early Judaism and Christianity* (Cambridge: Cambridge University Press, 1998), pp. 263-78.

29. Cited in Lieu, '"Parting of the Ways"', p. 103, who provides many insightful references to the history of discussion. On Melito, see *idem*, *Image and Reality*, pp. 199-240; Wilson, *Related Strangers*, pp. 241-56, who notes that Melito's strain

Irenaeus speaks of the Church as the synagogue of God (*Adv. Haer.* 3.6.1). Lastly, Tertullian says that the law was given by God because of the hardness of the Jews (*Adv. Marc.* 2.19), which observances have now been eliminated (*Adv. Marc.* 5.4),

b. *Apostasy by Christians*
Whereas the supersessionist view is one that is distinctly Christian, there is an equivalent Jewish position that also apparently developed early on and was widely held in the ancient world. It stands to reason that, as Christianity developed and began to attract more and more people both within and outside of Palestine, Jews would need to face their relationship with this group that still may have had some ties to the synagogue. The response of some Jews was to take what amounts to an anti-supersessionist view, that is, that Christians, by departing from the teaching and beliefs of Judaism, were apostate, and needed to be condemned as such.[30]

The evidence for this view is to be found in a number of ancient sources, some of it involving mirror reading of New Testament texts. Noted above was Paul's ejection from the synagogue in a number of cities where he did his missionary preaching, as recorded in Acts, and discussion of exclusion from the synagogue in John's Gospel, perhaps reflecting the situation in the last quarter of the first century. This scenario is apparently confirmed by Jewish sources of the time as well. In the Eighteen Benedictions, recited daily in the synagogue, a twelfth benediction was inserted, probably around 90 CE, written by Samuel the Small, a contemporary of Gamaliel II. Some scholars do not think that this was against Christians, and it may not have been exclusively directed against them at the start. However, on the basis of its wording in its historical context, as well as later comments by Justin Martyr (*Dialogue with Trypho the Jew* 16), Epiphanius (*Adv. Haer.* 29.9), and Jerome (*In Isa.* 5.18), and the discovery in 1898 of the text in a fragment from the Fustat Genizah, it appears that this benediction was

---

of anti-Judaism was to dominate Christianity from then on; *idem*, 'Passover, Easter, and Anti-Judaism: Melito of Sardis and Others', in Neusner and Frerichs (eds.), *'To See Ourselves'*, pp. 337-55, esp. pp. 343-53.

30. For an attempt to define apostasy, see J.M.G. Barclay, 'Who Was Considered an Apostate in the Jewish Diaspora?', in Stanton and Stroumsa (eds.), *Tolerance and Intolerance*, pp. 80-98. He notes that disputes over interpretation were often involved in such discussions (cf. our discussion of this above, pp. 38-39).

against Christians at least by the second century, if not earlier.[31] The fragment reads:

> For apostates let there be no hope, and the dominion of arrogance do thou speedily root out in our days: and let *nosrim* (Nazarenes) and *minim* (heretics) perish as in a moment, let them be blotted out of the book of the living and let them not be written with the righteous. Blessed art Thou, O Lord, who humblest the arrogant.[32]

The recitation of this benediction would have posed an insuperable challenge to any Christian still within the synagogue where it was recited, clearly labelling Christians as apostates. During the Bar Kokhba revolt also (c. 135 CE), there is some evidence, although much later, that Christians were compelled to be circumcised,[33] something that Jewish Christians may have been able to do, but that Gentile Christians rejected.

Other, later Jewish writers apparently held similarly strong views, labelling Christians as apostate to Judaism. *Contra Celsus*, Origen's response to the otherwise unknown Celsus, a notable Middle Platonist thinker from the second century, is written from a Christian standpoint, but perhaps gives insight into the actual thoughts and beliefs of at least one Jew of the time, who acts as one of Celsus's sources for his attack on the origins of Christianity. This Jew questions what was wrong with Christians, who 'left the law of your fathers, and, being deluded by that man whom we were speaking of just now, were quite ludicrously deceived and have deserted us for another name and another life?' (2.1). This Jew, if he is being accurately represented and quoted, sees Christianity as 'despising' its origins in Judaism, the only origin it can claim (2.4). Celsus himself repeats this same charge (5.33), describing

---

31. C.W. Dugmore, *The Influence of the Synagogue upon the Divine Office* (London: Faith Press, rev. edn, 1964), pp. 3-4; cf. McDonald, 'Anti-Judaism in the Early Church Fathers', pp. 246-47. For a contrary position, see R. Kimelman, 'Birkat Ha-Minim and the Lack of Evidence for an Anti-Christian Jewish Prayer in Late Antiquity', in E.P. Sanders with A.I. Baumgarten and A. Mendelson (eds.), *Jewish and Christian Self-Definition*. II. *Aspects of Judaism in the Graeco-Roman Period* (London: SCM Press, 1981), pp. 226-44.

32. Translation adapted from Dugmore, *Influence of the Synagogue*, p. 4, who traces the textual history, esp. in n. 1. The terms *nosrim* and *minim* are problematic, but probably point to Nazarenes being equated with followers of the Nazarene and *minim* with other kinds of heretics. Contra Lieu, ' "Parting of the Ways" ', p. 114.

33. See Eusebius, *Hist. Eccl.* 4.5.1-2.

Christians as those who have revolted against Judaism (3.5).[34] There is also the much later rabbinic tradition of anti-Christian statements found in the Talmud as well as the *Toledoth Jesu*. As discussed above, however, the direct evidence from Jews is disappointingly slender, probably because such writings did not survive well in the climate of post-Constantinian Christianity.[35]

c. *Roman Definition*

Whereas the first two positions represent views held by the most highly involved parties in the first centuries of the Common Era—Christians and Jews—they were not the only groups involved. Jews and Christians, whether distinguished or even distinguishable from each other in this earliest period or not, lived within the parameters of the Roman empire throughout the first several centuries of their relationship. It is understandable that the Romans themselves, including and perhaps especially those in authority who came into contact with the Jews and Christians, and who were called upon for rulings regarding their practices, would have a view on their relationship. A different essay could undoubtedly study in more detail the range of so-called pagan reaction to Christians and Jews, but we will concentrate here upon the reaction of those in official capacities. From the evidence that is available, it appears that the Romans themselves may have had a fairly clear view on the Jews and Christians.

Several factors should be considered here. The first is that there is a longstanding tradition in Roman and Greek antiquity of comments about the Jews, much of it negative. Undoubtedly, some of this had to do with their significant population throughout the Roman empire,

---

34. It is worth noting that Eusebius cites Porphyry, the polemicist against Christianity, as holding that Christians of Jewish descent 'have deserted the God honoured by the Jews and his precepts', and Christians from a pagan background as having 'deserted their ancestral ways and adopted the myths of the Jews, the enemies of humankind' (*Praep. Ev.* 1.2.3-4). This reflects the importance in Roman thought of the issue of loyalty to one's ancestral religion (cf. Cicero, *Flacc.* 28; G. La Piana, 'Foreign Groups in Ancient Rome during the First Centuries of the Empire', *HTR* 20 [1927], pp. 183-403 [325]).

35. For discussion of the issue of Jewish persecution of Christians, see J.M. Lieu, 'Accusations of Jewish Persecution in Early Christian Sources, with Particular Reference to Justin Martyr', in Stanton and Stroumsa (eds.), *Tolerance and Intolerance*, pp. 279-95.

totalling about 4 to 6 million out of 60 million,[36] and their practices such as circumcision (Tacitus, *Hist.* 5.1-13; Juvenal, *Satires* 1.3.10-16, 296; 2.5.542-47; 5.14.96-106; Seneca, cited in Augustine, *Civ.* 6.11), and so on, that clearly distinguished them from other religio-ethnic groups. Despite freedoms that the Jews enjoyed, and their own openness to others, they were apparently always held in some suspicion by the Romans, incurring a wealth of vitriolic and negative comment (e.g. Cicero, *Flacc.* 28.69; 60; Dio Cassius 37.16-17; cf. Josephus, *Apion* 2.79-96, 109-114). Compounding this was the fact that, within the first 150 years of the Common Era, there were three major revolts by the Jews (65–70 CE, 115–17 CE, 132–35 CE), and a number of expulsions of Jews from Rome (e.g. 19 CE and 41 CE, as well as 137 BCE) and even Jerusalem (135 CE, in the aftermath of the Bar Kokhba revolt).[37] Despite these negative comments about the Jews, however, these comments do not seem to have been applied to the Christians, certainly not the Gentile Christians. Even though Christianity clearly had its origin in Judaism, and the Jews were often the objects of mistrust and scurrilous comments, Christians do not seem to have been included in the scope of these comments or actions. As Judge says of the Christians, 'The Roman writers do not connect them with Judaism in any respect'.[38] Christians are commented upon in their own right. For example, Suetonius (*Nero* 16.2), in describing social disorders, lists Christians as practising 'a novel and threatening superstition',[39] as does Tacitus, who claims to not know how the superstition spreads, even though he knows it began in Judaea (*Ann.* 15.44.4; cf. book 5).[40]

---

36. R.L. Wilken, *The Christians as the Romans Saw Them* (New Haven: Yale University Press, 1984), p. 113.

37. For a number of important texts, see M.H. Williams, *The Jews among the Greeks and Romans: A Diaspora Sourcebook* (London: Gerald Duckworth, 1998), esp. pp. 98-99. On the expulsions of Jews from Rome, see H.D. Slingerland, *Claudian Policymaking and the Early Imperial Repression of Judaism at Rome* (SFSHJ, 160; Atlanta: Scholars Press, 1997).

38. E.A. Judge, 'Judaism and the Rise of Christianity: A Roman Perspective', *TynBul* 45 (1994), pp. 355-68 (359).

39. Cited in Judge, 'Judaism', p. 359.

40. J.D.G. Dunn, *The Partings of the Ways between Christianity and Judaism and their Significance for the Character of Christianity* (London: SCM Press; Philadelphia: Trinity Press International, 1991), p. 241, claims that the parallels between the descriptions of Jews and Christians points to Tacitus seeing the Christians as Jews. Judge, 'Judaism', p. 360 n. 4, points out that Tacitus's use of the

The second consideration is the early second-century correspondence between Pliny and Trajan regarding Christian practices. In *Ep*. 10.96, Pliny enquires of the emperor how he is to handle their trials, since he has never observed one before. He outlines his procedure:

> I interrogated them whether they were Christians; if they confessed it I repeated the question twice again, adding the threat of capital punishment; if they still persevered, I ordered them to be executed. For whatever the nature of their creed might be, I could at least feel no doubt that contumacy and inflexible obstinacy deserved chastisement (LCL).

As Judge points out, the question with Christians is not their alien practices, as it was with Jews, but several things that they do that seem to suggest insurrection, such as taking an oath and singing a hymn to Christ 'as to a God'. Hence Pliny compelled them to curse Christ and make offerings to Caesar. Trajan's response in *Ep*. 10.97 is that Pliny is correct in his procedure, but that Christians should not be pursued. According to Judge,

> Incomprehensible as the activities of Christians were, they could be tolerated providing (as Romans) they did not abandon their national duty of sacrifice to the Roman gods. The Romans had always understood and accepted that this was impossible for Jews, for whom exemption was secured. Why did they not see that the Christians stood in the same tradition, and were often themselves Jews into the bargain? There is no hint that anyone ever tried to suggest such a solution.[41]

A third factor is that this separation of Jews from Christians seems, according to this position, to have taken place early, as possibly indicated in the New Testament and from other first-century evidence. Three examples are worth noting. The first is the very name given to Christians. Acts 11.26 says that the name 'Christian' was first given in Antioch. The name would not have been invented by Jews, since it would have admitted the messianic claims of Jesus; more likely it was given by Romans, since the ending is a Latin one (*-ianus*) to designate members of a group, perhaps with some contempt. Judge speculates that the name may have arisen from questions posed as to the loyalties of these followers of Christ, and may similarly be reflected in Herod

phrase *genus hominum* ('a class of people') points to his not being able to correlate the group with any other.

41. Judge, 'Judaism', p. 361.

Agrippa II's response to Paul in Acts 26.28.[42] Further, Christians were not considered part of the imposition of payment of the *Fiscus Iudaicus*—the Jewish tax imposed after the defeat of Jerusalem in 70 CE (Dio Cassius 66.7.2; Suetonius, *Dom*. 12.2)—as were Jews, including those who were not circumcised but followed what might have appeared to be Jewish practices (see Dio Cassius 67.14).[43] When the compulsory tax was revoked in 96 CE,[44] the rules for who was a Jew were changed in a major way, because it made payment of the tax, and hence Jewish identity, voluntary.[45] If Christians identified with Judaism at this time, Judge wonders, why on the basis of Mt. 17.24-27 did they themselves not pay the tax, and hence avoid unnecessary persecution?[46] A possible exception to this separation of Christianity and Judaism in the minds of Romans is the incident of Claudius's banishment, in 41 or 49 CE,[47] of the Jews from Rome: 'Since the Jews constantly made disturbances at the instigation of Chrestus, he expelled them from Rome' (Suetonius, *Claud*. 25.4 [LCL]). Many biblical scholars think that this Chrestus is a reference to Christ, but this is not certain. The reasons are that the name is a very common one, no ancient source makes the identification with Christians (certainly not Suetonius himself!), and there is no indication in the New Testament that such conflict within the Jewish community over Christ had taken place this early (see Acts 18.2, where there is no indication of trouble when Paul meets up with Jewish refugees; 28.21).[48] The name may well have referred to any number of

42. Judge, 'Judaism', p. 363.

43. See Williams, *The Jews*, p. 104, citing her article, 'Domitian, the Jews and the "Judaizers"—A Simple Matter of *Cupiditas* and *Maiestas*?', *Historia* 39 (1990), pp. 196-211.

44. Nerva revoked the law in 96 CE and had the following inscription on the first three coins issued: 'calumnies removed of Jewish tax' (*fisci iudaici calumnia sublata*).

45. See M. Goodman, 'Nerva, the *Fiscus Judaicus* and Jewish Identity', *JRS* 79 (1989), pp. 40-44.

46. Judge, 'Judaism', p. 367.

47. Although traditionally placed in 49 CE, this date has been challenged in some recent work. Cf. G. Lüdemann, *Paul Apostle to the Gentiles: Studies in Chronology* (trans. F.S. Jones; Philadelphia: Fortress Press, 1984), pp. 164-71; and Slingerland, *Claudian Policymaking*, pp. 111-68, esp. 131-50.

48. See Judge, 'Judaism', pp. 361-62, citing *idem* and G.S.R. Thomas, 'The Origin of the Church at Rome: A New Solution', *Reformed Theological Review* 25 (1966), pp. 81-94; cf. Slingerland, *Claudian Policymaking*, pp. 151-68.

possible troublemakers.[49] Nevertheless, the result of the banishment was that the Jews were compelled to leave Rome, but there is no evidence that Christians were likewise forced to do so.

Conclusion

In conclusion, it is perhaps appropriate that we point to the future, and several ways in which this research could be further developed. In the first place, it seems that a logical next step would be a thorough-going analysis of modern positions on the split between Christianity and Judaism in terms of their use (and abuse) of the ancient evidence. In addition to this, it would be of interest to investigate the issues of ethnicity and theology in relation to the initial, intra-Christian, split, and, indeed, to develop the arguments which link this earlier internal split both to the later one between Christianity and Judaism, and to continuing controversies over theological (primarily christological) issues which flowed from this early split.

49. The tendency seems to be for biblical scholars to make the identification of Chrestus with Christ, but most classical scholars do not. Cf. Slingerland, *Claudian Policymaking*, pp. 151-68, for a detailed literary analysis.

WISDOM CHRISTOLOGY AND THE PARTINGS OF THE WAYS BETWEEN JUDAISM AND CHRISTIANITY

Crispin H.T. Fletcher-Louis

Introduction

The early Christian belief in Jesus' divinity is universally reckoned to have played a significant part in the partings of the ways between Judaism and Christianity. The varied theological expression of Jesus as somehow a unique manifestation of divinity and the giving of praise to his risen self, it is judged, marks a radical separation of Christianity from its parent faith. There are many issues in the study of Christology that require consideration in the pursuit of a precise understanding of the process and shape of that separation. I wish here to discuss, briefly, one of these.

It is widely held that Jewish Wisdom theology was a major stimulation towards, and resource for, the articulation of a Christology in which Jesus Messiah is given a divinity of cosmic and pre-existent scope. As far back as the book of Proverbs, as well as a rich tradition of late and post-biblical Jewish texts, Wisdom is personified as a pre-existent being who has been with God since creation. It is well known that, within the Gospels, particularly Matthew (11.19, 27-30) and John (1.1-18), Jesus is not merely a sage and purveyor of new wisdom, but is identified with Wisdom as her embodiment (see also Q 10.22; Lk. 13.31-34; 21.15 [cf. 11.49]). The extent and function of this Wisdom Christology is debated, but none denies its presence. Similarly, there are explicit statements in Pauline texts identifying Christ with Wisdom (1 Cor. 1.24), and in others a highly developed Christology is evidently expressed in language previously used of Wisdom (1 Cor. 8.5-6; Col. 1.15-20). That this form of Christology was widespread is clear from its presence in the opening verses of Hebrews (1.2-3) and possible influence upon sundry other passages.[1]

---

1. E.g. 1 Cor. 10.1-4; Rom. 10.6-10; Mt. 23.34 (par. Lk. 11.49); 1 Tim. 3.16.

The passages are widely discussed, and it is not my purpose to treat them here in detail. The fashion for seeing their background in gnostic speculation has now, rightly, passed. It is generally agreed that it is those Jewish passages where Wisdom is personified as a distinct individual that lie behind the New Testament texts. There is disagreement as to whether or not this personification is *merely* a literary one, with no intention of any high metaphysical claim to Wisdom's independence as a member of the heavenly world. It has been widely held that Wisdom in these texts is in fact a distinct hypostasis: meaning that we should take the personification literally and regard Wisdom as an independent entity or person, rather like an angel, with whom Jesus is then identified, while others, more recently, have questioned the usefulness of hypostasis terminology.

While there is this difference of opinion, there is universal *agreement* that within pre-Christian Judaism, Wisdom is *not* a goddess in her own right. She does not receive her own cult, as did the ancient Near Eastern goddess Ishtar-Astarte, the Egyptian Isis and Maat or, perhaps, the pre-exilic Israelite goddess Asherah. Neither, it is thought, is there any pre-Christian identification of Wisdom with a particular human individual. Various historical, pre-historical and eschatological figures are peculiarly endowed with Wisdom or act as her agents,[2] but the unequivocal identification which expresses an incarnational pattern of relationships is not present before Paul, the Gospel tradition and Hebrews. While this view may be taken positively to mean that Wisdom Christology is a significant theological achievement, it also means, of course, that it is unlikely to have been early. In his thorough survey of the genesis of early Christology, J.D.G. Dunn places a particular emphasis on the role of Wisdom in facilitating the movement towards a fully developed incarnational Christology.[3] Yet at the same time, he sees the identification of Wisdom with Jesus Christ as the culmination of a long process of theological and literary reflection upon the Gospel tradition. If there is a large conceptual gulf between a Jewish personified Wisdom and a Christian Wisdom embodied in Jesus of Nazareth, then it is also

---

2. For Adam and Wisdom, see Ezek. 28.12-13; *2 En.* 30.12. For the (Israelite) king and Wisdom, see, e.g., 1 Kgs 3.28; Isa. 11.2; 2 Sam. 14.20: the king 'has wisdom like the wisdom of the angel of God'; Prov. 1.10; 10.1; 25.1; Ezek. 28.12.

3. J.D.G. Dunn, *Christology in the Making: A New Testament Inquiry into the Origins of the Doctrine of Incarnation* (London: SCM Press, 1980), esp. pp. 163-268.

unlikely that such a gulf is going to have been crossed early in the development of Christian theology. Neither is it obvious what *theological* or other kind of rationale would motivate a Jewish Christian to have identified her saviour with a figure whose identity is strongly cosmogonic and cosmological.

While this has been the state of the question for some time, a fresh consideration of the relationship between the Jewish and the Christian Wisdom material is now required, given that recent work on Sirach has drawn attention to the equation of Wisdom with the high priest in his cultic office. New Testament scholarship has long been attentive to the fact that, in Sirach, Wisdom is identified with the Torah. This is, indeed, a particular feature of Sirach's contribution to the Wisdom tradition (see, esp., 24.23), and one which is significant given that, in at least one New Testament passage, Torah and Wisdom appear in close christological company (Mt. 11.25-30). More recent Sirach scholarship has sharpened up its understanding of the precise form in which Wisdom is identified with Torah in this work. Sirach, it is now clear, is a thoroughly priestly author for whom Wisdom is located not simply in Torah as written text, but in Torah actualized in the Jerusalem Temple cult and priesthood.[4] This Temple and priesthood focus comes to clearest expression in ch. 24's hymn to Wisdom, and in the climactic movement of both the whole book, and also the hymn in praise of the fathers (chs. 44–50)—in ch. 50's hymn in praise of the high priest Simon ben Onias. Discussion of Wisdom's identity and Sirach's role in the formation of early Christology has focused almost exclusively on the first of these two texts—ch. 24. However, chs. 24 and 50 are to be

---

4.   See L.G. Perdue, *Wisdom and Cult* (Missoula, MT: Scholars Press, 1977), pp. 188-211; H. Stadelmann, *Ben Sira als Schriftgelehrter: Eine Untersuchung zum Berufsbild des vor-makkabäischen Sofer unter Berücksichtigung seines Verhältnisses zu Priester-, Propheten- und Weisheitslehrertum* (WUNT, 2.6; Tübingen: J.C.B. Mohr [Paul Siebeck], 1980); S.M. Olyan, 'Ben Sira's Relationship to the Priesthood', *HTR* 80 (1987), pp. 261-86; C.T.R. Hayward, 'Sacrifice and World Order: Some Observations on Ben Sira's Attitude to the Temple Service', in S.W. Sykes (ed.), *Sacrifice and Redemption: Durham Essays in Theology* (Cambridge: Cambridge University Press, 1991), pp. 22-34; *idem*, *The Jewish Temple: A Non-Biblical Sourcebook* (London: Routledge, 1996), pp. 38-84; B.G. Wright, '"Fear the Lord and Honor the Priest": Ben Sira as Defender of the Jerusalem Priesthood', in P.C. Beentjes (ed.), *The Book of Ben Sira in Modern Research: Proceedings of the First International Ben Sira Conference 28–31 July 1996 Soesterberg, Netherlands* (Berlin: W. de Gruyter, 1997), pp. 189-222.

read in the light of one another, and the characterization of Wisdom in the first is mirrored by that of Simon in the second. Robert Hayward has recently highlighted the way that the vegetative symbolism used to describe Wisdom in Sir. 24.11-17 is used also of Simon in 50.8-12. The relationship can be laid out as follows:[5]

	Sirach 24		*Sirach 50*
vv. 8-11	Tabernacle image		
v. 10	'In the holy tent I ministered before him'	v. 5	Simon comes out of the sanctuary
v. 12	'I took root in an honoured people'	v. 8c	[Simon] 'like a green shoot'
v. 13a	'I grew tall like a *cedar in Lebanon*'	v. 8c	[Simon] 'like a green shoot *on Lebanon*'.
		v. 12c	[Simon] 'like a young *cedar on Lebanon*'
v. 13b	'like a *cypress* on the heights of Hermon'	v. 10b	[Simon] 'like a *cypress* towering in the clouds'
v. 13b	'I grew tall like a palm tree in Engedi'	v. 12c	(LXX) [the priests] are 'trunks of palm trees'
v. 14b	'like *rose bushes* in Jericho'	v. 8a	[Simon] 'like flower of *roses* in the days of new moon'
v. 14c	'like a fair *olive tree* in the field'	v. 10a	[Simon] 'like an *olive tree* laden with fruit'
v. 14c	'like a plane tree *beside water*'	v. 8b	[Simon] 'like lilies *beside a spring of water*'
v. 15	'like galbanum, onycha, and stacte, and like the odour of incense in the tent'	v. 9	'like fire and incense in the censer'

Now there is perhaps a temptation to take this as simply a poetic parallelism with no propositional claim that Wisdom is to be identified with Simon: Simon's beauty is merely comparable to that of Wisdom herself. However, Hayward has concluded that in some way Simon in his cultic office *embodies* divine Wisdom.[6] This is so because through-

---

5. Following Hayward, 'Sacrifice', p. 24, who provides relevant textual apparatus. See also his 'The New Jerusalem in the Wisdom of Jesus ben Sira', *SJOT* 6 (1992), pp. 123-38, esp. p. 127.

6. Hayward, 'Sacrifice', p. 23: 'the high priest and his colleagues, as they carry out the sacrificial service, perfectly embody that Wisdom which elsewhere he identifies with Torah'; *idem*, *Jewish Temple*, p. 52: 'Vested for service, Simon embodies

out these two chapters there are indications that the sanctuary and its liturgy is a reflection and actualization of the primaeval order which is properly Wisdom's. So, for example, in ch. 24, Wisdom takes up her home in Tabernacle and Temple (24.7-11) and brings with her the bounty of Eden and her life-giving waters (24.24-29).[7]

Hayward's discussion of this material throws open the question of the origins of the identification of Jesus Christ with Wisdom and the assumption that there is no precedent for such a hermeneutic in pre-Christian Judaism.

There are a couple of reasons why we can be sure that, as Hayward asserts, the high priest is the unique and perfect embodiment of Wisdom—her 'incarnation'—in Sirach 50. In the first place, such a highly exalted priestly anthropology is consistent with the identification of Simon with the anthropomorphic glory of God revealed to Ezekiel in his call vision (Ezek. 1.26-28). In Sirach Simon is

> like the rainbow which appears in the cloud (50.7b)
>
> וכקשת נראתה בענן (Geniza MS B)
>
> (cf. LXX καὶ ὡς τόξον φωτίζον ἐν νεφέλαις δόξης).

This is an explicit reference to the 'likeness of the Glory of the LORD' in Ezek. 1.28, who is also

> like the bow in a cloud on a rainy day
>
> MT כמראה הקשת אשר יהיה בענן ביום הגשם
>
> LXX ὡς ὅρασις τόξου ὅταν ᾖ ἐν τῇ νεφέλῃ ἐν ἡμέρᾳ ὑετοῦ.[8]

Secondly, if Wisdom has incarnated herself in the high priest, then this explains an otherwise puzzling statement in 24.10. There Wisdom says 'In the holy tent I ministered before him' (i.e. the Creator God). The

---

also something of that Wisdom which ben Sira identifies with Torah (24:23), the divine order undergirding all things' (cf. p. 78).

7.   For the identification between Wisdom and high priestly garb see also 6.29-31 and the discussion in Stadelmann, *Ben Sira als Schriftgelehrter*, pp. 50-51.

8.   This intertextuality is anticipated in the previous chapter by specific reference to Ezekiel's vision of the Glory (ὅρασιν δόξης) in 49.8. The deliberate evocation of Ezek. 1.28 is clear when one compares the description of the rainbow in the fourfold description of sun, moon, stars and rainbow in 43.1-12: while the focus on these four elements is parallel to 50.6-7, in the earlier passage the text makes nothing of the intertextuality with the Ezekiel verse.

language is overtly priestly. How can Wisdom have ministered as a priest in God's wilderness sanctuary? If Aaron and his sons embody Wisdom, then clearly she did so in the form of the human priesthood.

If this assessment of Wisdom and priesthood in Sirach is anywhere near the mark, it raises many other questions. In particular, since in Sir. 24.3-6 Wisdom is closely related to God in his creative action, perhaps as creatrix herself, does this mean also that the high priest is thought of as co-creator with God? Wisdom is both pre-existent and eternal for Sirach (24.9: 'Before the ages, in the beginning, he created me, and for all the ages I shall not cease to be'). Can this also be said of the high priest? With a view to the development of early Christology, can we be more precise about the way in which Wisdom is identified with the high priest, how this might have laid the foundations for the identification with Jesus Christ and whether, in fact, there are important points of difference between a sapiential high priesthood and Wisdom Christology?

First steps towards a proper appraisal of these issues can be made through an overview of the reworking of existing creation and Temple theologies in both chs. 24 and 50. In his discussion Hayward has pointed to the way in which the sacrificial liturgy in ch. 50 seems to recapitulate and bring creation to completion. This is implicit in the Edenic imagery of ch. 24: if Wisdom is a fountain of Edenic life in Jerusalem and her sanctuary, then, by the same token, the human actors within the Israelite cult are recreating Eden's fecundity. The priesthood's role as cosmogonic agent is most openly expressed in the grandson's Greek translation of Sirach's original work. In 50.19, the sacrificial offering is brought to its close with the people praying for mercy

> Until the order of the LORD was completed [ἕως συντελεσθῇ κόσμος κυρίου], and they had perfectly completed His service.

In the Greek, the word used for the liturgical order of the sacrifice (κόσμος) is that which also refers to the universe as a whole. This implies that the offering is related to 'the stability and order of the universe, the sacrifice in the Temple serving to establish to perfection God's order for the world'.[9] As Hayward points out, the Greek translator and his early readers would have heard here a clear allusion to the Greek version of the Priestly creation account which ends in Gen. 2.2 with the words: 'And the heavens and the earth were completed

9.   Hayward, *Jewish Temple*, p. 79.

[συνετελέσθησαν], and all their order [κόσμος]'.[10] Given that the high priest embodies Wisdom who is herself determinative of the *ordering* of the works of God's creation (24.3-6; cf. 42.21, 'The great works of His Wisdom he set in order [ἐκόσμησε]', and 16.27), Hayward concludes that, 'It is highly likely therefore that the high priest's completion of the order, *kosmos*, of the daily sacrifice, referred to in 50:19, belongs to the same sort of continuum as God's ordering of the works of creation'.[11] That is to say: here the high priest not only embodies Wisdom, he also acts as co-creator in as much as the temple service is itself symmetrical with God's original creative action. Is this an undeveloped hint of a Wisdom theology which anticipates the early Christian claim that Christ acts as co-creator and sustainer of the universe? Closer examination of Sirach 24 and 50 reveals that Hayward has brought to light what is in fact a sustained reflection on the creation and cult in which the high priest incarnates Wisdom and her cosmogonic action.

Sirach 24 and 50 and the Priestly Theology of Creation and Temple

A prerequisite for a full appreciation of the complex literary and theological intention of these chapters is a knowledge of the Priestly author's intratextuality in his account of creation in Genesis 1 and God's instructions to Moses for the building of the Tabernacle in Exodus 25–31 and 35–40. Recent discussion of this material has shown that they are closely related because the Tabernacle is a microcosm of the universe and the creation narrative is a thoroughly liturgical text.[12] In particular the seven days of creation in Genesis 1 are paired with God's seven speeches to Moses in Exodus 25–31. Each speech begins 'The LORD spoke to Moses' (Exod. 25.1; 30.11, 16, 22, 34; 31.11, 12) and introduces material which corresponds to the relevant day of creation. Most transparently, in the third speech (30.16-21) there is commanded

10. Hayward, *Jewish Temple*, p. 79.
11. Hayward, *Jewish Temple*, p. 80.
12. See J. Blenkinsopp, 'The Structure of P', *CBQ* 38 (1976), pp. 275-92; P.J. Kearney, 'Creation and Liturgy: The P Redaction of Exodus 25–40', *ZAW* 89 (1977), pp. 375-87; M. Weinfeld, 'Sabbath, Temple and the Enthronement of the Lord: The Problem of the *Sitz-im-Leben* of Gen. 1:1–2:3', in A. Caquot and M. Delcor (eds.), *Mélanges bibliques et orientaux en l'honneur de M. Henri Cazelles* (AOAT, 212; Neukirchen–Vluyn: Neukirchener Verlag, 1981), pp. 501-11.

the construction of the bronze laver. In the Solomonic Temple this is called simply the 'sea' and in P it matches the creation of the sea on the third day of creation in Gen. 1.9-11. Similarly, the seventh speech (31.12-17) stresses the importance of the Sabbath for Israel, just as Gen. 2.2-3 tells us how God rested on the seventh day. There is insufficient space here for a full exploration of the correspondences between the other parts, but it is enough, in interpreting Sirach 24 and 50, to know that Genesis 1 and Exodus 25–31 are two panels of a whole.[13]

Creation (Gen. 1.1–2.2)	Tabernacle (Exodus 25–31)
Day 1	*Speech 1* (Exod. 25.1–30.10)
heavens and the earth	tabernacle structure (= heavens and earth)
creation of light: evening and morning	tending of menorah, tamid sacrifice and incense offering (evening and morning) (27.20-21; 30.1-9)
Day 2	*Speech 2* (Exod. 30.11-16)
separation of upper and lower waters	(census and half shekel)
Day 3	*Speech 3* (Exod. 30.17-21)
separation of dry land and sea (1.9-10) vegetation (1.11-12)	bronze laver (the 'sea')
Day 4	*Speech 4* (Exod. 30.22-33)
sun, moon and stars	sacred anointing oil: myrrh, calamus, cinnamon, cassia
	anointing of cultic appurtenances and priests
Day 5	*Speech 5* (Exod. 30.34-38)
living creatures in the upper and lower realms	sacred incense: stacte, onycha, galbanum, frankincense
Day 6	*Speech 6* (Exod. 31.1-11)
land creatures and humankind (God's image)	Bezalel filled with God's spirit
Day 7	*Speech 7* (Exod. 31.12-17)
Sabbath	Sabbath

Hartmut Gese has briefly suggested that Sir. 24.3-6 follows the order of the first three days of creation as described in Genesis 1: the pre-creation chaos over which hovers God's primaeval spirit (Gen. 1.2; cf. Sir. 24.3); the creation of the 'intellectual light' (Gen. 1.3-5; cf. Sir. 24.4); the 'delimiting of the cosmos by the firmament and the abyss' (Gen. 1.6-8; cf. Sir. 24.5) and the ordering of land and sea (Gen. 1.9-10;

13. See Kearney, 'Creation', and Weinfeld, 'Sabbath', for further discussion.

cf. Sir. 24.6).[14] Though his comments have largely gone ignored, they can be developed considerably and, indeed, Sir. 24.3-22 as a whole emerges as a complex reflection upon Genesis 1 and Exodus 25–31.

Commentators universally recognize that in Sir. 24.3 there is an allusion to the creation by the word of God in Gen. 1.3 (cf. 1.6, 11, 14, etc.) and the spirit moving over the primaeval waters in Gen. 1.2.[15] In 24.4b Wisdom dwells in a pillar of cloud, which means she is identified with the cloud of fire which lights up the people's way in the wilderness (Exod. 13.21-22, etc.). Not only does this cloud provide light, its changing appearance also demarcates the boundary between day and night (Exod. 13.21-22; 40.38; Num. 14.14; Deut. 1.33; Neh. 9.12, 16, 19; Isa. 4.5), in a way parallel to the appearance of light on the first day of creation according to Genesis. As Gese notes, in the next verse Wisdom is located in the 'vault of heaven' and the 'depths of the abyss', the two upper and lower extremities created on day 2 according to Gen. 1.6-8.[16] In Sir. 24.6a Wisdom rules 'over the waves of the *sea*, over all the *earth*'. In the biblical mindset such ruling connotes demarcation of spheres of existence, which is precisely God's purpose in gathering together the waters to create the sea and dry land on the fourth day of creation (Gen. 1.9-10).[17]

The second act of creation on the third day—the creation of 'vegetation: plants yielding seed of every kind and trees of every kind bearing fruit with seed in it'—is the inspiration for the vegetative symbolism in

14. H. Gese, *Essays in Biblical Theology* (trans. K. Crim; Minneapolis: Augsburg, 1981), p. 196. Cf. *idem*, 'Wisdom, Son of Man, and the Origins of Christology: The Consistent Development of Biblical Theology', *HBT* 3 (1981), pp. 23-57 (32-33).

15. See, in particular, G.T. Sheppard, *Wisdom as a Hermeneutical Construct: A Study in the Sapientializing of the Old Testament* (BZAW, 151; Berlin: W. de Gruyter, 1980), pp. 22-27.

16. Gese, *Essays in Biblical Theology*, p. 196.

17. The creation of earth and sea is glossed with Wisdom's rule over 'every people and nation'. This is entirely appropriate given that the *Chaoskampf*, which lies behind Gen. 1.9-10 (cf. Ps. 104.7-9; Jer. 5.22; Job 38.8 and J. Day, *God's Conflict with the Dragon and the Sea: Echoes of a Canaanite Myth in the Old Testament* [University of Cambridge Oriental Publications, 35; Cambridge: Cambridge University Press, 1985], pp. 49-61), is regularly bound up with God's rule over not just creation, but also history and human communities (see, e.g., Isa. 17.12-14; 30.7; 51.9-11; Hab. 3.8-10, 15; Jer. 51.34; Ps. 87.4; Ezek. 29.3-5; 32.2-8; Dan. 7.2-14 and Day, *God's Conflict*, pp. 88-139, 151-78).

Sir. 24.12-17. However, before the author of the hymn comes to that fourth act of creation he signals that he is reading Genesis with an eye to Israel's cult, that is, to Exodus 25–40. In 24.7-11, Wisdom searches for a place of rest. She searches for what God achieved on the seventh day of creation and she finds it in Israel and the nation's two sanctuaries—one in the wilderness and one in Zion. Half-way through the sequence of creation the author flags up that he is about to switch to the Israelite cult as the sphere of God's creation which will ultimately give it completion and Wisdom her rest.

And so in what follows we are not told directly of the creation of sun, moon, stars and the living creatures of the fourth through sixth days. Instead, because our author knows very well the intratextuality between Genesis 1 and Exodus 25–31, he gives us in v. 15 those elements in the tabernacle order which correspond to the fourth and fifth days of creation: first he compares Wisdom's growth to the cinnamon, choice myrrh and fragrance of Israel's sacred incense (Sir. 24.15a-b par. Exod. 30.23: the fourth speech to Moses), and then to galbanum, onycha, stacte and frankincense of the sacred oil (Sir. 24.15c-d par. Exod. 30.34: the fifth speech to Moses). Finally the hymn climaxes with an invitation to Wisdom's banquet (24.19-22), which is reminiscent of God's abundant provision of food for humanity in Gen. 1.28-30. The final verse looks forward to the Edenic existence of Adam and Eve in Genesis 2–3 (which is developed in the rest of ch. 24). Wisdom proclaims: 'Whoever obeys me will not be put to shame, and those who work with me will not sin' (Sir. 24.22). In a chapter so redolent with themes from Genesis 1–3 this must be an allusion to the curse on humanity's labour on their exit from the garden (Gen. 3.19) and the first couple's freedom from shame before their temptation and fall (Gen. 2.25).[18] The hymn clearly has at its zenith the pre-lapsarian Adam and Eve, though it is not until Sirach 50 that the image of God of Genesis 1 is given full expression.

Clearly, then, Sirach has a detailed knowledge of the Priestly account of creation and tabernacle building and their cosmological interpenetration. Before turning to Sirach 50, where my attention ultimately lies, I must pause at this juncture to point out that, while commentators have

---

18. So rightly M. Barker, *The Great Angel: A Study of Israel's Second God* (London: SPCK, 1992), p. 58.

been unsure whether or not in this passage Wisdom is, in fact, co-creator with God, that cannot now be doubted: Wisdom's *curriculum vitae* is that of the creator God himself as prescribed by Genesis 1.

In Sirach 50, Wisdom has entered human history in high-priestly guise and her creative activity in accordance with Genesis 1 and Exodus 25–31 is recapitulated in the euergetism and cultic ministration of Simon ben Onias. In 50.1 Simon is responsible for repairing and fortifying God's house: a general statement which signals his care for the cosmos as a whole as it is ritually actualized in the temple-as-microcosm. In v. 2, he lays 'foundations for the high double walls, the high retaining walls for the temple enclosure'. The attention to foundations and high walls readily corresponds to the 'vault of heaven and...depths of the abyss' of 24.3 on the one hand and, on the other, the dome which separates the upper from the lower waters in Gen. 1.6-8. Next we are told that Simon builds 'a water cistern...a reservoir like the sea in circumference' (50.3), which obviously recalls the three passages Sir. 24.6a, Gen. 1.9-10 and Exod. 30.17-21. (Sirach could not have Simon making the bronze laver because there was already one of those, but, in any case, it was the symbolism of Simon's actions that concerns our author.)

Next Simon 'considered how to save his people from ruin, and fortified the city against siege' (50.4). The verse not only is a historical reference to Simon's astute political manoeuvres during the Seleucid–Ptolemaic conflict at the turn of the second century and the architectural improvements to the Temple complex after the triumph of Antiochus III, whom Simon had supported against the Ptolemies,[19] but it also corresponds to 24.6a where Wisdom 'held sway over every people and nation'.

These four verses all deal not with Simon the minister within the cult, but with Simon the leader on the political and religious stage. Verse 5 signals a change in perspective and what follows concerns his priestly activity within the sanctuary. In his exit from the 'house of the curtain' in vv. 6-7, Sirach's hero advances creation to its fourth day: he is 'like the morning star...the full moon...[and] the sun'. In his discussion of the intratextuality between creation and Tabernacle, Moshe Weinfeld has noted how important this verse is for seeing the priesthood—who are the focus of the fourth speech to Moses in Exod. 30.30—as symbols

---

19. See Josephus, *Ant.* 12.129-44.

of the heavenly bodies within the Temple-as-microcosm mindset.[20] In vv. 8-12, as we have seen, Simon actualizes the fecundity of Wisdom already described in 24.11-17. There is no specific mention of the anointing oil, which corresponded in ch 24 to the fourth day of creation, since we have now had explicit reference to the sun, moon and stars. However, the reference to the sacred incense of the fifth speech to Moses (Exod. 30.34-38) is retained, thereby demonstrating that Simon's recapitulation of creation includes the fifth day.

In the rest of the hymn in praise of Simon, there is described his offering of the sacrificial portions and his pouring the cup of the blood of the grape (vv. 12-15) followed by the people's response. Here, then, Simon makes an offering from the clean kinds of living creatures created on the sixth day of creation. Humanity's dominion over 'every living thing that moves upon the earth' (Gen. 1.28) is expressed in the offering up of life to its creator. This is probably the banquet to which all were invited by Wisdom in 24.19-22: the banquet which is sweeter than honey (cf. Lev. 2.11). Outside the sanctuary all this preparation of food and human activity would be regarded as work and thus liable to infringe the sabbath. However, within the sanctuary, which recreates the pre-lapsarian Eden, 'those who work in [Wisdom] will not sin' (24.22b).[21]

It should be clear by now that throughout this description of Simon's officiation he has acted as God's image.[22] He is identified with God's *kavod* (v. 7b) and his activity on both the wider political and more narrowly cultic stage is an actualization of both that of God himself in creation and Wisdom, God's co-creator. The identification of the high priest with Wisdom and the visible image of God makes sense within the text's understanding of the liturgical drama: the high priest plays the lead role in the re-enactment of creation which is the cult's defining dramatic performance. It is hardly surprising that when the author's grandson came to translate the Hebrew into Greek, he drew on the Greek translation of Gen. 2.2 in his version of Simon's completion of the liturgy (50.19b-c). With the high priest's completion of the sacrifice, creation is, likewise, completed.

---

20. Weinfeld, 'Sabbath', p. 507. He compares this with 1QSb 4.25 where the angelomorphic priest is the 'great luminary [מאור גדול]', i.e. the sun.

21. Cf. *Jub.* 50.10-11 and Mt. 12.5.

22. See Hayward, *Jewish Temple*, pp. 44-46 for Simon as the new Adam.

The Cultic Contours of New Testament Wisdom Christology

That the early Christian identification of Jesus with Wisdom is derived, in part, from the Jewish identification of the high priest with Wisdom is confirmed by the extent to which Wisdom Christology is bound up with the language of the cult in New Testament texts. A cursory glance at some of the Wisdom Christology texts makes this clear.

One of the most fully developed christological statements in the New Testament which is generally reckoned to owe its inspiration to Jewish Wisdom speculation is the hymn in Col. 1.15-20. Everything that is said about Christ in this hymn, apart perhaps from the cruciform and ecclesiological shape of its latter half, can be derived from Wisdom ideas in general and the cultic Wisdom theology we have laid out, in particular. In Sirach 50, Simon is 'the image of the invisible God': in so far as Simon plays the role of cosmogonic agent within the drama of the cultic microcosm it could be said that 'in Simon was created everything in heaven and on earth' (cf. Col. 1.16). In that Simon *precedes* the sequence of creation he achieves in Sirach 50 he may be said to be 'before all' (cf. v. 17) just as Wisdom, with whom he is identified, is the first work of God's creation (Prov. 8.22-23; Sir. 24.3, 9).

Commentators have struggled to find an explicit precedent for Christ as the sustaining nexus of creation as described in v. 17 ('in him all things hold together'). This is foreshadowed in pre-Christian logos speculation (e.g. Philo, *Rer. Div. Her.* 188; *Fug.* 112; *Plant.* 8; cf. Sir. 43.26 [Greek]), but not, it has seemed, in the language of Wisdom itself (though cf. Wis. 1.7). Because the cultic drama described in Sirach 50 is designed to 'recreate' the universe and guarantee its stability, it would also be true to say that 'in the high priest everything is held together'. Because Simon himself carries the visible image of creation (esp. vv. 5-12), and the high priestly garments were thought to represent the whole cosmos (Wis. 18.24; Philo, *Vit. Mos.* 2.117-26, 133-35, 143; Josephus, *Ant.* 3.180, 183-87) it can also be said that everything was created for him (cf. Col. 1.16 τὰ πάντα...εἰς αὐτὸν ἔκτισται). Because he is the embodiment of Wisdom, God's Glory *and* the whole cosmos finds its identity summed up in him, all the possible meanings of Col. 1.19's 'in him was pleased to dwell all the fullness [ἐν αὐτῷ εὐδόκησεν πᾶν τὸ πλήρωμα κατοικῆσαι]' may equally be said of Sirach's high priest. It is also true that Simon is the head of the body, the church (v. 18), so long as we mean by that ecclesial Israel (cf. esp.

Sir. 50.13, 20).[23] Though Simon does *not* make reconciliation through
his own blood on a cross, he is probably thought to bring reconciliation
to the cosmos (Col. 1.20) through the sacrificial blood of animals which
he offers (Sir. 50.12-15).

That the author of Colossians himself was aware of the overtly
sacrificial and cultic imagery of the language he has applied to Christ is
confirmed by the context which surrounds the setting of the hymn. For
a Jew to speak of 'redemption, the forgiveness of sins' (Col. 1.14) is to
call to mind a primary function of the Temple. In Col. 1.22, Christ
reconciles the readers of this letter through his death that he might act
as great high priest and 'present (them) holy and blameless and ir-
reproachable before him [παραστῆσαι ὑμᾶς ἁγίους καὶ ἀμώμους καὶ
ἀνεγκλήτους κατενώπιον αὐτοῦ]'. The language is overtly sacrificial.
Indeed, Jesus' own priestly ministry then becomes the model for Paul's:
he too suffers on behalf of (ὑπέρ) the body of Christ (1.24) in order that
he may 'present [παραστήσωμεν] every man perfect in Christ' (1.28),
just as any sacrificial lamb or goat is to be spotless and perfect. Ultimately, for this Christian author the Jewish cult and calendar is only a
'shadow' of that which it prefigures (2.16), but nonetheless it is that
cultic life which provides the prism through which his Christology is
refracted.

While commentators have offered various (competing) history-of-
religions backgrounds for the Colossians Christ hymn, they all ultimately derive from the theology and experience of the Jerusalem
Temple. Indeed, this is further consistent with the fact that it is otherwise reckoned that the Christology here is indebted specifically to
Genesis 1. Besides the reference to Gen. 1.26 in the 'image of God'
language of v. 15, N.T. Wright has recently shown how far the portrayal of Christ throughout this poem reflects different speculative
interpretative possibilities of the opening word of Genesis (בראשית).[24]

Turning to another text, we find a similar combination of Wisdom
and cultic theology in the Christology of Heb. 1.2-3. Hebrews 1.2c,
'through whom also he created the worlds', and 1.3a-b, 'He is the radiance [ἀπαύγασμα] of God's Glory and the exact imprint of God's very
being, and he sustains all things by his powerful word', are generally

23. For Israel as an ἐκκλησία see generally Deut. 4.10; 10.8; 23.10; 2 Chron.
23.10; Sir. 23.24; 24.2; 31.11; 39.10; 44.15; 46.7.
24. N.T. Wright, *The Climax of the Covenant: Christ and the Law in Pauline
Theology* (Edinburgh: T. & T. Clark, 1991), pp. 99-118.

reckoned to be an application of Wisdom speculation to Christ. The language of v. 2c recalls Wisdom as co-creator. Verse 3a perhaps relies on Wis. 7.26, where Wisdom is 'a radiance [ἀπαύγασμα] of eternal light, a spotless mirror of the working of God, and an image of his goodness'.[25]

In the remaining phrases of the proem and the main body of the homily, the author is preoccupied almost exclusively with a high priestly Christology. So, for example, the rest of 1.3 goes on to refer to Christ as the one who, having made a cleansing of sins, has sat down at the right hand of God. There is no real interest in Wisdom Christology in the rest of the letter, and commentators normally judge the Wisdom language in vv. 2c-3b to be a creative flurry, unrelated to the main burden of the homily, though perhaps echoing early Christian hymnody.

However, we can now see that, even if Wisdom is on stage, she is accompanied by the high priest from the very start of the performance. While the language of the Son as God's radiance in v. 3 may well echo Wis. 7.26, the fact that Christ is the radiance of *the Glory* points also to the equation of the high priest with the *kavod* in Sir. 50.7.[26] Similarly the creation through the Son (v. 2c) and the sustaining of the cosmos by his powerful word (v. 3b) evokes the ideology of the high priest as cosmogonic agent and liturgical recreator of the fabric of society and nature.

It is generally recognized that the Johannine prologue (1.1-18) has drawn upon Wisdom speculation.[27] Yet, that the author of this passage knew that Wisdom belonged to the cult and priesthood, and that

25. Cf. Philo, *Plant.* 18 on the logos.

26. For the language of 'radiance' used of the high priest see, e.g., *Ep. Arist.* 97: '...each stone pouring forth [ἀπαυγάζοντες] its own natural distinctive colour—quite indescribable'.

The normal secular meaning of χαρακτήρ is an impression on a signet ring, wax or a stamp seal (see H.W. Attridge, *The Epistle to the Hebrews: A Commentary on the Epistle to the Hebrews* [Hermeneia; Philadelphia: Fortress Press, 1989], pp. 43-44). Is there perhaps here an allusion to the language of the signet seal (חותם) used of the high priest's garments in Exod. 28.11, 21, 36; 39.6, 14, 30 and the sacral *Urmensch* in Ezek. 28.12?

27. See, in particular, Gese, *Essays in Biblical Theology*, pp. 190-22; J. Ashton, 'The Transformation of Wisdom: A Study of the Prologue of John's Gospel', *NTS* 32 (1986), pp. 161-86; and C.A. Evans, *Word and Glory: On the Exegetical and Theological Background of John's Prologue* (JSNTSup, 89; Sheffield: JSOT Press, 1993), pp. 83-145.

Genesis 1, upon which the opening stanza (vv. 1-5) relies so heavily, is a Temple text, is confirmed by the language of tabernacling in v. 14: 'the Word became flesh, and tabernacled [ἐσκήνωσεν] among us'. This is not simply a *verbal* echo of Sir. 24.8-10,[28] as commentators note, rather it is a *conceptual* recollection of a whole constellation of proto-incarnational themes within the Temple-Wisdom theology.[29] Not least among these themes is that of the priesthood as the source of light, which lies behind the language of Jn 1.4-5, 9.[30]

A fuller discussion of all those New Testament passages where Wisdom informs Christology would demonstrate the ubiquity of the assocation between Wisdom Christology and the Israelite cult. It can be no coincidence that a good many of those New Testament texts where a Wisdom Christology is developed are hymnic in character. While study of this hymnic form, and its implications for the tradition and conceptual history of each particular passage, has concentrated on possible settings in the life of the early church (baptism, Eucharist, and so on), we can now be fairly sure that the liturgical expression of the belief that Jesus is the embodiment of Wisdom will have grown out of the Jewish Temple cult, its worship experience and theology.

Conclusion

We have seen that, contrary to the general consensus, there *is* a precedent in pre-Christian Judaism for the identification of Wisdom with a particular human individual. In principle, the claim that Jesus Messiah

---

28. Sir. 24.8, 'he who created me rested my tent [σκηνήν] and said in Jacob make your dwelling [κατασκήνωσον]'; v. 10, 'In the holy tent [ἐν σκηνῇ ἁγίᾳ] I ministered before him'.

29. J. Fossum (*The Image of the Invisible God: Essays on the Influence of Jewish Mysticism on Early Christology* [NTOA, 30; Göttingen: Vandenhoeck & Ruprecht, 1995], pp. 109-33) is right to challenge the consensus that it is Wisdom speculation which provides the history-of-religions context for the Johannine prologue. However, his discussion of 'onomanology' is also a subsidiary element within the Temple mythology. God has chosen the Jerusalem cult as the locus of his Name—it is the high priest who wears the divine Name (cf., e.g., Sir. 50.20) and has the privilege of its utterance.

30. For the priesthood as the source of light see, e.g., Deut. 33.10 (LXX and Qumran MSS); Zech. 3.9; Sir. 50.5-7; *Ep. Arist.* 97; *T. Levi* 14.3; *T. Naph.* 5.1-4; *2 En.* 69.10; *3 En. 12*; 1QSb 4.27; 1Q29 and 4Q376; 4QpIsa[d] 5; 4QShirShabb[f] 23.2.9; Josephus, *Ant.* 3.184-87, 216-17.

was divine Wisdom would not have been a radically new claim for his earliest followers. Neither would it have been as odd as might be supposed for such Jewish believers to have claimed that, as Wisdom, Jesus was an agent of creation, the means by which creation has been and is sustained, and the ultimate goal of creation. That kind of thinking emerges not from abstract philosophical speculation, but from Israel's daily cultic life. So, too, to have Jesus be the head of the body, the Church, in a passage full of such Wisdom thinking is little more than an ecclesiological narrowing of the priestly ideology of high priest as embodiment of the people of God. (In Sirach 44–50, Simon stands at the apex of a long line of righteous heroes and is the 'pride of his people' [50.1], wearing, of course, their tribal names on his breastplate.)

There is, however, a radicalization of the tradition in a number of respects. First, while the anthropology implicit in the identification of Jesus with Wisdom would not in itself have been a problem, that Jesus of Nazareth was not the high priest would have. Furthermore, there is a sharp contrast between the identification of the high priest *in his cultic office* and Wisdom, on the one hand, and the identification of Jesus of Nazareth—with no real reference to any such stereotyped office—and Wisdom, on the other. Not Jesus a high priest in his sacred regalia, which only those of priestly lineage could have worn, but Jesus of Nazareth who lived *this particular life* issuing in a very particular kind of death—it is this *person*, early Christians claimed, who embodies Wisdom in all her fullness. Where, for example, the Wisdom hymn in Col. 1.15-20 has Jesus be the one who has made 'reconciliation [and] peace through the blood of his cross' (Col. 1.20), the particularity of *Jesus* as Wisdom comes starkly into focus. Jesus' atoning self-sacrifice should be seen as the counterpart to the Temple's animal sacrifice which is the climax of Simon ben Onias's act of cultic recreation. But, nevertheless, this is a qualitatively new sacrifice and ultimately a cause of the partings of the ways between Judaism and Christianity. It was this dimension of Christology, not the belief that a human being could embody and represent the One Creator God—in other words, not theological anthropology in purely abstract terms—which represented a significant shift in theological thinking for Jesus' Jewish disciples.

RESURRECTION IN JEWISH-CHRISTIAN APOCRYPHAL GOSPELS AND EARLY CHRISTIAN ART

Brook W.R. Pearson and Felicity Harley

1. *Introduction*

The New Testament records the events surrounding Jesus' resurrection from the dead in each of the four Gospels, with more truncated versions elsewhere (e.g. 'he was buried...he was raised on the third day in accordance with the scriptures...' [1 Cor. 15.4])[1]. However, not even the longer Gospel accounts tell us much about the actual resurrection event. Instead, we are told about the after-effects: for instance, in the Markan version of the resurrection (Mk 16.1-8), closely followed by Luke (23.56–24.11), the women who come to the tomb find Jesus already missing, and then speak with the angel(s) who, we might assume, took some part in the resurrection event itself, although neither Mark nor Luke actually spells this out for us. In fact, in Luke, it may very well be that his two angels (compared to Mark's one seated angel or 'young man') appear *after* the fact of the women's arrival.[2]

As has long been noticed, Matthew is much more detailed about the whole process. He is the only evangelist to include the story about the

---

1.   Unless otherwise noted, all biblical quotations are from the RSV.

2.   There is some disagreement over the interpretation of ἐπέστησαν in this verse. For discussion, see J.P Louw and E.A. Nida, *Greek–English Lexicon of the New Testament Based on Semantic Domains* (2 vols.; New York: United Bible Societies, 2nd edn, 1989), II, pp. 216, 725, domains 17.5 and 85.13, who include the interpretations, 'to be in proximity to something—"to be near, to be at, to be nearby"', and 'to stand at a particular place, often with the implication of suddenness—"to stand by, to stand at"', respectively. They give Lk. 4.39 as an example of the latter, and Mk 14.7, 2 Tim. 4.17 and Acts 22.20 as support for the former. Either way, Luke still gives no indication that these 'men' were involved in the resurrection.

guard placed on the tomb with the complicity of the Pharisees and Pilate (27.62-66), foreshadowing Matthew's other additional material regarding the post-resurrection bribery of the guards, who are paid to say that the disciples had come in the night and stolen the body away (28.11-15). However, although Matthew's 'angel of the Lord' (28.2) is clearly involved in the opening of the tomb ('an angel of the Lord descended from heaven and came and rolled back the stone and sat upon it' [28.2]), the following discourse is clear in its message that *the resurrection had already taken place*: ' "Do not be afraid; for I know that you seek Jesus who was crucified. He is not here; for he has risen, as he said"' (28.5-6). The implications of this sequence for the discussion of the nature of Jesus' post-resurrection body reflect the more detailed explanations offered in Lk. 24.36-43:

> As they were saying this, Jesus himself stood among them. But they were startled and frightened, and supposed that they saw a spirit. And he said to them, 'Why are you troubled, and why do questionings rise in your hearts? See my hands and my feet, that it is I myself; handle me, and see; for a spirit has not flesh and bones as you see that I have.' And while they still disbelieved for joy, and wondered, he said to them, 'Have you anything to eat?' They gave him a piece of broiled fish, and he took it and ate before them.

This is mirrored and expanded upon by John's Gospel,[3] which contains a number of such episodes in ch. 20, beginning with the oddly detailed (almost cinematic) passage where Peter and 'the other disciple' come running to the tomb only to find it empty, except for the linen burial clothes (the stone simply having been found by Mary Magdalene in 20.1 already rolled back). The 'other disciple' will not enter the tomb. However, when Peter arrives, he enters to find the 'napkin, which had been on his head, not lying with the linen cloths but rolled up in a place by itself' (20.7). This bit of detail seems to suggest that Jesus' resurrection, far from Matthew's seemingly spiritual event (the stone only being rolled back so that the women can enter and see the empty tomb), is an entirely physical one. Although we do not know who is

---

3.   By suggesting that there are similarities between John's Gospel and the Synoptics, we are in no way making a judgment on the relationship between John and the other three Gospels. In this instance, we are simply suggesting that this element is found in both traditions. Whether this is the result of a literary dependence is another question.

responsible for the rolling back of the stone in John, the state of Jesus' folded burial clothes gives us an impression of a man rising not spectacularly, walking through stones amid earthquakes and thunder (as one imagines from Matthew's account), but more like one who was rising from sleep. John clearly does not wish, in his emphasis on the physicality of the resurrection, to sacrifice the spiritual nature of the risen Jesus: when Mary sees him (thinking he is a gardener) outside the tomb, Jesus warns her not to 'hold [him], for [he has] not yet ascended to the Father' (20.17). Following this event, we have the unique Johannine giving of the Spirit, mission and control of forgiveness (20.21-23), which, in combination with the events in ch. 21, seems to reflect those events described in Lk. 24.36-43. In addition, there is the programmatic story of Thomas the twin (20.24-29), who doubts and then believes. This story stands as a paradigm of what *not* to do as believers in subsequent generations, when there was no possibility of having doubts assuaged by physical contact with the risen Jesus. That John does not record that Thomas actually touched Jesus simply underscores this point.

By the second century, with dependence only on the canonical Gospel texts, one would have the following elements upon which to draw in a reconstruction of the resurrection:

- Jesus is buried in a tomb in a garden
- There are guards at the tomb (Matthew only)
- The tomb is sealed (Matthew only)
- Following the Sabbath, women (or only Mary Magdalene, as in John) come to the tomb to embalm his body, wondering how they might get the stone rolled away
- Arriving at the tomb, they either (following Mark, Luke and John) find the tomb open and empty, or (following Matthew) witness the rolling away of the stone
- Either there is an angel or there are two angels present
- Jesus is nowhere to be found (excepting John's scene of Mary Magdalene's subsequent encounter with him in the garden)

From the standpoint of a narrator trying to tell *what* exactly happened at the resurrection event, or indeed *how* it was accomplished, it is only Matthew who breaks ranks and gives us some detail about the stone, but neither he nor John, with his intimate portrait of rolled-up burial clothes, actually describes the resurrection event. We are treated only to the events immediately preceding (that is, the death and burial) and proceeding from the resurrection event itself (various appearances, the ascension, etc.).

In view of these results, gleaned from a brief survey of the Gospel accounts, it is our purpose to examine two strands within early Christianity, both of which take up and develop the resurrection topos, but in entirely different ways. While these two strands are both Christian, it is our hypothesis that the differences between these two ways of treating the resurrection are the result of the internal split within early Christianity between Jewish and Gentile Christianity. In short, our argument is that, given the level of detail in the literary development of the resurrection story from the second century (which seems to have come to fruition in Jewish-Christian circles), one might be tempted to expect that such developments would be included in the early stages of Christian artistic representation of the same events. As briefly explored in section 3, this does not take place. Hence, we might further hypothesize that this may represent yet another front upon which the conflict between Jewish and Gentile Christianity took place. As space does not allow for a detailed treatment of this secondary hypothesis, we limit ourselves here to the initial observation of the dissimilarity between these two strands by way of a gathering and presentation of the evidence, as well as a detailed exposition of the way in which the literary strand may represent elements of Jewish-Christian tradition from the post-apostolic era.

2. *The Resurrection and Related Topoi in Early Non-Canonical Christian Literature*

As we shall see in section 3, a harmonized canonical picture of the resurrection (with a clear preference for Matthew's version) seems to lie behind virtually all of the details of resurrection scenes in early Christian art, with almost no extra features. This reticence to embellish is not universal, however, in early Christianity. For instance, consider the resurrection narrative of the probably second-century *Gospel of Peter* 39–40:

> And in the night when the Lord's day was drawing on, as the soldiers were on guard, two and two in each watch, there was a great voice in heaven, and they saw the heavens opened, and two men descend thence with great radiance, and they stood over the tomb. But that stone which had been cast at the door rolled away of itself and withdrew to one side, and the tomb was opened, and both the young men entered.

When those soldiers saw this, they aroused the centurion and the
elders (for they also were present on guard); and as they were relating
what they had seen, again they beheld three men coming out of the tomb,
and two of them were supporting the third, and a cross was following
them:[4] and the heads of the two men reached to the heaven, but the head
of Him who was being led along by them was higher than the heavens.

This scene, by turns seen as late and dependent on the canonical
Gospels, or asserted to be earlier than and independent from them,[5]

4.   On this scene, cf. J. Daniélou, *The Development of Christian Doctrine
before the Council of Nicaea. I. The Theology of Jewish Christianity* (trans. and ed.
J.A. Baker; London: Darton, Longman & Todd, 1964), pp. 266-67. Daniélou connects the (re-)vivified Cross to other Jewish-Christian texts, including *Bar.* 12.1
(which he suggests, on the basis of a similar quotation in Gregory of Nyssa, *Testi-
monia adversus Iudaeos* 44.213D, is a Jewish-Christian midrash of Jeremiah), a
Sahidic Coptic fragment (see his p. 266 n. 5) and even possibly the *Odes* 23.14. Cf.
also J. Fossum, 'Ascensio, Metamorphosis: The "Transfiguration" of Jesus in the
Synoptic Gospels', in idem, *The Image of the Invisible God: Essays on the Influence
of Jewish Mysticism on Early Christology* (NTOA, 30; Freiburg: Universitätsverlag; Göttingen: Vandenhoeck & Ruprecht, 1995), pp. 71-94, esp. 88-89, where
he discusses the identity of the two attending figures, and suggests that they were
not, indeed, supporting the third, but are rather simply his attendants.
5.   The interchange on the dependence of this gospel on, or its independence
from, the canonical Gospels has continued since its first publication in 1892 (U.
Boriant, 'Fragments du texte grec du livre d'Enoch et de quelques écrits attribués à
Saint Pierre', *Mémoires publiés par les membres de la mission archéologique
française au Caire* 9.1 [1892], pp. 137-42). For full chronological bibliography to
1994, see C.A. Evans, *Life of Jesus Research: An Annotated Bibliography* (NTTS,
24; Leiden: E.J. Brill, 2nd edn, 1996), pp. 263-66. Most recently defended in J.D.
Crossan's *The Cross that Spoke: The Origins of the Passion Narrative* (San Francisco: Harper & Row, 1987), the idea that the *Gospel of Peter* depends on a source
other than the canonical Gospels was first argued by A. von Harnack in his *Bruch-
stücke des Evangeliums und der Apokalypse des Petrus* (TU, 9; Leipzig: J.C. Hin-
richs, 1893), and followed 30 years later by P. Gardner-Smith in 'The Gospel of
Peter', *JTS* 27 (1925–26), pp. 255-71 and 'The Date of the Gospel of Peter', *JTS* 27
(1925–26), pp. 401-407. While Harnack and Gardner-Smith's position on the
gospel received much criticism at the time, the recent discovery of two papyrus
fragments has revitalized discussion of the gospel. One of these is almost certainly
part of the *Gospel of Peter*, and dates from as early as the end of the second century
(*P. Oxy.* 2949; cf. D. Lührmann, 'POx 2949: EvPt 3–5 in einer Handschrift des 2./3.
Jahrhunderts', *ZNW* 72 [1981], pp. 216-22), and the second, less sure in its identification (and not overlapping with any section of the ninth-century Akhmim amulet
gospel fragment which forms our longer version) is *P. Oxy.* 4009 (see D. Lührmann, 'POx 4009: Ein neues Fragment des Petrus-evangeliums?', *NovT* 35 [1993],

contains certain elements consistent with several passages in other non-canonical early Christian sources, namely, the gigantic proportions of the angelic and Christ figures, and the way in which the exact role of angels in the resurrection scene is made explicit.[6] *Ascension of Isaiah* 3.15-16 (end of the first century[7]), describes how the angel Michael and 'the Angel of the Holy Spirit' open the tomb and carry Christ forth. (The 'Angel of the Holy Spirit' is also described as being involved in aiding the ascent of individuals through the heavens in 7.23.) In addition to this, Hermas, *Sim.* 9.12.8 describes (perhaps significantly, *not* in a resurrection scene) the Son of God (who is the 'Glorious Man' of the *Similitudes*) being supported by six angels on each side.[8] Earlier, in *Sim.* 9.6.1, the 'Glorious Man' is described as 'a man so tall that he rose above the tower', which is previously described as 'higher than the mountains and the square, so as to contain the whole of the world' (*Sim.* 9.2.1). Another passage of apparent significance in connection to this is Hippolytus, *Ref.* 9.13.2-3, which tells the story of how Elchasai[9]

pp. 390-410). The paradigm suggested for the material contained within the resurrection scene of *Gospel of Peter* in this essay is somewhat of an equivocation of both positions: if based on an earlier 'source', this 'source' is, at best, to be identified as the theology of the Jewish-Christian mystical tradition within the early Church. That the canonical Gospels, while varying somewhat in their details, agree entirely that the resurrection of Jesus was a bodily event (despite the problems with the Matthaean narrative) is not necessarily the result of a competing 'source', but rather a competing theology.

6.   Daniélou (*Jewish Christianity*, pp. 254-55) suggests that 'Christ is borne up on a throne formed of angels', and that the 'imagery here is in fact that of the *merkaba*, the heavenly chariot formed of angels... It is patently Jewish in character, and derives from the oldest stratum of Jewish Christianity, that of Palestine.'

7.   See M.A. Knibb, 'Martyrdom and Ascension of Isaiah', *OTP*, II, pp. 143-76 (149).

8.   Note C.A. Gieschen, *Angelomorphic Christology: Antecedents and Early Evidence* (AGJU, 42; Leiden: E.J. Brill, 1998), p. 240, where he suggests that the two angels supporting the resurrected one in the *Gospel of Peter* are reminiscent of the 'Jewish idea that the one who is ascending was to be accompanied or met by two heavenly beings or angels'. On the same page, in n. 28, he cites Hermas, *Vis.* 1.4.3, where the lady who is the personification of the Church is borne away into heaven supported by two angels; *2 En.* 1.4-9; and even the transfiguration account of Mk 9.2. Cf. Fossum, 'Ascensio, Metamorphosis'. See also Daniélou's characterization of Christ's ascent into heaven in the *Gospel of Peter* as a Merkabah event (above, n. 6).

9.   Elchasai is discussed in Hippolytus in connection with the Nazarene Chris-

received his revelation, describing the Son of God and the Holy Spirit as massive angelic figures.

It is remarkable to note the similarities between these texts, and the various details upon which they agree.[10] There would seem to be reason to believe that this developed picture of various spiritual and angelic figures has its roots in the Jewish strand of the early Church—in connection with various mystical traditions brought into the Church from Judaism. In particular, it would seem that these texts point towards an interpretation of the resurrection (and its christological implications) which owes its details in some degree to the developing traditions of Merkabah mysticism (based on the throne-room visions of such passages as Ezekiel 1 and Isaiah 6) and, perhaps, the nascent Shi'ur Qomah ('measure of the stature [of God]') speculations which often accompany Merkabah mystical ideas. There are at least two issues, however, which need to be raised in connection with such a hypothesis: (a) how the development of Merkabah mysticism and Shi'ur Qomah concepts in wider Judaism fits with their apparent place within early (Jewish-)Christianity, and (b) how this fits with the idea of conflict between Jewish and Gentile factions in earliest Christianity.

a. *The Development of Shi'ur Qomah Speculation*
The discussion of Shi'ur Qomah literature and concepts is still in its infancy. Up until the last decade, the texts which bear the name *Shi'ur Qomah* were still being published and identified.[11] In the last decade, errors in dating the texts were not uncommon, and their provenance and origin are still in debate. What is universally agreed is that all of our

tians, but this is likely an incorrect connection. See R.A. Pritz, *Nazarene Jewish Christianity: From the End of the New Testament Period until its Disappearance in the Fourth Century* (SPB, 37; Jerusalem: Magnes Press; Leiden: E.J. Brill, 1988), p. 36, and n. 9 for bibliography on Elchasai. See also J. Irmscher, 'The Book of Elchasai', in W. Schneelmelcher (ed.), *New Testament Apocrypha. II. Writings Relating to the Apostles, Apocalypses and Related Subjects* (trans. and ed. R. McL. Wilson; Louisville, KY: Westminster/John Knox Press; Cambridge: James Clarke, 1992), pp. 685-90; and Daniélou, *Jewish Christianity*, pp. 64-67.

10. Daniélou (*Jewish Christianity*, pp. 64-67) especially notes the similarity between the theology of Elchasai, the *Gospel of Peter* and *Hermas*.

11. See, for instance, M.S. Cohen, *The Shi'ur Qomah: Liturgy and Theurgy in Pre-Kabbalistic Jewish Mysticism* (Lanham, MD: University Press of America, 1983).

extant MSS of the *Shi'ur Qomah* are no earlier than the eleventh or twelfth centuries.[12]

The origins of this literature, however, are not so clear. The consensus in recent scholarship (following the pioneering early work of Gershom Scholem) is that the Shi'ur Qomah literature has its genesis in the post-Talmudic era, and has no cognate in earlier Jewish (or Christian) literature. It seems, however, that there is some equivocation in the literature on this topic as to whether, when we are speaking of Shi'ur Qomah, we are speaking of the literary 'Ur-text' of the later documents called *Shi'ur Qomah*, or of the *ideas* that underlie these later documents. The argument of this paper is that, although the literary form of the Shi'ur Qomah literature may not have achieved the shape of the later documents until sometime in the post-Talmudic or gaonic period, the ideas that underlie it must come from a much earlier period. Indeed, it is the very presence of the texts at issue in this part of the paper which seem to be some of the best evidence for the early existence of Shi'ur Qomah ideas. As Pieter van der Horst negatively states:

> The strongest argument in favour of a much earlier dating [of Shi'ur Qomah literature or ideas] seems to be the supposed influence of *SQ* on Elchasai, a Jewish-Christian prophet from about 100 C.E., who describes an angel, most probably Christ, of enormous dimensions, 96 miles long, 24 miles wide, etc... But quite apart from the fact that the 96 miles of Elchasai and the 100.000.000.000 [i.e. one hundred billion] parasangs[13]

12. For a good example of the (understandable) confusion surrounding this literature, see P. van der Horst, 'The Measurement of the Body: A Chapter in the History of Jewish Mysticism', in D. van der Plas (ed.), *Effigies Dei: Essays on the History of Religions* (Studies in the History of Religions, 51; Leiden: E.J. Brill, 1987), pp. 56-68, where he identifies his text as tenth century, but, when republished in his *Essays on the Jewish World of Early Christianity* (NTOA, 14; Freiburg: Universitätsverlag; Göttingen: Vandenhoeck & Ruprecht, 1990), pp. 123-35, he notes on pp. 14-15 of the introduction to the book that he used this date in his initial publication of the document following the example of Cohen (who published it for the first time in *The Shi'ur Qomah*), but that, upon correction by Peter Schäfer, he had to admit that the text was actually eighteenth century!

13. A parasang = 3 miles; 1 mile = 10,000 ells; 1 ell = 3 small fingers. Each small finger is the small finger of God, each of which fills the whole world! See discussion in I. Gruenwald, *Apocalyptic and Merkavah Mysticism* (AGJU, 14; Leiden: E.J. Brill, 1980), p. 214. The Elchasite measurement of '96 miles long, 24 miles wide, etc.' might also be taken somewhat differently if the 'mile' measurement itself can be used in such a way.

of *SQ* are really incomparable quantities, the other essential *SQ* element, the names of God's limbs, is wholly lacking in Elchasai.[14] Although certainty is impossible in this matter, it is safe, for the time being, to date *SQ* to the early post-Talmudic or gaonic period.[15]

However, another Christian text that at no time seems to have been brought to bear on this discussion is Hermas, *Sim.* 9.6.1, mentioned above. This text would seem to suggest that, despite the objections raised to it by van der Horst, the disparity between Elchasai's measurements and the later 10^{10} parasangs of Shi'ur Qomah literature is somewhat ameliorated in this earlier material, and that these massive figures are part of an earlier continuum of speculation, despite the absence of names for the divine limbs, which is so important for later material. In addition, from non-Christian Jewish literature, Fossum notes that, in the shorter recension (B) of *Testament of Abraham* 10, 'the Man [i.e. Adam or Abel] is described as being of exceedingly great stature and wearing three golden crowns. The ascription of immense stature to the Man apparently must be seen in the light of the Merkabah mystics' descriptions of שיעור קומה',[16] a text which E.P. Sanders, in the introduction to his *Old Testament Pseudepigrapha* translation of this text, assigns to the last quarter of the first century CE, suggesting that, despite a few later Christian additions, it 'remains unmistakably Jewish'.[17]

In the light of this, Cohen's remark is well taken:

> The central problem in research on the text of the *Shi'ur Qomah* is the lateness of the manuscript sources. Scholars who argue for an early date for the text must realize that they are conducting their research over the long and silent centuries that divide the supposed date of composition from our earliest manuscript. Of course, the same is the case for nearly all, or almost all, Jewish literature that has survived from antiquity, so it

---

14. Van der Horst, 'The Measurement of the Body', p. 124; and p. 131 n. 7 (to this quotation) criticizes J.M. Baumgarten ('The Book of Elkasai and Merkabah Mysticism', *JSJ* 17 [1986], pp. 212-23) for ignoring this.

15. Horst, 'The Measurement of the Body', p. 125.

16. J.E. Fossum, *The Name of God and the Angel of the Lord: Samaritan and Jewish Concepts of Intermediation and the Origin of Gnosticism* (WUNT, 36; Mohr Siebeck, 1985), p. 277 n. 55.

17. E.P. Sanders, 'Testament of Abraham', *OTP*, I, p. 875. However, note the caution of J.R. Levison, *Portraits of Adam in Early Judaism: From Sirach to 2 Baruch* (JSPSup, 1; Sheffield: JSOT Press, 1988), p. 30, who decides against its inclusion in his study on the grounds that its date is not certain.

is hardly the case that a lack of early manuscript support rules out an early date for a text.[18]

An additional text which has been brought to bear on this question is Irenaeus, *Adv. Haer.* 1.14.1-9, in which the theology of a certain Marcus is discussed. It seems that Marcus, an early gnostic, had discussed the makeup of the 'Body of Truth', where the limbs are made out of letters of the Greek alphabet. Scholem argues that this is a parallel to one of the central features of the later Shi'ur Qomah literature.[19] As van der Horst states:

> The *SQ* literature...is characterized by an excessive indulgence in an almost provocative anthropomorphism, which is the reason why there has always been bitter antagonism against it in more rationalistic Jewish circles. The name *Shiur Qomah* itself, meaning 'the measurement of the body' (*sc.* of God), indicates that it is really God's body, in all its parts and members, that the mystic wanted to become familiar with.[20]

Cohen, after thorough analysis of the passage and its possible cognates in the Shi'ur Qomah literature, rightly rejects the close parallel that is argued for by Scholem. However, he does allow that, 'Although Scholem's parallel between the Shi'ur Qomah and Marcus may not be that exact, there are other gnostic authors of a relatively early period that might, in fact, provide parallels to the description of God in the Shi'ur Qomah, and specifically to the aspect of gigantism'.[21] After citing Elchasai and the Elchasites as mentioned in Hippolytus, Origen and Epiphanius, and quoting the passage from Hippolytus, he goes on:

> If Scholem's second century date for the Shi'ur Qomah is correct, then it is not implausible that it was composed in response to this sort of gigantistic speculation regarding Jesus. Certainly, this seems more likely than taking a Jewish text as a reaction (or even as a development) of Marcus' alphabet mysticism.[22]

This seems to be a particularly difficult interpretation, for it would suggest that there was an independent mystical development within

---

18. Cohen, *Shi'ur Qomah*, pp. 30-31.
19. G. Scholem, *Jewish Gnosticism, Merkabah Mysticism, and Talmudic Tradition* (New York: The Jewish Theological Seminary of America, 2nd edn, 1965), pp. 37-38.
20. Van der Horst, 'The Measurement of the Body', p. 124.
21. Cohen, *Shi'ur Qomah*, pp. 38-39 n. 64 (to p. 25).
22. Cohen, *Shi'ur Qomah*, p. 39 n. 64 (to p. 25).

early Christianity which somehow was seen as important enough by later Jewish mystics (whose access to the Christian material here presented must surely have been extremely limited) to combat it with the invention of Shi'ur Qomah literature and concepts. It is difficult to imagine the process by which this might have taken place, and it ignores the clear presence within earlier Jewish literature of gigantism in the discussion of angelic and divine figures. We have already mentioned *T. Abr.* B 10, with the massive Adam/Abel figure (whose importance especially in the Christology of Paul ought not be forgotten in this connection[23]), but a further text, adduced by van der Horst, would also suggest that, at the earliest stages of Merkabah mysticism, the implications of the *size* of God and divine things must have been apparent. In two articles,[24] van der Horst argues that the difficult passage in *Ezek. Trag.*, *Exodus* fragment 6, where Moses receives a vision of the throne of God in a dream, and then has this interpreted (in a somewhat surprising manner) by his father-in-law, is actually the earliest extant postbiblical example of Merkabah speculation.[25] Van der Horst's support for this interpretation of *Ezek. Trag.*, *Exodus* makes one particular

---

23. Cf., e.g., Rom. 5; 1 Cor. 15; but note the cautions of Levison, *Portraits of Adam*, pp. 13-23, with regard to the understanding of Adam in Second Temple Jewish literature in the light of Paul's particular 'take' on this figure in relation to Christ.

24. P.W. van der Horst, 'Moses' Throne Vision in Ezekiel the Dramatist', in *idem*, *Essays on the Jewish World of Early Christianity*, pp. 63-71 (originally published in *JJS* 34 [1983], pp. 21-29), and 'Some Notes on the *Exagoge* of Ezekiel', in *idem*, *Essays on the Jewish World of Early Christianity*, pp. 72-93, esp. pp. 82-85 (originally published in *Mnemosyne* 37 [1984], pp. 354-75), responding to H. Jacobson, *The Exagoge of Ezekiel* (Cambridge: Cambridge University Press, 1983); see also D.T. Runia, 'God and Man in Philo of Alexandria', *JTS* NS 39 (1988), pp. 49-75, esp. pp. 49-53. C.R. Holladay (*Fragments from Hellenistic Jewish Authors. II. Poets* [SBLTT, 30; SBLPS, 12; Atlanta: Scholars Press, 1989], p. 318) has also lent (tentative) support to van der Horst's interpretation.

25. 'On Sinai's peak I saw what seemed a throne so great in size it touched the clouds of heaven. Upon it sat a man of noble mien, crowned, and with a sceptre in one hand, while with the other he beckoned me. I made approach and stood before the throne. He handed over the sceptre and he bade me mount the throne, and gave to me the crown; then he himself withdrew from off the throne. I gazed upon the whole earth round about; things under it, and high above the skies. Then at my feet a multitude of stars fell down, and I their number reckoned up. They passed before me like armed ranks of men. Then I in terror woke from the dream' (a slightly modified version of Robertson's rather Shakespearean translation of ll. 68-82 in R.G. Robertson, 'Ezekiel the Tragedian', *OTP*, II, pp. 803-19).

aspect of the key passage stand out: the very *size* of the divine throne. It is described as 'a throne so great in size it touched the clouds of heaven' (ll. 68-69). Surely such massive proportions *must* have eventually led to discussion of the size of the figures associated with such furniture.[26] It is by now also fairly widely recognized that mystical ascent to the throne room of God was practised at Qumran.[27] Various texts from Qumran show this quite clearly (e.g. the various biblical MSS of Ezekiel, 4QpsEzek[a'], 4QM[a] 11 i), but the most obvious evidence has come in the form of the so-called 'Songs of the Sabbath Sacrifice' or 'Angelic Liturgy',[28] which depend heavily on Ezekiel's throne-chariot visions. Van der Horst's hypothesis concerning the existence of Merkabah speculation in Ezekiel hardly seems radical in the light of the existence of this tradition at this stage in the development of the Qumran community.

It would seem that the most reasonable picture of the development of Shi'ur Qomah *concepts*—and not necessarily the developed literature of the later period—in the Second Temple period would follow a line delineated from early (pre-Christian) Jewish speculation on the Throne of God as it appears in various Old Testament texts (Ezek. 1, Isa. 6, Dan. 7, etc.), together with speculations relating to the various angelic figures in relationship to God, as well, apparently, as speculations on the size or stature of such figures and of God himself.[29]

26. Cf. discussion in Fossum, 'Ascensio, Metamorphosis', p. 75, where he also notes the gigantic throne of the heavenly ruler in *3 En.* C 48.8 (in MS K), which is a particularly interesting connection in the light of the explicitly Merkabah mystical character of *3 Enoch*; and Jacobson, *Exagoge*, p. 200 n. 4 (to p. 90): 'Ezekiel's emphasis on the great size of the throne (and evidently of the man) is probably significant', but he is not convinced that this holds any special significance in the light of gigantism in other dream-sequences from antiquity.

27. For brief discussion of this, in relation to Paul, see J.M. Scott, 'Throne-Chariot Mysticism in Qumran and in Paul', in C.A. Evans and P.W. Flint (eds.), *Eschatology, Messianism, and the Dead Sea Scrolls* (Studies in the Dead Sea Scrolls and Related Literature; Grand Rapids: Eerdmans, 1997), pp. 101-19, esp. pp. 103-104.

28. Now discussed thoroughly in C. Newsom, *Songs of the Sabbath Sacrifice: A Critical Edition* (HSS, 27; Atlanta: Scholars Press, 1985); *idem*, 'Merkabah Exegesis in the Qumran Sabbath Shirot', *JJS* 38 (1987), pp. 11-30. The 'Songs' are made up of eight fragmentary MSS: 4Q400–407, and are dated to the early- to mid-first century BCE.

29. On the various angelic figures associated closely with God, see Fossum, *The*

b. *Conflict between Jewish and Gentile Christians in the Earliest Church*
The consensus now generally held is that, in the earliest period of Christianity, the Jesus movement and the earliest Church were part of a multi-faceted Judaism (or, as it is often written, Judaisms), with much variation among its constituent parts. Only later did Christianity emerge as a movement independent of Judaism. However, the split between Judaism and Christianity is of less interest in this earlier period than is the split within the Christian movement itself, drawn largely along ethno-cultural lines, between Gentile and Jewish Christianity. This thesis, first defended by F.C. Baur and the Tübingen School, has been revived in recent years by the British scholar Michael Goulder.[30] Goulder's formulation of this theory rests on three key arguments: (1) 'The line for Paul does not run between two religions, Judaism and Christianity. It runs between those whose faith is in the gospel of the cross of Christ, Pauline Christians, and those whose trust is in the works of the law, whether they call themselves Jews or Christians.'[31] (2) 'The Petrine Christian leaders were delivering halakha as under inspiration of the Spirit, "words of wisdom" interpreted from the Bible... It is the delivery of *dibre hôkmah*, which are not (Paul says) divine law at all, but are mere human cleverness, taught in the Church as the Tannaim taught them in Judaism.'[32] In further work, Goulder suggests that this non-Pauline group (or groups) was, at least in places, connected with mystical practices in keeping with Jewish mysticism, specifically Merkabah-related visions.[33] (3) There were christological differences between Paul and the Paulines on the one hand, who held to

Name of God and the Angel of the Lord, and the work of his recent doctoral student, Gieschen, *Angelomorphic Christology*.

30. See S.E. Porter and B.W.R. Pearson, 'Ancient Understandings of the Christian–Jewish Split', pp. 36-51, in this volume.

31. M.D. Goulder, '2 Cor. 6:14–7:1 as an Integral Part of 2 Corinthians', *NovT* 36 (1994), pp. 47-57 (56).

32. M.D. Goulder, 'ΣΟΦΙΑ in 1 Corinthians', *NTS* 37 (1991), pp. 516-34 (523). See also *idem*, 'Vision and Knowledge', *JSNT* 56 (1994), pp. 53-71, esp. pp. 58-65.

33. M.D. Goulder, 'John 1.1–2.12 and the Synoptics', in A. Denaux (ed.), *John and the Synoptics* (BETL, 101; Leuven: Leuven University Press/Peeters, 1992), pp. 201-37 (212): 'Its members not only gave their devotion to the Law, but also experienced visions in which they were taken up to the Throne of God and given angelic instructions on its interpretation'. Cf. *idem*, 'The Visionaries of Laodicea', *JSNT* 43 (1991), pp. 15-39, esp. p. 33.

an incarnationalist Christology, and the Jerusalem church and its followers, on the other, who held to an early docetism or possessionistic
Christology.[34]

In the light of this theory, it is striking that many features of the
resurrection account in the *Gospel of Peter* seem also to have been
influenced by, for instance, Merkabah mysticism and possibly a nascent
Shi'ur Qomah speculation. Contrary to a picture such as Scott draws,
where Merkabah speculation runs throughout Paul's writings,[35] this
paradigm would suggest that such elements have their place more
firmly in the non-Pauline mission and its descendants than in Paul, and
that their presence should suggest to us a Jewish- (or Jerusalem, or
Jacobite) Christian rather than Gentile- (or Pauline) Christian origin.
The *Gospel of Peter* (and its supporting texts such as *Hermas* and Elchasai) clearly owes much of its developed imagery to this early Jewish
Christianity, and to developing mystical speculation.

3. The Resurrection in Early Christian Art

As outlined above, the canonical records of the resurrection were supplemented in ensuing literary traditions with additional narrative
details. These embellishments could constitute the wholesale interpola-
tion of new elements, such as the *Gospel of Peter*'s description of the

34. See M.D. Goulder, *A Tale of Two Missions* (London: SCM Press, 1994), esp.
Chs. 14 and 15; *idem*, 'A Poor Man's Christology', *NTS* 45 (1999), pp. 332-48.

35. Scott, 'Throne-Chariot Mysticism'. One of Scott's key assumptions is that
Paul's reference to the 'man he knew who ascended to the third heaven' is Paul
himself. Supporters of this position include G. Scholem, 'The Four Who Entered
Paradise and Paul's Ascension to Paradise', in *idem*, *Jewish Gnosticism* (New
York: Jewish Theological Seminary, 2nd edn, 1965), pp. 14-19; C.R.A. Morray-
Jones, 'Paradise Revisited (2 Cor 12:1-12): The Jewish Mystical Background of
Paul's Apostolate', *HTR* 86 (1993), pp. 177-217, 265-92; and A.F. Segal, 'Paul and
the Beginning of Jewish Mysticism', in J.J. Collins and M. Fishbane (eds.), *Death,
Ecstasy and Other Worldly Journeys* (Albany, NY: SUNY Press, 1995), pp. 95-
122. There is, however, a strong contingent who would see the issue the other way
around, and argue that Paul is *not* indeed talking of himself. Cf. P. Schäfer, 'New
Testament and Hekhalot Literature: The Journey into Heaven in Paul and Merkabah
Mysticism', *JJS* 35 (1984), pp. 19-35; A. Goshen-Gottstein, 'Four Entered Paradise
Revisited', *HTR* 88 (1995), pp. 69-133 (in response to Morray-Jones, 'Paradise
Revisited'). This is also one of the arguments upon which Goulder builds his interpretation of Paul's attitude towards Jewish mystical practice (cf. Goulder, 'ΣΟΦΙΑ
in 1 Corinthians', p. 525; *idem*, *Tale of Two Missions*, pp. 49-50).

talking cross following three figures out of the tomb, or the conspicuous emphasis on visual details, notably with respect to the size of the risen Christ and the angels accompanying him. Given the highly visual nature of these additions, one might expect to see their eventual translation into the resurrection imagery developed in the early Church. Yet, as the ensuing glimpse of art in the early Christian period will suffice to show (c. 200–500 CE),[36] artists and/or their patrons remained seemingly uninfluenced by the embellishments provided in the later literary sources. Instead, their pictorializations of the resurrection effected a comparable, but not necessarily purloined, conservatism of detail as evinced in the canonical records.

While questions relating to the specific circumstances of Christ's rising were unequivocally avoided,[37] artists did approach the subject almost from the inception of Christian artistic expression around 200 CE, and successfully utilized more than one image for its visual expression.[38] In their preference for the expression of broader soteriological themes rather than the delineation of Christ's own resurrection, artists developed a repertoire of enigmatic images and symbols for inclusion within pre-Constantinian funereal iconographies. The image of the phoenix, legendary in ancient literature as capable of regenerating itself out of its decomposing remains, was appropriated by both writers and artists as an allegory of Christian, and of Christ's own,

36. In art historical terms, the chronological parameters of the 'Early Christian' period are defined as 200–500 CE. Cf. M.C. Murray, *Rebirth and Afterlife: A Study of the Transmutation of Some Pagan Imagery in Early Christian Funerary Art* (British Archaeological Reports, International Series, 100; Oxford: British Archaeological Society, 1981), pp. 5-8. See also P. Finney, *The Invisible God* (Oxford: Oxford University Press, 1994), Ch. 5.

37. A. Kartsonis, in her seminal work on the birth, growth and dissemination of material figurations of the resurrection up to the eleventh century (*Anastasis: The Making of an Image* [Princeton, NJ: Princeton University Press, 1986], p. 28), has shown how careful early Christian artists were to avoid literal representations of Christ rising to new life, regardless of the source of patronage, function or intended usage of the artefact bearing a visual allusion to the resurrection.

38. Previous studies of early resurrection iconography include: J. Villette, *La résurrection du Christ dans l'art chrétien du II. au VII. siècle* (Paris: H. Laurens, 1957); B. Brenk, *Tradition und Neuerung in der christlichen Kunst des ersten Jahrtausends* (Wiener byzantinische Studien, 3; Vienna: Böhlau in Kommission, 1966); A. Grabar, *Christian Iconography: A Study of its Origins* (London: Thames & Hudson, 1980), pp. 123-27; Kartsonis, *Anastasis*, pp. 19-39.

resurrection.[39] Similarly, scriptural episodes interpreted as antetypes of Jesus' rising or as typological parallels were inserted as visual substitutes: Jonah's encounter with the whale, construed as presaging the ultimate resurrection of Jesus, appeared frequently in the catacombs and on sarcophagi of the third and fourth centuries,[40] as did the New Testament miracle of the raising of Lazarus.[41] The visual impact of the latter was in fact drawn from several underlying meanings: as an illustration of God's fulfilled promise of eternal life, shown through the death-destroying action of his son Jesus; a message of hope for all believers in the anticipated general resurrection of the dead at the day of judgment; and as a prefiguring of the Passion and resurrection of Jesus himself.

Following the peace of the Church (313 CE), artists devised a yet more striking visual reference to the resurrection, an emblem that in its admixture of representationalism and symbolism encapsulated both the death and rising of Jesus while still managing to avoid a literal depiction of both events.[42] The motif appeared on fourth-century Roman

39. The image of the phoenix, as a means of communicating the mystery of the resurrection of the flesh, was taken up in literature as early as the late first century with *1 Clem.* 1.25-26. For an incised visual representation from the catacomb of Callistus, Rome, see P.C. Finney, 'Phoenix', in E. Ferguson (ed.), *Encyclopedia of Early Christianity* (2 vols.; Garland Reference Library of the Humanities, 1839; New York: Garland, 2nd edn, 1997), II, pp. 918-19.

40. The parallelism between Jonah in the stomach of the whale (Jon. 1.17) and Jesus in the tomb had of course been pointed out by Jesus himself (Mt. 12.39-40). The Jonah story was generally depicted in early Christian art as a trilogy: Jonah expunged from the boat; cast up by the monster; and finally resting under the gourd vine, e.g. a sarcophagus in the Museo Pio Cristiano, dated around 290, whereon Lazarus also appears (see K. Weitzmann [ed.], *Age of Spirituality: Catalogue* [New York: The Metropolitan Museum of Art, 1979], cat. no. 361).

41. The earliest pictorial formula of the raising of Lazarus shows Jesus holding a staff, and his friend, partly covered or wrapped in a shroud, standing in the doorway of an *aedicula*, e.g. a late third-century wall painting in the catacomb of SS. Pietro and Marcellino, Rome (A. Grabar, *The Beginnings of Christian Art 200–395* [trans. S. Gilbert and J. Emmons; London: Thames & Hudson, 1967], no. 22; cf. G. Schiller, *Iconography of Christian Art* (2 vols.; trans. J. Seligman; London: Lund Humphries, 1971), I, pp. 181-83. Also regarding the evolution of the scene, see F. Albertson, 'An Isiac Model for the Raising of Lazarus in Early Christian Art', *JAC* 38 (1995), pp. 123-32.

42. The earliest extant passion sarcophagus is that formerly in the Lateran (inv. no. 171) and now in the Museo Pio Cristiano, Vatican City, Italy, dated c. 340

passion sarcophagi, and commonly comprised an image of a triumphal cross, surmounted by the crown of victory encircling a Chi-Rho, and flanked by two standing or sleeping soldiers. With the symbolic cross-trophy a reference to the crucifixion, and the soldiers reminiscent of the Matthaean guard at the tomb, it remained the central and climacteric motif in sarcophagal passion narratives until around the mid-fourth century.[43] A rare iconographical variant saw the soldiers substituted for an abbreviated depiction of Mary's approach to the tomb, the inclusion of which conceivably prepared the way for more explicit pictorial-izations of post-resurrection events at the sepulchre.[44]

While this crucifixion/resurrection emblem successfully introduced canonical narrative elements into the visual realm, it also provided a tangible symbol of the risen Jesus: the cross-trophy rising above either the soldiers or the women at the tomb might also have functioned as an allusion to, and possible visual substitute for, the risen person of Christ.[45] Such a reading of the conjunction of cross and tomb is particularly germane for understanding a fragmentary stone relief in the Dumbarton Oaks collection.[46] There, the placement of the powerful cross before the open entrance to the tomb forms an explicit reference to the risen Jesus, and is temptingly reminiscent of the cross at the resurrection site in the *Gospel of Peter*. However, despite the intimation of Christ's risen-presence in this way, one does not find in art the triune elements of tomb–Jesus–cross as the author of this gospel conceives of such a combination.[47]

(E. Kitzinger, *Byzantine Art in the Making: Main Lines of Stylistic Development in Mediterranean Art 3rd–7th Century* [Cambridge, MA: Harvard University Press, 5th edn, 1995], fig. 44).

43. The literature on the motif is vast. See briefly Grabar, *Christian Iconography*, pp. 124-25; Kartsonis, *Anastasis*, p. 25; Schiller, *Iconography*, II, p. 5.

44. As on a columnar sarcophagus from Aix, cited by A. Soper, 'The Italo-Gallic School of Early Christian Art', *Art Bulletin* 20 (1938), pp. 145-92 (188). See further, n. 57 below.

45. Villette, *La résurrection*, pp. 43-44.

46. Dumbarton Oaks Collection, Harvard University (Acc. no. 38.56. Height 67 cm, width 57 cm); said to have come from Syria. First published by P.A. Underwood, 'The Fountain of Life in Manuscripts of the Gospels', *Dumbarton Oaks Papers* 5 (1950), pp. 43-138, esp. p. 91 and figs. 39 and 40. Cf. Kartsonis, *Anastasis*, pp. 25-26 and 32, who discusses the relief in connection with the central motif of the passion sarcophagi.

47. The inclusion of the cross within a resurrection narrative of the date of the

It is highly likely that the artistic interest in the discovery of the empty tomb as a visual allusion to the resurrection of Jesus surfaced in the East during the first third of the third century CE. A frieze in the baptistery of the Christian *domus ecclesiae* at Dura Europos, depicting a procession of five women towards a large white pedimented structure, is traditionally construed as the women approaching and entering the sepulchre on Easter morning.[48] If this identification is correct, it constitutes the earliest surviving figurative reference to the resurrection of Jesus in Christian art.[49]

Without detailing the finer points of the identification debate, it is important to recognize several features that, if accepted as a representation of the Marian cortege, render this portrayal highly unusual. First, the number of women (five) does not relate to any of the canonical Gospel narratives, which specify the presence of one to three women,[50] a discrepancy Kraeling attempted to reconcile by appealing to the harmonization of Tatian's *Diatessaron* as a possible source for both the iconographical peculiarity and the sequential nature of the frieze.[51] An

Gospel of Peter is certainly striking in the light of the fact that, as a visual motif, the cross is not linked explicitly to the crucifixion in Christian art prior to the appearance of the passion sarcophagi (c. 340 CE; see above, n. 42).

48. Grabar, *Christian Iconography*, p. 124. The frescoes are dated to around 240 CE. For a visual reproduction of the north-wall frieze and other images from the decorative programme, see Grabar, *Beginnings of Christian Art*, pls. 59-63. Cf. C.H. Kraeling, *The Excavations at Dura-Europos: Final Report*. VIII.2. *The Christian Building* (New Haven: Dura-Europos Publications, 1967). A hypothetically reconstructed view of the baptistery's decorative programme (after Kraeling) is given in A.J. Wharton, *Refiguring the Post Classical City: Dura Europos, Jerash, Jerusalem and Ravenna* (Cambridge: Cambridge University Press, 1995), p. 52 fig. 17.

49. The identification of the fresco as the women at the tomb, first made by Henry Seyrig in 1932, is now generally accepted. See Kraeling, *Excavations*, VIII. 2, pp. 80-88, 190-97, 231; cf. A. Grabar, 'La fresque des saintes femmes au tombeau à Doura', in *idem, L'art de la fin de l'Antiquité et du Moyen Age* (3 vols.; Paris: Collège de France, 1968), I, pp. 517-28. Alternative readings have identified the figures as the wise and foolish virgins of Mt. 25.1-13. See Kraeling, *Excavations*, VIII.2, p. 81 n. 1; cf. Wharton, *Refiguring*, pp. 53, 59-60.

50. Mt. 28.1 mentions two; Mk 16.1 three; Jn 20.1 one. Lk. 24.1 does not specify the number (or identity).

51. Kraeling (*Excavations*, VIII.2, pp. 86-88, 196) thought that the frieze reflected the triune narrative composition of Tatian's harmonization of the Gospels—a text well known in Syria until the fifth century, and of which a fragment was discovered at Dura Europos (pp. 114-16). For comment, see Wharton,

additional problem is the depiction of the interior of the tomb, in accordance with the Markan (16.5) and Lukan (24.3) narratives, which describe the women entering the sepulchre. Such an internal view is conspicuously rare in early Christian art. A third problem is the absence of a figurative representation of an angel. This absence is remarkable, not simply when one considers the emphasis on a physical angelic presence inside the tomb in both Mark (one angel, Mk 16.5) and Luke (two angels, Lk. 24.4) but also the later Johannine tradition, which describes Mary Magdalene looking inside—but not entering—the tomb and seeing two angels (Jn 20.11-12).[52]

To accommodate these iconographic peculiarities, the details of the Dura fresco might be seen to synthesize the various narrative elements contained in the four canonical Gospel accounts, whether effecting the synthesis themselves or drawing on extra-canonical sources such as the *Diatessaron*. By comparison, later Western and Eastern artists would seem to have favoured the Matthaean resurrection narrative, in which Mary Magdalene and Mary Mother of James and Joseph do not enter the sepulchre, but meet an angel outside who informs them of the resurrection (cf. Mt. 27.56). It is this post-resurrection scene, mentioned above as making its debut on Western passion sarcophagi in the fourth century, which appeared perhaps most notably on ivory reliefs carved for wealthy patrons in the fourth and fifth centuries. The number of women shown approaching the tomb could vary from the canonical two to three, with an angel/Christ-like figure usually shown seated by the

Refiguring, p. 54. A. Perkins (*The Art of Dura-Europos* [Oxford: Clarendon Press, 1973], p. 54) reiterates this notion that the frieze presents a deliberate coalescence of the Gospel accounts, although she does not comment on the possibility that the artists used the *Diatessaron* as a source of reference for the blending of narrative detail.

52. One theory to offset the figurative absence was J. Villette's reading, accepted by Kraeling, of the two stars surmounting either corner of the sarcophagus as symbolic references to an angelic presence. Kraeling, *Excavations*, VIII.2, pp. 81-83. In comparison, M. Rostovtzeff (*Dura Europos and its Art* [Oxford: Clarendon Press, 1938], p. 132) interprets them as stars of hope. With regard to the figurative absence of an angel or angels, it should be noted that winged angels did not appear in Christian art until the fourth century—a phenomenon most recently explored by N. Ricklefs in his paper, 'How the Angel Found its Wings', delivered at the eleventh Conference of the Australian Association for Byzantine Studies, Macquarie University, Sydney, 16–18 July 1999.

open entrance.[53] For instance, on the Munich ivory panel, dated around 400 CE, three women approach a wingless-angel/Christ figure, who sits before the tomb and extends his left hand in the sign of benediction.[54]

A variation on the approach of the women sees them kneeling before the figure at the tomb and taking his feet, according to the episode described in Mt. 28.9-10. On an ivory panel in Milan, dated 400 CE, the seated figure is nimbate, and holds a scroll in his right hand while still extending his left hand in the sign of benediction.[55] This portrayal led Weitzmann to interpret the scene as a conflation of the angelic announcement the later episode of Jesus appearing to the Marys.[56] The earlier episode described in Mt. 28.1-9, in which the women depart from the angel and are met by Jesus, was depicted on a fourth-century Roman sarcophagus from the Palazzo del Duca di Ceri in Borgo Vecchio (now lost): thereon, beneath the arms of the cross-trophy, two women kneel before a standing Christ and worship him.[57] On the carved wooden doors of St Sabina, Rome, dated c. 430 CE, the two episodes are depicted on separate panels: the first showing the angel appearing to two women; the second displaying the resurrected Jesus standing before them.[58] Hence artists took the liberty of condensing or perhaps emphasizing certain narrative elements, conceivably in accordance with their own knowledge of a particular canonical version or versions, or even

53. On the sarcophagus of St Celso in Milan, a levitating winged-figure appears peeping over the roof of the sepulchre. Cf. Soper, 'Italo-Gallic School', p. 188.

54. Bayerisches Nationalmuseum at Munich; late fourth or early fifth century. Cf. Kitzinger, *Byzantine Art*, p. 39 fig. 76.

55. Milan, Castello Sforzesco, Civiche Raccolte d'Arte applicata ed Incisioni, Avori 9; measuring 30.7 × 13.4 cm. Formerly in the Trivulzio Collection. Weitzmann (ed.), *Age of Spirituality*, pp. 504-505; Kitzinger, *Byzantine Art*, p. 40.

56. Weitzmann's theory is mentioned by G. Vikan in his entry on the ivory in Weitzmann (ed.), *Age of Spirituality*, p. 505 cat. no. 453.

57. Soper ('Italo-Gallic School', p. 188) claims that the episode actually entered Roman iconography on this sarcophagus. The sarcophagus is preserved in a drawing by A. Bosio. See F.W. Deichmann, B.G. Bovini and H. Brandenburg (eds.), *Repertorium der christlich-antiken Sarkophage*. I. *Rom und Ostia* (Wiesbaden: Franz Steiner, 1967), pp. 388-89 cat. no. 933, pl. 149, with bibliography. The scene appears on the Servannes sarcophagus with three women. Cf. F. Gerke, *Die Zeitbestimmung der Passionssarkophage* (Berlin: W. de Gruyter, 1940), pl. 17, figs. 70 and 71.

58. G. Jeremias, *Die Holztür der Basilika S. Sabina in Rom* (Tübingen: Ernst Wasmuth, 1980), pp. 63-66, pls. 53 and 56.

from their memory of a previously seen prototype. For example, on the resurrection panel in the series of ivory passion reliefs from the Maskell Collection in the British Museum, the tomb-scene is reduced to include only two women and two soldiers, with the notable exclusion of the angel.[59] The customary procession of the Marys towards the sepulchre is also abandoned in favour of a symmetrical division of the four characters in seated positions on either side of the entrance.

Ivory plaque: Two Marys and soldiers at the empty sepulchre (M&LA 56,6–23,6). By courtesy of the Trustees of the British Museum.

59. London, British Museum (M&LA 56,6–23,6), 75 mm × 99 mm. The series, comprising four reliefs, is probably of Roman provenance and dated between 420 and 430 CE. The four panels depict in turn: (1) Pilate washing his hands, Christ on the road to Calvary, Peter's denial; (2) the death of Judas and the crucifixion; (3) the Marys at the sepulchre; (4) the incredulity of Thomas. For discussion and bibliography, cf. D. Buckton (ed.), *Byzantium: Treasures of Byzantine Art and Culture from British Collections* (London: British Museum Press, 1994), pp. 58-59 cat. no. 45.

Despite the experimentation with and development of the pious women iconography, the meaning of preceding scriptural allusions to Jesus' resurrection was not lost to new generations of artists and their audiences. On both the London and the Milan ivories, Lazarus is depicted on the open doors of the sepulchre, an appearance reinforcing and indeed underpinning the solemnity of the eyewitness testimony provided by the women. The women's testimony could be further underscored by the incorporation of later narrative episodes such as the incredulity of Thomas, which appears on one of the aforementioned Maskell passion reliefs.

It should also be noted that, while each of the four Gospels attests to the resurrection of Jesus as a physical happening—not a vision, apparition or supernatural appearance—the protagonist remains conspicuously absent from their narratives. The only exception is the Johannine inclusion of the encounter between Jesus and Mary Magdalene in the garden (Jn 20.14-17), which may have been pictorialized in such visual instances as the Milan ivory. In most examples, however, as on the London ivory, the actuality of the bodily resurrection of Jesus is attested not in a literal depiction of his risen body, but in the emptiness of the tomb, which gradually came to form something of an iconographic shorthand for the resurrection in the early Christian period.[60]

As this brief overview of early Christian art reveals, the adamant exclusion of a literal figuration of the resurrection from the earliest visual art allowed for the development of alternative symbols, typological parallels and antetypes as substitutes. These proved immensely popular in funerary contexts as a means of evoking the Christian belief in resurrection without having to depict Jesus' own rising. Beyond the utilization of these alternatives, formative experimentations with literal expressions of the resurrection event continued to circumnavigate both theological and practical problems relating to the depiction of the bodily form of the risen Jesus and the means of his rise from death. While a non-symbolic representation of the resurrection had conceivably been attempted at Dura at the beginning of the third century, such depictions were rare at this date. The female approach to the tomb was a more common reference, with the development of passion cycles on

60. Grabar (*Christian Iconography*, p. 124) calls this type of iconography 'juridical and evangelical (because, like the Gospels, it evoked the dogma by showing the story of the eyewitnesses to the Resurrection)'.

sarcophagi occurring around the mid-fourth century. In both the East and the West, this historical substitute with the subsequent angelic revelation (Mt. 28.10//Mk 15.46–16.8//Lk. 23.55–24.8//Jn 20.1-8) remained the most popular visual alternative to a literal rendering of the resurrection from the third to sixth centuries, alluding to and under-scoring the historical veracity of the rising of Jesus.[61]

4. *Conclusions*

Our conclusions may be found in the following six points: (1) The embellishment of the resurrection of Jesus as found in especially the *Gospel of Peter* and Hermas (with other early Christian texts supplying support for various details) is the result of the interaction between Jewish-Christian mystical beliefs and practices and the canonical Gospel texts. (2) Speculations in early Judaism regarding the measure of the stature of God (Shi'ur Qomah) pre-date Christianity. (3) This Jewish-Christian or Jewish-influenced picture of the resurrection does not seem to have been reflected in the art of the Early Christian period—to the point that angels are often simply absent, and certainly do not seem to be pro-active in the resurrection. (4) The most popular 'resurrection' scenes in early Christian art are, like the canonical Gospels, post-resurrection ones. (5) The resurrection in early Christian art, as in the fourth Gospel, is emphasized as a fleshly one. (6) The Gospel of Matthew seems to have been the favoured version of the resurrection in *both the non-canonical texts to which we alluded above, and the visual representations of the resurrection in early Christian art.*

While the artistic absence of details concerning the actual exit of Jesus from the sepulchre would seem to be linked to the corresponding descriptive restraint of the canonical resurrection narratives, we would be mistaken to cite this as the main point of influence. In the case of the crucifixion, for instance, the canonical Gospels provide various points of narrative detail that fail to appear in artistic translations of the event in the early period. The restraint in depicting the resurrection might

---

61. The subject was ultimately superseded by the descent into hell iconography, the oldest extant instances of which occur in the early eighth century. Cf. Grabar, *Christian Iconography*, pp. 125-26; Kartsonis, *Anastasis*, pp. 29-31 and 69-81.

thus be seen to relate to various factors, including theological reservations regarding the form of the risen Jesus.[62] In addition, it is not impossible that the discretion of artists in their attempts to pictorialize the resurrection might relate to their rejection of the details provided by the extra-canonical writers, just as conceivably as it might reflect their wholesale adoption of the canonical versions.

62. Kartsonis (*Anastasis*, p. 39) mentions doctrinal traps attendant to the depiction of the resurrection, traps relating to the fact that a Christology of Christ's death had not yet been fully defined.

1 ENOCH AMONG JEWS AND CHRISTIANS:
A FRINGE CONNECTION?

Lawrence VanBeek

One of the ways to find connections between groups of peoples is the literature they use to define themselves. Connections can be expressed through actual titled works, or simply through the use of common genres. Particular sectors of Judaism and Christianity had just such a connection in the Enochic literature.

The intrigue of *1 Enoch*, and particularly *The Book of the Watchers*, is that it appears to have been highly regarded by the Essenes and was adopted and used by some New Testament authors as well as some Apostolic and some Church Fathers. *1 Enoch* then fell into disuse by the power parties, or at least literary groups within both Judaism and Christianity. The 'Enochic Christians' had much in common with 'Enochic Jews'. Although there are strong disagreements between the groups, the similarities in authority, angelology and ethics (or at least decorum) are telling of their commitment to the literature.

This essay will focus on the common use of *1 Enoch* by the Essenes and Christians, its priority and its demise and its effect on the communities who used it. I will also explore how literature helps to bring an unconscious cohesiveness to two groups that appear to be fundamentally different.

Jewish Use of 1 Enoch

1 Enoch *and* Jubilees

1 Enoch appears to have had a prominent place in *Jubilees* and the Qumran literature, which attest to the authority given to some of the Enochic corpus.[1] *Jubilees* was dependent upon *1 Enoch*, but was not

---

1. We could also include the *Testament of Naphtali* from the *Testaments of the Twelve Patriarchs*, possibly written about the same time as the Dead Sea Scrolls, c.

exclusively dependent upon it. Several works[2] have discussed the person of Enoch in the apocalyptic literature, as well as antecedents of Enoch in other literature. Heinrich Zimern (1902) and Pierre Grelot (1958) see a comparison of Enoch in Berossus's *Babyloniaca* (c. 280 BCE), where Enoch is identified with King Euedoranchos (Zimern 1902: 530-43). H. Ludin Jansen (1939) saw a comparison between Enoch and the Babylonian Ea, and with other figures associated with Ea such as Gilgamesh. James VanderKam sees parallels and possible antecedents of Enoch the culture bringer with Taautos (Thouth to the Egyptians, Thoth to the Alexandrians), the Phoenician culture bringer (1984: 182), and supports the figure of Enoch being a Jewish version of the Mesopotamian diviner-king Enmeduranki (1984: 116). The main value of these works—particularly Grelot and VanderKam—is, for the purpose of this essay, that they show *Jubilees* as not solely dependent on the Enoch literature. What needs to be shown is that, even if *Jubilees* is not completely dependent upon the Enoch literature, it is dependent to some degree, and sees *1 Enoch*, particularly *The Book of the Watchers*, as authoritative.

Although it is true that *Jub.* 4.16-25 gives a portrait of Enoch that goes beyond what is found in *The Book of the Watchers*, *The Book of Dreams* and the *Astronomical Book* of *1 Enoch* (VanderKam 1984: 180-83), *Jubilees* is partly dependent upon these sources and considers them to be authoritative.[3] *Jubilees* uses *1 Enoch* in 4.16-25; 5.1-12; 7.21-22; and 21.10.

Along with *Jubilees'* use of *1 Enoch*, there are some passages that give Enoch credit for having written authoritative words. *Jubilees* 4.17-18 says:

> [Enoch] was the first of mankind who were born on the earth who learned (the art of) writing...who wrote down in a book the signs of the sky in accord with the fixed pattern of their months so that mankind would know the seasons of the years according to the fixed patterns of each of their months...[he] made known the days of the years; the months he arranged, and related the Sabbaths of the years.

150 BCE (Kee 1983: 778), which mentions the watchers being responsible for the flood in 3.5.

2.   These works are critiqued in VanderKam 1984: 11-20.

3.   This is still the case even if, as VanderKam suggests, the writers of the Enochic literature had no scruples against incorporating (with modifications) pagan mythological material into their books (1984: 188).

These words point to the *Astronomical Book* in *1 Enoch*, and tie them in with the patriarch Enoch, showing the author of *Jubilees'* belief in the authority of the *Astronomical Book.*

Jubilees 4.19 says: 'While he slept he saw in a vision what has happened and what will occur—how things will happen for mankind during their history until the day of judgement. He saw everything and understood. He wrote a testimony for himself and placed it upon the earth against all mankind and for their history.' These words are a summary of *1 Enoch* 1–36 generally and point specifically to the proem and central theme of *1 Enoch* as shown in *1 En.* 1.1-9. *Jubilees* 21.10 says:

> Eat its meat during that day and on the next day: but the sun is not to set on the next day until it is eaten. It is not to be left over until the third day because it is not acceptable to him. For it was not pleasing and is therefore commanded. All who eat it will bring guilt upon themselves because this is the way I found [it] written in the book of my ancestors, in the words of Enoch and the words of Noah.

These words again point to the writings of Enoch,[4] and show that the author of *Jubilees* considered all three parts of *1 Enoch* pre-dating *Jubilees* as authoritative for himself and his audience.

The Use of 1 Enoch at Qumran

The Qumran community considered parts of *1 Enoch* to be authoritative, and also appears to have considered *Jubilees* to be authoritative.[5] Fifteen copies[6] of *Jubilees* were found in five caves at Qumran. The number of copies alone may not be enough to show the value of the book at Qumran, but there is enough when that evidence is added to the direct mention of *Jubilees* in the *Damascus Document*[7] (García Mar-

---

4.   'The words of Noah' may also point to the *Noah Apocryphon.*

5.   Lawrence Schiffman (1990) suggests that the people of Qumran were Sadducees, and Norman Golb (1989) suggests that the caves were not part of Qumran but were a depository for documents hidden by people from Jerusalem escaping Romans in the first Jewish Revolt. For a critique of these views, see VanderKam (1994: 92-97). Though the identification of the Qumran people is still a matter of some debate; I agree with VanderKam (1994: 71-98) that the Essenes are still the best case for the inhabitants of Qumran and for the authors of some and collectors of the works known as the Dead Sea Scrolls.

6.   VanderKam suggests that there may have been 16 copies (1989b: 153).

7.   VanderKam mentions that CD 10.7-10 may also refer to *Jub.* 23.11 and 4Q228 in the statement about the age limit for judges being 65 years old, 'for this is the way it is written in the division of the days' (1989b: 154).

tínez 1996: 39). CD 16.2b-4a states: 'And the exact interpretation of their ages about the blindness of Israel in all these matters, behold, it is defined in the book of the divisions of the periods into their Jubilees and their weeks'. The 'Book of the Divisions of the Periods into their Jubilees and Weeks' is a reference to the book of *Jub.* 1.1: 'These are the words regarding the divisions of the times of the law and of the testimony, of the events of the years, of the weeks of their jubilees throughout all the years of eternity as he related [them] to Moses on Sinai when he went up to receive the stone tablets—the law and the commandments...'

Another point showing that the Qumran documents considered *Jubilees* to be authoritative is that the book of *Jubilees*, as VanderKam says, 'blatantly advertises itself as divine revelation' (1994: 153). *Jubilees* 1.7 says, 'now write the entire message which I am telling you today...'; 1.8 says, 'then this testimony will serve as evidence'. These words point to a revelation beyond the Pentateuch, because they claim to be evidence to the descendants of Abraham, Isaac and Jacob after they turn and serve foreign gods. If Qumran, or at least some members of that community, used a book that claimed to be revelation, then they must have to some degree accepted the claims of the book to which they allude. However, VanderKam points out that there is evidence that 4QpGen[a] shows that the '*Jubilees* = chronology' of the flood was not accepted by all the documents at Qumran. Some calendrical texts used a schematic lunar calendar that *Jubilees* condemned, so not all the documents from Qumran agreed with all the details of *Jubilees* (VanderKam 1994: 154-55). Still, if the majority of the Qumran community saw *Jubilees* as authoritative and *Jubilees* used parts of *1 Enoch* as authoritative, then this would be at least one factor in seeing *1 Enoch* as authoritative at Qumran.

Fragments of four books of *1 Enoch*—*The Book of the Watchers*, *The Book of Dreams*, the *Astronomical Book* and *The Epistles of Enoch*—were found in four caves at Qumran. *The Similitudes (Parables)* is missing from Qumran but *The Book of the Giants* (which is not part of the extant Ethiopic book of *1 Enoch*) was found there. (See García Martinez [1996: 467-519] for the specific locations of the fragments.) No part of *1 Enoch* was found in caves 3, 5, 7,[8] or 8, 10 and 11, while

---

8.   Recently Ernest A. Munro, Jr (1997: 307-12) and Emil Puech (1997: 313-23) have argued that cave 7 contains seven fragments in Greek from *1 En.* 100, 103

caves 1, 2, 4 and 6 contained parts of *1 Enoch*. Though Qumran documents do not introduce *1 Enoch* in the authoritative manner that they do *Jubilees*, there are three factors that make *1 Enoch* appear to have had authority at Qumran. First, the number of extant fragments from different copies of sections of the book. Secondly, like *Jubilees*, parts of *1 Enoch* claim for themselves revelation through God's angels. Thirdly, some of the angel stories that expand on the story of Gen. 6.1-4 can be traced to *The Book of the Watchers*, or at least to *Jubilees*, which gets its story of the angels marrying the daughters of men from *The Book of the Watchers*.

1 Enoch 1.1-3; 12.4; 13.7; 14.8; 15.1-2; and 16.2 all show a consciousness of revelation from God or the angels. There are conversations with Uriel, Raphael, Raguel and Michael (who are said to be holy angels) in 21.4-10; 22.6; 23.4; 24.6; 27; 32; and 33. There are also places where Enoch is aware of revelatory visions. The dream visions begin with and say throughout either 'I saw', or 'I looked and understood' (83.1-2; 85.1; 86.1; 87.1; 88.1; 89.2-3, 21, 51, 57; 91.1, 8, 9, 14, 15, 17, 20, 26, 29, 34, 36, 37). The letters also suggest self-consciousness of revelation in 93.2.[9] There is too much evidence for the self-consciousness of revelation in *1 Enoch* for *Jubilees*, the *Genesis Apocryphon* or the *Damascus Document* to use it without their knowing that it claimed authority for itself; and if they were willing to use it with that knowledge, they likely agreed with it. CD 2.16b-19[10] says,

> For many wandered off for these matters; brave heroes yielded on account of them from ancient times until now. For having walked in the stubbornness of their hearts the Watchers of heaven fell; on account of it they were caught, for they did not follow the precepts of God. And their sons whose height was like that of cedars and whose bodies were like mountains fell.

This portion of the *Damascus Document* is not verbatim *1 En.* 7.2 (Black 1985: 28): 'And they became pregnant by them and bore great

---

and 105. (Munro says they all come from 103.3-4, 7-8.)

9. *The Similitudes* also show a self-consciousness of revelation, but since they have not been found at Qumran, they are not included here.

10. This portion is found at Qumran in fragments: 4Q270 (4QD^e), which is fairly broken and does not include the information about the size of the sons of the Watchers from CD 2.19; and 4Q267 (4QD^b), now part of 4Q266 (4QD^a); this fragment is very broken, but does mention 'mountains' in v. 19.

giants of three thousand cubits; and there were [not] born upon the earth off-spring [which grew to their strength]'.[11]

However, the sentiment is the same in *1 En.* 7.2 and CD 2.16-19. The *Damascus Document* likely did not get this information from *Jubilees*, since the extant accounts of *Jubilees* do not contain information on the size of the giants, so it is probable that the information on the size of the giants in CD 2.16-19 is a loose rendition of *1 En.* 7.2.

The *Genesis Apocryphon* (1Q20apGen 2.1-18) tells a story about Enoch's grandson Lamech. Lamech is angry with his wife Bitenosh because she is pregnant and he fears that the watchers have made her pregnant and that her son will be one of the giants. Bitenosh swears that she was not made pregnant by 'any foreigner, or watcher, or son of heaven' (v. 16). In 2.18-26, Lamech has his father Methuselah seek out the advice of his father Enoch. This story is not contained in Genesis or in *Jubilees*, but it is a fairly close rendition of *1 Enoch* 106–107 (except that Lamech's wife Bitenosh is mentioned by name only in *Jub.* 4.28 and not in *1 Enoch* or the Genesis account); therefore, the story in the *Genesis Apocryphon* could be built upon both *Jubilees* 4 and *1 Enoch* 106–107. The *Genesis Apocryphon* also mentions the written work of Enoch in 19.25: 'I read in front of them the [book] of the words of Enoch [...]', after which the text is fragmented and vague, and does not *necessarily* point to *1 Enoch*, but *1 Enoch* is our most likely candidate for the words read here.

1 Enoch *in Jewish Literature outside Qumran*

1 Enoch does not show up a great deal in the Jewish literature outside of the material of the Dead Sea Scrolls found at Qumran, but there is some evidence for it.[12] *1 Enoch* is referred to in *Testament of Reuben* 5:

---

11. 2Q20 does not show the size of the offspring. *The Book of the Giants* fragments at Qumran closely connect the giants with the nephilim, but do not mention their size.

12. Gabrielle Boccaccini (1998) argues that the Essenes mentioned by Philo and Josephus were committed to the Enochic corpus, part of which was rejected by the Qumran community on the basis of its deterministic stance and the Enoch literature's interest in free will of humans and angels. Boccaccini includes in the Enoch corpus: the Temple Scroll, books of *1 Enoch*, and the *Testaments of the Twelve Patriarchs*. He says that Qumran accepted the earlier Enochic literature but turned away from the later books, particularly *The Letter of Enoch* and the *Testaments of the Twelve Patriarchs*.

Women are evil my children... It was thus they allured the Watchers before the flood; for, as a result of seeing them continually these [Watchers] lusted after one another, and they conceived the act in their minds and changed themselves into the shape of men and appeared to them [the women] when they were having intercourse with their husbands. And the women lusting in their minds after their phantom forms, gave birth to giants.

The *Testament of Reuben* either uses *1 Enoch* or one of the books that uses *1 Enoch*. The *Testament of Reuben*, however, does not follow the same line of responsibility. The *Testament of Reuben* makes the women responsible for the actions of the watchers; this is also different from the Christian authors who make the angels responsible.[13] *Testament of Reuben* 5 may be Christian, but the story is from a Jewish source and does not deviate at all from the purpose of the book.[14] *1 Enoch* and *Jubilees* make the watchers responsible, and Gen. 6.1-4 does not assign responsibility to anyone or even openly suggest that anything unrighteous has been done.

Testament of Naphtali 3.5–4.1 mentions that the watchers changed their order and the Lord cursed them at the flood, and 'mentions that I have read in the writing of Enoch that you yourselves will forsake the Lord'. The provenance of the *Testament of Naphtali* is the same as that of *Testament of Reuben* except that a copy of the *Testament of Naphtali* (though possibly different from the *Testament of Naphtali* in the *Testaments of the Twelve Patriarchs*) was discovered in the caves at Qumran. The *Testament of Naphtali* does mention the watchers, and though it does not mention sexual sin, it concentrates on the watchers changing their order.

13. There is one possible exception. In *2 Apol.* 5, Justin Martyr says 'the angels transgressed this order and were enticed by women'. From what Justin says, it is uncertain whether the responsibility lies with the watchers or the women, though the watchers is more likely.

14. The study of the provenance of the *Testaments of the Twelve Patriarchs* has had a varied history. H. Dixon Slingerland's (1977: 112-14) thorough review of the study on the *Testaments of the Twelve Patriarchs* concludes that they were either composed or redacted by a Christian community. M. de Jonge (1984: 508-12) agrees with Slingerland that the *Testaments of the Twelve Patriarchs* are Christian, but does allow that there were other testaments in Hebrew and Aramaic and that there is a Jewish background to the *Testaments of the Twelve Patriarchs*.

Targum Pseudo-Jonathan[15] mentions the names Shemhazai and Azazel, the chief angels of the watcher, and the story found in *1 En.* 6.3 and Gen. 6.4. *Targum Pseudo-Jonathan* 5.24, speaking of Enoch, says 'and he was called Metatron, the Great Scribe'. The connection with Metatron seems to come from after 425 CE (Maher 1992). This at least says that Enoch traditions were not completely ignored or crept back into favour (to a minor extent) in Jewish literature after Augustine was rejecting portions of *1 Enoch* in Christian literature.

Summary
Jubilees used *1 Enoch* as authoritative literature, and Qumran used both *Jubilees* and some of the books of *1 Enoch* authoritatively; so for at least one segment of Judaism—the Qumran Essenes—some books of *1 Enoch* were authoritative literature. The watcher story shows up several times in the literature at Qumran, and then the hard evidence for the story disappears from Jewish literature except for the *Testaments of the Twelve Patriarchs*, which have an uncertain provenance. The re-emergence of the story in *Targum Pseudo-Jonathan* is puzzling. After Qumran, *1 Enoch* was picked up by Christians who seemed to honour or disparage it in turn until the time of Augustine, who openly denied the possibility of the watcher story.

Christian Use of 1 Enoch

Jude, 2 Peter and the Apostolic and Church Fathers give evidence to the place of *1 Enoch* in the first three centuries of the Church. 2 Peter follows Jude in using *1 Enoch* as authoritative literature. The Apostolic and Church Fathers' views on *1 Enoch* vary, but it is an important sign of the importance of *1 Enoch* that the Church debated the authority of *1 Enoch* in the centuries following the New Testament. The vast majority of the allusions are from the watcher story.

The New Testament
2 Peter apparently alludes to the book of *1 Enoch* in 2.4,[16] by using Jude 6: 'For if God did not spare angels who sinned but cast them into

---

15. Maher (1992: 11-12) lists four scholars that date *Targum Pseudo-Jonathan* after the seventh century CE.
16. Charles (1913: 180-81) lists a great many other portions of the New Testament that may borrow language from *1 Enoch*, but these are all very small

the darkness of Tartarus to be kept for judgement' (2 Pet. 2.4); 'but the angels who did not keep their own domain but left their own abode He has kept unto the judgement of the great day in eternal bonds under darkness' (Jude 6). Several modern commentators argue that the author of 2 Peter has followed Jude 6 on this (Bauckham 1983: 248; Side-bottom 1982: 68, 113; Neyrey 1993: 197).[17] Bauckham (1983: 246) says that 2 Peter is partially dependent on Jude 6, but is independently drawing on paraenetic tradition that also lies behind Jude 5–7. The paraenetic traditions are in Sir. 16.7-10; CD 2.17–3.12; *3 Macc.* 2.4-7; *T. Naph.* 3.4-5; *m. Sanh.* 10.3.[18] Sirach was written in the first quarter of the second century BCE (Skehan and Di Lella 1987: 10). The *Damascus Document* is a document written at some point in the second century BCE to the first century CE; *3 Maccabees* is from the third century BCE.[19] E. Bickerman (in Collins 1984: 347-48) suggests that *T. Naph.* 5.8 was written before the expulsion of the Syrians in 141 BCE, and the parallels with the Qumran scrolls may reflect the early Hasmonean period, but there is also much paraenetic material that could come from any time in the Hellenistic or Roman era. As we have seen, most of this paraenetic material that 2 Peter is seen to have used relies on either *Jubilees* or portions of *1 Enoch*. If this is true, then at least two New Testament books—2 Peter and Jude—use *1 Enoch* as an important source for their material.

Bauckham (1983: 247) contends that 2 Peter was unfamiliar with the text of *1 Enoch*, for the echoes of *1 Enoch* in Jude 6 are lost in 2 Pet. 2.4. However, 2 Peter puts the story of the flood for the destruction of the ancient world and the salvation of Noah directly after the story from the watchers, which is what the book of *Jubilees* does in 5.1-11. This ties the flood directly to the judgment due to the corruption of people,

references and many could come from other portions of the Old Testament. Two interesting ones, however, are Rev. 14.20, 'blood came out even to the horses bridles' (cf. *1 En.* 100.3: 'the horse shall walk up to the breast in the blood of sinners'); and Rom. 8.38; Eph. 1.21; Col. 1.16, 'angels...principalities...powers' (cf. *1 En.* 61.10 'angels of power and...angels of principalities').

17. Norman Hillyer (1992: 19) sees a common source for Jude and 2 Peter. Stott (1995: 160) sees 2 Peter as being earlier than Jude.

18. For a study of these passages, see Berger (1970: 1-47) and Schlosser (1973: 13-36). Bauckham (1983: 46) mentions that Lührmann (1972: 131) corrects Berger's view on Sir. 16.6-10.

19. See Nickelsburg 1984: 33, 80.

which came from the corrupt angels (watchers) and their sons the giants. The flood was still against mankind, for the watchers were bound in the depths of the earth for the great judgment and the giants killed each other.

Genesis 6.1-4 tells a similar story, putting the story of the sons of God marrying the daughters of men and creating the nephilim just before the story of the flood. However, the Genesis account does not include the aspect of the watchers being bound in the depths of the earth until the day of the great judgment, which *Jub.* 5.10 and 2 Pet. 2.4 include.[20] Both 2 Peter and *Jub.* 5.1-11 are shortened versions or capsules of *1 Enoch* 6–11, where the deluge of *1 En.* 10.10 is a direct result of the activities of the watchers corrupting mankind in *1 Enoch* 6–10.[21] 2 Peter's purpose was different from but dependent on Jude,[22] but the author may possibly have known the story of the watchers from sources other than Jude. Most importantly for our purpose, the *Book of the Watchers* did underlie 2 Pet. 2.4-5 just as it did Jude 6 and 14.

2 Peter 1.20, 21 and 3.2 add strength to the argument of the authority of the watcher tradition from *1 Enoch*. Though the meaning of these verses is disputed, most scholars hold that 2 Peter is referring to the words of Old Testament prophets. *1 Enoch* stands alongside portions of the Old Testament in the midst of 2 Peter's argument, which relies on the authority of Old Testament prophetic words.

There is fair bit of debate as to the meaning of τὸν προφητικὸν λόγον (the prophetic word) in 2 Pet. 1.19. Bauckham (1983: 224) outlines the views as: (1) Old Testament messianic prophecy; (2) the entire Old Testament understood as messianic prophecy; (3) a specific Old Testament prophecy; (4) Old Testament and New Testament prophecies; (5) 2 Pet. 1.20–2.19; and (6) the transfiguration itself as a prophecy of the parousia. Bauckham (1983: 224) prefers a modified version of (2), which would say that that the eschatological message is based on 1.19, which refers to Old Testament prophecy, and 1.16-18, which refers to their own eyewitness account mentioned in 1.16-18. Other

---

20. CD 2.17–3.12 also includes the story of the watchers just before the story of the flood.

21. Note that *3 Macc.* 2.4 and *T. Naph.* 3.5 also connect the watchers with the flood.

22. Jude's argument is against those who fell from grace or disobeyed God. 2 Peter's argument is for God's just judgment (Neyrey 1993: 198-99).

than Neyrey (1993: 178-82), who holds to (6), all allow that τὸν προφητικὸν λόγον points to the Old Testament prophecies. Even Neyrey allows this, in that the emphasis he makes is because the 'issue is not the source of the prophecy but its interpretation' and he allows that 3.2 points to 'holy prophets' who seem also to be the Old Testament prophets (Neyrey 1993: 182).

Though there is some trouble with the exact interpretation of 2 Pet. 1.20-21, it is clear that 'prophecy of scripture' (1.20) and 'A prophecy...men of God being carried along by the Holy Spirit spoke' (1.21) point to the authoritative words of prophets; and that 2 Pet. 3.2, 'to remember the words having been previously spoken by the holy prophets', points to the words of authoritative prophets before the New Testament writers since 'and by your apostles' distinguishes the apostles separately.[23]

2 Peter 1.20, 21 and 3.2 show a view of Old Testament prophets' words being authoritative for the author of 2 Peter. Sandwiched in these verses that show a high view of the Old Testament is a portion from *The Book of the Watchers*. It would appear that the author of 2 Peter would also have a high regard for *The Book of the Watchers*, either from personal knowledge, or, as Bauckham (1983: 246) has suggested, from others (such as Jude 6) who showed a personal knowledge of the book. 2 Peter uses the watcher story as an example of God's ability to punish the unrighteous, but he is not so interested in the details of the story as the outcome for the watchers, who are treated as real examples.

Jude also uses *1 Enoch* authoritatively. The introduction, 'and to these ones even Enoch the seventh from Adam prophesied saying', shows that Jude considered the words of Jude 14, and the book of *1 Enoch* from which they came, to be authoritative. This is shown in two ways: first, Jude used an introductory formula which resembles that of several portions of the New Testament, particularly Mt. 15.7 and Mk 7.6; secondly, Jude pointed to the fulfilment of a prophet's words in Jude's own time, which is also common in the New Testament writings.

---

23. Sidebottom (1982: 118) would disagree and says that both prophets and apostles in 2 Pet. 3.2 point to New Testament writers since there is no mention of Old Testament proof texts to follow; both Bauckham (1983: 283) and Neyrey (1993: 227) counter Sidebottom, saying that there is a distinction that prophets refer to ancient prophets and the commandment of 'our lord and saviour' points to the words of the New Testament apostles.

B.B. Warfield (1982: 843-44),[24] in an article on inspiration, shows some of the formulas used to introduce works that were considered 'Scripture' by the New Testament authors. Warfield does give preference to the term 'it is written' or 'it is said', but these are by no means the only terms used. Often the term 'it is written' is used (Mt. 4.4; Mk 1.2; Lk. 24.46), and sometimes 'according to the scriptures' is used (1 Cor. 15–16; Acts 8.35; 17.3; 26.22; Rom. 1.17; 3.4, 10; 4.17; 11.26; 14.11; 1 Cor. 1.19; 2.9; 3.19; 15.45; Gal. 3.10; 13; 4.22, 27). He also mentions, 'Therefore, as the Holy Spirit says, Today when you hear his voice' (Heb. 3.7 quoting Ps. 95.7); and '…who by the mouth of our father David, thy servant did say by the Holy Spirit, "why did the Gentiles rage…?"' (Acts 4.25 quoting Ps. 2.1). Sometimes 'it is said' replaces 'it is written' (Heb. 3.15; Rom. 4.18; also Lk. 4.12 replaces the 'it is written' of Matthew). Warfield, therefore, correctly leaves some room here for other introductory formulas and evidence for other introductory formulas for inspired writings.

It would appear also that Jude would consider Enoch and his words as historical. Bruce Metzger (1951: 306) says that the New Testament frequently recognizes the instrumentality of human authors such as Moses, David, Isaiah, Jeremiah, Daniel, Hosea, Joel and Enoch.[25] Metzger's words correspond with what was said earlier about introductory formulas being varied and referring to authoritative individuals as well as works, or at least referring to the individuals to whom the authoritative works are ascribed. Many of these formulas use forms of λέγω (I say) which Jude also uses. Most of the λέγω formulas point to the prophet Isaiah (Rom. 9.27; 10.19; Jn 12.38, 39; Mt. 3.3; 4.14; 8.17; 12.17; Acts 28.25, 26), but other prophets are mentioned also (e.g. Jeremiah in Mt. 2.17; Mt. 27.9 is interesting, in that it ascribes to Jeremiah a prophecy from Zech. 11.12, 13). The book of Hosea is mentioned in Rom. 9.25 (rather than the prophet himself), but generally, individuals are mentioned for the works that are ascribed to them and most of the references point to fulfilments in the days of the New Testament writers, similar to the way Jude remarks about an individual prophet whose words are fulfilled in his day.

---

24. Also see Warfield's chapter '"It says:" "Scripture says:" "God says:"' (1948: 299-351).

25. Metzger (1987: 303) lists the passages where individuals are referred to by a variety of formulas.

In a couple of instances the formulas used in the New Testament to refer to a prophet from an authoritative book closely resemble the wording of Jude 14. In Mt. 13.14, prophecy is in the form of a noun rather than a verb, but the sentiment is similar to Jude and again the prediction of Isaiah is said to be fulfilled in the people of Matthew's day.[26] The second instance, in Mt. 15.7, has ὑποκριταί, καλῶς ἐπροφή-τευσεν περὶ ὑμῶν Ἡσαΐας λέγων ('hypocrites, well Isaiah prophesied concerning you, saying...'); which is almost the same formula used in Jude 14, προεφήτευσεν δὲ καὶ τούτοις ἕβδομος ἀπὸ Ἀδὰμ Ἐνὼχ λέγων ('to these even Enoch the seventh from Adam prophesied, saying...'). A parallel to Mt. 15.7 in Mk 7.6 adds 'as it is written', both of which point to a prophecy from an authoritative book, even though one has the term 'as it is written' and the other uses 'says'. More importantly both passages use the word 'prophesied' in a similar manner to Jude 14, so Jude's formula is not unique to him. Jude's formula also resembles that of other Jewish literature. Metzger (1951: 299) mentions that in the Mishnah שנאמר ('it is written', or 'for it is written') is the most often used formula with over 300 occurrences.

Qumran also had a number of ways of introducing such material (Bauckham 1990: 227). Bauckham's example of 4QAges (4Q180) shows the use of pesher on an apocryphal work, similar to the pesharim Qumran uses for other scriptural works. This is comparable, he suggests, to Jude's use of pesher for an apocryphal work. Joseph Fitzmyer (1960: 303), in a work examining the quotation formulas in the *Damascus Document*, the *Manual of Discipline*, the *War Scroll* and *Florilegium*, noted that the New Testament tended to use the formulas of fulfilment or realization, where such formulas are almost non-existent at Qumran, likely because Qumran was looking forward, whereas the New Testament was looking at the culmination of events in Christ. As Fitzmyer mentions, F.F. Bruce (1988: 64) said 'the New Testament interpretation of the Old Testament is not only eschatological, but also Christological. Jude does this seeing the fulfilment of Enoch's words in his present day (v. 14).[27] Fitzmyer (1960: 305) then shows that the use

---

26. Kaiser (1985: 212-13; also 43-44) also deals with the problem of past particularity having present significance for the New Testament writers. Gundry mentions that the use of ἀναπληροῦν (fulfil) suggests that there was a consciousness that the text had a meaning for Isaiah's day as well as a meaning for the New Testament times (Gundry 1975: 213).

27. Fitzmyer (1960: 305) lists four types of quotations at Qumran and in the

of the formula 'as God has said by means of the prophet Isaiah'[28] from CD 4.15 is a reference to the *Testament of Levi* in the Greek *Testaments of the Twelve Patriarchs*, but concludes that the introductory formula needs not make it canonical like the books that are found in later canonical lists. The formula alone may not be enough, but in the case of *1 Enoch*, where such a formula is combined with other evidence, then the case becomes much stronger.

A strict adherence to two or three introductory formulas does not fit the evidence of the Mishnah, Qumran or, most importantly for our purposes, the New Testament. In addition, there is ample evidence from the New Testament to suggest that Jude's introduction formula to the quotation he attributes to Enoch fits the introductory formula that is used of several prophets to which Old Testament books are ascribed, particularly the formula of Mt. 15.7 and Mk 7.6. The evidence suggests, as Bauckham claimed, that Jude intended the words of Enoch in v. 14 to be considered inspired prophecy. Jude 6 alludes to the watcher story and v. 14 quotes from *1 Enoch*, both of which seem intended to show that judgment upon the opponents of Jude's audience is imminent and certain.

Apostolic and Church Fathers
Several of the Apostolic and Church Fathers saw *1 Enoch* as authoritative.[29] *1 Enoch* is mentioned in *Barn.* 4.3; 16.5; Justin Martyr, *2 Apologia* 5; Clement of Alexandria, *Strom.* 5.1.10; Origen, *Contra Celsum* 5, 52; Tertullian, *De cultu fem.* 1.3.50; and Didymus the Blind. Bigg summarizes the view of *1 Enoch* by the Church Fathers:

> In short, at the time when Barnabas wrote, Enoch was held to be an inspired book, it retained this reputation more or less throughout the second century, and from that date onward was emphatically condemned and the ground of the condemnation was its attribution of carnal lust to heavenly beings (1946: 309).

New Testament: (1) literal or historical; (2) modernized; (3) accommodation; (4) eschatological. Jude's reference fits the eschatological type of quotation. For treatments of the use of the Old Testament in the New Testament, see Beale (1994) and Kaiser (1985: 43-57; 212-13).

28. García Martínez (1996: 35) places the expression in CD 4.13.

29. VanderKam (1996: 34-102) gives a thorough review of the watcher story in Christian literature, including the gnostic literature.

The epistle of *Barnabas* is an anonymous work to an uncertain, likely Egyptian, audience. It has an uncertain date from either the first century, based on the ch. 6 reference to the ten kings, or to about 132 CE based on the reference to the rebuilding of the temple in ch. 16. Neither of these dates is without difficulty, but a date of late first or early second century CE is suitable (Lake 1977: 337-38; Coxe 1885: 133; Staniforth 1968: 189-90; Grant 1964: 78-79). The letter was quoted as Scripture by Clement of Alexandria, but was not considered so highly by Jerome (Kraft 1978: 263).

Barnabas 4.3 says, 'the first offence is near concerning which it is written, as Enoch said, "For unto this the master has shortened the seasons and the days"'. 'It is written, as Enoch said' fits very well with the New Testament introductory formula used of authoritative works. After using the introductory formula, the epistle makes an editorial comment based loosely on Enochic writings. Kraft (1965) suggests that two weak candidates for the passage are *1 En.* 89.61-64; 90.17; or *2 En.* 34.1-3. It is odd, but not without precedent, that such a specific formula is followed by such a loose rendering (cf. Mt. 27.9, discussed above, where Matthew introduces Jeremiah, but quotes Zechariah). It is also possible, though not likely, that *Barnabas* is quoting a portion not extant today or, somewhat more likely, a portion by a work other than Enoch. What is important, however, is the introductory formula and that the author used the name of a work, suggesting that the author would have considered his source to be authoritative. *Barnabas* 16.5 is said by Grant (1964: 77) to be a direct quotation from *1 Enoch* 89, which would fit nicely with its preceding paragraph, since it is introduced with the words, 'for it says in scripture'. Unfortunately, *1 Enoch* 89, though related to the symbolism of *Barn.* 16.5, does not contain a direct quotation, but *Barn.* 16.5 might be a summary of *1 En.* 89.45-77. There is mention of a tower in 89.50, 54, 67, of the Lord abandoning his sheep in 89.54-56, and of sheep of the pasture in 89.54, all of which are present in *Barn.* 16.5. Another problem, though not insurmountable, is that *1 Enoch* 89 is not particularly eschatological; it refers to the period of the Judges to the time of Alexander the Great (Black 1985: 78-80). However, authors of the New Testament sometimes interpreted a prophet's words for their own time, such as the use of Isa. 7.14 being interpreted as pointing to Jesus Christ. In summary, it would appear, though not conclusively, that the author of *Barnabas* was aware of the book of *1 Enoch*, and used it as Scripture.

Justin Martyr (fl. c. mid-second century) uses *1 Enoch*'s account of
the angels in *2 Apologia* 5: 'The angels transgressed this order and were
enticed by women and begat children, the ones which are called
demons; and enslaved the remaining human race to themselves, partly
through magic writings and partly through fears and the punishment
they brought, and partly through teaching them to offer sacrifices and
incense and drink offerings of which they needed after they were
enslaved by lustful passions'. Where Justin got these exact words is
uncertain, but they can be traced to *The Book of the Watchers*. '[T]he
angels transgressed this order and were enticed by women' points to
1 En. 6.1. Justin mentions that the children were of the women and
angels were δαίμονες (demons), which is not found in Jude or 2 Peter.
He also states that the angels subdued men by μαγικῶν γραφῶν (magic
writings), which is not quite the same as *1 En.* 8.3 which says that
Semhazah taught spell-binding, and Hermoni taught the loosing of
spells, magic, sorcery and sophistry. *1 Enoch* 7 mentions that the offspring of the angels devoured man, but not that the angels in particular
brought fear. Justin's account varies according to his purpose, but
shows a clear reliance on the book of *1 Enoch*, or on some source that
itself relied on *1 Enoch*.

Clement of Alexandria (150–214 CE) was versed in philosophy, archaeology, poetry, mythology and literature. He often used anthologies
and florilegia, but also clearly knew the Scriptures—he quotes the Old
Testament around 1500 times, and the New Testament around 2000
times—as well as classical literature, with over 360 citations (Quasten
1954a: 5-6). *Stromata* is one of Clement of Alexandria's theological
writings. He mentions Enoch in *Strom.* 5.1.10, 2. Clement uses Philo as
a source in *Stromata*, calling him a Pythagorean who proved the antiquity of Jewish philosophy (*Strom.* 1.135.3; Grant 1988: 180-81).
Clement, *Strom.* 5.1.10 says that the philosophers were thieves taking
their principle dogmas from Moses and the prophets. After this, he adds
a portion of *1 Enoch* from *The Book of the Watchers*:

> To which we shall add that angels who had obtained the superior rank,
> having sunk into pleasures, told to the women the secrets which had
> come to their knowledge; while the rest of the angels concealed them, or
> rather, kept them against the coming of the Lord. Thence emanated the
> doctrine of providence, and the revelation of high things; and prophecy
> having already been imparted to the philosophers of the Greeks, the
> treatment of dogma arose among the philosophers, sometimes true when

they hit the mark, sometimes erroneous when they comprehended not the secret of the prophetic allegory.

Clement uses the words of an ancient to show that Greek philosophers retrieved their ideas from earlier prophets, of which, presumably, Enoch was one. Later, Photius (*Lexicon* 109) blames Clement in severe terms for adopting the account of angelic sin (Bigg 1946: 309).

Tertullian (155–220 CE) became a Christian in 193 CE (Quasten: 1954a: 246-47; Barnes 1985: 1-2).[30] He mentions *1 Enoch* in *De cultu fem.* 1.2, 3.[31] In 1.2, Tertullian speaks at length of ornaments and make-up on women being traced back to the fallen angels' dealing with women in *The Book of the Watchers*. He mentions 'those angels, who rushed from heaven on the daughters of men' and then says that they taught the women about metallurgy and eye make-up and jewellery (from the metallurgy). Because the angels were ill masters, they taught lustful things. He then interprets the watchers story for his own, saying, 'women who possessed angels (as husbands) could desire nothing more', but that they became worse for their lusts. Tertullian stated that men would judge angels because of the actions of the watchers. There is much that could be said about Tertullian's feelings on make-up or his interpretative skills and methods, but what is important here is that Tertullian used the watcher story as an actual event to support his own thesis. In 1.3, Tertullian defends the genuineness of the prophecy of Enoch:

> I am aware that the Scripture of Enoch which has assigned this order (of action) to angels is not received by some because it is not admitted into the Jewish canon either. I suppose they did not think that, having survived the deluge, it could have safely survived that world-wide calamity, the abolisher of all things. If that is their reason then let them recall to their memory that Noah, the survivor of the deluge was a great grandson of Enoch himself, and he, of course, had heard and remembered, from domestic renown and hereditary tradition, concerning his own great-grandfather's 'grace in the sight of god', and concerning all his preachings since Enoch had given no other charge to Methuselah than that he should hand on the knowledge of them to his posterity... If Noah had not

---

30. Coxe (1963: 3-5) felt that Tertullian was born 145 CE and died about 240 CE.

31. There are other mentions of *1 Enoch* in Tertullian's writings: *Orat.* 12.5; *De cultu fem.* 7.1-4, but these two could also point to Gen. 6.1-4. *Apol.* 35.12 also mentions *1 Enoch* (see Daniélou 1977: 162-67).

> had this by so short a route there would still be this to warrant our assertion of this scripture: he could have equally renewed it under the Spirit's inspiration... Jewish literature is generally agreed to have been restored through Ezra... By the Jews it may now seem to have been rejected for that reason just like all the other (portions) nearly which tell of Christ... To these contradictions is added the fact that Enoch possesses a testimony in the Apostle Jude.

This portion shows the very strong sentiment by Tertullian that (for him) *1 Enoch* was inspired Scripture.[32] Important also is his belief that Jude considered it to be Scripture. Tertullian shows us that, at the same time that Origen was rejecting *1 Enoch*, others were strongly defending its inspiration. Origen said that *1 Enoch* was 'generally' not accepted by the churches as Scripture, but there were those who would defend its status while recognizing that by the second century the 'Jews' were rejecting it.

Origen (185–254 CE) mentions *1 Enoch* in his argument with Celsus. All that is known of Celsus's *Logos alethes*, or 'True Account' (c. 178 CE[33]), is from Origen's lengthy quotation in his *Contra Celsum* from c. 248 CE (Grant 1988: 133, 136). Celsus took some of his points straight from the Academy (a group of Plato's successors who opposed all Stoic doctrines), against which Origen would argue the normative Stoic doctrine, or, if Celsus argued from a Stoic position, Origen would argue using the Academy's argument (Chadwick 1965: x-xi). What is more important for the argument of this paper is that Origen follows some of his predecessors such as Clement,[34] Justin, Tatian, Theophilus and Athenagoras in using the traditional apologetic developed in the Hellenistic synagogue which shows that Moses and the prophets were earlier than the Greek philosophers and therefore a source of their learning (Chadwick 1965: ix). In *Cels.* 5.52-53 Origen quotes Celsus's argument: 'If they say that [God] is the only one, they would be convicted of telling lies and contradicting themselves. For they say that others have also often come, and, in fact, sixty or seventy at once, who became evil and were punished by being cast under the earth in chains.'

32. Tertullian also makes a clear reference to *1 Enoch* in *De idololatria* 4 and 9.
33. Chadwick (1965: xxiv-xxviii) gives the arguments for the date of Celsus and concludes that it was written between 177–80 CE.
34. Munck contended that Origen was a pupil of Clement of Alexandria (1933: 224-29). Though Chadwick disagrees with this, he does agree that Origen was influenced by Clement (1965: 9).

Origen argues in 5.54 that, 'Celsus misunderstood what was written in the book of Enoch'. This at least tells us that Origen was familiar with a book he called the book of Enoch, which contained Celsus's argument from what is presently known as *The Book of the Watchers*. Origen goes on to say, 'the books entitled Enoch are not generally held to be divine by the churches'. Origen knew that many churches, of his association anyway, were inclined to disregard Enoch. 'Generally' implies that there was some argument in Origen's day as to the inspiration of *1 Enoch*. Origen does not here directly give his opinion on the book, but suggests in 5.55 that he himself is uncertain as to 'the truth…about the Sons of God who desired the daughters of men'.

In *De prin.* 1.3.3, Origen shows a distinction between his view of *1 Enoch* and Scripture. He gives a quotation from Hermas and then says, 'And in a book of Enoch we also have similar descriptions. But up to the present time we have been able to find no statement in holy scripture.'

After the second century CE, as has been pointed out by Bigg (1946: 309), *1 Enoch* was condemned due to its position on the carnal lust of heavenly beings.[35] The main reason for the decline of the use of *1 Enoch* is its explicit terms about the actions of the angels in Gen. 6.1-4—a position that both Jude and 2 Peter defend.

Conclusion

The works of 2 Peter and the Apostolic and Church Fathers mentioned above show that *1 Enoch* was argued by factions of the Church to be authoritative. That there was debate at all shows the prominence of the book through the first three centuries of the Common Era. After Augustine, there is little mention of *1 Enoch* in Christian literature; and after Qumran, there is little mention of *1 Enoch* in Jewish literature. The power parties or at least the prolific parties either suppress or ignore the book, but the continued use of *1 Enoch* and the Watcher story shows a connection between the thought of the two groups. This cohesiveness was ignored or denied by those who would eventually become the 'keepers of truth'.

35. Charles (1913: 184) also notes that Augustine (of Hippo) condemned the book in *Civ.* 15.23.4; 18.38, and then the book is explicitly condemned in *Apost. Const.* 6.16 and after that fell into disuse in the Western Church, except in Georgius Syncellus's *Chronographia*, which preserves fragments of it.

SELECT BIBLIOGRAPHY

Barnes, T.D.
    1985   *Tertullian* (Oxford: Clarendon Press),
Bauckham, R.
    1983   *Jude, 2 Peter* (WBC, 50; Waco, TX: Word Books).
    1990   *Jude and the Relatives of Jesus in the Early Church* (Edinburgh: T. & T. Clark).
Beale, G.K.
    1994   *The Right Doctrine from the Wrong Texts: Essays on the Use of the Old Testament in the New* (Grand Rapids: Baker Book House).
Berger, K.
    1970   'Hertherzigkeit und Gottes Gesetz, die Vorgeschichte des anti-judischen Vorwerts in MC 10:5', *ZNW* 61: 1-47.
Bigg, C.
    1946   *The Epistles of St Peter and St Jude* (ICC; Edinburgh: T. & T. Clark).
Black, M.
    1985   *The Book of Enoch or 1 Enoch* (Leiden: E.J. Brill).
Boccaccini, G.
    1998   *Beyond the Essene Hypothesis* (Grand Rapids: Eerdmans).
Bruce, F.F.
    1988   *The Canon of Scripture* (Downers Grove, IL: InterVarsity Press).
Campenhausen, H. von
    1955   *The Fathers of the Greek Church* (trans. S. Godman; New York: Pantheon Books).
Chadwick, H.
    1965   *Origen Contra Celsum* (Cambridge: Cambridge University Press).
Charles, R.H.
    1913   *The Apocrypha and Pseudepigrapha of the Old Testament*, II (Oxford: Clarendon Press).
Collins, J.J.
    1984   'Testaments', in M.E. Stone (ed.), *Jewish Writings of the Second Temple Period* (Philadelphia: Fortress Press; Assen: Van Gorcum, 1984): 331-44.
Coxe, A.C.
    1885   *The Apostolic Father with Justin Martyr and Irenaeus* (ANF, 1; repr., Grand Rapids: Zondervan).
    1963   *The Writings of the Fathers down to AD 325* (ANF, 3; Grand Rapids: Zondervan).
Daniélou, J.
    1977   'The Origins of Latin Christianity', in D. Smith and J.A. Baker (trans.), *An Early Christian Doctrine before the Council of Nicea*, III (London: Westminster Press).
Fitzmyer, J.A.
    1960   'The Use of Explicit Old Testament Quotations in Qumran Literature and in the New Testament', *NTS* 7: 297-333.

García Martínez, F.
    1996   *The Dead Sea Scrolls Translated* (ed. W. Watson; Leiden: E.J. Brill).
Golb, N.
    1989   'The Dead Sea Scrolls: A New Perspective', *The American Scholar* 58: 177-207.
Grant, R.
    1964   'An Introduction', in *idem* (ed.), *The Apostolic Fathers: A New Translation and Commentary*, I (New York: Thomas Nelson & Sons).
Grant, R.M.
    1988   *Greek Apologists of the Second Century* (Philadelphia: Westminster Press).
Grelot, P.
    1958   'La legende d'Henoch dans les apocrypha et la Bible: Origine et signification', *RSR* 46: 181-220.
Gundry, R.H.
    1975   *The Use of the Old Testament in St Matthew's Gospel* (Leiden: E.J. Brill).
Hillyer, N.
    1992   *1 and 2 Peter, Jude* (Peabody, MA: Hendrickson).
Jansen, H.L.
    1939   *Die Henochgestalt: Eine vergleichende religionsgeschichtliche Untersuchung* (Norske Videnskaps-Akademi i Oslo II. Hist.-Filos. klase 1; Oslo: Dybwad).
Jonge, M. de
    1984   'The Testaments of the Twelve Patriarchs', in H.F.D. Sparks (ed.), *The Old Testament Apocryphal Literature* (Oxford: Clarendon Press).
Kaiser, W.C.
    1985   *The Use of the Old Testament in the New* (Chicago: Moody Press).
Kee, H.
    1983   'Testaments of the Twelve Patriarchs', OTP, II: 775-828.
Knibb, M.A.
    1978   *The Ethiopic Book of Enoch* (Oxford: Clarendon Press).
Kraft, R.A.
    1965   'Barnabas and the Didache', in R. Grant (ed.), *The Apostolic Fathers: A New Translation and Commentary*, I (New York: Thomas Nelson & Sons).
    1978   'The Letter of Barnabas', in J. Sparks (ed.), *The Apostolic Fathers* (Nashville: Thomas Nelson).
Lake, K.
    1977   *The Apostolic Fathers* (LCL; Cambridge, MA: Harvard University Press).
Lührmann, D.
    1972   'Noah and Lot (Lk 17:26-29)—ein Nachtrag', *ZNW* 63: 130-33.
Maher, M.
    1992   *Targum Pseudo-Jonathan: Genesis* (Collegeville, MN: Liturgical Press).
Metzger, B.
    1951   'The Formulas Introducing Quotations of Scripture in the New Testament and the Mishnah', *JBL* 70: 297-307.
    1987   *The Canon of the New Testament* (Oxford: Clarendon Press).

Munck, J.
    1933   'Untersuchungen über Klemens von Alexandria', *Forschungen zur Kirchen und Geistesgeschichte* 2: 224-95.
Munro, E.A., Jr
    1997   'The Greek of Enoch from Qumran Cave 7 (7Q4, 7Q8, &7Q12 = 7Qen gr) = Enoch 103: 3-4, 7-8', *RevQ* 18: 307-12.
Neyrey, J.H.
    1993   *2 Peter, Jude* (AB, 37c; New York: Doubleday).
Nickelsburg, G.W.
    1984   'The Bible Written and Expanded', in M. Stone (ed.), *Jewish Writings of the Second Temple Period* (Philadelphia: Fortress Press), pp. 90-97.
Puech, E.
    1997   'Sept fragments de la lettre d'Henoch (1 Hen 100, 103 et 105) dans la grotte 7 de Qumran (=7QHen gr)', *RevQ* 18: 313-23.
Quasten J.
    1954a   *Patrology*, I (Westminster, MD: The Newman Press).
    1954b   *Patrology*, II (Westminster, MD: The Newman Press).
Schiffman, L.
    1990   'The New Halakhik Letter (4QMMT) and the Origins of the Dead Sea Sect', *BA* 53: 64-73.
Schlosser, J.
    1973   'Les jours de Noe et de Lot: Apropos de Luc, 17:26-3', *RB* 18: 1-36.
Sidebottom, E.M.
    1982   *James, Jude, 2 Peter* (NCBC; Grand Rapids: Eerdmans).
Skehan, P., and A. Di Lella
    1987   *The Wisdom of Ben Sirach* (New York: Doubleday).
Slingerland, H.D.
    1977   *The Testaments of the Twelve Patriarchs: A Critical Historical Research* (SBLMS, 21; Atlanta: Scholars Press).
    1992   *The Testaments of the Twelve Patriarchs* (SBLMS, 12; Atlanta: Scholars Press).
Staniforth, M.
    1968   *Early Christian Writings* (Harmondsworth: Penguin Books).
Stott, J.
    1995   *The Message of 2 Peter and Jude* (Leicester: Inter-Varsity Press).
VanderKam, J.C.
    1977   *Textual and Historical Studies in the Book of Jubilees* (Missoula, MT: Scholars Press).
    1984   *Enoch and the Growth of an Apocalyptic Tradition* (CBQMS, 16; Washington, DC: Catholic Biblical Association).
    1989a   'The Book of Jubilees: A Critical Text', in *CSCO*, Vol. 510.
    1989b   'The Book of Jubilees: A Critical Text', in *CSCO*, Vol. 511.
    1994   *The Dead Sea Scrolls Today* (Grand Rapids: Eerdmans).
    1996   '1 Enoch, Enochic Motifs, and Enoch in Early Christian Literature, in J. VanderKam and W. Adler (eds.), *The Jewish Apocalyptic Heritage in Early Christianity* (Assen: Van Gorcum).
Van Winden, J.C.M.
    1971   *An Early Christian Philosopher* (Leiden: E.J. Brill).

Vaughan, C., and T.D. Lea
    1988   *I, II Peter, and Jude* (Grand Rapids: Zondervan).
Warfield, B.B.
    1948   *The Inspiration and Authority of the Bible* (Grand Rapids: Baker Book
             House).
    1982   'Inspiration', *International Standard Bible Encyclopedia*, II, pp. 839-49.
Williamson G.A. (trans.)
    1965   *Eusebius: The History of the Church* (Harmondsworth: Penguin Books).
    1984   *Eusebius: The History of the Church* (New York: Dorset Press).
Wintermute, O.S.
    1983   'Jubilees', *OTP*, II, pp. 35-42.
Zimern, H.
    1901   *Beiträge zur Kenntnis der babylonischen Religion: Die Beschwörungs-*
             tafeln Surpu, Ritualtafeln für den Wahrsager, Beschwörer und Sänger
             (Assyriologische bibliothek, 12; Leipzig: J.C. Hinrichs).

THE CONCEPT OF 'WORKS OF THE LAW' IN
JEWISH AND CHRISTIAN LITERATURE

Jacqueline C.R. de Roo

Introduction

Many scholars have debated Paul's meaning when he uses the expression 'works of the law' (ἔργα νόμου) in his letters. The phrase appears eight times in Romans and Galatians: Rom. 3.20, 28; Gal. 2.16 (3×); 3.2, 5, 10.[1] A question directly related to the meaning of 'works of the law' is: 'Why does Paul say that no one will be justified by "works of the law"?' Several different interpretations have been given. Some have argued that the term 'works of the law' in Pauline literature has a positive meaning: it implies the fulfillment of God's requirements. 'Works of the law' do not justify, because nobody can fulfill the law perfectly (with the exception of Jesus Christ). Both Jew and Greek are unable to do this, because of their sinful nature.[2] Others have argued that 'works of the law' is used by Paul in a negative sense: it refers to the sinful attempts of humans to earn their own salvation, that is, to their self-righteous deeds.[3] According to L. Gaston, the phrase 'works of the law'

---

1. The phrase ἔργα νόμου occurs nine times in the Textus Receptus: it has it in Rom. 9.32 as well.

2. Examples of scholars who have argued for this interpretation are C.E.B. Cranfield, ' "The Works of the Law" in the Epistle to the Romans', *JSNT* 43 (1991), pp. 89-101; *idem, Romans 1–8* (ICC; Edinburgh: T. & T. Clark, 1979), pp. 197-99; D. Moo, *Romans 1–8* (WEC; Chicago: Moody, 1991), pp. 208-218; *idem*, ' "Law", "Works of the Law", and Legalism in Paul', *WTJ* 45 (1983), pp. 73-100; T.R. Schreiner, ' "Works of Law" in Paul', *NovT* 33 (1991), pp. 217-44.

3. Examples of scholars who have argued for this interpretation are G. Bertram, 'ἔργον', *TDNT*, II, pp. 635-55, esp. p. 651; H.D. Betz, *A Commentary on Paul's Letter to the Churches in Galatia* (Hermeneia; Philadelphia: Fortress Press, 1979), p. 146; E.D.W. Burton, *A Critical and Exegetical Commentary on the Epistle to the Galatians* (ICC; Edinburgh: T. & T. Clark, 1921), p. 120: D.P. Fuller, 'Paul and

in Pauline literature is a subjective genitive. Paul is thinking of the works produced by the law, for example, bringing a curse (Gal. 3.21), causing guilt (Rom. 3.19), revealing sin (Rom. 3.20), and increasing sin (Rom. 5.20). The law does not save. On the contrary, it brings condemnation. It works in such a way that it creates a situation from which humankind needs to be saved.[4]

Gaston's theory has received little acceptance among scholars.[5] The first two interpretations mentioned above have both been fairly widely accepted, although the latter of these two is rapidly decreasing in popularity due to E.P. Sanders's influencial work which describes first-century Judaism as a religion in which grace played a central role. Fairly recently, J.D.G. Dunn has come up with an innovative theory on the meaning of ἔργα νόμου which is partially based on Sanders's new insights into Second Temple Judaism. His theory is becoming increasingly popular.

Sanders's Influence on Dunn's Interpretation of 'Works of the Law'

The underlying philosophy of Dunn's theory on ἔργα νόμου is to be found in Sanders's description of Judaism, even though Dunn disagrees with Sanders on several points.[6] In 1977, Sanders's most famous book was published, entitled *Paul and Palestinian Judaism*.[7] In this work, Sanders looks at 'patterns of religion' found in Palestinian Judaism.

"the Works of the Law" ', *WTJ* 38 (1975), pp. 32-33; E. Käsemann, *Commentary on Romans* (trans. G.W. Bromiley; Grand Rapids: Eerdmans, 1980), p. 103.

4. L. Gaston, ' "Works of Law" as a Subjective Genitive', *SR* 13 (1984), pp. 39-46.

5. J.A. Fitzmyer rightly observes that the occurrence of the phrase 'works of the law' in 4QMMT (see discussion below) rules out Gaston's theory as a possible interpretation of this expression. See J.A. Fitzmyer, *According to Paul: Studies in the Theology of the Apostle* (New York: Paulist Press, 1993), p. 23; *idem, Romans* (AB, 33; London: Geoffrey Chapman, 1993), p. 338.

6. It is not the purpose of this essay to discuss the disagreements between Sanders and Dunn, as Dunn himself points these out in several of his works. See J.D.G. Dunn, 'The New Perspective on Paul', *BJRL* 65.2 (1983), pp. 95-103; *idem*, 'Works of the Law and the Curse of the Law (Galatians 3.10-14)', *NTS* 31 (1985), pp. 523-42. Despite these disagreements, Sanders has still had an important impact on Dunn's work.

7. E.P. Sanders, *Paul and Palestinian Judaism: A Comparison of Patterns of Religion* (Philadelphia: Fortress Press, 1977).

The expression 'pattern of religion' is peculiar to Sanders. He defines it as 'the description of how a religion is perceived by its adherents to *function*'—'*how getting in and staying in are understood:* the way in which a religion is understood to admit and retain members...'[8] Sanders finds a common pattern of religion in Palestinian Judaism which he calls 'covenantal nomism'. God chose Israel, made a covenant with them and gave them the law. 'The law implies both God's promise to maintain the election and the requirement to obey.' God will reward obedience to the law, but will punish transgression. The law also supplies a means of atonement for the penitent sinner. This is God's way of forgiving a sinner who repents. The result of atonement is 'the maintenance or re-establishment of the covenantal relationship'. Salvation belongs to 'all those who are maintained in the covenant by obedience, atonement and God's mercy'.[9] An important point is that this covenantal relationship is 'established by God's mercy'. It is 'maintained by the individual's obedience and repentance and by God's forgiveness'.[10]

Therefore, Sanders argues, it is wrong to characterize Judaism 'as a religion of legalistic works-righteousness', a view which Christians in particular have promoted.[11] The Judaism of the time of Jesus and Paul 'kept grace and works in the right perspective'. God's mercy plays an important role in 'covenantal nomism': it is the basis of the covenantal relationship.[12]

---

8. Sanders, *Paul and Palestinian Judaism*, p. 17 (his emphasis). Sanders goes on to say that a 'pattern of religion' is largely related to the concepts which belong to 'soteriology' in systematic theology, though he would not equate the two. For a complete overview of Sanders's definition of 'pattern of religion', see pp. 16-18.

9. Sanders, *Paul and Palestinian Judaism*, p. 422.

10. Sanders, *Paul and Palestinian Judaism*, p. 235.

11. Sanders, *Paul and Palestinian Judaism*, p. 59.

12. Sanders, *Paul and Palestinian Judaism*, pp. 423-27. Sanders comes to this description of covenantal nomism within Judaism by analyzing various Jewish sources such as Tannaitic literature, the Dead Sea Scrolls, the Apocrypha (Ben Sira) and the Pseudepigrapha (*1 Enoch, Jubilees, Psalms of Solomon*). According to Sanders, the only Jewish source in which we do not find this pattern of covenantal nomism is *4 Ezra*. In *4 Ezra* we indeed find 'a religion of individual self-righteousness' in which the religious system of covenantal nomism is not at work any more. *4 Ezra* is characterized by 'legalistic perfectionism'. However, its religious pattern is not characteristic of Judaism in general and has been wrongly used to support the idea that first-century Judaism was legalistic in nature, so Sanders contends (*Paul and Palestinian Judaism*, pp. 409-18).

Dunn believes that Sanders deserves an accolade for 'breaking the mould of Pauline studies':[13] 'Sanders has given us an unrivalled opportunity to look at Paul afresh, to shift our perspective back from the 16th century to the first century...to see Paul properly within his own context.'[14] Dunn agrees with Sanders that, on the basis of Pauline literature, many biblical scholars have drawn a false picture of Judaism as being legalistic. Like Sanders, Dunn thinks that Paul's writings have been erroneously read in the light of Lutheran theology, which emphasizes the antithesis between justification by self-righteous deeds versus justification by grace.[15] According to Dunn, this wrong notion of Judaism has led to misinterpretations of Paul's concept of 'works of the law'.

Dunn's Interpretation of 'Works of the Law'

Dunn's view on 'Paul and the law', in particular on 'works of the law', focuses on 'the social function of the law', as he himself expresses.[16] In his attempt to define the phrase ἔργα νόμου, Dunn begins by explaining that every social group has various characteristics and features which lead to the group's self-definition and distinguish it from other groups. Those belonging to the group will tend evidently to think of the group and their membership of it in terms of these characteristics and features, including any particular beliefs and practices. These characteristics often become *identity* and *boundary* markers. The concepts of identity and boundary are closely linked together. It is particularly the boundary—that is, what distinguishes a group from other groups—which gives the sense of identity. Especially when a group feels itself under threat, it will emphasize its boundaries in order to preserve its unity. A group in danger of survival tends to be preoccupied with bodily rituals and purity.[17]

13. Dunn, 'New Perspective', p. 97.

14. Dunn, 'New Perspective', p. 100.

15. Dunn, 'New Perspective', p. 98. Dunn gives credit to Krister Stendahl for giving the same warning about misreading Paul's writings in the light of Luther's theology. See K. Stendahl, 'The Apostle Paul and the Introspective Conscience of the West', *HTR* 61 (1963), pp. 199-215, reprinted in his *Paul among Jews and Gentiles* (London: SCM Press, 1977), pp. 78-96.

16. Dunn, 'Curse of the Law', pp. 523-24.

17. Dunn ('Curse of the Law', p. 524) refers to the works of the sociologists H. Mol, *Identity and the Sacred* (Oxford: Basil Blackwell, 1976), pp. 57-58, 233

We see this phenomenon very clearly in the Judaism of the post-exilic period. 1 Maccabees 1.60-63 recounts how, during the reign of the Seleucid ruler Antiochus IV Epiphanes, a decree was issued to put to death everybody who was involved in circumcising children and everybody who refused to eat unclean food. Here we see clearly the identity and boundary markers: circumcision and purity laws concerning food. Therefore, Dunn contends, it is not surprising that these same two issues are dealt with in Paul's letter to the Galatians (2.1-14). For, since the Maccabean period, these two legal obligations had been fundamental to the Jewish identity. They marked off the Jew as a member of God's people with whom he had made a covenant. These rituals created a distinction between Israel and the surrounding nations, between Jews and Gentiles.

The Jews suffered persecution not only during the reign of Antiochus IV Epiphanes, but also during the Roman occupation of Palestine. Galatians 2 describes the events which took place when the national and religious identity of Judaism was again under threat. The political situation in Judea during this period was very tense: in 40 CE Emperor Caligula attempted to have his own statue placed in the Temple of Jerusalem.[18] During this period there was an increasing need for the Jewish people to affirm their identity by emphasizing the importance of their distinctive Jewish boundary markers. To understand this social function of the law during the time of Paul, Dunn contends, will help us to understand the meaning of the phrase 'works of the law'.[19]

According to Dunn, it is precisely the expression ἔργα νόμου with which Paul chose to denote these distinctive Jewish boundary markers in the form of legal requirements which characterize the practitioner as belonging to 'the people of the law, the covenant people, the Jewish nation'.[20] A good rendering of ἔργα νόμου would be 'service of the

---

and M. Douglas, *Purity and Danger* (London: Routledge & Kegan Paul, 1966), pp. 62-65, 128.

18. Dunn, 'Curse of the Law', pp. 524-27. *idem, The Partings of the Ways between Christianity and Judaism and their Significance for the Character of Christianity* (London: SCM Press; Philadelphia: Trinity Press International, 1991), pp. 126-27, 305. Dunn refers to Israel's history as described by the ancient authors Philo, *Leg. Gai.* 184–338; Josephus, *War* 2.184-203; *Ant.* 18.261-309; Tacitus, *Hist.* 5.9.

19. Dunn, 'Curse of the Law', pp. 524-27.

20. Dunn, 'Curse of the Law', p. 527.

law'[21] or 'nomistic service'.[22] It does not refer to deeds already accomplished, but to 'obligations laid down by the law, the religious system determined by the law'.[23]

It is in Gal. 2.16 that Paul introduces the phrase ἔργα νόμου for the first time. According to Dunn, it obviously refers back to the matters of legal dispute spoken of in the preceding verses: circumcision and food laws (2.1-14). The issue is 'whether to be justified by faith in Jesus Christ requires also observance of these "works", whether...it is possible to conceive of a membership of the covenant people which is not characterized precisely by these works'. Paul is protesting against those who promoted the view that 'works of the law', identity badges such as circumcision and food laws, 'were an essential concomitant of membership of Israel's covenant', a view which resulted in 'shutting out' Gentiles.[24]

Dunn's interpretation of ἔργα νόμου affects his reading of Paul's letter to the Romans. In Romans, Paul introduces the phrase ἔργα νόμου at the conclusion of the first main section of his treatise (3.19-20).[25] Romans 3.19-20 emphasizes the universality of the indictment of 1.18-32. According to Dunn, the way Paul draws up the universal indictment is as follows: In 1.18-32, he describes humanity's sinfulness as a whole, but in a way which is peculiar to 'Jewish polemic against Gentile idolatry'.[26] From 2.1 and onwards, Paul's primary concern is to show that the Jew is as much a sinner as the Gentile and, therefore, falls under the same condemnation. The person spoken of in 2.1-3 who passes judgment on another is 'the Jew' who condemns 'the Gentile'. Paul attacks what he views as the typically Jewish attitude. 'The Jew' feels

---

21. Dunn ('Curse of the Law', pp. 527, 540) is referring here to E. Lohmeyer's translation of ἔργα νόμου in German as 'Dienst des Gesetzes' or 'Gesetzesdienst' in *Probleme paulinischer Theologie* (Stuttgart: W. Kohlhammer, n.d.), p. 67; reprinted under the same title in *ZNW* 28 (1929), pp. 177-207.

22. Dunn ('Curse of the Law', pp. 527, 540) is referring here to J.B. Tyson's translation of ἔργα νόμου in ' "Works of Law" in Galatians', *JBL* 92 (1973), pp. 423-31 (424-25).

23. Dunn, *Partings of the Ways*, p. 136; see also 'Curse of the Law', pp. 527-28 and *idem*, *Romans 1–8* (WBC, 38A; Dallas: Word Books, 1988), p. 154.

24. J.D.G. Dunn, *The Theology of Paul the Apostle* (Grand Rapids: Eerdmans, 1998), pp. 361-62.

25. Dunn, 'Curse of the Law', p. 528.

26. J.D.G. Dunn, 'Yet Once More—"The Works of the Law": A Response', *JSNT* 46 (1992), pp. 99-117 (104-105).

superior to the Gentile and, as a consequence, does not see his own sins (such as listed in 1.29-32) while condemning the Gentiles' homosexual practices (1.23-27).[27] Paul criticizes the attitude of 'the Jew' toward the law: we are the chosen people of God, the people of the covenant, the people of the law. The boasting of the Jew which Paul criticizes in 2.17-24 and 3.27-29 is 'the boasting in Israel's privilege and distinctiveness' as attested by its identity badges, 'works of the law'. As in Galatians, Paul is protesting against the idea that 'God is God of Jews only'.[28]

Dunn's final conclusion is that Paul's statement that 'no one will be justified by works of the law' should not be interpreted as a polemic against a supposed Jewish notion (which, as Sanders has demonstrated, did not exist in Judaism) that they could earn their own salvation by doing good works. According to Dunn, it is clear 'that "works of the law" do not denote any attempt to earn favor with God'. Rather, so Dunn contends, Paul is reacting against the Jewish assumption of privileged status as God's people as certified by identity markers, that is, 'works of the law'.[29]

Dunn's Use of Qumran Texts to Support his Interpretation of 'Works of the Law'

In order to support his interpretation of ἔργα νόμου in the Pauline epistles, Dunn brings in three Qumran texts which contain Hebrew equivalents to the Greek phrase ἔργα νόμου. The first one is the famous, or maybe I should say notorious, 4QMMT which, according to Dunn, particularly well supports his interpretation. 4QMMT is generally believed to be a letter written by a leader of the Qumran community to those who were not abiding by their interpretation of the law (their precise identity is uncertain). The Qumran interpretation of the law is spelled out in 'a series of distinctive *halakhic* rulings',[30] which, accord-

---

27. Dunn, *Romans 1–8*, pp. 89-90. Dunn believes that this interpretation of 2.1-3 may explain the order of the polemic in 1.18-32. 'Having played to the gallery of Jewish assurance of moral superiority over the Gentile, [Paul] then broadened out his description of human corruption in order to provide a base for his attack on that very assurance' (p. 90).

28. Dunn, *Theology of Paul*, p. 363.

29. Dunn, 'Yet Once More', pp. 109-110.

30. J.D.G. Dunn, 'Intra-Jewish Polemic in Galatians', *JBL* 112 (1993), pp. 459-77 (467).

ing to Dunn, the author refers to at the end of the letter as מקצת מעשי
התורה 'some works of the law' (C 27), encouraging his addressees to
perform them. In 4QMMT it is very clear, so Dunn argues, that 'works
of the law' were 'identity badges', separating the members of the
Qumran community from outsiders. Likewise, he goes on, the Pauline
expression ἔργα νόμου should be interpreted as 'identity badges',
separating Jews from Christians. The second equivalent to ἔργα νόμου
Dunn brings into the discussion is found in 4Q174, col. 3,[31] line 7:
תורה מעשי, 'works of law' which are to be offered in the Temple consisting of human beings (most likely a reference to the Qumran community). He believes that מעשי תורה in 4Q174 is synonymous to מעשי
התורה in 4QMMT, marking out the Qumran community 'in its distinctiveness from outsiders and enemies'. Dunn also observes that 1QS
5.20-24 and 6.18, which contain the phrase מעשיו בתורה, describe
how the community member was tested on ' "his deeds with regard
to the law", his "observance of the law" as understood within the
community'.[32]

Dunn's Clarification/Modification of his Interpretation of 'Works of the Law'

In his article 'Yet Once More—"The Works of the Law"', Dunn
attempts to clarify his interpretation of the term 'works of the law',
claiming to have been misinterpreted by fellow scholars such as Cranfield. Cranfield, in his article ' "The Works of the Law"', criticizes
Dunn's interpretation of ἔργα νόμου in 'a special restricted sense' by
refuting Dunn's exegesis of the passages in Romans in which the
phrase occurs. Cranfield concludes that ἔργα νόμου must be interpreted
as obedience to the law in general (as opposed to giving it a restricted
meaning).[33]

In this later article Dunn 'clarifies' (I would say modifies) his view as
follows:

> 'Works of the law' characterize the whole mind set of 'covenantal nom-
> ism'—that is, the conviction that status within the covenant (= righteous-
> ness) is maintained by doing what the law requires ('works of the law').
> Circumcision and food laws in particular come into play simply (!)

31. Formerly col. 1.
32. Dunn, *Partings of the Ways*, p. 136; *idem*, 'Intra-Jewish Polemic', p. 467.
33. Cranfield, ' "The Works of the Law"', pp. 89-101.

because they provided the key test cases for most Jews of Paul's time… So, 'works of the law' are *not* to be understood in a special restricted sense, but in a general sense given particular point by certain crucial issues and disputes.[34]

Dunn also states that 'Cranfield's criticism loses its point', because he does not deny 'that "work(s) of the law" means "works required by the law"'.[35] In a subsequent article Dunn tells his readers:

This is not to say, as I have been understood to say, that by 'works of law' Paul meant only such obligations as the food laws (and circumcision and sabbath observance). It is simply that the larger commitment and sense of obligation to live within the terms laid down by the law, to perform works of the law came to focus in particular test cases like circumcision and food laws.[36]

Again, in discussing the evidence from Qumran, Dunn attempts to clarify his definition of 'works of the law':

מעשי התורה ('deeds of the law') were, of course, understood by the Qumran covenanters to mean all that the law required of the loyal covenanter. But 'all that the law required of the loyal covenanter' really meant in practice Qumran's sectarian understanding of what the law required. In other words, 'deeds of the law' denoted precisely that understanding of the law's requirements which distinguished the Qumran covenanters from their fellow Jews. This is confirmed by the appearance of 4QMMT, a document which takes its name from this very phrase (*Miqsat Ma'aseh Ha-Torah*, 'The Sum of the Deeds of the Law'),[37] and

34. Dunn, 'Yet Once More', pp. 100-101 (his emphasis).
35. Dunn, 'Yet Once More', p. 105.
36. Dunn, 'Intra-Jewish Polemic', p. 466.
37. Dunn is inconsistent in his translation of the word מקצת, which he renders both as 'the sum of' (see his 'Yet Once More', p. 103) and as 'some of' (see his '4QMMT and Galatians', *NTS* 43 [1997], pp. 147-53 [150]). Ironically, the former translation is the antonym of the latter. Seifrid also translates מקצת with 'the sum of' (see M.A. Seifrid, 'Blind Alleys in the Controversy over the Paul of History', *TynBul* 45 [1994], pp. 73-95 [81]). The word מקצת occurs no less often than six times in 4QMMT (B 1, 59, 80; C 20, 27, 30). It stands in construct relationship with five different words or phrases: מקצת דבריניו (B 1; C 30), מקצת [ע]צמות (B 59), מקצתהכהנים (B 80), מקצת הברכות והקללות (C 20) and מקצתמעשי התורה (C 27). The word מקצת is an Aramaism and a combination of two words: קצת and מן. Jastrow's lexicon of the Talmud lists the meanings: 'a part, partially, in some cases' (see M. Jastrow, *A Dictionary of the Targumim, the Talmud Babli and Yerushalmi, and the Midrashic Literature* [2 vols.; New York: Pardes, 1950 (1903)], II, p. 832). In Dan. 2.42, it is written as two separate words and also means 'some of, part of'.

which makes it clear that מעשי תורה come to focus in particular *halakhic* disputes—those points of *halakhic* disputes where the Qumran covenanters differed from other Jews, including particularly, it would appear, the Pharisees...[38]

The Vagueness of Dunn's Interpretation of 'Works of the Law'

The main difficulty with Dunn's view is its vagueness as expressed in its many ambiguities and inconsistencies. In order to understand Dunn's view, it is important to realize that he offers a modification of it in his later articles without entirely admitting it. After all, in one of his earlier articles, Dunn uses the word 'restricted' in reference to 'works of the law': 'The phrase "works of the law" in Gal. 2.16 is, in fact, a fairly restricted one'.[39] Moreover, Dunn says in his discussion of the term 'works of the law' in the book of Romans that 'it is the social function of *ritual* which is in view, circumcision as a badge of Jewish identity'.[40] The word 'ritual' suggests a restriction, excluding the ethical by implication. It is striking that Dunn uses different terminology in his later articles. He avoids the term 'ritual' and seems to replace it with the word *halakhic*. Nevertheless, all of the 'identity badges' Dunn observes, both in Pauline and Qumran literature, are cultic as opposed to ethical in nature.

Dunn makes some significant observations, but fails to give a clear answer to several important questions which are crucial to a right understanding of the concept of 'works of the law', in both Pauline and Qumran literature. The remainder of this essay will address the following issues while discussing Dunn's theory and showing its weaknesses:

The conflated word מקצת is relatively rare in the Hebrew Bible, but appears in Dan. 1.2 and Neh. 7.69. There is no evidence that 'the sum of' is a possible rendering for מקצת. In 4QMMT, it is clear that מקצת is used as a synonym for the preposition מן 'from, a selection of', since the phrase מקצת דברינו 'some of our pronouncements' in C 30, as represented in 4Q398, has the textual variant מדברינו in 4Q399. Moreover, neither in the Hebrew Bible, nor in rabbinic writings does מקצת ever mean 'the sum of'.

38. Dunn, 'Yet Once More', pp. 103-104. Dunn often claims that his colleagues have misrepresented his view. Therefore, in discussing Dunn's view, I give relatively long quotations in order to avoid any misunderstanding or misrepresentation.

39. Dunn, 'New Perspective', p. 111.

40. Dunn, 'Curse of the Law', p. 530 (emphasis added).

(a)   If 'works of the law' are 'identity badges', as Dunn argues, are they Jewish national identity badges, separating Jews from Gentiles, or identity badges which separate Jews from Jews?

(b)   Is the phrase 'works of the law' found in 4Q174?

(c)   Dunn makes a connection between מעשׂן (ה)תורה 'works of the law' in 4Q174 and 4QMMT and מעשׂיו בתורה in the community rule. What are the implications of this important connection?

(d)   Are 'works of the law' ethical or cultic in nature?

(e)   Are 'works of the law' 'works performed' or 'works prescribed'? In other words, are they deeds or precepts? Assuming that מעשׂי תורה in 4Q174 is synonymous with התורה מעשׂי in 4QMMT, what is the implication of this equation?

(f)   Did Jews of the Second Temple period think of 'works of the law' as meritorious?

Although an attempt will be made to address these questions in the above mentioned order, the reader should be aware that they are interrelated, and, therefore, overlap is inevitable. Since others (in particular Cranfield, but also Moo and Schreiner)[41] have already criticized Dunn by giving a detailed analysis of Paul's letters to the Romans and Galatians in which ἔργα νόμου occurs, I will focus on Dunn's use of Qumran texts to support his interpretation of 'works of the law'.[42]

If 'Works of the Law' Are 'Identity Badges', of What Nature Are They?
Dunn's definition of 'works of the law' is rather vague. In Galatians and Romans, 'works of the law' refer to rules or practices that distinguish Jews from Gentiles, or so he argues. According to Dunn, they are religious, but also national identity markers. For the Jews, 'the works of the law demonstrate[d] national identity, constitute[d] national righteousness'.[43] In 4QMMT, so Dunn contends, they refer to rules or practices that distinguish Jews from other Jews. Therefore, in the case of 4QMMT, 'works of the law' cannot be national identity markers at all. They could not, for example, include the ritual practice of circumcision which, according to Dunn, Paul refers to when he speaks of 'works

41. See bibliography above in n. 2.

42. While the main focus of this essay is Dunn's theory on 'works of the law', at times it will be necessary to discuss related issues which have not been addressed by Dunn.

43. Dunn, 'Curse of the Law', p. 530.

of the law'. It could never have been an issue of dispute among Jews (for example, the two parties described in 4QMMT), simply because all Jews believed in the practice of circumcision. It seems that Dunn's interpretation of the term 'works of the law' allows for a change in its meaning depending on the context in which it occurs. In Romans and Galatians, 'works of the law' are *Jewish national* identity markers, in 4QMMT they are not. Such a definition is vague and inconsistent. Moreover, a different analysis of the Qumran texts will show that 'works of the law' does not denote 'identity badges'.

Is the Phrase 'Works of the Law' Found in 4Q174?
I believe that Dunn is right in viewing מעשי תורה (4Q174) and מעשי התורה (4QMMT) as synonymous, although he does not demonstrate why this is so. It is by no means self-evident, because the reading מעשי תורה in 4Q174 3.7 is uncertain. There is an important textual problem: the noun attached to the construct form of מעשים (that is, מעשי) is not clear and has been read by some scholars as תודה, written with a daleth,[44] while others have taken it as תורה, written with a resh.[45] The resultant phrases are מעשי תודה 'works of thanksgiving' and מעשי תורה 'works of law' respectively. The sentence in which the phrase in

44. M.B. Bachmann, '4QMMT und Galaterbrief, מעשי התורה und ΕΡΓΑ NOMOY', *ZNW* 89 (1998), pp. 91-113 (100); G.J. Brooke, *Exegesis at Qumran: 4QFlorilegium in its Jewish Context* (JSOTSup, 29; Sheffield: JSOT Press, 1985), p. 92; F. García Martínez, '4QMMT in a Qumran Context', in J. Kampen and M.J. Bernstein (eds.), *Reading 4QMMT: New Perspectives on Qumran Law and History* (SBL Symposium Series, 2; Atlanta: Scholars Press, 1996), pp. 15-28 (24); E. Puech, *La croyance des esséniens en la vie future: Immortalité, résurrection, vie éternelle? Histoire d'une croyance dans le judaisme ancien* (2 vols.; EB NS, 22; Paris: J. Gabalda, 1993), II, p. 578; J. Strugnell, 'Note en marge du volume V des "Discoveries in the Judaean Desert of Jordan" ', *RevQ* 7 (1969–71), pp. 163-276 (221).

45. J. Allegro, *Qumran Cave 4. I. 4Q158–4Q186* (DJD, 5; Oxford: Clarendon Press, 1968), pp. 53-54; Fitzmyer, *According to Paul*, pp. 20-21; S.D. Fraade, 'Interpretive Authority in the Studying Community at Qumran', *JJS* 44 (1993), pp. 46-69, here p. 63; Moo, *Romans 1–8*, p. 209; *idem*, 'Legalism in Paul', p. 91; P.J. Tomson, 'Halachische Brieven uit de Oudheid: Qumran, Paulus en de Talmoed', *Nederlands Theologisch Tijdschrift* 46 (1992), pp. 284-301, here p. 289; J.C. VanderKam, *The Dead Sea Scrolls Today* (Grand Rapids: Eerdmans, 1994), p. 51; G. Vermes, *The Dead Sea Scrolls in English* (Harmondsworth: Penguin Books, 4th edn, 1995), p. 353; M.O. Wise, '4QFlorilegium and the Temple of Adam', *RevQ* 15 (1991), pp. 103-32 (105).

question occurs is as follows: 'And he [God] said to build for him a temple consisting of human beings in which to make go up in smoke to him before him works of thanksgiving/law'. Several scholars have argued for either תודה or תורה on palaeographical grounds. Puech, having looked at a photograph of PAM 41.807,[46] seems entirely convinced that a *daleth* should be read.[47] Fitzmyer, with 'a glance' at plate 19, comes to the opposite conclusion: it is not a *daleth*, but a resh.[48] Obviously, it is difficult to decide solely, if at all, on palaeographical grounds whether one should read תודה or תורה, because the third letter in the word has been too damaged. Therefore, in this particular case context should be the main guide.

Scholars in favor of the reading מעשי תודה 'works of thanksgiving' refer to Amos 4.5 and Ps. 141.2 in order to support their view. In 4Q174 3.7 the works are to be offered up in smoke to God. The Hebrew verb for 'to offer up in smoke' is קטר. In Amos 4.5, the verb קטר is used in combination with the noun תודה: קטר מחמץ תודה 'offer a sacrifice of thanksgiving'. According to Brooke, this favors the reading מעשי תודה.[49] In Ps. 141.2, the psalmist wishes his prayer to be like incense (קטרת) before God and the lifting of his hands as an evening sacrifice. Here prayer is an act of praise and pictured as incense rising before God, so Grelot argues in favor of the reading מעשי תודה, which he renders as 'oeuvres de louange' (deeds of praise).[50] Puech believes the cultic context of 4Q174 is an indication that מעשי תודה should be read. He also argues that the absence of the article prefixed to the noun in question tells us that it cannot be תורה, because in 4QMMT the phrase מעשי התורה does have the article.[51]

The arguments Brooke and Grelot offer to support the reading מעשי תודה are not convincing in comparison to similar, but stronger arguments which can be given in favor of the reading מעשי תורה. The combination of עשה or מעשה and תודה occurs neither elsewhere in the Dead Sea Scrolls, nor in the Hebrew Bible. The combination of עשה or מעשה and תורה, on the other hand, is found in several Qumran sectarian

---

46. This photograph is reproduced in Allegro, *Qumran Cave 4*, I, pl. 19.
47. Puech, *La croyance des esséniens*, II, p. 578.
48. Fitzmyer, *According to Paul*, p. 20.
49. Brooke, *Exegesis at Qumran*, p. 268.
50. P. Grelot, 'Les oeuvres de la loi (à propos de 4Q394-398)', *RevQ* 16 (1994), pp. 441-48 (445). 'Praise' is an acceptable rendering for תודה (see BDB, p. 392).
51. Puech, *La croyance des esséniens*, p. 578.

documents, even in 4Q174 itself! 4Q174 4.2 speaks of the remnant who will do the whole of the law (ועשׂו את כול התורה). Moreover, in 1QpHab 7.11, 'men of fidelity' are described as 'doers of the law (עושׂי התורה)'. The same phrase is found in 1QpHab 8.1; 12.4; 4QpPs[a] 1–2.2.14, 22. An important variant of the phrase occurs in 11QT 56.3: ועשׂיתה על פי התורה 'and you shall do according to the law'. Also, in 1QS 6.18, the novice's works with regard to the law (מעשׂיו בתורה) are examined (see also 5.21, 23; 6.14; CD 13.11).[52] The almost identical phrase, מעשׂי התורה 'works of the law', found in 4QMMT, strengthens the possibility that 4Q174 speaks of מעשׂי תורה, rather than מעשׂי תודה.[53]

Puech believes that we should read תודה instead of תורה, because the context of 4Q174 is cultic. However, the context of 4QMMT, in which the phrase מעשׂי התורה occurs, is also cultic. The 'works' spoken of in section B are cultic, relating to purity. Many of these describe the proper way to sacrifice. Moreover, there are other striking similarities between 4Q174 and 4QMMT which strengthen the idea of a connection between the two documents and, consequently, the possibility that both speak of 'works of the law'.[54]

Puech argues that the absence of the article prefixed to the noun in question tells us that it cannot be תורה, because in 4QMMT C 27, the phrase מעשׂי התורה does have the article. Therefore, in his opinion, one must read מעשׂי תודה. However, תורה and התורה are often used as synonyms. First, in the Hebrew Bible, God's law is many times referred

---

52. All these combinations of תורה with עשׂ have been observed by Fitzmyer (*According to Paul*, p. 21), except the one in 4Q174 4.2.

53. Fitzmyer, *According to Paul*, p. 21; Fraade, 'Interpretive Authority', p. 63.

54. The most important resemblances between 4Q174 and 4QMMT are the following: (1) 4Q174 speaks of a remnant 'doing the whole law (ושׂו את כול התורה)' (4.2), and the author of 4QMMT encourages his addressee(s) to do 'works of the law (מעשׂי התורה)', so in both documents we see the combination of the root עשׂה and תורה, regardless of whether we read מעשׂי תורה in 4Q174 3.7, or not; (2) an important theme in 4Q174 and 4QMMT is 'the last days (אחרית הימים)', this phrase being repeated several times in both documents and seeming to be connected to the idea of obedience to the law (4Q174 3.2, 12 [partly reconstructed], 15, 19; 5.3 [partly reconstructed]; 4QMMT C 14, 21); (3) both documents contain a quotation or allusion to Dan. 12.10 in their description of אחרית הימים 'the last days' (4Q174 4.3; 4QMMT C 22); (4) both documents speak of a sacrificial cult, whether actual or spiritualized; (5) both documents refer to David (4Q174 3.7, 11, 12, 13; 4QMMT C 10, 18, 25).

to as התורה,[55] but also as תורה.[56] The cases where תורה is used instead of התורה are mostly found in prophetic literature. 4Q174 quotes and exegetes many passages found in the prophets. Moreover, in the book of Psalms, the only occurrence of the word תורה in the absolute state[57] does not have the article. As 4Q174 expounds several passages from the Psalms,[58] it should not surprise us to find in 4Q174 the word תורה without the article, referring to God's law. Secondly, in 4QMMT C 26-28, התורה and תורה are used as synonyms, in close proximity to each other:

> Now we have written to you about some works of the law [מקצת מעשי
> התורה], those which we determined would be beneficial to you and to
> your people, because we have seen [that] you possess insight and knowl-
> edge of the law [ערמה ומדע תורה].

This suggests that the expressions מעשי התורה and מעשי תורה are synonymous as well. In short, there seems to be strong evidence that the reading מעשי תורה 'works of law' in 4Q174 3.7 is preferable to מעשי תודה 'works of thanksgiving', and that מעשי תורה is used as a synonym of מעשי התורה.[59] This has significant implications for under-

---

55. E.g. Exod. 24.12; Deut. 1.5; 4.8, 44; 17.18, 19; 27.3, 8, 26, 58, 61; 29.21, 29; 30.10; 31.9, 11, 12, 24, 26, 46.

56. Deut. 33.4; Isa. 2.3; 8.6, 20; 42.21; 51.4; Jer. 18.18; Ezek. 7.26; Mic. 4.2; Hab. 1.4; Zeph. 3.4; Hag. 2.11; Mal. 2.7; Ps. 78.5; Job 22.22; Prov. 6.23; 28.4 (2×), 7, 9; 29.18; Lam. 2.9; Neh. 9.14; 2 Chron. 15.3.

57. Of course, the construct noun תורה never has the article. All such occurrences of תורה have been disregarded.

58. The author of 4Q174 quotes many biblical passages in an attempt to shed light on what will happen 'in the last days'. These are 2 Sam. 7.10-14 (3.1-2, 8, 10-11), Exod. 15.17-18 (3.3), Amos 9.11 (3.12), Ps. 1.1 (3.14), Isa. 8.11 (3.15-16), Ezek. 37.23 (3.16-17), Ps. 2.1 (3.18-20), Dan. 12.10 (4.4a), Ps. 5.2-3a (5.2) and Isa. 65.22-23 (6.1-3). The author interprets these passages as references to the future of his own community 'in the last days'. See M.O. Wise, 'The Last Days: A Commentary on Selected Verses (4Q174)', in M.O. Wise, M.G. Abegg, Jr and E.M. Cook (eds.), *The Dead Sea Scrolls: A New Translation* (San Francisco: HarperSan-Francisco, 1996), pp. 225-28.

59. A. Dupont-Sommer also reads מעשי תורה, yet he does not take מעשי to be the plural masculine construct form of the noun מעשה 'work'. He takes מעשי to be a qal active participle masculine plural (in construct) of the verb עשה 'to do, to practise', preceded by the preposition *min*, and translates the phrase מעשי תורה with 'parmi ceux qui pratiquent la Loi' which is the English equivalent of 'among those who do (practise) the law'. See A. Dupont-Sommer, *Les écrits esséniens*

standing the function of מעשי התורה in 4QMMT C 27 which will be discussed below.[60]

What Is the Connection between מעשי(ה)תורה 'Works of the Law' and מעשיו בתורה?

Dunn is right in observing a close connection between מעשי(ה)תורה and 1QS 5.21-24 and 6.18 where the phrase מעשיו בתורה occurs in connection with the examination of the novice by the full members of the community. He correctly defines the latter phrase as 'his deeds in reference to the Torah'[61] or 'his deeds with regard to the law'.[62] Several scholars either have given an imprecise translation of this phrase or have mistakenly assumed that מעשיו בתורה is virtually synonymous with מעשי(ה)תורה, except that it specifies the doer of works of the law (that is, the novice). The key question is: 'How should the preposition *bet* be rendered?' M.O. Wise obviously had a difficult time deciding on its meaning, because he is inconsistent in his translation of the phrase מעשיו בתורה: in 1QS 5.21 he renders it as 'his works vis-à-vis the Law', whereas in 6.18 as 'his works of the Law'.[63] The first translation is

découverts près de la Mer Mortre (Paris: Payot, 1959), p. 325. Grelot ('Les oeuvres de la loi', p. 443) seems somewhat suspicious in his initial response to Dupont-Sommer's translation of מעשי: 'On pouvait toutefois s'étonner de la *scriptio defectiva* pour עשי', but immediately afterwards he adds: 'Mais dans cette langue qui tend vers l'hébreu rabbinique, les règles peuvent être flottantes'. However, I believe that Grelot's initial suspicion is justifiable. In the Hebrew Bible, the qal active participle masculine plural (in construct) of עשה is always עשי (Exod. 35.35; 36.8; 2 Kgs 12.11, 14, 15; 22.5, 9; 24.16; Mal. 3.15; Est. 3.9; 9.3; 2 Chron. 24.13), except in two cases where the longer form עושי is used (2 Chron. 26.13 and 34.17). However, the presence of this longer form עושי is not an exception to the rule in Qumran literature (1QS 8.3; 1QSb 1.1; 1QpHab 7.11; 8.1; 1QM 12.11; 19.3; 4Qp Ps^a 2.5, 14; 4QTohD 1.5). As E. Tov has observed, the orthography in 4Q174 is typically Qumranian. See E. Tov, 'The Orthography and Language of the Hebrew Scrolls Found at Qumran and the Origin of these Scrolls', *Textus* 13 (1986), pp. 31-57. So one would expect the qal active participle masculine plural (in construct) of the verb עשה to be written עושי instead of עשי. Therefore, Dupont-Sommer's translation of מעשי תורה is highly unlikely. The preferable rendering for מעשי תורה in 4Q174 3.7 is 'works of law'.

60. See the discussion below in the section headed: Are 'Works of the Law' Works Performed or Works Prescribed?, pp. 135-41.

61. Dunn, *Partings of the Ways*, p. 136.

62. Dunn, 'Intra-Jewish Polemic', p. 467.

63. M.O. Wise, 'Charter of a Jewish Sectarian Association: 1QS, 4Q255-264a,

preferable. F. García Martínez incorrectly translates מעשיובתורה both in
5.21 and 6.18 as 'his works according to the law', although he rightly
observes that 'the deeds of the aspirant member…are examined to see if
they are according to the law'.[64]

It is important to take into account the force of the verb דרש in 1QS
5.20 'to inquire about, to question, to examine' and the verb שאל in
6.18 which has a similar meaning 'to ask about, to inquire about'. The
verb דרש also occurs in 6.14. In 6.14, which resembles 5.21 and 6.18,
we read that a leader of the community was supposed to examine (דרש)
the works of the novice (מעשיו 'his works'). The word מעשיו here is not
modified in any way. The noun מעשים when unmodified is neutral: it
can have either a positive or a negative meaning. In 6.14, the 'works' of
the novice which are to be examined are all his works. These could
have included both good and bad ones. Whether they were good or
bad—that is, in accordance or not in accordance with the law—was
exactly what needed to be determined. Likewise, in 5.21 and 6.18, the
works of the novice are to be examined. Here the word בתורה follows
מעשיו, making explicit that the works of the novice were to be compared to what was prescribed in the law.[65] So context makes clear that
the proper translation of מעשיו בתורה is 'his works vis-à-vis the law,
with regard to the law' as opposed to 'his works of the law', because it
would not make sense to examine a person's works if they were already
in accordance with the law. The leaders of the Qumran community
wanted evidence that the novice was performing 'works of the law',
because they viewed themselves as a holy temple in which good works
were offered as sacrifices to God (cf. 4Q174 3.7).[66]

Curiously enough, although Dunn makes the connection between
מעשי(ה)תורה in 4QMMT and 4Q174, and מעשיו בתורה in the Community Rule, he fails to draw out the full implications by ignoring the
context in which the latter expression occurs. I disagree with Dunn's
statement that מעשי תורה' come to focus in particular *halakhic*

5Q11', in Wise, Abegg, Jr and Cook (eds.), *The Dead Sea Scrolls*, pp. 123-43 (133-
35).

    64. García Martínez, '4QMMT in a Qumran Context', p. 24.
    65. It is interesting that 1QS 5.24 has a textual variant in 1QS[d]: ומעשיהם in 1QS
5.24 is ומעשיהם בתורה in 1QS[d].
    66. See J.C. de Roo, 'David's Deeds in the Dead Sea Scrolls', *DSD* 6 (1999),
pp. 44-65.

disputes—those points of *halakhic* disputes where the Qumran covenanters differed from other Jews, including particularly, it would
appear, the Pharisees'.[67] A close reading of the Community Rule
reveals that, in this document, 'works of the law' come to focus in ethical issues rather than ritual matters on which the Qumranites differed
with outsiders.

In 1QS 6.13-23 rules are given as to when and how a novice may be
fully *included* into the community. Those who wanted to join the
Qumran community were not immediately admitted, but needed to
undergo a period of testing before they could become full members.
There needed to be evidence that they were performing 'works of the
law'. Becoming part of the community was a gradual process. Only
after having spent a period of time in the community would one be considered for partaking in the 'pure meal of the congregation' and for
participating in shared ownership (6.16-17, 20, 22).

In the immediately following section (1QS 6.24–7.25), rules are
given as to when and how a backsliding member should be *excluded*
from the community. A backsliding member who did not behave in
accordance with the law, and thus failed to perform 'works of the law',
could be excluded again. When we read 6.24–7.25, we notice that
members are punished and at times excluded on the basis of unethical
behavior. Most of the sins spelled out relate to inconsideration of one's
fellow human being. Many of them relate to sinning in speech. The
smaller sins, such as 'speaking foolishly' or 'interrupting one's companion' (7.9-10), would not lead to exclusion, but only to a reduced
portion of food for a certain period of time.[68] However, some sins did
lead to exclusion, either from the company of other members in the
community for a limited period or from the community as a whole for
good. Just as becoming part of the community was a gradual process,
so was being excluded. Although the mildest form of punishment, a
reduced ratio of food by one quarter (6.25), was not a way of exclusion
as such, it may have symbolized it by reminding the transgressor of
what would await him if he continued sinning. For those who had
committed more serious offenses, the next form of punishment was
exclusion from the 'pure meal of the congregation' (literally 'the purity

67. Dunn, 'Yet Once More', pp. 103-104.
68. In 1QS 6.25 we are told explicitly that the punishment is a reduced ration of
food by a quarter.

of the many', in Hebrew טהרת רבים, 6.25; 7.3, 16, 19).[69] This was a
more severe form of punishment, because it meant not being a full
member any more and it was a reminder what would await the transgressor if he kept on sinning. The severest form of punishment was
expulsion from the community forever (7.1-2, 16-17).

It is important to read 1QS 6.24–7.25 in the light of the immediately
preceding passage 6.13-23. In 6.13-23, rules are given as to when and
how and to what degree a member should be included into the community. One could only gain full membership by performing 'works of the
law, works in accordance with the law [מעשׂי(ה)(ה)תורה]'. Therefore, the
novice's works with regard to the law (מעשׂיו בתורה) needed to be
examined. In 6.24–7.25, rules are also given as to when and how and to
what degree a member should be excluded from the community. One
could be excluded if one failed to perform 'works in accordance with
the law'. The failures mentioned all relate to ethical behavior, specifically actions which hurt one's companion or which show disrespect for
those in authority. Answering one's companion with obstinacy or
answering him impatiently (6.25-26), holding unjustly a grudge against
him (7.8), interrupting him (7.9-10) and showing oneself naked in his
presence (7.12) were to be punished by giving the offender less food.
Lying about one's property (6.25), speaking in anger to the priests (7.2-
3) or insulting or slandering one's companion (7.4, 15-16) were to lead
to exclusion from the pure meal of the congregation.

To come back to Dunn's formulation of 'works of the law', in the
Community Rule, performance of 'works of the law' does indeed determine whether one may become or remain a (full) member of the community. Yet, in 1QS 6–7, the focus is surely not on those *halakhic* disputes on which the Qumran covenanters differed from other Jews.
Being considerate toward one's companion was presumably not a characteristic peculiar to the Qumranites. It cannot be perceived as a sectarian 'identity badge', distinguishing the Qumranites from outsiders and
surely not from the Pharisees. In fact, being considerate toward each
other was a feature which the Pharisees shared with the Qumranites.
Josephus informs us that the Pharisees were affectionate with one
another and cultivated harmonious relations with the people (*War* 2). A
detailed analysis of 1QS 6–7 demonstrates that 'works of the law'

---

69. It seems that exclusion from the 'pure meal' automatically meant receiving
less food.

cannot be defined as identity badges, distinguishing one group from another.

Are 'Works of the Law' Actual or Spiritual Sacrifices, Cultic or Ethical Deeds?

It has been a matter of scholarly debate whether the sacrificial cult spoken of in 4Q174 was actual or spiritual. This is an essential issue for our consideration, because a spiritualization of the sacrificial cult would be able to convey the importance of ethical behavior through cultic imagery. I believe there is strong evidence that it was spiritualized.

The issue has been so controversial due to the difficulties scholars encountered in interpreting the crucial line, 3.6b-7a, where we read: ויאמר לבנות לוא מקדש אדם להיות מקטירים בוא לוא לפניו מעשי תורה ('And he said to build for him a temple consisting of human beings in which to make go up in smoke to him before him works of law').[70] The expression מקדש אדם does not occur anywhere else in the Dead Sea Scrolls, nor in the Hebrew Bible. It is likely that מקדש אדם means 'temple of human beings', that is, consisting of human beings, and refers to the Qumran community, that is, the *Yahad*. First, the typical Qumranian word *Yahad*, which is generally believed to refer to the Qumran community or a part thereof, occurs in 3.17. Secondly, in 1QS 8, the council of the *Yahad* is described as a temple: 'a house of holiness [בית קודש] for Israel' and 'a most holy place [קודש קודשים] for Aaron' (ll. 5-6).[71] In both 1QS 8 and 4Q174, we clearly find elements which speak of a sacrificial cult. In 1QS 8.9-10, the council of the *Yahad* are 'to offer [hiphil of קרב] a sweet fragrance [ריח ניחוח]... They will be an acceptable offering, atoning for the land (והיו לרצון לכפר בעד הארץ)'. Likewise, in 4Q174 3.6b-7a, 'a temple consisting of human beings' is supposed to be built for God in order to sacrifice to him 'works of law'. Both in 1QS 8 and 4Q174, the temple is a symbolic representation of the community, it is not actual. In 1QS 8.10, the community itself is

---

70. This English translation of 4Q174 3.7 is somewhat awkward (i.e. 'to him before him'). However, I have given a fairly literal translation of these lines in order not to lose any of the ideas they express: לוא 'to him' emphasizes that the 'works' offered are for God, לפניו 'before him' conveys the idea that these sacrifices are made in his presence.

71. By way of comparing 4Q174 with 1QS 8, several scholars have come to the conclusion that the מקדש אדם is 'the council of the *Yahad*', i.e. the Qumran community. See Wise, '4QFlorilegium', p. 108.

pictured as an offering. So this offering is not actual, but symbolic. Also, 4Q174 4.2 speaks of the remnant, that is, the *Yahad*, as performing the *whole* law (ועשׂו את כול התורה), suggesting that the 'works of the law' (מעשׂי תורה, notice the recurrence of the root עשׂה and the noun תורה) were not limited to actual sacrifices or other cultic deeds, but comprised spiritual sacrifices, ethical actions. The emphasis on performance of the *whole* law is a clear indication that 4Q174 was written to stimulate obedience to the law in general and not, as Dunn argues, specifically obedience to those rulings on which the community differed from outsiders.

Moreover, an important sentence in the *Damascus Document* seems to indicate that in 4Q174 3.7 the 'works of law' going up in smoke to God are spiritual as opposed to actual sacrifices. In CD 5.5b-6a we read: ויעלו מעשׂי דויד מלבד דם אוריה ויעזבם לו אל ('And the works of David rose up, except for the blood [murder] of Uriah, and God left them to him'). Elsewhere I have argued in the light of 4Q174 3.7 that the verb ויעלו in CD 5.5 is either a qal (וַיַּעֲלוּ) or a hophal (וַיֻּעֲלוּ), and best translated as 'and they were offered'. A good rendering of the full sentence would be: 'And David's deeds were offered (as sacrifices to God), except for the murder of Uriah, and God remembered them to David's benefit'. The first part of the sentence is a clear allusion to 1 Kgs 15.5, where we read: 'David did that which was right in the eyes of Yahweh and he did not turn aside from anything that he commanded him all the days of his life, except with regard to the matter of Uriah the Hittite'. The deeds of David which went up to God as sacrifices were 'works of the law'. David's 'works' refer not specifically to sacrificial or other cultic deeds, although these would have been included, but to good deeds in general. This is suggested by the exception-clause 'except for the murder of Uriah'. David murdered Uriah in order to be able to marry the beautiful Bathsheba who was expecting a child by him.[72] The biblical narrator tells us in 2 Sam. 11.26 that 'the thing David had done was evil in the eyes of Yahweh'.[73] This deed of David was not a deed offered to God. The murdering of a person is an act which falls under the ethical as opposed to the cultic realm. This

72. See 2 Sam. 11–12.
73. Cf. 2 Sam. 12.9. The verb עשׂה 'to do' in 2 Sam. 11.26 is from the same root as the noun מעשׂים 'works'.

suggests that David's 'works of the law' which went up as sacrifices to God included ethical deeds.[74]

Both 1QS 6–7 and CD 5.5b-6a show that 'works of the law' include ethical deeds and in these passages they come into focus in the discussion of ethical behavior. The ideology behind Dunn's theory on 'works of the law' is the concern that Judaism should not be pictured as 'legalistic'. Judaism, Dunn argues, did not perform 'works' in order to gain salvation, or in order to be blessed in the afterlife. The Jews knew that they could not obey the law perfectly, but trusted that their membership in God's covenant, as attested in their Jewish 'identity badges' ('works of the law'), would ensure their final aquittal.[75] Ironically, while making every attempt to combat the idea that Judaism was 'legalistic', Dunn seems to promote one form of legalism by reducing the concept of 'works of the law' to a mere emphasis on ritual observances. He wrongly pictures Second Temple Judaism as accentuating the ritual rather than the ethical requirements of the law. Although it is true that rituals were significant to the Jews, we also have evidence from the Dead Sea Scrolls that 'ethical behavior' was important to them. Indeed, 4QMMT focuses on rituals, but 1QS 6–7 emphasizes the importance of ethical obedience to the law. CD 5.5b-6a, read in the light of 4Q174, shows that Jews, in this case the Qumranites, conveyed the significance of good moral deeds by the use of cultic imagery, suggesting that for them the ritual and the ethical were not two separate categories, but inseparable in their minds. Therefore, they used one and the same phrase to denote obedience to the divinely given requirements in both the cultic and ethical realm, namely the phrase 'works of the law'.[76]

---

74. For example, David shows mercy and kindness (חסד) to the lame Mephibosheth, the son of his friend Jonathan, but also the grandson of his enemy Saul (2 Sam. 9). This is one of the good deeds of David. Cf. C.A. Evans, 'David in the Dead Sea Scrolls', in S.E. Porter and C.A. Evans (eds.), *The Scrolls and the Scriptures: Qumran Fifty Years After* (RILP, 3; JSPSup, 26; Sheffield: Sheffield Academic Press, 1997), pp. 183-97 (189). For a more elaborate discussion of this issue, see de Roo, 'David's Deeds in the Dead Sea Scrolls', pp. 57, 61-63.

75. Dunn, 'Yet Once More', p. 109; *idem, Partings of the Ways*, pp. 136-38.

76. Interestingly, at Qumran those who were morally impure were considered to be cultically impure as well: in case of serious moral transgression, they were not allowed to have meals with the other members (cf. 1QS 6.24–7.25 and discussion above). Again, this demonstrates how the ethical and the cultic were intertwined in the minds of the Qumranites.

The evidence from the Qumran literature discussed above shows that 'works of the law' did not function as 'identity badges'. It also demonstrates that 'works of the law' is sometimes used in the discussion of ritual practices (although this is not what the phrase itself stands for),[77] but at other times the focus is on ethical behavior. The same shift in focus can be observed in Paul's usage of the phrase ἔργα νόμου. In Galatians 2, Paul uses the expression 'works of the law' in his discussion of whether Christians need to practice circumcision and abide by particular foodlaws. In Romans 4, on the other hand, we have a clear example of Paul speaking of 'works of the law'—particularly in reference to ethical deeds. In 4.6, 'David speaks of the blessing upon the man to whom God reckons righteousness apart from works [Δαυὶδ λέγει τὸν μακαρισμὸν τοῦ ἀνθρώπου ᾧ ὁ θεὸς λογίζεται δικαιοσύνην χωρὶς ἔργων]'. The verbal and conceptual parallels with Paul's words in the preceding paragraph are striking: 'For we maintain that a man is justified by faith apart from works of the law [λογιζόμεθα γὰρ δικαιοῦσθαι πίστει ἄνθρωπον χωρὶς ἔργων νόμου]' (3.28). In the light of 3.28, it is evident that ἔργων, 'works', in 4.6 is a shorter way of saying ἔργα νόμου, 'works of the law'. A quotation from Ps. 32.1-2 follows: 'Blessed are those whose lawless deeds have been forgiven, and whose sins have been covered. Blessed is the man whose sin the Lord will not take into account' (Rom. 4.7-8). In Ps. 32.3-5, the psalmist, whom Paul evidently takes to be David, is speaking of his own sin. So in Rom. 4.6-8, David's 'righteousness apart from works (of the law)' is described as 'the blessing of forgiveness for lawless deeds and sins'. In other words, David's lack of works of the law is described as sin. Therefore, 'works of the law' here must be the opposite of sin, that is, actions done in obedience to God's commandments.[78] We know from 2 Samuel 11–12 that David failed to obey God in the ethical realm: he committed adultery with Bathsheba and murdered her husband. In Paul's mind, this would have been the sin the psalmist referred to in Psalm 32. So in Rom. 4.6-8, 'works of the law', or the lack of them, come into focus in the discussion of ethical behavior.

Are 'Works of the Law' Works Performed or Works Prescribed?
Dunn always renders the phrase ἔργα νόμου as 'works of the law'. While he refers to them as 'identity confirming/boundary defining

---

77. See discussion below.
78. Schreiner, '"Works of Law" in Paul', p. 229.

acts',[79] he also emphasizes that they do 'not denote actions already accomplished, so much as obligations laid down by the law...'[80] Elsewhere he defines 'works of the law' as 'regulations prescribed by the law'.[81] Although Dunn does not use the word 'precepts' in these instances, this is how one could capture succinctly the phrases 'obligations laid down by the law' and 'regulations prescribed by the law'. Yet is there not an important difference between 'acts' and 'precepts'? The difference is crucial in a context which discusses soteriological questions. 'Acts' are works already accomplished, and, therefore, a person can be judged by his acts. Yet 'precepts' only prescribe the works which ought to be done. What direct role could they play in attaining righteousness?

In discussing the parallels between 4QMMT and Galatians, Dunn says in reference to the phrase מעשי התורה in 4QMMT C 27 that

> the closeness of the parallel with Paul's phrase, ἔργα νόμου, has unfortunately been obscured by the translations so far adopted—'the precepts of the Torah' (Qimron C 27; Martínez 113), 'observances of the law' (Vermes). Eisenman and Wise render the phrase as 'works of the law' (so also Abegg); but the weight of the other translators is likely to count against the Eisenman and Wise version. However, 'deed' or 'act' is the most natural meaning for מעשה.[82]

On the one hand, Dunn prefers the translation 'works of the law', because it brings out the Pauline parallel and is closer to the natural meaning of מעשה (deed, act). In the following paragraph Dunn makes a statement which states that he is hesitant to discard the translations given by Qimron, García Martínez and Vermes: he views the phrase (מקצת) מעשי התורה in 4QMMT C 27 'as a summary reference to a series of legal/halakhic rulings/practices', namely those mentioned in section B.[83]

Dunn comes to this conclusion by misinterpreting the function of מעשים in 4QMMT. Curiously enough, Dunn rightly observes that '"deed" or "act" is the most natural meaning for מעשה'.[84] He even refers to several Qumran passages (including 4Q174 3.7 where we

79. Dunn, *Partings of the Ways*, p. 137 (emphasis added).
80. Dunn, *Partings of the Ways*, p. 136.
81. Dunn, 'New Perspective', p. 111.
82. Dunn, '4QMMT', p. 150.
83. Dunn, '4QMMT', p. 150.
84. Dunn, '4QMMT', p. 150.

encounter the phrase מעשי תורה and the word מעשיהם in 4QMMT C 23!) to support this statement. In addition to the passages Dunn mentions, we could refer to any other Qumran text containing the word מעשה in order to show that it always carries the meaning 'act' or 'deed' as opposed to 'precept', 'ruling' or the like.[85] Unfortunately, Dunn fails to draw out the full implications of his own observation. He assumes too quickly (like most scholars who have commented on 4QMMT) that the phrase מקצת מעשי התורה in 4QMMT C 27 refers to the *halakhot* listed in section B.

The word מעשים occurs three times in 4QMMT (B 2, C 23 and 27). Its first occurrence is in the opening paragraph of section B, which makes virtually all scholars, including the editors, assume that it introduces the following list of *halakhot*.[86] However, the context is so fragmentary (the words immediately preceding מעשים and many of those following have been lost), that it is impossible to demonstrate this. In

---

85. The singular form of מעשה occurs in CD 12.18; 1QS 3.25; 4.4; 1QM 5.4, 5, 6, 14; 7.11; 1QH 5.12, 16; 8.20; 15.13; 18.18; 4Q299, frag. 2, col. 1, l. 18; col. 2, ll. 3, 6, 10, 15; frag. 34, col. 1, l. 2; 4Q418, frag. 159, col. 2, l. 4; frag. 238, col. 1, l. 2; 4Q509, frag. 8, col. 3, l. 1; 11QT 43.16, 17; 50.17. The plural form of מעשי occurs in CD 1.1, 2, 10; 2.1, 7-8, 14-15; 4.6; 5.5, 16; 6.8; 13.7-8, 11; 20.3, 6; 1QS 1.5, 19, 21; 2.5, 7; 3.14, 22; 4.3-4, 10, 15-16, 20, 23, 25; 5.18-19, 19, 21, 23, 24; 6.14, 17, 18; 8.18; 10.17; 11.16, 20; 1QSa 1.18, 22; 1QSb 2.27; 3.27; 1QpHab 10.12; 12.8; 1QM 5.5, 7, 8, 9 (2×), 10, 11; 10.8, 14; 11.4; 13.1, 2, 9; 14.12; 15.9; 1QH 4.18, 19; 5.9, 10, 14, 25; 6.7, 16; 7.20; 8.17; 9.6, 7, 9, 26, 27, 30, 33; 10.3; 11.12, 17, 23; 12.8, 17, 20, 31, 32; 13.16, 36; 14.9; 15.32; 18.11, 36; 19.4, 24, 30; 23.13; 1QH, frag. 3, col. 1, ll. 10, 16; 1Q34bis, frag. 3, col. 2, l. 7; 4Q162 [= 4QpIs[b]], col. 2, l. 4; 4Q169 [= 4QpN], frags. 3-4, col. 3, l. 3; 4Q174, frag. 1, col. 3, l. 7; 4Q286, frag. 1, col. 2, l. 6; 4Q288, frag. 1, col. 1, l. 13; 4Q300, frag. 1, col. 1, l. 3; 4Q301, frag. 1, col. 1, l. 3; 4Q374, frag. 2, col. 2, l. 3; 4Q384, frag. 8, col. 1, ll. 1, 3; 4Q385, frag. 36, col. 2, l. 2; 4QMMT B 2; C 23, 27; 4Q400, frag. 1, col. 1, l. 5; 4Q402, frag. 4, l. 11; 4Q403, frag. 1, col. 1, l. 35; 4Q405, frag. 19, l. 6; frag. 20, col. 2, l. 10; frag. 23, col. 2, ll. 7, 9, 10; 4Q418, frag. 81, col. 1, l. 7; frag. 102, col. 1, l. 2; frag. 123, col. 2, l. 6; frag. 148, col. 1, l. 3; col. 2, l. 8; frag. 158, col. 1, l. 4; frag. 198, col. 1, l. 2; 4Q427, frag. 7, col. 2, l. 13; 4Q434, frag. 1, col. 1, l. 3; 4Q491, frags. 8-10, col. 1, l. 10; 4Q509, frags. 97-98, l. 9; 4Q511, frag. 10, col. 1, l. 10; frag. 18, col. 2, l. 7; frags. 48+, col. 2, l. 5; frag. 63, col. 3, ll. 2, 3; col. 4, l. 1; 4Q512, frags. 1-6, l. 15; 11QPs [= 11Q5], col. 22, l. 10; col. 24, l. 9; col. 28, ll. 6, 7; 11QT 59.3. In all of these occurrences, the word מעשה clearly expresses 'work(s) performed' or 'the product(s) of work', rather than 'works prescribed (i.e. precepts)'.

86. E. Qimron and J. Strugnell, *Qumran Cave 4.* V. *Miqsat Ma'ase ha-Torah* (DJD, 10; Oxford: Clarendon Press, 1994), p. 139.

fact, context is so unclear, that we do not even know for sure whether
the word מעשים is a noun. It may equally well be a qal active masculine
plural participle from the verb עשה (עשׂים), preceded by the preposition
min. The two other occurrences of מעשים are found in a context which
has been relatively well preserved:

> Think of the kings of Israel and consider their works [מעשׂיהם] carefully:
> for he who feared [the La]w was delivered from troubles; and these were
> the se[ek]ers of the law (*vacat*), those whose sins [were for]given. Re-
> member David, he was a man of good works [חסדים], and was delivered
> from many troubles and forgiven. We have written to you about some
> (examples) of works of the law [מקצת מעשׂי התורה], because we con-
> sidered it beneficial to you and to your people (C 23b-27).

García Martínez has rightly observed that, in C 23, מעשׂים clearly
means 'works' as opposed to 'precepts', as the third masculine plural
suffix indicates (cf. 1QS 6.18).[87] Even Qimron and Strugnell, who give
מעשׂים the rendering 'precepts' in C 27, translate מעשׂיהם in C 23 as
'their deeds', recognizing that these are works performed as opposed to
prescribed.[88] García Martínez rightly criticizes Qimron and Strugnell
for being inconsistent in their rendering of מעשׂים: in C 23 it clearly
means 'works', therefore, in C 27 it must be rendered as 'works' too.[89]
Dunn recognizes the validity of this observation, but still holds on to
the idea that מקצת מעשׂי התורה must refer to the precepts in section B.

Yet in the light of 4Q174 3.7, the only other Qumran document
which contains the phrase 'works of the law', it would be more
reasonable to contend that 'works of the law' is an idiom to denote
'works performed—as opposed to prescribed—in obedience to God's
law'. In 4Q174, 'works of the law' are pictured as sacrifices made to
God by his people, the Qumran community. It is amazing how
influential the interpretation of 'works of the law' in 4QMMT has been
on 4Q174, resulting in curious translations of מעשׂי תורה. For instance,
S.D. Fraade, believing מעשׂי תורה and מעשׂי התורה to be synonymous,
translates מעשׂי תורה in 4Q174 with 'precepts of Torah'.[90] However,
how should we picture the offering of 'precepts of Torah'? Clearly, in
4Q174 the actual performance of good deeds, deeds pleasing to God, is
in view.

87. García Martínez, '4QMMT', p. 25.
88. Qimron and Strugnell, *Qumran Cave 4*, V, p. 61.
89. García Martínez, '4QMMT', p. 25.
90. Fraade, 'Interpretive Authority', p. 63.

There is no need to give a different meaning to the phrase 'works of the law' in 4QMMT: here too it clearly refers to works accomplished. As mentioned above, in Qumran literature the word מעשׂים always carries the meaning 'works performed' rather than 'works prescribed'. Simply changing the translation of מעשׂיהתורה 'precepts of the Torah' given by Qimron and Strugnell into 'works of the law' does not clarify the function of the phrase in 4QMMT, if one does not recognize that 'works of the law' are 'works accomplished in accordance with the law' as opposed to 'works prescribed'. If the author of 4QMMT had wanted to refer in C 27 to the precepts mentioned in section B, he would not have used the phrase מעשׂיהתורה, but words like מצוות or חוקים which are frequently used in Qumran literature to denote 'precepts'.[91]

Moreover, as has been observed above, in 4QMMT C 23, מעשׂים clearly means 'works performed'. The proximity of מקצת מעשׂי התורה (C 27) to מעשׂיהם (C 23) suggests that there is a direct connection between 'some of the works of the law' and 'the works' done by the kings. Looking at the immediate context in which מקצת מעשׂי התורה occurs, it would be natural to take it as a direct reference to the deeds performed by pious kings, mentioned in C 23–26, as opposed to a summary statement which refers to the *halakhot* described in section B.[92]

91. For the usage of the word מצווה, see CD 2.18, 21; 3.2, 8, 12; 5.21; 8.19; 9.7; 19.2, 5, 32; 1QSb 1.1; 1QpHab 5.5; 4QpHos[a] 2.4; 4QTestim 1.4 (quoting Deut. 5.28-29); 4QpGen[c] 1.3; 11QT 55.13; 59.16. For the usage of the word חוקים, see CD 5.12; 9.1; 12.20; 19.6, 14; 20.11, 29, 30, 33; 1QS 1.7, 12, 15; 3.8; 5.7, 11, 20, 22; 9.12; 10.10; 1QSa 1.5, 7; 1QSb 3.24; 1QpHab 8.10; 1QH 6.5; 7.12; 8.24. Qimron and Strugnell (*Qumran Cave 4*, V, p. 139) state that 'the Dead Sea sectarians did not employ the term halakhot' to refer to the rulings in 4QMMT B, because it 'was used by their opponents'. Instead, so they argue, the Dead Sea sectarians used the phrase מעשׂיהתורה. Yet Qimron and Strugnell fail to explain why the author of 4QMMT would not have used one of the frequently occurring nouns for 'precepts' in the Dead Sea Scrolls, מצווה or חוקים.

92. Although García Martínez ('4QMMT', pp. 25-26) comes fairly close to this interpretation, he still draws too close a connection between מקצת מעשׂי התורה and the precepts listed in section B: ' "We have written to you some of the works of the law" then becomes a perfect summary of MMT: a collection of some of the practices, of the works, which according to the prescription of the law should be done in order to be rewarded'. Bachmann ('4QMMT und Galaterbrief', pp. 91-113) has also drawn attention to the inconsistency of scholars in showing a connection between מעשׂי התורה (C 27) and מעשׂיהם (C 23) in their translations, while still arguing that מעשׂי התורה refers to the rulings of section B. He criticizes in particular Dunn for

There were those kings in Israel whose actions showed that they feared the law, that they were seekers of the law. King David is singled out as the epitome of kingly piety, being described as a אִישׁ חֲסָדִים ('a man of good deeds'). When the author of 4QMMT tells his addressee 'we have written to you about some of the works of the law', he is in fact saying: we have reminded you of examples ('some') of 'works of the law' performed by people, in other words, of some exemplary lives led in obedience to God's law. He says that he has written about the right actions performed by exemplary kings (that is, they sought the law [l. 24] and performed 'good deeds' [חֲסָדִים, l. 25]) 'to your benefit and to the benefit of your people' (l. 27). The author believes that these descriptions of proper behavior are beneficial to his addressees, because they would view their heroic kings as examples, whose lives of obedience to God's law they must imitate.

It is surely not accidental that the author of 4QMMT singles out David as an example of piety, describing him as 'a man of good deeds' (אִישׁ חֲסָדִים, l. 25). During his lifetime, David offered works of the law to God, in other words, he led a life of obedience to God's law. Nevertheless, he did fall into sin when he committed adultery with Bathsheba and, afterwards, killed her husband to be able to marry her (CD 5.5b-6a; 1 Kgs 15.5; cf. 2 Samuel 11–12). Yet God forgave him for this (4QMMT C 26), because he repented (cf. 2 Sam. 12.13). Although not mentioned explicitly, it is implied that the author of 4QMMT wants his addressees to follow David's example in this regard too. In his opinion,

---

using 'merkwürdingen Doppelungen' ('ambiguous expressions') such as 'rulings/ practices' (p. 102). In his attempt to be consistent, Bachmann comes to the opposite conclusion to the one drawn in this essay. He stresses that a clear distinction should be made between מַעֲשִׂים modified by a suffix (as in C 23) on the one hand, and מַעֲשִׂים unmodified (as in B 2) or modified by the word תורה (as in C 27) on the other hand. In the latter case, so Bachmann argues, the word מַעֲשִׂים does not carry the meaning 'deeds' any longer, but 'rulings'. Although I disagree with Bachmann, I appreciate his attempt to give a precise definition of 'works of the law'. He contends that מעשׂי התורה and ἔργα νόμου should be rendered as 'Halakhot' or 'Tora-Regelungen', and emphasizes that they are not 'works performed': '[Es geht] nicht um menschliches Tun, sondern um Tora-Gebote' (p. 110). See also *idem*, 'Rechtfertigung und Gesetzeswerke bei Paulus', *TZ* 49.1 (1993), pp. 1-33, esp. 26. The main error Bachmann makes is that he reads מעשׂי תודה 'Werke des Dank-opfers', in 4Q174 3.7, following Grelot and Kuhn, and, as a result, fails to see the connection between 4QMMT C 27, 4Q174 3.7 and CD 5.5b-6a ('4QMMT und Galaterbrief', p. 100; 'Rechtfertigung', p. 29).

they sinned by violating the rules mentioned in section B. The author wants his addressees to repent from their sin, like their heroic king David did. So, there surely is a connection between the precepts listed in section B and the 'works of the law' (deeds of obedience) spoken of in section C. The 'works of the law' performed by the kings (that is, their seeking of the law, their good deeds [חסדים], and, implied, their acts of repentance) should encourage the addressees to follow these exemplary patterns of obedient behavior by repenting from sin and abiding by the right (that is, Qumranic) interpretation of the law as described in section B.

It is evident that, in both 4Q174 and 4QMMT, the phrase 'works of the law (מעשׂי[ה]תורה)' denotes 'works performed in obedience to God's law', rather than 'works prescribed'. CD 5.5b-6a, read in the light of 4Q174, tells us that 'works of the law' is an expression to describe obedience in general, the devotion of one's entire life to God, the sacrificing of oneself.[93] Likewise, in 4QMMT, 'works of the law' refers to the obedient lifestyle of the good Israelite kings, their 'fearing of the law' and their 'seeking of the law', that is, their desire to know what God wanted them to do, and their 'good deeds (חסדים)'. 'Works of the law' expresses all of these: fearing, seeking and practicing the law; in short, it stands for living in obedience to God's law.

Likewise, Paul clearly uses the phrase ἔργα νόμου to denote works performed rather than prescribed. As several New Testament scholars have convincingly demonstrated, the reason why 'works of the law' do not justify in Paul's thinking is because they 'are not forthcoming'.[94] The problem is disobedience on the part of all humans, both Jew and Greek. No one is excluded because of humanity's sinful nature.[95] In other words, 'works of the law' is the opposite of sin and stands for obedience.[96] How else could obedience be defined as the actual *performance* of good deeds?

---

93. In 1QS 8.9-10, which also speaks of the Qumran community as a temple, the members of the community are to sacrifice themselves. See also de Roo, 'David's Deeds in the Dead Sea Scrolls', pp. 50-51.

94. Cf. Cranfield, *Romans 1–8*, p. 198.

95. Of course, the exception which would have been in Paul's mind is the person Jesus Christ.

96. Cranfield, '"The Works of the Law"', pp. 89-101; *idem, Romans 1–8*, pp. 197-99; Moo, *Romans 1–8*, pp. 208-18; *idem*, 'Legalism in Paul', pp. 73-100; Schreiner, '"Works of Law" in Paul', pp. 217-44.

Did Jews of the Second Temple Period Think of 'Works of the Law' as Meritorious?

Dunn uses Qumran texts in order to support his view that 'works of the law' were not thought of by Jews of the Second Temple period as meritorious. Yet Dunn seems to have difficulties in entirely moving away from this notion, as the following quotation shows:

> I very much doubt, therefore, whether Rom. 4.4-5 is rightly to be understood as accusing Paul's fellow Jews of thinking they could achieve or earn acceptance by God by means of their own efforts and hard work. Since the typical Jewish mind set was of those who perceived themselves as *already* within the bounds of God's covenant grace, in that crucial sense there was nothing to be earned! Though it was certainly a status to be documented and maintained over against Gentile sinners by works of the law. And that attitude *is not so very far* [my emphasis] from the attitude of the merit-earner of Professor Cranfield's interpretation. But the two are *not* the same, and the extent of the disagreement between Professor Cranfield and myself shows *how far apart they actually are* [my emphasis].[97]

Again, we sense the influence of Sanders on Dunn: Sanders also stresses that Jews of the Second Temple period viewed themselves as belonging to God's covenant by grace, and, therefore, could not have thought of their deeds as merit-earning. Yet, Dunn adds, this favored status that the Jews held needed to be maintained by works of the law. He rightly admits (at least initially!) that this 'attitude *is not so very far* from the attitude of the merit-earner'. Indeed, it is not. Even if Sanders's portrayal of Judaism was correct, works which are necessary to 'stay in' can still be characterized as meritorious.[98]

Moreover, the evidence from Qumran literature suggests that Jews, in this case the Qumranites, viewed their 'works of the law', their 'good works', as meritorious. In 4Q174 3.7, the Qumran community is pictured as a spiritual temple in which 'works of the law' are offered as sacrifices to God. CD 5.5b-6a, read in the light of 4Q174, makes clear that these 'works of the law' were thought of as deserving God's favor. The 'good deeds' which David offered to God were left to him in the sense that God reckoned them to him as meritorious. God rewarded

---

97. Dunn, 'Yet Once More', p. 113.

98. Moo (*Romans 1–8*, p. 216) aptly states: 'It is clear that works, even in Sanders's view, play a necessary and instrumental role in salvation'. Of course, Sanders himself does not perceive it this way.

David for his good deeds by remembering them in his dealings with the house of Judah, of which he safeguarded a remnant for himself (cf. 2 Samuel 7; 1 Kgs 11.13, 34; 2 Kgs 8.19; 19.30). According to the Qumranite way of thinking, God remembered David's deserving deeds and, for David's sake, he preserved a remnant which became their community. Following the example of their hero David, the Qumran community offered 'works of the law' as sacrifices to God, believing that God would reward them for their good deeds, just as he blessed David.[99] Likewise, the author of 4QMMT tells his addressees that 'works of the law', in other words, doing what is right and good in God's eyes, will result in being reckoned as righteous (C 23–32). Is it accidental that David is mentioned by name as a great example of piety, being described as a חסדים איש, 'a man of good deeds'? Surely not! The Qumranites believed, as the *Damascus Document* reveals, that David merited God's favor by his 'works of the law'.

Conclusion

This essay has attempted to discuss the relevance of Qumran texts for understanding the concept of 'works of the law' in Pauline literature. The focus has been on Dunn's use of these texts to support the idea that 'works of the law' are 'identity badges', separating Jews from Gentiles. There are several reasons why this notion should be abandoned. The chief weakness of Dunn's view is its inconsistency. According to Dunn, 'works of the law' in Paul's letters are Jewish *national* identity badges, separating Jews from Gentiles, but in 4QMMT they are identity badges *separating Jews from Jews*.

Moreover, Dunn's definition of 'works of the law' appears to be illogical in another way. On the one hand, he posits that 'works of the law' are all deeds in accordance with God's law. On the other hand, he argues that 'works of the law' are 'identity badges' and come to focus in *halakhic* disputes. An issue related to this is that all the 'identity badges' observed by Dunn are cultic in nature, as opposed to ethical. In one of his earlier articles, Dunn explicitly states in relation to the concept of 'works of the law' that the ritual is in view, although in his later articles he seems to replace the word ritual with the word *halakhic*. My treatment of 1QS 6–7 and CD 5.5b-6a shows that 'works of the law'

---

99. De Roo, 'David's Deeds in the Dead Sea Scrolls', pp. 63-65.

included ethical deeds, and came into focus in the discussion of ethical behavior. Also, a detailed analysis of 1QS 6–7 suggests that 'works of the law' cannot be defined as 'identity badges', and surely not as 'identity markers' which distinguished the Qumranites from the Pharisees. Equally significant is the emphasis in 4Q174 on performance of the *whole* law (4.2). It is a clear indication that 4Q174 was written to stimulate obedience to the law in general (the performance of 'works of the law', cf. 3.7) and not, as Dunn argues, specifically obedience to those rulings on which the community differed from outsiders.

Dunn uses 4QMMT in particular to support his idea that 'works of the law' are 'identity badges'. He fails to make a clear distinction between works performed and works prescribed. He can never decide whether to call 'works of the law' 'acts', 'works', 'practices' or 'rulings'. Dunn wrongly uses 4QMMT to demonstrate that 'works of the law' means works prescribed, viewing מקצת מעשי התורה as a summary reference to the *halakhot* mentioned in section B. My analysis of 4QMMT in the light of 4Q174 and CD 5.5b-6a shows that מקצת מעשי התורה is in all likelihood a direct reference to the deeds performed by pious kings, mentioned in C 23–26. It does not refer to the *halakhot* which distinguished the Qumranites from outsiders, and, therefore, Dunn's use of 4QMMT to demonstrate that 'works of the law' are 'identity badges' is invalid.

The evidence from Qumran literature strongly suggests that Jews of the Second Temple period (in this case the Qumranites) viewed 'works of the law' as meritorious. The author of 4QMMT tells his addressees that 'works of the law', that is, doing what is right and good in God's eyes, will result in being reckoned as righteousness (C 23–32). He mentions David as an example of obedience (C 25), because the Qumranites believed that David earned God's favor by offering to him 'works of the law' (CD 5.5b-6a). In the light of the Qumran literature, it is not difficult to believe that Paul was polemicizing against a prevalent Jewish notion that it was possible to be justified in God's eyes by performing good works (that is, works in obedience to God's law). The evidence from the Qumran texts weakens Dunn's interpretation of 'works of the law' rather than supports it.

WAS PAUL A GOOD JEW?*
FUNDAMENTAL ISSUES IN A CURRENT DEBATE

Stanley E. Porter

1. *Introduction*

William Wrede was, to my knowledge, the first to say that 'Paul is to be regarded as the *second founder of Christianity'*—at the least, he is the best known for saying out loud what many have thought.[1] This is an understanding and interpretation of the formative work of the apostle to the Gentiles that seems more profoundly true every time the primary texts of the New Testament are analysed regarding the development of early Christianity.[2] Since Paul was the second founder of Christianity— perhaps even, arguably, the *first* founder, depending upon one's view of whether Jesus intended formally to found a group of followers—and since this form of Christianity ultimately became the basis of Western Christianity,[3] his Christianity is rightly not often called into question. He was a follower of Christ, and hence what soon became known as a Christian,[4] or a good Christian (to follow the format of my title),

---

* My title is noticeably similar to that of M. Barth, 'St Paul—A Good Jew', *HBT* 1 (1979), pp. 7-45, but does not conclude similarly.

1. W. Wrede, *Paul* (trans. E. Lummis; London: Philip Green, 1907), p. 179 (emphasis in the original).

2. On the issue of the separation of Christianity and Judaism, including reference to relevant bibliography, see S.E. Porter and B.W.R. Pearson, 'Why the Split? Christians and Jews by the Fourth Century', *Journal of Greco-Roman Christianity and Judaism* 1 (forthcoming 2000), a summary of part of which appears in this volume as 'Ancient Understandings of the Christian–Jewish Split', pp. 36-51.

3. See W.H. Frend, *The Rise of Christianity* (Philadelphia: Fortress Press, 1984), esp. pp. 85-117.

4. Those who became known as Christians were originally called a number of different things, including followers of the Way, disciples, etc. Acts 11.26 records that it was at Antioch that these people were called Christians, an appellation that

because to a large extent he defined what it meant to be one. Not everything Paul said has been easy to interpret (cf. 2 Pet. 3.16), and significant debate still surrounds a number of significant issues to which Paul speaks,[5] but his Christian status is secure. In the light of this situation, however, the question of how good a *Jew* Paul was often fades from view.

The importance of this question—was Paul a good Jew?—rests in the fact that, of course, by birth or ethnically Paul was himself Jewish (Phil. 3.5-6; cf. 1 Cor. 9.20; 2 Cor. 11.22, 24; Gal. 2.15),[6] and, according to the information to which we have access, was reared and trained as a Pharisaic Jew (Phil. 3.5),[7] regardless of whatever other training he also received.[8] This training as a Pharisee, probably in Jerusalem under

appears to have caught on within and without the group (e.g. Josephus, *Ant.* 18.64; 1 Pet. 4.16). Whether this is what Christians called themselves or were called by others remains a point of dispute, although E.A. Judge has made a convincing case for this being an early sign of the Romans distinguishing between Jews and Christians, in 'Judaism and the Rise of Christianity: A Roman Perspective', *TynBul* 45.2 (1994), pp. 355-68, esp. pp. 363-64. See also J.A. Fitzmyer, *The Acts of the Apostles* (AB, 31; New York: Doubleday, 1998), pp. 477-78, with bibliography on pp. 478-79.

5.   As will be noted below, these issues are not only confined to the more popular ones, such as the role of women in the church, homosexuality, or speaking in tongues, but also involve more theologically central concepts, some of which are discussed below.

6.   Paul's Jewishness is also much depicted in the book of Acts (but Acts is not required to show that Paul was a Jew). The evidence ranges from his disputing in the synagogues to his personal statements regarding his life. See Acts 7.58; 9.1; 13.5, 14; 14.1; 16.3; 17.1, 10, 17; 18.4, 19, 26; 19.8, 34; 21.39; 22.3, 19; 24.12; 26.11. For a recent discussion of the relationship between the Paul of his letters and the Paul of Acts, with assessment of some of the arguments against the reliability of Acts in reconstructing the life and teaching of Paul, see S.E. Porter, *The Paul of Acts: Essays in Literary Criticism, Rhetoric, and Theology* (WUNT, 115; Tübingen: Mohr Siebeck, 1999), esp. pp. 187-206. I will concentrate here upon the Pauline letters, but will also mention Acts where important, since I do not believe that a firm disjunction should be made between the letters and Acts for the purposes of historical reconstruction.

7.   M. Hengel with R. Deines, *The Pre-Christian Paul* (trans. J. Bowden; London: SCM Press, 1991), pp. 1-17; cf. also M. Hengel, 'The Pre-Christian Paul', in J. Lieu, J. North and T. Rajak (eds.), *The Jews among Pagans and Christians in the Roman Empire* (London: Routledge, 1992), pp. 29-33.

8.   The purpose here is not to discuss the life of Paul. Suffice it to say that he was born in Tarsus of Cilicia (Acts 21.39; 22.3), a city of significance in the

Gamaliel I (Acts 21.39, although this verse is difficult),[9] set him upon his course of behaviour. However, on his way to Damascus to persecute Hellenistic Jewish Christians,[10] Paul claims to have been confronted by the risen Christ (Acts 9.1-9; 22.3-11; 26.9-18).[11] This episode transformed the enthusiastic persecutor of the Church (Gal. 1.13) into an equally, if not more, enthusiastic follower of the risen Christ. According to the consensus of contemporary New Testament scholarship, Paul's conversion[12] was instrumental in establishing his missionary purpose as the apostle to the Gentiles (Gal. 1.16), a vocation he took seriously right up to the end of his life.[13] This active proselytization for

Graeco-Roman world, as well as a city with a significant Diaspora Jewish population. On Tarsus, see the ancient writers Strabo, 14.5.8-15 and Dio Chrysostom, *Or.* 32–34; and the modern treatments of A.H.M. Jones, *Cities of the Eastern Roman Provinces* (Oxford: Clarendon Press, 1937), esp. pp. 192-215, who treats the whole of Cilicia; and W.M. Ramsay, *The Cities of St Paul: Their Influence on his Life and Thought* (London: Hodder & Stoughton, 1907), pp. 85-244. On education in the ancient world, see H.I. Marrou, *A History of Education in Antiquity* (trans. G. Lamb; London: Sheed & Ward, 1956), pp. 242-313.

9.   For a recent discussion of this highly problematic verse, see Hengel with Deines, *Pre-Christian Paul*, pp. 18-39; cf. pp. 54-62.

10.   See Hengel with Deines, *Pre-Christian Paul*, pp. 63-86; cf. *idem*, 'The Pre-Christian Paul', pp. 43-48. For a contrasting position, see J. Taylor, 'Why Did Paul Persecute the Church?', in G.N. Stanton and G.G. Stroumsa (eds.), *Tolerance and Intolerance in Early Judaism and Christianity* (Cambridge: Cambridge University Press, 1998), pp. 99-120, esp. 110-13.

11.   On these three accounts, see the recent treatment of D. Marguerat, 'Saul's Conversion (Acts 9, 22, 26) and the Multiplication of Narrative in Acts', in C.M. Tuckett (ed.), *Luke's Literary Achievement: Collected Essays* (JSNTSup, 116; Sheffield: Sheffield Academic Press, 1995), pp. 127-55.

12.   On Paul's conversion, within the context of other kinds of religious conversion, see A.D. Nock, *Conversion: The Old and the New in Religion from Alexander the Great to Augustine of Hippo* (Oxford: Clarendon Press, 1933); A.F. Segal, *Paul the Convert: The Apostolate and Apostasy of Saul the Pharisee* (New Haven: Yale University Press, 1990); and J.D.G. Dunn, 'Paul's Conversion—A Light to Twentieth Century Disputes', in J. Ådna, S.J. Hafemann and O. Hofius (eds.), *Evangelium—Schriftauslegung—Kirche: Festschrift für Peter Stuhlmacher zum 65. Geburtstag* (Göttingen: Vandenhoeck & Ruprecht, 1997), pp. 77-85; *idem*, *The Theology of Paul the Apostle* (Grand Rapids: Eerdmans, 1998), pp. 347-53; *idem*, 'Paul: Apostate or Apostle of Israel?', *ZNW* 89 (1998), pp. 256-71, esp. pp. 259-60; cf. also *idem*, *The Epistle to the Galatians* (BNTC; Peabody, MA: Hendrickson, 1993), pp. 55-62.

13.   See S. Kim, *The Origin of Paul's Gospel* (WUNT, 2.4; Tübingen: Mohr

the cause of Christ was apparently untypical of Jewish proselytization practices of the time.[14] That it was on behalf of a figure probably seen by most Jews who had heard of him as just another deluded messianic pretender,[15] and not 'Lord' as Paul describes him, leads to the inevitable question—was Paul a *good* Jew?

Asking this question implies that one has a clear idea of what it meant to be a good Jew in the first part of the first century, and that Paul can be judged against such a standard. As I shall attempt to show, asking this question is itself highly problematic. A number of further issues are also raised by this analysis, however. For example, would we be examining whether Paul thought of himself as a good Jew, or would we be assessing whether his contemporaries—distinguishing between Jews, Jewish-Christians and Gentiles (Christian or otherwise)—thought he was a good Jew? The answer might well vary with the group being considered. Would we be attempting to answer this question from the perspective of the first-century person, or from that of the late twentieth century, with full benefit of historical distance and hindsight? Again, the answer might vary, in the light of the development of Christianity,

Siebeck, 1981; repr. Grand Rapids: Eerdmans, 1982), even though he probably overstates the case that virtually everything in Paul's thought stems from his conversion (certainly his attempts to ground this equation in the Greek tense-forms is to be questioned); C.K. Barrett, *Paul: An Introduction to his Thought* (London: Chapman, 1994), p. 10. For a discussion of recent scholarship on Paul's conversion and its influence on him, see J. Plevnik, *What are They Saying about Paul?* (New York: Paulist Press, 1986), pp. 5-27.

14. See S. McKnight, *A Light to the Gentiles: Jewish Missionary Activity in the Second Temple Period* (Minneapolis: Fortress Press, 1991), esp. pp. 1-2, for a brief survey of the literature; M. Goodman, 'Jewish Proselytizing in the First Century', in Lieu, North and Rajak (eds.), *Jews among Pagans and Christians*, pp. 53-78; and I. Levinskaya, *The Book of Acts in its First Century Setting. V. Diaspora Setting* (Grand Rapids: Eerdmans, 1996), pp. 19-49. The opposite position is represented by D. Georgi, *The Opponents of Paul in Second Corinthians* (Philadelphia: Fortress Press, 1986 [1964]), pp. 83-228; L.H. Feldman, *Jew and Gentile in the Ancient World: Attitudes and Interactions from Alexander to Justinian* (Princeton, NJ: Princeton University Press, 1993), pp. 288-341; cf. pp. 342-415; with a critique of Feldman by L.V. Rutgers, *The Hidden Heritage of Diaspora Judaism* (Leuven: Peeters, 1998), pp. 199-234.

15. Dunn ('Paul's Conversion', p. 82) argues that recognition of Jesus as Messiah may not have been as contentious to many Jews of the first century as many scholars have thought. However, he neglects such references as 1 Cor. 1.23 and Gal. 3.13, and the evidence regarding other messianic aspirants (see below).

and Paul's role in this development. In other words, asking the question of whether Paul was a good Jew is far easier than answering it.

2. *Defining Judaism in Recent Research*

In order to come to terms with the question of whether Paul was a good Jew, one must first examine what constitutes Judaism. There has been much discussion of this topic, a summary of which will help to set the question of this essay in its proper setting.[16]

A major view for the best part of last and this century, both among Christian and Jewish scholars, has been that first-century Judaism was a relatively homogeneous religious group, one that could be fairly easily and well defined on the basis of the rabbinic writings, in particular the Mishnah and the Talmud (especially the Babylonian, but also the Palestinian), and hence described in terms of normative Judaism. This form of Judaism was often equated with Pharisaism, since it is the Pharisees who ultimately developed into what we now call rabbinic Judaism. A line of virtually unbroken continuity was drawn from Judaism as it was developed and exemplified by Ezra upon the return from Exile in the fifth century BCE to the second and third centuries CE. This Judaism was said to be based upon a tradition that combined use of the Hebrew Bible and a set of oral traditions. Since Jesus, and later Paul, were often depicted in contrast with the Pharisees, it seemed to be a rather straightforward enterprise to compare this Judaism with the Jesus of the Gospels and the Paul of Acts and the letters, and to draw some fairly well-defined similarities and differences between the two. Other expressions of Judaism were known to those promoting such a view, such as the Sadducees and the Essenes, but these groups tended to be viewed as something out of the mainstream, and not representative of this

16. I am indebted to several works for the perspective to follow. Chief among these is that of P.-A. Bernheim, *James, Brother of Jesus* (trans. J. Bowden; London: SCM Press; Philadelphia: Trinity Press International, 1997), esp. pp. 47-49, with notes, pp. 280-81. See also G.G. Porton, 'Diversity in Postbiblical Judaism', in R.A. Kraft and G.W.E. Nickelsburg (eds.), *Early Judaism and its Modern Interpreters* (Philadelphia: Fortress Press; Atlanta: Scholars Press, 1986), pp. 57-80; Dunn, 'Paul's Conversion', pp. 77-85; Rutgers, *Hidden Heritage of Diaspora Judaism*, esp. pp. 24-28. On methodological questions, see S.J.D. Cohen, 'The Political and Social History of the Jews in Greco-Roman Antiquity: The State of the Question', in Kraft and Nickelsburg (eds.), *Early Judaism and its Modern Interpreters*, pp. 31-56.

normative Judaism. These other groups were even viewed as aberrant or quaint or isolated groups, for example, off in the desert with their own small following. This synthetic view of Judaism has been promoted by a number of scholars who have been highly influential in discussion for much of the nineteenth and twentieth centuries. They include the important volumes by Schürer on the history of the Jewish people,[17] the work of Herford,[18] the three-volume work of Moore,[19] W.D. Davies's book on Paul,[20] the highly influential book of Jeremias on Jerusalem,[21] Schoeps's work on Paul,[22] Urbach's *The Sages*,[23] and the edited volume of Safrai and Stern on the Jewish people in the first century,[24] among many others that could be cited.[25] (Note how many of the titles on Judaism place them in an overtly Christian context—'age of Jesus Christ' or 'time of Jesus'.) Recognizing that the concept of normativity may be too monolithic, Sanders prefers to speak of 'common' Judaism in his *Judaism: Practice and Belief 63 BCE–66 CE*.[26]

17. E. Schürer, *A History of the Jewish People in the Time of Jesus Christ* (5 vols.; Edinburgh: T. & T. Clark, 1885–90). The same perspective is also found in the revision of this work, E. Schürer, *The History of the Jewish People in the Time of Jesus Christ (175 B.C.–A.D. 135)* (3 vols.; rev. and ed. G. Vermes *et al.*; Edinburgh: T. & T. Clark, 1973–87).

18. R.T. Herford, 'The Significance of Pharisaism', in *idem*, *Judaism and the Beginnings of Christianity* (London: Routledge, 1923), pp. 125-66.

19. G.F. Moore, *Judaism in the First Centuries of the Christian Era: The Age of the Tannaim* (3 vols.; Cambridge, MA: Harvard University Press, 1927–30).

20. W.D. Davies, *Paul and Rabbinic Judaism: Some Rabbinic Elements in Pauline Theology* (Philadelphia: Fortress Press, 4th edn, 1980 [1948]).

21. J. Jeremias, *Jerusalem in the Time of Jesus: An Investigation into Economic and Social Conditions during the New Testament Period* (trans. F.H. Cave and C.H. Cave; Philadelphia: Fortress Press, 1969 [1962]).

22. H.J. Schoeps, *Paul: The Theology of the Apostle in the Light of Jewish Religious History* (trans. H. Knight; Philadelphia: Westminster Press, 1961 [1959]).

23. E.E. Urbach, *The Sages: Their Concepts and Beliefs* (2 vols.; trans. I. Abrahams; Jerusalem: Magnes Press, 1975).

24. S. Safrai and M. Stern (eds.), *The Jewish People in the First Century* (CRINT, 2; Assen: Van Gorcum; Philadelphia: Fortress Press, 1976).

25. See, e.g., M. McNamara, *Palestinian Judaism and the New Testament* (Good News Studies, 4; Wilmington, DE: Michael Glazier, 1983), pp. 159-204, esp. p. 163.

26. E.P. Sanders, *Judaism: Practice and Belief 63 BCE–66 CE* (London: SCM Press; Philadelphia: Trinity Press International, 1992); cf. R. Deines, *Die Pharisäer* (WUNT, 101; Tübingen: Mohr Siebeck, 1997), esp. pp. 534-55.

After he acknowledges that Judaism of the time was 'dynamic and diverse',[27] he then goes on to define this common Judaism. He says that '"normal" or "common" Judaism was what the priests and the people agreed on'. He takes this form of Judaism as common to the Jews of the Greek-speaking Diaspora—hence the world of Paul's origins—and to those in Palestine. The fact that this section of his book is 158 pages, and is the central section of the volume, gives some indication that Sanders wishes this to be seen as the heart of Judaism.

The weaknesses in this approach to characterizing Judaism are several, and have been noted often. One is the primary evidence on which the characterization is based. There are so few sources for the Pharisees and what they believed. The three sources of information for the Pharisees, none of them primary sources and none without a definite inclination (*Tendenz*), are Josephus (esp. *War* 2.162-63, 166; *Ant.* 18.12-15), the New Testament, and the rabbinic literature. Josephus is contradictory in his accounts, and does not acknowledge his sources, the New Testament seems to depict the Pharisees primarily as an opposition party, and the rabbinic literature is often ambiguous.[28] In addition, the rabbinic writings are in many, if not most, instances too late to serve as direct historical evidence for the first century, at least before the first (66–70 CE) or second (132–135 CE) Jewish revolts.[29] Another objection concerns the historical reconstruction of a virtually unbroken

---

27. Sanders, *Judaism*, p. 3.

28. See L.L. Grabbe, *Judaism from Cyrus to Hadrian* (London: SCM Press, 1992), pp. 467-84, with bibliography. Cf. also J. Neusner, 'Josephus' Pharisees: A Complete Repertoire', in L.H. Feldman and G. Hata (eds.), *Josephus, Judaism, and Christianity* (Detroit: Wayne State University Press, 1987), pp. 274-92; *idem, Judaism in the Beginning of Christianity* (London: SPCK, 1984), pp. 45-61; and S.J.D. Cohen, 'Were Pharisees and Rabbis the Leaders of Communal Prayer and Torah Study in Antiquity? The Evidence of the New Testament, Josephus, and the Church Fathers', in W.G. Dever and J.E. Wright (eds.), *The Echoes of Many Texts: Reflections on Jewish and Christian Traditions. Essays in Honor of Lou H. Silberman* (BJS, 313; Atlanta: Scholars Press, 1997), pp. 99-114.

29. The issue of dating of the rabbinic material is addressed in J. Neusner, '"Judaism" after Moore: A Programmatic Statement', *JJS* 31 (1980), pp. 141-56; *idem*, 'New Problems, New Solutions: Current Events in Rabbinic Studies', in *idem, Method and Meaning in Ancient Judaism, Third Series* (Chico, CA: Scholars Press, 1981), pp. 61-81; P.S. Alexander, 'Rabbinic Judaism and the New Testament', *ZNW* 74 (1983), pp. 237-46; B. Chilton, *A Galilean Rabbi and his Bible: Jesus' Own Interpretation of Isaiah* (London: SPCK, 1984), esp. pp. 13-35.

line of continuity between Ezra and rabbinic Judaism. This clearly looks back from the vantage of later history, without appreciating the great diversity that existed in Jewish thought and life, and the great developments[30] caused by such things as Greek rule, the Maccabean revolt and Hasmonean dynasty, the conquest of the Romans, and the first and second revolts.[31] A third objection concerns what is made of the other Jewish groups at the time. In the light of the further discoveries around the Dead Sea, including those of the Qumran community,[32] there is simply more evidence of groups with their own distinctives that must be taken into account. A final objection is the equation of Palestinian and Diaspora Judaism, and how much can be inferred about the latter on the basis of the former, an equation that is necessary for this theory. This relation has been the focus of much recent discussion (see below).

As a result of these problems with the first definition of Judaism, a second interpretation has emerged. Despite the willingness to place Diaspora and Palestinian Jews in the same category ('normative' or 'common' Judaism), there still was a tendency among scholars who endorsed such a characterization to focus their description on Palestine.[33] Jews of the Diaspora were frequently seen to be in many ways distinct from those in Palestine,[34] undoubtedly due to the fact that they

30. I hesitate to call these disruptions, since that term implies continuity.

31. See P. Schäfer, 'Der vorrabbinische Pharisäismus', in M. Hengel and U. Heckel (eds.), *Paulus und das antike Judentum* (WUNT, 58; Tübingen: Mohr Siebeck, 1991), pp. 125-71; cf. *idem, The History of the Jews in Antiquity: The Jews of Palestine from Alexander the Great to the Arab Conquest* (Luxembourg: Harwood, 1995); A.R.C. Leaney, *The Jewish and Christian World 200 BC to AD 200* (Cambridge: Cambridge University Press, 1984).

32. See J.J. Collins, 'Jesus, Messianism and the Dead Sea Scrolls', in J.H. Charlesworth, H. Lichtenberger and G.S. Oegema (eds.), *Qumran-Messianism: Studies on the Messianic Expectations in the Dead Sea Scrolls* (Tübingen: Mohr Siebeck, 1998), p. 101.

33. A brief history of this discussion is found in J.M.G. Barclay, *Jews in the Mediterranean Diaspora: From Alexander to Trajan (323 BCE–117 CE)* (Edinburgh: T. & T. Clark, 1996), pp. 4-9.

34. The epitome of this distinctiveness is illustrated by E.R. Goodenough, *Jewish Symbols in the Greco-Roman Period* (13 vols.; Princeton, NJ: Princeton University Press, 1953–68), with a summary in vol. 12 (1965). A summary of the set is found in *idem, Jewish Symbols in the Greco-Roman Period* (ed. J. Neusner; Princeton, NJ: Princeton University Press, abridged edn, 1988). See also W.R. Farmer, *Maccabees, Zealots, and Josephus: An Inquiry into Jewish Nationalism in the*

did not live in the Holy Land,[35] had chosen to settle and live elsewhere, had come under a variety of Hellenistic influences, and contented themselves with sending a Temple tax and perhaps making an occasional trip to Jerusalem to the Temple. Their living outside of the Holy Land almost certainly meant that they were more subject to religious syncretism, or at least had to contend more fervently with the temptations to abandon Judaism that were represented by the various other religions and other Hellenistic influences of the Graeco-Roman world. Despite the fact that three or four times the number of Jews lived in the Diaspora than in Palestine, this stereotype was also seen as in some ways an argument for analysis of Palestinian Judaism as representing the essential heart of what defined true Judaism. Again, this Palestinian Judaism was often depicted on the basis of typifications of the Pharisees using the later rabbinic sources.[36]

This modification of the first viewpoint has also been subject to criticism. Much of the criticism in response to the first view discussed above applies here as well, along with some further criticisms that ought to be noted, most concentrating on what is said about Palestine. The discoveries of other writings in the Dead Sea area have given evidence of far more diversity within Jewish thought even in Palestine. Important here are, of course, the various scrolls of the Qumran community (probably Essene material), but also important are the documents of other Jews in the area, such as those who lived further east (e.g. Nabataea) and were involved in the second Jewish revolt. Some of the Pseudepigrapha and other literature produced in and around Palestine also attests to this diversity.[37] The archaeological evidence, which has revealed a greater range of features at various sites even within

Greco-Roman Period (New York: Columbia University Press, 1956).

35. I realize that this term is somewhat anachronistic, but a special view of the Land has long been a belief of at least some Jews. See W.D. Davies, *The Gospel and the Land: Early Christianity and Jewish Territorial Doctrine* (Berkeley: University of California Press, 1974; repr. Sheffield: Sheffield Academic Press, 1994), pp. 3-158; *idem*, 'Reflections on the Territorial Dimension of Judaism', in *idem*, *Pauline Studies* (London: SPCK, 1984), pp. 49-71; and now I.M. Gafni, *Land, Center and Diaspora: Jewish Constructs in Late Antiquity* (JSPSup, 21; Sheffield: Sheffield Academic Press, 1997), esp. pp. 19-57.

36. See E.P. Sanders, *Jewish Law from Jesus to the Mishnah: Five Studies* (London: SCM Press; Philadelphia: Trinity Press International, 1990), esp. pp. 255-56.

37. See Porton, 'Diversity in Postbiblical Judaism', pp. 60-73.

Palestine than previous scholarship has recognized, must also be considered. For example, synagogal architecture shows much greater diversity than once was thought to be the case.[38] The primary texts often cited in support of such a reconstruction raise further objections. The new light that has been shed upon some strains of Jewish belief within Palestine in the first century by the Qumran documents provides evidence for a complex set of messianic expectations, with possibly two messiahs being expected by that group.[39] This belief perhaps also influenced the concept of two messiahs (one from Judah and the other from Levi) in the *Testaments of the Twelve Patriarchs*.[40] The later rabbinic texts seem to show that what one might call a normative rabbinic belief did not develop until the third or fourth centuries CE, leaving no certain line by which to retrovert and reconstruct Jewish belief in Palestine in the first century, preceding the two Jewish revolts. Morton Smith,[41] Neusner,[42] and Boccaccini[43] have emphasized this re-

38. E.M. Meyers and A.T. Kraabel, 'Archaeology, Iconography, and Nonliterary Written Remains', in Kraft and Nickelsburg (eds.), *Early Judaism and its Modern Interpreters*, pp. 177-83; cf. A.T. Kraabel, 'The Diaspora Synagogue: Archaeological and Epigraphic Evidence since Sukenik', *ANRW*, II, pp. 477-510. See also A.R. Petersen, 'The Archaeology of Khirbet Qumran', in F.H. Cryer and T.L. Thompson (eds.), *Qumran between the Old and New Testaments* (JSOTSup, 290; Copenhagen International Seminar, 6; Sheffield: Sheffield Academic Press, 1998), pp. 249-60.

39. See K.G. Kuhn, 'The Two Messiahs of Aaron and Israel', in K. Stendahl with J.H. Charlesworth (eds.), *The Scrolls and the New Testament* (New York: Crossroad, rev. edn, 1992 [1957]), pp. 54-64; J.J. Collins, 'Messiahs in Context: Method in the Study of Messianism in the Dead Sea Scrolls', in M. Wise, N. Gold, J.J. Collins and D.G. Pardee (eds.), *Methods of Investigation of the Dead Sea Scrolls and the Khirbet Qumran Site: Present Realities and Future Prospects* (Annals of the New York Academy of Sciences, 722; New York: New York Academy of Sciences, 1994), pp. 213-31; G.S. Oegema, 'Messianic Expectations in the Qumran Writings: Theses on their Development', in Charlesworth, Lichtenberger and Oegema *et al.* (eds.), *Qumran-Messianism*, pp. 53-82.

40. Besides Kuhn, 'The Two Messiahs of Aaron and Israel', pp. 54-64, see also H.D. Slingerland, *The Testaments of the Twelve Patriarchs: A Critical History of Research* (Missoula, MT: Scholars Press, 1977), *passim*; J.J. Collins, 'Testaments', in M.E. Stone (ed.), *Jewish Writings of the Second Temple Period: Apocrypha, Pseudepigrapha, Qumran Sectarian Writings, Philo, Josephus* (CRINT, 2.2; Assen: Van Gorcum; Philadelphia: Fortress Press, 1984), pp. 325-55, esp. p. 338.

41. M. Smith, *Palestinian Parties and Politics that Shaped the Old Testament* (New York: Columbia University Press, 1971; repr. London: SCM Press, 1987),

assessment of the Jewish, especially Palestinian, situation.

A third perspective, and second modification on the first major position above, examines the distinction between Diaspora and Palestinian Judaism. As I have noted, in the first position there is a begrudging lumping together of Diaspora and Palestinian Judaism, while maintaining a sceptical view of the purity of Diaspora Judaism. The second position draws the distinction between the two more strongly, while concentrating upon Palestinian Judaism. This third position returns to the question of the distinction, but wishes to place emphasis upon the larger context of the Graeco-Roman world, and sees continuity amid the change from Persian province to Greek and then Roman domination. Following the work of such scholars as Bickerman,[44] Tcherikover,[45] and, most recently, Hengel,[46] there has been a recognition in some circles that the Judaism of the first century, whether in Palestine or the Diaspora, was in various ways and to varying degrees, but clearly in most respects, Hellenized Judaism. Despite the attempts of some scholars to claim that Palestinian Judaism had resisted Hellenistic cultural

esp. pp. 43-61; this chapter repr. in M.E. Stone and D. Satran (eds.), *Emerging Judaism: Studies on the Fourth and Third Centuries B.C.E.* (Minneapolis: Fortress Press, 1989), pp. 103-128 (a volume with contributions also by Bickerman, Cross, Stone, Tcherikover, Momigliano and Hengel).

42. From his extensive writings, see J. Neusner, *Studying Classical Judaism: A Primer* (Louisville, KY: Westminster/John Knox Press, 1991), esp. pp. 27-36; cf. *idem, Judaism in the Beginning of Christianity* (London: SPCK, 1984).

43. G. Boccaccini, *Middle Judaism: Jewish Thought 300 B.C.E. to 200 C.E.* (Minneapolis: Fortress Press, 1991).

44. E.J. Bickerman, *The Jews in the Greek Age* (Cambridge, MA: Harvard University Press, 1988); cf. *idem, From Ezra to the Last of the Maccabees: Foundations of Postbiblical Judaism* (New York: Schocken Books, 1962); *idem, Four Strange Books of the Bible* (New York: Schocken Books, 1967); and *idem, The God of the Maccabees: Studies on the Meaning and Origin of the Maccabean Revolt* (SJLA, 32; Leiden: E.J. Brill, 1979).

45. V. Tcherikover, *Hellenistic Civilization and the Jews* (trans. S. Applebaum; New York: Atheneum, 1975 [1959]); cf. also *idem*, 'Palestine under the Ptolemies (A Contribution to the Study of the Zenon Papyri)', *Mizraim* 4–5 (1937), pp. 9-90.

46. M. Hengel, *Judaism and Hellenism* (2 vols.; trans. J. Bowden; Philadelphia: Fortress Press, 1974 [1966]); *idem, Jews, Greeks and Barbarians: Aspects of the Hellenization of Judaism in the Pre-Christian Period* (trans. J. Bowden; London: SCM Press, 1980 [1976]); *idem* with C. Markschies, *The 'Hellenization' of Judaea in the First Century after Christ* (trans. J. Bowden; London: SCM Press; Philadelphia: Trinity Press International, 1989).

incursions from the surrounding Graeco-Roman world, these scholars have maintained that even Judaism in Palestinian was thoroughly Hellenized.[47] Thus the Graeco-Roman world becomes the context within which any form of Judaism must be examined. This influence of Hellenism, however, is not to be seen as a late development. Hengel, along with Millar, claims that there were numerous Hellenistic influences upon Palestinian Judaism that pre-dated the first century, reaching back even before the conquests of Alexander III (the Great). This Hellenism was continued through the reigns of the Diadochi or Hellenistic kings, and then by the Romans. The result was that Palestine became a fertile ground for much Greek and Hellenistic Jewish thought and writing, including work in the Greek language. It has also been shown, by such scholars as Kraabel and Barclay,[48] that Judaism in the Diaspora, rather than being a degenerate and unproductive Judaism looking to Palestine for its inspiration and religious fervour, was in fact a creative and robust form of Judaism, but reflecting the Hellenistic influences of the Graeco-Roman world in which it too was situated.

A final perspective on this question of what constitutes Judaism has now come to the fore, so much so that it seems to control recent discussion. This position, first, recognizes a large degree of continuity between Palestinian and Diaspora Judaism (although not perhaps fully accepting the Hellenistic influences for which Hengel argues) and, secondly, sees the Judaism of the first century as highly diverse and in a process of development and even change in the light of the cultural, historical and theological factors of the time.[49] These factors include the

47. See F. Millar, 'The Problem of Hellenistic Syria', in A. Kuhrt and S. Sherwin-White (eds.), *Hellenism in the East* (London: Gerald Duckworth, 1987), pp. 110-33; and *idem*, *The Roman Near East 31 BC–AD 337* (Cambridge, MA: Harvard University Press, 1993), esp. pp. 337-86.

48. For example, A.T. Kraabel, 'The Roman Diaspora: Six Questionable Assumptions', *JJS* 33 (1982), pp. 445-64; *idem*, 'Synagoga Caeca: Systematic Distortion in Gentile Interpretations of Evidence for Judaism in the Early Christian Period', in J. Neusner and E.S. Frerichs (eds.), *'To See Ourselves as Others See Us': Christians, Jews, 'Others' in Late Antiquity* (Chico, CA: Scholars Press, 1985), pp. 219-46; Barclay, *Jews in the Mediterranean Diaspora*, esp. pp. 82-102.

49. The number who now hold to this view in varying ways is large. See, for example, Cohen, 'Political and Social History', pp. 31-56; Porton, 'Diversity in Postbiblical Judaism', pp. 57-80; Grabbe, *Judaism from Cyrus to Hadrian, passim*; N.T. Wright, *The New Testament and the People of God* (London: SPCK, 1992), pp. 145-338.

transition from Herodian rule to direct rule of the Romans, the formative process that resulted in the Jewish Scriptures (which involved Greek as much as Hebrew documents), the obvious divisions that existed or were taking place, such as those between the Pharisees and Sadducees (as well as other groups, such as the Essenes of the Qumran community), and the political events that led up to the first Jewish revolt, and then eventually to the second. Within this religious and cultural environment, the Pharisees were apparently an influential group, at least with many of the people, who respected their piety and attempts to interpret the Scriptures in the world in which they lived.[50] They were not the only group with influence and power, however. The Sadducees seemed to have had more influence with the ruling authorities, and controlled the Sanhedrin.[51] Nevertheless, an increasing number of scholars are recognizing that the amount of primary evidence for this reconstruction is quite small. Many scholars have become doubtful that it is possible to reconstruct what would have constituted Pharisaic teachings and beliefs, especially on the basis of the much later rabbinical writings. As a result, writers in the first century either side of the turn of the eras are increasingly being consulted in an attempt to understand this world. These ancient authors include what we now call the Apocrypha and Pseudepigrapha, the Qumran writings, and the New Testament, as well as other Jewish writers of the time such as Philo and Josephus.

There are also a number of points of criticism that should be raised regarding this position as well. The tendency for this latest perspective is, in many circles, to speak not of Judaism, but of *Judaisms*, using the plural.[52] Thus we have Pharisaic Judaism, Essenic Judaism, Sadducean Judaism, etc., and taken together they constitute the Judaisms of the first century. There is much validity in such a terminological distinction, because it reminds us that these various Jewish groups cannot

---

50. See Bernheim, *James*, p. 48 n. 10, who notes that the influence of Pharisaism must have been much higher than their numbers warranted, as attested by 4QMMT (see below). The history of their study is discussed in Deines, *Die Pharisäer, passim*; and H.-G. Waubke, *Die Pharisäer in der protestantischen Bibelwissenschaft des 19. Jahrhunderts* (WUNT, 107; Tübingen: Mohr Siebeck, 1998); cf. D.A. Renwick, *Paul, the Temple, and the Presence of God* (BJS, 224; Atlanta: Scholars Press, 1991), pp. 5-23.

51. See Porton, 'Diversity in Postbiblical Judaism', pp. 66-68.

52. For example, Neusner, *Studying Classical Judaism*, p. 35.

necessarily be equated. However, an important distinction is lost by making such a differentiation—the one between Judaism and other religious cults of the Roman world. Why is it that all of these groups are referred to as Judaisms, and such groups as the Isis cult, for example, are not?[53] This logically implies that there is something that these Judaisms have more in common with each other than with other groups of the time, hence Sanders's term 'common' Judaism. A second point is that there is still a tendency for this model to emphasize Palestinian Judaism, even if it recognizes diversity among the groups in that area.[54] The result is that discussion of this Judaism is often in terms of what are characterized as distinctly Semitic features, such as that Jews in Palestine spoke Aramaic, used certain scriptural texts, and believed particular things regarding Palestinian Jewish laws and customs. The fact of the matter is that Jews even in Palestine spoke a number of languages. Some of them spoke Aramaic, to be sure, but others spoke Greek, some may have even spoken Hebrew, and many, if not most, were probably bi- or even tri-lingual.[55] Their scriptural texts reflected this multiglossic linguistic situation. Even within Palestine there were religious texts written in or translated into Greek (e.g. 1 and 2 Maccabees), besides Semitic languages, and the Greek Bible (what is called the Septuagint) was also used at the same time as Aramaic interpretive traditions were developing (the targums).[56] This position needs to incorporate the diversity of Jewish belief and expression from outside of Palestine as well. There too there is potential for diverse expression of Jewish belief, with Roman Judaism facing a different set of specific problems than Judaism in Asia Minor. For example, the developing emperor cult, which seems to have spread from east to west, would have affected these two areas differently.[57] We unfortunately have

53. Bernheim, *James*, p. 49; cf. Sanders, *Jewish Law*, pp. 255-56; Boccaccini, *Middle Judaism*, pp. 18-21.

54. For example, Sanders, *Jewish Law, passim*.

55. See S.E. Porter, 'Did Jesus Ever Teach in Greek? A Look at Scholarly Opinion and the Evidence', in *idem, Studies in the Greek New Testament: Theory and Practice* (SBG, 6; New York: Peter Lang, 1996), pp. 139-71.

56. On the targums, see J. Bowker, *The Targums and Rabbinic Literature: An Introduction to Jewish Interpretations of Scripture* (Cambridge: Cambridge University Press, 1969), pp. 3-92; M. McNamara, *Targum and Testament. Aramaic Paraphrases of the Hebrew Bible: A Light on the New Testament* (Grand Rapids: Eerdmans, 1968), esp. pp. 79-89; Chilton, *A Galilean Rabbi and his Bible*, pp. 35-56.

57. For primary sources, see L.R. Taylor, *The Divinity of the Roman Emperor*

limited evidence for Judaism of this period in most areas of the Diaspora.[58] As Barclay's recent study has shown, there is a limited number of areas in the Mediterranean world of the time that have enough evidence to give an adequate characterization of Judaism outside of Palestine: Egypt, Cyrenaica, Syria, the province of Asia, and Rome.[59] Lastly, despite the inclusion of a wider range of evidence in the historical reconstruction, for few of these religious texts and writers, however, is it clear what their relationship is to the groups being discussed. For example, Philo writes from a clearly apologetic stance, but his allegorical exegetical method is noticeably different from much other Jewish interpretative literature of the time (although it is probably much closer to much Hellenistic interpretation of sacred texts).[60] Josephus is anything but a straightforward reporter of the facts of the situation, since he is concentrating upon the events of the first revolt, in the light of Jewish history.[61] Many of the pseudepigraphal works, despite

(Middletown, CN: American Philological Association, 1931; repr. Atlanta: Scholars Press, n.d.), pp. 267-83; and V. Ehrenberg and A.H.M. Jones, *Documents Illustrating the Reigns of Augustus and Tiberius* (Oxford: Clarendon Press, 2nd edn, 1955), pp. 81-97. For recent discussion, see L.J. Kreitzer, *Striking New Images: Roman Imperial Coinage and the New Testament World* (JSNTSup, 134; Sheffield: Sheffield Academic Press, 1996), pp. 69-98. See also D.N. Schowalter, *The Emperor and the Gods: Images from the Time of Trajan* (HDR, 28; Minneapolis: Fortress Press, 1993); A. Brent, 'Ignatius of Antioch and the Imperial Cult', *VC* 52 (1998), pp. 30-58.

58. Hengel, *Jews, Greeks and Barbarians*, p. 51; cf. Rutgers, *Hidden Heritage of Diaspora Judaism*, p. 41.

59. Barclay, *Jews in the Mediterranean Diaspora, passim*. Cf. Levinskaya, *Diaspora Setting*, pp. 127-93, where she looks at Antioch, Asia Minor, Macedonia and Achaia, and Rome.

60. C.D. Stanley, *Paul and the Language of Scripture: Citation Technique in the Pauline Epistles and Contemporary Literature* (SNTSMS, 74; Cambridge: Cambridge University Press, 1992), pp. 323-36; cf. R. Lamberton, *Homer the Theologian: Neoplatonist Allegorical Reading and the Growth of the Epic Tradition* (Berkeley: University of California Press, 1986), esp. pp. 44-54.

61. See, e.g., the essays in Part 1 of Feldman and Hata (eds.), *Josephus, Judaism, and Christianity*, pp. 71-129; T. Rajak, *Josephus: The Historian and his Society* (Philadelphia: Fortress Press, 1983), pp. 78-103; P. Bilde, *Flavius Josephus between Jerusalem and Rome: His Life, his Works, and their Importance* (JSPSup, 2; Sheffield: JSOT Press, 1988), pp. 173-82; S. Mason, 'Should Any Wish to Enquire Further (*Ant.* 1.25): The Aim and Audience of Josephus's *Judean Antiquities/Life*', in *idem* (ed.), *Understanding Josephus: Seven Perspectives* (JSPSup,

various attributions, defy identification with particular groups (some, but clearly not all, of the Dead Sea Scrolls being an exception).[62] The New Testament is in many respects the source that appears to be at least the most transparent for giving insight into various forms of Jewish belief in the first century, but many of the episodes are highly contentious, with the Pharisees, for example, appearing as Jesus' and Paul's adversaries in many instances.

Thus, although a consensus is emerging regarding how to speak of Jewish expression and belief in the first century, no single characterization has commanded universal assent, and even the most popular one has a number of problems that are still not adequately resolved.

3. An Attempt to Decide whether Paul Was a Good Jew

In answering the question of whether Paul was a good Jew, it is appropriate first to return to some basic issues that must be entered into the discussion, before attempting to formulate an answer, even a tentative one.

One of the most basic issues in the debate over whether Paul was a good Jew must begin with the meaning of the words 'Jew' and 'Judaism'.[63] The term 'Jew' (יהודי) was originally used in a few instances to indicate a person who was a member of the tribe of Judah

32; Sheffield: Sheffield Academic Press, 1998), pp. 64-103; and J.S. McLaren, *Turbulent Times? Josephus and Scholarship on Judaea in the First Century CE* (JSPSup, 29; Sheffield: Sheffield Academic Press, 1998).

62. On the origin of some of this writing, see Hengel with Markschies, *'Hellenization' of Judaea*, pp. 24-29; on the difficulty in noting the origin of at least one text from Qumran, see J.C.R. de Roo, 'Is 4Q525 a Qumran Sectarian Document?', in S.E. Porter and C.A. Evans (eds.), *The Scrolls and the Scriptures: Qumran Fifty Years After* (JSPSup, 26; Sheffield: Sheffield Academic Press, 1997), pp. 338-67.

63. Bernheim, *James*, p. 49; S.J.D. Cohen, 'Religion, Ethnicity, and "Hellenism" in the Emergence of Jewish Identity in Maccabean Palestine', in P. Bilde, T. Engberg-Pedersen, L. Hannestad and J. Zahle (eds.), *Religion and Religious Practice in the Seleucid Kingdom* (Studies in Hellenistic Civilization, 1; Aarhus: Aarhus University Press, 1990), pp. 204-209; developed in S.J.D. Cohen, *The Beginnings of Jewishness: Boundaries, Varieties, Uncertainties* (Berkeley: University of California Press, 1999), pp. 69-106, who provides many of the examples cited below. Cf. J.D.G. Dunn, 'Who Did Paul Think He Was? A Study of Jewish Christian Identity', *NTS* 45 (1999), pp. 174-93, esp. pp. 179-89, where he includes discussion of 'Hebrew' and 'Israelite', as well.

(2 Kgs 16.6; 25.5), and then later increased in frequency of use in the sixth to fourth centuries BCE to refer to an inhabitant of Judaea (Jeremiah, Ezra, Nehemiah, Esther, with numerous instances), and then to a member of the nation of those from Judaea (Nehemiah). The use of the term ('Ιουδαῖος) for a member of the tribe of Judah apparently had disappeared by Roman times (see Josephus, *Ant.* 11.173), while the third use continued at least until the late first century CE (e.g. 1 Macc. 8.23; 10.25; 11.30, 33; 13.36; 15.2; Josephus, *Apion* 1.179; *Ant.* 12.135-36; 14.117, 259; 19.281; *CPJ* 151). This term, even in its second or third senses, was not the most popular self-designation of what we would now call the Jews, since they tended to prefer various designations such as 'children of Israel', 'house of Israel' and 'people of Israel'. In the second century BCE, however, the concept 'Jew' underwent significant semantic expansion from an ethnic and geographical designation to a functional one, referring to what many have labelled 'a way of life', following the distinction of Josephus (*Apion* 2.210). It began to be used of followers of Yahweh (see 1 and 2 Maccabees for numerous instances). Cohen contends that the 'dual identity is a product of the Maccabean period, because it was only then that an "ethnic" or "national" self-definition was supplemented by a "cultural" or "religious" self-definition'. A question must be raised regarding the nature of this self-definition. Cohen contends that 'the Hellenistic world not only served as the foil against which the Jews redefined themselves, but also provided the conceptions that were essential to the new Jewish self-definition'.[64] His initial disjunction is probably not a proper one, however. The Maccabaean revolt was probably not against Hellenism *per se*; it was more likely against foreign oppression, a growing wealthy aristocracy (i.e. it was a class struggle), curtailment of religious freedom and self-determination, and perversion of the Law and transformation of the Temple.[65] At best, the revolt was against *perceived* Hellenistic excess, as represented by the actions of the high priests

---

64. Cohen, 'Religion, Ethnicity, and "Hellenism"', p. 204; see also Schürer, *History of the Jewish People*, rev. edn, I, pp. 147-48; Bernheim, *James*, p. 49; Dunn, 'Paul's Conversion', p. 87; *idem*, 'Who Did Paul Think He Was?', pp. 180-82; *idem*, *Theology of Paul*, p. 347.

65. See D.M. Rhoads, *Israel in Revolution: 6–74 C.E. A Political History Based on the Writings of Josephus* (Philadelphia: Fortress Press, 1976), pp. 21-22; cf. J. Sievers, *The Hasmoneans and their Supporters: from Mattathias to the Death of John Hyrcanus I* (SFSHJ, 6; Atlanta: Scholars Press, 1990), esp. pp. 157-58.

Jason and Menelaus, and of Antiochus IV Epiphanes, who renamed Yahweh as Zeus (2 Macc. 6.2)—in fact, the political and religious reasons were to the fore.[66]

The term 'Judaism' (Ἰουδαϊσμός), a Greek formulation, is used for the first time in the late second century BCE in 2 Maccabees (2.21; 8.1; 14.38 [2×]; cf. *4 Macc.* 4.26).[67] The passages in 2 Maccabees are formulated in a clearly Greek way. In 2 Macc. 2.21, in a formulation reminiscent of the Greeks, the author refers to those faithfully following Judaism as opposed to the barbarians, paralleling the Jews with the Greeks as distinct from all others.[68] In 2 Macc. 8.1, Judaism is used of the whole of the people, of whom the Maccabees are a part. In 2 Macc. 14.38, the author speaks categorically of one having practised Judaism exposing himself 'body and soul' to danger for the sake of Judaism, not mingling with Gentiles.[69] These are the only apparent uses of the term pre-dating Paul's use in Gal. 1.13-14 (2×), even though it became relatively frequent in later Christian literature (e.g. Athanasius, Basilius, Epiphanius, Eusebius, Gregory Nazianzus, Ignatius, John Chrysostom, and Origen).[70]

One can see from this brief survey above that there is bound to be confusion with the use of the term 'Jew', since it is one that has been used historically by both those within and without the group itself. But

66. See D.J. Harrington, *The Maccabean Revolt: Anatomy of a Biblical Revolution* (Old Testament Studies, 1; Wilmington, DE: Michael Glazier, 1988), pp. 92-97; Grabbe, *Judaism from Cyrus to Hadrian*, pp. 248-56; who summarize the various positions on this highly contentious issue.

67. Bernheim, *James*, p. 49; Dunn ('Paul's Conversion', p. 86 n. 27) cites *CII* I.537 as 'within and prior to our period' (referring to the time of Paul). This inscription, however, is probably dated to the third or fourth century CE, and so is not relevant. The epitaph is translated (and dated) in M.H. Williams, *The Jews among the Greeks and Romans: A Diasporan Sourcebook* (London: Gerald Duckworth, 1998), p. 47. It is also to be noted that the term Hellenism (Ἑλληνισμός) appears for the first time in 2 Macc. 4.13.

68. See J.A. Goldstein, *II Maccabees* (AB, 41A; Garden City, NY: Doubleday, 1983), p. 192.

69. The dichotomy of body and soul is a typically Hellenistic philosophical formulation. See A.A. Long, *Hellenistic Philosophy: Stoics, Epicureans, Sceptics* (London: Gerald Duckworth, 2nd edn, 1986), esp. pp. 50-51, 152-54.

70. It is possible that seeing Judaism as a term opposed to Hellenism was a concept that can be attributable to later Christian writers. For example, Athanasius, *Contra Sabellianos* 28.96.44, refers to Judaism being opposed to Hellenism, neither being pious but both being outside the truth.

what of the term 'Judaism'? It is not a term that has a long history before its use in the first century CE by Paul.

Bernheim says that the notion of a Jew has three elements: ethnic, territorial and socio-cultural, varying in degrees of importance depending upon the time period.[71] This definition illustrates the difficulty of coming to terms with the question posed in this essay. For Jews of the first century, the territorial dimension surely had diminished in importance, with the vast majority of Jews (fully three-fourths) living outside of Palestine.[72] As we have seen above in the survey of characterizations of Judaism, determining the socio-cultural factors is also highly problematic, since there were a number of distinguishable Jewish groups, even if they did have a number of beliefs and practices in common. This leaves ethnicity as the only truly unifying factor (especially with resistance to proselytization), and the ethnic dimension was still in effect as a common unifying bond (Josephus, *Ant.* 14.259; 19.251; *CPJ* 151; various inscriptions from Ephesus from the second and third centuries: *CII* II.745, 746; cf. in Latin Ambrosiaster, *Liber Quaestionum* 81).[73] If this last one is the criterion for determining whether Paul was a Jew, then he clearly was, from beginning to end. As he clearly states in Phil. 3.5, he was circumcised on the eighth day, and was of the 'people of Israel', specifically of the 'tribe of Benjamin'.[74] But was he a *good* Jew?

Rather than concentrating on defining what it means to be 'good', I wish here to emphasize a different dimension of the problem, allowing a functional definition of 'good' to emerge from the discussion. The

71. Bernheim, *James*, p. 50. Cf. D.R. Schwartz, *Studies in the Jewish Background of Christianity* (WUNT, 60; Tübingen: Mohr Siebeck, 1992).

72. The issue of whether the Jews were 'at home' in the Diaspora has been highly contentious. Those who argue that Jews were integrated into their surroundings include A.T. Kraabel ('Unity and Diversity among Diaspora Synagogues', in L.I. Levine [ed.], *The Synagogue in Late Antiquity* [Philadelphia: American Schools of Oriental Research, 1987], pp. 49-60) and those who argue that Jews were uncomfortable in their surroundings include Rutgers (*Hidden Heritage of Diaspora Judaism*, esp. pp. 19-24). For a recent discussion of these positions, see J.M. Scott, 'Exile and the Self-Understanding of Diaspora Jews in the Greco-Roman Period', in *idem* (ed.), *Exile: Old Testament, Jewish, and Christian Conceptions* (JSJSup, 56; Leiden: E.J. Brill, 1997), pp. 173-218.

73. See Cohen, 'Religion, Ethnicity, and "Hellenism"', pp. 205-206; Schürer, *History of the Jewish People*, rev. edn, III, p. 23.

74. For a discussion of this passage, see Hengel with Deines, *Pre-Christian Paul*, pp. 25-26.

dimension that seems important is in relation to which *form* of Judaism Paul followed. If we are asking whether Paul was a good Essenic or Qumranic or Sadducean Jew, then the question must be answered negatively. No, he was not a good any of those Jews. The reason is clear. He was not a good Essenic or Qumranic or Sadducean Jew because he did not attempt to be so, and was not affiliated with those forms of Judaism, but with Pharisaism.[75] One might just as well argue that this is asking the wrong question. In other words, one cannot ask whether Paul was a 'good' any of these types of Jew, because he was not aligned with any of them nor was attempting to be.

It is only in terms of Pharisaic Judaism that the question can be asked with the possibility of obtaining either a positive or a negative answer. Was Paul a good Pharisaic Jew? Here we could open the door and enter into the major point of contention in Pauline studies of the last 20 plus years. Although with antecedents in previous research, Sanders is credited with instigating the recent discussion of Paul's understanding of Judaism, followed in various ways by such notables as Dunn, Räisänen, and Wright, among a host of others.[76] This has come to be known as the

---

75. See Hengel with Deines, *Pre-Christian Paul*, pp. 40-53; *idem*, 'The Pre-Christian Paul', pp. 39-41. Cf. W.A. Meeks, *The First Urban Christians: The Social World of the Apostle Paul* (New Haven: Yale University Press, 1983), p. 33.

76. For a selection of the most important works, see E.P. Sanders, *Paul and Palestinian Judaism: A Comparison of Patterns of Religion* (Philadelphia: Fortress Press, 1977); *idem*, *Paul, the Law, and the Jewish People* (Philadelphia: Fortress Press, 1983); *idem*, *Paul* (Past Masters; Oxford: Oxford University Press, 1991). Among others, see J.D.G. Dunn, 'The New Perspective on Paul', *BJRL* 65 (1983), pp. 95-122; repr. in *idem*, *Jesus, Paul and the Law: Studies in Mark and Galatians* (London: SPCK, 1990), pp. 183-214, with other essays; *idem*, *Romans* (2 vols.; WBC, 38A, B; Dallas: Word Books, 1988); *idem*, *The Theology of Paul's Letter to the Galatians* (Cambridge: Cambridge University Press, 1993); *idem* (ed.), *Paul and the Mosaic Law* (WUNT, 89; Tübingen: Mohr Siebeck, 1996), where those on both sides participate; H. Räisänen, *Paul and the Law* (WUNT, 29; Tübingen: Mohr Siebeck, 1983; repr. Philadelphia: Fortress Press, 1986); *idem*, *Jesus, Paul and Torah: Collected Essays* (trans. D.E. Orton; JSNTSup, 43; Sheffield: JSOT Press, 1992); F. Watson, *Paul, Judaism and the Gentiles: A Sociological Approach* (SNTSMS, 56; Cambridge: Cambridge University Press, 1986); P.J. Tomson, *Paul and the Jewish Law: Halakha in the Letters of the Apostle to the Gentiles* (Assen: Van Gorcum; Minneapolis: Fortress Press, 1990); N.T. Wright, *The Climax of the Covenant: Christ and the Law in Pauline Theology* (Edinburgh: T. & T. Clark, 1991); T.L. Donaldson, *Paul and the Gentiles: Remapping the Apostle's Convictional World* (Minneapolis: Fortress Press, 1997).

'New Perspective on Paul', as Dunn has characterized it. This re-interpretation of Paul has been widely disputed by a host of interpreters, who have themselves accepted refined forms of the traditional position.[77] In a distinctive sense, whether one accepts the new perspective or holds on to the old, the question of whether Paul was a good Pharisaic Jew remains unanswered. There is a place within each perspective for Paul to see himself as a good Jew, since Paul is not actually addressing the issue of his own relation to Judaism, but the relation of Judaism to its larger scriptural and interpretative traditions. According to the new perspective, the lines of differentiation between Paul and Judaism seem to evaporate. It is impossible to characterize or define in specific terms the type of Judaism to which Paul was responding in his letters, such as Galatians, but in any event Paul is responding within the parameters of the 'covenantal nomism' of the day, even if he rejects the Jewish boundary markers, such as circumcision, food laws and sabbath observance (although these may apply more to Gentiles than to Jews).[78] According to the traditional perspective, the answer to the question is perhaps more difficult to answer. What is clear is that there is a distinction drawn between Paul's beliefs regarding justification, faith and works and what his Judaizing opponents at, for example, Galatia were promoting. In that sense, he is at odds with the Judaism that he confronts, whatever type it may have been. But does that mean that he did not see himself as a good Pharisaic Jew?

From the perspective of other Pharisees, who did not accept Christ as the resurrected Messiah, as Paul did, it is entirely possible that the answer would have been that he was not a good Jew. However, from

77. As a small list of examples, see H. Hübner, *Law in Paul's Thought: A Contribution to the Development of Pauline Theology* (SNTW; trans. J.C.G. Greig; Edinburgh: T. & T. Clark, 1984 [1978]); S. Westerholm, *Israel's Law and the Church's Faith: Paul and his Recent Interpreters* (Grand Rapids: Eerdmans, 1988); B.L. Martin, *Christ and the Law in Paul* (NovTSup, 62; Leiden: E.J. Brill, 1989); M.A. Seifrid, *Justification by Faith: The Origin and Development of a Central Pauline Theme* (NovTSup, 68; Leiden: E.J. Brill, 1992); T.R. Schreiner, *The Law and its Fulfillment: A Pauline Theology of Law* (Grand Rapids: Baker Book House, 1993); F. Thielman, *Paul and the Law: A Contextual Approach* (Downers Grove, IL: InterVarsity Press, 1994); cf. *idem*, *From Plight to Solution: A Jewish Framework for Understanding Paul's View of the Law in Romans and Galatians* (NovTSup, 61; Leiden: E.J. Brill, 1989).

78. See Dunn, 'Paul: Apostate or Apostle of Israel?', pp. 261-69, for readings of Galatians and Romans in the light of this issue and perspective.

Paul's perspective, he was one who saw Jesus as the risen Christ, the one who came as fulfilment of expectation of the Messiah.[79] Messianic expectation among various branches of Judaism was relatively common at the turn of the eras, and in this regard Paul does not distinguish himself from other Jews.[80] He does not even distinguish himself by accepting a particular figure as Messiah. Josephus records a range of people who were proclaimed or proclaimed themselves as Messiah (*Ant.* 17.285), and were followed by others, from Judas of Sepphoris (son of Hezekiah the 'brigand chief') in 4 BCE to Ben Kosiba in 132 CE.[81] If the kind of works righteousness that Paul rejects had come to distinguish Judaism, then that dimension of it was being rejected by Paul. However, that does not mean that he had necessarily abandoned everything connected with this form of Judaism. One of the distinguishing features of Paul's apostleship to the Gentiles seems to have been his development of a theology for the Gentiles that did not require submission to Jewish law, but that simply required acceptance of Jesus as the Lord and Christ. This was, in Paul's understanding, the same for both Jews

79. See J. Klausner, *From Jesus to Paul* (trans. W.F. Stinespring; New York: Macmillan, 1943), p. 591.

80. On Messianic expectation in Judaism, see A. Chester, 'Jewish Messianic Expectations and Mediatorial Figures and Pauline Christianity', in Hengel and Heckel (eds.), *Paulus und das antike Judentum*, pp. 17-89; A. Laato, *A Star is Rising: The Historical Development of the Old Testament Royal Ideology and the Rise of the Jewish Messianic Expectations* (International Studies in Formative Christianity and Judaism, 5; Atlanta: Scholars Press, 1997); W. Horbury, *Jewish Messianism and the Cult of Christ* (London: SCM Press, 1998), esp. pp. 36-63; cf. G.S. Oegema, *The Anointed and his People: Messianic Expectations from the Maccabees to Bar Kochba* (JSPSup, 27; Sheffield: Sheffield Academic Press, 1998), esp. pp. 103-195.

81. See C.A. Evans, *Jesus and his Contemporaries: Contemporary Studies* (AGJU, 25; Leiden: E.J. Brill, 1995), pp. 53-81; M. Hengel, *The Zealots: Investigations into the Jewish Freedom Movement in the Period from Herod I until 70 A.D.* (trans. D. Smith; Edinburgh: T. & T. Clark, 1989 [1976]), pp. 290-302, 330-41, 358-66; and B.W.R. Pearson, 'Dry Bones in the Judean Desert: The Messiah of Ephraim, Ezekiel 37, and the Post-Revolutionary Followers of Bar Kokhba', *JSJ* 29.2 (1998), pp. 192-201. Cf. Rhoads, *Israel in Revolution*, pp. 47-148. For debate whether many of these figures were messianic pretenders, see M. de Jonge, *Christology in Context: The Earliest Christian Response to Jesus* (Philadelphia: Westminster Press, 1988), pp. 163-65, responding to R.A. Horsley and J.S. Hanson, *Bandits, Prophets, and Messiahs: Popular Movements at the time of Jesus* (San Francisco: Harper & Row, 1986), pp. 88-134.

and Gentiles. Nevertheless, with the publication of 4QMMT,[82] and its implications for Paul's characterization of Judaism in, for example, Galatians 2–3 as accurately reflecting a Judaism that had a place for works righteousness, the traditional position would seem to have re-established its claims. In this case, Paul is not a Jew like those he characterizes as depending upon works of the law for their justification. But would Paul have said as a result that he was not a good Jew, Pharisaic or otherwise?[83]

A potentially more enlightening perspective would be to examine what Paul specifically says about himself in relation to Judaism in Gal. 1.13-14, the only place where he actually uses the term 'Judaism'.[84] Paul speaks of 'my former life in Judaism, how I persecuted the church of God violently and tried to destroy it; and I advanced in Judaism beyond many of my own age among my people, so extremely zealous was I for the traditions of my fathers'. The formulation certainly looks like Paul is claiming that his former life, before his being called by God and having his Son revealed (Gal. 1.15), was 'in Judaism', with the implication that his later life was not. Dunn has argued that this is, indeed, what these verses seem to be saying, but that the term 'Judaism' is more complex:

> the 'Judaism' of which [Paul] speaks is not the Judaism of modern historical and sociological analysis. It is the 'inside' view of first century Judaism, or rather, of a particular understanding and practice of the ancestral religion of the Jews in the first half of the first century CE. Indeed, it would perhaps be more accurate to speak of Pharisaic Judaism as that from which Paul turned in his conversion.[85]

---

82. For a useful translation of this important document, see R. Eisenman and M. Wise, *The Dead Sea Scrolls Uncovered* (Shaftesbury, England: Element, 1992), pp. 182-84; cf. now J. Kampen and M.J. Bernstein (eds.), *Reading 4QMMT: New Perspectives on Qumran Law and History* (Symposium, 2; Atlanta: Scholars Press, 1996), especially the chapter by Kampen, '4QMMT and New Testament Studies', pp. 129-44.

83. At this point, I will not appeal to passages in Acts that might shed light on this situation. For example, in Acts 23.6-10, when appearing before high priest, Paul clearly identifies himself as a Pharisee (v. 6).

84. It is surprising how little attention is given to this passage in a variety of scholarly discussions of the question of Paul's Judaism. Many discussions focus on a number of other passages, such as those that are often thought to be anti-Judaistic, such as 1 Thess. 2.14-16, or those that are concerned with the Law.

85. Dunn, 'Paul's Conversion', p. 88; cf. *idem*, *Theology of Paul*, p. 348; *idem*,

Dunn provides three strands of evidence for this position. The first is his understanding of how the term 'Judaism' is used contemporary with and before Paul, to indicate factional tendencies by the Jews, who at the time of the Maccabaean revolt were attempting to 'defend the distinctive national identity given them by their ancestral religion'.[86] The second strand is in terms of how Paul depicts himself in the rest of Gal. 1.13-14, in particular his zeal as expressing fervency for preserving these factional distinctives. The third is Paul's mission to the Gentiles, the heart of his conversion, in which he recognized that the 'good news of Jesus Messiah was for the Gentiles'.[87] This complements Paul's earlier fervent conviction that Hellenistic Jews were to be prevented from believing in Jesus Messiah.

Each of Dunn's strands of argumentation requires further analysis. First, his interpretation of the use of 'Judaism' by contemporary and earlier writers is not borne out by the evidence cited above. From a modern perspective, we can agree that the group that led the Maccabaean revolt did not comprise all of the Jews, but represented a small group within the populace. However, the texts that use the term are probably not best interpreted in that way. In the instances of the use of 'Judaism' in 2 Maccabees and in *4 Maccabees,* twice it seems to be a term inclusive of Judaism as a whole (2 Macc. 8.1; *4 Macc.* 4.26), and twice there is a clear opposition between Judaism and its opponents,[88] represented by such terms as barbarians (2 Macc. 2.21) or Gentiles (2 Macc. 14.38). There is no evidence here that the term barbarians is used to depict other Jews.[89] This interpretation is confirmed by Paul's use of the cognate verb form (ἰουδαΐζειν) in Gal. 2.14 when opposing Peter, defining it as 'living Jewishly' (Ἰουδαϊκῶς ζῆς), apparently to characterize a distinctively Jewish practice, not a faction of it (Peter

The Partings of the Ways between Christianity and Judaism and their Significance for the Character of Christianity (London: SCM Press; Philadelphia: Trinity Press International, 1991), pp. 148-49; *idem,* 'Paul: Apostate or Apostle of Israel?', pp. 260-61; *idem,* 'Who Did Paul Think He Was?', p. 184.

86. Dunn, 'Paul's Conversion', p. 86; cf. *idem, Theology of Paul,* p. 347; *idem,* 'Paul: Apostate or Apostle of Israel?', pp. 260-61; *idem,* 'Who Did Paul Think He Was?', p. 184.

87. Dunn, 'Paul's Conversion', p. 90; cf. *idem, Theology of Paul,* p. 353.

88. See R.N. Longenecker, *Galatians* (WBC, 41; Dallas: Word Books, 1990), p. 27.

89. Contra Dunn, 'Who Did Paul Think He Was?', p. 184, who draws selective parallels between Gal. 1.13-14 and 2 Maccabees.

was not a Pharisee).[90] Secondly, it is true that Paul goes on to depict himself in Galatians 1 in terms similar to his description of himself in Phil. 3.6 as a Pharisee. However, in the light of Dunn's first argument not apparently holding, it cannot be said that Paul's fervency or zeal is directed merely at preserving factional distinctives. Fervent observance of the law was a characteristic of much Judaism of the period, as is attested in a wide range of evidence (Josephus, *Ant.* 12.271, with reference to Mattathias being zealous for the customs/laws of the fathers; 1 Macc. 2.26, 27, 50; 2 Macc. 4.2; *4 Macc.* 18.12; Philo, *Spec. Leg.* 1.30; 2.253; *Abr.* 60; *Virt.* 175; besides Acts 21.20; 22.3).[91] The 'traditions of my fathers', when spoken of in terms of zeal, might appear at first glance to refer to Pharisaism, and some scholars have taken it that way.[92] However, contemporary usage may indicate otherwise. For example, as noted above, Josephus speaks of Mattathias being zealous for the customs or laws of the fathers (*Ant.* 12.271) and even of the traditions followed by the Pharisees as coming from the fathers (*Ant.* 13.297), both passages extending the phrase beyond its being simply a reference to Pharisaism. In the light of Paul's apparent contrast here between Judaism and his current life, the phrase probably refers to 'the Jewish tradition of the Torah as a whole', that is, his national traditions, a concept that 'is frequent in Hellenistic Judaism', rather than to a factional tradition such as Pharisaism.[93] This analysis fits well with Paul's writing to the Gentile Galatians (the phrase 'among my people' [ἐν τῷ γένει μου] probably refers ethnically to the Jews as a people,

90. F.F. Bruce, *The Epistle to the Galatians* (NIGTC; Grand Rapids: Eerdmans, 1982), p. 90.

91. See H.D. Betz, *Galatians* (Hermeneia; Philadelphia: Fortress Press, 1979), p. 68, esp. n. 121.

92. See, e.g., J.B. Lightfoot, *Saint Paul's Epistle to the Galatians* (London: Macmillan, 1892), p. 81; Bruce, *Galatians*, p. 91. H. Lietzmann, *An die Galater* (HNT, 10; Tübingen: Mohr Siebeck, 3rd edn, 1932), p. 7, claims that it means the traditions of the rabbis, which Paul as a Pharisee would have eagerly guarded—this position is anachronistic, as noted above.

93. Betz, *Galatians*, p. 68, esp. n. 118; J.L. Martyn, *Galatians* (AB, 33A; New York: Doubleday, 1997), p. 155 (see *idem*, 'Galatians, an Anti-Judaic Document?', in *idem, Theological Issues in the Letters of Paul* [SNTW; Edinburgh: T. & T. Clark, 1997], p. 80); cf. F.J. Matera, *Galatians* (SP, 9; Collegeville, MN: Liturgical, 1992), p. 59. See also G. Schrenk, 'πατήρ, κ.τ.λ.', *TDNT*, V, pp. 1014-1015, 1021-22, who cites a range of evidence for similar phrasing, although he takes Gal. 1.14 as referring to Paul's immediate father.

not to the Pharisees, confirming a Gentile audience for the book).[94] Paul makes a distinction between this former period (using the word ποτε, 'formerly', in Gal. 1.13), and a later one (in v. 15, using the words ὅτε δέ ['but when']). Although these transition words may point to continuity, with one period following on from the previous one, Martyn has shown that it is better to see a sharp contrast between the two periods of Paul's life.[95] Thirdly, the question of Paul's mission to the Gentiles does not seem to support Dunn's case, since it was not a distinctive of Pharisaic Judaism to believe in a coming Messiah.

Thus, on the basis of brief analysis of Gal. 1.13-14, Dunn is partly correct to say that Paul is rejecting a particularly *Pharisaic* Judaism, but Paul seems to be going further and, at least in these verses, rejecting the beliefs and practices that characterized Judaism as a whole. As Witherington says of this passage,

> Here Judaism is contrasted with living a life in accord with the Gospel and within the assembly of God. To be sure, Paul continues to regard himself as ethnically a Jew, so that he can speak of his kinsmen and kinswomen according to the flesh, or of 'my people' (cf. 1.14; 2.15), but his point is that he is no longer a part of the social and religious and political system known as Judaism.[96]

4. *Conclusion*

Much of this essay has been an attempt to clarify terminology in an attempt to get closer to answering the question posed at the outset—was Paul a good Jew? Insofar as this question can be answered in ethnic terms, it seems to me beyond question that Paul was an ethnic Jew all of his life. He was born a Jew and remained one. However, for most

---

94. See E.D.W. Burton, *A Critical and Exegetical Commentary on the Epistle to the Galatians* (ICC; Edinburgh: T. & T. Clark, 1920), p. 48; Lightfoot, *Saint Paul's Epistle*, p. 81.

95. Martyn, *Galatians*, pp. 153-54, 161-62.

96. B. Witherington, III, *Grace in Galatia: A Commentary on St Paul's Letter to the Galatians* (Edinburgh: T. & T. Clark, 1998), p. 98; cf. *idem*, *The Paul Quest: The Renewed Search for the Jew of Tarsus* (Downers Grove, IL: InterVarsity Press, 1998), pp. 56-60. See also R.H. Gundry, 'Grace, Works, and Staying Saved in Paul', *Bib* 66 (1985), pp. 1-38, esp. pp. 36-37; J.M.G. Barclay, 'Who was Considered an Apostate in the Jewish Diaspora?', in Stanton and Stroumsa (eds.), *Tolerance and Intolerance in Early Judaism and Christianity*, pp. 80-98, esp. 89-90.

scholars, the question seems to involve much more than the ethnic question, but becomes inextricably linked to questions of theology, that is, belief and practice. In that sense, we must recognize that in many instances the question is inappropriate to ask of Paul, or must be answered clearly in the negative, since he did not appear to identify himself with a number of branches of Judaism, but only with Pharisaic Judaism. We also must recognize that in the eyes of a good number of Jews of his time, including many Pharisaic Jews who did not recognize Jesus as Messiah, the answer to our question must have surely been in the negative. In Paul's eyes, however, in terms of the Pharisaic Judaism in which he was trained, the situation is much more complex. Paul appears to have rejected the structures of belief of much Judaism of his time, including Pharisaism, but saw Jesus as the Christ or Messiah, something which for him became central to Christian faith. Rather than rejecting Judaism outright, he saw Jesus as a fulfilment of its messianic expectations, and the justification that he saw as effected through his death and resurrection as confirming God's graciousness towards his people, including the Jews, but also now including the Gentiles.[97]

97. See Burton, *Galatians*, p. 44.

MOSES AND HEBREWS 3.1-6: APPROACH OR AVOIDANCE?

Cynthia Long Westfall

1. *Introduction*

The book of Hebrews is presented by some New Testament scholars as a first-century Christian polemic or apologetic argument which targeted Jewish converts who were tempted to revert to Judaism or to Judaize the gospel. Whereas Galatians is directed towards Judaizers in issues related to the Gentiles, Hebrews is thought to strike out at Judaism and to attempt to detach Jewish Christians from a Jewish angelology as well as an attachment to Moses, the work of the conquest, and the sacrificial system.

Philip E. Hughes presents an outline that is representative of a broad number of New Testament scholars.[1] He bases his view on the author's repeated use of κρείττων ('better'):

1. Christ superior to the Prophets, 1.1-3
2. Christ superior to the Angels, 1.4–2.18
3. Christ superior to Moses, 3.1–4.13
4. Christ superior to Aaron, 4.14–10.18
5. Christ superior as a new and living way, 10.19–12.29
6. Concluding exhortations, requests and greetings, 12.30–13.25

The force of the argument would be to convince Jewish Christians that they should not revert back to Judaism, because of Christ's superiority to the central figures of the Jewish faith. This view has not gone unchallenged. H. Attridge argues:

---

1. P.E. Hughes, *A Commentary on the Epistle to the Hebrews* (Grand Rapids: Eerdmans, 1977). For scholars who hold similar views, cf. G.W. Buchanan, *To the Hebrews* (Garden City, NY: Doubleday, 1976), p. 57; P. Ellingworth, *The Epistle to the Hebrews* (London: Epworth Press, 1991), p. 27; B.F. Westcott, *The Epistle to the Hebrews* (repr.; Grand Rapids: Eerdmans, 1965), p. 72.

> If it is the work's aim to wean the addressees from Judaism, it is remark-
> able how small a role an appeal to keep free from the Israel of the flesh
> plays in the explicit hortatory segments of the text. Only in the warning
> of 13:9 does the author seems to draw an explicit practical consequence
> from his anti-traditional language... A clear warning against conversion
> or relapse it is not.[2]

As far as the passages that relate to Moses and the Old Covenant,
Attridge and W.L. Lane contend that the author of Hebrews was establishing a parallel between Jesus and Moses.[3]

This essay will focus on Heb. 3.1-6, which is the key place in the
epistle in which Moses is mentioned that could be construed as a polemic directed against him.[4] The objective is to determine whether the
message of the passage supports a polemic against Judaism. Polemics
involve an aggressive attack or a corrective refutation of error. They are
controversial disputes. In a polemic, one would expect some kind of
pejorative statement identifying either an error, the persons who are the
source of the error, or the people who had been led astray by the error.[5]
The assumption is that a polemic involves some kind of criticism. The
message of 3.1-6 will be determined by describing the logical relationship between the passage's clauses, examining the topic of the passage,
locating the prominent or emphatic material, and finally examining the
text in relationship to its surrounding text (co-text).

---

2.   H. Attridge, 'Paranesis in a Homily (λόγος παρακλήσεως): The Possible
Location of, and Socialization in, the "Epistle to the Hebrews"', *Semeia* 50 (1990),
pp. 209-26 (220-21).

3.   H. Attridge, *The Epistle to the Hebrews* (Philadelphia: Fortress Press, 1989),
p. 104; W.L. Lane, *Hebrews 1–8* (WBC, 47A; Dallas: Word Books, 1991), p. 73.

4.   J. Swetnam suggests that 3.1-6 is 'a key passage from the standpoint of discovery' at the present stage of research in the epistle. He was referring to its role in
the structure of the text ('The Structure of Hebrews 1,1–3, 6', *Melita Theologica* 43
[1992], pp. 58-66 [58]). Moses is also mentioned in 7.14, 8.5, 11.23, 11.24 and
12.21. Of these verses, only 12.21 could be considered as polemic in nature, inasmuch as the readers have been brought to a mountain that is favorably contrasted
with the mountain to which Moses brought the Israelites.

5.   The other New Testament writers tend to have a low tolerance for error, and
do not employ euphemism when combatting it. Error is described as 'another gospel' (Gal. 1.6), 'strange doctrines' (1 Tim. 1.3), and 'another Jesus' (2 Cor. 11.4).
The perpetrators of error are described as 'antichrists' (1 Jn 2.18), 'Satan's synagogue' (Rev. 2.9), 'false teachers' (2 Pet. 2.1), and 'hypocrites' (Mt. 23.13). Those
who had been deceived by Judaizers, for instance, were chided by Paul: 'You foolish Galatians, who bewitched you?' (Gal. 3.1).

2. *Methodology*

The passage will be analyzed with methods taken from discourse analysis, which is a linguistics-based study of language above the sentence level. The particular approach to discourse analysis that will be used is developed from systemic linguistics, which was developed by M.A.K. Halliday, R. Hasan, and the so-called Birmingham school.[6] Two of the distinguishing features of the approach are that the analysis of language should be textually based, and that form and meaning are inseparable.[7] J. Sinclair summarizes the textually based approach with the injunction 'Trust the text'.[8] Trusting the text entails the assumption that the author has a purpose in the way he or she structures the text and that the formal features do reflect meaning and should affect interpretation.

a. *The Logical Relationship between the Clauses*
The logical relationships between clauses can be described in terms of their 'interdependency' and 'expansion'. These relationships are determined both formally and semantically. The starting point for the formal analysis of the logical relationships between the clauses is the 'signposting', or discourse markers, that are utilized by authors.[9] Authors use words such as articles, conjunctions, deictic indicators, adverbs and prepositions as intersentential signals. One difference between English and Hellenistic Greek is that intersentential conjunctions are far more common, and are not typically restricted to transitional locations. Therefore, although Hellenistic Greek lacks orthographic marking of units such as paragraphs, sections and chapters, the use of particles to

---

6. For a brief summary of discourse analysis based on Halliday's systemic linguistics, see J.T. Reed, 'Discourse Analysis', in S.E. Porter (ed.), *Handbook to Exegesis of the New Testament* (NTTS, 25; Leiden: E.J. Brill, 1997), pp. 189-217.

7. See M. Stubbs, 'Introduction', in M. Baker, G. Francis and E. Tognini-Boneli (eds.), *Text and Technology: In Honour of John Sinclair* (Philadelphia: John Benjamins, 1993), p. 2. Stubbs summarizes nine points that are central to much of the British school of linguistics.

8. J.M. Sinclair, 'Trust the Text', in M. Davies and L. Ravelli (eds.), *Advances in Systemic Linguistics: Recent Theory and Practice* (London: Pinter, 1992), pp. 5-19.

9. M. Hoey, *Signalling in Discourse* (Birmingham: University of Birmingham, 1979); the term 'discourse markers' originates in D. Schiffrin, *Discourse Markers* (Cambridge: Cambridge University Press, 1987).

mark the relationships between the sentences or clause complexes is very common.[10]

Interdependency between clauses has two recognized categories: coordination and subordination. Parataxis is the coordination between two independent clauses that are joined together on an equal footing. It is signaled by conjunctions such as καί (and), ἀλλά (but) and μέν...δέ (on the one hand...on the other hand). Hypotaxis is the subordination of one element to another signaled by conjunctions such as ἵνα (explanatory), εἰ (if...then), and ὅτι (discourse content).[11] Non-finite verbs (participles and infinitives) are also subordinate with rare exceptions.[12] Prepositonal, adverbial or adjectival phrases are subordinate by definition.

Some conjunctions between two independent clauses may signal that the logical relationship is not on an equal footing. Certain conjunctions or phrases may indicate that a following independent clause is support material such as τοῦτο ἐστιν (in other words), μάλλον (more, at least), and γάρ (for, in explanation). Other conjunctions, such as the so-called inferential particles (such as οὖν, ὅθεν and διό), often signal a conclusion, abstract or summary. These particles signal a logical discontinuity, emphasis or dominance, in that they can 'imply the conclusion of a process of reasoning'.[13] This kind of function indicates that a clause is a 'main idea'.

10. J. Blomqvist, *Greek Particles in Hellenistic Prose* (Lund: C.W.K. Gleerup, 1969), pp. 146-47. J. Blomqvist observes: '[Connective particles] were also very important to hellenistic prose writers, for it is obvious that these writers carefully indicated the relations between the sentences and strived to bring the short clauses together in big coherent complexes where every stage in the argumentation or exposition was clearly defined... Such words also directed the attention of the reader to the opening of the clause and showed him what he might expect to find in the following words. The desire of the writers explains why connective particles were still extensively used.'

11. M.A.K. Halliday, *Functional Grammar* (London: Edward Arnold, 1985), pp. 218-35. Cf. J.T. Reed, *A Discourse Analysis of Philippians: Method and Rhetoric in the Debate over Literary Integrity* (JSNTSup, 136; SNTG, 3; Sheffield: Sheffield Academic Press, 1997), p. 90; S.E. Porter and M.B. O'Donnell, *Discourse Analysis and the New Testament* (forthcoming), Ch. 4.

12. D. Wallace, *Greek Grammar beyond the Basics: An Exegetical Syntax of the New Testament* (Grand Rapids: Zondervan, 1996), p. 650. The absolute and imperatival use of the participle and infinitive is described as functioning 'as though they were finite verbs', since they are not formally dependent on any other verb.

13. J.P. Louw and E.A. Nida, *Greek–English Lexicon of the New Testament Based on Semantic Domains* (2 vols.; New York: United Bible Societies, 2nd edn,

Interdependency may also be shown when there is asyndeton, which is the absence of a conjunction or subordinating word or phrase. It occurs when 'the INTERPRETATION of some element in the discourse is dependent on that of another. The one PRESUPPOSES the other, in the sense that it cannot be effectively decoded except by recourse to it.'[14] This is called an endophoric tie, and includes referential relations such as anaphora, cataphora, substitution and ellipsis.

Expansion and projection are two general types of clausal relations that Halliday calls 'logico-semantic relations'.[15] Expansion involves elaborating, extending or enhancing, and projection involves quotations. In elaboration, a subsequent clause does not introduce a new element, but restates, clarifies, refines or adds an attribute or comment to an element that is already there. In extension, 'one clause extends the other by adding something new to it',[16] which could be an addition, replacement or alternative. In enhancement, a clause enhances the meaning of another by reference to things such as time, place, manner, cause or condition. The three kinds of expansion can either be coordinating or subordinating.

The expansion relations show which clauses, or parts of clauses, are supported by greater detail. Material that is supported by elaboration is more emphatic or prominent than the support material, unless the support material is explicitly signaled as prominent. These logical relations may exist not only between clauses and clause complexes, but also larger units such as paragraphs (a cohesive group of clauses and clause clusters) and sections (a cohesive group of paragraphs). A discourse

---

1989), I, p. 783. Cf. Schiffrin, *Discourse Markers*, p. 191. Her argument about 'so' as a marker of result and 'because' as a marker of cause relates to οὖν, ὅθεν and διό as markers of result: '*So* and *because* are grammatical signals of main and subordinate clauses, respectively, and this grammatical difference is reflected in the discourse use: *because* is a marker of subordinate idea units and *so* is a complementary marker of main idea units. Before I show this, however, it is important to define "subordinate" and "main" in discourse. Such designations depend on both the functional and referential organization of talk. From a functional perspective, subordinate material is that which has a secondary role in relation to a more encompassing focus of joint attention and activity' (Schiffrin's italics).

14. M.A.K. Halliday and R. Hasan, *Cohesion in English* (London: Longmans, 1976), p. 33.

15. Halliday, *Functional Grammar*, pp. 225-39. See also the charts in Reed, *Discourse Analysis of Philippians*, pp. 91-93.

16. Halliday, *Functional Grammar*, p. 230.

marker at the beginning of a paragraph can signal the relationship of the whole paragraph to the preceding material.

b. *Topic and Information Flow*

Topic refers to what a speaker or writer is talking about in a given unit. Two ways to discover possible topics are (1) analyzing chain interaction, and (2) studying the linear information flow. Chain interaction involves the identification of key semantic chains in a unit. Semantic chains consist of participant chains and lexical chains.[17] Participants are the actors or recipients of processes (material, mental or relational), and the modifiers of substantives.[18] Participant chains are expressed by co-referential ties. The use of reference to participants includes anaphora, cataphora, substitution and ellipsis so that a chain includes direct references to the participants, the use of pronouns (anaphora and cataphora) and the inclusion of a participant in the person and number of a given verb.

Lexical chains are expressed by various forms of repetition, including reiteration, groups of words from the same semantic domain, labeling and categorization.[19] Reiteration tends to be particularly emphatic. It is the repetition of the same lexical item, allowing for variations in declension. Lexical reiteration may not always involve the same referent. For instance, in word plays and in some forms of categorization or labeling, the referent changes and the lexical reiteration expresses or creates a relationship between the referents. Words from the same semantic domain are groups of words that have associated meanings.[20] Authors will create links within a paragraph by using words that are closely associated, such as 'doctor' and 'sickness' or where one item includes another, such as 'animal' and 'bear'. Labeling and categorization are closely associated, where a writer or speaker creates non-

---

17. Reed, *Discourse Analysis of Philippians*, pp. 100-101. Reed is particularly interested in tracing interacting chains at the level of discourse, and thus identifying 'central tokens' at the global level.

18. Halliday, *Functional Grammar*, Ch. 5. Material processes are the processes of doing, mental processes are the processes of sensing, and relational processes are the processes of being.

19. For an extensive discussion on repetition, see M. Hoey, *Patterns of Lexis in Text* (Oxford: Oxford University Press, 1991), Ch. 3.

20. See Louw and Nida, *Greek–English Lexicon*, I. Louw and Nida have classified the New Testament vocabulary into domains and subdomains based on their meaning.

lexical categories by placing things in the same pile, or calling them by the same name.

In chain interaction, participant chains may interact with each other, lexical chains may co-occur with each other, and participant chains may interact with lexical chains. Such interaction makes a significant contribution to the *cohesion* of text. Cohesion consists of the formal links within a passage or discourse that make it 'hang together' internally.[21] Along with discourse markers and other patterns that set apart one chunk of discourse from the rest, stretches and shifts in chain interaction signal topic boundaries. When we speak of 'topic', we are usually referring to what Brown and Yule[22] call the 'topic entity', which is the 'main character/object/idea' notion. The chains that include the largest number of items and/or that interact the most with other chains as well as items that are not in a chain would be a consideration for the topic entity. However, an analysis of chain interaction will not be appropriate for every paragraph. Sometimes the logical relationships, the information flow, and prominence will play a greater role than lexical repetition.

Describing the information flow involves taking into account the linearization process. The author must produce a starting point and an end point for a given discourse and for each chunk or unit that he or she creates within it. That starting point is the 'theme'.[23] Its function is to connect back with the previous discourse, and to serve as a point of departure for further development. At the clause level, it 'gives the clause its character as a message'.[24] Brown and Yule as well as Halliday recognize thematization at all levels of discourse.[25] The starting

21. Halliday and Hasan, *Cohesion*, pp. 4-5.
22. Y. Brown and G. Yule, *Discourse Analysis* (Cambridge: Cambridge University Press, 1983), p. 137.
23. Halliday, *Functional Grammar*, Ch. 3.
24. Halliday, *Functional Grammar*, p. 37.
25. Brown and Yule, *Discourse Analysis*, pp. 133-34: 'We may talk in general of *thematisation* as a discoursal rather than simply a sentential process. What the speaker or writer puts first will influence the interpretation of everything that follows. Thus a title will influence the interpretation of the text which follows it. The first sentence of the first paragraph will constrain the interpretation not only of the paragraph, but also of the rest of the text. That is, we assume that every sentence forms part of a developing, cumulative instruction which tells us how to construct a coherent representation.'
Halliday agrees, 'Above the clause, the same principle lies behind the organization of paragraphs in written discourse; the "topic sentence" of a paragraph is

point of a paragraph or discourse has semantic significance, but it does not always indicate mainline material. Sometimes the author places the most important point first, but other times, as a point of departure, it may be the first step in a process, or the least important point in a progression towards the main point.

Every paragraph also has a destination or an endpoint. Its function is to conclude the unit and to point the way forward to the rest of the discourse. It may correspond at the paragraph level to Longacre's concept of 'discourse peaking' in genres that contain episodes with a climax, parables, conclusions of processes, inductive reasoning, or other patterns of mental progression.[26] Like the theme of the paragraph, the destination may or may not be mainline material. However, the way that the author chooses to begin a paragraph or unit, and the way he or she chooses to end it are semantically significant. As Brown and Yule observe, 'Our interpretation of *what* a speaker is talking about is inevitably based on *how* he structures what he is saying'.[27]

The study of thematization presupposes and compliments the author's organization of the discourse into paragraphs or units. Writers control the presentation and flow of the discourse by grouping related material together, and the use of some form of variation such as partitions, breaks or shifts. This helps the writer organize information, and helps the reader to process the message by breaking the material up so that it is possible to assimilate longer stretches of discourse. In many written languages, the 'chunking' of discourse is signaled orthographically with indentation and often the use of titles, headings and subheadings.[28] We

---

nothing other than its Theme' (*Functional Grammar*, p. 54). However, the 'topic sentence' is only one of many realizations of thematization, and the two terms are not synonymous. The topic sentence or main clause may occur in the middle or end of a paragraph as a conclusion, but the theme is always first in the paragraph.

26. R.E. Longacre, *The Grammar of Discourse* (New York: Plenum Press, 2nd edn, 1996), p. 37, indicates that discourse entails peaks below the discourse level such as Gen. 7.17-24 and Gen. 9.1-17. See also K. Callow, 'Patterns of Thematic Development in I Corinthians 5:1-13', in D.A. Black *et al.* (eds.), *Linguistics and New Testament Interpretation: Essays on Discourse Analysis* (Nashville: Broadman Press, 1992), pp. 194-206 (196-97). She talks of a 'graded increase in prominence as we move away from fact towards volition and action' in describing a 'purposive chain' and mental progression, where prominence at the end of the unit coincides with the main clause.

27. Brown and Yule, *Discourse Analysis*, p. 94.

28. Brown and Yule, *Discourse Analysis*, p. 140: 'There are, of course,

have no evidence that the author of Hebrews or other Hellenistic writers utilized orthographic divisions or headings. However, writers and speakers utilize other tools that produce patterns of groupings in texts. The grouping of material is produced by the use of cohesion and variation in the grammar and lexis. Cohesion in the paragraph is not only produced by continuity of the topic, but also by consistency in grammatical patterns.[29] Paragraph shifts are signaled by variations in these patterns and the patterned use of certain particles as discourse markers.

c. *Main Clauses and Prominence within Units*

Authors highlight clauses or clause complexes as being 'main' or 'central'.[30] Main clauses are central at the level of discourse in which they are functioning, and relate most closely to the purpose of the unit. They are highlighted or marked by prominence and a semantic relationship with the rest of the passage. The author may highlight a clause/ clause complex that is main in a given paragraph (cluster of adjacent sentences), but he or she may highlight another clause that is the main clause for a number of paragraphs, or central for the entire discourse.

Prominence is also known as emphasis, grounding, relevance or

many...easily recognisable thematisation devices used in the organisation of discourse structure. Placing headings and sub-headings within a text is a common thematisation device in technical or public-information documents... What these thematisation devices have in common is not only the way they provide "starting points" for paragraphs in a text, but also their contribution to dividing up a whole text into smaller chunks. This "chunking" effect is one of the most basic of those achieved by thematisation in discourse.'

29. S.H. Levinsohn, *Discourse Features of New Testament Greek* (Dallas: SIL, 1992), pp. 191-92. Levinsohn suggests that the boundaries of a paragraph are defined on semantic grounds, and that formal features are 'supporting evidence only'. It is odd that he devotes only a page to discussing 'single theme' as the primary criterion for determining a sentence, and then devotes ten pages to describing the 'supporting evidence'. The 'single theme' (topic entity) of a paragraph is not always self-evident, and the formal features are also a realization and indication of the message. Furthermore, writers may 'partition' a discourse with some pattern of variation where there is no discernable topic-shift (see Brown and Yule, *Discourse Analysis*, p. 95). Also, a writer may join two topics in one sentence that would seem better to belong to two different paragraphs.

30. 'Main' or 'central' clauses are often referred to as 'thematic'. Cf. Reed, *Discourse Analysis of Philippians*, p. 107; Callow, 'Patterns of Thematic Development', p. 195.

salience. It is signaled by formal and semantic features in the discourse which set apart or elevate some of the content.[31] The formal features include the use of variation of grammar, discourse markers, word order, deixis, emphatic words or phrases, and repetition. They also include grammatical choices that are marked in the language system, such as the use of the present or perfect tense-form as opposed to the aorist.[32] Semantic prominence or conceptual emphasis involves devices such as the use of extra words and vividness, the crowding of the stage[33] and the use of logical relationships that distinguish between mainline material and support material.[34]

Prominence in discourse and linguistic categories is sometimes described in terms of figure, background, foreground and frontground, utilizing terms borrowed from the visual perception of spatial relations.[35] These are useful descriptive terms, but the actual text, like a real landscape or any other subject of art, is composed of intricate contours. Prominence is relative at the various levels of the discourse, and serves various functions.[36] There is emphasis at the level of sentence, paragraph, section and discourse, and many clauses within a given paragraph will have some measure of emphasis. However, authors highlight

31. Reed, *Discourse Analysis of Philippians*, pp. 105-19. Reed defines prominence as 'those semantic and grammatical elements of discourse that serve to set aside certain subjects, ideas or motifs of the author as more or less semantically and pragmatically significant than others' (p. 106). The 'more or less' is misleading, since the basic function of prominence is to make something more signficant, not less significant.

32. See S.E. Porter, *Verbal Aspect in the Greek of the New Testament, with Reference to Tense and Mood* (SBG, 1; New York: Peter Lang, 1989), p. 198: 'When a Greek speaker narrated events, the Aorist, used alongside the Imperfect, formed the basis for carrying the narrative, with the historic Present used for selecting processes for emphasis (the most heavily-marked Perfect was available as well).'

33. Longacre, *Grammar of Discourse*, p. 40.

34. Longacre, *Grammar of Discourse*, pp. 21-28; L. Neeley, 'A Discourse Analysis of Hebrews', *OPTAT* 1.3–4 (1987), pp. 1-146, esp. 4-5.

35. For figure and ground, see S. Wallace, 'Figure and Ground: The Interrelationships of Linguistic Categories', in P. Hopper (ed.), *Tense-Aspect: Between Semantics and Pragmatics* (Amsterdam: Benjamins, 1982), pp. 201-23. A simplified description of background, foreground and frontground is in S.E. Porter, *Idioms of the Greek New Testament* (BLG, 2; Sheffield: Sheffield Academic Press, 1992), pp. 22-23.

36. Brown and Yule, *Discourse Analysis*, p. 134.

the clauses that are central to the message with clusters of indicators that create 'zones of turbulence',[37] so that one can refer to one clause as more prominent in the paragraph than another on the basis of a confluence of emphatic indicators.

d. *The Relationship of the Text to the Co-text*
The co-text is text that surrounds the passage. Both the interpretation of individual lexical items and the interpretation of utterances in the discourse are constrained by their co-text. Brown and Yule write:

> For the moment the main point we are concerned to make is to stress the power of co-text in constraining interpretation. Even in the absence of information about place and time of original utterance, even in the absence of information about the speaker/writer and his intended recipient, it is often possible to reconstruct at least some part of the physical context and to arrive at some interpretation of the text. The more co-text there is, in general, the more secure the interpretation is. Text creates its own context.[38]

This observation is particularly pertinent in the case of Hebrews, in which there is a complete absence of information about the original place, time, writer and recipients of the discourse. Fortunately, the discourse is large. In order to arrive at the meaning of 3.1-6, it is important to examine how the text creates its own context in terms of what precedes the passage. It is also important to determine how the passage under consideration has in turn created a context for what follows in the text.

Co-text is also crucial in determining the domain of prominence of a given emphatic element. Reed defines the domain of prominence in the following way:

> The domain of prominence [is] the extent to which a linguistic element maintains its degree of prominence... The domain of prominence may or may not extend throughout the whole discourse, but it will extend to some extent. The domain of an element's prominence reveals its relative importance in the discourse. In New Testament discourse, the domain of prominence may consist of the phrase (e.g. headword of a prepositional

---

37. 'Zones of turbulence' is a term utilized by Longacre, *Grammar of Discourse*, p. 38. The 'cluster concept' is described in Wallace, 'Figure and Ground', p. 216.
38. Brown and Yule, *Discourse Analysis*, pp. 49-50.

phrase), clause (e.g. rheme), paragraph (e.g. verbal aspect) or the entire discourse (e.g. epistolary formulas).[39]

The domain of prominence of a clause, clause cluster or paragraph within the discourse must be determined not only by the relationship to the immediate co-text, but also by whether its content is repeated in other parts of the discourse. The domain of prominence within a section is often determined by the continuation of dominant semantic chains beyond the paragraph shift. The domain of prominence at the level of discourse is determined by whether the material is repeated in other sections of the discourse. Often, the 'zone of turbulence' created by the indicators of prominence will form a peak in the discourse that corresponds to the role that the material plays in the discourse. That is, material that is dominant at the section level will tend to have a greater number of indicators of prominence than material that is dominant at the paragraph level. However, the repetition of a given element has a cumulative effect on its relative prominence in subsequent paragraphs and sections.

In the following sections, it will be shown how the preceding two chapters constrain the interpretation of Heb. 3.1-6. The logical relationship indicated by the conjunction at the seam in 3.1, as well as the links between preceding semantic chains and any other form of repetition, will be examined. Then, the relationship between 3.1-6 and 3.7-15 will be studied. The focus will be on the logical relationship indicated by the conjunction at the seam in 3.7, and whether any semantic chains are continued or initiated. The way in which the passage's prominent clauses play a part beyond its boundaries will indicate whether the material has a domain of prominence at the level of paragraph, section or discourse.

3. *The Logical Relationships in Hebrews 3.1-6*

The point of departure for the passage is 3.1. The readers are the grammatical subject, or the intended sensors of the cognitive process of thinking intently.[40] The author identifies the readers with the nominative of direct address as 'holy brothers and sisters', and 'partners of a heavenly calling'. The imperative verb directs them to think intently

---

39. Reed, *Discourse Analysis of Philippians*, p. 108.
40. See Halliday, *Functional Grammar*, pp. 112-19, for a description of the terms for mental processes.

about Jesus. The author also elaborates twice on Jesus' identity, adding 'the apostle and high priest of our confession'.

The relationship between 3.2 and 3.1 is a further elaboration on Jesus' identity in the form of a comparison. 3.2 is connected to 3.1 with a participle, a non-finite verb that is grammatically subordinate to 3.1. The comparison states that Jesus is faithful to the one who appointed him, as Moses was in his house. There are several implications that can be drawn. Although the readers are the point of departure for the passage, Jesus is specifically focused on through elaboration. The comparison is subordinate to 3.1, and functions as support material. The starting point of the comparison focuses on how Jesus and Moses are alike: 'Jesus is faithful [in all his house] like Moses was [faithful] in his house'.[41]

There is an extension to the comparison in 3.3 that functions as 'subtraction'. Halliday gives the meaning of subtraction as 'X but not all X'.[42] In 3.2, the author states that Jesus was like Moses in that he was faithful in his house. In 3.3, he qualifies the comparison, by stating that they are not alike in the degree of glory that they should receive. The conjunction γάρ signals an explanation, and the logical relationship could be glossed in the subtraction relationship as 'except': 'Jesus was faithful [in his house] like Moses was [faithful] in his house, except this one [Jesus] is worthy of greater glory than Moses'. The author continues with a coordinating elaboration: 'to the extent that a builder has more honor than his house'. It is possible that the exception in 3.3 could be in either a coordinating or subordinating relationship to 3.2, though the explanatory γάρ would suggest subordination. It is not probable, however, that 3.1 or 3.2 is subordinate to 3.3.

The author further elaborates both the similarity and the difference between Jesus and Moses by clarifying the relationships of the participants in the comparison. In 3.4, with an explanatory γάρ, he identifies God as the builder of both houses: 'Every house is built by someone,

41. For a discussion of alternate readings of 'his house', see P. Ellingworth, *Commentary on Hebrews* (NIGTC; Grand Rapids: Eerdmans, 1993), p. 201. Ellingworth states that αὐτοῦ in 3.1 could mean (1) God's, (2) Christ's or (3) Moses'. Ellingworth suggests that God's house is the best choice, but the antecedent of αὐτοῦ would most naturally be Moses. As Ellingworth notes, this creates the existence of two houses, but, rather than weakening the contrast between Moses and Jesus, it becomes the point of the contrast.

42. Halliday, *Functional Grammar*, p. 230.

but the builder of all is God'. The relationships of Moses and Jesus to God are coordinated with a καί, and they are coordinated to each other in 3.5 and 3.6 with a μέν...δέ construction: 'And Moses was faithful on the one hand in his entire house as a servant in order to witness to what was to be said. On the other hand, Jesus is faithful over his house as a son.' The cultural context could supply the rest of the correlation that a son and heir is given respect from his household that reflects the father's status.[43] Yet, the focus on faithfulness continues the force of the comparison. There is a surprising addition to the list of participants in 3.6b: 'We are [Jesus'] house if we hold on to the confidence and pride of hope'. This clause is attached to the preceding clause with οὗ, which is an endophoric tie to Christ. It also parallels the identification of the other participants. However, the clause is not completely parallel, because it lacks a coordinating conjunction. Also, since Jesus' house is identified, not all of the participants are specified at this point. To complete the parallel, there would need to be a mention of Moses' house: the Israelites in the wilderness generation. The parallel relationship between the readers and the Israelites in the wilderness generation is made explicit in 3.7-15.

The logical relationships within the passage demonstrate that the comparisons and contrasts between Jesus and Moses are subordinate to 3.1. The contrast in 3.3 which states that Jesus is worthy of more glory than Moses can possibly be coordinating with the comparison in 3.2, but it is not made more central as an idea as far as the conjunctive relationship is concerned. On the other hand, there is a considerable amount of elaboration and clarification as to why Jesus is worthy of glory, though the comparison of how they are alike receives equal elaboration. The elaboration is balanced with the comparison, which is an indication of parallelism: both Moses and Jesus are faithful over their houses, and both houses are built by God. Since the similarity between Moses and Jesus is placed before the contrast and continues to be developed, it appears that typology is at least as much in the author's mind as superiority.

---

43. See, e.g., the parable of the vineyard and tenants in Mt. 21.33-36, Mk 12.1-12, and Lk. 20.9-18. After the tenants had killed or mistreated a number of servants, the father was convinced, 'Surely they will respect my son'. The respect and honor for the father as an owner or builder was expected to be imputed to the son.

4. *The Topic of Hebrews 3.1-6*

The topic entity is what is being talked about in the passage. Sometimes it is assumed that the grammatical subject of the individual sentences must be the topic of a paragraph, but the grammatical subject can vary considerably as it does in this passage. Repetition is a far more reliable guide, since it not only takes into account the grammatical subject, but also other references.

Although 3.1 and 3.2-6 are joined grammatically, they have little apparent lexical cohesion. In contrast, 3.2-6 has an unusual amount of lexical cohesion. The terms 'house' (6×), 'Moses' (3×), and 'faith' (2×) are reiterated in the passage. The repetition of 'faith' in 2.17, 3.2 and 3.5 provides some cohesion with the preceding co-text in 2.5-18, but 'faith' hardly dominates either passage.[44] The passage is instead dominated by two identity chains that interact with each other and with the reiterative chain. The identity chain of Jesus has eight references, and the identity chain of Moses has five references. The reiterative chain of οἶκος occurs six times, and interacts with all of the participants, including God in 3.4. The fact that the word is reiterated so many times within five verses without pronominalization gives it semantic weight and identifies it as a key to the topic.[45] Furthermore the identification as 'house' as a key to the topic will help to account for 3.4, which is often labeled as a digression, since it does not directly interact with the participant chains of Jesus and Moses.

The identification of believers as Jesus' house in 3.6 further links the comparison with 3.1. In 3.1, the readers are identified as partners with Christ in a holy calling. In 3.6, the word 'house' is substituted for the word 'partners', and is used as the basis of the comparison of the readers with the relationship between Moses and his followers. Therefore,

---

44. A. Vanhoye, *Structure and Message of the Epistle to the Hebrews* (Rome: Pontifical Biblical Institute, 1989), pp. 24-26; and Lane, *Hebrews 1–8*, p. 69, see the antonyms πίστις and ἀπιστία as dominating 3.1–4.14. The antonyms are used 7 times altogether in the 33 verses. However, the comparisons between Moses and Jesus and the Israelites and the readers are primary identity chains; faithful (Jesus and Moses) versus unfaithful (the wilderness generation) is one of several lexical chains with which the participants interact, and serves to warn the readers not to become like the Israelites.

45. Ellingworth, *Commentary on Hebrews*, p. 196, agrees: 'The key term in this section is clearly οἶκος'.

the author has placed the readers and himself in the same category as 'house'. A semantic chain based on categorization emerges which dominates the passage, and also reflects the theme or point of departure of the passage: 'holy brothers and sisters, partners of a heavenly calling'. Furthermore, it also reflects the endpoint of the passage in 3.6: 'We are his house if we hold on to confidence and the pride of our hope'. The topic entity that best accounts for the passage is the readers' partnership with Jesus, which is introduced in 3.1 and enhanced by a comparison.[46]

5. *Prominence and Main Clauses*

The theme of the unit is 3.1. As the point of departure, it is prominent by definition. It is joined to the preceding co-text with ὅθεν (from which fact), an inferential particle which expresses a causal relationship with the preceding material. As will be shown below, it marks a conclusion or summary and signals that the material is logically dominant. However, there are other indicators of prominence that create a clustering effect that makes 3.1 a main clause.[47] The author directly addresses the readers for the first time in 3.1 with the nominative of direct address: ἀδελφοὶ ἅγιοι, κλήσεως ἐπουρανίου μέτοχοι. The direct address is prominent because it grabs the readers' attention and highlights their identity.[48] The use of extra words to describe the readers and Jesus is a primary feature of the sentence, and also produces prominence. The command to 'think intently' creates an interpersonal involvement of the readers with information that could have been presented in the indicative as a proposition.[49] In addition to the numerous

46. See Halliday, *Functional Grammar*, pp. 232-39, where he discusses enhancement. Comparison signaled by 'as' or 'like' is classified as enhancing clauses of manner.

47. 'Cluster effect' is a term to describe numerous contributing influences of prominence in Wallace, 'Figure and Ground', p. 216.

48. Wallace writes, 'People tend to place themselves at the center of attention' ('Figure and Ground', p. 213).

49. D. Tannen, *Talking Voices: Repetition, Dialogue and Imagery in Conversational Discourse* (Cambridge: Cambridge University Press, 1987). Tannen describes involvement strategies in conversation, observing that writing elaborates on strategies that are spontaneous in conversation. These strategies both reflect and create interpersonal involvement which binds people to the material. She contrasts direct

indicators of prominence in 3.1, both the readers' identity and Jesus' identity are further supported by the comparison and contrast between Jesus and Moses in 3.2-6. The comparison and contrast structurally elaborates on Jesus, but 3.6 clarifies that the readers' identity has also received at least equal elaboration. The identification of the believers as Jesus' house shows that all the above references to house belonged to the same category as the readers.

The starting point for the comparison in 3.2 is grammatically subordinate and unemphatic. However, the comparison itself contains some relative prominence. Moses would be a subject of special interest if the readers are Jewish. Also, the comparison is marked by the repetition of a pattern that is similar, though not identical, to the comparison of Jesus with angels in chs. 1 and 2. Both involve a comparison of a lesser with a greater, or what Halliday and Hasan call 'particular comparison'.[50] Jesus is said to be superior, which is expressed with comparative adjectives (κρείττων, πλείων). Both also emphasize the fact that Jesus is the son of God. However, in the comparison with angels, the starting point and continuing emphasis is on contrasts rather than on any likenesses. The similarity between the two comparisons creates texture in the discourse.[51] The studies based on rhetorical analysis which suggest that Hebrews is epideictic rhetoric are close to the mark as far as the interpretation of 3.1-6 is concerned. Epideictic rhetoric involves the praise or blame of a person, thing or quality based on accepted values. Harold W. Attridge,[52] David E. Aune,[53] Clifton Black II,[54] and Thomas Olbricht[55] have noted the abundance of comparisons of Christ with entities as a distinguishing feature of the discourse. In 3.1-6, Moses is a highly respected person with whom Jesus is favorably compared. How-

---

speech and third-person report, asserting that direct speech is more vivid and more effective (p. 25).

50. Halliday and Hasan, *Cohesion*, p. 81.

51. The texture of the discourse is how the discourse functions as a unity (Halliday and Hasan, *Cohesion*, p. 2).

52. Attridge, *Hebrews*, p. 14. See *idem*, 'Paraenesis in a Homily', p. 214.

53. D.E. Aune, *The New Testament in its Literary Environment* (LEC, Philadelphia: Westminster Press, 1987), p. 212.

54. C.C. Black, II, 'The Rhetorical Form of the Hellenistic Jewish and Early Christian Sermon: A Response to Lawrence Wills', *HTR* 81 (1988), pp. 1-18 (5).

55. T.H. Olbricht, 'Hebrews as Amplification', in S.E. Porter and T.H. Olbricht (eds.), *Rhetoric and the New Testament: Essays from the 1992 Heidelberg Conference* (JSNTSup, 90; Sheffield: Sheffield Academic Press, 1993), pp. 375-87.

ever, none of the statements about Moses is marked as a main clause. They are not marked as main clauses by logical relationship, nor by a confluence of other indicators of prominence.[56]

The lexical development formed around οἶκος clearly marks 3.1-6 as a package of information. The development is concluded in 3.6b, which indicates a logical prominence of destination or conclusion. It has several other indicators of prominence that set it apart as a main clause in relationship to the comparison. Direct references to the readers are prominent because people tend to place themselves in the center of attention.[57] The author's use of the first-person plural pronoun and two first-person plural verbs involves interpersonal markers that make the information prominent by involving himself and the readers. Further-more, the clause is the only finite clause in the passage that is not linked specifically by a conjunction. The variation of omitting a conjunction also adds to its emphasis.

The most emphatic material in the unit is 3.1. The concluding identi-fication of the readers and author as Jesus' house is best seen in a rela-tionship of expository apposition to their identity in 3.1 as 'partners in a heavenly calling'.[58] They are partners in Jesus' heavenly calling, or by another name, they are his house. They are sharers in the same sense that the Israelites were sharers in Moses' calling. The concluding identi-fication is transitional, because it shifts the focus of the text from Jesus (the focus of the first two chapters) to the readers and to certain impli-cations of their partnership with Jesus, which shall be shown below. The focus on the identity of the readers is consistent with the author's thematic point of departure: 'holy brothers and sisters, partners in a heavenly calling'. In this unit, the author signaled the topic entity by placing it first.

56. There is a perfect in 3.3: ἠξίωται. This places emphasis on Jesus being worthy of more honor than Moses, but the emphasis is relative. It does not neces-sarily emphasize the contrast over the general comparison, since the general com-parison was emphatic as the point of departure.

57. See n. 55.

58. Expository apposition is one of the additive conjunctive relations which are shown on Halliday and Hasan's chart in *Cohesion*, p. 242, and explained on p. 248. It would be explicitly expressed by 'that is', 'I mean', 'in other words', 'to put it another way' or 'by another (alternative) name'. The readers' identity might be paraphrased as: 'You are sharers of Jesus' heavenly calling. In other words, you are members of his house in the same way as the Israelites were members of Moses' house.'

6. *Relation of the Passage to the Co-text*

As was suggested on p. 185, to arrive at the meaning of 3.1-6, one must examine how the text creates its own context in terms of what precedes the passage in chs. 1 and 2. It is also important to determine how that passage in turn creates a context for what follows. The constraint of the co-text is made more powerful by the fact that both 3.1-6 and 3.7-19 are joined to their co-text by inferential particles that show the preceding material is leading up to the following summary, conclusion or inference.

a. *The Relationship of 3.1-6 to Chapters 1–2*

The clause in 3.1 is joined to the previous passage with the conjunction ὅθεν, which is glossed as 'from which fact',[59] and expresses a causal relation.[60] The conjunction signals a summary or a conclusion. The grounds, basis or reason for 3.1 would be found somewhere in 1.1–2.18.

The identification of the readers as 'holy brothers and sisters' is introduced in the previous passage. The readers are identified as ἅγιος in 2.11, and a semantic chain develops the readers' identity as ἀδελφοί in 2.10, 11, 12, 13, 14 and 17. The semantic chain emphasizes the readers' relationship with Jesus as well as the author. The concept of the heavenly calling is given less development. However, the explanation of the quotation of Ps. 8.4-6 in Heb. 2.9-10 states that Jesus is the forerunner or trailblazer of the believers' salvation, crowned with glory and honor, who is bringing many sons and daughters to glory. In other words, the 'glory' with which Jesus is crowned is depicted as a kind of destination to which he leads his followers. Therefore, glory would be at least a part of the heavenly calling which Jesus shares with believers. There has already been a reference to believers being partners or sharers with Jesus. In 2.14, Jesus is described as sharing (μετέσχεν) in the children's humanity. The identification of believers as partners (μέτοχοι) in a heavenly calling is the other side of the coin.

---

59. BAGD, p. 555, Louw and Nida, *Greek–English Lexicon*, I, p. 780. The latter describe ὅθεν as a marker of cause or reason with focus upon the source.

60. Halliday and Hasan, *Cohesion*, pp. 256-61. Halliday and Hasan classify conjunctions in four groups: additive, adversative, causal and temporal (see their chart, pp. 242-43).

The grounds for the application of the titles 'apostle' and 'high priest' to Jesus are found in the previous passage. Based on external and internal evidence, it is most likely that the author is introducing these titles with reference to Jesus to the readers for the first time. The titles are unusual: 'apostle' is not applied to Jesus in any other New Testament passage, and 'high priest' is applied to Jesus only in Hebrews.[61] The internal evidence is the introduction that the author gives to ἀπόστολος before using the term, and the lengthy proof of Jesus' high priesthood in chs. 5 and 7–10. It is not likely that the application of the title 'apostle' to Jesus would raise any eyebrows, but the designation of Jesus as a high priest had to be explained and defended because of the exclusive claim to priesthood of the Levitic cultus.

The extensive use of words from the same semantic domain as ἀπόστολος forms two semantic chains in chs. 1 and 2 that constrain its interpretation in 3.1.[62] Though the word 'apostle' does not occur, two other nouns from similar semantic domains form a participant chain: ἄγγελος (1.4, 5, 13; 2.2, 5, 7, 9, 16) and προφήτης (1.1). All three words are used for messengers who speak for God.[63] The 'son' is also emphatically categorized as a messenger whom God spoke through in the paragraph theme in 1.2. There are as many as 19 references to the 'son' in ch. 1, counting the extensive anaphora. The use of the verbs ἀποστέλλω (1.14),[64] λαλέω (1.1, 2) and λέγω (1.5, 6, 7, 13) forms a

---

61. Ellingworth, *Commentary on Hebrews*, p. 199.

62. It forms an 'endophoric tie' which is a general name for reference within a text (Halliday and Hasan, *Cohesion*, p. 33). Labeling it as an endophoric tie implies that the interpretation of 3.1 is not possible without recourse to chs. 1 and 2.

63. Louw and Nida, *Greek–English Lexicon*, indicate that the semantic domains for ἀπόστολος are 53.74 (apostle) and 33.194 (messenger). The semantic domain for προφήτης is 53.79 (one who speaks for God). The semantic domains for ἄγγελος are 33.195 (messenger) and 12.28 (angel). Though 'messenger' is not given as a meaning for προφήτης, its meaning as one who speaks for God indicates a collocation between the terms. Justin Martyr reflects the close relationship of ἄγγελος and ἀπόστολος as messenger in *1 Apol.* 63.5: 'Now the Word of God is His Son, as we have said before. And he is called Angel and Apostle; for he declares whatever we ought to know, and is sent forth to declare whatever is revealed.' See also P.R. Carrell, *Jesus and the Angels: Angelology and the Christology of the Apocalypse of John* (Cambridge: Cambridge University Press, 1997), p. 110; C.A. Gieschen, *Angelomorphic Christology: Antecedents and Early Evidence* (AGJU; Leiden: E.J. Brill, 1998), pp. 176-80.

64. It is interesting that the word ἀποστέλλω is applied to angels in this verse.

chain of verbal processes. First, the fact that God spoke 'in these last days' through his son is tied in with the series of remarks which God spoke in the string of quotations in ch. 1—all but one of them to the son (1.5a, 5b, 6, 8-9, 10-12, 13). Secondly, the verb εἶπεν is omitted through ellipsis but is the cohesive tie between the quotations in 1.5b, and λέγει is omitted through ellipsis in the same way in 1.8 and 10. In the majority of the clauses where the participant chain of messengers interacts with the process chain of saying, the messengers are recipients, and God is the 'sayer'. Therefore, there are two participant chains and a process chain which interact with each other, primarily in the first chapter. One participant chain is God, and the other is the son and the prophets and angels who are his messengers. The messages that are spoken to and through the son are favorably contrasted with the messages spoken to and through God's other messengers. Throughout the chapter, it is clear that the son is the ultimate messenger as he is presented in 1.1-2: 'God spoke to the forefathers at various times and by various means through the prophets, and in these last days he has spoken to us in his son'.[65]

In 2.1-4, the author applies the fact that the son is God's ultimate messenger as shown in ch. 1. Since Jesus is God's ultimate spokesperson, it is necessary for the readers to pay closer attention to the salvation proclaimed (λαλεῖσθαι) by him than they did to the Law proclaimed (λαληθείς) by angels.[66] Therefore, the particular comparison of a lesser to a greater between the angels and Jesus in 1.5-14 provides the grounds for the conclusion in 2.1-4.

In the following paragraph, there is at least one more reference to Jesus as a messenger. He is the implied subject of the verb ἀπαγγελῶ (2.12): 'I will proclaim your name to my brothers and sisters'. There is probably also a connection with ἀρχηγός (2.10), which indicates unique leadership.[67] However, the reference to the process of speech and the

---

65. Swetnam, 'Hebrews 1,1–3,6', p. 62, sees ἀπόστολος as primarily looking forward to 3.2-6, though he does see a connection with chs. 1 and 2.

66. There was a contemporary belief that angels delivered the law to Moses, as F.F. Bruce observes in *The Epistle to the Hebrews* (Grand Rapids: Eerdmans, 1990), p. 258.

67. W.L. Lane, *Hebrews 9–13* (WBC, 47B; Dallas: Word Books, 1991), p. 84, sees a leadership motif of which ἀπόστολος and ἀρχηγός are a part, but that motif would be secondary in the first two chapters. Ellingworth also connects the two terms (*Commentary on Hebrews*, p. 348). ἀρχηγός also occurs in 12.12, and only

use of angels as a basis of comparison in 2.5-18 does not indicate the topic entity. They primarily function to create cohesion with 1.1–2.4.

The basis for Jesus' identification as high priest is provided in 2.5-18. As in 3.1, the particle ὅθεν in 2.17 is causal, which indicates that the assertion that Jesus is a high priest is a conclusion that has its basis in the preceding co-text. The content in 2.5-16 supports the conclusion by showing that humanity's sharing in Jesus' dominion is based on Jesus' sharing in humanity. His identification with humanity in suffering and temptation enabled him to become a merciful and faithful high priest. Jesus' identification with humanity was nothing new to the readers. However, as mentioned above, the designation of Jesus as high priest in 2.17-18 introduces a new doctrine which the author will define and defend at length in the discourse's long central exposition in 7.4–10.18.[68]

The connections between chs. 1–2 and 3.1-6 occur primarily in 3.1. However, the use of particular comparison in 3.3-6 also creates coherence with the preceding co-text, and there is an association between the final phrase in 3.6 and 2.1, involving holding on to the confession of hope. The domain of prominence of 3.1 is extensive. It summarizes the two primary topic entities of the preceding co-text, which constrains the understanding of the verse's terminology.[69] Jesus' two unusual titles encapsulate two main topics of the discourse. As an apostle, he is the ultimate spokesperson (1.1-2), and he proclaimed the confession on to which the readers must cling without drifting away (2.1; 4.14; 10.23). In addition, as an apostle, he continues to speak 'today' (3.7, 15; 4.7; 12.24-25), and they must not refuse to respond to him. As a high priest, he has led the way for them into the Holy of Holies and the presence of God (4.14-16; 6.19-20; 10.19-22). When introducing the two offices,

---

two other times in the New Testament (Acts 3.15 and 5.3).

68. As B. Lindars suggested in 'The Rhetorical Structure of Hebrews', *NTS* 35 (1989), pp. 382-406 (392 n. 1): 'The author slips in a concept which he will use later in the argument. It does not therefore have to be already familiar.'

69. There is a debate as to whether 3.1 looks backwards or forwards. However, others have seen it as summarizing the previous two chapters. F.J. Delitzsch, *Commentary on the Epistle to the Hebrews* (trans. T.L. Kingsburg; Minneapolis: Klock & Klock, 1978), p. 153, states, 'In these few weighty words all the preceding thoughts of our epistle recur'. Lane agrees (*Hebrews 1–8*, p. 75), observing that the two designations for Jesus 'simply sum up the presentation of Jesus in 1:1–2:18 as the one through whom God proclaimed the definitive word of salvation and made propitiation for the sins of the people'.

the author exhorts the readers directly to think intently about Jesus in these two new ways in the light of the fact that they share his heavenly calling. The readers' identity has comparatively less development in the first two chapters. Instead, it is developed more fully in this paragraph and the following co-text. It continues to be developed in the rest of the discourse, as discussed below. The repetition of these topics throughout the discourse demonstrates that the domain of prominence of 3.1 is global.

b. *The Relationship of 3.7-15 to 3.1-6*
At least one of the functions of 3.1-6 is that it sets the stage, or provides the basis for a series of prohibitions and imperatives in 3.7-15. The paragraph is joined to the co-text by διό, another inferential particle, which Louw and Nida describe as a 'relatively emphatic marker of result, usually denoting the fact that the inference is self-evident'.[70] Like ὅθεν, it marks a result, conclusion or inference, and suggests that the following material may have logical dominance. The paragraph in 3.1-6 poses many challenges, but perhaps the greatest challenge to commentators has been to explain in a convincing way how 3.7-15 is a self-evident result of 3.1-6. The transition seems to be abrupt, and the relationship between 3.6 and 3.7 is often ignored or explained inadequately.[71]

It is interesting that a quotation of a prohibition from Ps. 95.7-11 follows the διό. The quotation is introduced by καθὼς λέγει τὸ πνεῦμα τὸ ἅγιον, which indicates that the Holy Spirit is addressing this psalm directly to the readers.[72] The command is, 'Today, if you hear his voice

70. Louw and Nida, *Greek–English Lexicon*, p. 783.

71. For example, Ellingworth, *Commentary on Hebrews*, p. 213, asserts, 'In NT terms, there is an implied contrast between the trustworthiness of Jesus (3.1-6) and the disobedient unbelief which characterized God's people in the past and threatens them now.' However, since the comparison or contrast in 3.1-6 is between Moses and Jesus, it is hard to see how the reader is led to see a contrast between Jesus and the wilderness generation. Furthermore, all the the explicit contrasts in 3.7–4.11 are made between the wilderness generation and the hearers.

72. Lane, *Hebrews 1–8*, p. 85, supports the same interpretation for dubious reasons, interpreting the present tense of λέγει as indicating time. Buchanan, *To the Hebrews*, p. 61, agrees for better reasons: 'The "just as" indicates that the author was speaking to his generation in the same way and in the same words as the Holy Spirit'. D. Guthrie, *The Letter to the Hebrews* (Grand Rapids: Eerdmans, 1983), p. 103, asserts that the author 'sees the opening *Today* as significant, allowing him to

do not harden your hearts'. The use of a quotation as a direct command is unusual, but the author clearly uses the same technique in 12.5.[73] Furthermore, in v. 13, he asserts that it is still 'called today', meaning that the warning is in force and applies to the readers. The rest of the quotation is framed semantically and structurally around the prohibition 'do not harden your hearts'. The prohibition is followed by the enhancement of a negative example or analogy which is introduced by the particle ὡς ('like' or 'as') in 3.8. Readers are directly admonished not to be like the Israelites 'in the rebellion', which is a reference to the wilderness generation that followed Moses. The information in 3.8b-11 provides the context of the time, place and circumstances of a previous episode in Israel's history where the followers of Moses provoked God.

The author follows the quotation with an elaboration of two positive commands that parallel the prohibition. The readers are commanded to watch for an unbelieving and unfaithful heart, and to exhort each other while it is still called 'today' (3.11-12). Then the author combines three strands from the preceding co-text to complete a series of commands. The author makes an explicit connection with 3.1 and 3.6, and then the initial prohibition is restated in 3.14-15: 'We have become partners [μέτοχοι] of Christ' (3.1), if we hold fast (κατάσχωμεν) to our original conviction until the end is secure (3.6). While it is still called 'Today', if you hear his voice, do not harden your hearts as they did in the wilderness' (3.7-8). The selective repetition together with the marked return to the first-person plural indicates that these two verses serve as a kind of summary.[74] Though the summary lacks the confluence of indicators of prominence that marked 3.1, it serves as a signpost indicating how 3.1-6 and 3.7-15 are interpreted together. The focus is on the nature of the partnership and how it is based on maintaining the confession which they had heard and accepted in the past, and responding

apply the words to his present readers'. Ellingworth, *Commentary on Hebrews*, p. 217, is more reticent in his observations, merely stating that 'The grammatical construction is probably διὸ...μὴ σκληρύνητε rather than the more remote διὸ... βλέπετε', and leaves his readers to draw their own conclusions.

73. Heb. 12.5 reads, 'and you have forgotten the exhortation which is addressed to you as children, "My child, do not belittle the Lord's discipline, nor faint when you are rebuked by him"'. Since the imperative from the quotation is described as 'addressed to you', there is little question that the author is applying it directly.

74. It is important to note that vv. 12-13 are structurally indivisible from vv. 14-15, since the four verses form a periodic sentence (Lane, *Hebrews 1–8*, p. 84).

in the present to the voice of Jesus, the apostle of the faith.

The interpretation of 3.7-15 is constrained by 3.1-6, because the comparison between Jesus' relationship with his house and Moses' relationship with his house lays the groundwork to draw a further correlation. The parallel relationship between the two houses enables the author to use the Israelites' disobedience as a relevant warning to the readers. The readers are in a situation that is comparable to the Israelites during the rebellion. They are in danger of hardening their hearts to what Jesus is saying to them in a time of crisis. The analogy between the followers of Moses and the readers which is set up in 3.1-6 is extended into ch. 4, where the author presents the opportunity of entering the rest as still being open. Therefore, the readers' partnership with Jesus is portrayed as having the same danger and the same opportunity as the Israelites' partnership with Moses.

Whereas the preceding co-text in chs. 1 and 2 was primarily linked to the description of Jesus in 3.1, the following co-text in 3.7-15 is explicitly linked to the readers' identity in 3.1 and 3.6b. The comparison between Moses and Jesus in 3.2-6a is not developed further. Moses is not mentioned again until 7.14, and then he is not compared directly to Jesus. The terminology pertaining to 'house' is similarly abandoned, and the word οἶκος does not appear again until ch. 8 in an Old Testament quotation about the house of Israel. Jesus does not appear as a theme of a clause until ch. 5, though the readers' partnership with him (3.14) and the appeal to listen to him is emphasized through repetition. The author continues to refer to Jesus' apostleship in the following passage through the repetition of the refrain 'Today if you hear his voice' (3.7, 15; 4.7), as well as the description of the word of God in 4.12-13. Jesus' identity as a high priest is resumed at the end of the section in 4.14. The application of his high priesthood to the readers' calling is further developed in the material that follows 10.19.

Therefore, the domain of prominence of the different elements in 3.1-6 varies. All of the elements in 3.1 are prominent at the level of discourse, which is consistent with the confluence of indicators of emphasis at that point. Besides being prominent at the global level of discourse, the verse has a pivotal relationship to the surrounding co-text. The identification of the offices of Jesus summarizes the first two chapters, while the thematic identification of the readers provides the topic entity for the next two chapters. On the other hand, the following comparison and contrast of Jesus with Moses in 3.2-6a is support material that is not developed beyond the passage's boundaries, which is consistent with the relatively low prominence of the material. The relatively emphatic conclusion in 3.6b, which correlates the readers with the Israelites, serves as a main clause at the paragraph level in a more narrow sense than 3.1, since it specifies the point of the comparison. It provides the basis for the application of the prohibition in 3.7-8 to the readers, so that point of the comparison serves as support material for the following paragraph. In contrast, the prohibition in 3.7-8 has a domain of prominence that is more extensive. It not only is supported by the previous paragraph, but is also supported by elaboration and repetition in 3.15 and 4.5, so that it serves as a main clause at the section level.

7. Conclusion

The analysis of the logical relationships between the clauses in 3.1-6 reveals that the comparison and contrast between Moses and Jesus in 3.2-6 are support material for 3.1, which contains the identity of the readers and the titles of Jesus. The topic entity of the passage is the readers' identity as partners with Jesus in terms of being members of his house. Their relationship with Jesus is illustrated or elaborated by a comparison of Moses' relationship with his house. There are two places in the passage that have a confluence of prominent indicators: 3.1 and 3.6b. They serve as the point of departure and the destination of the paragraph. The theme in 3.1 which identifies the topic entity is relatively more prominent than the destination in 3.6, which reveals the point of the comparison. The relationship of the passage to the co-text reveals that the relative prominence in the passage corresponds to the domain of prominence of the two verses. The material in 3.1 is pivotal for a larger section of material. The titles of Jesus summarize the topic entities in chs. 1 and 2, while the identity of the readers provides the thematic point of departure for chs. 3 and 4. Furthermore, the topics of Jesus as high priest and apostle and the readers as partners in a heavenly calling are prominent at the discourse level, since they are developed throughout the discourse. The semantic domain of the identification of the readers as Jesus' house in 3.6b is local. It provides the point of the comparison in 3.2-6a, and specifies the grounds for the commands in 3.7-15. The passage is transitional and sets up a parallel between the readers and the Israelites who followed Moses to show that the readers faced the same danger and opportunity that the Israelites faced.

In view of the subsequent development, the similarities between Jesus and Moses are the intended focus of the comparison. This fits in well with the linearization of the passage, where the similarity is stated first and then qualified with a subtraction. The statement and elaboration that Jesus is worthy of more glory serves to intensify the force of the comparison of the readers with the Israelites in their increased responsibility to respond to him.

As to this passage being polemic in nature, particular comparisons in epideictic rhetoric are not pejorative. In this comparison, Moses is a highly respected individual and leader who functions as a type of Christ, rather than the target of a polemic. The passage lacks the kind of polemic language that characterizes the attack and refutation of error. According to 3.7-15, the danger that the readers face is not the error of inappropriate association with the central figures of the Jewish faith. Rather, it is the error of refusing to listen to God who spoke through those figures in the past and who is now speaking to them through his son.

Christ's status and function are amplified and clarified through the comparison with Moses, as well as the comparison with angels and prophets. However, 3.1-6 shifts the focus from Jesus to the readers. The following co-text draws the readers to interact with the implications that Jesus' apostleship has on their partnership with him. Many translations and Greek New Testaments such as the *UBSGNT* subtitle 3.1-6 as 'Jesus Superior to Moses'. This contributes to a misunderstanding about the nature of the material. It takes the least prominent material in the passage, and moves it into a powerful thematic position. The consequent reading of the passage lacks coherence. The superiority of Jesus over Moses cannot account for all of the material in the passage and results in a tendency to explain parts of the passage such as vv. 2b and 4 as parentheses.[75] Furthermore, the following co-text in 3.7-15 becomes a non sequitur. On the other hand, if the subheading read 'Partners of a Heavenly Calling', it would reflect the theme which the author chose, and would suggest a topic entity that can better account for the material in the passage.

---

75. Cf. Lane, *Hebrews 1–8*, pp. 71-74 for a discussion of the coherence of the passage and how it has been challenged.

MISGUIDED MISSALS: IS EARLY CHRISTIAN MUSIC JEWISH OR IS IT GRAECO-ROMAN?

Wendy J. Porter

1. *Introduction*

The word 'missal' and its homophone 'missile' serve here as a point of observation. The first missal, the book that contains all the texts that are said or sung at Mass for the entire year,[1] was not developed until the tenth to the thirteenth centuries,[2] but is used here in a broad sense as an authoritative document that identifies the words and musical texts of even the earliest Christian liturgy, the theoretical canon that concerns musicologists and liturgists. 'Misguided' missals in this sense suggests the possibility that Church tradition has not accurately reflected the music of the early Church in its canon of music for the liturgy. For instance, while scholars are dependent on early sources—writings from the Jewish or the Graeco-Roman perspective—there is always a question of accurate interpretation of these sources. Similarly, documents that have actual musical notation of any sort are extremely limited in

---

1. W. Apel, *Gregorian Chant* (Bloomington, IN: Indiana University Press, 1990 [1958]), p. 15, writes that the missal contains 'the complete liturgical texts, of the musical items as well as of the prayers, lessons from Scriptures, psalms, etc.', with the Missal (or *Missale*) being specifically for the Mass. Its companion book, the Gradual (or *Graduale*), contains the actual chants for the Mass.

2. See, e.g., D.M. Hope, 'Liturgical Books', in C. Jones, G. Wainwright and E. Yarnold (eds.), *The Study of Liturgy* (London: SPCK, 1978; repr. with corrections, 1983), pp. 65-69 (67); also in the same volume, C. Howell, 'From Trent to Vatican II', pp. 241-48; see also a brief historical summary, including introduction to the liturgical books, in N. Sandon (ed.), *The Use of Salisbury: The Ordinary of the Mass* (Antico Church Music; Newton Abbott, Devon: Tabitha Phillips, 1984), p. vi; and F.H. Dickinson (ed.), *Missale ad usum insignis et praeclarae ecclesiae Sarum* (Burntisland: Pitsligo; Oxford and London: J. Parker, 1861–83), p. iii, where he writes in the preface that 'the Missal is the most important book', although it 'is not complete without...the Gradual, giving the ancient music of the Missal'.

number, and it is entirely possible that none existed in the earliest period of the Christian churches.

The second 'missile', a twentieth-century weapon of war, has perhaps entered the equation in attempts to define the elusive parameters of what may have existed musically in the early Christian Church. 'Misguided' missiles in this sense suggests that scholars who concentrate on discrediting the opposing view as to influences on early Christian music may be misdirecting their energies, for undoubtedly both Jewish and Graeco-Roman influences must be acknowledged.

For my purposes, homophonic words that can provide musical reference to the early Church and simultaneously conjure up imagery of twentieth-century disputes are useful. The debate—is early Christian music Jewish or is it Graeco-Roman?—perhaps has more overtones of the second kind of missile than the first, for prejudices sometimes have interfered with a judicious approach to the subject. The twentieth-century discussion of music of the early Church often consists of scholars presenting views that they perhaps *wish* to be true, for particular theological or religious reasons, although exclusive positions frequently cannot be substantiated. The current view sees the influence on the music of the early Christian Church as Jewish, with a majority of New Testament scholars promoting this view, and it is futile to argue that there was no influence of Jewish culture and belief on early Christianity, for it grew to some degree directly out of Judaism. On the other hand, to argue against Greek influence is equally unfounded, for the young Church was situated fully within the Hellenized culture of the Graeco-Roman world. Several scholars through musical and liturgical investigation have gone against the common consensus and have reintroduced the influence of Graeco-Roman culture. To my mind, there is some disparity between those who focus on the arguments and those who are inclined to take adamant positions or aggressive postures, rather than addressing the data and the arguments. Similarly, there is some question as to whether the direction of the present-day discussion is misguided, for the evidence suggests neither one single influence nor the other, but, rather, an uncomfortable mix of at least these two musical cultures.[3]

3. A third element of this discussion could include the dichotomy of the term 'Graeco-Roman' itself, where the Greek side of things is often treated. This is in part because there has been little known about Roman music, and, further, a perception that it was fairly barbaric, which may represent simply a lack of informa-

2. *Difficulties in Investigating Early Christian Music*

While the prevailing perception of the early Christian Church is that it was a singing Church, references in the New Testament to music are not numerous.[4] There is virtually nothing to indicate the actual notation or sound of the music and many inferences must be drawn by the reader who is particularly interested in the music of the early Church. This lack of material is sometimes the basis for unfounded assumptions, because although there is little to substantiate them, there is also little to disprove them. Edwin Hatch summarizes the problems associated with this kind of inquiry, by identifying two of the most significant problems:

> The one is the tendency to overrate the value of the evidence that has survived... The other is the tendency to under-estimate the importance of the opinions that have disappeared from sight, or which we know only in the form and to the extent of their quotation by their opponents.[5]

For instance, many scholars have accepted the idea that musical instruments were banned both from the early Church and from the Jewish synagogue on account of their 'worldly nature'. Some believe they were banned throughout the first century; others, that they were banned only after the destruction of the Temple as a way of expressing disapproval. Eric Werner writes:

> Rabbinic sources explain the strict prohibition of any instrumental music in the Synagogue as an expression of mourning for the loss of the Temple and land, but the present writer has been able to show that a certain animosity against all instrumental music existed well before the fall of the Temple... It seems that this enmity towards instrumental music

---

tion. See, e.g., J.E. Scott, 'Roman Music', in E. Wellesz (ed.), *Ancient and Oriental Music* (The New Oxford History of Music, 1; London: Oxford University Press, 1957; repr. 1966), pp. 404-20.

4.　See a summary in W.S. Smith, *Musical Aspects of the New Testament* (Amsterdam: W. Ten Have, 1962), pp. 59-65.

5.　E. Hatch, *The Influence of Greek Ideas and Usage upon the Christian Church* (The Hibbert Lectures, 1888; London: Williams & Norgate, 1890; repr. as *The Influence of Greek Ideas on Christianity* [New York: Harper & Brothers, 1957]), p. 10. Although these were part of lectures given in 1888, the fact that they were deemed important enough to reprint in 1957 and still stand as sound judgments for historical inquiry says much about the quality of Hatch's contribution to scholarship.

was a defence against the musical and orgiastic mystery cults in which Syrian and Mesopotamian Jews not infrequently participated... The primitive Christian community held the same view, as we know from apostolic and post-apostolic literature: instrumental music was thought unfit for religious services.[6]

One of the difficulties with the latter part of this statement is that most of the literature that expresses a view against instrumental music was written several centuries later than the early period of Christianity and may not express the views that were held in the first or second century. The lack of early documents is a problem that is common to the period, but assertions that are made on much later evidence must be subjected to some scrutiny.

There is evident animosity between some Jews and non-Jews in the first centuries after Christ that can be seen in various writings. Werner writes that 'Concerning the music of Hellenism, the Rabbinic position was unequivocal: they viewed it with the greatest suspicion, rightly connecting it with the orgiastic cults of Asia Minor... The early Church held, at least in the first two centuries, exactly the same principles as normative Judaism.'[7] Werner cites ecclesiastical authorities that provide evidence of an anti-Jewish position; for instance, Diodorus of Tarsus 'complained bitterly that the Church was imitating Jewish songs and asked of what use the many Hebrew words and Psalmodies could be'.[8] However, Diodorus lived in the fourth century CE (died c. 390), so this is not a definite indication of the trend in the earliest days of the Christian Church. Similarly, Chrysostom 'warned Christians against imitating Jewish practices and customs' and is stingingly anti-Jewish and sarcastic in his perspective, citing Mt. 9.23-24 first to make his point:

And when Jesus came to the ruler's house, and saw the aulos players, and the crowd making a tumult, he said, 'Depart; for the girl is not dead but sleeping'. And they laughed at him. Noble tokens, these, of the rulers of the synagogue—auloi and cymbals raising a dirge in the hour of her death.[9]

---

6. E. Werner, 'The Music of Post-Biblical Judaism', in Wellesz (ed.), *Ancient and Oriental Music*, pp. 313-35 (315).

7. E. Werner, 'The Conflict between Hellenism and Judaism in the Music of the Early Christian Church', *HUCA* 20 (1947), pp. 407-70 (457).

8. Werner, 'Conflict between Hellenism and Judaism', p. 458.

9. John Chrysostom, *In Matthaeum*, Hom. 11.7 (*PG* LVII, col. 200), cited in J. McKinnon (ed.), *Music in Early Christian Literature* (Cambridge Studies in the

But, again, Chrysostom lived in the fourth century (c. 347–407), so it is difficult to ascertain whether fourth-century patterns duplicate or even represent those of the earliest two centuries.[10]

Undoubtedly there was reciprocal antagonism between at least some of the Jews and non-Jews, but these statements do not necessarily represent all those involved in the discussion in the first century, again, because what is thought to be known about both the sentiments of the people involved and the actual music of the early Christian Church can be read back only from much later documents. Werner, for example, speaks of tenth-century documents in referring to the Jewish musical traditions, which means that they are removed from the period of interest here by almost 1000 years. While it can reasonably be argued that music did not change much in the first millennium, this is still a very long period of time. In his defence of the Jewish tradition found in the music of the Church, but the lack of sources until the tenth or even eleventh centuries, Werner poses the question that the reader might ask:

> How is it possible that we possess 14 fully written pieces of ancient Greek music, and not a scratch of Hebrew? The explanation is simple: The Greeks had a system of notation, based upon the alphabet, which identified each tone with a letter—hence our naming of tones after letters, a, b, c, d, e, and so on. We Jews did not use symbols for each tone, but for each whole phrase. Indeed it would have been rather difficult to break up one of those florid, richly embellished Hebrew melodies into single tones. Thus, from the practical point of view the cantillation marks of Jews, Syrians, Armenians, Byzantians, and those of the early Roman Church were more practical, more appropriate to the style of the music, which they symbolized, but alas, much less faithful than the comparatively clumsy Greek characters.[11]

The explanation may be simple, as Werner says, but it does not entirely solve the problem of the lack of documentation to support his hypotheses for the dominant influence of Hebrew music on the music of the early Christian Church—that problem remains.

An example from a biblical scholar that shows the course of the discussion is found in C.W. Dugmore's preface to the 1964 reprint of his 1944 book, *The Influence of the Synagogue upon the Divine Office*. He

---

Literature of Music; Cambridge: Cambridge University Press, 1987), p. 84 n. 178.

10. Werner, 'Conflict between Hellenism and Judaism', p. 459.

11. E. Werner, 'The Oldest Sources of Synagogal Chant', *PAAJR* 16 (1947), pp. 225-32 (225-26).

includes revealing statements that have a bearing on the development of the discussion of this essay:

> The original preface was necessarily 'dated' and has been omitted. The 'Introduction', which has also been omitted, drew attention to the older emphasis on the influence of the Mystery Religions and of Hellenism upon the worship and theology of the primitive Church, and sought to redress the balance of this nineteenth-century approach (whilst recognizing the contribution of Greece) by stressing the influence of Judaism and, especially, of the Synagogue to the development of early Christian worship. This view has found increasing support in the intervening years.[12]

While genuine attempts have been made to counterbalance the bias of some past scholars regarding the music of the Church,[13] nonetheless, the attempt cannot be a substitute for genuine investigation on either side of the equation. Dugmore himself mentions factors that show the influences of both cultures, even if not always directly related to music. For example, he speaks of 'the pre-Christian elements of the liturgy of the Synagogue' being the reading and exposition of the Scriptures, and the reference in Acts 17.2 to the Berean Jews who had daily access to them, saying that this 'suggests that in the synagogues of the Dispersion access could be had to the rolls of Scripture (Greek) at any time, just as, presumably, was the case in the synagogues in Palestine'.[14]

In another vein, a factor that contributes to the difficulties of studying early Christian music is summarized by Alec Harman. He describes the beginning of the fourth century, with the division of the Roman Empire into east and west, and further liturgical divisions that resulted in five main groups of the Christian Church. In the east, these were Syrian, Byzantine and Egyptian, all retaining the Greek language, and in the west, Roman and Gallican, using the Latin language.[15]

---

12. C.W. Dugmore, *The Influence of the Synagogue upon the Divine Office* (London: Faith Press, 1964 [1944]), p. v.

13. Several offenders are conveniently identified by Eric Werner in *The Sacred Bridge: The Interdependence of Liturgy and Music in Synagogue and Church during the First Millennium* (2 vols.; vol. I: London: Dennis Dobson; New York: Columbia University Press, 1959; vol. II: New York: Ktav, 1984), II, p. 262 n. 92, where he commends the efforts of one scholar whose 'approach does not, fortunately, hark back to Wellhausen's, Lagarde's, or Baumstark's wilful and one-sided neglect of the contemporary Judaistic scholarship'.

14. Dugmore, *Influence of the Synagogue*, p. 71.

15. A. Harman, *Man and his Music: The Story of Musical Experience in the*

Tracing these five, with their various offshoots, back to their earliest roots has been something only recently engaged in with any great success, by the collaboration of scholars from various related areas of study, including musicology, theology, historiography and linguistics. The focus in the twentieth century has been on discovering the Jewish roots of the music of the early Church. Harman states:

> We do not know who composed these melodies, but some of them were certainly adapted from Greek and Jewish sources and possibly from folk-song also. Which had the greater influence, Greek or Jewish music, was a bone of contention until recently, but although Greek was the accepted language in most of the churches during the early years—hence the words 'eucharist' and 'kyrie eleison' ('Lord have mercy'—originally a hymn to the Greek sun-god!), which were retained even after the Roman Church had changed over to Latin—and although the Church Fathers were greatly influenced by Greek thought, it now seems certain that Christian chant owes more to the Jewish synagogue than to the Greek temple. For one thing, the chant melodies as they have come down to us are much more closely allied to Jewish than to Greek music, and as the texts are nearly all taken from the psalms (which are of course Jewish, not Christian) it seems very probable that many of the psalm melodies themselves were adapted from those used in the synagogue. In fact, it has been shown that many such tunes sung to-day by Jewish communities who have been completely isolated since pre-Christian times are strikingly similar to those of the Christian Church. Furthermore, the different ways of singing the psalms were the same in both church and synagogue; these are now called direct, responsorial, and antiphonal psalmody.[16]

This statement may well summarize the current view, but it raises questions as it answers others. For instance, what examples of Greek chant does he refer to for comparison? What corpus does he use that defines that 'the texts are nearly all taken from the psalms (which are of course Jewish, not Christian)', and does he mean in the latter, 'Jewish, not *Greek*'? How can it be determined that it is (1) 'very probable that many of the psalm melodies themselves were adapted from those used in the synagogue' and (2) 'the different ways of singing the psalms were the same in both church and synagogue'?[17] Harman states that

---

West. I. *Medieval and Early Renaissace Music (up to 1525)* (London: Barrie & Rockliff, 1962), pp. 4-5.

16. Harman, *Man and his Music*, I, p. 5.

17. See discussion below on psalmody in the ancient and first-century synagogue.

'Another important type of chant was the hymn, also of Jewish origin but influenced to some extent by Greek models. The first Christian hymns were written (in Greek) for the eastern churches...'[18] The first statement, that the hymn was of Jewish origin, is hard to substantiate, as the term itself is a Greek word, with Greek hymns well known for hundreds of years before the time of Christ. Similarly, the second statement, that the 'first Christian hymns were written (in Greek)', raises some questions in this regard, especially noting that Harman places 'in Greek' in parentheses.

Questions also arise as a result of statements by A. Sendrey on the Jewish writer, Philo (c. 20 BCE–c. 40 CE), whose life would have spanned the life of Christ. Sendrey says:

> His numerous historical and philosophical essays, both large and small, reveal, on the whole, a good understanding of the general musical culture of his time. But his treatment of the subject is completely under the spell of the musical theory and philosophy of the Hellenes. Facts concerning the music of his own people are almost entirely missing in his writings.[19]

While Sendrey's concern is that Philo, as a Jewish writer, discusses little of the Jewish heritage of music, what is perhaps more significant is that three of Sendrey's own statements in his summary underline the predominance of Greek influence on music at that time. First, Sendrey admits that Philo has a good understanding of the general musical culture of his time. Secondly, he assumes that Philo Judaeus's writing is 'under the spell' of the Hellenes, which suggests that Hellenistic music and musical theory were in fact the most dominant or compelling at the time. Thirdly, he states that facts about the Jewish music 'are almost entirely missing in his writings', which again supports the case for a largely Hellenistic approach to music at the time of Philo's writing. The three statements that Sendrey has commented on in fact indicate that Philo is quite consistent in his representation of the music at the turn of the millennium and during the life of Christ; therefore, Philo's statements may in fact support the case for the Greek or Graeco-Roman influence on the soon-to-be-formed Christian Church.

These are only a few of the problems faced when dealing with the material related to the music of the early Christian Church. More could be mentioned, but these should suffice to show the nature of the inquiry

18. Harman, *Man and his Music*, I, p. 6.
19. A. Sendrey, *Music in Ancient Israel* (London: Vision, 1969), p. 62.

and the difficulties that scholars of either persuasion must or should face. At the very least, it is difficult, perhaps impossible, to ascertain which influence was the very first, although this seems to be at the heart of the debate.

3. *Is Early Christian Music Jewish?*

Over the last 100 years, there has been a tremendous increase in scholarly writing about the heritage of Judaism in the music of the early Christian Church, most notably and comprehensively by Eric Werner in two volumes, both entitled *The Sacred Bridge: The Interdependence of Liturgy and Music in Synagogue and Church during the First Millennium*, as well as numerous articles.[20] Werner's work is monumental and impossible to ignore—he presents intuitive hypotheses that have gained credibility as more information has come to light, as well as assimilating data in a way that has revolutionized this area of inquiry. However, his work is sometimes coloured by emotive language and backlashing tendencies (not that they are without some provocation) against earlier studies of scholars who ignored Jewish influences and contemporary Jewish scholarship. R.T. Beckwith reminds the reader that 'At its origin, Christianity was a Jewish religion. Jesus Christ was a Jew, and his first followers were Jews.'[21] It should come as no surprise to find an overlap of Judaism with Christianity and numerous imprints of a Jewish heritage in the musical traditions of the Christian Church.

In the preface to the first volume of *The Sacred Bridge*, Werner freely admits that in the study of liturgy, liturgical music and the necessary accompanying interpretation of historical documents, 'Prejudice cannot be fully avoided, it being an intrinsic part of genuine religious conviction'.[22] This prejudice shows itself in his own article on 'Music' in *The Interpreter's Dictionary of the Bible*, where he writes: 'Indeed, all evidence points to the chant and music of the primitive church as practically identical with the customs and traditions of the synagogue',[23] making it seem very clear-cut, which it is not.[24] Numerous

---

20. Some of which are reprinted in E. Werner, *Three Ages of Musical Thought: Essays on Ethics and Aesthetics* (New York: Da Capo Press, 1981).

21. R.T. Beckwith, 'The Jewish Background to Christian Worship', in Jones, Wainwright and Yarnold (eds.), *The Study of Liturgy*, pp. 39-51 (39).

22. Werner, *The Sacred Bridge*, I, p. xv.

23. E. Werner, 'Music', *IDB*, III, pp. 457-69 (466).

24. See references to J. McKinnon and J.A. Smith below, n. 26.

biblical scholars state with confidence that the tradition of the synagogue was carried on into the Christian Church, but there is an increasing number of questions in this regard. One scholar writes that from the
earliest times people sang psalms 'following the practice of the synagogue',[25] but what this practice may have been is unknown, as there is
no record of psalm-singing, at least in the ancient synagogue.[26] R.P.
Martin says that the 'Church was cradled in Judaism, and borrowed
many of its forms of worship from the Temple and synagogue',
although he says he must 'admit that there is some doubt as to the
extent to which the singing of divine praises had developed in the
Palestinian synagogues of the first century'.[27] Another writer refers to
the 'natural continuity of responsorial psalmody from synagogue to
church'.[28] Again, this assumption is possible but undocumented. Dom
Gregory Dix gives an outline of the Christian synaxis (order of liturgy
to precede the Eucharist), stating that it was followed everywhere.[29]
Specifically included in his list is psalmody, but P.F. Bradshaw points
out that these elements of the Christian synaxis are found only with
certainty in fourth-century documents, and it is unknown if the fourth-
century practices reflected the primitive practices of the early Church.[30]
In contrast to the outline referred to by Dix, B. Reicke's reconstruction
of the normal worship on a sabbath makes no mention of music.[31]

25. A. Robertson, 'Psalmody', in J.G. Davies (ed.), *A Dictionary of Liturgy and
Worship* (London: SCM Press, 1972), p. 326.

26. See J. McKinnon, 'On the Question of Psalmody in the Ancient Syna-
gogue', in E. Fenlon (ed.), *Early Music History: Studies in Medieval and Early
Modern Music*, VI (Cambridge: Cambridge University Press, 1986), pp. 159-91.
See also J.A. Smith, 'The Ancient Synagogue, the Early Church and Singing',
Music & Letters 65.1 (1984), pp. 1-16.

27. R.P. Martin, *Worship in the Early Church* (Grand Rapids: Eerdmans, 1964),
p. 40.

28. T.H. Connolly, 'Responsorial Psalmody', in S. Sadie (ed.), *The New Grove
Dictionary of Music and Musicians* (20 vols.; London: Macmillan, 1980), XV,
p. 759.

29. Dom Gregory Dix, *The Shape of the Liturgy* (Westminster: Dacre Press,
1954 [1945]), p. 38.

30. P.F. Bradshaw, *The Search for the Origins of Christian Worship: Sources
and Methods for the Study of Early Liturgy* (Oxford: Oxford University Press,
1992), pp. 137-38.

31. B. Reicke, *The New Testament Era: The World of the Bible from 500 B.C.
to A.D. 100* (trans. D.E. Green; Philadelphia: Fortress Press, 1968). H. Ulrich and
P.A. Pisk, *A History of Music and Musical Style* (New York: Harcourt, Brace &

Evidence that Werner compiles throughout his two volumes of *The Sacred Bridge* serves only to verify that the earliest traditions that are known seem to correspond to *later* Jewish chant, but there is little knowledge of how those came to be interwoven in the early centuries of the Christian Church, or of what influences Jewish chant may have absorbed.[32]

Judging from these various statements, it appears that many scholars have followed the assumption that the solitary source for the musical-liturgical traditions of the Christian Church is the Jewish synagogue and/or temple. However, just as Werner denounces those who have in the past come from an 'all-Hellenistic approach',[33] so he himself virtually excludes reference to, or acknowledgment of, influences other than Jewish in what clearly was a period of multiple influences. Werner clearly denounces scholars who do not follow his own presuppositions. There is no mincing of words for those who have not cited his own work favourably,[34] although he clearly rejects the work of James

World, 1963), p. 39, writing from a musical perspective, take a much more conservative view than do biblical scholars, proposing that 'As early as the third century, psalm-singing was a well-established part—perhaps the main element—of the Christian ritual'.

32. W.S. Smith, *Musical Aspects*, e.g., writes: 'Jewish musical practice, of course, did not escape the syncretistic influences of Oriental and Hellenic cultures in the centuries preceding the Christian era. The liturgy of the dispersion synagogues especially was affected. The mere fact that the texts were sung in Greek language must have brought about some modification of the traditional music. Also, if analogy with later processes is of any value at this point, it is well known that the music of more recent Jews has been strongly colored by the music native to the lands in which they were living' (p. 7).

33. Werner, *The Sacred Bridge*, I, p. 28.

34. See, e.g., Werner, *The Sacred Bridge*, II, p. 219 n. 69. He refers to 'Mr. McKinnon's study, *The Church Fathers and Musical Instruments*', saying the following: 'The author had limited himself to a few selected Fathers, mostly of the Western Church; also his knowledge is rather limited. The Syrian, Armenian, and most of the Byzantine Fathers have—luckily—escaped his attention, not to mention the rabbinic authorities. So has my study, "If I Speak in the Voices of Angels..." [actually Werner's article is entitled "If I Speak in the Tongues of Men...", see below, n. 41] escaped his attention, where St. Paul's hostile attitude to all instruments is shown and explained, although this occurs in a document *before* the fall of the Temple. Nor has the author taken cognizance of my study, "The Conflict between Hellenism and Judaism..."' Later in the same volume, it appears to be McKinnon again who receives attention, although not by name this time. Werner

McKinnon, who presents evidence that calls into question the viability of a strictly Jewish position on early Christian music.[35] Werner rarely makes reference to such works and certainly never in a positive light.

In Werner's discussion about the languages of prayer in the synagogues, he admits that

> In the Jewish Church at least three idioms were considered: Hebrew, Aramaic, and Greek. Hebrew was then, in the second century A.D., all but a dead language. Its use was confined to religious and legal discussions, to scholarly expositions, and to prayer... [I]n the apostolic and post-apostolic centuries Aramaic prayers were at least used as often as were Hebrew. This, however, does not hold true for all of Palestine; in Caesarea, for example, the language of the Synagogue was Greek... In the entire Diaspora the language of the synagogues was Greek.[36]

Here he freely acknowledges the predominance of the Greek language, and yet elsewhere denies that there could have been Greek influence of any significance on the music of the early Church. Werner further states:

> Moreover, we must not forget that there was a Greek synagogue in Jerusalem itself, where most of the prayers were recited in the Koine (Greek vernacular). These regional synagogues in Jerusalem contributed much to the uniformity of liturgical tradition throughout the Diaspora, since their authority was unquestionable.[37]

writes that there is evidence that 'seems to demonstrate the well-established function of a number of synagogues in Palestine at least a century before Christ. If certain scholars have more recently overlooked these facts in order to be "newsworthy", and claim that there is no evidence of a synagogue before the fall of the Temple (in 70 C.E.), they are either ignorant, or less than honest, or both' (p. 236 n. 119). If it is McKinnon who is the recipient of the latter criticism, which it seems to be, it is a bit puzzling, for I have seen no reference in his work to the idea that there was no synagogue, nor even well-established synagogues, before 70 CE, rather, that there is some question as to the role that music had in them until this time. His documentation implies that the synagogue remained a place for study of the Scriptures, but not for services that included a full liturgy with psalmody.

35. It should be noted that McKinnon's work addresses the argumentation or lack of documentation for a particular position, but I have not found instances of him attacking the person who represents the argument. This, however, is not to say that Werner may not be accurate in his criticism of McKinnon's selective evidence and possibly limited broader scope of knowledge of the subject.

36. Werner, *The Sacred Bridge*, I, p. 28.

37. Werner, *The Sacred Bridge*, I, p. 29.

He points out that

> In no way different was the attitude of the early Church toward the language of prayer. The Apostles used all three languages according to their respective environments, and if one interprets in a rationalistic manner I Cor. 14:16 ('...Wherefore let him that speaketh in an unknown tongue pray that he may interpret...'), one may regard the entire passage as a plea for the unlimited use of the Greek vernacular in worship. This principle was generally accepted...[38]

Here he freely recognizes the predominance of the Greek language in both the Jewish synagogue and the Christian Church, yet refuses to permit the possibility of its influence.

Again, Werner writes: 'The entire terminology of the Synagogue, whether referring to its dignitaries or to the conduct of the service, is familiarly understood in the New Testament; the original Hebrew terms were simply translated into Greek'.[39] But the wording of this sentence within which Werner places his premise that the Christian liturgy and ultimately its music are almost exclusively Jewish in origin is belied by the fact that the institution within which these forms were said to originate is itself called by a Greek term, 'synagogue'. Although this is well known by every New Testament scholar, and certainly by any person who attended the early synagogues, Werner ignores that even within the confines of a Jewish institution there is evidence that the Graeco-Roman environment had an influence on it. Interestingly, at this point Werner admits that 'Our knowledge of the Synagogue liturgy at the time of Jesus is very limited, since most of the descriptive sources originated in the following centuries'.[40] Later changes in the synagogue seem to have been implemented to counteract the creeping influence of Graeco-Roman culture, a sure acknowledgment of the intensity of its influence.

Without question, Werner brings his own unique perspicacity to the discussion of vocal music versus instrumental music in the early Church. He comments that the primacy of vocal music over instrumental music is so completely established that it is not often realized that this position was not a consistent one throughout the history of the early Christian Church. Equally, he points out that 'it would be a bold inference if we were to assume that there was no instrumental music in the

---

38. Werner, *The Sacred Bridge*, I, p. 29.
39. Werner, *The Sacred Bridge*, I, p. 2.
40. Werner, *The Sacred Bridge*, I, pp. 2-3.

liturgy of the Early Church. Quite to the contrary! Why all these outbursts, why all this frenzied searching for all kinds of reasons to justify
the prohibition of instrumental music, if there was actually no violation
of these injunctions?'[41] Werner cites two of the main reasons com
monly given for the Christian avoidance of instrumental music: first, its
association with pagan cults and, secondly, its association with Jewish
sacrificial rites. However, if the synagogue banished instrumental music
after the destruction of the Temple in 70 CE, and if the Christian Church
avoided use of them for the above-mentioned reasons, it is interesting
to note that Christian and Jewish practices coincided exactly, but for
entirely different reasons. Regarding musical instruments, Werner says,
'Rabbinic and patristic literature should be used only with great caution;
while the texts deal mainly with the music of the temple—in an ideal-
izing fashion—they were written at least 150 years after the temple's
destruction. Many, if not all, of them rely upon hearsay.'[42]

An example of the selective nature by which certain kinds of evidence can be presented and biases maintained can be seen in the work
of a respected scholar in the field of Jewish music, in particular, A. Sendrey. Sendrey discusses several of the early attestations to Jewish
instruments during the time of the early Christian Church, including
reference to a coin of Bar Kokhba. His explanation of the instruments
depicted on this coin is not entirely convincing, for he tries to show that
what looks like the aulos,[43] an instrument that is not viewed favourably
by the Jewish leaders,[44] is actually a pair of trumpets. He begins by

---

41. Werner, *The Sacred Bridge*, I, pp. 316-17 (317); it is a good point. However, see also his article, ' "If I Speak in the Tongues of Men...": St Paul's Attitude
to Music', *Journal of the American Musicological Society* 13 (1960), pp. 18-23, in
which he argues that it is clearly evident that Paul despised musical instruments; I
find his arguments unconvincing on this point, but intriguing, nonetheless.

42. E. Werner, 'Musical Instruments', *IDB*, III, pp. 469-76 (470).

43. For description and discussion of the aulos, a reedpipe or oboe that is played
in pairs, see J.W. McKinnon and R. Anderson, 'Aulos', in S. Sadie (ed.), *The New
Grove Dictionary of Musical Instruments* (2 vols.; London: Macmillan, 1984), I,
pp. 85-87; and S. Michaelides, 'Aulos', in *idem*, *The Music of Ancient Greece: An
Encyclopaedia* (London: Faber & Faber, 1978), pp. 42-46.

44. See Werner, ' "If I Speak in the Tongues of Men..." ', p. 19: 'The rabbis
held a particularly low opinion of certain instruments: the *halil* (a primitive clarinet,
or a kind of αὐλός)'. For discussion of the aulos in relation to the New Testament
church at Corinth, see W.J. Porter, 'λαλέω: A Word about Women, Music and Sen-
suality in the Early Church', in M.A. Hayes, W.J. Porter and D. Tombs (eds.),

saying that the coin 'shows a pair of trumpets; they are designed in such a shortened and clumsy fashion that it is somewhat difficult to reconstruct their original shape'. He continues,

> Nevertheless, we maintain that they are reproductions of the sacred trumpets of the Temple. In these numismatic designs the exact shape of the depicted instruments was only of a secondary importance; the main objective must have been a patriotic demonstration, on coins issued by the victorious national hero, of a sacred symbol of the Jewish religion. The oboe (*halil*) was far from having the same symbolic meaning for the Jews as the *hazozerot* [sacred trumpets], the use of which was instituted by the commandment of the Lord Himself (Num. 10:2)... The fact that on the coins *two* instruments are represented, is an unmistakable sign that they are the sacred trumpets.[45]

Sendrey briefly refers to Curt Sachs, mentioning but downplaying that Sachs thinks that they do not represent trumpets, but oboes.[46] Sachs's own words are:

> Among the Jewish coins stamped during Bar Kokba's revolt against Emperor Hadrian (132–135 A.D.), some show pairs of wind instruments. Numismaticians call them trumpets, or even trombones; but this is incorrect. The stout shape, the reedlike top, the disk that supports the lips, and the bell are all features of the modern Arabian oboe *zamr* and its relatives. Consequently, this oboe existed in Jewish Palestine at the beginning of the second century A.D.

What the coin seems to represent, therefore, is not the sacred trumpets that Sendrey would like them to represent, but more likely that ubiquitous instrument with the questionable reputation, the Greek-named 'aulos'.[47]

The difficulty that Sendrey has in accepting that something other than the sacred trumpets could be represented on these coins, and the

Religion and Sexuality (RILP, 4; Studies in Theology and Sexuality, 2; Sheffield: Sheffield Academic Press, 1998), pp. 101-124.

45. Sendrey, *Music in Ancient Israel*, pp. 64-65.

46. C. Sachs, *The History of Musical Instruments* (New York: W.W. Norton, 1940; London: J.M. Dent & Sons, 1942), p. 120; see also p. 248.

47. Having referred to the instrument by its Greek name, however, is not to suggest that the Jewish musical tradition does not have its own early reference to a similar instrument. Sendrey includes in his own book a reference to (and photograph of) a bronze figurine (c. 1300–1200 BCE) of a Jewish flute-girl playing a double oboe (Sendrey, *Music in Ancient Israel*, p. 310 and illustration no. 36, p. 68).

assumption that he makes in determining that they 'must be' the sacred instruments, may call into question other statements and assumptions in this discussion. More significantly, it shows the nature of the problem of determining facts when prior assumptions are in place. Some of these same tendencies have been seen in the arguments of Werner, who, although he admits to the predominance of the Greek language in the synagogue and further admits that little is known of the liturgy of the synagogue in the first few centuries and little of the Jewish music, still asserts the dominance of Jewish influence on early Christian music. He seems to have almost single-handedly taken upon himself to engage in a battle of Judaism over Hellenism, not entirely unlike the one he describes in his article, 'The Conflict between Hellenism and Judaism in the Music of the Early Christian Church'. Few scholars have made such an impact upon the study of Jewish origins of early Christian music, but perhaps no one has seen it so clearly as a battle, either. The question of what comprised the music of the early Church is still open to dispute; perhaps more questionable are some of the assertions or assumptions made by Werner in particular, as well as some others who hold the same positions, in his aggressive posture to influence the view we have of early Christian music.

4. *Is Early Christian Music Graeco-Roman?*

As I have mentioned in the section above, several recent scholars have opposed the idea that there has simply been an ongoing tradition from Jewish synagogue to Christian Church. In James McKinnon's research into the early rabbinical writings and other contemporaneous literature, he, for instance, found no evidence to support the idea that instruments were banned in the synagogue. However, he similarly found no positive information to suggest that musical instruments were ever employed in the ancient synagogue. As a result of his research, he further concluded that the central element of the service, the simple declamation of Scripture, had no call for the use of instruments in any case.[48] In other research into the perspectives of the Church Fathers, McKinnon clearly shows the prejudice that is evident in someone such as John Chrysostom, but also shows that too much has been made of this in some ways.

48. J. McKinnon, 'The Exclusion of Musical Instruments from the Ancient Synagogue', *Proceedings of the Royal Musical Association* 106 (1979–80), pp. 77-87.

For instance, he introduces the example of Chrysostom's polemic against musical instruments that shows an 'extravagant manner' of expression: 'John Chrysostom...refers to musical instruments along with dancing and obscene songs as the "devil's garbage", and on another occasion declares that, "Where the aulos is, there, by no means, is Christ"'.[49] However, regarding the relationship of musical instruments to singing, McKinnon points out that

> Music historians have tended to assume that there is a direct connection, that is, that ecclesiastical authorities consciously strove to maintain their music free from incursion of musical instruments. There is little evidence of this in the sources however. What one observes is that there are two separate phenomena: a consistent condemnation of instruments in the contexts cited above, and an ecclesiastical psalmody obviously free of instrumental involvement... The truth remains that the polemic against musical instruments and the vocal performance of early Christian psalmody were—for whatever reasons—unrelated in the minds of the church fathers.[50]

McKinnon's approach to the literature is to raise questions in areas that are considered certainties by others. This is seen in his opinion that, in regard to Christianity, the destruction of the Temple happened too late to have influenced synagogal music and hence have any real bearing on the early history of Christian music, although there would have been a parallel in the history of both the music of Judaism and Christianity. He suggests that by the end of antiquity, there would have been two equal factors in the music of the Christian Church: 'the Hebraic inheritance of psalmody and the Hellenic inheritance of musical theory'.[51]

In 1984, J.A. Smith published an article in which he raised the prior question to the one that asks if there was instrumental accompaniment to the singing in the synagogue, that is, was there *singing* in the ancient synagogue? And if not, is there any reason to assume that the music of the early Church was simply an extension of that of the synagogue? Smith speaks disparagingly of the scholar who 'stretches historical credibility to absurd limits by reading back elements of fourth-century

---

49. McKinnon (ed.), *Music in Early Christian Literature*, p. 1.

50. McKinnon (ed.), *Music in Early Christian Literature*, p. 3.

51. J. McKinnon, 'Early Western Civilization', in *idem* (ed.), *Antiquity and the Middle Ages: From Ancient Greece to the 15th Century* (Man and Music; Basingstoke, Hants: Macmillan, 1990), pp. 1-44, esp. pp. 1-12 (12).

Christian practice into the first century and then assuming their synagogal origin'.[52] He states: 'The result of such speculative retrojection... has been to give the false impression that the first-century synagogue service was more highly developed than the evidence from the contemporary sources suggests'.[53] Smith points out that there have been recent studies, namely that of McKinnon, that call into question the long-held assumption that there was singing in the ancient synagogue, and that there was any formal psalmody in the first-century synagogue. McKinnon writes that the notion that 'psalmody flourished in the ancient synagogue is a notion created primarily by Christian liturgical and musical historians',[54] and that there is only one group of scholars who have 'failed to claim an important role for psalmody in the ancient synagogue: Jewish liturgical historians. They have little to say on the matter for the simple reason that the primary sources provide no occasion to discuss it.'[55] P.F. Bradshaw, also, says that

> Liturgical and musical historians have tended to assert confidently that psalmody was a standard part of the early synagogue... There is, however, an almost total lack of documentary evidence for the inclusion of psalms in synagogue worship. The Mishnah lists a psalm for each of the seven days of the week (24, 48, 82, 94, 81, 93, 92) which was sung by the Levites at the Temple sacrifices (*Tamid* 7.4), and at the important festivals the *Hallel* (Pss. 113-118) accompanied the sacrifices. But while the *Hallel* seems to have been taken over into the domestic Passover meal at an early date, and apparently also into the festal synagogue liturgy, the first mention of the adoption of the daily psalms in the synagogue is not until the eighth century.[56]

At this juncture, McKinnon's investigation reminds us that, according to Jewish writings, the Hallel was not sung, as is often thought, but it was recited.[57]

---

52. J.A. Smith, 'Ancient Synagogue', p. 2.

53. J.A. Smith, 'Ancient Synagogue', p. 2.

54. McKinnon, 'Question of Psalmody', p. 180.

55. McKinnon, 'Question of Psalmody', p. 182. But also see W.S. Smith, *Musical Aspects*, p. 10, who writes: 'The convertible usage of "sing" and "say" is not uncommon to the O.T', and that the 'same lack of precision' can be found in dealing with the New Testament.

56. Bradshaw, *Search for the Origins*, pp. 22-23. See also McKinnon (ed.), *Music in Early Christian Literature*, who presents the texts in chronological order.

57. McKinnon, 'Question of Psalmody', pp. 184-85. In his 'Early Western Civilization', he suggests that in 'Judaism the psalmody that accompanied sacrifice

It is noteworthy that these three scholars are not suggesting that early Christian music was not influenced by Jewish culture and religious practice, but are calling into question assumptions that have made it into the mainstream of current thinking, assumptions that are possibly unfounded. An example of these kinds of assumptions can be seen in the article on 'Music' in *The Anchor Bible Dictionary*, for if even *some* of the observations of the above-mentioned scholars are accurate, this article would need to be reassessed as accurately representing the state of the discussion. While such articles do not necessarily claim to represent original research, they are often used as the source of basic information for biblical scholars who work in related areas, but who are not necessarily specialists in music or liturgy. Opinions that may be totally unfounded are thus introduced into the mainstream of the subject. In the article mentioned, the writer makes statements such as (1) 'It was in the synagogue, however, that music continued to flourish and serve as an emotional and didactic aid to the maintenance of Judaism', (2) 'the writers of the NT and the founders of the new Christian movement very likely adopted what they knew of synagogue music to their own worship', and (3) 'The borrowing from synagogue worship of both hymn and chorus singing added the emotional, communal feeling needed to help build the new movement'.[58] While these statements are obviously couched in tentative language, there is some question whether they can be substantiated at all. Nonetheless, they seem to represent a common (mis?)perception of music in the New Testament.

However, at the beginning of the twentieth century, there were the opposite kinds of assumptions being made to those just cited. For instance, in the first volume of *The Oxford History of Music* (1901), H.E. Wooldridge made the kind of statement that could be seen to justify Werner's aggressive stance. Wooldridge spoke of 'expecting' the music of the Christian ritual to resemble Graeco-Roman practice and immediately followed these words with the statement: 'we find these

---

in the late Temple was music in the fullest sense, but the psalms recited in the synagogues, and in the early Christian gatherings as well, were more scripture than song. They were no doubt recited with some sort of cantillation, but so was all scripture; it would take several centuries in each of the religions before psalmody became music in a selfconscious sense' (p. 10). Cf. again W.S. Smith, *Musical Aspects*, p. 10 n. 38.

58. V.H. Matthews, 'Music in the Bible', *ABD*, IV, p. 934.

expectations fully justified'.[59] If one were to use Wooldridge's statement as the gauge for the general state of the discussion, it would seem that there was little investigation into anything besides a Graeco-Roman perspective in the late nineteenth century and the early part of the twentieth century. When the volume was published in 1901, Grenfell's and Hunt's edition of the earliest Christian hymn, *P. Oxy.* 1786, published in 1922, was still some years away. As it is still the earliest known fragment of a Christian hymn with musical notation,[60] it is difficult to know what material would have constituted a study of the music of the early Christian Church to justify Wooldridge's remarks.

Here, again, it must be pointed out that Werner himself participates in the same kind of presentation but from the opposite stance. For instance, in his 13-page article on 'Music' in *The Interpreter's Dictionary of the Bible*, one-half of one page deals with how the music of the New Testament has fused with Hellenistic music, and even under that heading the bulk of the material is an argument for the Semitic influence seen in the music; in his bibliography, there is little mention of those works that would represent a Graeco-Roman influence on this music.[61] While obviously much discussion has taken place about the music of the Jewish synagogue and its influence on the early Christian Church, with advocates of the Jewish heritage not infrequently citing evidence of synagogal practice as an indication of the Jewish influence, it must be acknowledged, as mentioned earlier, that the very fact that the word for these Jewish gathering-places is Greek in origin—'synagogue'—suggests an environment where boundaries are not as distinct as many would like them to be, nor influences as definite as their various proponents might wish to present them. There can be little doubt that there were Hellenistic or Graeco-Roman influences on both the Jewish synagogue and the early Christian Church, as well as Jewish influences.

New Testament 'hymns' also provoke discussion along these lines. Whether they were actually hymns to be sung is not part of my discussion in this paper, but the hymn-like or poetic nature of some of these

---

59. H.E. Wooldridge, *The Oxford History of Music.* I. *The Polyphonic Period. Part I: Method of Musical Art, 330–1330* (Oxford: Clarendon Press, 1901), p. 25.

60. B.P. Grenfell and A.S. Hunt, 'Christian Hymn with Musical Notation', in *The Oxyrhynchus Papyri*, XV (Egypt Exploration Society Graeco-Roman Memoirs; London: Egypt Exploration Society, 1922), no. 1786, pp. 21-25.

61. Werner, 'Music', p. 469.

passages allows for a brief inclusion of them here. R.P. Martin holds to the common position that the early Church took over from the Temple and synagogue the use of hymns and psalms.[62] However, he also refers to Jewish-Christian fragments of hymnic praise in 1 Tim. 1.17 and identifies a mix of influences here: the phrase 'King of the ages' he describes as an exact phrase used at Jewish table prayers and in synagogue praise, but 'for ever and ever' as a Greek phrase.[63] Both phrases are significant in the terminology of the Christian Church and are still used in this context. J. Jeremias refers to the latter as 'a Greek expression which helps to anchor the doxology of 1 Timothy in the Church life of some Greek-speaking Hebrew Christian community',[64] again an acknowledgment of a confluence of cultures. Kraeling and Mowry, in their discussion of the 'confessional hymn' in 1 Tim. 3.16, say that they think the structure is oriental (and they think the music must have been oriental), but admit that the parallelism is Hellenistic in its rhetorical construction.[65] While those who might argue for an Aramaic background for texts such as these—based apparently on the ease with which they can be re-translated into Aramaic, although constructing a hypothetical Aramaic text from which to work seems to introduce numerous dubious factors and difficulties—also seem to argue for the strictly Jewish influence on the music, there is an undeniable tendency in these (potentially) musical texts to have characteristics that are also Hellenistic. Here one can see the difficulty in maintaining that a single influence shaped the music of early Christianity. Similarly, Kraeling and Mowry discuss the nature of the hymn in Phil. 2.6-11, and suggest that the construction is completely remote from Jewish psalmody; the text, which is a hymn to Christ, is entirely out of keeping with Jewish tradition, but the rhythm is not quantitative but accentual, suggesting an oriental melody and not a Greek mode.[66] Whether they are right or wrong, they acknowledge that the evidence does not point to a single pure tradition, but to a mix of traditions, Jewish and non-Jewish. To

---

62. Martin, *Worship in the Early Church*, p. 45.

63. Martin, *Worship in the Early Church*, p. 45.

64. J. Jeremias, *Die Briefe an Timotheus und Titus* (Göttingen: Vandenhoeck & Ruprecht, 1953), p. 13, cited in translation in Martin, *Worship in the Early Church*, p. 46.

65. C.H. Kraeling and L. Mowry, 'Music in the Bible', in Wellesz (ed.), *Ancient and Oriental Music*, pp. 283-312 (308).

66. Kraeling and Mowry, 'Music in the Bible', p. 309.

ignore one or the other is to ignore a great number of important details and facts.

5. *Is the Earliest Notated Christian Hymn Jewish or Graeco-Roman?*

One final example is *P. Oxy.* 1786, which continues to be one of the most fascinating documents for the study of music in the early centuries of the Christian Church. Greek hymns before the time of Christ were commonly known, being sung to a god or gods, but this is the first known hymn with musical notation to have reference to the Christ of Christianity.[67] The *P. Oxy.* 1786 hymn dates from the late third century. M.L. West, dealing specifically with this document, says:

> This hymn...is perhaps the latest in date of the known texts recorded in the ancient Greek notation. At the same time it is by a considerable interval the oldest surviving example of music used in Christian worship. It is therefore a matter of some interest to determine, if possible, to what musical tradition it belongs... Egon Wellesz...denied that the music of the hymn was of genuinely Greek character, and stated decisively that it represented a new ecclesiastical music modelled on patterns deriving from Jewish or Syriac hymnody. He thought that the hymn might even be a translation from a Jewish or Syriac original.[68]

West argues that Wellesz's position is mistaken 'and that those who see the hymn as eminently a product of Greek tradition are on altogether stronger ground'.[69] Werner writes that

> Hellenistic chant, as we know from its remnants, limited itself to a strictly syllabic relation of word and tone. Thus, one syllable corresponded to one and only one tone, a principle which naturally excludes any melismatic nonsyllabic motifs. The Oxyrhynchus Hymn breaks with

---

67. Music at the time of Christ is thought by many to have consisted mainly of unaccompanied melody, which has later come to be known as plainsong or plainchant. Three styles characterized this vocal music: (1) syllabic, usually with one note per syllable; (2) neumatic or group, with two or three notes per syllable; and (3) melismatic, with more notes or groups of notes per syllable. Ulrich and Pisk, *History of Music and Musical Style*, p. 27.

68. M.L. West, 'Analecta Musica', *ZPE* 92 (1992), pp. 1-54 (47). One of Wellesz's statements along this line is in E. Wellesz, 'The Interpretation of Plainchant', *Music & Letters* 44 (1963), pp. 343-49 (347), where he speaks of 'Christian chant, which is of Syro-Palestinian origin and was in no way connected with Greek or Roman music'.

69. West, 'Analecta Musica', p. 47.

this principle, especially in the four Amens, which are placed at the end of verses. Thus, the Semitic element of so-called 'punctuating melismata' has entered into a basically Hellenistic structure. A Hebrew heritage, the melismatic formulas, is recognizable in a hymn of the Gentile church...[70]

Werner's statement at this point is not an unreasonable proposal; however, A.W.J. Holleman, following Werner, believes that the papyrus was simply a failed exercise in applying Greek musical notation to an already existing hymn. He says that the papyrus is 'a demonstration of the inadequacy, and at least as regards the rhythmical signs, of the fundamental error of using the existing Greek notation for Christian music'.[71] Again, however, it must be added that there is no documentation for the early notation of Jewish music at this time, the earliest documents coming from around the tenth century CE.

West says, 'The fact that the hymn is expertly recorded in the Greek notation itself suggests a composer with a Greek musical education, which had probably included the study of Mesomedes's works. He is a Christian, but his religious outlook may have been formed in a syncretistic atmosphere...'[72] West further argues the Graeco-Roman relationship of this fragment of music based on the poet's use of a Homeric expression, adapted by Callimachus to Zeus, later used by Clement and Origen to apply to the Christian God.[73] He says, 'It was this Alexandrian confluence of Christian doctrine with Hellenic culture that put the title at our hymnodist's disposal. The continuing influence of Greek poetic tradition betrays itself' in his use of forms of the words.[74]

West argues that scholars who claim that the music stems from oriental principles of composition, both downplay the anapaestic character of the music and elevate the fact that a syllable is set to two or three notes.[75] West points out that there are several texts

70. Werner, 'Music', pp. 467-68.

71. A.W.J. Holleman, 'The Oxyrhynchus Papyrus 1786 and the Relationship between Ancient Greek and Early Christian Music', *VC* 26 (1972), pp. 1-17 (11).

72. West, 'Analecta Musica', p. 50. For brief introductory discussion on Mesomedes, see H. Leichtentritt, *Music, History, and Ideas* (Cambridge, MA: Harvard University Press, 1938), pp. 20-21.

73. The reconstructed title to which West refers is δωτὴρ μόνος πάντων ἀγαθῶν.

74. West, 'Analecta Musica', pp. 50-51.

75. West, 'Analecta Musica', p. 52.

from the Roman period such as the Oslo and Michigan papyri...and the Oxyrhynchus papyri 2436...and 3161, which show that Greek music in the second and third centuries was becoming increasingly florid. If this tendency is slightly more developed in the Christian hymn than in the other texts, it is no more so than might be expected in view of the hymn's date. Individually the melisms it contains are no more extravagant than those seen in the Michigan papyrus, which is dated to the second century.[76]

Elsewhere, he similarly states: 'I can see no feature of the music that cannot be illustrated from the foregoing documents of the art as it existed in the second- and third-century Empire. It is only a little further along the path towards ever greater ornament, as might be expected from its date.'[77]

West therefore refutes the assertion of Wellesz that, because the music consists of a series of melodic formulas, which Wellesz states are unknown in Greek music, it must be from the Middle East. West responds that in fact melodic formulas were well known in Greek music, as evidenced by several musical fragments, and that knowledge of the melodies of the Middle East is not nearly as well documented. In most cases where there is any kind of documentation, it is by reconstructed melodies from 'widely separated Jewish communities in the modern era'.[78] Rather than simply asserting a single line of influence, however, West writes that 'whatever Byzantine ecclesiastical music may have owed to liturgical tradition going back to the Primitive Church (and ultimately to Jewish chant), there is nothing implausible in its also owing something to earlier Greek music'.[79] This is the point at which many biblical scholars depart, for at present it seems—according to my reading of the state of the discussion—that those who argue for a

76. West, 'Analecta Musica', p. 52.
77. M.L. West, *Ancient Greek Music* (Oxford: Clarendon Press, 1992), p. 325.
78. West, 'Analecta Musica', p. 52.
79. West, 'Analecta Musica', p. 53. G. Reese (*Music in the Middle Ages* [London: J.M. Dent, 1941 (1940)]) writes that the 'famous Oxyrhynchos hymn... has been held to show traits linking Christian Chant with the music of Greek paganism, both through its stylistic features and through the Greek notation in which it survives' (p. 115), and he admits that the 'rarity of ancient melodies makes it impossible to determine whether the Hebrew influence or the Greco-Roman was the stronger', and 'that both influences were at work' (p. 115, but see all of pp. 114-15 and n. 4). His position here supports the one that is most tenable—that both perspectives must be represented.

Jewish influence feel compelled to argue that it is an exclusive influence, while those who argue for a Graeco-Roman influence acknowledge that there are at least these two significant influences on the music of the early Church, that is, both Jewish and Graeco-Roman. W.S. Smith's balanced conclusion is that there is 'one obvious and certain lesson to be learned from the extant data—the fact of variety'.[80] The clear picture seems to be that there is no clear picture; instead, there is an intermingling of cultural and religious influences on the music of the early Christian Church.

6. *Conclusion*

In looking at the general state of the research into whether the music of the early Church was Jewish or Graeco-Roman, there does seem to be a sense of misguided effort, and possibly some lack of genuine inquiry. This is particularly apparent on the part of those who either adamantly argue for or unquestioningly assume a single influence on early Christian music. From my analysis of the research into this subject, it seems that few scholars accept the less clearly defined categories of multiple influences; the majority are not willing to concede that overlapping forces were at work on this aspect of the early Church. Some scholars admit at one point that there was more than one force shaping the music, but then ignore those statements when it is convenient to do so. After looking at these various examples, I think it would be an overstatement to say that there is a genuine battle over the canon of musical texts that comprise early Christian music and the dominant influences that shaped it, but it would not be an overstatement to say that the direction of the discussion seems to be aimed more at other scholars than at their arguments. There is resistance to acknowledging multiple influences, perhaps inversely proportionate to the resistance that Werner felt in the past towards Jewish influences and Jewish scholarship. This field of study is highly complex, enough to require every informed contribution and contributor. I think it is clear that both Jewish and Graeco-Roman culture had an influence on the music of the early Christian Church, which is one of the reasons that its study has been so difficult—one must be expert in many areas at once. Certainly Eric Werner has raised the level of inquiry; he has both engaged in and

80. W.S. Smith, *Musical Aspects*, p. 58.

called for comprehensive comparative approaches that have revolutionized the discipline. However, in spite of a desire on the parts of some to
find a true lineage in one direction or another, it seems that in order for
scholarship in this area to really move forward, biblical scholars,
musicologists, historians and liturgists must accept that the relationship
of at least these two cultures—Jewish and Graeco-Roman—resulted in
a synthesis that was neither exactly one culture nor the other, but
incorporated aspects of both in a new approach to music that corresponded to the new faith of Christianity itself.

JEWS AND CHRISTIANS IN ANTIOCH AT THE END OF THE FOURTH CENTURY

Pieter W. van der Horst

In this short chapter I want to focus on a brief but significant period in the history of Jewish–Christian relationships. It deals with the situation in Antioch (in Syria) in the eighth decade of the fourth century. It happens to be the case that, from that decade, we possess two documents from Antioch; each sheds light on the relations between the large Jewish and Christian communities in that city, but in a very different way. The most interesting aspect of these documents is that they demonstrate the strong influence of Judaism upon Christianity in this city, and the consequential blurring of the distinction between the two religions in the minds of a great many believers.

Clear evidence of this is, first, the eight notorious homilies against the Jews by John Chrysostom in the year 386/387.[1] This John was a Christian scholar who lived c. 347–407 CE. He was ordained priest in 386 in Antioch by Bishop Flavian, who appointed him to devote special attention to preaching (his ability in this was so great that it earned him the nickname Chrysostom, 'the one with the golden mouth'). His

---

1. The text can be found in *PG*, XLVIII, cols. 843-942. See further R.L. Wilken, *John Chrysostom and the Jews: Rhetoric and Reality in the Late 4th Century* (Berkeley: University of California Press, 1983), still the best study of the subject in English; cf. also W.A. Meeks and R.L. Wilken, *Jews and Christians in Antioch in the First Four Centuries of the Common Era* (Missoula, MT: Scholars Press, 1978), pp. 83-126. R. Brändle, 'Christen und Juden in Antiochien in den Jahren 386/87: Ein Beitrag zur Geschichte altkirchlicher Judenfeindschaft', *Judaica* 43 (1987), pp. 142-60, has a useful bibliography. See now especially R. Brändle and V. Jegher-Bucher, *Johannes Chrysostomus: Acht Reden gegen Juden* (Stuttgart: Hiersemann Verlag, 1995), which contains a German translation with an excellent introduction and commentary.

preaching was directed especially to the instruction and moral reformation of the nominally Christian society of his day. In the eight long sermons under consideration (the *Homilies*), delivered six months after his ordination, we hear Chrysostom's vehement invectives against Christians who go to the synagogue on sabbath and on Jewish high holidays, who say Jewish prayers, who undergo the Jewish rite of circumcision, who celebrate Jewish Pesach, who keep Jewish food laws, who fast together with the Jews on the Day of Atonement, etc. These were not marginal renegades who came to church only infrequently, rather 'From John's comments, they appear to be regular members of his congregation who thought they could remain members of the Church while observing Jewish rites and customs'.[2] In their mind that was not contradictory; Paul's distinction between law and grace did not constitute a problem for them. But Chrysostom tries to dissuade his parishioners from keeping all these practices by a variety of rhetorical means, the most important of which is blackening the Jews and their synagogal meetings.

Let me give just a few examples of his terminology and imagery.[3] First, Judaism as a dangerous disease:

> Another more terrible sickness beckons and our tongue must be turned to heal a disease which is flourishing in the body of the church... What is this sickness? The festivals of the wretched and miserable Jews which follow one after another—Trumpets, Booths, the Fasts[4]—are about to take place. And many who belong to us and say that they believe in our teaching attend their festivals and even share in their celebrations and join in their fasts. It is this evil practice that I now wish to drive from the church... If those who are sick with Judaism are not healed now, when the Jewish festivals are near, I am afraid that some, out of misguided habit and gross ignorance, will share in their transgressions (*Hom.* 1).

2. Wilken, *John Chrysostom and the Jews*, pp. 75-76.

3. The examples are taken from Wilken, *John Chrysostom and the Jews*, pp. 116-23. An English translation of all eight homilies can be found in P.W. Harkins, *Saint John Chrysostom: Discourses against Judaizing Christians* (The Fathers of the Church: A New Translation, 68; Washington: Catholic University of America Press, 1979).

4. Most probably Rosh ha-Shana (New Year), Sukkot (Feast of Tabernacles), and Yom Kippur (Day of Atonement). The three feasts were all celebrated within a month of each other (usually September–October).

Secondly, the Jews as ravenous wolves:

> Those sorry Jews, most miserable of all men, are about to hold a fast and it is necessary to protect the flock of Christ. As long as a wild beast is not causing trouble, shepherds lie down under an oak tree or a pine to play the flute, allowing the sheep to graze wherever they want. But when they realize that *wolves* are about to attack, they immediately throw down their flute, grab their sling, lay aside the shepherd's pipe, arm themselves with clubs and stones, and stand before the flock shouting with a loud and booming voice... So also we, in the days just past, were frolicking about in the exegesis of the Scriptures as in a meadow not touching on anything contentious because no one was troubling us. But since today the Jews, who are more troublesome than any wolves, are about to encircle our sheep, it is necessary to arm ourselves for battle so that none of our sheep become prey to wild beasts (*Hom.* 4).

The venom of this rhetoric becomes all the more apparent when we realize that it suggests that the Jews were active in persuading Christians to abandon the church and join the synagogue, whereas it is most probable that in reality it was the Christians themselves who were willingly seeking contact with the synagogal community. Chrysostom's rhetoric 'is intended to picture the Jews in the worst possible light to frighten Christians so that they will not attend the synagogue'.[5] The same motive underlies Chrysostom's depiction of the Jewish character as concerned with 'rapacity, greed, betrayal of the poor, thefts, and keeping of brothels'.[6]

What all this makes abundantly clear is that, as late as the final decades of the fourth century, many Christians in the city of Antioch were being strongly attracted by Judaism. If the Jews were painted so black, it was because they appeared not sufficiently unattractive to too many Christians. 'The most compelling reason for anti-Semitism was the religious vitality of Judaism.'[7] How strong this vitality was in Asia Minor and Syria is very much evident from several canons of the council of Laodicea (Phrygia) which was held not long before Chrysostom's sermons, somewhere in the third quarter of the fourth century.[8]

5.   Wilken, *John Chrysostom and the Jews*, p. 119.
6.   All quotations are from various parts of *Hom.* 1 and 4.
7.   M. Simon, *Verus Israel: A Study of the Relations between Christians and Jews in the Roman Empire (AD 135–425)* (Oxford: Oxford University Press, 1986), p. 232. Cf. also E.M. Smallwood, *The Jews Under Roman Rule* (SJLA, 20; Leiden: E.J. Brill, 1976), p. 508.
8.   The exact date of this synod is unknown, though most scholars seem

In canon 29 it is stated: 'It is forbidden that Christians live like Jews (*joudaïzein*) and rest on sabbath; they should work on that day. They should prefer the Lord's day to rest on, if possible, since they are Christians. If they turn out to be judaizers, let them be accursed (*anathema*) by Christ.' Canon 38 runs as follows: 'It is forbidden to take unleavened bread from the Jews or to participate in their godless acts'. Canon 37 forbids any participation in the festivals of the Jews or heretics, and canon 36 warns the clergy against making *phylakteria*, which are probably *tefillin* (that is, the small boxes containing scriptural verses bound on forehead and arm during Jewish prayers), which were also used as magical apotropaic amulets.[9] These canons can only be explained on the assumption that keeping the sabbath, celebrating Pesach and other Jewish religious festivals, and so on, were not marginal events, but were frequently occurring and tenacious phenomena among Christians in Asia Minor and elsewhere in the second half of the fourth century. John Chrysostom's (and also the Syrian Church Father Aphraat's)[10] testimonies make it highly probable that this assumption is correct. Only the fact that Judaism continued to make itself strongly felt and to be effectively influential throughout the first five centuries of our era makes it explicable that during these centuries there was a persistent tradition of judaizing in the church which defied all the anathemas of the church authorities. Marcel Simon put it well: 'The anti-Jewish bias of official ecclesiastical circles was counterbalanced by equally marked pro-Jewish sentiments among the laity and among some of the clergy too. Or rather, it is the existence of the pro-Jewish sentiments among the laity that is the real explanation of Christian anti-Semitism.'[11]

---

inclined to date this meeting to the sixth decade of the fourth century. The text of the canons can be found in E.J. Jonkers, *Acta et symbola conciliorum quae saeculo quarto habita sunt* (Textus minores, 19; Leiden: E.J. Brill, 1954), pp. 86-96.

9.   On the great reputation of Jewish magic in antiquity, see Simon, *Verus Israel*, pp. 339-68, esp. p. 361 on the magical use of phylacteries/tefillin. Some scholars regard also canon 35 (against *angelolatreia*) as directed against judaizing practice.

10.   On Aphraat, see J. Neusner, *Judaism, Christianity, and Zoroastrianism in Talmudic Babylonia* (Lanham, MD: University Press of America, 1986), pp. 199-228.

11.   Simon, *Verus Israel*, p. 232.

We can only guess at the causes or the reasons for the attraction which Judaism exercised upon both pagan and Christian minds and for the strength of its influence.[12] That Jews could present their religion as an enlightened philosophy with lofty ethics will certainly have made Judaism one of the more attractive of the Eastern cults in the Roman Empire. The rather detailed code of behaviour that Scripture and halakha contained must have been envisioned as a stabilizing factor in life by a good many people. The colourful and vivid synagogue services were to many a much more pleasant spectacle than the often lengthy and rather dull Christian services.[13] Also, the Jewish charitable institutions will have been a source of attraction. For many Christians, the argument that the commandments in the Torah were, after all, God's words may have carried more weight than the often tortuous argumentations to the effect that God had abolished his own law. For many pagans and Christians, the antiquity of Judaism was a very important factor—we should not forget that throughout antiquity it was an unquestioned axiom that the oldest is the best, including religious matters.[14] Be that as it may, not only in Asia Minor and Syria but also in the rest of the Empire, Judaism and Christianity struggled with one another over the pagan soul. In the practical sphere, the two religions fought over the pagan clientele that Judaism had built up for itself and whose attention the Church tried to gain.

John Chrysostom's vituperative and vitriolic sermons against judaizing Christians and Jews eloquently testify to this struggle, but we have to bear in mind that they had a nefarious *Wirkungsgeschichte*: they fomented hatred against Jews and Judaism in an unprecedented manner. 'They are not only a compendium of many of the themes that emerged in the Christian polemic against Judaism, but have also had an enormous influence on later Christian attitudes towards the Jews.'[15]

---

12. For an extensive discussion of the topic of 'The Attractions of the Jews', see L.H. Feldman, *Jew and Gentile in the Ancient World* (Princeton, NJ: Princeton University Press, 1993), pp. 177-287. Wilken, *John Chrysostom and the Jews*, pp. 66-94, also deals with this topic.

13. See W. Kinzig, '"Non-Separation": Closeness and Co-operation between Jews and Christians in the Fourth Century', *VC* 45 (1991), pp. 27-53 (39).

14. See P.W. van der Horst, 'Plato's Fear as a Topic in Early Christian Apologetics', *Journal of Early Christian Studies* 6 (1998), pp. 1-14.

15. Wilken, *John Chrysostom and the Jews*, p. xv.

The *Apostolic Constitutions* is another important document written shortly after 380 in Antioch, which also happens to be the nearest contemporary document to the homilies of Chrysostom that we have. The *Apostolic Constitutions* is a collection of materials on ecclesiastical law that is widely believed to have been compiled in Syria in the two final decades of the fourth century, probably by the same (semi-)Arian author who interpolated the letters of Ignatius of Antioch and wrote the Arian commentary on Job.[16] Its potential relevance for the study of Chrysostom's homilies is hardly taken into account in the modern literature on Chrysostom's sermons. Chrysostom's main point of criticism of his own religious flock is that many Christians attend services in the synagogues of Antioch, pray the Jewish prayers, and so on, for which he threatens his co-religionists with the worst possible consequences. What the *Apostolic Constitutions* demonstrate is that in the same period, probably in one of the other churches of Antioch,[17] a very different strategy was adopted: no terrible threats, but a tactical move to obviate the needs of these so-called judaizers by incorporating elements of the synagogal liturgy into the the liturgy of the church. To be sure, the anonymous author of this document also urged Christians to avoid Jewish festivals and dissuaded even bishops and presbyters to join the Jews in their fasts and feasts (*Apost. Const.* 8.47.70; cf. 2.61, 5.17)! But in book 7 of the *Apostolic Constitutions* we find a set of six (out of seven) originally Jewish prayers which, after having undergone some christianizing editing, were taken over from the synagogal prayer book (even though the tendency of the *Apostolic Constitutions* as a whole is not at all pro-Jewish). These prayers are demonstrably Greek versions

16. The best recent discussion of the *Apostolic Constitutions* is the almost 200 pages of introduction to the SC edition by M. Metzger, *Les constitutions apostoliques* (3 vols.; SC; Paris: Cerf, 1985–87), I, pp. 13-93, and II, pp. 10-110. Volume 3 contains text and French translation of books 7 and 8 into which the prayer texts under discussion have been incorporated. See further B. Steimer, *Vertex Traditionis: Die Gattung der altchristlichen Kirchenordnungen* (Berlin: W. de Gruyter, 1992), pp. 114-33; E.M. Synek, *'Dieses Gesetz ist gut, heilig, es zwingt nicht...': Zum Gesetzesbegriff der Apostolischen Konstitutionen* (Kirche und Recht, 21; Vienna: Plöchl-Druck, 1997). Steimer and Synek have good bibliographies of the older publications on the *Apostolic Constitutions*.

17. On the deep splits that marked the Christian community in Antioch, see the remarks by Kinzig, '"Non-Separation"', p. 36, and the Introduction in Harkins, *Saint John Chrysostom*.

of the 7 *berakhot* of the Eighteen Benedictions for the sabbath,[18] as is now generally recognized. 'If you can't beat them, join them!' the compiler seems to have thought. The relevance of comparing Chrysostom's sermons to the *Apostolic Constitutions* may be clear: both authors have to cope with the same situation, but they do so in strikingly different ways. Whereas the highly rhetorically gifted Church Father puts all his skills into the scales in order to scare the members of his community away from their judaizing practices, the anonymous compiler apparently takes the needs of his co-religionists much more seriously, and is willing to make a compromise with them. They are allowed to continue their use of Jewish prayers, but within the Christian community and with Christian elements added. So the anonymous compiler of the *Apostolic Constitutions* can be seen to have not only a more tactical, but also a more pastoral approach. What a difference there is between the slanderous language of Chrysostom and the way in which the compiler of the *Apostolic Constitutions* invites his co-religionist to pray:

> Our eternal Saviour, King of the Gods, the one who alone is almighty and Lord, God of all beings, and God of our holy and blameless fathers who were before us, God of Abraham, Isaac and Jacob, who is merciful and compassionate, patient and abundant in mercy, to whom every heart appears as naked and (to whom) every secret thought is revealed. To you the souls of the righteous cry out, upon you the devout have put their hopeful trust... Defender of the offspring of Abraham, blessed are you forever! (*Apost. Const.* 7.33).

Or from another prayer:

> Lord almighty, you created the world [*through Christ*][19] and you have instituted the sabbath in memory of this—for it was on that day that you rested from your works—for training in your laws. You have also

---

18.   See D. Fiensy, *Prayers Alleged to Be Jewish: An Examination of the Constitutiones Apostolorum* (Chico, CA: Scholars Press, 1985). The best edition of the text of these prayers is to be found in Metzger, *Les constitutions apostoliques*, III, pp. 66-95. It should be borne in mind that in the diaspora (and even sometimes in Palestine) the synagogue services were conducted in Greek.

19.   On these and other Christian interpolations, and the question of how to distinguish the Christian redaction from the Jewish 'Grundschrift' in these texts see my forthcoming commentary, in the Commentaries on Early Jewish Literature series (Berlin: W. de Gruyter, forthcoming). Cf. P.W. van der Horst, 'The Greek Synagogue Prayers in the Apostolic Constitutions, Book 7', in J. Tabory (ed.),

ordained festivals for the gladdening of our souls, so that we may be reminded of the Wisdom created by you... For you, O Lord, you also led our fathers out of the land of Egypt, and you saved them from an iron furnace and from clay and the making of bricks, you redeemed them from the hands of Pharaoh and his underlings, and you led them through the sea as through dry land, and in the desert you endured their manners (and presented them) with all sorts of good things. You gave them the Law of the ten words spoken by your voice and written by your hand, and you commanded them to keep the sabbath (*Apost. Const.* 7.36).

To be sure, at the end of this prayer the Christian interpolator has added that 'the Lord's day surpasses all this!' However, even in spite of this clumsily appended correction meant to prevent the Christians from abandoning the celebration of Sunday altogether, it is clear that the Jewish prayer for the sanctification of the shabbat in the Jewish liturgy, the *Qiddush* or *Qedushat ha-Yom*, is here an integral part of a Christian liturgy.

We know from other sources that in the early centuries of the Common Era Antioch had a very large and vibrant Jewish community, of which Josephus had already written that 'they were constantly attracting to their religious ceremonies multitudes of Greeks' (*War* 7.45).[20] Not long after Josephus wrote these words, Ignatius, one of the first bishops of Antioch, at the beginning of the second century made some remarks in his letters that strongly suggest that he was upset by the fact that several Christians in his community were adopting Jewish practices, evidently under the influence of the local Jewish community (*Magn.* 8.1-2; *Phil.* 6.1). From John Chrysostom we learn that this situation persisted two and a half centuries after Ignatius.[21] There was a

From Qumran to Cairo: Studies in the History of Prayer (Jerusalem: Orhot, 1999), pp. 19-46.

20. On the Jews of ancient Antioch, see C.H. Kraeling, 'The Jewish Community at Antioch', *JBL* 51 (1932), pp. 130-60; G. Downey, *A History of Antioch in Syria from Seleucus to the Arab Conquest* (Princeton, NJ: Princeton University Press, 1961), pp. 447-49, and most recently J. Hahn, 'Die jüdische Gemeinde im spätantiken Antiochia', in R. Jütte and A.P. Kustermann (eds.), *Jüdische Gemeinden und Organisationsformen von der Antike bis zur Gegenwart* (Vienna: Böhlau, 1996), pp. 57-89.

21. For a discussion of possible evidence for the period between Ignatius and Chrysostom, see Fiensy, *Prayers*, pp. 218-19. For two rich donations by the leaders of the Jewish community of Antioch to the synagogue of Apamea from the year 391 CE see the inscriptions in B. Lifshitz, *Donateurs et fondateurs dans les synagogues juives* (Paris: J. Gabalda, 1967), nos. 38 and 39. Also several tomb inscrip-

thriving Jewish community that had lived there for more than six and a half centuries (twice as long as the Christians), a community of which one of the members most probably was the son of the Jewish patriarch in Palestine, who studied in Antioch with the famous pagan orator Libanius (who had always spoken with respect of the Jews). In this connection it is telling that in the five or six years after Chrysostom's sermons Libanius carried on an extensive correspondence with this Jewish patriarch (Gamaliel), whom he apparently befriended.[22] In these circumstances, with a powerful and self-conscious Jewish community that had good relationships with pagans[23] and a strong influence upon Christian believers—and this was not a unique situation!—it was a wise tactical move to incorporate Jewish prayers into the Christian liturgy. If there existed a real and tenacious need among Christians in Antioch for using Jewish liturgical material, which was one of the reasons why they went to the synagogue on sabbath, then the best thing church leadership could do was to see to it that the prayers the members of his community said in the synagogue could also be said by them in the church—albeit with some modifications—so that the need of these members was met and the risk of losing them to the synagogue was lessened. This may have been much more effective than John Chrysostom's aggressive policy, a policy that, as he himself indirectly admitted some ten years later, had been far from successful (see his *Hom. in Ep. ad Tit.* 3.2 = *PG*, LXII, col. 679).[24]

tions in the famous catacombs in Beth She'arim (Galilee, third–fourth centuries CE) are of leading Antiochene Jews.

22. See the texts and translations in M. Stern, *Greek and Latin Authors on Jews and Judaism* (3 vols.; Jerusalem: Israel Academy of Arts and Sciences, 1980), II, pp. 580-600.

23. See the statement by Hahn ('Die jüdische Gemeinde', p. 71) 'daß die jüdische Gemeinde von Antiochia nach dem Erscheinungsbild ihrer Elite zur Zeit des Libanios eine blühende, außerordentlich wohlhabende und hellenisierte Gemeinschaft darstellte, die im Leben der Stadt und deren weiterem Umfeld ein deutliches Profil besaß, sich hierbei in ihrer sozialen Umgebung vorbehaltslos und selbstbewußt einfügte und dennoch eine unverkennbar jüdische Identität bewahrte'. The relationship between Jews and Gentiles in Antioch had not always been good, however. Especially in the first century CE there was much tension with occasional outbursts of violence; see M. Hengel and A.M. Schwemer, *Paul between Damascus and Antioch* (London: SCM Press; Louisville, KY: Westminster/John Knox Press, 1997), pp. 183-91.

24. See Hahn, 'Die jüdische Gemeinde', p. 76. Hahn speaks of the paradoxical

Now it could of course be argued, as indeed one of the investigators of this document has recently done, that the compiler of the *Apostolic Constitutions* did not incorporate these Jewish prayers into a Christian liturgical setting by christianizing them, but that this had already been done in one of its sources. We do know that the *Apostolic Constitutions* is indeed a compilation of older material, for it contains three major sources that we know: the *Didascalia Apostolorum*[25] (books 1–6); the *Didache*[26] (7.1-32); and the *Traditio Apostolica* (or *Diataxeis of the Holy Apostles*) by Hippolytus[27] (8.3-45) (and there are some other sources too). Since some of his major sources are known to us (cf. the *Didache* and the *Didascalia*), we are in a position to see the compiler at work. He does not take over the text of his sources unaltered. We can observe omissions, additions, insertions, corrections, etc. Sometimes these are minor; at other times they are major redrafts.[28] This teaches us two things. First, the anonymous author was not a slavish compiler: he made all kinds of changes in his material, as befitted his purposes, and he did so also in prayer material. That is to say that this man was perfectly capable of redrafting the Jewish prayer texts himself so as to make them fit for use in a Christian setting. Secondly, the majority of the sources he used had a Syrian provenance, which is not surprising for an author who worked in Antioch. Therefore the set of Jewish prayer texts may well have belonged to his sources of Syrian provenance. That implies that, even if we assume for the sake of argument that it was not the compiler himself who adopted and adapted these prayers—so that we can no longer treat it as an Antiochian document from the 380s—we still have to deal with a situation in which in a Syrian context this process has taken place, albeit now at an earlier date. That would not make it a less interesting case. It still would enable us to envisage a situation in which a Christian community in Syria that was in contact with the local Jewish community took over synagogal shabbat prayers in order to use them in their weekly services in the

situation that the Jewish community of Antioch could be so influential and powerful exactly because the church was so weak and had so little inner coherence (laity and clergy were continuously at odds with each other).

25. First half of the third century, Syria.

26. End of the first or beginning of the second century, Syria.

27. Beginning of the third century, Rome.

28. For our purposes, it is important to see, for instance, that the prayers in *Did.* 9–10 have been thoroughly modified in *Apost. Const.* 7.25-27.

church with some modifications. So what remains is the difference in approach between Chrysostom and this source, the difference between frontal attack and unbridled polemics, with all its baneful consequences, on the one hand,[29] and the more accommodating, or, rather, 'ecumenical' approach of the *Apostolic Constitutions'* source, on the other. If we look for an ancient model of Jewish–Christian encounters that is helpful in inspiring mutual respect and in building bridges, we can no doubt learn more from the *Apostolic Constitutions* than from Chrysostom, whose famous 'golden mouth' spouted so much venom.[30]

29. For many other instances of this kind of literature, see especially H. Schreckenberg, *Die christlichen Adversus-Judaeos-Texte und ihr literarisches und historisches Umfeld (1.–11. Jh.)* (Frankfurt: Peter Lang, 2nd edn, 1990). On pp. 320-29, Schreckenberg discusses Chrysostom.

30. I owe many thanks to the editors of this volume who were so kind as to check my English.

'THIS STONE SHALL BE A WITNESS' (JOSHUA 24.27):
JEWS, CHRISTIANS AND INSCRIPTIONS
IN EARLY MEDIAEVAL GAUL

Mark Handley

Perhaps the greatest obstacle for anyone attempting to study the Jewish communities of early mediaeval Gaul and their relations with the surrounding Christian communities is the nature of the sources available to us. Without exception, for the period of the fifth to the seventh centuries, the written sources consist of councils, laws,[1] hagiography and history. All of these were written by Christians for a Christian audience. We do not have a single text written by a Jew; nor do we have a text written for a Jewish audience. Archaeology, for this period, is also of little help.[2] We have no examples of an excavated synagogue, and in contrast to Spain, Italy and North Africa, no examples of a Jewish cemetery, or even Jewish burials.[3] It is also difficult, without the chance survival of wall paintings, to imagine a means of distinguishing a Jewish house from any other house. We are faced, therefore, with a distinct lack of Jewish texts, buildings and burials. Given this situation, it is remarkable that the small corpus of Jewish inscriptions from early mediaeval Gaul has been so little studied.[4] This corpus is arguably our

---

1.   These are all collected, edited and translated in A. Linder (ed.), *The Jews in the Legal Sources of the Early Middle Ages* (Detroit: Wayne State University Press, 1997).

2.   For later in the middle ages, see G. Nahon, 'L'archéologie juive de la France médiévale', *Archéologie médiévale* 5 (1975), pp. 139-59.

3.   For a Jewish burial on Majorca, see D. Noy (ed.), *The Jewish Inscriptions of Western Europe*. I. *Italy (excluding the City of Rome), Spain and Gaul* (Cambridge: Cambridge University Press, 1993), pp. 238-39; for Venusa see, pp. 61-149 pl. 2; and for North Africa see Y. Le Bohec, 'Inscriptions juives et judaïsantes de l'Afrique Romaine', *Antiquités Africaines* 17 (1981), pp. 165-207.

4.   Full bibliographies in Noy (ed.), *Jewish Inscriptions*, I.

only body of material 'written' for a Jewish audience. It is also almost our only evidence for diaspora Jewish attitudes in Gaul to burial and commemoration, the language(s) used by Jews, and Jewish literacy. Some have argued that the Jewish inscriptions of the early mediaeval West can tell us nothing about Jewish–Christian relations.[5] In contrast to this, an analysis of the formulas, palaeography, language and decoration of these inscriptions provides us with a great deal of evidence for relations between the Jewish and Christian communities of early mediaeval Gaul.

The corpus, however, is small. There are only four Jewish-Latin inscriptions in Gaul from between the fourth and the seventh centuries. Of these, one is a seal inscribed only with a menorah and the name Ianuarius from fourth-century Avignon,[6] and another is a ring from sixth-century Bordeaux inscribed with a menorah and the name Aster.[7] This leaves us with only two monumental Jewish-Latin inscriptions from early mediaeval Gaul. The first of these is from Visigothic Gaul and the city of Narbonne, and the second, while also from southern Gaul, is from the Frankish town of Auch.[8] There are no inscriptions in Hebrew from Gaul until later than the period covered in this essay, and even then there are only three from before the tenth century: two from eighth- or ninth-century Arles commemorating a Juda and a Meir,[9] and another from tenth-century Vienne commemorating a Samuel.[10] Compared even to neighbouring Spain which has 15 Jewish inscriptions,[11] our corpus is small. Early mediaeval Italy and North Africa, by contrast, have much larger corpora,[12] although here too more could be done

5. N. Roth, *Jews, Visigoths and Muslims in Medieval Spain: Cooperation and Conflict* (Leiden: E.J. Brill, 1994), p. 40.

6. Noy (ed.), *Jewish Inscriptions*, I, no. 190, pp. 266-67.

7. Noy (ed.), *Jewish Inscriptions*, I, no. 192, pp. 270-72.

8. Noy (ed.), *Jewish Inscriptions*, I, nos. 189, 191, pp. 263-66, 267-70.

9. Noy (ed.), *Jewish Inscriptions*, I, nos. 198-99, pp. 281-82.

10. Noy (ed.), *Jewish Inscriptions*, I, no. 200, p. 283.

11. Noy (ed.), *Jewish Inscriptions*, I, nos. 177-88, 197, pp. 238-62, 278-81.

12. Noy (ed.), *Jewish Inscriptions*, I, nos. 1-162, 169-76, and *idem* (ed.), *The Jewish Inscriptions of Western Europe*. II. *The City of Rome* (Cambridge: Cambridge University Press, 1995); Le Bohec, 'Inscriptions juives', pp. 165-207; and F. Vattioni, 'Una iscrizione guidaica di Leptis Magna', *Antiquités Africaines* 19 (1983), pp. 63-64; see also G. Lüderitz (ed.), *Corpus jüdischer Zeugnisse aus der Cyrenaika* (Wiesbaden: L. Reichert, 1983).

to use this material to inform us of relations between Jews and Christians.[13]

Given the data collected above, what is most required before we can begin to look at the inscriptions themselves is context. First and foremost this must be provided by looking at the Christian inscriptions of Gaul. All too often, Jewish inscriptions are seen in isolation, compared only to other Jewish inscriptions. Yet it is becoming increasingly clear that a large part of the context for the Jewish epigraphy of any given locale is provided by the non-Jewish inscriptions of that region and less by the Jewish inscriptions of elsewhere.[14] Context can also be provided by the Christian written sources of Gaul, and what they have to tell us about Jewish–Christian relations.

In the fifth to seventh centuries, a total of 13 councils in Gaul enacted canons concerning Jews. We might think that this would provide us with a wealth of information concerning Jewish–Christian relations. Unfortunately this is not the case. One of the many achievements of the work by Linder has been to show the extremely formulaic nature of much of this legislation.[15] Thus six councils enacted canons against dining with Jews,[16] six enacted legislation concerning the ownership of Christian slaves by Jews,[17] while five and four councils respectively enacted canons against Jews being placed in a position of authority over Christians,[18] and on the conversion of Christians, largely slaves, to Judaism.[19] Three councils also enacted against Jewish–Christian mar-

---

13. The exception to this being the excellent studies of L.V. Rutgers, *The Jews in Late Ancient Rome: Evidence of Cultural Interaction in the Roman Diaspora* (Leiden: E.J. Brill, 1995), and, on a smaller scale, D. Noy, 'The Jewish Communities of Leontopolis and Venosa', in J.W. van Henten and P.W. van der Horst (eds.), *Studies in Early Jewish Epigraphy* (Leiden: E.J. Brill, 1994), pp. 162-82.

14. This is the great benefit of the works cited above in n. 13.

15. Cf. Linder (ed.), *Jews in the Legal Sources*, pp. 465-82.

16. Vannes (461–491), Agde (506), Epaone (517), Clermont (535), Macon (581–583), Clichy (626–627); cf. Linder (ed.), *Jews in the Legal Sources*, pp. 466-69, 474-75, 479-80.

17. Orleans III (533), Orleans IV (541), Macon, Clichy, Rheims (630), Chalon (647–653); cf. Linder (ed.), *Jews in the Legal Sources*, pp. 469, 472, 475-76, 479-82.

18. Clermont, Macon, Paris (614), Clichy, Rheims; cf. Linder (ed.), *Jews in the Legal Sources*, pp. 470, 474, 478-81.

19. Orleans IV, Macon, Clichy and Rheims; cf. Linder (ed.), *Jews in the Legal Sources*, pp. 472-73, 476, 479-81.

riages.[20] The problem with much of this conciliar legislation is that, to a certain extent, we cannot tell how much it refers to relations between Jews and Christians of a specific time and place, and how much it is a function of what Christian clerics at council thought should be included in a collection of canons. This is supported by the inclusion of anti-Jewish canons in the *Collectio Canonum Hibernensis*, a collection put together in Ireland around 800 CE, a period in which it is extremely unlikely that there were any Jews in Ireland.[21] This does not make the canons any less useful for the study of Christian views of Jews, but it does limit the extent to which we can see the canons as related to any specific Jewish community, and to relations between actual people, rather than between monolithic religious blocs.

The only Gallic council that seems to stand out from these 'traditional' enactments was that of Narbonne in 589.[22] Here we actually get a sense of Jews forming an integral part of the population of the town. Thus canon 4 forbids anyone 'whether freeborn or slave, Goth, Roman, Syrian, Greek or Jew' from working on a Sunday, and canon 14 bans 'Goth, Roman, Syrian, Greek or Jew' from consulting soothsayers. Canon 9 is of more interest because it deals singularly with Jews:

> It is decreed above anything else that the Jews should not be allowed to sing psalms while accompanying the dead, but they shall accompany the dead and put them to rest according to their usage and ancient custom. If they should dare to do otherwise they shall pay the city count six ounces of gold.

This is our only source to mention Jewish burial practice in early mediaeval Gaul.[23] From it we can see that the bishops of Visigothic Gaul were not happy with Jews singing psalms at funerals, perhaps

---

20. Orleans II (533), Clermont, Orleans III; cf. Linder (ed.), *Jews in the Legal Sources*, pp. 469-71. On this subject also see H. Sivan, 'Rabinnics and Roman Law: Jewish–Gentile/Christian Marriage in Late Antiquity', *REJ* 156 (1997), pp. 59-100.

21. Linder (ed.), *Jews in the Legal Sources*, pp. 594-95. Quite apart from stating that 'It was appropriate that they [Jews] should be killed on the very same days on which they crucified the savior', this collection equates Jews with the lowest of the low—heretics and Britons.

22. Cf. Linder (ed.), *Jews in the Legal Sources*, pp. 476-78.

23. See S. Katz, *The Jews in the Visigothic and Frankish Kingdoms of Spain and Gaul* (Cambridge, MA: Medieval Academy of America, 1937), p. 76; and J. Juster, *The Legal Condition of the Jews under the Visigothic Kings* (updated A.M. Rabello; Jerusalem: Israel Law Review Association, 1976), pp. 564-65.

because this was also an integral part of the Christian funeral service.[24] The bishops did not have a problem with specifically Jewish burial rites, indeed they appear to encourage Jewish 'ancient custom'. Rather they seem to be attempting a more complete distinction between Jewish and Christian burial ritual. It is an unanswerable question, yet one cannot but wonder what the bishops of southern Gaul thought 'ancient' Jewish burial custom consisted of, and indeed just how 'ancient' this was.

The secular laws and enactments of Frankish Gaul have little to say about Jews.[25] However, the laws of the Visigothic kingdom, of which Narbonne was part, are notorious for their extremely harsh and oppressive anti-Jewish and indeed anti-semitic legislation.[26] To give some sense of these laws, we can note a law of King Ervig that required Jews who were travelling through the kingdom to present themselves at each town or village to the local bishop or priest. Before they could move on, this cleric had to write a letter declaring that the sabbath had not been celebrated and that only the company of good Christians had been kept. If a Jew returned from travels without letters from each of the stops he or she made, they were to be flogged with 100 lashes.[27] Moreover, to ensure that no Jew could claim ignorance of such laws, it was also decreed that the laws were to be read out to all Jews, and that they were to have a copy of these laws on them at all time. The surviving manuscripts end with the chilling note: 'The above laws were read to all the Jews in the church of Saint Mary in Toledo on the sixth day before the calends of February of the first felicific year of the reign of our glorious Lord Erviga the king'.[28] Arguments about the nature of early mediaeval law and the extent to which it was made manifest within society appear to fade in front of this all too real state-sponsored oppression.

The literary, non-legal, sources can also tell us much about Jewish–Christian relations in early mediaeval Gaul. Thus the *Life of Caesarius*

---

24. For the importance of psalms in Christian funeral processions, see F. Paxton, *Christianizing Death: The Creation of a Ritual Process in Early Medieval Europe* (Ithaca, NY: Cornell University Press, 1990), pp. 39, 41, 43.

25. These can be found in Linder (ed.), *Jews in the Legal Sources*, pp. 207-208, 343-44.

26. For an edition and translation of all the Visigothic Jewish legislation see Linder (ed.), *Jews in the Legal Sources*, pp. 257-332. For one of many examples of laws relating to converted Jews see pp. 281-84.

27. See Linder (ed.), *Jews in the Legal Sources*, pp. 321-23.

28. Linder (ed.), *Jews in the Legal Sources*, pp. 331-32.

of Arles tells us of a section of the wall of Arles aportioned to the Jewish community to defend during a siege,[29] while other sources mention Jews as trusted messengers (for example, Sidonius, *Ep.* 3.4.1; 4.5.1). We also hear of Jews at the Merovingian court,[30] and of the destruction of synagogues.[31] The most infamous episode is the forced conversion or expulsion of the Jewish community at Clermont in 576,[32] recorded by both Gregory of Tours and Venantius Fortunatus, and so reminiscent of the forced conversion of the Jews of Minorca in the fifth century.[33] Jews appear quite regularly in the works of Gregory,[34] and from him we can get an impression of a fairly large and widespread population, albeit one subjected to occasional acts of violence and oppression. From another source, we also hear of Jews being converted by Sulpicius of Bourges,[35] and from Gregory the Great we hear of Jews being forcibly led to baptism in Marseilles.[36]

29. See B. Krusch (ed.), *Vita Caesarii Episcopi Arelatensis* I.31, in *MGH, SRM*, III (Hanover: Hahnian, 1896), and W.E. Klingshirn (ed. and trans.), *Caesarius of Arles: Life, Testament, Letters* (Liverpool: Liverpool University Press, 1994), p. 24.

30. See B. Krusch and W. Levison (eds.), Gregory of Tours, *Decem Libri Historiarum*, VI.5, VI.17, in *MGH, SRM*, I.1 (Hanover: Hahnian, 1885), and L. Thorpe (ed. and trans.), *Gregory of Tours: The History of the Franks* (Harmondsworth: Penguin Books, 1974), pp. 330-33, 347-48.

31. *Decem Libri Historiarum* 8.1 (Krusch and Levison [eds.], *Gregory of Tours*, p. 433).

32. F. Leo (ed.), *Venanti Honori Clementiani Fortunati Opera Poetica*, in *MGH, AA*, IV.1 (Berlin: Weidmann, 1881), *Carmina* 5.5, *Decem Libri Historiarum* 5.11, and Krusch and Levison (eds.), *Gregory of Tours*, pp. 265-67. On this episode, see W. Goffart, 'The Conversions of Avitus of Clermont, and Similar Passages in Gregory of Tours', in J. Neusner and E.R. Frerichs (eds.), *'To See Ourselves as Others See Us': Christians, Jews, 'Others' in Late Antiquity* (Chico, CA: Scholars Press, 1985), pp. 473-97, and B. Brennan, 'The Conversion of the Jews of Clermont in AD 576', *JTS* 36 (1985), pp. 321-37.

33. See S. Bradbury (ed.), *Severus of Minorca: Letter on the Conversion of the Jews* (Oxford: Oxford University Press, 1996).

34. See B. Blumenkranz, *Les auteurs chrétiens latins du moyen age sur les juifs et le judaïsme* (The Hague: Mouton, 1963), pp. 67-73, and A. Keely, 'Arians and Jews in the *Histories* of Gregory of Tours', *Journal of Medieval History* 23.2 (1997), pp. 103-115, and the articles cited above in n. 32.

35. B. Krusch (ed.), *Vita s. Sulpitii Bituricensis*, IV, in *MGH, SRM*, IV (Hanover: Hahnian, 1902), pp. 374-75.

36. See Linder (ed.), *Jews in the Legal Sources*, pp. 418-19.

Literary references to the spoken or written language of the Jews of early mediaeval Gaul are extremely limited. In part, however, this lack of evidence is telling us something. In all the references we have to Jews in Gaul, debating, talking, writing and travelling, we do not have a single reference to the use of an interpreter. The one possible reference to the use of Hebrew is, moreover, problematic. Gregory of Tours states that upon entry to Orleans, King Guntram was met 'by large delegations from every segment of the population, carrying bells and banners, and intoning acclamations in their particular languages'. From this we might surmise that the Jewish delegation acclaimed Guntram in Hebrew, yet the words Gregory quotes are Latin.[37] To make the situation all the more complex, it has been argued that the Latin words Gregory quotes come from a Jewish prayer.[38] It is difficult to know what to make of this evidence.[39]

The lack of other evidence for language use encourages us to use the evidence supplied by the inscriptions. The inscription from Auch reads in Latin script:

IN DEI NOMINE S(AN)C(T)O
PELEGER QUI IC BENNID
D(EU)S ESTO C[U]M IPSO. OCOLI
INVIDIOSI CREPEN\<T\> DE D(E)I
DONUM IONA FECET

---

37. *Decem Libri Historiarum* 8.1 (Goffart, 'The Conversions', p. 297).

38. N. Coulet, 'De l'intégration à l'exclusion: La place des Juifs dans le cérémonies d'entrée solennelle au moyen âge', *Annales: Economies, sociétés, civilisations* 34 (1979), pp. 672-83 (674).

39. Without getting too entwined in a discussion of Jewish-Latin Scriptures, it needs to be stated that the argument based upon a presumption that the Visigothic kings would not have required Jewish Scriptures to be deposited for inspection if they were in Greek or Hebrew—therefore they were in Latin—is utterly unconvincing. For this see Roth, *Jews, Visigoths and Muslims*, pp. 24-25. Moreover the arguments based on a supposed echo of the Vulgate in a Jewish inscription from Rome (for which see A. Deissmann, *Light from the Ancient East* [London: Hodder & Stoughton, 4th edn, 1927], p. 447) would require evidence that the inscription was not produced in a Christian epigraphic workshop. On the other hand, the conclusion of T. Rajak, 'Inscription and Context: Reading the Jewish Catacombs of Rome', in van Henten and van der Horst (eds.), *Studies in Early Jewish Epigraphy*, pp. 226-41 (232), that 'there is no direct evidence for a Latin Jewish Bible', seems to overlook the evidence of Severus of Minorca that Jews and Christians sang the psalms together (see Bradbury [ed.] *Severus of Minorca*, Ch. 13, pp. 92-93).

This was followed by SHALOM in Hebrew as well as a shofar, a menorah and the lulab. Noy translates this as, 'In the holy name of God. The foreigner who comes here, may God be with him. May envious eyes burst. From the gifts of God, Jona made (this). Peace', and argues that it records the building of either a synagogue, or more likely some sort of accommodation for visitors.[40] In terms of language, the first thing that can be noticed is the use of IC for *hic* showing the loss of the initial H that would eventually lead to French *ici*. The spelling of FECET for *fecit* is another example of post-classical Latin pronunciation finding orthographic representation, as is OCOLI for *oculi*, showing the common confusion of U and O. The word BENNID, however, has caused problems for a number of interpreters. Noy, the most recent editor, concludes that this is not a name, but rather a form of the verb VENIT,[41] which, if he is right (and I think he is), shows confusion of B for V and D for T, as well as gemination, or doubling, of the N.[42] We can conclude, therefore, that the spelling of this inscription was chosen in order to represent post-classical spoken Latin.

The inscription from Narbonne reads,

```
IC REQUIESCUNT
IN PACE BENE MEMORI
<T>RES FILI D(OMI)NI PARAGORI
DE FILIO CONDAM D(OMI)NI SA
PAUDI ID ES<T> IUS<T>US MA
TRONA ET DULCIORELLA QUI
VIXSERUNT IUSTUS ANNO
XXX MATRONA ANN(O)S XX DULCI
ORELA ANNOS VIIII
OBUERUN<T> ANNOS SECUNDO D(O)M(IN)I EGICANI / REGIS
```

Before the IC is a menorah, and the third to the last line ends with 'Peace upon Israel' in Hebrew. This is clearly an epitaph for three

---

40. See Noy (ed.), *Jewish Inscriptions*, I, pp. 267-70.

41. See Noy (ed.), *Jewish Inscriptions*, I, pp. 268-69.

42. Examples of B for V include E. Le Blant (ed.), *Inscriptions chrétiennes de la Gaule antérieures au VIIIe siècle* (2 vols.; Paris: Imprimerie Nationale, 1856–65), nos. 541, 613A and 616B, the last two of which come from Narbonne, and N. Gauthier (ed.), *Recueil des inscriptions chrétiennes de la Gaule. I. Première belgique* (Paris: CNRS, 1975), no. 228. For confusion of T for D, see J. Vives (ed.), *Inscripciones cristianas de la España romana y visigoda* (Barcelona: A.G. Poussa, 2nd edn, 1969), no. 48. For examples of gemination of N, see Gauthier (ed.), *Première belgique*, nos. 49, 178.

siblings, and Noy has translated it as; 'Here rest in peace, remembered for good, the three children of Lord Paragorius, grandchild(ren) of the late Lord Sapaudus; that is Justus, Matrona and Dulciorella. They lived: Justus 30 years, Matrona 20 years, Dulciorella 9 years. Peace upon Israel. They died in the second year of Lord Egica the king.'[43] Once again, therefore, we can see the use of IC for *hic*, but we also have CONDAM for *quondam*, with this being an example of the post-classical sound-change that saw *quinque* in Latin become *cinq* in French and *cinque* in Italian. The final such example is the use of VIXSERUNT for *vixerunt*. This is a common spelling in late antiquity and the early Middle Ages,[44] and again is an attempt to represent through orthography the sounds of spoken Latin.[45]

Our inscriptions supply us with considerable evidence for spoken Latin, but little evidence for knowledge of Hebrew. Hebrew tags such as those found on these inscriptions are known elsewhere and have been described as 'decorative' and 'of little significance' when it comes to assessing language use.[46] We can conclude, therefore, that the use of *shalom* on an otherwise Latin inscription cannot be taken as evidence for knowledge of Hebrew, just as *alpha* and *omega* on the Latin-Christian inscriptions of Gaul cannot be taken as evidence for knowledge of Greek. The evidence of the inscriptions indicates that the Jews of southern Gaul spoke the same Latin as their Christian neighbours.

How were these inscriptions produced? This is not a question that has been asked before. Normally, Jewish inscriptions are seen only in the context of other Jewish inscriptions. It has to be remembered, however, that whereas we have two Jewish inscriptions from Gaul, we have over 2300 Christian inscriptions. I would argue that these provide much of the context for our Jewish inscriptions, and that comparison with these

---

43. Noy (ed.), *Jewish Inscriptions*, I, p. 263. It should also be pointed out that there are four mistakes in the inscription. The first three are the use of I instead of T, while the last involved the carving of an R instead of a T. Such errors are relatively common.

44. We have 25 examples from early mediaeval Gaul and Spain of the misspelling of *vixit* with either *vixsit* or *vixset*.

45. On inscriptions representing such sound changes, see J. Kramer, 'Zwischen Latein und Moselromanisch: Die Gondorfer Grabinschrift für Mauricius', *ZPE* 118 (1997), pp. 281-86.

46. Rajak, 'Inscription and Context', p. 230.

gives us our best chance of using inscriptions as evidence for Jewish–Christian relations.

In order to answer 'How were Jewish inscriptions produced?', we must first ask how Christian inscriptions were produced.[47] It can be argued that the urban Christian inscriptions of early mediaeval Gaul were very largely produced within workshops attached to particular cemeteries, and that these workshops adopted particular, local and identifiable styles. Thus from the cemetery of St Mathias in Trier we find a particular form of T with a wavy top-stroke, and a particular abbreviation of an I within a D for DI(ES). These are not found from the other cemetery in Trier.[48] From the cemetery of St Gervasius in Vienne we find a style in which gridlines, final crosses, and reference to the resurrection is common, again traits not found elsewhere in Vienne.[49] Local styles could extend to formulas such as the use of IN HUNC TITULUM and BENE MEMORIAE in Mainz.[50] Other evidence points to the use of model-books for inscriptions.[51] Most famously we have the inscription from Algeria which reads HIC IACET PUER NOMINANDI— *Here lies the boy, put his name in.*[52] From Gaul we have the epigraphic formulary from Jouarre discussed by Bernard Bischoff,[53] and the possible survival of a sixth-century formulary in a ninth-century Lyon manuscript.[54] Most importantly we also have the evidence of the

47. The following is summarized from the chapter on 'Producing Inscriptions' in M.A. Handley, 'The Early Medieval Inscriptions of Britain, Gaul and Spain: Studies in Function and Culture' (PhD thesis, Cambridge University, 1998), pp. 201-54.

48. See Gauthier (ed.), *Première belgique*, pp. 27-31.

49. Handley, 'The Early Medieval Inscriptions', pp. 216-18.

50. Handley, 'The Early Medieval Inscriptions', p. 114. For the inscriptions of Mainz, see W. Boppert (ed.), *Die Frühchristlichen Inschriften des Mittelrhein-gebeites* (Mainz am Rhein: von Zabern, 1971).

51. For model-books in the Classical period, see R. Cagnat, 'Sur les manuels professionels des graveurs d'inscriptions romaines', *Revue Philologique* 13 (1889), pp. 51-65.

52. *L'année épigraphique* (1931), no. 112.

53. B. Bischoff, 'Epitaphienformeln für Äbtissinen (Achtes Jahrhundert)', in *idem, Anecdota novissima: Texte des Vierten bis Sechzehnten Jahrhunderts* (Stuttgart: A. Hiersemann, 1984), pp. 150-53.

54. M.A. Handley, 'Epitaphs, Models and Texts: A Carolingian Collection of Late Antique Inscriptions from Burgundy', in A. Cooley (ed.), *Inscriptions and their Afterlife* (London: Bulletin of the Institute of Classical Studies, Supplementary Series, forthcoming).

inscriptions from Arles. The vast majority of Arlesian inscriptions that survive intact begin with something like HIC IN PACE REQUIESCIT BONE MEMORIAE; this is followed by the name of the commemorand, a statement of how old they were, and finally the recording of the day of death. The formulaic nature of the epigraphic record enables us suspect that a model-book was being used. Thankfully one unfinished inscription survives that allows us to prove this. The inscription reads:[55]

HIC IN PACE REQUI
ESCIT BON(E) M(EMORIAE) LEONI
DIUS QUI VIXIT
ANNUS PL(US) M(INUS)
ET OBIIT SUB DIE

      INDICTIO
NE

The formulaic words have been carved, but the personal details of age and day of death have been left blank. We are able to conclude, therefore, that many of the inscriptions had been started, and the local formulas added, even before a customer had walked into the workshop to say that their parent had died yesterday aged about 50.

We do not have large enough numbers of inscriptions from Narbonne, or Auch, to be able to undertake this sort of analysis. Yet by looking for parallels for the letter-forms and formulas of our two Jewish inscriptions among the larger corpus of Christian inscriptions, we should be able to ascertain whether it is likely that they were produced within the same workshops. With this in mind, we can turn to the palaeography of our two inscriptions. The distinctive letter-forms of the Auch inscription are the angular, almost triangular D, an R with a short oblique 'foot', an A with an angled cross-bar, a minuscule q, a half-uncial G, an O with two 'antennae', and an F with a forked ascender. The first three of these letter-forms are very common and are readily found elsewhere in south-western Gaul.[56] The minuscule q was

---

55. E. Le Blant (ed.), *Nouveau recueil des inscriptions chrétiennes de la Gaule antérieures au VIIIe siècle* (Paris: Imprimerie Nationale, 1892), no. 174.

56. Examples with this A and this D include E. Espérandieu (ed.), *Inscriptions latines de Gaule (Narbonnaise)* (Paris: E. Leroux, 1929), no. 605, illustrated in C. Landes (ed.), *Les derniers Romains en Septimanie IVe–VIIIe siècles* (Lattes: Imago, 1988), p. 228, and Le Blant (ed.), *Nouveau recueil*, no. 298. The R and A in particular are found on hundreds of other inscriptions, the D only becomes more common from the seventh century.

common in this region,[57] while the particular forms of O and F can also be paralleled.[58] Only the half-uncial G is difficult to parallel, although it is found on our other inscription from Narbonne, as well as further afield in Gaul. The minuscule q, angle-bar A, short 'foot' R, and angular D are also found on the Narbonne inscription. Other letter-forms from Narbonne not shared between the two are the angular U with an ascender that extends downward, the backwards N where the cross-stroke goes from bottom left to top right, a B with two quite separate bows, an M with curved, rather than angular arches, a lozenge-shaped O, and a minuscule D with an ascender that bends to the left over the bow. Once again parallels within the Christian corpus are easy to find for all of these.[59] Palaeographically there is nothing to distinguish our two Jewish inscriptions from the mass of Christian inscriptions that surrounded them.

Turning to the evidence of the texts themselves, it must be said that building inscriptions are not common in Gaul in the early Middle Ages, with the result that parallels for the wording used at Auch are difficult to find.[60] The epitaph from Narbonne, however, is quite different. The funerary formula HIC REQUIESCIT IN PACE BONE MEMORIAE, and other variations on this theme, are extremely common in the early Middle Ages. In total we have over 270 such inscriptions from elsewhere in Gaul, not to mention further examples from Spain, Italy, North Africa and Britain. Of course the inscription does not read *bone memoriae* but BENE MEMORI. This is potentially significant for it has been argued that the use of *bene* in this way is particularly common on

---

57. For example, Le Blant (ed.), *Inscriptions chrétiennes de la Gaule*, no. 601, from Toulouse, and *idem* (ed.), *Nouveau recueil*, no. 295 from Eaunes in the same province as Auch, and Espérandieu (ed.), *Inscriptions latines de Gaule*, no. 606, illustrated in Landes (ed.), *Les derniers Romains*, p. 229.

58. Le Blant (ed.), *Nouveau recueil*, no. 298, and *idem* (ed.), *Inscriptions chrétiennes de la Gaule*, no. 601 respectively.

59. To cite just a few examples, the angular U and minuscule D are found in Espérandieu (ed.), *Inscriptions chrétiennes de la Gaule*, no. 601, the backwards N in Le Blant (ed.), *Nouveau receuil*, no. 309, the curved M in Le Blant (ed.), *Nouveau recueil*, no. 295 and *idem* (ed.), *Inscriptions chrétiennes de la Gaule*, no. 613A. The B with separate bows and the lozenge-shaped O are so common as to be easily found anywhere in Gaul.

60. See Noy (ed.), *Jewish Inscriptions*, I, p. 270, for some parallels from elsewhere.

Jewish epitaphs, and indeed that the version *benememorius* is exclusively Jewish.[61] It has already been stated that the use of *bene* was common on the Christian inscriptions of the city of Mainz.[62] Moreover, it is found on Christian epitaphs elsewhere in Gaul, as well as Italy.[63] The variants used include *bene memoria, bene memoriae, bene memorie, bene memorio, bene memorus,* and indeed we have epitaphs of two priests with the supposedly exclusively Jewish form *benememorius*.[64] I would argue, therefore, that the use of *bene* did not denote Jewishness, and that the use of this formula on a Jewish epitaph from Narbonne in no way marks it out as being different from the Christian inscriptions of that city.[65]

Two other aspects of the inscription from Narbonne are worth dwelling on. The first is the presence of ages for the deceased. It has recently been argued that the practice of age-recording was 'not of Oriental origin', and that when we find Jews of the Diaspora recording age at death, it is a sign of 'outside influence'.[66] Recording the age-at-death was certainly common in Gaul, where we find a total of 678 such inscriptions. We can argue, therefore, that the recording of the ages of Justus, Matrona and Dulciorella provides a further point of comparison between this inscription and the Christian inscriptions around it.

The final aspect is the presence of a regnal date on this inscription. The use of dating systems on epitaphs is quite widespread in the early

---

61. See P.W. van der Horst, *Ancient Jewish Epitaphs: An Introductory Survey of a Millennium of Jewish Funerary Epigraphy (300 B.C.E.–700 C.E.)* (Kampen: Kok, 1991), p. 65, and Noy (ed.), *Jewish Inscriptions,* I, p. 2.

62. Boppert (ed.), *Die frühchristlichen Inschriften,* nos. Adalharius, Badegiselus, Gaereholdus, Pertram and Roteldis.

63. For Italy, see, e.g., G. Mennella and G. Coccoluto (eds.), *Inscriptiones christianae italianae. IX. Regio IX, Ligura reliqua tras et cis Appeninum* (Bari: Edipuglia, 1995), no. 5, and G. Binazzi (ed.), *Inscriptiones christianae italianae. VI. Regio VI, Umbria* (Bari: Edipuglia, 1989), no. 24; and for Gaul, see Le Blant (ed.), *Nouveau recueil,* nos. 157, 309, 426; *L'année épigraphique* (1983), no. 704; and F. Descombes (ed.), *Recueil des inscriptions chrétiennes de la Gaule. XV. Viennoise du Nord* (Paris: CNRS, 1985), nos. 266, 269.

64. Boppert (ed.), *Die frühchristlichen Inschriften,* no. Badegiselus, and P. Rugo (ed.), *Le iscrizioni dei sec. VI-II-VIII esistenti in Italia. II. Venezia e Istria* (Citadella: Bertonella, 1975), no. 37.

65. Le Blant (ed.), *Nouveau recueil,* no. 309, with *bene memoria* from the same province as Narbonne.

66. Rutgers, *The Jews in Late Ancient Rome,* pp. 100-107, especially p. 107.

Middle Ages, and could vary from the continued use of Roman provincial eras in Spain,[67] to consular and post-consular dates in the kingdom of Burgundy.[68] Regnal dating, the citing of the year of the reign of the king, was also quite common. The use of such dating systems should be seen as assertions of political allegiance. Such acts were not compulsory, and it is only ever a minority that are so dated. In Visigothic Gaul, we find regnal dates on more than 15 inscriptions with the series beginning in 496.[69] The last Christian inscription from Visigothic Gaul to use a regnal date is dated to the year 589.[70] The epitaph of Justus and his sisters is the first such inscription in Visigothic Gaul for over 100 years. Given the background of harsh anti-Jewish, and indeed anti-Semitic, legislation in the Visigothic kingdom, this public statement of some sort of allegiance to the king may seem a strange act for a Jewish family. We simply cannot know the background to this action. We have no other information on Jewish attitudes to the Visigothic kings. While it may be tempting to see this as an act of appeasement, along similar lines to Robin Lane Fox's statement that the vast majority of early Christians actively avoided martyrdom,[71] all we can be confident of is that the recording of a regnal date was a political act.

In terms of language, palaeography, formulas, and information included, the Jewish inscriptions of Gaul are indistinguishable from the Christian inscriptions. We have seen that the Christian inscriptions of Gaul were produced from model-books in workshops attached to particular churches and cemeteries. I would argue that the Jewish inscriptions of Auch and Narbonne were produced in these same workshops. What, however, are we to make of this, and how does this bear upon Jewish–Christian relations? Are we to conclude that Jewish–Christian relations were sufficiently cordial that no one saw a problem with Jews

---

67. See M.A. Handley, 'Tiempo e identidad: La datación por la Eva en las inscripciones de la España Tardormana y Visigoda', *Iberia* 2 (1999), pp. 191-201.

68. See M.A. Handley, 'Inscribing Time and Identity: The Uses of Consular Dating in the Kingdom of Burgundy', in S. Mitchell and S. Greatrex (eds.), *Race, Religion and Culture in Late Antiquity A.D. 300–600* (Swansea: Classical Press of Wales, forthcoming 2001; London: Gerald Duckworth, forthcoming 2002).

69. Descombes (ed.), *Inscriptions chrétiennes de la Gaule*, XV, no. 482.

70. Le Blant (ed.), *Inscriptions latines de Gaule*, no. 669.

71. R. Lane Fox, 'Literacy and Power in Early Christianity', in A. Bowman and G. Woolf (eds.), *Literacy and Power in the Ancient World* (Cambridge: Cambridge University Press, 1994), pp. 126-48 (139).

using the same workshops, and having similar epitaphs and inscriptions? Or are we to conclude that restrictions on Jewish actions, and restrictions on expressions of Jewish identity were so stringent that Jews were forced to use Christian workshops, and adopt a largely Christian form of commemoration? Should we conclude that the addition of stray pieces of Hebrew, and of the menorah and other decoration (perhaps after the event), was a means of circumventing such restrictions, or instead that they were an acceptable expression of Jewish identity? Indeed, should we conclude that the burial formulas were not themselves perceived as being specifically Christian—that it was decoration and location, along with the rituals of burial, that made a particular epitaph and person Christian or Jewish? Our corpus is simply not large enough to enable us to answer these, and other questions, with any certainty. If we turn briefly to the better documented Jewish community at Rome we can see that Rutgers has argued that the Jewish community used the standard epitaphs, sarcophagi and paintings of the wider pagan and then Christian community. The Jews of Rome distinguished themselves in burial solely by the use of specifically Jewish catacombs, and by the addition of specifically Jewish elements such as Hebrew, the menorah or the ethrog.[72] Despite the lack of Jewish burial archaeology in Gaul, a similar situation can easily be imagined. Certainly our two inscriptions, one recording the erection and donation of a building, the other recording the untimely deaths of three siblings, both have Jewish decorative elements, as well as Hebrew. Whatever else we can say, the use of Hebrew and of Jewish decorative elements was a public statement of Jewish identity. Indeed, it is what defines these inscriptions as Jewish. Such is the similarity between these and other inscriptions of the region that without these features we would have no way of detecting 'Jewishness'.

Walter Goffart has argued that Jews were the only recognized religious minority in the early Middle Ages. This recognition stemmed from the assumption that Jews would all one day convert, and indeed it was seen as the duty of bishops and priests to advance that day. This delicate balancing act between temporary recognition and desired conversion occasionally but consistently turned into outright aggression and oppression.[73] It is these tips in the scale that we find in our sources with Minorca, Clermont and Visigothic Spain in the fifth, sixth and

72. Rutgers, *The Jews in Late Ancient Rome*, pp. 50-99.
73. Goffart, 'The Conversion', pp. 314-17.

seventh centuries respectively. I would argue that the surviving Jewish inscriptions give us some inkling of when the scales were in balance. They show us times and places where the public expression of Jewish identity was both permitted and sought after. The Jewish inscriptions of western Europe form an extremely valuable source, and one which still has much to offer. In terms of Jewish–Christian relations, however, we can see that the Jewish inscriptions of Gaul were the product of the same workshops as the Christian inscriptions. Language, palaeography and formulas were largely identical. That Jews used these workshops, and that they retained the desire and ability to proclaim themselves as being Jewish, allows us to state that, as well as providing evidence for the use of literacy and of spoken Latin, the Jewish inscriptions of Gaul speak to us of recognition. Perhaps begrudging, perhaps temporary, but nonetheless recognition.

'COLONIZING THE OLD TESTAMENT' OR 'REPRESENTING CHRISTIAN INTERESTS ABROAD': JEWISH–CHRISTIAN RELATIONS ACROSS OLD TESTAMENT TERRITORY

Yvonne Sherwood

In biblical studies...supersessionism...plays out rather like colonialism: Jews have not managed their scriptural territory rightly, and it is therefore the right of Christianity to take it over, renaming it 'Old Testament'.[1]

There is no more interesting question of the present day than that of what is to be done with the world's land which is lying unimproved; whether it shall go to the great power that is willing to turn it to account, or remain with its original owner, who fails to understand its value.[2]

> Take up the White Man's Burden—
> In patience to abide,
> To veil the threat of terror
> and check the show of pride;
> By open speech and simple,
> An hundred times made plain.
> To seek another's profit,
> And work another's gain.[3]

I am English. Now I can see that this does not count as a major confession but it seems to be important in this case. I live in something called the Commonwealth—a term that suggests some kind of commonality, an equal sharing of wealth, but that masks the exploitation of the British colonies and the underdevelopment that is a legacy of imperialism. I am

1. T.K. Beal, *The Book of Hiding: Gender, Ethnicity, Annihilation and Esther* (London and New York: Routledge, 1997), p. 5.

2. Richard Harding Davis, writing in Honduras, three years before the United Fruit Company was established (*Three Gringos in Venezuela and Central America* [New York: Harper, 1896]).

3. R. Kipling, 'The White Man's Burden' (1899), in *idem, Complete Verse* (New York: Doubleday, 1989), p. 322. Reprinted by permission of A.P. Watt Ltd on behalf of the National Trust for Places of Historic Interest or Natural Beauty.

a resident of Great Britain—formerly much greater, now shrivelled and retracted, emblematized in Britannia who once buoyantly rode the waves. The fact that I want to deflate her, to picture her as a cartoonish cellulite Queen coasting on a boogie board in a Union Jack swimsuit, does not mean that my head is not still crammed with a nostalgic mental landscape of the Empire, the Raj and Rudyard Kipling. Irony transforms, but does not exorcise ghosts; Raymond Williams is right when he says that the effects of colonialism on the English imagination 'have gone deeper than can easily be traced'.[4]

My mental landscape is also overwhelmingly Christian. Not just in the sense that a certain twee sense of middle-class Englishness is made up of church spires and teas and vicars, or that Christianity is still the official state religion, epitomized in the Church of England, but in the sense that a typically English secularity defines itself against a Protestant Christian heritage. My own history is also (unusually) Christian: I grew up worshipping in a small village Baptist church, where William Carey was something of a hero,[5] and where, very occasionally, we had missionaries for tea (let the reader understand). The extent to which I 'practise' seems hardly relevant in this respect, for it is my understanding that dominant ideologies do not need to be rehearsed to be sustained. For me, the language, idioms and symbols of Christianity are home-ground, and Judaism will always be an Other—idealized, denigrated, compared and contrasted, but always construed in some sense alongside or against Christianity.

And in this respect I am pleased to report that I am reassuringly normal. For, as the structuralists and poststructuralists keep telling us, the Western mind sinks naturally into antitheses, into contrasts between Self and Other, civilized and savage, male and female, home and

---

4. R. Williams, *The Country and the City* (New York: Oxford University Press, 1973), p. 281.

5. William Carey, a Calvinist and a Baptist, founded the Baptist Missionary Society in 1792. As a child, I read a book extolling him as a hero. Now I'm reading Sugirtharajah and Dharmaraj, who point out how, unlike some of his contemporaries, he failed to protest against colonial expansion, and who argue that 'his unwillingness to speak against the political and economic evils of the colonial government had missional and monetary aims' (R.S. Sugirtharajah, 'A Postcolonial Exploration of Collusion and Construction in Biblical Interpretation', in *idem* [ed.], *The Postcolonial Bible* [Bible and Postcolonialism, 1; Sheffield: Sheffield Academic Press, 1998], pp. 91-116; J.S. Dharmaraj, *Colonialism and Mission: Postcolonial Reflections* [Delhi: ISPCK, 1993], p. 53).

abroad.[6] Instinctively we make our others into a negative image of the Self: the rational male is supported by an emotional female. Conversely (and it's symptomatic that we think in converses), when Self or home-ground becomes distasteful, our first instinct is to demonize the Self, idealize the Other, flip over the hierarchy and start again.

This tendency to produce our world in binaries runs deep throughout Western history. It is there in the Bible: in the oppositions between Jacob and Esau, Isaac and Ishmael, good brother and bad brother, Israelite and Edomite, Jew and Gentile, Sarah and Hagar (Gal. 4.22-31); it is there in the genesis of the Moabites, Ammonites and Canaanites in the sordid nexus of incest, nakedness and curse (Gen. 9.20-28; 19.30-38).[7] And it is there in the projection of the inhabitants of the land of Canaan as, variously, monstrous giants, thorns or scourges requiring wholesale extraction, invisible non-presences in an empty land—images that have all been conscripted in the service of colonial enterprises across the globe.[8] The Other is a projection of our own

---

6.   It also tends to use huge imperialistic abstractions like 'the Western Mind'.

7.   This point was first made, as far as I know, not by a biblical critic but by the cultural critic Hayden White. White links the rhetorical debasement of the Other to the crisis of self-definition in times of socio-cultural stress. He explores how Genesis sets up a tension between the Israelites and the accursed races, marked by savagery or physical aberration in size and colour (H. White, *Tropics of Discourse: Essays in Cultural Criticism* [Baltimore: Johns Hopkins University Press, 1978], p. 162). Similarly, the cultural theorist Jeffrey Cohen has pointed to Num. 13 as the 'most famous example' of 'the exaggeration of cultural difference into monstrous aberration': 'The aboriginal inhabitants of Canaan', he writes, 'are envisioned as menacing giants to justify the Hebrew colonisation of the Promised Land'; and 'representing an anterior culture as monstrous justifies its displacement or extermination by rendering the act heroic' (J.J. Cohen, 'Monster Culture [Seven Theses]', in *idem* [ed.], *Monster Theory* [Minneapolis: University of Minnesota Press, 1996], pp. 3-25 [7-8]). It is still unusual to find this kind of ideological critique in mainstream biblical studies, and commentaries on the book of Genesis or Joshua tend to maintain a studied silence. But, for a recent, trenchant discussion of the issues, see R. Schwartz, *The Curse of Cain: The Violent Legacy of Monotheism* (Chicago: University of Chicago Press, 1997).

8.   See, e.g., Gen. 13.14-17; Num. 33.50-56; Deut. 20.16-18; Josh. 23.12-13; 24.11-13; 1 Sam.15.2-3. The exploration of the complicity between the Bible and colonial discourse is just beginning in biblical studies (see Sugirtharajah [ed.], *The Postcolonial Bible*; D.M. Gunn, 'Colonialism and the Vagaries of Scripture: Te Kooti in Canaan [A Story of Bible and Dispossession in Aotearoa/New Zealand]',

anxiety, a way of enforcing borders: as J. Fabian puts it, 'our ways of making the Other are ways of making ourselves'.[9] No man or nation is an island, as Donne famously proclaimed, but around the conceptual island that is my England, my Christian England, is a sea of Others keeping her sense of herself afloat.

So is there any way out of this habitual, violent reflex of the mind? A range of philosophers from Coleridge to Levinas to Derrida suggest 'negative capability', counter-intuitive reading, empathy with the face of the Other, deconstructing 'violent hierarchies'. But there is a sense in which the conceptual realignment of our world has been going on, in a blander, less theorized sense for centuries, in the quiet rearrangement of our world that takes place in metaphor. Metaphors 'carry over' senses from one sphere to another; they confuse categories, put words in unexpected new relationships. Metaphors are the unsensationalized stagehands of our thought processes—lugging and shifting the scenery of our mental landscape.[10]

In this brief essay I want to probe a new and strange-seeming metaphor, with the aim of dislocating some of my habits of thought. The metaphor I'm exploring is the idea of *inner-biblical colonization*: that is, I am comparing the way Christianity aligns its Self in relationship to

in T. Linafelt and T.K. Beal [eds.], *God in the Fray: A Tribute to Walter Brueggemann* [Minneapolis: Fortress Press, 1998], pp. 127-42; and M. Prior, *The Bible and Colonialism: A Moral Critique* [The Biblical Seminar, 48; Sheffield: Sheffield Academic Press, 1997]—a groundbreaking study that is nevertheless disturbing in its focus on Zionism as the iconic instance of nationalism). For a wonderful—and disturbing—exploration of 'murder' as the condition of self-definition and meaning in the Hebrew Bible, see D.N. Fewell, 'Imagination, Method and Murder: Un/Framing the Face of Post-Exilic Israel', in T.K. Beal and D.M. Gunn (eds.), *Reading Bibles, Writing Bodies: Identity and the Book* (Biblical Limits; London: Routledge, 1997), pp. 132-52.

9.   J. Fabian, 'Presence and Representation: The Other and Anthropological Writing', *Critical Inquiry* 16 (1989), pp. 753-72 (756).

10.   Michel de Certeau makes a similar point regarding stories. Playing with the connection between metaphor and the root *metapherein* ('to transfer') he writes: 'In modern Athens, the vehicles of mass transporation are called *metaphorai*. To go to work or come home, one takes a "metaphor"—a bus or train. Stories could also take this noble name: every day they traverse and organise places, they select and link them together; they make trajectories and itineraries out of them. They are spatial trajectories' (M. de Certeau, 'Spatial Stories', in *idem, The Practice of Everyday Life* [trans. S.F. Randall; Berkeley: University of California Press, 1984], pp. 115-30 [115]).

the Jew and the Old Testament, to the way in which an imperial England conceptualizes itself in relation to the annexed territories and their indigenous population. It needs to be said at the outset that the metaphor has many weaknesses, many points of dissimilarity; no metaphor runs on all four legs at once, said Coleridge sagely, and this one sometimes runs on two, and sometimes hops or even limps.[11] Still, it

11. At this point the footnotes begin to play rather a key role. This essay is thinking metaphorically, and metaphor is always an exercise in conjunction *and disjunction*. So I shall be using footnotes to support and prop up the main text (long footnotes, stacking sources and evidences, providing impressively deep foundations) *and* to point out places where the metaphor unravels (contra conventional academic wisdom, and self-presentations of that wisdom, I see dissonance as part of the experiment, and detailing it, showing where the metaphor limps, will hopefully prevent the main text from congealing into some kind of cartoonish caricature). The metaphor walks, I think, and allows me to make progress, because plundering insights from a more developed field of critique—Postcolonial Studies—allows me to say and theorize things that are only beginning to be noticed and theorized in my own discipline. It limps in the sense that, in the attempt to weld the analogy together, I inevitably homogenize: I lump Jewish others and colonial others together, conscripting the latter as signifers, and I give a skewed impression of Old Testament studies, inevitably focusing on its more explicitly Christian and anti-Jewish manifestations. Paradoxically, even as it attempts to highlight the supreme self-confidence of the Christian 'Metropolis' or centre, and its damaging side-effects, the metaphor also *obscures* the real issue—anti-Judaism and supersessionism in *contemporary* Old Testament commentary. Perhaps what is needed at this point is simply a catalogue of examples, boldly showing why, when preparing course bibliographies, I spend as much time emphatically *not* recommending books as recommending them. Lest the point of the metaphor gets lost in colonial tropes and analogies, I at least try to document the evidence as fully as possible, *down here*, in footnotes. Here are some examples, found in one hour on the university library shelves that my students (or at least some of them) regularly peruse. Gordon Wenham on Leviticus: 'Leviticus used to be the first book that Jewish children studied in the synagogue. In the modern Church it tends to be the last part of the Bible anyone looks at seriously' (G.J. Wenham, *The Book of Leviticus* (Grand Rapids: Eerdmans, 1985 [1979]). Though this is evidently not Wenham's intention, the statement unfortunately reinforces perceptions of a Judaism preoccupied with sacrifice, and sets up an antithesis between synagogue and 'modern Church'. W. Gladstone Watson on Joel: 'When Joel thinks of…victory as the glorification of the Jews and the destruction of the Gentiles, he shows that he is but a child of his age, sharing its limitations and prejudices. He has failed to grasp the universality of the grace of God… His view is also vastly opposed to that of Paul and the general attitude of the NT. 'Joel', in F.C. Eiselen, E. Lewis and D.G. Downey [eds.], *The Abingdon Bible Commentary* [New York: Abingdon Press, 1929], pp. 768-74

helps me to articulate a sense of profound discomfort that I feel working in the field of Old Testament/Hebrew Bible, and that is only
gauchely and awkwardly expressed by calling myself a lecturer in Old
Testament and Hebrew Bible.

The colonial metaphor is not my own: it was first suggested by
Timothy Beal in his work on the book of Esther. Beal explores how in
Christian commentary (and the bulk of Old Testament commentary *is*
implicitly or explicitly Christian), the book of Esther has been seen as a
repository of a vindictiveness, a nationalism, an earthiness and a sen-

---

[770]). Robert Rogers on the Suffering Servant: 'I personally accept and also make
my own a fine testimony of George Adam Smith, which is in these words: "It may
relieve the air of electricity, which is apt to charge it at the discussion of so classic a
passage as this...if we at once assert, what none but prejudiced Jews have ever
denied, that his great prophecy...was fulfilled in One Person, Jesus of Nazareth, and
achieved all its details by him alone"' ('Isaiah', in Eiselen, Lewis and Downey
[eds.], *The Abingdon Bible Commentary,* pp. 628-76 [665]). W. Neil on 'the situation in Palestine after the return from the exile', and the book of Jonah's role in
that situation: the attempt 'to reproduce in Palestine the splendid isolationism of
Jewry, which had developed during the Exile, had borne bitter fruit... The Jews
were the people; all Gentiles were to be hated and shunned. The book of Jonah
therefore finds its place in the OT as the work of an unknown writer of the fourth
century BC who in a little tale of the lesson which Yahweh taught to the harsh and
intolerant Jew, protested against this travesty of the message of Second Isaiah, and
saught to persuade his countrymen that God's love is wide enough and deep enough
to include the hated Gentile' ('Jonah', *IDB,* IV, pp. 964-66 [965-66]). Derek Kidner
on Ezra–Nehemiah: 'The rebuilding of the wall almost asks to be seen as a symbol
of Israel's separatism: the material expression of a siege mentality. While this is not
altogether fair, since the wall had been torn down in a campaign of slander and
intimidation and rebuilt in a spirit of faith, it is true that Nehemiah used it not only
for physical protection but for spiritual quarantine, to defend the sabbath from
violation'; and 'In short what we see in Ezra–Nehemiah is an Israel cut down to the
roots, but drawing new vitality from its neglected source of nourishment in the
Mosaic law and already showing signs, by its new concern for purity, of growing
into the Judaism which we meet, for better and worse, in the New Testament' (D.
Kidner, *Ezra and Nehemiah* [TOTC; Leicester: Inter-Varsity Press, 1979], p. 23).
These quotations do nothing to discourage stereotyped perceptions of the Jew as
xenophobic, entangled in blood and sacrifice, burdened by law, insular, and
altogether dwarfed by the religion of the New Testament. And clearly, the detailed
critique of Jewish stereotypes by New Testament scholars, and the awareness that
these are a product of polemic, rather than a snapshot of reality, has not yet fully
permeated Old Testament studies, where New Testament stereotypes are commonly
replicated in discussions of Old Testament texts.

suality that is seen as characteristically 'Jewish' as opposed to 'Christian'.[12] Thus the book of Esther has contributed to the formation of

12. To give a flavour of some of the commentary against which Beal is reacting, here is a selective sample. Luther (on 2 Maccabees and Esther): 'I am so hostile to this book and to Esther that I could wish that they did not exist at all, for they judaize too much and have much pagan impropriety' (*Table Talk*, cit. Beal, *The Book of Hiding*, p. 6). H.G.A. Ewald: 'Its story knows nothing of high and pure truths. In it we fall as if from heaven to earth' (*History of Israel* [London: Longman, Green, 1869], p. 197, cit. Beal, *The Book of Hiding*, p. 7). Lewis Bayles Paton (after detailing the shortcomings of all the characters in the book, the sensual despotism of Ahasuerus, the bloodthirstiness and sexual immorality of Esther the concubine, the self-interest of Mordecai): '[the author] gloats over the wealth and the triumph of his heroes and is oblivious to their moral shortcomings. Morally Esther falls far below the general level of the Old Testament and even the Apocrypha' (*The Book of Esther* [ICC; New York: Charles Scribner's Sons, 1908], p. 96, cit. Beal, *The Book of Hiding*, pp. 7-8). O. Eissfeldt: 'The fact that in spite of all the objections which would militate against its acceptance, it was nevertheless taken into the canon, is in the last resort to be explained from the close connection between Jewish religion and the Jewish national spirit. A book which was so closely bound up with the national spirit, and which indeed the people regarded as a source of its power, could not be excluded by the religion which was bound up with it. This we can understand. But *Christianity, extending as it does over all peoples and races*, has neither occasion nor justification for holding onto it. For Christianity Luther's remark should be determinative...' (*The Old Testament: An Introduction* [trans. P.R. Ackroyd; Oxford: Basil Blackwell, 1965 [1934], pp. 511-12; emphasis added). B. Anderson: 'Esther is an emphatically Jewish book' which sounds a 'discordant note...in the ears of those accustomed to hearing the Christian gospel' ('The Place of the Book of Esther in the Christian Bible', *JR* 30 (1950), pp. 32-43 [32], cit. Beal, *The Book of Hiding*, p. 8). W.L. Northridge: 'The intensity of the hatred which the book reveals is indicated in 9.13-16, where demand is made for a second butchery of the non-Jewish population. Here, and in 8.7-14, we see Jewish vindictiveness at its worst.' However, the book 'serves a useful purpose in setting the contrast between the unworthy elements in Judaism and the Christian spirit of love to all, even to one's enemies' (from an introduction published in 1937, cited in C.G. Montefiore and H. Loewe, *A Rabbinic Anthology* [Philadelphia: Jewish Publication Society of America, 1963 [1938], pp. 614-15). Montefiore and Loewe's anthology, written in 1938, makes for haunting reading. Anticipating the arguments of this essay by about 50 years, they write of the 'human love of foils and contrasts' that makes the Jewish a 'foil' for the Christian, and they observe how 'Esther has become the most Jewish book in the OT, and Jonah the least'. They explain Purim (at worst, Haman is a sort of 'Jewish Guy Fawkes'), and they critique the linguistic advantage of Christianity (for according to the dictionary a 'Christian' is by definition both moral and mild). But most hauntingly, in essays written after

Christian identity by offering the *antithesis* of Christian identity, or, as Beal puts it, Esther has become a kind of Christian colony, 'a dark continent into which images of the Jew are projected as quintessentially not us'.[13] Beal also adds, provocatively, that Esther is the book that offers the most caricatured depictions of Jewishness, and that 'Esther is the remotest "Jewish" outpost within the Christian Old Testament'.[14]

Lurking behind Beal's study of Esther, then, is a sense of an Old Testament map, or globe, of which Esther forms one—very distinctive and symptomatic—part. I sense the map that Beal is referring to because when I first emigrated to Biblical Studies from English Litera-ture I too learned to navigate the globe of the Old Testament, to under-stand the larger cartography of the imagination that lurks beneath and structures the meticulous scholarly prose. The Old Testament is full of fractures and fissures and 'struggling contradictions':[15] it is woven from different sources, and is made up from a collection of different textual fabrics that 'will not take the same theological dye'.[16] Judaism and Christianity both extricate themselves from some portions of the Word, and create a huge, glossed living space from others.[17] In the case of

---

Kristalnacht but before the Second World War, they argue that Jews and Christians 'both live in glass houses and therefore should not throw stones', and ask in a rhetorical flourish, should religion be characterized by its worst elements—should Hitler, for example, be classed as typically 'Christian'?

13. Beal, *The Book of Hiding*, p. 5.

14. Beal, *The Book of Hiding*, p. 12.

15. W. Eichrodt, *Theology of the Old Testament* (2 vols.; London: SCM Press, 1961), I, p. 490.

16. M.C. Calloway, 'Canonical Criticism', in S.L. McKenzie and S.R. Haynes (eds.), *To Each its Own Meaning: An Introduction to Biblical Criticisms and their Application* (Louisville, KY: Westminster/John Knox Press, 1993), pp. 121-34 (122).

17. Jewish and Christian traditions are similar in the sense that they tend to explain the most violent or seemingly unjust passages in the Old Testament/ Tanakh, to improve the reputation of heroes, and to betray a profound discomfort with the passages in which God or Israel seem to act most cruelly towards their enemies. For example, in rabbinic Judaism, Pharaoh is given five warnings before God hardens his heart (*Exod. R.* 9.9), 'an eye for an eye and a tooth for a tooth' is adjusted to monetary compensation, and the triumphalist Song of the Sea (Exod. 15) undergoes divine censorship, as Yhwh protests: 'My handiwork is drowning in the Sea and you presume to sing praises' (*b. Meg.* 10b). As Montefiore notes, Judaism as well as Christianity displays that 'delightful inconsistency so customary in human nature' whereby 'bad' biblical passages are 'theoretically unrepudiated'

Christianity, the textual territories tend to be hierarchized and organized—and the theological or ideological map that emerges is as simple, and complex, as the map of the British Empire. It is simple because every book or territory tends to be read in relation to 'home', and a default dichotomy is set up between home and abroad, New and Old Testament. But it is complex in the sense that Abroad, the realm of the Other, is not monolithic, but is structured by a complex set of gradations, contrasts and internal contradictions. On a map of the British Empire 'the colonies' may all be coloured pink, but they take up different, distinct places on the ideological spectrum. The white colonies (Australia, Canada) are closer to us, the black and Asian colonies (Rhodesia, India) are further away; Africa is the 'heart of darkness', the 'dark continent'; India is a country that 'no mind can take hold of',[18] and the disorientating Orient, seductively feminized, mascaraed, veiled, is a veritable 'porno-tropics of the imagination', a 'magic lantern of the mind' onto which Europe projects its forbidden sexual desires and fears.[19] Similarly an Old Testament topography charts our Pocohontases and our Calibans, our noble savages, our Pals, our monstrous Others, our places of dark seductive allure.[20] At the dark extremities of the

---

but also 'carefully ignored, or ingeniously, if not very ingeniously, explained away' (C.G. Montefiore, 'The Use of the Adjectives "Jewish" and "Christian" in England', in Montefiore and Loewe, *A Rabbinic Anthology*, pp. 609-16 [613-14]).

18. E.M. Forster, *A Passage to India* (New York: Harcourt, Brace & World, 1952), p. 136. Compare Hegel's assertion that India is a place of confusion, where the sensuous object 'is not liberated by free power of the Spirit into a beautiful form, but is expanded into the immeasurable and the undefined, and the Divine is thereby made bizarre, confused, ridiculous' (G.W.F. Hegel, *Lectures on the Philosphy of History 1830–31* [trans. J. Sibree; New York: Dover, 1956], p. 141).

19. A. McClintock, *Imperial Leather: Race, Gender and Sexuality in the Colonial Contest* (London: Routledge, 1995), p. 22.

20. E. Said's catalogue of the cultural repertoire of Orientalism suggests that the imaginative space of the Orient overlaps with the imaginative space of the Old Testament *and vice versa*: 'In the depths of this Oriental stage', he writes, 'stands a prodigious cultural repertoire whose individual items evoke a fabulously rich world: the Sphinx, Cleopatra, *Eden*, Troy, *Sodom and Gomorrah*, Astarte, Isis and Osiris, *Sheba*, Babylon, the Genii, *the Magi, Nineveh*, Prester John, Mahomet, and dozens more; settings in some cases names only half-imagined, half-known; monsters, devils, heroes, terrors, pleasures, desires' (*Orientalism: Western Conceptions of the Orient* [Harmondsworth: Penguin Books, 1995], p. 63; emphasis added). You only have to look at lavish Hollywood productions like *Esther and the King*, or equally lavish descriptions of the rites of sacred prostitution, to see that, for the

imagination lie our Indias, our Africas, our dark Continents—Ezra–Nehemiah, Esther, Joshua, Leviticus, 'the Law'[21]—which all have their own very distinctive, and conflicted, 'poetics of space'.[22] At the other end of the spectrum lie the Servant Songs, Ruth, Jonah, the pre-exilic prophets, Second Isaiah—so like us, so like home, that they are virtually *Translations of the Gospel into the Hebrew Tongue.* The lie of the conceptual land is clearly laid out for the student in textbooks such as Anderson's *The Living World of the Old Testament,* where Esther is placed at the 'opposite extreme' to Jonah and Second Isaiah, and where the 'wide vistas' of Second Isaiah or Jonah are contrasted with Esther's 'provincial and vindictive spirit'.[23] Thus the noble books and their primitive antitheses mark the two ends of the spectrum—and most books take up their places somewhere in between.[24]

'scholarly' and 'popular' imagination alike, the Old Testament has acted as a projection of the desires and fears outlawed at 'home'. Certainly in my colonized and Christianized imagination, the allure of the Old Testament has had something to do with a sense of the exotic, the seductive, the savage-as-attractive, which is probably why the nexus of the exotic—of Vashti, Sheba, Esther, Beauty Queens, perfumes, exotic oils, the Song of Songs—now appeals as a highly alluring area of study. But, for the moment, I will have to leave it beckoning, fluttering its mascaraed lashes at me beyond the edges of the essay, and get on with the business of writing this one.

21. The list of unsatisfactory, residual texts varies from author to author, but usually includes the same core texts. For R.H. Pfeiffer, for example, the dark remainder includes 'The Jewish exclusivism of Nehemiah and the sanguine apocalyptic dreams of Jehovah's extermination of the Gentiles (Ez. 38–39, Joel, Obadiah and the like)' (*Introduction to the Old Testament* [London: A. & C. Black, 1952], p. 589).

22. The phrase 'poetics of space' comes from G. Bachélard, *The Poetics of Space* (trans. M. Jolas; New York: Orion Press, 1964). On the way in which the annexed territories become an empty space for the colonial imagination, see, e.g., V.Y. Mudimbe, *The Invention of Africa: Gnosis, Philosophy and the Order of Knowledge* (Bloomington: Indiana University Press, 1988).

23. B.W. Anderson, *The Living World of the Old Testament* (London: Longman, 1988), pp. 607, 610.

24. Already a whole set of qualifications are needed to bolster the metaphor and keep it from crumbling. Though Old Testament theology and commentary tends to hierarchize texts, the misfit texts, the strange dark texts are by no means always 'othered' as 'Jewish'. A whole strain of scholarship during the late nineteenth and early twentieth centuries, for example, analysed the 'Religion of the Semites' drawing on the work of colonial anthropologists (see, e.g., W. Robertson Smith, *Lectures on the Religion of the Semites* [London: Routledge, 1996 (1889)] and W.O.E. Oesterley and T.H. Robinson, *Hebrew Religion: Its Origin and*

The logic of Empire is the logic of appropriation, of 'stretch[ing] the taut tight skin of the nation over the gigantic body of the Empire'.[25] Similarly, there is a tendency, particularly with the most familiar, noble texts of the Old Testament, to domesticate them, to stretch the taut tight skin of Christianity over them, to make their ideological landscapes as much like home as possible. Just as Stanley, looking out for the first time over the country of Ukawendi near Lake Tanganyika, imagined 'a church spire' and 'a score of pretty cottages' instead of 'tamarinds' and 'gum trees',[26] and Thomas Babington Macaulay looked out over India

---

Development [London: SPCK, 1996 (1937)]). In a classic post-Enlightenment move, texts that were manifestly incompatible with standards of Western civilization, Western rationalism and Western Christianity (such as the violent destruction of Achan's whole family in Judg. 7) were explained using terms borrowed from colonial discourse (the whole family was destroyed because the primitive believed in 'corporate personality' and could not distinguish between the individual and the group). Similarly, stories of talking snakes and crude anthropomorphic presentations of God were ascribed to a sub-strata of folk-tale and primitive religion. Such studies suggest a different kind of reciprocity between biblical studies, colonialism and anthropology (the so-called 'handmaiden of colonialism'), but also show that the antithesis between Christian and Jew is only one means of ordering (and controlling) Old Testament material. Similarly, there are other misfit texts that are perceived as hovering on the very edges of the canon, but that have not habitually been categorized as 'Jewish'—for example the book of Ecclesiastes. T.C. Vreizen, for example, is uncomfortable with Esther, which is a 'revelation of the spirit of the Jewish people' and Ecclesiastes which is a 'revelation of the spirit of the age' (*An Outline of Old Testament Theology* [Oxford: Basil Blackwell, 1958], p. 89): the distinction suggests that it is only the violent, nationalistic, particularistic texts that are classically percieved as Jewish. An exception is A.J. Grieve who, writing in 1919, concludes that 'we are justified in seeing in Qoheleth, not exactly a Sadducee, but a herald of Saducceeism, a representation of the temper of the outlook out of which that unlovely school developed' ('Ecclesiastes', in A.S. Peake [ed.], *A Commentary on the Bible* [London: Nelson & Sons, 1919], pp. 411-17 [411-12]). Incidentally, under a section entitled 'Value', Grieve makes it absolutely clear how dark, quintessentially Jewish texts work in the Christian canon: 'Ecclesiastes has the qualities of its defects. Not without Divine Providence has this book been included in the Canon of Scripture. It shows better than any other the need for the incarnation, it forms a most effective background for the Good News...' (p. 412).

25. B. Anderson, *Imagined Communities: Reflections on the Origin and Spread of Nationalism* (London: Verso, 1991), p. 101.

26. N.R. Bennett (ed.), *Stanley's Dispatches to the New York Herald* (Boston: Boston University Press, 1970), pp. 75-76. For a discussion of the colonial desire to turn the foreign into the image of home, and its consequences, see A. Crosby, *Eco-*

and longed to create a 'class of persons, Indian in blood and colour, but English in taste, in morals, in opinions and intellect',[27] so biblical critics similarly graft 'imperial [Christian] structures on alien scaffolding'[28] ('As so often', writes Leslie Allen of Jonah, 'the effect of this Old Testament book is to lay a foundation upon which the New can build'[29]). The book of Jonah is like the parable of the Good Samaritan, Rom. 3.29, Jn 3.16 and the showdown between Jesus and the narrow-minded Pharisees;[30] the Suffering Servant, in a wonderful conflation of missionary rhetoric and New Testament language, is one who goes through Gethsemane and is 'called to be a light to the Heathen'.[31] Like annexed territories, the Old Testament texts are perceived as 'voids' into which the colonizers can 'pour their own ideas'[32]—and the net effect is as strange as honeysuckle Englishness grafted into the heart of Africa.

It is a common feature of colonial rhetoric that it eradicates mutuality and 'transfers the locus of desire onto the colonised object'.[33] The Empire does not need the colonies—the colonies need the Empire: the undeveloped land begs for the *cultivation* of Empire, as does the undeveloped native, who typically beseeches Imperial tutelage, Imperial order, Imperial government. Though annexing foreign territory obviously serves British nationalism and British interests, nationalism and interests are displaced onto the colonized. The indigenous population is habitually described as 'selfish'—either self-consciously, or unwittingly

logical Imperialism: The Biological Expansion of Europe 900–1900 (Cambridge: Cambridge University Press, 1986), pp. 196-216.

27. T.B. Macaulay, 'Minute on Indian Education' (1835), in J. Clive (ed.), *Selected Writings* (Chicago: University of Chicago Press, 1972), pp. 244-50 (249).

28. A. Loomba, *Colonialism/Postcolonialism* (London: Routledge, 1998), p. 67.

29. L. Allen, *The Books of Joel, Obadiah, Jonah and Micah* (London: Hodder & Stoughton, 1976), p. 194.

30. See, e.g., W. Rudolph, *Joel, Obadiah, Jonah und Micah* (Gütersloh: Gerd Mohn, 1971), p. 371; Allen, *The Books*, p. 180. Rudolph deems Jonah a very *'christlichen'* book, and claims that it captures the very *'quintessenz des Evangeliums'*.

31. C.R. North, *Isaiah 40–55: Introduction and Commentary* (London: SCM Press, 1959), table of contents.

32. E. Said, *Culture and Imperialism* (New York: Vintage, 1993), p. 349.

33. D. Spurr, *The Rhetoric of Empire: Colonial Discourse in Journalism, Travel Writing and Imperial Administration* (Durham, NC: Duke University Press, 1993), p. 28.

so, in the sense that they are 'lazy'[34]—because they hoard their rich natural resources and keep them from the rest of civilization. Frederick Lugard, the British Governor General of Nigeria, expressed the view that 'The tropics are the heritage of mankind, and…the races which inhabit them [do not have] a right to deny their bounties to those who need them';[35] Albert Sarraut, governor of French Indochina, commented on the perversity of global distribution—the way in which intellectual wealth was located in Europe, but 'natural wealth' was locked up in 'territories occupied by backward races who, not knowing how to profit by it themselves, are even less capable of releasing it to the great circular current that nourishes the ever-growing needs of humanity'.[36] It

---

34. The African and West Indian were commonly regarded as childlike and sunk in tropical indolence: the school textbook, Nelson's *The World and its Peoples* (c. 1907) described the African as 'an overgrown child, vain, self-indulgent, and fond of idleness'; C.R.L. Fletcher and R. Kipling's *A School History of England* (Garden City, NY: Doubleday, Page & Co., 1911) characterized the negro as 'lazy, vicious, and incapable of serious improvement, or of work except under compulsion' and recommends that 'a few bananas will sustain the life of a negro quite sufficiently' (both school textbooks are cited in J.M. MacKenzie, *Propaganda and Empire: The Manipulation of British Public Opinion 1880–1960* [Manchester: Manchester University Press, 1990], p. 184). For examples of how similar ideas were mapped onto the Malays, Filipinos and Javanese, see S.H. Alatas, *The Myth of the Lazy Native: A Study of the Image of the Malays, Filipinos and Javanese from the Sixteenth to the Twentieth Century and its Function in the Ideology of Colonial Capitalism* (London: Frank Cass, 1977). For example, Alatas cites the professional opinion of the economic historian Clive Day (1904) that 'nothing less than immediate material enjoyment will stir [the Javanese] from their indolent routine' (Alatas, *The Myth of the Lazy Native*, p. 62).

35. F. Lugard, *The Dual Mandate in British Tropical Africa* (London: Frank Cass, 1922), pp. 60-61.

36. According to colonial logic, by a perverse twist of fate, there appears to have been an error regarding divine distribution of national resources. Albert Sarraut, Governor General of French Indochina in 1911–14 and 1917–19, later Minister of Colonies, commented on how nature's 'double abundance' of intellectual and material resources seem to have come adrift from one another: 'While in a narrow corner of the world nature has concentrated in white Europe the powers of invention, the means of progress, and the dynamic of scientific advancement, the greatest accumulation of natural wealth is locked up in territories occupied by backward races who, not knowing how to profit by it themselves, are even less capable of releasing it to the great circular current that nourishes the ever-growing needs of humanity' (A. Sarraut, *Grandeur et servitude coloniales* [Paris: Saggitaire, 1931], p. 109).

falls to the colonizer, then, to nourish humanity—to take up the White Man's burden and the 'trusteeship of the weaker races'[37] —to boldly do battle with the pride, nationalisms,[38] weaknesses and ineptitudes that would prevent riches circulating to the rest of civilization.

Now if we map this rhetoric onto the field of Old Testament studies, some telling correspondences begin to emerge. For, occasionally surfacing between the carefully chosen words and neat erudition of scholarship, are traces of a similarly skewed, 'colonial' metanarrative. The introductory student text *The Living World of the Old Testament* critiques the 'legalistic' preoccupation with Torah that became a fundamental 'weakness' in Judaism[39]—the observation can be traced back to Wellhausen, for whom postexilic Judaism was the iconic and reprehensible example of institutionalized, stagnant religion.[40] Deep in the heart

37. The phrase 'the trusteeship of the weaker races' was frequently used in the British parliament during the colonial era (see Spurr, *The Rhetoric of Empire*, p. 114).

38. For example, the British Governor of Egypt 1882–1907, Lord Cromer Evelyn Baring (appropriately known as 'over-Baring'), rejected Egyptian demands for a self-sustaining sovereignty on the grounds that 'the real future of Egypt lies not in the direction of a narrow nationalism which will only embrace native Egyptians...but rather in that of an enlarged cosmopolitanism' (cit. Said, *Orientalism*, p. 37).

39. Anderson, *The Living World of the Old Testament*, p. 538. The heading of the section is 'The Weaknesses of Judaism' and Anderson claims that 'Devotion to the Torah easily lapsed into legalism, the fruit of which was a complaining bitterness about one's lot or a proud self-righteousness—notes that sometimes are heard in the Psalms. The Torah could become so overladen with minutiae or so twisted by clever legal interpretation that it could be used as a means of escaping from God's demand—an accusation that Jesus made against the scribes and Pharisees of his day (Matt. 15.1-9)... We have only to read the New Testament to become aware of this weakness within Judaism... Preoccupation with the Torah seemed to stifle the spirit of prophecy.' Though Anderson adds that 'the rabbis of the post-biblical period at times were just as severe in their criticism of the dangers and corruptions to which the Jewish faith was exposed', the picture of postexilic Judaism as 'corrupt' and 'weak' is clear. Anderson's comments amply demonstrate how forays into the Old Testament from the New Testament as metropolis, base or home, so easily locate negative New Testament stereotypes of Jews within Old Testament texts.

40. J. Wellhausen idealized ancient Israelite religion in stark contrast to postexilic Judaism. Clearly, anti-Judaism finds its way into Wellhausen's work and, arguably, structures his hugely influential thesis. In the *Prolegomena*, Wellhausen condemns the fundamentally 'Jewish' invention that ignores 'objective truth' to

of Old Testament studies, then, there is a sense, to borrow the words of Lugard and Sarraut, that postexilic Judaism becomes 'incapable of releasing [its] natural wealth' to the great circular current that nourishes the ever-growing needs of humanity', that bounties were locked up, unfairly denied to those who need them.[41] True, this scholarly legacy is

pass off later traditions as 'Mosaic', and compares this tendency to the rabbis—'the audacious inventors of history' (*Prolegomena to the History of Israel* [London: A. & C. Black, 1885], p. 161). He goes on to denounce the complex lists of temple functionaries, furnishings and genealogies in 1 Chron. 22–29 as 'artificial', 'monotonous' and a 'horrible example of the statistical phantasy of the Jews which revels in vast sums of money on paper' (*Prolegomena*, p. 166). For condemnation of anti-Judaism in Wellhausen's work, see S. Schechter, 'Higher Criticism—Higher Anti-Semitism', in his *Seminary Addresses and Other Papers* (Cincinnati: Ark Publishing, 1915), pp. 36-37; J.D. Levenson, *The Hebrew Bible, the Old Testament and Historical Criticism* (New Haven: Yale University Press, 1993); L. Silberman, 'Wellhausen and Judaism', *Semeia* 25 (1983), pp. 75-82. For the counter-argument that Wellhausen's dominant influence is not anti-Semitism but Romanticism, with its attendant hatred of institutionalized religion, see J. Barton, 'Wellhausen's Prolegomena to the History of Israel: Influences and Effects', in D. Smith-Christopher (ed.), *Text and Experience: Towards a Cultural Exegesis of the Bible* (The Biblical Seminar, 35; Sheffield: Sheffield Academic Press, 1995), pp. 316-29. (Personally I find that the two arguments do not negate, but rather reinforce one another. For it is crucial, surely, that in the Romantic condemnation of insitutionalized religion, Wellhausen seizes on Judaism as the iconic example.)

41. The big names of Old Testament studies—Noth, von Rad, Koch, and Eichrodt—can sound remarkably like Baring, Kipling, Lugard and Sarraut, as they take on a disturbingly imperious tone. M.L. Noth, *The History of Israel* (London: A. & C. Black, 1960), p. 454: 'Thus ended the ghastly epilogue of Israel's history' ('ghastly' is such an appropriately Etonesque translation, making Noth sound more like a colonial governor than he perhaps does in the German). K. Koch: 'It is well known that for any self-respecting Old Testament scholar, the real Old Testament comes to an end with Deutero-Isaiah, or at the latest with Ezra. Everything which comes after that is Judaism and is of no interest' ('Sühne und Sündenvergebung um die Wende von der exilischen zur nachexilischen Zeit', *EvT* 26 [1966], pp. 217-39). W. Eichrodt: 'It was not until in later Judaism a religion of harsh observances had replaced the religion of the Old Testament that the sabbath changed from a blessing to a burdensome duty...real worship of God [was] stifled under the heaping of detailed commands from which the spirit has fled... The living fellowship between God and man shrivelled up into a mere correct observance of the legal regulations... The affirmation of the law as the revelation of God's personal will was lost' (Theology of the Old Testament [2 vols.; Philadelphia: Westminster Press, 1961], I, p. 333, II, p. 348 n. 1, I, pp. 168, 218; cited by J.D. Levenson, *The Hebrew Bible, the Old Testament and Historical Criticism* [Louisville: Westminster/ John

sometimes perpetuated innocently, but then innocence, as Graham Greene so aptly put it, can be like a 'dumb leper who has lost his bell, wandering the earth, meaning no harm'. And not only is there a sense that textual-theological territory is not being managed rightly, but the texts themselves, as rendered in commentary, *proclaim their own need for tutelage and colonization*. Just as the colonizing powers pictured the colonies as needing them and anticipating their (inevitable, benevolent) coming, so the Old Testament is constantly waiting for and demonstrating its need for the New administration. And this need is expressed both negatively and positively (and with different levels of subtlety and intention). A typically 'Jewish' Jonah, for example—lazy, bungling, clownish, unable to respond to simple tasks, unable to see God's purpose, even bloodthirsty and violent—is the very image of pre-colonial chaos that the European comes to ameliorate.[42]

Knox, 1993], p. 19. G. Von Rad: 'The end was reached at the point where the law became an absolute quantity, that is, when it ceased to be understood as the saving ordinance of a special racial group (the cultic community of Israel) linked to it by the facts of history, and when it stepped out of this function of service and became a dictate which *imperiously* called into being its own community' (*Old Testament Theology* [2 vols.; New York: Harper & Row, 1965], I, p. 201; my emphasis—I find the use of the adverb 'imperiously' ironic in the extreme). I am grateful to S.C. Reif for pointing out the Noth, von Rad and Eichrodt references in his essay on 'Jews, Hebraists and "Old Testament" Studies', presented to the Society for Old Testament Study winter conference, Birmingham, 5 January 1999).

42. Again the supporting quotations just need to be stockpiled. Jonah is commonly perceived as 'a type of the narrow, blind, prejudiced and fanatic Jews' (J.A. Bewer, 'Critical and Exegetical Commentary on Jonah', in H.G. Mitchell, J.H. Powis Smith and J.A. Bewer, *A Critical and Exegetical Commentary on Haggai, Zechariah, Malachi and Jonah* [ICC; Edinburgh: T. & T. Clark, 1912], pp. 3-65 [64]), or a 'first-class expansionist ("Israel First")' (J.S. Meek and W. Pierson Merrill, 'Jonah', *IB*, VI, pp. 875-94 [876]). According to *The New Bible Dictionary*, 'The readiness of the people of Nineveh to repent was a salutary lesson to the Jews, who were renowned for their stubbornness and lack of faith' (D.F. Payne, 'Jonah', in J.D. Douglas [ed.], *The New Bible Dictionary* [Leicester: Inter-Varsity Press, 1962], pp. 652-54 [653]), while Pfeiffer asserts that: 'The contemptible attitude of some Jews in the time of the author, represented by Jonah's bitter disappointment when Jehovah in his mercy failed to destroy Nineveh, is stigmatised in God's stinging rebuke to Jonah' (*Introduction to the Old Testament*, p. 588). Read almost as an allegory of supersession, the book of Jonah subjects 'Israel's prerogative' to 'bitter ridicule' (H.W. Wolff, *Obadiah and Jonah* [Hermeneia; trans. M. Kohl; Minneapolis: Augsburg, 1988], p. 119) and exposes the 'untenability of the understanding of the ways of God that was then prevalent in Israel' (E.M. Good, 'Jonah: The

Meanwhile the books of Ezra and Nehemiah look for 'consummation'[43] in the Christianity that will remove the legalistic 'burden' from its shoulders,[44] and make it more effective, and postexilic Judaism in general looks to the 'strength' that will remedy its 'weakness', the civilization that will correct its 'ghastliness'. The metaphors used—the stronger lifting the weaker up, healing weaknesses, removing burdens—are all tropes of imperial discourse.[45] And while the 'inhospital-

---

Absurdity of God', in *idem, Irony in the Old Testament* [London: SPCK, 1965], p. 54). And as well as attracting all the usual adjectives that go along with the anti-Semitic stereotype, Jonah is typically characterized as 'good-for-nothing' (Wolff, *Obadiah and Jonah*, p. 109), as 'self-centred and lazy' (J.C. Holbert, 'Deliverance Belongs to YHWH: Satire in the Book of Jonah', *JSOT* 21 [1981], pp. 59-81 [70]), as 'mulish' (G. von Rad, *God at Work in Israel* [trans. J.H. Marks; Nashville: Abingdon Press, 1980], p. 76), 'monstrous' (von Rad, *God at Work*, p. 66) and 'ludicrous' (M. Burrows, 'The Literary Character of the Book of Jonah', in H.T. Frank and W.L. Reed [eds.], *Translating and Understanding the Old Testament: Essays in Honour of H.G. May* [Nashville: Abingdon Press, 1970], pp. 82-105 [86])—adjectives which make him strikingly similar to colonial Others who are also not up to managing their God-given territory. For critiques of anti-Judaism in Jonah studies, see E.J. Bickerman, 'Les deux erreurs du prophète Jonas', *RHPR* 45 (1965), pp. 232-64; F.W. Golka, 'Jonaexegese und Antijudaismus', *Kirche und Israel* 1 (1986), pp. 51-61; Y.M. Sherwood, 'Rocking the Boat: Jonah and the New Historicism', *BibInt* 5.4 (1997), pp. 364-402 (388-402); and *idem*, 'Cross-Currents in the Book of Jonah: Some Jewish and Cultural Midrashim on a Traditional Text', *BibInt* 6.1 (1998), pp. 49-79 (49-61).

43. F.C. Fensham, *The Books of Ezra and Nehemiah* (Grand Rapids: Eerdmans, 1982), p. 19.

44. Kidner, *Ezra and Nehemiah*, p. 268.

45. David Spurr's excellent study *The Rhetoric of Empire* gives numerous examples, but for my purposes a few will suffice. Albert Sarraut supplies a fabulously bumptious conflation of all the healing, helping, life-saving qualities of the colonizer: 'Without us, without our intervention...these indigenous populations would still be abandoned to misery and abjection; epidemics, massive endemic diseases, and famine would continue to decimate them; infant mortality would still wipe out half their offspring; petty kings and corrupt chiefs would still sacrifice them to vicious caprice; their minds would still be degraded by the practice of base superstition and barbarous custom; and they would perish from misery in the midst of unexploited wealth' (*Grandeur et servitude coloniales*, p. 117). And W.H. Elliott of the London Missionary Society obligingly supplies a wonderfully vivid illustration of the burden-carrying colonizer: for him the typical 'missionary position' involves 'pulling *them* up' with a 'rope of sympathy' while 'they' try to 'pull [the missionary] down' into the 'horrible pit of miry clay' (cited in A.C. Cairns, *Prelude*

ity' and 'bigotry'[46] of Jonah and the Ezra–Nehemites negatively proclaim the need for a new government, so more civilized Old Testament
personae and passages proclaim their need in a more positive sense.
Even before the New Testament arrives, the Old Testament is already
filling up with missionaries (the temporal paradox is as acute as in the
Fathers, where, in a strange de-temporalized synchrony, the New
Testament retrospectively casts a shadow, which is the Old). The Suffering Servant is 'called to be a light to the Heathen', and the book of
Jonah, which has a 'missionary message',[47] is busy outlining 'Israel's
mission to be a light to the Gentiles' and trying to get Jonah to go to
one of the most difficult of 'mission fields'.[48] Just as the motif of Paul's
missionary journeys first emerges in the eighteenth century, etching on
the biblical texts the journeys of emergent missionary societies,[49] so in
the eighteenth and nineteenth centuries, missionary texts and messages
begin to appear in the Old Testament, and the language of the light to
the nations and the universal mission takes on new (colonial) reson-
ances. And just as those who have received an English education are,
according to Macaulay, expected to feel alienated from the darker
realms of their own culture and religion,[50] so the missionized (and mis-
sionizing) texts of the Old Testament tend to detach themselves from,
and evangelize, their weaker, darker, fellow texts. A first-prize winning
essay written in 1841 by an Indian student at Hindu College Calcutta

to *Imperialism: British Reactions to Central African Society, 1840–1890* [London:
Routledge, 1965], p. 67).

46. On the 'bigotry' of Jonah, see, e.g., A.D. Martin, cit. S.D.F. Gotein, 'Some
Observations on Jonah', *JPOS* 17 (1937), pp. 63-77 (66).

47. So H.H. Rowley, *The Missionary Message of the Old Testament* (lectures
given in 1944 to the Baptist Missionary Society; London: Carey Press, 1948); R.
Payne, 'The Prophet Jonah: Reluctant Messenger and Intercessor', *ExpTim* 100
(1988), pp. 131-34.

48. A.S. Peake, 'Jonah', in Peake (ed.), *A Commentary*, pp. 556-58 (556).

49. See Sugirtharajah, 'A Postcolonial Exploration'.

50. Macaulay, who was of the opinion that 'a single shelf of a good European
library is worth the whole native literature of India and Arabia', envisaged a process
of mental miscegenation by which the educated classes would become, to all intents
and purposes, culturally English and Christian. 'No Hindu', he wrote, 'who has
received an English education ever remains sincerely attached to his religion. It is
my firm belief...that if our plans of education are followed up, there will not be a
single idolater among the respectable classes in Bengal thirty years hence' (cit.
Anderson, *Imagined Communities*, p. 91).

gushingly exults in how 'the science and religion of Christendom' is now poised to 'capture the Citadel of Hinduism', and exhorts those who have 'drunk from the beauty' of English culture to awake their 'poor fellow countrymen'.[51] Similarly, Second Isaiah, Ruth, Jonah (having trained successfully at Western Christian college) produce gushing, prize-winning theses, extolling the virtues of the superior culture, forcing the other lesser texts into a position of cultural cringe.[52] By prioritizing texts that seem to crane their heads above the parapet of the Old Testament and catch a glimpse of the New, commentary, on the whole, does nothing to dissuade Christian students from the preconception that the Old Testament is only and always the trailer to the main film, the support act before the curtain of the New Testament goes up and Jesus Christ enters onto the world stage. In the moral spatial order of the Old Testament, the New Testament is the central, authorizing (colonial) ego, and the gospel and 'churches' are already strategically planted in the receptive textual places where they most effectively take root.

Thus, just as colonial discourse congeals in bulk caricatures—the 'untruthful and uncourageous Hindu', the 'illogical Oriental', the 'barbarous Turk'[53]—so Old Testament studies produce their own characteristic Other—the 'nationalistic, legalistic, post-exilic Jew'. And this Other, like colonialism's Others, is anthropologically observed, scientifically catalogued, and pinned down in globalizing, universalizing statements. But the story is not this simple: the 'Jew' is not just monochrome or negative—he is both the *antithesis* and the *virtual double* of

---

51. Quoted in B.P. Majumdar, *First Fruits of English Education* (Calcutta: Bookland Private, 1973), p. 201.

52. The Macaulayish thesis of the book of Ruth, for example (at least as rendered by one reasonably contemporary commentary) is that 'the particularism of the Jews is shallow and selfish' and that it is a 'stance that should be surrendered to a more hospitable attitude' (H.J. Flanders, R.W. Crapp and D.A. Smith, *People of the Covenant: An Introduction to the Old Testament* [New York: Ronald Press, 1973], p. 470). I am grateful to Julia O'Brien for pointing out this example in her article 'On Saying "No" to a Prophet', in J. Capel Anderson and J.L. Staley (eds.), *Taking it Personally: Autobiographical Biblical Criticism* (Semeia, 72; Atlanta: Scholars Press, 1995), pp. 111-21 (119).

53. Orientals, according to Lord Cromer, 'could not learn to walk on pavements, could not tell the truth, and could not use logic', while the governors of Bengal were convinced that the 'Hindu is inherently untruthful and lacks moral courage' (cit. Said, *Culture and Imperialism*, p. 182).

the Christian self.[54] And in this sense he is like the colonial Others who span the spectrum from the virtual image of the colonizer to his absolute antithesis. Because colonialism assumes a Hegelian model of evolution (Europe is at the pinnacle, the other nations crawl or limp along behind), colonial discourse longs to 'efface difference and gather the colonised into the folds of an all-embracing civilisation'.[55] But at the same time, it needs to emphasize racial and cultural difference as a means of establishing superiority—it needs to keep the line between Self and Other intact. This fundamental paradox at the heart of colonial discourse means that the Other is on a continuum with the European self (like us, but *not quite*)[56] but is also radically, emphatically Other. Fredrick Lugard, Governor of Nigeria, divided the natives into three classes: primitive tribes, advanced communities, and English-educated, Europeanized Africans—so different to their fellow Africans that it was as if they were 'of a different race'.[57]

54. Linda Hutcheon, for example, observes how 'Doubleness and difference are established by colonialism in its paradoxical move to enforce cultural sameness while, at the same time, producing differentiations and discriminations', and speaks of the 'doubleness of the coloniser in relation to the colonised either as model or antithesis' ('Circling the Downspout of Empire', in B. Ashcroft, G. Griffiths and H. Tiffin [eds.], *The Post-Colonial Studies Reader* [London: Routledge, 1995], pp. 130-35 [134]).

55. Spurr, *The Rhetoric of Empire*, p. 32.

56. And it is absolutely essential to keep the 'not quite' in place. According to one British educationalist, the native coming into contact with high culture for the first time is like a 'clown' clomping in 'hobnail boots' through the 'lady's boudoir' of British culture (the metaphor is that of one H.G. Robinson, cited by C. Baldick, *The Social Mission of English Criticism* [Oxford: Clarendon Press, 1983]; p. 66). And however well he succeeds in aping European culture, an element of the clownish must always remain in place. In Kipling's *Kim*, for example, the native anthropologist, though bright and educated, is always a little gauche, a little caricatured. Even the most educated among the colonized retain something comically not-quite-white (or right) about them, and are still tainted by what Said calls the idea of the 'ontologically funny native' (Said, *Culture and Imperialism*, p. 185).

57. Lugard, cit. Spurr, *The Rhetoric of Empire*, p. 68. This experience of double alienation is painfully recounted, from another continent, by Bipin Chandra Pal in 1932: 'In mind and manners [the Indian magistrate] was as much an Englishman as any Englishman. It was no small sacrifice for him, because in this way he completely estranged himself from the society of his own people and became socially and morally a pariah among them... He was as much a stranger in his own native land as the European residents in the country'—and yet, and this was also the

And this is a helpful, if disturbing, way of looking at Christian relations with the 'Jew' as Other. For if Others are not merely opposites—if they are related to the Self by a relation of 'conjunction and disjunction'[58]—then the Jew is the quintessential Other of Christianity. The Jew stands at the origin of Christianity and represents the dangerous possibility of its denial; the Christian narrative of self depends on 'him', and yet if 'he' retains his distinctiveness, then that same narrative is under threat.[59] The Jew is habitually placed on a continuum with Christianity in the strange hyphenated hybrid 'the Judaeo-Christian',[60] but is also, equally habitually, physically and conceptually ghettoized, segregated, annihilated beyond Christian borders. And just as this symbolic tension is clearly manifest in history, so it is also reflected in the spatial distribution of the Old Testament. You can see it

unspoken part of Macaulay's vision, he was sentenced to service in his own country, and only in his own country, and was denied access to the uppermost peaks of the Raj (B.C. Pal, *Memories of my Life and Times* [Calcutta: Bipin Chandra Pal Institute, 1973], pp. 331-32).

58. De Certeau, 'Spatial Stories', p. 127. Jonathan Dollimore expresses the conjunction/disjunction between self and other brilliantly in the statement that 'to be against (opposed to) is also to be against (close up, in proximity to) or in other words, up against' (J. Dollimore, *Sexual Dissidence: Augustine to Wilde/Freud to Foucault* [Oxford: Clarendon Press, 1991], p. 229). And again this is a formulation that maps provocatively onto the field of Christian–Jewish relations.

59. For a discussion of how 'in the complex and contradictory fabric of Western Christian culture...the Jew has functioned alternately as its conscience, its alter ego, its abject, its Other', see T. Garb, 'Modernity, Identity, Textuality', in L. Nochlin and T. Garb (eds.), *The Jew in the Text: Modernity and the Construction of Identity* (London: Thames & Hudson, 1995) pp. 20-30 (20-21).

60. My own feeling about the term 'Judaeo-Christian' is that it is a dangerous homogenization that suggests that the Judaeo and the Christian exist on a harmonious continuum, that they are two halves of a unity that congenially share one tradition, vaguely thought of as biblical culture or monotheism. In practice, when the 'Judaeo' and the Christian exist together, I suspect that the Christian gobbles the 'Judaeo' up, and that what is distinctive about the 'Judaeo' (in terms of history, belief and culture) is effaced. Ironically, an example of this can be found in postcolonial criticism, where the centre of colonial power is described as 'Judaeo-Christian' Europe (Said, e.g., speaks of the 'Judaeo-Christian triumphalism' of imperialism [*Culture and Imperialism*, p. 367]). For a critique of this assumption, which effaces the Jew as the Other within Europe, see M. Grossman, 'The Violence of the Hyphen in Judaeo-Christian', *Social Text* 22 (1989), pp. 115-22, and J. Boyarin, *Storm from Paradise: The Politics of Jewish Memory* (Minneapolis: University of Minnesota Press, 1992).

on a macro-scale in the spectrum of Christian uses of the 'Old'—
ranging from the Church Fathers' sense of the Old as New in shadow-
form, to Harnack's suggestion that the Old, senile muttering, dribbling
Testament, should be forcibly retired, or printed after the New as an
appendix[61]—and you can see it on a micro-scale in the way in which a
single biblical book struggles to contain both retrogressive and progressive forces.[62] You can see it in the way in which 'the Jew' functions
both as Christian *antithesis*—as, to quote one commentator, 'a
psychological and religious monster'[63]—*and* as virtual Christian
double—the author of Jonah, for example, is a 'singularly Enlightened
(or broad-minded) Jew',[64] 'a pre-Christian Christian',[65] as Jonathan
Magonet ironically puts it (so different to his other fellow Jews that it is

61. A. von Harnack, *Marcion: Das Evangelium vom fremden Gott* (Darmstadt:
Wissenschaftliche Buchgesellschaft, 1960 [1921]). Von Harnack's opinion was
merely the extreme but logical culmination of a post-Enlightenment dissatisfaction
with the Old Testament as a primitive and savage text.

62. For example, if we unpick the comments of F. Charles Fensham, cited earlier in this study (see n. 44), it becomes clear that Judaism is *both* foundational,
almost us ('[The exile] was the starting point of a new form of religious life known
as Judaism, which found its consummation in the coming of Christ') *and* legalisti-
cally antithetical ('A new era of Jewish worship has started, worship according to
prescribed legal principles. It was only with the coming of Christ and the interpretation of his coming by Paul that another new era was commenced in which the
legal burden was removed from the shoulders of mankind [sic] and the center of
religion placed in his vicarious suffering on the cross' (Fensham, *The Books of Ezra
and Nehemiah*, pp. 19, 268). Thus Ezra–Nehemiah, Janus-like, is both forward and
backward looking. The book of Jonah is similarly riven, though the positive and
negative qualities are more clearly distributed: Jonah the book is a virtual proto-
gospel, and the author (the book personified?) is an 'enlightened Jew'; but Jonah
the character is 'Jewish' in the most negative sense of the word. No book in the Old
Testament canon has a simple, 'negative' identity—the identity of every book is in
some sense conflicted. Even Esther, arguably the darkest of Old Testament texts,
has defenders who want to redeem it: A. Duff, for example, with the help of the
LXX, argues that this is not a light, pious, and conventionally sacred text ('Esther',
in Peake [ed.], *A Commentary,* pp. 336-40).

63. Von Rad, *God at Work*, p. 66.

64. A.W. Krahmer describes Jonah as an 'enlightened [*aufgeklärte*] Jew' (*His-
torische-kritische Untersuchung über das Buch Jonas* [Cassel, 1839]) and F.A.
Malony describes the author of Jonah as a 'singularly broad-minded Jew' (*Journal
of the Transactions of the Victoria Institute* 69 [1937], pp. 243-47 [246]). Malony's
view is quoted with approval by Allen, *The Books*, p. 179.

65. J. Magonet, 'Jonah', *ABD*, III, pp. 936-42 (941).

as if he were 'of a different race'). You can see it in the strange double identity of the 'P' source document—the source that gives us access to postexilic (and therefore the most immediately pre-Christian) Judaism, and that is responsible *both* for the refined, monotheistic transcendental faith of Genesis 1, and for genealogies, catalogues and lapsed and retrogressive legalism.[66] And you can see it in the way in which Christian commentators both *denounce* and *deny* the savagery and primitivism of the Old Testament, for the Old is inextricably bound up with the New, the Judaeo with the Christian.[67] Judaism is Christianity's double and antithesis—on the same evolutionary trajectory, but yet ultimately incapable of crossing colonial (or intertestamental) border lines. And, although Judaism is theoretically Christianity's 'parent', it is frequently placed in the position of child. As Ania Loomba observes, 'the white man's burden was conceived as a parental one',[68] of looking after, disciplining, correcting, teaching. And in a strange temporal reversal (analogous to the missionaries who are somehow already in Old Testament territory), Christian commentary (anxiously?) reverses the parent–child relationship, and chastises, teaches, and even disciplines, a growing Judaism-as-child.

But the point is, whether he functions as virtual proto-Christian, or monstrous savage Other, the 'Jew' in Old Testament commentary is still largely a projection of the Christian imagination. Like the colo-

66. Whatever 'P' may be able to tell us about the sources of the Pentateuch, it certainly seems to intimate something of Christianity's double-edged relation with Judaism. Those who, like me, find it difficult to imagine a group who are on the one hand so retrogressive and legalistic, and yet on the other hand so capable of sublime religious insight, may like to compare this riven, schizoid P with perceptions of Judaism.

67. Harold Eilberg-Schwarz argues that anthropological studies of the Old Testament and comparisons with other primitive religions were shortlived because, in order to maintain its 'superiority to other religious traditions', Christianity had to deploy a 'variety of defensive strategies to deny or trivialize the presence of savage elements in Judaism' (*The Savage in Judaism: An Anthropology of Israelite Religion and Ancient Judaism* [Bloomington: Indiana University Press, 1990], p. 49). But Eilberg-Schwarz's study downplays, in my opinion dangerously, how Christianity will, at times, acknowledge and even relish the savagery of the Old Testament, and displace it onto the spectre of postexilic Judaism. And it is this two-sided response—protecting that with which our identity is bound up, denigrating that which our identity sets itself against—that is so characteristic of Christianity's riven relationship with Judaism.

68. Loomba, *Colonialism/Postcolonialism*, p. 217.

nized Other, he tends to 'drown in an anonymous collectivity',[69] to undergo what Aimé Césaire calls 'thingification',[70] to be subsumed in a colonizing discourse that 'swallows up complexity'.[71] When I read globalizing statements such as '[Jews at that time were] renowned for their stubbornness or lack of faith',[72] or read a description of 'flinty-hearted [postexilic] Judaism' that had 'jealously sunk into itself',[73] I hear (among other things) echoes of Said's claim that 'There is a convergence between the great geographical scope of the empires, especially the British one, and universalising cultural discourses'.[74] I am struck by the irony of a group with universalism and civilization on its side, using a very skewed universalism, and violent rhetoric, to condemn the Other for violence and nationalism.[75] No one is denying that there are violent, problematic, passages in the Old Testament/ Hebrew Bible, but these are difficult dark places for both Christianity and Judaism—in Christian discourse the contrast between universalism and particularism so often collapses into a contrast between Us and Them:

---

69. A. Memmi, *The Colonizer and the Colonized* (Boston: Beacon Press, 1967), p. 88.

70. A. Césaire, *Discourse on Colonialism* (New York: Monthly Review Press, 1972), p. 21.

71. Loomba, *Colonialism/Postcolonialism*, p. 249.

72. Payne, 'Jonah', in Douglas (ed.), *The New Bible Dictionary*, p. 653.

73. Peake, 'Jonah', p. 556.

74. Said, *Culture and Imperialism*, p. 126.

75. Recent critiques of universalist/Christian anti-Judaism sound strikingly similar to post-colonial critiques of 'a universalism that is Eurocentric in the extreme' and the 'insidious universalism that connected culture with imperialism' (Said, *Culture and Imperialism*, pp. 51, 336). For example, Tamar Garb has written provocatively on 'universalist' anti-Judaism: 'The secularising and universalising dream [of the Enlightenment] whilst purporting to be inclusive and democratising, resembled the proselytising ethos of the Christian missionaries in a fundamental way. It was premised on an eradication of difference that was by no means reciprocal. There was no negotiation of a new shared culture for Christians and Jews, involving a give and take, a symbiosis or universal respect. Rather Jews were expected to discard their cultural specificity for a more "rational", "modern", "universal" identity and thereby enter into the "common culture of man"' (Garb, 'Modernity, Identity, Textuality', p. 24). The similarity between Garb's critique and post-colonial criticism suggests that Jews and colonial others are similarly (and paradoxically) situated as that which is outside the 'universal' and against which the 'universal' is defined. In other words they are the 'unthought', that which, when thought, causes the 'universalist' centre to collapse.

the open vistas of Second Isaiah belong to Us, and welcome Us; the narrow closed-off territory of Esther typically belongs to Them.

'The rebuilding of the wall [in Ezra–Nehemiah]', writes Derek Kidner, 'almost asks to be seen as a symbol of Israel's separatism'.[76] Because biblical scholars have so often mapped Christianity as 'open vistas' and Judaism as 'wall-building',[77] it is appropriate to tell a different spatial story—the story of Christian colonists erecting their own churches, 'Gethsemanes', and New Testament analogies in Old Testament space, and stereotyping the 'Jew' as part of an unthinkingly expansionist 'universalism'. This is not, however, a simple parable with a facile point—something like 'imperial Christian forces should pull out of Old Testament territory, rename it Tanakh, and give a genuinely Jewish book back to the Jewish people'.[78] My point is rather a point of observation—that Christian commentary, *in practice*, on my bookshelves, so often sinks into a supersessionist logic as natural, and as unthought, as the logic of imperialism.[79]

76. Kidner, *Ezra and Nehemiah*, p. 23.

77. In some strains of commentary the motif of the wall-builder becomes iconic of the postexilic Jew. Paul Trudinger, for example, sees the book of Jonah as a lesson for the 'wall-builders' who 'feather their own nest' (P. Trudinger, 'Jonah: A Post-Exilic Verbal Cartoon?', *The Downside Review* [1989], pp. 142-43 [143]).

78. At this point the colonial metaphor, which just about staggered/limped/ hopped to the end of the essay, falls down, exhausted. For one of the problems with it is that it tends to imply, by analogy, that the indigeneous population of the 'Old Testament' is Jewish. This is a very dangerous assumption—indeed it is this assumption, and the tendency to conflate biblical Judaeans, post-biblical Jews and New Testament Jewish stereotypes in a horrible caricatured gloop, that lies at the root of many of the problems discussed in this essay.

79. For me the most disturbing examples of anti-Judaism in commentary are those that are trying to remedy overt anti-Semitism in the wake of the Second World War, but that in fact demonstrate how deep the logic of supersession goes. Often this produces a strange mixture of apologetic for Judaism and a lingering condemnation of Judaism's inferiority and inadequacy. Bernhard Anderson's article 'The Place of the Book of Esther in the Christian Bible' tries to combat Christian dimissal of Esther as a 'Judaising text', but at the same time maintains the idea of Jewish separatism, which, in an 'action-reaction chemical equation', incites persecution, which in turn creates Judaism (for a trenchant critique of what is at stake in this article, see Beal, *The Book of Hiding*, pp. 8-12). The contrast is even starker in an address given by H.H. Rowley (an equally prestigious and venerated Old Testament scholar) to the Baptist Missionary Society in 1944 and published in 1948. Rowley goes on at length about the 'greatness' of Judaism, and gives several rea-

And so—as in all post-colonial and post-modern retellings—the civilized centre becomes 'one of the dark places of the earth'.[80] And this time I know what it is like to be at the centre[81]—to inhabit a textual commonwealth in which textual wealth/space/value is certainly not common, nor equally distributed, and where my centre, my norm, takes the lion's share.

One last thought (before my limping, struggling metaphor entirely collapses). John Stuart Mill, in his *Principles of Political Economy*, describes 'these outlying possessions of ours' as little market gardens, or local shops—symbolically and economically subordinate 'place[s] where England finds it convenient to carry out the production of sugar, coffee and a few other tropical commodities'[82]—and the legacy of this attitude is clearly skewed- or under-development.[83] And, as I look out over the exhausted theological diamond-mine of the Servant Songs, the hugely overploughed territory of Jonah, the relatively untouched landscape of Obadiah and Nahum, I wonder what the globe of the Old Testament would look like if it had not been distributed according to

sons why we should 'have no stones to throw at it', the chief of which is that 'Christianity was a growth out of Judaism, not a revolt against it, and if Judaism had been essentially evil, it would not have had so much to pass onto its daughter faith' (Rowley, *Missionary Message*, p. 79). Judaism is redeemed not by its own character (in Rowley's article all the old stereotypes are firmly in place) but through the testimony of the (sweet) daughter-faith—that is, the only redemption that he can work for Judaism has to be through the logic of supercession.

80. The phrase is from J. Conrad, *Heart of Darkness* (Harmondsworth: Penguin Books, 1972 [1902]), p. 49.

81. As opposed to, say, feminist criticism, in which I occupy the periphery, critiquing the centre from outside. I have to say, standing here on the Mount of Englishness and Christianness, it is quite clear to me that I stand at the epistemic centre, that I carry the conviction, in whatever, dilute form, that, as Seeley put it, 'my treasure of truth forms the nucleus of civilisation' and is 'more sterling' than the others' (*The Expansion of England* [Chicago: University of Chicago Press, 1971 (1884)] p. 193). Which I guess makes me confused as to why those who stand at other centres, centres I do not occupy, take so much persuading...

82. J. Stuart Mill, *Principles of Political Economy* (2 vols.; ed. J.M. Robson; Toronto: University of Toronto Press, 1965), III, p. 693. Mill's statement is, of course, a perfect illustration of the complicity between colonialism and capitalism, and the way in which the 'business of Empire' depends on the 'Empire of business'.

83. See N. Smith, *Uneven Development: Nature, Capital and the Production of Space* (Oxford: Basil Blackwell, 1984).

the *Principles of Theological Economy*. How would the land of our discipline lie if the territory had not been organized according to its relative usefulness[84] to the Christian Metropolitan centre? How would we map and teach these texts if the 'Jewish' were brought in as more than the othered, stereotyped side-effect or 'foil' of the Christian?

84. Rubbing culture's nose in the mud of politics is never a pleasant activity, and some may resent the New Historicist move that brings Christian theology/ commentary out of its transcendental supra-political zone, and implies that its activities are comparable to the mercantile exploits of, say, the East India Company. But critics often seem to beg, or, in Kidner's terms, 'ask for', the utilitarian/economic analogy: Grieve, for example, includes a section on 'value' in his discussion of Ecclesiastes ('Ecclesiastes', p. 412 n. 30) and W.L. Northridge is quite explicit about how Esther 'serves a useful purpose' in the Christian economy (cit. Montefiore and Loewe, *A Rabbinic Anthology*; cf. p. 615).

Part II
CHRISTIAN–JEWISH RELATIONS IN THE MODERN WORLD

'INHABITING WHAT REMAINS OF JUDAISM': JEWISHNESS
AND ALTERITY IN THE FICTION OF PHILIP ROTH,
SAUL BELLOW, AND BERNARD MALAMUD

Kevin McCarron

'The time will come when we are people again, and not just Jews.'
Philip Roth, *The Ghost Writer*

The literary critic Stan Smith begins his book *A Sadly Contracted Hero* by noting: 'Post-war [American] writing has celebrated the emergence of the Jew from the ghetto into the mainstream of American life. Leslie Fiedler even calls one of his chapters in *Waiting for the End* "Zion as Main Street"…'[1] In his book *The Modern American Novel*, Malcolm Bradbury writes: 'The rise of Jewish-American fiction in the years immediately after the Second World War was the development of a tradition that went back to the 1890s and to writers like Abraham Cahan. But its remarkable efflorescence…indicates the extraordinary revival and indeed the new dominance of this tradition in post-war American culture.'[2] In an essay called 'Some New Jewish Stereotypes', originally given as a speech in 1961 at Chicago's Loyola University, Philip Roth writes: 'I find that I am suddenly living in a country in which the Jew has come to be—or is allowed for now to think he is—a cultural hero'.[3]

One of the most pre-eminent Jewish-American writers of the postwar years, Saul Bellow, wrote an introduction for the poet John Berryman's autobiographical novel *Recovery*. In Berryman's book, the alcoholic protagonist, symbolically named Alan Severance, is 'drying out' in a recovery clinic. While reviewing his life, Severance realizes that he

---

1.   Stan Smith, *A Sadly Contracted Hero* (Durham: British Association for American Studies, 1981), p. 9.
2.   Malcolm Bradbury, *The Modern American Novel* (Oxford: Oxford University Press, 1992), p. 168.
3.   Philip Roth, *Reading Myself and Others* (London: Corgi, 1975), p. 125.

wishes for nothing more in life than to reject Christianity and become a Jew. An entry in Severance's journal reads: *'To become a Jew*—the wonder of my life—*it's possible*... Rabbi Mandel is coming at 2:30. My uneasiness w. Xtianity came to a head in Mass w George this morning... Left and came to my room and incredibly thought of *becoming a Jew.'*[4] Although such a desire might seem to support Roth's observation that in the immediate postwar years, perhaps against all the odds, the Jew has become 'a cultural hero', the novel makes it clear that Severance sees Judaism as a metaphor for oppression, alienation and exile. He wishes to become a Jew primarily because Judaism offers the promise of continued exclusion, not incorporation. In addition, Severance persistently equates the God of Judaism with his own father: harsh, uncommunicative and punitive.

The basic contention of this essay is that the Jew has been widely perceived, not necessarily portrayed, in postwar American fiction as a metaphor for contemporary intellectual angst, as exemplary of the intelligent, enlightened, religious scepticism of the modern age. This is, among other reasons, the result of persistent attempts in writing about the Holocaust to represent Auschwitz metonymically as the paradigmatic, exemplary *event* of our time. In addition, the primacy of ethics within Judaism has proved particularly congenial to a postwar age which increasingly regards religion less as an experiential category which admits the numinous and the supernatural—indeed is predicated upon them—and more as a formal framework for the dissemination of ethical imperatives. Finally, I want to suggest that the form of Jewish-American fiction is especially appropriate for the issues raised by Saul Bellow, Philip Roth, and Bernard Malamud, the writers whose work I will be focusing on in the course of the essay.

I have taken my title, 'Inhabiting What Remains of Judaism', from that exemplary unpicker of metaphors Jacques Derrida, who writes in *Circumfession* that he is one who is 'inhabiting what remains of Judaism'.[5] In his essay 'Thinking about Fire: Derrida and Judaism', Steven Shakespeare assumes that Derrida is referring to himself; that, born a Jew, Derrida now 'inhabits' what remains of his own Judaism. However, it is also possible that Derrida believes himself to be living within

---

4.   John Berryman, *Recovery* (New York: Farrar, Straus & Giroux, 1973), p. 72.

5.   Cited in Steven Shakespeare, 'Thinking about Fire: Derrida And Judaism', *Literature & Theology* 12.3 (1998), pp. 242-55 (242).

a culture that now contains only the vestiges of Judaism. For what does remain? What does it mean, particularly after Auschwitz, to be a Jew? Bryan Cheyette and Laura Marcus write: ' "the Jew" signifies a multitude of incommensurable categories. For this reason, Jews were historically appropriated by the most disparate of ideologies.'[6] Max Silverman writes:

> 'Jew' is one of the most malleable signifiers. Over the ages, it has been the name given to an extraordinary and bewildering number of conceptions. Frequently—too frequently?—'Jew' has been employed allegorically to represent some human 'truth' or other: the transcendent nature of Christ within whom *even* Jews can be saved; the transcendent nature of the Third Reich which can purify itself of the 'filth' of society. The one common and persistent preoccupation here is the construction of a 'jewish question', the resolution of which will ensure the well-being of society. 'Jew' is the site on which unruly desire and ambivalence can, supposedly, be transformed into a coherent and univocal discourse.[7]

Obviously enough, there is unlikely to be any 'eternal truth' about the Jews any more than there is likely to be about anyone or anything else, but here, precisely, is the impasse faced by most Jewish characters in the novels I now wish to discuss: on the one hand, historical and theological certainty, and on the other a desacralized, contemporary universe in which all meanings are arbitrary and all writing *about* meaning is itself under the constant threat of erasure.

For the French writer Jean-Francis Lyotard, the very word 'Jew' is now too unstable a signifier to be useful. He proposes 'the jews': lower case, always in inverted commas, and argues for this typology in *Heidegger and 'the jews'* thus: 'Lower-case to say that I am to say that I am not thinking of a nation. Plural to signify that it is not a political figure or subject (Zionism), nor a religious one (Judaism), nor a philosophical one (Hebraic thought) that I am invoking with this name. Quotation marks to avoid confusion of these "jews" with the real jews.'[8] Considerably clearer about what 'the jews' are not than what they are, Lyotard turns 'the jews' into a metaphor, distinguishing them from 'real

---

6.   Bryan Cheyette and Laura Marcus (eds.), *Modernity, Culture and 'the Jew'* (Oxford: Polity Press, 1998), p. 5.

7.   M. Silverman, 'Re-figuring "the Jew" in Frane', in Cheyette and Marcus (eds.), *Modernity*, pp. 197-207 (197).

8.   Cited in G. Bennington, 'Lyotard and "the Jews" ', in Cheyette and Marcus (eds.), *Modernity*, pp. 188-96 (192).

jews'. Geoffrey Bennington's observation that Lyotard's construction is 'Not just a metaphor'[9] is surely correct, but nevertheless, that it is more than a metaphor acknowledges that it is, essentially, a metaphor. The metaphorical drive concluding in metonymy, the substitution of the part for the whole, seems to be a characteristic feature of writing both about Jews and by Jews. The Jew, however written, always carries a surplus of meaning, is always over-determined, is never able to transcend context, hence, perhaps, Nathan Zuckerman's fantastic description of himself in the final lines of Philip Roth's novel *The Counterlife*: 'A Jew without Jews, with Judaism, without Zionism, without Jewishness, without a temple or any army or even a pistol, a Jew clearly without a home, just the object itself, like a glass or an apple'.[10]

However, as Zuckerman himself knows well, to be a Jew is to be in a position of radical alterity, a position determined by Christianity. Cheyette and Marcus write of the work of Zygmunt Bauman: 'In contrast to the construction of ambivalence as an undifferentiated characteristic of colonial discourse, Bauman believes Jews to be *sui generis* or "unlike the others" because of their historical relationship to Christendom'.[11] Bauman himself writes of 'allosemitism', the practice of setting the Jews apart as people radically different from all others, needing separate concepts to describe and comprehend them: 'I suggest that the allosemitism endemic to western Civilization is to a decisive extent the legacy of Christendom'.[12] Anti-Semitism is, inevitably, a recurrent motif in postwar Jewish-American fiction and, like 'Jewishness' itself, is a complex phenomenon within literature of the period overall. In his autobiography *Black Boy*, the African-American writer Richard Wright remembers growing up in the American South: 'All of us black people who lived in the neighborhood hated Jews, not because they exploited us, but because we had been taught at home and in Sunday School that Jews were "Christ Killers"'.[13] Conversely, in Bernard Malamud's novel *The Tenants*, the black writer Willie Spearpoint writes a fantasy about black ghetto guerrillas exterminating the Jews in New York City, which the Jewish writer, Harry Lesser, discovers, as he seems intended to do,

9.   Bennington, 'Lyotard and "the Jews"', in Cheyette and Marcus, p. 193.

10. P. Roth, *The Counterlife* (Harmondsworth: Penguin Books, 1986), p. 328.

11. Cheyette and Marcus (eds.), *Modernity*, p. 10.

12. Z. Bauman, 'Allosemitism: Promodern, Modern, Postmodern', in Cheyette and Marcus (eds.), *Modernity*, pp. 143-56 (148).

13. R. Wright, *Black Boy* (London: Longman, 1970), p. 52.

while in his apartment: 'Working quickly in small squads, the guerrillas round up and line up a dozen wailing, hand-wringing Zionists, Goldberg among them, in front of his Liquor Emporium, and shoot them dead with pistols'.[14] Spearpoint's anti-Semitism is economically based. He is convinced 'Jew money-men' rule the world, a conviction which, ironically, links him to American white supremacists, who construct Jews in precisely the same way. Anti-Semitism is one of Malamud's primary concerns, and he is the master of the imaginary pogrom, but his fable 'The Jew Bird' is a scathing critique of Jewish anti-Semitism while also a brilliantly comic narrative. In this story, a bird flies into the New York apartment of Harry Cohen and his family, and begins to speak. He informs them he is fleeing anti-Semites because he is a 'Jew Bird':

> Cohen laughed heartily. 'What do you mean by that?' The bird began dovening. He prayed without Book or tallith, but with passion. Edie bowed her head though not Cohen. And Maurie rocked back and forth with the prayer, looking up with one wide-open eye.
> When the prayer was done Cohen remarked, 'No hat, no phylacteries?'
> 'I am an old radical.'[15]

As the story progresses, Cohen begins to hate the bird and eventually flings him from the window to his death. The fundamental absurdity of the fable's story-line precisely parallels the absurd position of the Jewish anti-Semite.

Malamud's 1966 novel *The Fixer* is the definitive text of the period on the subject of Jewish–Christian relations. *The Fixer* is set in the pogroms of Tsarist Russia before the First World War. Jakov Bok leaves his tiny village seeking a new life in St Petersburg, only to be falsely accused of the ritual murder of a Christian child. The novel is clearly based on the infamous Mendel Bellis case: the Black Hundred, in an attempt to start a pogrom, helped fabricate the charge of ritual murder against the innocent Bellis when a young boy was found horribly murdered. Among the book's most striking features is the virulence of the anti-Semitic views expressed throughout the novel. As Bok is rowed across the river, the Russian boatman, mistaking him for a Latvian, tells him of his 'solution' to the Jewish problem:

14. B. Malamud, *The Tenants* (London: Methuen, 1971), pp. 219-20.
15. B. Malamud, 'The Jewbird', in his *Idiots First* (London: Methuen, 1964), pp. 95-96.

'When the church bells begin to ring we move on the Zhidy quarter, which you can tell by the stink, routing them out of wherever they're hiding—in attics, cellars, or ratholes—bashing in their brains, stabbing their herring-filled guts, shooting off their snotty noses, no exception made for young or old, because if you spare any they breed like rats and then the job's to do all over again. And when we've slaughtered the whole cursed tribe of them…we'll pile up the corpses and soak them with benzine and light fires that people will enjoy all over the world. Then when that's done we hose the stinking ashes away and divide the roubles and jewels and silver and furs and all the other loot they stole… You can take my word—the time's not far off when everything I say, we will do, because our Lord, who they crucified, wants his rightful revenge.'

He dropped an oar and crossed himself.[16]

It is, of course, quite impossible to read this novel without thinking of Nazi Germany and the death camps, and the ways in which the boatman's wicked prophecies were fulfilled.

The Fixer, although written from a traditional omniscient viewpoint, mingles omniscient observation with Bok's own thoughts; his dreams and fantasies, including one of shooting the Tsar, are never announced as such, thereby creating a narrative which disconcertingly interweaves differing narrative modes to create a world which is bewilderingly both real and fantastic. This, too, is a characteristic feature of Jewish-American writing of the period. Frank D. McConnell writes of Saul Bellow's writing, for example: 'To read Bellow intelligently we must call into serious question our time-honored prejudices about the nature of "realism" and "fantasy" as varieties of narrative… The fantastic and the realistic modes are carefully and continually intermingled in his tales.'[17] Metonymy occupies a privileged position within *The Fixer*. While in jail, Bok realizes, in an epiphanic moment: 'To the goyim what one Jew is is what they all are. If the fixer stands accused of murdering one of their children, so does the rest of the tribe. Since the crucifixion the crime of the Christ-killer is the crime of all Jews. "His blood be on us and our children." '[18]

16. B. Malamud, *The Fixer* (London: Eyre & Spottiswoode, 1966), pp. 34-35.

17. F.D. McConnell, *Four Postwar American Novelists* (Chicago: University of Chicago Press, 1977), p. 7.

18. Malamud, *The Fixer*, p. 288.

This understanding of metonymic perception is connected, as I suggested earlier, to the pervasive postwar practice of seeing the Holocaust, and particularly Auschwitz, as metaphor. Max Silverman writes:

> The Holocaust is once again the main resource mobilized for allegorically overdetermining 'the Jew'. If…some use the Holocaust as a trope in which 'the Jew' is the marker of 'the other' to modernity's Christo- and logo-centrism, others are equally vociferous in making the Holocaust the fixed and unalterable measure of Jewish identity in the form of justification of *all* future Jewish action.[19]

In a recently published article in the *Times Literary Supplement*, Michael Bernstein writes that after the Second World War

> the Shoah alone remained as the century's—indeed humanity's—pre-eminent incarnation of annihilatory monstrousness. Metonymically figured as the site of extermination, Auschwitz gave to the sense of gathering evil that has haunted Western consciousness throughout the first half of this century 'a local habitation and a name' and it is as that habitation and that name, not as some never-before imagined moral and conceptual black hole, that it has been possible to talk about the Shoah at all.[20]

Cheyette and Marcus similarly note of Lyotard's writings: ' "jews" for Lyotard are reduced to a form of placelessness and indeterminacy which is, in the end, metonymically signified by the name "Auschwitz"'.[21] The Jews as metaphor; Auschwitz as metonymy: from the confluence a dreadful irony emerges. A ubiquitous, and far from unexpected, theme within Holocaust narratives is the loss of religious faith in the presence of such truly appalling evil. Ironically, within modern American fiction, the genocide of the Jews utterly refutes the promise of an omnipotent, beneficent Creator and it is the Jewish character who is invited to interrogate the absence left behind by this vanished, Christian, God.

Within the discipline of literary criticism, it is remarkable how persistently and how effortlessly Jewish characters are transformed into allegorical representations of contemporary spiritual alienation. Stan Smith, for example, writes: 'In fact, the emancipated Jew has become the

19. Silverman, 'Re-Figuring', p. 203.

20. M.A. Bernstein, 'Homage to the Extreme: The Shoah and the Rhetoric of Catastrophe', *Times Literary Supplement* (6 March 1998), p. 6.

21. Cheyette and Marcus (eds.), *Modernity*, p. 13.

symbol of a universal condition'.[22] Howard Harper writes of Tommy Wilhelm, the protagonist of Saul Bellow's *Seize the Day* (1956): 'Wilhelm is modern man, caught in the classical dilemma of the absurd: the irreconcilable conflict between the human need for unity or rational order in life and the ultimate incomprehensibility of the universe around and within him...'[23] However much the contemporary reader might like Wilhelm to be 'modern man', this would be true only if 'modern man' has been raised a Jew, and has a crazy Jewish father. Later, Harper writes of the protagonist, Moses Herzog, of Bellow's eponymous novel *Herzog* (1964): 'Herzog's is the typical crisis of the contemporary intellectual'.[24] Well, sure—if the typical contemporary intellectual has been raised in a Jewish family so kosher it gives its children names like Moses. To suggest that the Jew is an allegory of contemporary universality is, quite clearly, an effacement of Jewish specificity. Cheyette and Marcus note that Max Silverman criticizes the work of Lyotard, as well as that of Jean-Luc Nancy and Phillippe Lacoue-Labarthe, because at the core of their work there is 'an unresolved paradox as they employ an ethnic allegory to signify a supposedly universal site of otherness or strangeness'.[25] Clearly, Silverman's criticism here can be applied to the reading of literary texts. I would suggest that the fiction itself actually resists all such attempts to view Jewish characters as representative of contemporary spiritual alienation, and would like to consider the issue of circumcision within some of these texts to suggest that it is the condition of being a Jew, precisely and specifically a Jew, in contemporary America which provides their central dynamic.

I want to contrast three 'accounts', so to speak, of circumcision, a particularly radical signifier of the difference between Jews and Christians. In a recently published essay, Eric L. Santner writes:

> Beyond all its often inconsistent and unstable cultural meanings, circumcision confronts us with a paradoxical site where a vast universality crosses over into embodied particularity, where the authority of a cultural institution attaches itself to the force of an enunciation and bodily

22. Smith, *A Sadly Constructed Hero*, p. 12.

23. H.M. Harper, *Desperate Faith: A Study of Bellow, Salinger, Mailer, Baldwin and Updike* (Chapel Hill, NC: University of North Carolina Press, 1967), p. 36.

24. Harper, *Desperate Faith*, p. 52.

25. Cheyette and Marcus (eds.), *Modernity*, pp. 12-13.

inscription. The 'savage' and 'primitive' practice of circumcision might thus be understood as a locus of knowledge about the workings of symbolic power, the ways in which such power is ultimately dependent on a certain intensification of the human body.[26]

In the final paragraph of Bernard Malamud's 1959 novel *The Assistant*, Malamud writes of one of his central characters, the Gentile Frank Alpine: 'One day in April Frank went to the hospital and had himself circumcised. For a couple of days he dragged himself around with a pain between his legs. The pain enraged and inspired him. After Passover he came a Jew.'[27] Santner's understanding of circumcision is persuasive and comprehensive but, necessarily, he has little interest in what the act of circumcision might *mean* to the circumcised subject, or what it might *feel* like to be circumcised. A primary difference between these two understandings of circumcision resides, it seems to me, in Malamud's imaginative reconstruction of the physical and spiritual significance of the act upon the circumcised individual. Prosaic though Malamud's prose is here, indeed it is rarely so prosaic, it is artfully constructed. It is noticeable, for example, that Malamud employs an active construction, 'Had himself circumcised', rather than say 'he was circumcised'. Note, too, the demotic 'a couple of days', which universalizes and demystifies the act, and the powerful and somewhat puzzling phrase 'enraged and inspired him'. Enraged him against what, or whom? Inspired him to do what, emulate whom? This passage, precisely because of its artful construction, is able to imply that one function of circumcision is to provide a template for suffering; the act itself serves as a constant reminder not only that one is different, but that with difference comes pain, and that, furthermore, pain has a purpose.

In Roth's *The Counterlife*, the issue of circumcision threatens to destroy the marriage of Nathan Zuckerman and his Christian wife, Maria, who is opposed to the practice. Maria has already noted, in an imaginary interview: 'he [Zuckerman] had tremendous ambivalence about a Christian woman. I was a Christian woman.'[28] In a letter, which he may or may not post, written to Maria, a woman who may or may not be 'real', Zuckerman writes:

26. E.L. Santner, 'My Own Private Germany: Daniel Paul Schreber's Secret History of Modernity', in Cheyette and Marcus (eds.), *Modernity*, pp. 40-62 (47).

27. B. Malamud, *The Assistant* (London: Eyre & Spottiswoode, 1959), p. 222.

28. Roth, *The Counterlife*, p. 247.

The pastoral stops here and it stops with circumcision. That delicate surgery should be performed upon the penis of a brand-new boy seems to you the very cornerstone of human irrationality, and maybe it is... But why not look at it another way? I know that touting circumcision is entirely anti-Lamaze and the thinking these days that wants to debrutalize birth and culminates in delivering the child in water in order not even to startle him. Circumcision is startling, all right, particularly when performed by a garlicked old man upon the glory of a newborn body, but then maybe that's what the Jews had in mind and what makes the act seem quintessentially Jewish and the mark of their reality. Circumcision makes it clear as can be that you are here and not there, that you are out and not in—also that you're mine and not theirs. There is no way around it: you enter history through my history and me. Circumcision is everything that the pastoral is not and, to my mind, reinforces what the world is about, which isn't strifeless unity. Quite convincingly, circumcision gives the lie to the womb-dream of life in the beautiful state of innocent prehistory, the appealing idyll of living 'naturally', unencumbered by man-made ritual. To be born is to lose all that. The heavy hand of human values falls upon you right at the start, marking your genitals as its own. Inasmuch as one invents one's meanings, along with impersonating one's selves, this is the meaning I propose for that rite.[29]

Although generally perceived as an initiatory rite, one that comes at the beginning, it is noticeable that both Malamud and Roth conclude their novels with the issue of circumcision. It may be of particular interest to the literary critic that while Zuckerman is able to claim license for circumcision by suggesting 'maybe that's what the Jews had in mind', he feels equally able to invest his own meanings, without reference to history and tradition. Clearly, for both Roth and Malamud, circumcision is metaphor quite as much as reality, indeed it is a metaphor *for* reality.

Although difference is indeed inscribed in the flesh by the act of circumcision, and although, in my view, the Jewish character in American fiction remains a Jew first and foremost, it is true that the Jewish character, to some extent, can effectively represent the alienated, contemporary human condition. This is not, however, because these characters having 'lost' their religious faith, but not their spiritual aspirations, represent a contemporary, post-Auschwitz, human condition, as the critics cited above suggest, but the very opposite: they are representative of contemporary religious attitudes because they cannot reject

29. Roth, *The Counterlife*, p. 327.

Judaism, at the very centre of which lies estrangement, alienation and even the possibility of atheism. The philosopher Emmanuel Levinas, himself, of course, Jewish, has written extensively on the subject of Judaism, and in his book *Difficult Freedom* suggests that the key role of Judaism in history has been to create 'a type of man who lives in a demystified, disenchanted world'.[30] It should be noted, however, that while Levinas speaks in general terms about Judaism, this is essentially rabbinical Judaism, as opposed to Hasidic Judaism. The element of popular mysticism which he perceives as central to Hasidic Judaism is an anathema to Levinas, who stresses the superiority of rabbinical Judaism, with its emphasis on the Jewish sacred texts, on hermeneutics and exegesis. Levinas writes, again in *Difficult Freedom*: 'Judaism has decharmed the world, contesting the notion that religions apparently evolved out of enthusiasm and the sacred. Judaism remains foreign to any offensive return of these forms of human elevation. It denounces them as the essence of idolatry.'[31] Indeed, he goes so far as to say that Judaism lies close, by its very nature, to atheism: 'The rigorous affirmation of human independence, of its intelligent presence to an intelligible reality, the destruction of the numinous concept of the sacred, entail the risk of atheism. That risk must be run.'[32] God is not encountered directly in Judaism, as he is in Christianity, through the incarnation, but approached in the ethical relationship with the Other. Colin Davis writes: 'Judaism thus turns out to be a concrete, practical religion, concerned with immediately relevant questions of individual behaviour and social justice'.[33]

It is, then, not at all surprising that it is Jewish characters, with their complete lack of interest in the miraculous complemented by their zealous interest in ethics, who dominate American literary culture in the immediate postwar years. Nathan Zuckerman's thoughts during a carol service indicate a profound, and typical, scepticism about the mysteries central to Christianity:

> Jewishly, I still thought, what *do* they need all this stuff for? Why do they need these wise men and all these choruses of angels?... Though frankly I've always felt that the place where Christianity gets dangerously, vulgarly obsessed with the miraculous is Easter, the Nativity has

30. Cited in C. Davis, *Levinas* (Oxford: Polity Press, 1996), p. 102.
31. Davis, *Levinas*, p. 102.
32. Davis, *Levinas*, p. 104.
33. Davis, *Levinas*, p. 105.

always struck me as a close second to the Resurrection in nakedly
addressing the most childish need. Holy shepherds and starry skies,
blessed angels and a virgin's womb…[34]

Zuckerman's own concerns, of course, are rational, practical, ethical.

Malamud is more interested in the unusual and the mysterious than
either Roth or Bellow. Marcus Klein writes: 'The radiant artifacts of
Bernard Malamud's fiction have been the shrouds and the graves of
Jews… His guides to the spirit have been, characteristically, scrawny
old Jews, skeletal *nudniks*, the agents of oblique commands and Yiddish paradoxes, whose very presence is a visitation.'[35] Later, he writes:
'His talent is for the extraordinary, for annunciations and epipha-
nies…'[36] However, and perhaps paradoxically, he is also the most concerned of the three writers with ethics. Roth, one of Malamud's
shrewdest critics, writes: '*The Assistant* is a manifestation of ethical
Jewhood…'[37] Malamud's interest in the fantastic should not be confused with an interest in the miraculous, a very different ontological
category. In his *Autobiographical and Social Essays*, Rudolph Otto
writes: 'Aesthetics is not religion'.[38] Equally, ethics is not religion
either, but for an increasing number of people ethics is indeed religion—the two terms have achieved contemporary synonymity.

The preoccupation with ethics within fiction of the period is striking
and the Jewish character, particularly when placed against a Christian,
is invariably associated with ethical issues. Frank D. McConnell notes,
for example, of Bellow: 'His Jews, at least his Jewish Jews, tend to be
carriers of ethical sensitivity, of high seriousness, of morality and
responsibility; while his gentiles (and his deracinated, "assimilated"
Jews) tend to represent triumphs or disasters of the elemental, the sensual, the self-indulgent'.[39] Marcus Klein writes of Malamud's work:
'His constant and his total moral message is, quite simply, the necessity
in this world of accepting moral obligation'.[40] Tony Tanner writes of

---

34. Roth, *The Counterlife*, p. 102.
35. M. Klein, *After Alienation: American Novels in Mid-Century* (Chicago: University of Chicago Press, 1978), p. 247.
36. Klein, *After Alienation*, p. 250.
37. Roth, *Reading Myself and Others*, p. 211.
38. Cited in E.J. Ziolkowski, 'The Study of Religions and Literature', *Literature
& Theology* 12.3 (1998), pp. 305-25 (310).
39. McConnell, *Four Postwar American Novelists*, p. 17.
40. Klein, *After Alienation*, p. 252.

Bellow's protagonist Asa Leventhal in Bellow's 1947 novel *The Victim*: 'Leventhal comes to a "kind of recognition" of man's responsibilities, his relationship with other men'.[41] At Zuckerman's funeral, in Roth's *The Counterlife*, his publisher says in his eulogy of one of Zuckerman's fictional characters, Carnovsky: 'the real ethical life has, for all its sacrifices, its authentic spiritual rewards... Judaism at a higher level than he has access to does offer real ethical rewards to its students.'[42] A funeral oration is also at the centre of *The Assistant*, although here it is given by a rabbi and at its centre lies a subtle analysis of the difference between the spirit and the law. The rabbi addresses the mourners at Morris Bober's funeral:

> When a Jew dies who asks if he is a Jew? He is a Jew, we don't ask. There are many ways to be a Jew... Morris Bober was to me a true Jew because he lived in the Jewish experience, which he remembered, and with the Jewish heart. Maybe not to our formal tradition—for this I don't excuse him—but he was true to the spirit of our life—to want for others that which he wants also for himself... He wanted for his beloved child a better existence than he had. For such reasons he was a Jew.[43]

For the rabbi, Morris Bober was a Jew because he wanted a better existence for his child than he had himself. If this is a criterion for Jewishness, then surely there are very few parents who are not Jews. It is remarkable how often readers of *The Assistant* assume the rabbi is expressing Malamud's views when virtually every other incident in the novel suggests otherwise. Bober is a Jew because, above everything else, he is honest, and because he understands that to engage in an ethical relationship with others is to invite suffering, and to be forced to endure it. In a fascinating discussion with Frank he defends himself against the observation that he isn't kosher:

> To some Jews is this important but not to me. Nobody will tell me that I am not Jewish because I put in my mouth once in a while, when my mouth is dry, a piece of ham. But they will tell me and I will believe them, if I forget the Law. This means to do what is right, to be honest, to be good. This means to other people. Our life is hard enough. Why should we hurt somebody else? For everybody should be the best, not

---

41. T. Tanner, *Saul Bellow* (Edinburgh: Oliver & Boyd, 1965), p. 31.
42. Roth, *The Counterlife*, p. 213.
43. Malamud, *The Assistant*, pp. 207-208.

only for you and me. We ain't animals. This is why we need the Law. This is what a Jew believes.[44]

This is a position not radically dissimilar from the political implications of existentialism. It is unsurprising that the work of Bellow, Malamud and Roth should have proved so congenial to a postwar age which has little interest in the numinous or the supernatural elements of religion and has, perhaps inevitably, displaced it as a subject worthy of serious consideration with an interest in more practical anxieties about morality and ethics.

However, I want to conclude by referring to Malamud's *The Fixer*. As Bok sits in his cell he thinks: 'What was being a Jew but an everlasting curse? He was sick of their history, destiny, blood guilt.'[45] Then he reads the Old Testament: 'he read longer and faster, gripped by the narrative of the joyous and frenzied Hebrews, doing business, fighting wars, sinning and worshipping—whatever they were doing always engaged in talk with the huffing-puffing God, who tried to sound, maybe out of envy, like a human being'.[46] Eventually, Bok realizes: 'God envies the Jews: it's a rich life'.[47] On the evidence of the fiction evaluted in this chapter, one could also legitimately repeat that last sentence of Malamud's: 'It's a rich life'.

44. Malamud, *The Assistant*, p. 115.
45. Malamud, *The Fixer*, p. 241.
46. Malamud, *The Fixer*, pp. 255-56.
47. Malamud, *The Fixer*, p. 254.

THE STATEMENT: A LITERARY-HISTORICAL REFLECTION ON CATHOLIC–JEWISH RELATIONS

Liam Gearon

Introduction

There is a historical and inescapable relationship between religion and writing within literate cultures.[1] An extensive literature of commentary now exists which continues to explore this relationship both in generic terms[2] and with reference to specific religious texts or Scriptures.[3] Integral to this is the complex of theological concerns within 'secular' literature, in drama, poetry and the novel.[4] This essay examines this interface of religion and literature in Brian Moore's 1995 novel, *The Statement*,[5] which reflects the concern of this present volume, that is, Christian (here specifically Catholic)–Jewish relations.

1.   See S. Prickett, 'Orality, Literacy and the Idea of the Spiritual', in L. Gearon (ed.), *English Literature, Theology and the Curriculum* (London: Cassell, 1999), pp. 35-43.

2.   See the following: T. Wright, *Literature and Theology* (Oxford: Basil Blackwell, 1988); B. Ingraffia, *Postmodern Theory and Biblical Theology: Vanquishing God's Shadow* (Cambridge: Cambridge University Press, 1995); J. Milbank, *The World Made Strange: Theology, Language and Culture* (Oxford: Basil Blackwell, 1997); cf. C. Pickstock, *After Writing: On the Liturgical Consummation of Philosophy* (Oxford: Basil Blackwell, 1998); Gearon (ed.), *English Literature*.

3.   For example, see W.C. Smith, *What is Scripture? A Comparative Approach* (London: SCM Press, 1993); also N. Frye, *The Great Code: The Bible and Literature* (London: Routledge & Kegan Paul, 1982); D. Jasper, 'How Can We Read the Bible?', in Gearon (ed.), *English Literature*, pp. 9-26.

4.   Gearon (ed.), *English Literature*.

5.   B. Moore, *The Statement* (London: Bloomsbury, 1996 [1995]). References to this are cited in the text.

With a considerable body of criticism accrued on his work since the publication of *The Lonely Passion of Judith Hearne* in 1955,[6] Moore has often (rather surprisingly) been neglected within the context of the 'Catholic novel'.[7] Moore's distinctive contribution here has been the breadth of portrayal of Catholic thinking within his fiction, spanning many aspects of pre- and post-Vatican II Catholicism.[8]

Specific indications of an interest in Jewish–Catholic relations surface in Moore's early work. For instance, in *The Luck of Ginger Coffey*,[9] published in 1960, James Francis Coffey, like Moore an Irish immigrant to Canada, associates Irish Catholicism with anti-Semitism. This stance matches pre-Vatican II Catholic thinking on Catholic–Jewish relations, the traditional 'Teaching of Contempt'.[10] Coffey's personal rejection of Catholicism seems, though, to distance himself from such an anti-Jewish stance: 'He did not agree with many of his countrymen in their attitude to the Jews. None of his best friends were Jews, but that was no reason to dislike Jews was it?'[11]

6.   B. Moore, *Judith Hearne* (London: Andre Deutsch, 1955). The following are major studies of Moore's fiction and include bibliographical sources: H. Dahlie, *Brian Moore* (Toronto: Copp Clark, 1969); *idem*, *Brian Moore* (Boston: Twayne Publishers, 1981); J. O'Donoghue, *Brian Moore: A Critical Study* (Dublin: Gill & Macmillan, 1990); R. Sullivan, *A Matter of Faith: The Fiction of Brian Moore* (Westport, CT: Greenwood Press, 1996); D. Sampson, *Brian Moore: The Chameleon Novelist* (Dublin: Marino, 1998).

7.   See, e.g., T. Woodman, *Faithful Fictions: The Catholic Novel in British Literature* (Milton Keynes: Open University Press, 1991); P. Sherry, 'The End of the Catholic Novel?', *Literature & Theology* 9 (1995), pp. 165-78; cf. T. Brown, 'Show Me a Sign: The Religious Imagination of Brian Moore', *Irish University Review* 18 (1988), pp. 37-49, and P. Gallagher, 'Religion as Favourite Metaphor: Moore's Recent Fiction', *Irish University Review* 18 (1998), pp. 50-58.

8.   L. Gearon, 'The Writing of Catholic Worlds: Landscape and the Portrayal of Catholicism in the Novels of Brian Moore', in Gearon (ed.), *English Literature*, pp. 266-311.

9.   B. Moore, *The Luck of Ginger Coffey* (London: Andre Deutsch, 1960; repr., London: Flamingo, 1994).

10.   J. Cardinal Willebrands, 'Christians and Jews: A New Vision', in A. Stacpoole (ed.), *Vatican II by Those Who Were There* (London: Geoffrey Chapman), pp. 220-36.

11.   Moore, *The Luck*, p. 31.

In *An Answer from Limbo*,[12] a work published in 1962, the year when the Second Vatican Council opened, the protagonist, Brendan Tierney, is also an Irish immigrant who has further distanced himself from his Catholic roots. Such distance is shown most markedly by the contrast between Brendan and his Irish Catholic mother. Brendan asks his mother to come to New York to childmind his two children while his wife works to support him in his struggle to complete his first, supposedly great novel. On her arrival in New York from Ireland, though, Tierney's mother immediately causes offence to Jane, Brendan's part-Jewish wife. Thus, Brendan's mother comments on her son's changed appearance:

> 'Sure, I didn't know him at all, when he met me', she said, smiling.
> 'With those dark glasses on him I took him for some Jew man.'
> 'Mamma, Jane's mother is part Jewish.'[13]

Brendan attempts to defend his mother by way of conciliation but the subsequent conversation with Jane also highlights alleged Jewish prejudice against Christians:

> 'Well, she didn't really mean any harm, you know. It's not her fault either. She just doesn't know any Jews.'
> 'She does now.'
> 'Come off it Jane, you're not Jewish.'
> 'I'm one quarter Jewish. And your children are one eighth Jewish, remember. What's going to happen if she fills them full of anti-semitism?'
> 'She won't. I'll speak to her. Let's be fair, darling. Remember your grandmother and *her* remarks about the drunken *goyim*.'
> 'That's different. My grandmother had cause.'
> 'Your mother came from a backward environment, that was why she thought all Christians were drunks. And my mother comes from a backward environment too. Same thing.'[14]

In his early fiction, though, particularly early North American novels like *The Luck of Ginger Coffey* and *An Answer from Limbo*, the novelist is more keen to explore the relation between religious and *secular* worldviews (principally that encounter between Catholic Ireland and a liberal North America), rather than inter-religious difference.

---

    12. B. Moore, *An Answer from Limbo* (London: Andre Deutsch, 1963; repr., London: Flamingo, 1994).
    13. Moore, *An Answer*, p. 38.
    14. Moore, *An Answer*, p. 39.

In later fiction, the relations between Catholicism and other ideological and religious worldviews are explored more fully. In *The Colour of Blood*,[15] for example, Moore examines relations between the east European Catholic Church and an atheistic, communist regime, while in *No Other Life*[16] Moore examines the interaction of revolutionary Marxism and Christianity in liberation theology. Moore's later fiction develops a concern with inter-*faith* relations too. His novel *Catholics*[17] thus begins his first fully fledged treatment of Vatican II theology on a range of issues, including liturgical reform, ecumenism but also inter-faith dialogue.[18] Catholic encounter with other *religious* worldviews is seen more strikingly in later American novels such as the portrayal of seventeenth-century Jesuit missionary Canada in *Black Robe*.[19] Most recently, Moore's final novel *The Magician's Wife*[20] deals with the encounter between an imperialist, nineteenth-century French Catholicism and Islam in colonial Algeria.

One of the most sensitive and yet controversial treatments of Catholic inter-faith relations, though, is in Moore's 1995 novel, *The Statement*, a work which is a literary-historical reflection on Catholicism in Vichy France and the subsequent postwar period. Within this novel, Moore effectively integrates developments in post-Vatican II Catholic thinking as well as in social and political attitudes within France. To adapt terms made familiar by Lyotard and literary theory,[21] Moore's fiction here invokes an intertextual relationship with the grandnarratives of theology and ideology.

15. B. Moore, *The Colour of Blood* (London: Jonathan Cape, 1987).

16. B. Moore, *No Other Life* (London: Bloomsbury, 1993).

17. B. Moore, *Catholics* (London: Jonathan Cape, 1972).

18. In A. Flannery (ed.), *Vatican Council II: The Conciliar and Post Conciliar Documents* (Dublin: Dominican Publications, 1992), see, respectively, *The Constitution on the Sacred Liturgy* (Vatican II, *Sacrosanctum concilium*, 4 December 1963), pp. 1-36; *Decree on Ecumenism* (Vatican II, *Unitatis redintegratio*, 21 November 1964), pp. 452-70; *Declaration on the Relationship of the Church to Non-Christian Religions* (Vatican II, *Nostra aetate*, 28 October 1965), pp. 738-42.

19. B. Moore, *Black Robe* (London: Jonathan Cape, 1985).

20. B. Moore, *The Magician's Wife* (London: Bloomsbury, 1997).

21. J.-F. Lyotard, *The Postmodern Condition: A Report on Knowledge* (Manchester: Manchester University Press, 1984).

The Statement: A Literary-Historical Reflection
on Catholic–Jewish Relations

The Plot: Narrative and Grandnarrative

In terms of the portrayal of Catholicism, *The Statement* is an important novel which focuses upon key theological issues for the Church, that of Catholic–Jewish relations, and more broadly Catholic theological understanding of religious plurality. The narrative shifts between 1940s Vichy France and the 1980s, a time-frame which not only spans the major phase of Moore's own career as a novelist, but also marks developments from pre- to post-Vatican II Roman Catholic thinking. Significantly, the period was characterized by a move away from the traditional 'Teaching of Contempt' of Catholics towards Judaism to a more conciliatory stance.

The changes are most noted in four documents arising from the Second Vatican Council and the post-Conciliar period. The four documents are: *Declaration on the Relationship of the Church to Non-Christian Religions* (*Nostra aetate*, 28 October 1965, Ecumenical Council Vatican II); *Guidelines and Suggestions for Implementing the Conciliar Declaration* (*Nostra aetate*, 1 December 1974, Vatican Commission for Religious Relations with the Jews); *Notes on the Correct Way to Present the Jews and Judaism in Preaching and Catechesis in the Roman Catholic Church* (24 June 1985, Vatican Commission for Religious Relations with the Jews); *We Remember: A Reflection on the Shoah* (16 March 1998, Vatican Commission for Religious Relations with the Jews).

The Statement opens with a strong evocation of France from the perspective of the anonymous would-be assassin, 'R'. The assassin's quarry is Pierre Brossard, a wartime Nazi collaborator in Vichy France. Moore based this character directly on the figure of Paul Touvier and the plot of the novel mirrors in essence the patterns of postwar political (religious and secular) collusion which allowed the historical Paul Touvier to escape justice for over 40 years.[22] One early assumption in the novel is that the assassin is part of a Jewish conspiracy to track down and kill those who have escaped justice for their crimes against humanity; another assumption is that 'It was a known fact that the Church was involved' (p. 2). Brossard, however, manages to kill his

22. See Sampson, *Brian Moore*, pp. 286-88.

first potential assassin and this early death reveals what turns out to be a false Jewish-Canadian identity and the nature of 'The Statement' itself, the paper to be pinned to the murdered Brossard:

THE STATEMENT
COMMITTEE FOR JUSTICE FOR THE
JEWISH VICTIMS OF DOMBEY

> This man is Pierre Brossard, former Chief of the Second Section of the Marseille region of the milice, condemned to death in absentia by French courts, in 1944 and again in 1946, and further charged with a crime against humanity in the murder of 14 Jews at Dombey, Alpes-Maritimes, 15 June 1944. After 44 years of delays, legal prevarications, and the complicity of the Catholic Church in hiding Brossard from justice, the dead are now avenged. This case is closed (p. 7).

This statement seemingly confirms the reader's likely assumptions from the first pages of the novel.

Influenced by the fiction of the late Graham Greene, Moore uses a sub-genre of writing which he has identified as the 'metaphysical thriller'.[23] In this instance, a complex series of narrative twists extend the novel's plot to incorporate wider conflict between and *within* competing grandnarratives. Simplistically, there is a narrative/grandnarrative dialectic between the protectors and pursuers of Brossard. The significant *protectors* of Brossard are those high in French political office as well as extreme conservatives within the Church. The notable *pursuers* of Brossard include representatives of French justice and a *reformed* Church hierarchy. Within this metaphysical thriller, which largely mirrors the Touvier incident except for Brossard's eventual assassination, protectors and pursuers highlight ideological and theological shifts in French political and Catholic ecclesiastical history.

The Protectors

Brossard's protectors become apparent through a complex series of geographical moves through France. Shifts in landscape and setting, as Brossard searches for an ever elusive security, reflect different sides of ideological and religious debate. Associating monasticism with political and religious conservatism, Moore's reactionary forces within the Church are those that demonstrate independence from changes within

23. See Sampson, *Brian Moore*, p. 242.

the post-Vatican II Catholicism: in Salon du Provence is Dom Vladimir Gorkakov of Abbaye de St Cros; in Aix, Dom Andres Vergnes of Prieure de St Christophe; in Cannes, Abbe Fessard (p. 84); in Armijnon, Dom Henri Armijnon, the Carmelite Abbey St Michel des Monts at Villefranche (pp. 88, 119), and finally in Nice, Dom Olivier Villedieu of the Prieure de la Fraternité St Donat (pp. 190, 193, 195). In fear of either imminent capture or assassination, Brossard's passage from monastery to monastery provides the reader with the opportunity to hear the voice of the political right within the French Church.[24] Thus, for instance, the Abbot addresses Father Blaise, the Abbot's liberal *père hospitalier*:

> ...under the Marechal Petain, France was given a chance to revoke the errors, the weakness and selfishness, of the Third Republic, that regime that caused us to lose the war to the Germans. Of course, it was a sad time. I'm not denying it. Part of the country was occupied, but you must remember there was a large free zone, the zone of the Vichy Government, the Marechal's government, which was giving us the hope of a new co-operation between our country and Germany. Under the Marechal, we were led away from selfish materialism and those democratic parliaments that preached a false equality back to the Catholic values we were brought up in: the family, the nation, the Church. But when the Germans lost the war, all that was finished. Stalin's communist armies overran Europe. The enemies of religion came back in force (p. 73).

Establishing within his fiction an intertextual space which is both literary and theological, Moore explicitly integrates the historical context of Vatican II within the narrative moves of *The Statement*. Thus the Prieure Fraternité of St Donat, Dom Olivier, has chosen to follow Monsignor Lefebvre, 'the former Archbishop of Dakar who believed that, with the abandonment of the Latin mass and the changes that followed Vatican II, Rome was no longer the true Church' (p. 175). Active resistance to post-Conciliar liturgical change is thus portrayed as a mark of political extremism. Dom Olivier's pre-Vatican II liturgical conservatism is associated with the perniciousness of classical Christian anti-Semitism, the association of the Jews with evil personified in the form of the devil, as he explains to the man he had sheltered for so many years:

24. For an accessible account of this period, see R. Price, *A Concise History of France* (Cambridge: Cambridge University Press, new edn, 1997), pp. 244-77.

Pierre, one of the reasons we have lost the true path is the Devil, more than at any other time in history, has managed to conceal his ways and works. The people have forgotten that the Evil One exists. And, alas, the Church, the Papal Church, has not seen fit to remind them of his existence. If, indeed, the Papal Church believes that the Devil still exists. I am not sure of that, as I am not sure of anything in connection with present-day Rome... We know, and we have always known, that the Jews do not have the interests of France at heart and that they are still willing to sow dissension and feelings of guilt and blame, more than forty years after the German Occupation. I see that lust for vengeance as inspired by the Devil (p. 195).

Brossard concurs, reflecting with unrepentant anti-Semitism that the 'Devil isn't someone with a cloven hoof and a forked tail. The Devil is the Jews' (p. 207). With Brossard's greatest public advocate, Monsignor le Moyne (pp. 42-43), innocent of crimes but duped by a revisionist view of Holocaust history ('The numbers of the dead are exaggerated no doubt, but what matter?', p. 44), Moore seemingly presents a fairly damning picture of postwar Catholic involvement in perpetuating prejudicial attitudes to Judaism. However, with his portrayal of Brossard's pursuers, such a simplistic picture is modified if not fully overturned.

The Pursuers
If Brossard's flight around the south of France, then, is charted by Moore as a complex ideological and theological landscape, Brossard's protectors are only one face of this map of French political and Catholic ecclesiastical life. Thus, postwar *political* reform and post-Vatican II *Church* reform are shown as having radically altered the ideological and theological landscape of France. The literal and metaphorical territory which allowed Brossard to escape justice is shown to have been reduced exponentially; though, to extend the metaphor, a territory of ideological and theological extremism remains which is personified by figures like Le Pen in politics and Lefebvre in theology. Massed against Brossard are those representative forces which would seek redress for the injustices of France's and the Church's wartime and postwar past.

One major change to France's theological map is the post-Vatican II Catholic Church itself. Thus Archbishop Delavigne's commission, consisting of an independent group of secular, university historians, attempts to provide evidence of ecclesiastical culpability, though not legal judgment, on Church involvement with Jewish persecution. This Commission might be said to parallel the Commission for the Religious Relations with the Jews behind the most recent Vatican statement on Catholic–Jewish relations, *We Remember: A Reflection on the Shoah*. With openness towards the Vatican's 'murky' record, including the acknowledgment of 'the post-war Vatican passports issued to Nazis to help them escape to South America' (p. 66), one of the independent historians, Professor Valentin, speaks for Cardinal Delavigne and the Commission to the investigating magistrate: 'I feel that Cardinal Delavigne is sincere when he says he set up the investigation because he believes a wrong that is brought out into the open is preferable to a declaration of innocence, which is suspect' (p. 66). Recognizing the diversity of post-Vatican II Catholicism, he states that the 'Church is not monolithic, particularly in France' (p. 66), implying the persistence of pre-Vatican II attitudes within the post-Vatican II Church. Representative of such progressive–conservative diversity, Brossard's protectors are indicative of these unreformed elements within the Church. Indeed, unreformed elements in the post-Vatican II Church provide the wider critique of the Church's past, one of indifference as much as active persecution. As one monk comments to a pro-Brossard supporter, the Church 'forgives itself for its silence when thousands of Jew were sent to their deaths' (p. 154). Response to recent publications from the Vatican on Catholic–Jewish relations would indicate that much ground still needs to be covered before full reconciliation, statements from the Vatican being described by critics as 'a bridge too short'.[25] Still, Delavigne's position does mark the major shift in Catholic inter-faith relations since the Second Vatican Council, particularly from *Nostra aetate*.

If the acceptable *public* face, though, of Catholic–Jewish relations changed with pronouncements of the Second Vatican Council and post-Conciliar Church,[26] political change in postwar France is portrayed as lacking such a definitive break with the past.[27] The new state *juge*

25. Editorial, *The Tablet* (21 March 1998), p. 371; also pp. 390-91. This was in response to the Vatican publication of *We Remember: A Reflection on the Shoah*, 16 March 1998, by the Commission for Religious Relations with the Jews. See also R. Hill, *The Tablet* (21 March 1998), pp. 372-73.

26. See E.J. Fisher and L. Klenicki (eds.), *In our Time: The Flowering of Jewish–Catholic Dialogue* (New York: Paulist Press, 1990).

27. On the rise of the National Front in France, see Price, *A Concise History of France*, pp. 350-53, 356, 358, 369.

d'instruction investigating the Brossard case, Madame Annemarie Livi, surmises that Church protection of Brossard might be part of the wider context of continuing, mainstream political support within France (pp. 36, 122-23).[28] The novel thus sets the case of Brossard against other postwar trials such as that of Klaus Barbie but, since the likely assassins of Brossard cannot be traced to 'one of the well-known Nazi-hunters like the Klarsfelds or the Wiesenthal Centre' (p. 123), this provides an additional clue to culpability within the French political hierarchy. Moore hereby integrates competing political ideologies (as well as competing Catholic theologies) into his novel, providing a meta-text for the analysis of postwar French political and ecclesiastical history.

Here we have the crux: Colonel Roux, one of Livi's fellow investigators, reveals that 'other Frenchmen are similarly charged but have never been brought to trial. But if Brossard is caught and tried, their trial can't be put off any longer. So, to sum up Madame, I don't believe the Church alone had the power to help Brossard escape the police and the courts over a forty-year period' (p. 67). Significant here is Commissioner Vionnet, who had arranged the immediate postwar release of Brossard for information received, a means of covering up a 'question about deportation orders signed by someone high up in the *prefecture* in Paris'. Politically most sensitive, though, is the place of Maurice de Grandville, former 'Paris prefect of Police under de Gaulle':

> Now eighty years old, with a record of past action requiring judicial investigation, which, over the years, had accumulated thirty tomes of evidence, without his ever spending a night in prison, he had outlived the statute of limitations on his former deeds. Except one, the one that had shadowed his long career. In the years of the German Occupation, as Secretary General of the *prefecture* of the Gironde, he had facilitated his SS colleagues by organising a series of French deportation trains which sent sixteen hundred people, including two hundred and forty children,

---

28. The magistrate's early comments to Colonel Roux help clarify this: 'I've been told that it concerns the relations between the Commissariat of Police and the Vichy regime. It's a matter of record that the French police were pro-Petain and collaborated with the German occupiers in deporting Jews to German concentration camps... The gendarmerie, on the other hand, were sympathetic to the Resistance and to the de Gaulle forces fighting outside France. As a result the gendarmerie has a clean record in the matter of collaboration with the Germans. The Commissariat of Police does not' (p. 36). It is for this reason that, in the novel, the investigation of Brossard is transferred from the police to the army.

to their deaths in Nazi extermination camps. For this action there was no
statute of limitations. The crime against humanity (p. 183).

It is de Grandville's money, channelled by retired Commissioner
Vionnet and Inspector Pochon in the French police, which has been
supporting Brossard financially while certain monasteries have provided physical shelter. De Grandville, fearing Brossard's revelations on
capture, has thus arranged for the latter's assassination. Aware of public
knowledge of Church complicity with Brossard and expecting no public
surprise if a Jewish group is found to be responsible for killing Brossard, it is de Grandville who is behind 'the statement' which would
point, incorrectly, to Jewish involvement in the death of Brossard and
confirm Church complicity.

Conclusion

The complexities of this metaphysical thriller are greater for its trans-
historical plot, and, to borrow from Lyotard,[29] for the manner in which
the grandnarratives of politics and religion merge within Brossard's
much smaller story. Perhaps controversially, Moore sees the Church as
an easy target whose post-Vatican II reforms can be ignored by anti-
ecclesiastical public prejudice, while racial intolerance is seen as
endemic to French political life. The former Prefect's involvement in
the repression of Algerian protest which led to independence in 1962 is
indicative of this. There is thus a cruel irony in the use made by de
Grandville of an Algerian to kill an old Nazi collaborator. Indeed 'T',
the second would-be assassin of Brossard, himself assumes de
Grandville is Jewish. Importantly, though, through the character and
background of the second failed assassin, 'T', Moore further highlights
the contentious issue of immigration in modern day France, a social history which presents Catholic–Jewish prejudice and persecution within
the wider context of racial conflict and cultural intolerance. Here 'T'
looks at the photograph of the young Brossard and reflects on his earlier
meeting with de Grandville in the context of his own immigrant family
history:

> Now he's supposed to be seventy, he should be dead, he's part of
> history. The *milice*. Those days are old movies, that's all, Nazi uniforms,
> propeller bombers, *Casablanca* with Ingrid Bergman, and chez nous,

29. Lyotard, *The Postmodern Condition*.

Rommel in the desert with his tanks, and the Americans landing at Algiers. Papa was a little kid in the Arab quarter in Oran, he saw Rommel's tanks on the run, then the winners, Americans, French, British, parading through the streets, he loved that, he loved uniforms, Papa, he wanted to be a soldier, not the ones in France, not Vichy, not the ones this guy fought for, but de Gaulle's. Not that it mattered. No matter which French side you fight for, the French will fuck you, like they did Papa, who couldn't wait to grow up and join the French army, yes, in '55, signing on in Algiers, he was twenty years old, and they filled him full of lies, he was to be a Harkis, part of an elite commando, auxiliary troops, riding camels, encamped beside the French, Papa was in the top commando, the Georges, Muslims against French officers, fighting for Salan and the junta against the FLN, our own brothers. I wonder if that rich Jew officer tonight knew I'm the son of a Harkis. No, he wouldn't know that. I'm not dark, like Papa. I can always pass for French (pp. 32-33).

Elsewhere in the novel similar themes are presented. For example, talking with Monsignor le Moyne, arch-advocate of Brossard, 'the winegrower' Bouchard, returning 'obsessively to the subject of immigrant population', blames the Muslim element in his son's school for the boy's involvement with drugs: 'Le Pen is right', he said. 'Send them back where they came from. What do you think Father? Wouldn't you vote for Le Pen, if you were me?' (pp. 44-45).

France, though, becomes a prison for Brossard as, trapped by memory, political changes in French society and theological shifts in Church culture, his demise becomes inevitable. Residual pre-Vatican II attitudes and post-Vatican II developments in Catholic thinking on Catholic–Jewish relations are thus mirrored within *The Statement* when his (still undiscovered) political protectors take direct responsibility for his assassination. (Brossard is killed by Inspector Pochon, one of his former protectors.) In the last lines of the narrative, we are left with Pierre Brossard's final and unrepentant stream of consciousness which, at least in part, reflects too a collective, if reformed, *conscience* within the Catholic Church:

Pain consumed him but through it he struggled to say, at last, that prayer the Church had taught him, that true act of contrition for his crimes. But he could feel no contrition. He had never felt contrite for the acts of his life. And, now when he asked God's pardon, God chose to show him fourteen dead Jews (p. 218).

If Brossard is finally unrepentant for both his crimes and his anti-Semitic attitudes, his death at the hands of right-wing, former political protectors marks a public separation of such ideological and theological extremes. Wartime collaboration between Church and Vichy government had been possible because of loosely shared and perhaps unsystematic anti-Semitic attitudes, the classical 'teaching of contempt' which historically marked Jewish–Catholic relations. If in postwar France anti-Semitic and more broadly racist ideology remains prominent through figures such as Le Pen and the French National Front, then post-Vatican II, it is an ideology which the Church can no longer support theologically.

AFTER FAGIN: JEWISHNESS AND CHILDREN'S LITERATURE

Pat Pinsent

Introduction: Literature of the Past

Standing over [the sausages], with a toasting fork in his hand, was a very
old, shrivelled Jew, whose villainous-looking and repulsive face was
obscured by a quantity of matted red hair.[1]

This description provides the first sight that the reader of an unabridged
version of Dickens's classic novel has of perhaps his most notorious
character, Fagin. It is far from clear whether the point of view the
reader shares is that of the eponymous hero—how did Oliver know
Fagin was a Jew?—or if it is wholly that of the narrator. Modern,
abridged, children's versions of this text tend to remove its anti-
Semitism by always referring to the character by his name only, but it
would be rash to ignore the effect of Dickens's hostile portrayal of
Jewishness on generations of young readers. In particular, the ugliness,
the red hair, and the use of the toasting fork are all traditional signifiers
of the devil, as indeed is the title 'the old gentleman', with which Dickens often endows Fagin. This is no coincidence, since we know that, at
the time when he was writing this book, Dickens was reading Defoe's
History of the Devil. How far Dickens himself was aware of his anti-
Semitism it is difficult to be sure. We do know, however, that this character was based on a notorious Jewish fence, Ikey Solomon. It is, of
course, quite likely that some of the money-lenders and pawnbrokers to
whom Charles's father John had frequent recourse, and whom the
young Charles may have blamed for encouraging his father's propensity
to debt, were Jewish. We also know that Dickens named this character
after Bob Fagin, a boy who befriended him in the childhood experience
he never ceased to lament: working in his relative's 'blacking factory'

---

1. C. Dickens, *Oliver Twist* (Harmondsworth: Penguin Books, 1962 [1837–
39]), Ch. 8, p. 105).

when his father was in a debtor's prison. The young Dickens was so afraid of sinking into the mire of lowlife London, and becoming like Bob Fagin, that he later repaid his kindness by notoriety. As Ackroyd says, 'Although it seems that even by Dickens' own account Bob Fagin was gentle and considerate to him, his very presence evoked a horror greater than any gratitude Dickens might have felt—the horror of being a part of the poor'.[2] I have no information, however, as to the racial antecedents of the original Bob Fagin.

Oliver Twist was not, of course, specifically written for children. However, because of its young central character, it has certainly been appropriated by young readers, and additionally made into films and musicals. Dickens was writing near the culmination of a long tradition of anti-Semitic writing, from the fourteenth-century *Prioress's Tale* by Chaucer to sixteenth-century plays such as Marlowe's *The Jew of Malta* and Shakespeare's *The Merchant of Venice*. All of these are deeply influenced by social factors, notably the unpopularity of the nevertheless necessary figure of the Jewish money-lender in a period when usury was forbidden by the Christian Church.[3]

There are implicit and at times explicit racist assumptions in the adventure stories of John Buchan and Dornford Yates, and even in T.S. Eliot's *The Waste Land*, but of the Jewish characters created in these and other books, probably only Shylock and Fagin are really accessible to children. Evidence of anti-Semitism within literature likely to be

---

2.   P. Ackroyd, *Dickens* (London: Guild Publishing, 1990), p. 78. Information about Dickens's life has been derived from this source, as well as E. Hobsbaum, *A Reader's Guide to Charles Dickens* (London: Thames & Hudson, 1972), esp. Chs. 3 and 12.

3.   Other nineteenth-century novels testify to the prevalence of descriptions of Jews as rich and associated with money-lending. Sir Walter Scott's *Ivanhoe* (1820), set in the twelfth century, portrays Isaac of York in a dismal panic which the Palmer, the titular character himself in disguise, admits is justified: 'You have cause for your terror, considering how your brethren have been used, in order to extort from them their hoards'. Thackeray, in the mid-nineteenth-century *Vanity Fair* (1848), has the penurious Rawdon Crawley exclaim: 'Before I was married I didn't care what bills I put my name to, and so long as Moses would wait or Levy would renew for three months, I kept on never minding'. However relatively harmless this kind of image might be, it fuelled more dangerous ideas: 'L'image du "Juif riche", de la "finance juive" cosmopolite, sans frontière et sans patrie, alimente l'antisémitisme moderne' (J. Tarnero, *Le racisme* [Toulouse: Editions Milan, 1998]), p. 8.

regarded as suitable for children comes in a relatively little known tale, 'The Jew in the Thornbush', included by the Grimm brothers in the second volume (1815) of their first collection, from a 1618 source.[4] This is the story of a faithful but naïve servant who is paid off by his master at the inadequate rate of a farthing for each of the three years he has worked. He gives this money to a dwarf in exchange for being granted three wishes: for a gun that hits everything he aims at, for a fiddle that will make everyone dance, and for the power to make people grant him anything he requests. Next he meets 'a Jew with a long goatee, who was standing and listening to the song of a bird perched high on top of a tree'; the Jew longs to possess the bird. The servant kills it and orders the Jew to collect the corpse which has fallen into a thornbush. When he is stuck in the bush, the servant plays the fiddle, the Jew dances, so that 'the thorns ripped the Jew's coat to shreds, combed his goatee, and scratched and pricked his entire body'. The motive for the servant's vindictiveness is disclosed: 'You've skinned plenty of people, so now the thorns will give you some of your own treatment in return'. In order to escape, the Jew gives the servant a bag of gold; he then goes on to attempt to bring the servant to justice. The servant is condemned to death, but is granted his last request: to play his fiddle. Everyone is forced to dance to the music, so the judge agrees to release the servant if he stops fiddling. This isn't the end, however, for:

> The good servant was moved by this plea, put down his fiddle, hung it around his neck again, and climbed down the ladder. Then he went over to the Jew, who was lying on the ground and gasping for breath, and said, 'You lousy swindler, confess and tell us where you got the money from, or I'll take the fiddle from my neck and begin playing again.'
>
> 'I stole it, I stole it!' he screamed, 'but you earned it honestly.'
>
> Then the judge had the Jew led up to the gallows, and he was hanged as a thief.[5]

This rather unpleasant little story really typifies anti-Semitism in seventeenth-century Europe, and it is interesting to note how the servant is constantly referred to as 'good', presumably not only for his years of faithful service, but also for his exposure of the Jew as a thief.

---

4.   Brothers Grimm, 'The Jew in the Thornbush', in their *Complete Fairy Tales* (trans. and ed. J. Zipes; New York: Bantam, 1987), pp. 398-402.

5.   Brothers Grimm, 'The Jew in the Thornbush', pp. 400-402.

The Jew is given a stereotypical appearance with the goatee, is made to look foolish in his dancing and grovelling, and is finally condemned by society for, we must assume (given the lack of detail in the story), having fulfilled a necessary but unpopular role as a money-lender. This surely means that the story, if printed at all, needs to be associated with explanatory footnotes relating it to the prejudice of its period. My own copy of the story is in an American edition of 1987, translated by the eminent fairy-tale scholar, Jack Zipes. Despite a dedication to his daughter, it is presumably intended for adults. More recently, an edition of Grimms' tales including this story was published in Britain; an observant person noticed it in the junior section of a bookshop and drew it to the attention of various bodies who have been investigating as to whether it infringes the Public Order Act of 1886. The publishers exonerated themselves from any blame by claiming that the edition concerned was produced solely for academic study. The problem, which cannot easily be solved, is obviously one of audience—how to ensure a story is available to an adult audience but does not have the potential to induce wrong attitudes in a young audience.

When we look at literature more specifically written for children than fairy-tales, the situation becomes still more complex. Not only are such authors writing from their own basis within society, they are often also consciously or unconsciously trying to influence the opinions or behaviour of young readers. It is probably impossible for any adult to write a book for children 'innocently', and it is certainly impossible to do so on such a potentially inflammatory subject. Attitudes will surface and questions arise about what some people call equality issues and others term political correctness.

It is only in recent years that people are likely to have this kind of awareness of the potential to cause offence. When E. Nesbit's *The Story of the Amulet* was published in 1906, its caricature of Jewish financiers would have been regarded by most adults as harmless fun. The children who are the focal characters of the story have inadvertently brought the Queen of Babylon to London, where she has supplied many poor people with food before arriving at the Stock Exchange. There we see such obviously Jewish characters as Mr Rosenbaum, Lionel Cohen and Mr Levinstein, the last of whom, in what I assume to be a heavily Yiddish accent, says, 'I think it is chust a ver' bad tream;…all along Bishopsgate I haf seen the gommon people have their hants full of food—*goot* food. Oh yes, without doubt a very bad tream!'[6]

Nesbit is taking advantage of the stereotype of the Jew as making money from exploiting the ordinary people, and I imagine few of her original readers would have been very worried about this, though to her credit she docs not identify these characters as Jewish other than by their names; probably few children, then or now, would be aware of her prejudice. Nevertheless, I suspect writers today would find themselves in difficulty with their publishers if they tried to include such a scene.

Not all books portraying Jewish characters present them as evil, however, but there seem to be relatively few among the 'classics', whether of children's or of adult literature, which permit such characters to be simply ordinary. The Jewish characters in George Eliot's *Daniel Deronda* (1876) have an aura of mystery about them,[7] while by contrast it seems likely that the pitiably poor Hummel family in Alcott's *Little Women* (1868) may be Jewish—they are certainly German-speaking immigrants.[8]

Twentieth-Century Children's Literature

I have felt it necessary to present a context of earlier literature for my scrutiny of more contemporary children's literature. Most of the books I am looking at are English originals, which means I have had to give little attention to some significant children's books in German.[9] It is difficult to draw a firm boundary round 'children's literature'; I shall use the term to apply to texts which appears to have been written with a primary audience in mind of young people under about 18. The books that are relevant to my current enquiry are, by the nature of things, within a broadly 'realist' mode; contemporary fantasy tends to exclude any descriptions which could enable us to identify the racial origins of

6. E. Nesbit, *The Story of the Amulet* (Harmondsworth: Penguin Books, 1959 [1906]), p. 151.

7. George Eliot's *Daniel Deronda* (1876) portrays the titular character as being fascinated by Judaism, which he later discovers, through the mysterious and exotic Mira, is his parental inheritance.

8. L. Alcott, *Little Women* (Oxford: Oxford University Press, 1994 [1868]), Ch. 2.

9. See G. Lathey, *The Impossible Legacy: Identity and Purpose in Autobiographical Children's Fiction Set in the Third Reich and the Second World War* (Bern: Peter Lang, 1999) for fuller information about both English and German books about the war.

characters. Some of the books I shall mention could, however, be regarded as examples of 'magic realism', in their depiction of impossible events within an otherwise realist picture. The genre of realism includes adventure, school, family and historical stories. Some books set in today's society introduce an element of what is sometimes termed 'gritty realism'—the encounter with problems such as drug taking, poverty and death.

In looking at sensitive subjects such as race and prejudice, it is always interesting to reflect on the extent to which authors, consciously or unconsciously, reveal their own biases. Peter Hollindale[10] suggests that ideology is revealed in two possible ways: the author may explicitly seek to persuade readers towards his or her point of view, or may implicitly accept current ideas without question. Still more difficult to pin down is the way in which the use of language, again unquestioned, may convey atttitudes towards a subject. Whereas in the past, deliberate anti-Semitism may well have led to explicitly hostile portrayals of Jewish characters, explicit ideology today is more likely to lead to a rather over-didactic presentation of the evils of anti-Semitism, as indeed we shall see. Unquestioning acceptance of the prejudices of the times is, I would suggest, what we find in the work of Dickens and Nesbit, but relatively little of it is apparent today. An interesting example, however, occurs in a book for young adults by the Australian writer, Ruth Park, whose *The Harp in the South* (1948) depicts a central character from an Irish background, Roie, falling in love with a crippled Jewish lad who gets her pregnant, but is so overwhelmed by his feelings of inadequacy that he cannot help her. Perhaps fortunately, she loses the baby. She muses: 'Had she really been in love with the Jewish boy, so shallow, so emotionally brittle, his mind clouded with the selfishness engendered by his deformity?'[11] I can imagine other groups also being worried about the assumptions revealed here; I am not of course denying that a Jewish boy with a club foot may be emotionally immature, but I feel that Park, who may even be basing the character on someone known to her, is nevertheless unnecessarily slanting her writing by an unquestioning acceptance of preconceived ideas. Clearly Roie's viewpoint is not necessarily that of the author, but no corrective

10. P. Hollindale, *Ideology and the Children's Book* (Stroud: Thimble, 1988).

11. R. Park, *The Harp in the South* (Harmondsworth: Penguin Books, 1951 [1948]), p. 186.

seems to be implied within the text. That Park is not automatically racist, despite her reference elsewhere to 'a buck nigger' (p. 70), is revealed by the fact that Roie eventually finds happiness with a man who is half Aborigine. What seems more likely is that at this relatively early date, and early stage in her own career, Park has not been forced to question her implicit assumptions.

Instances of unquestioning acceptance of the anti-Semitism of the English language, where terms such as Jew or Hebrew were often used in the past to indicate meanness, are less easy to pinpoint, but I suspect they have become much fewer since the Second World War.

The active, rather than incidental, portrayal of Jewish characters and themes in children's books of the last 50 years or so may for convenience be divided into (1) didactic treatment in books displaying the evils of prejudice; (2) a presentation from the inside of issues very specific to the Jewish community; and, the largest category and one needing treatment on its own, (3) the Second World War and the Holocaust, whether treated directly or indirectly.

Books Exposing the Evil of Prejudice

I want to start with two examples of non-Jewish authors whose books reveal a clear intention to warn their young readers against the evils of prejudice; interestingly, both of these writers appear to be Roman Catholic. *Tunes for Bears to Dance to* (1992), by the American writer, Robert Cormier,[12] is about Henry, who earns some money by working in a grocery shop; the owner is prepared to pay him to smash up a model village created by an elderly man, and his motivation seems entirely anti-Semitic:

> 'Why was it so important to smash the old man's village? Why do you hate him so much?'
> 'He's a Jew', the grocer said. As if that explained it all (p. 88).

Since the grocer has already been revealed as an unpleasant character, while the reader is involved with the fortunes of Henry and sees him as deeply disturbed by this kind of hatred, there seems little doubt as to Cormier's intention of warning his young readers against this kind of bias.

12. R. Cormier, *Tunes for Bears to Dance to* (London: HarperCollins, 1994 [1992]).

Antonia Forest's *End of Term* (1959)[13] is one of several in a series about a girls' boarding school, Kingscote. Different volumes focus on various of the five members of the Marlow family who attend it. In this case, twins Nicola and Lawrie are involved with the usual vicissitudes of the netball team, but the main theme is the end-of-term play. Forest's didactic aims are partly concerned with aspects such as the need for truth and 'fair play', but she is obviously also anxious to provide information about religion, in this case both Catholicism and Judaism. Nicola Marlow becomes friendly with a Jewish girl, whom Forest first describes as she is observed by Nicola:

> Miranda's clever little Jewish face, with its brilliantly blue eyes, thin aquiline nose, and short dark hair which curled like a diving duck's crest. She might be rather an interesting person to be friends with (p. 33).

The friendship becomes established as Miranda gives Nicola 'one of the quick and vividly interested looks to which Nicola was to become accustomed' (p. 34). Thus the Jewish girl is presented as attractive and intelligent, so that the reader is ready to share her point of view of the school Nativity play, in which it is felt she cannot participate. A rather unpleasant girl explains, 'Well of course you can't. You're Jewish.' When Miranda answers that all the characters in the play were also Jewish, Lawrie responds 'Nonsense. You're just making it up', but eventually, perhaps like the young reader, she learns that she is wrong (pp. 63-64).

Miranda is constantly presented as an attractive character; her family is rich, and she is kind to a girl who has family trouble. Thus when she reveals that she has experienced prejudice, the reader is prepared not only to believe her but also to appreciate the wrongness of it. We meet Miranda again in *The Attic Term* (1976),[14] and while this book does not add much further information about Judaism, the writer does use it as a medium through which to express her very traditional, pre-Vatican II, Catholic position. Forest seems to be one of a small minority of authors of the second half of the twentieth century who are prepared to discuss religion in a children's book; this rarity is the direct opposite of the prevalence of such books in the nineteenth century.

Another attempt to dispel prejudice, and also to convey information about the situation of Jewish people during the war is provided by an

---

13. A. Forest, *End of Term* (London: Faber & Faber, 1972 [1959]).
14. A. Forest, *The Attic Term* (London: Faber & Faber, 1976).

author of Jewish background, Adèle Geras, in *A Candle in the Dark* (1995).[15] This is part of a series which claims: 'Each book in this series tells you what it was like to live at a different time in history'. It focuses on a small Jewish girl, Clara, and her brother Maxi, who come in 1938 to stay with an English family. The daughter Phyllis is confronted with a prejudiced classmate who cites her mother as authority for the statements, 'You can depend on Jewish people to exaggerate' (p. 20) and 'All Jews [are] rich' (p. 67). Phyllis therefore has to choose between Clara and Eileen, and she chooses Clara: 'Suddenly she no longer cared whether or not Eileen was her best friend' (p. 81). Phyllis, and the reader, also learn about the Jewish Hannukah celebrations, while the reader is provided with an afterword: 'Between December 1938 and August 1939 ten thousand children came to Britain... Nine thousand of them never saw their parents again' (p. 86). In the light of this, the happy ending—Clara and Maxi reunited in England with their parents—could seem a little forced. Although this is a relatively slight book (more of the nature of a history textbook than a novel in its own right) it does display Geras's interest in the portrayal of personal relationships.

Jewish Life and Identity

In addition to the above, there are books whose authors, while equally didactic in their aims, are writing from a perspective within Judaism and intend to educate their readers, Jewish and non-Jewish alike, about aspects of Jewish life in relation to the world at large. These books, while equally didactic in their aims, are very different from those of Cormier and Forest, though inevitably less so from that of Geras. The exploration of the nature of Jewish identity becomes a major focus, and the whole question of the importance of specific aspects of practice looms large.

Lynne Reid Banks's *One More River* (1973)[16] describes how a Canadian Jewish family, the Shelbys (originally Stupinskys), decide to relocate on a kibbutz in Israel, and the effect of this move on the daughter, Lesley. The issue of religious practice, which served to indicate distinctiveness in Gentile countries such as Canada, but which some characters see as no longer necessary within the secular state of Israel,

15. A. Geras, *A Candle in the Dark* (London: A. & C. Black, 1995).
16. L. Reid Banks, *One More River* (Harmondsworth: Penguin Books, 1980 [1973]).

is fully explored, and another major theme is relationships between Jews and Arabs. Lesley illicitly meets, and is attracted to, an Arab boy, Mustapha, but by the end of the novel she realizes that they will grow up never to meet again. The ending has a mixed effect; the happy side is that Lesley and her parents have become acclimatized to Israel, and are notably less materialistic than they were in their Canadian days, but the young reader is expected to have sufficient maturity to accept the impossibility of lasting relationships between members of warring groups. The final words concern Mustapha: 'He didn't in the least know why, but his tears, his awful sense of loss, told him that he and that girl he would never see again were the two most important people in the world' (p. 249).

Iris Rosofsky's *Miriam* (1988)[17] also makes heavy demands on the young reader's ability to cope without a happy ending, as shortly before the end of the book the central character has lost her dearly loved, and very Orthodox, brother Moshe. When she is reunited with her cousin, Rosie, she is forced to confront the question of cultural identity within the secular but residually Christian world of New York. The acceptance of festivals such as Christmas and Thanksgiving is particularly problematical for Miriam; she feels that Rosie has reappeared in her life, not so much 'out of love and a desire to renew our friendship', but rather 'to show me how far beyond [religion] she had advanced'. Miriam decides that on the one hand 'I could no longer accept on blind faith all those commandments and traditions I used to accept when I was a child' but on the other that 'I couldn't follow Rosie's way, either. Life without the Holy One, a single day without blessing His Name when I lay down to sleep and when I woke again to life, would be unthinkable.' To negotiate between these extremes, Miriam feels, 'I wanted Moshele to give me the answer. But the silence was palpable' (pp. 185-88).

Books about War and Holocaust
The bleakness of the endings of these last two books, by Jewish authors, is perhaps a reflection of the difficulties posed by the question of assimilation and the problem of maintaining a distinctly Jewish identity. Fear is often expressed today that, even independently of the religious aspects, distinctive cultural features which have helped to

17. I. Rosofsky, *Miriam* (London: William Collins, 1989 [1988]).

establish uniqueness are threatened by assimilation into society. The factor which often seems to be central to maintaining Jewish identity is the remembrance of the Holocaust. Since the Second World War, the shadow of this mass slaughter and the way it has affected Jews through-out the diaspora is inescapable in the majority of books with Jewish characters. Questions therefore arise about not only the suitability of this kind of material for a young audience, but also the need for extreme care in treating such a theme without cheapening it.

While all such books have a strong dependence on the facts of the historical situation, there is a basic division between those that make direct use of the experience, either of the writers themselves or of close family members, and those that, while remaining true to the events, have attempted to transmute these into a more shaped fictional narrative.

The haziness of the boundary between fact and fiction is particularly apparent in the many autobiographical or biographical narratives that have been offered to young readers in recent years. The progenitor of many of these texts is, of course, Anne Frank's *The Diary of a Young Girl*, first published in 1947.[18] The provenance of many of these later books in real-life experience is usually indicated in the blurb. On the back of Judith Kerr's *When Hitler Stole Pink Rabbit* (1971)[19] we are told: 'Judith Kerr was born in Berlin and left Germany in 1933 to escape the Nazis. Her novels are based on her own experience', while Johanna Reiss's *The Upstairs Room* (1972),[20] the account of two Jewish sisters hiding in occupied Holland, is described as 'Based on the author's own childhood experiences'. In both of these novels, the central character is slightly distanced from the author by the adoption of a different name for the central persona, Anna and Annie respectively. Size of print and style of writing suggest that Kerr's intended audience is somewhat younger than that for some of the other books mentioned. Early in the book she dispels racial stereotypes; Anna's friend Elspeth says: 'If you look the same as everyone else and you don't go to a special church, how do you know you *are* Jewish?' Anna replies: 'I suppose it's because my mother and father are Jews, and I suppose their mothers and fathers were too' (p. 9). Later it becomes even more evident that

18. A. Frank, *The Diary of a Young Girl: The Definitive Edition* (Harmonds-worth: Viking, 1995 [1947]).

19. J. Kerr, *When Hitler Stole Pink Rabbit* (London: William Collins, 1971).

20. J. Reiss, *The Upstairs Room* (Oxford: Oxford University Press, 1972).

her family is not Orthodox, when in the relative safety of France they celebrate Christmas, without any mention being made of Hannukah (p. 153). Nevertheless, while on holiday in Switzerland they encounter anti-Semitism from a German family.

The situation of the young Annie and her sister Sini in occupied Holland is far less secure, as like the Frank family they are hidden by courageous Dutch people. Unlike the Franks, they emerge unscathed, though physically weakened by their long and at times threatened incarceration, during which Annie learns from a newspaper about the very real danger she has been in: 'Of course I had known that there were camps. That's where those trains took you. But I hadn't known that they were like this, that Hitler had told his soldiers to murder Jews any time they felt like it.' She goes on to give an account of the gas ovens and concludes, 'Now I knew why I was here, why I shouldn't stand close to the window in the front room' (p. 96).

Unlike the transmutation of their experiences into fiction carried out by Kerr and Reiss, Ilse Koehn's *Mischling: Second Degree—My Childhood in Nazi Germany* (1977)[21] is described on the back of the book as 'Real Life', and the protagonist bears the author's name. By contrast, in Hans Peter Richter's *Friedrich* (1961),[22] which, unlike the others, was written in German, no such claims appear to be made for their identity of the author and the nameless first-person narrator despite their being the same age as each other. Also unlike the others, the standpoint of this last book is that of a non-Jewish child, often puzzled and distressed about what happens to his Jewish friend whose plight is central to the plot. This perspective allows Richter more opportunity to display the variety of attitudes towards the Jews held by ordinary people in Nazi Germany than is the case where narrators or focal characters are themselves Jewish and have to learn such attitudes more incidentally.

Another book heavily dependent on the experiences of a survivor, though less specifically for a young audience, is Art Spiegelman's *Maus* (1986),[23] where the memories of the cartoonist's father provide the central plot, framed by a somewhat argumentative discourse

21. I. Koehn, *Mischling: Second Degree—My Childhood in Nazi Germany* (Harmondsworth: Penguin Books, 1981 [1977]).

22. H.P. Richter, *Friedrich* (trans. E. Kroll; Harmondsworth: Penguin Books, 1987 [1961]).

23. A. Spiegelman, *Maus: A Survivor's Tale* (Harmondsworth: Penguin Books, 1987 [1986]).

between the father and the son in 'present-day' America.

All that is possible here is to indicate the abundance of this kind of material, and to suggest that it raises complex issues concerned with the nature of fictional writing and of history. In these narratives, authors are clearly inventing conversations of which they could not possibly have perfect recall, and selecting from a mass of material incidents which are of interest and excitement. They are manifestly shaping, probably most successfully when it appears most artless, the randomness of life. Aristotle claimed that fiction, by its universality, was truer than history,[24] and while the kind of literature about which he was talking was very different, I think there are some grounds for the contention that apart from actual diaries (and even those are shaped to some extent), the most effective narratives are those which have most been shaped by their authors, as appears to have been the case in Richter's *Friedrich*.

All the books to which I have referred so far have given both their readers and their characters information about concentration camps, rather than setting any of the action within them. To some extent, this arises from the autobiographical nature of many of the narratives; while we do have examples of children's art drawn from these camps, we do not have many instances of survivors writing about their experiences as children within them.[25] Nevertheless, there are some examples of children's books which do take on board this kind of material, though in each instance the authors have found it necessary to distance themselves by some kind of imposed convention in order to approach the real horror of the central situation. Interestingly, two of the most poignant examples are picture books, thus discrediting any assumptions that such texts are designated for young children. Neither Robert Innocenti's *Rose Blanche* (1985) nor M. Wild's *Let the Celebrations Begin* (1991)[26] has an explicit reference to the people they depict within the

24. In *Poetics* C.2.3 Aristotle says: 'Poetry…is more philosophic and of greater significance than history, for its statements are of the nature rather of universals, whereas those of history are particulars' (*Aristotle's Poetics* [trans. J. Warrington; London: Dent, 1963], p. 17).

25. Survivors like Bruno Bettelheim and Primo Levi, while affected by their experiences to the extent of both ultimately committing suicide, and having a strong interest in fiction, nevertheless do not appear to have felt able to express this experience in a mode appropriate to young readers. There is much concentration camp art from children (for instance in one of the Jewish museums in Prague) but little written material from young children.

26. R. Innocenti, *Rose Blanche* (London: Jonathan Cape, 1985) and M. Wild,

concentration camps as being Jewish; the focus of the former is on a young girl who discovers the camp in the woods and who is tragically killed just before liberation, while the latter focuses on the desperate plight of those in the camps and the pathos of their attempts to live in some kind of normality.

Two books by Jane Yolen, an American Jewish writer with a notable interest in fairy-tales,[27] take the step into the concentration camps which many other writers avoid. *The Devil's Arithmetic* (1988) seems to envisage a reader at least ten years old, while *Briar Rose* (1992)[28] is aimed at young adults. Both books use well-established literary conventions to approach the subject: the earlier book employs a prism of time travel and *Briar Rose* makes use of the structure and motifs of the fairy-tale to tell a story which would otherwise be too painful.

The Devil's Arithmetic is the story of Hannah, a young Jewish girl who is bored by the 'remembering' involved in the celebration of the Passover. When she opens the door so that the prophet Elijah may be imagined to make his entrance, she finds herself conveyed back to a Polish village in 1942 and subsequently to Auschwitz. When she is restored to her own time, she realizes that she has met family members, including her grandfather, in this setting. Although the story is competently told, and Yolen's didactic intentions are manifest, it is difficult to avoid the feeling that there is a kind of cheapening of the painful material in the use of the time travel device. Perhaps Yolen's attempt to render this subject accessible to younger children is a hopeless endeavour; certainly I find the book less moving than for instance Innocenti's *Rose Blanche*. I do not have the same reserves about *Briar Rose*, however. This may be because the nature of fairy-tale, which is rich in symbolism and very frequently the subject of interpretation by the great psychologists, lends itself to dealing with issues of life and death,

---

Let the Celebrations Begin (London: Bodley Head, 1991). A. Holm, *I am David* (trans L.W. Kingsland; London: Methuen, 1965; originally published as *David* (Denmark: Gyldendal, 1963), is the story of an escapee from a concentration camp, but despite a sympathetic portrayal of Judaism, it is made clear that he himself is not Jewish.

27. She has written both critically and creatively about fairy-tales; perhaps her most influential article is 'America's *Cinderella*', *Children's Literature in Education* 8 (1977), pp. 21-27, which is often quoted by theorists on the subject; cf. J. Zipes, *Fairy Tales and the Art of Subversion* (London: Routledge, 1991), p. 43.

28. J. Yolen, *The Devil's Arithmetic* (Harmondsworth: Penguin Books, 1990 [1988]); *idem, Briar Rose* (Basingstoke: Macmillan, 1994 [1992]).

cruelty and suffering, in a way that time travel fantasy never can. The epigraph to this text is a quotation from Jack Zipes's *Spells of Enchantment*:

> [B]oth the oral and the literary forms of the fairy tale are grounded in history: they emanate from specific struggles to humanize bestial and barbaric forces, which have terrorized our minds and communities in concrete ways, threatening to destroy free will and human compassion. The fairy tale sets out to conquer this concrete terror through metaphors.[29]

Yolen's scholarship in this area eminently qualifies her for this kind of venture.

The fairy-tale framework for *Briar Rose* is the Grimms' story by that name, sometimes also known as *Sleeping Beauty*, a story which obviously holds a good deal of fascination for Yolen.[30] Additionally to this central tale, hints of other motifs may be detected: the protagonist, Rebecca, is the youngest and, to the reader, the most attractive, of three sisters, and her quest for the 'castle' which her apparently senile grandmother, Gemma, claims to have left her, provides the central theme of the book. Forests and woodcutters also loom large in the story. The clues on which Rebecca bases her search are some souvenirs her grandmother has kept in a box, and her grandmother's rather idiosyncratic version of the fairy-tale; in it, only the princess (with whom Gemma identifies) is awakened from sleep by the handsome prince, while all the rest sleep on in a sleep of death (cf. p. 38). The quest leads Rebecca to the site of Chelmno, an extermination camp in Poland where she meets Josef Potocki, who gives her access to her grandmother's story. Josef tells of how he, and the leader of his resistance group, nicknamed Avenger, were witnesses to the gassing of a band of prisoners in a van, and their interment in an open pit in the forest:

> Then the Avenger cried out, 'Look! Someone is moving!'
>
> At first Josef thought it must be because of the dark, because of the shadows, because of their fear. Then he had an even darker thought that the gasses bodies exude when decomposing must be rising up from the earlier dead. But Avenger was, after all, a medical student and surely he would know all that. Besides, he had already leaped down into that

---

29. J. Zipes (ed.), *Spells of Enchantment: The Wondrous Fairy Tales of Western Culture* (New York: Viking, 1991).

30. J. Yolen, *The Sleeping Beauty* (New York: Knopf, 1986).

hellish pit, pushing the stiffening bodies aside. And when he stood up again, shakily, on the backs and breasts and sides of slaughtered people, he held a single body in his arms.

It was a young woman and, even in the quickening dark, Josef could see that her arm was moving sluggishly, that her face had an odd pattern of roses on the cheeks.

Avenger handed up the body to Josef...but...the girl had stopped breathing. Josef could feel her die in his arms. So he laid her down on the ground and, putting his mouth on hers, the taste of vomit bitter on his lips, he tried to give her breath.[31]

Rebecca comes to realize that the young woman was her grandmother, and that this 'kiss of life' was to her the kiss of Prince Charming in the fairy-tale. For a moment she wonders if Josef was the grandfather she never knew, but he tells her that the reason that he himself had earlier been in a camp was that he was gay, and that the avenger had become the husband of the rescued woman, whom he termed 'The Princess'.

Thus Yolen makes a convincing link between the old story, with its mystery and even potential horror, and the appalling events of the Holocaust. There is no danger of her trivializing it, and, while some might well query as to the suitability of the material even for the 'young adult', I think many teenage readers could well find it an illuminating and disturbing encounter with events about which they should know. Among the many enthusiastic testimonials to her success which are printed inside the book and on the cover, perhaps the most telling is that from Jack Zipes:

There are few writers capable of using the fairy-tale form to write about *all* the ramifications of the holocaust, and Jane Yolen is one of them. Her novel is not only a superb accomplishment but also an important social statement.

By contrast, in a recent German children's book, Gudrun Pausewang's *The Final Journey* (1992),[32] there is no softening and no distancing. Alice, a young Jewish girl who has been told nothing about Nazi persecution, finds herself, with her grandfather, in a crowded truck heading towards Auschwitz. The book enacts her gradually developing awareness of their plight, but even at the end she does not realize that

31. Yolen, *Briar Rose*, p. 173.

32. G. Pausewang, *Reise im August* (Ravensburg: O. Maier, 1992; ET *The Final Journey* [trans. P. Crampton; Harmondsworth: Penguin Books, 1996]).

gas, not water, is what will be emitted from what she thinks are the cleansing showers at the end of the journey. This is possibly the harshest portrayal yet of the unmitigated horrors of the Holocaust, and its aim is clearly to inform the younger generation of these.

The last few years have seen an increase in the number of books about the Second World War, and, in particular, the topic of the plight of Jewish Holocaust victims. The French theorist Michel Foucault claims that history 'is always written from the perspective of the present; history fulfils a need of the present'.[33] The question then arises as to what need of the present has given rise to this compulsion to ensure that young people are made aware of their heritage.

Conclusion

My survey of children's fiction written from or about a Jewish perspective is far from exhaustive, but even so I think I can say with conviction that far fewer books have been written in the last 20 years that highlight Jewish issues than those that focus on black characters. It may be that this arises from the general reluctance of children's writers to engage with the question of religious identity, though I suspect there are more recent books which take on the allied issue of Muslim identity and practice. There are today many distinguished English writers who have a Jewish background—Adèle Geras and Michael Rosen notable among them. Geras has indeed written and spoken about her Jewish background, but it does not appear to enter into some of her most important children's novels, such as her Egerton Hall trilogy. Perhaps the main issue today is not how to portray Jewish characters and traditions, but rather what should be done by teachers to help readers, Jewish and non-Jewish alike, to read critically those books from the past that display prejudice.

From my small-scale study, however, I would dare to claim that there are substantial differences between Jewish and non-Jewish writers. The latter often seem most concerned with the question of prejudice and educating their audience to avoid it, while those who have been brought up in the Jewish community evidence the vigour of its continuing traditions, even when some of these have been much affected by long contact with those from Christian origins.[34] In earlier literature, Jewish characters often tended to be seen as threatening, mysterious or exotic, or even sometimes pathetic, while today, if their origins are mentioned, non-Jewish writers sometimes seem to feel the need to 'explain' them. It is only writers who can take Jewishness as a norm, like Yolen and Rosofsky, who can succeed in making such characters distinctive by means of their personalities, rather than by their racial or religious origins.

34. M. Hilton, *The Christian Effect on Jewish Life* (London: SCM Press, 1994), makes clear how much Jewish celebrations, notably that of Hannukah (Ch. 1), have been influenced by Christian festivals.

IMAGES OF ANTI-SEMITISM IN NINETEENTH- AND TWENTIETH-CENTURY POPULAR CULTURE

Irene Wise

Cabaret was written more than 30 years ago, but the score (music by John Kander and lyrics by Fred Ebb) remains as powerful as ever. A particular clip from Bob Fosse's film version shows Joel Grey as the Master of Ceremonies, singing on stage to a gorilla, pleading for the audience to love the animal as much as he does: 'If you could see her through my eyes'. The provocative last line—'she doesn't look Jewish at all'—still shocks and is often cut from recordings and changed to something bland. But what an enduring image! The pirouetting gorilla is both comic and tragic: it is a larger-than-life version of the dark, hirsute stereotype of the Jew.

Even now, we find it unusual when a Jew breaks the familiar mould. We think we know who is Jewish. We easily recognize the Jewishness of, say, Dustin Hoffman, Peter Sellars or Woody Allen (even though he changed his name from Allen Koningsberg)—but Lawrence Harvey and Harrison Ford might come as a bit of a surprise. Even more of a surprise is Paul Newman or—for heaven's sake!—Fred Astaire, but then, they only had Jewish *fathers*, so that makes them only a bit Jewish—or Jew-*ish*. The biggest surprise of all has to be *Shakespeare in Love*'s Gwyneth Paltrow, described by critics as an 'ice maiden' for her portrayal of Estella in *Great Expectations*. Paltrow's persona owes more to the New England country club than to the old-country shtetl; as one journalist said, she seems to have been 'cloned into a Wasp' and is 'so assimilated that it's easier to believe she's a Kennedy than a Jew'.[1] At least Liz Taylor had the chutzpah to seem as Jewish as she looked, even before she converted. Gwyneth Paltrow's waspish demeanour

---

1. E. Forrest, 'What Ever Happened to the Jewish Princess'?, *The Guardian* (12 May 1997), G2, p. 8.

actually beats that of Lauren Bacall, whose cool beauty fooled Howard Hawks, despite the director refusing to employ Jews.

I have chosen to begin lightheartedly, but also I think it is useful to bear in mind all these people that do break through the stereotype. We can all conjure up those famous Hollywood faces.

In this brief essay, I will examine a few negative representations of the Jew in popular literature for children, young people and adults. The sources are mainly British and German, covering the years 1860 to the present day, but the focus is mainly twentieth-century Germany and Victorian and Edwardian England. Most of this printed material was aimed at young people or children, and, as you might expect, a lot of it was published in Nazi Germany, around the time that *Cabaret* is set.

Fibel für die Deutsche Jugend (Tales for German Youth) is a picture-book for infants, dating from 1941 (See Fig. 1). One can see how little girls were encouraged to admire their brothers marching in uniform. This book was designed as an early reading book for infants, a primer to be used in school. Figure 1 is obviously an instruction page for learning about the letter T. The rhyme accompanying this picture is innocuous:

> *Trum, trum, trum!*
> *There they march,*
> *Always in time,*
> *One, two, one, two.*
> *Teo is amongst them.*
> *Dieter is too. Trommel.*
> *Trum, trum, trum!*

The words below the verse are straightforward vocabulary—hard, soft, and so on. It could almost be any children's primer from any period—but not quite. The flag in the picture belongs to the SS, the militarized Stormtroopers, the Blackshirts (the uniform that Mosley's fascist party copied in Britain). The little girl in the foreground heralds the marchers with the Nazi salute. The verse is harmless enough, but this book also includes an anti-Semitic counting rhyme, ending with the words: 'one for you, one for me and the Jew gets none'.

Why did the Nazis take such trouble with infants' first reading books? Obviously, it was a chance to indoctrinate 300,000 children from the moment that they started to read primers[2]—but there was

---

2.   Christa Kamenetsky, *Children's Literature in Hitler's Germany: The Cul-*

Figure 1. *Fibel für die Deutsche Jugend* (Tales for German Youth) (Berlin: Deutscher Schulbuchverlag, 1941) p. 45. From the catalogue *Lesen Lernen: ABC—Bücher Fibeln und Lernmittel aus drei Jahrhunderten* (Oldenburg: Stadmuseum Oldenburg, 1982), p. 61. Reproducd by permission of BIS Universität Oldenburg, Germany.

more to it. When a young child takes their reading book home, the parents look at it with them. So the party knew that with primers, they could get the message across to the whole family.[3]

tural Policy of National Socialism (Athens, OH: Ohio State University Press, 1984), p. 174.

3. Kamenetsky, *Children's Literature*, p. 184.

Official Nazi literature focused on the countryside and totally neglected the urban environment. So much so, that there there were not enough German books to bridge the gap. By the early 1930s, nearly two-thirds of the population lived in towns and cities and wanted to read literature that reflected their way of life. Recognizing this deficiency, the party allowed certain books by English and American writers. Ironically, then, foreign socially critical writers were allowed to be read in translation. Books by Steinbeck were allowed, for example, and Galsworthy, because they showed up the corruption in American and English societies.[4]

One English book officially recommended in Nazi Germany was *The Citadel*, by A.J. Cronin.[5] First published in July 1937, *The Sunday Express* greeted it with a rapturous review: 'A remarkable book—one of the most vigorous attacks on the medical profession ever published... It is a sincere, absorbing and moving book.'[6]

Cronin does indeed expose Harley Street malpractice and provides an exciting story. The book could even be read as a compelling argument for a sound national health service, which was not then in existence for Britain. However, the Nazis promoted this book for another reason, too: it has several anti-Semitic references. The hero is Andrew, a young medic, who is tempted for a while by the extravagant lifestyle of a group of corrupt doctors. There are several allusions to one of the dishonest doctors being Jewish. We are given this information in the most ambivalent manner. We are told, for example, that Deedman is 'slight, dark-eyed, with a clever Jewish face' (p. 212) and that his wife has 'a pretty, almost oriental bloom' (p. 211). Andrew wants to be part of this circle of rich, well-dressed surgeons. His wife, though, wants none of it, and for a while her steadfast morality causes a rift in their marriage. It is significant, I think, that her name is Christine and that during this time she rediscovers her Christian religion. The contrast between Christian morality and supposed Jewish amorality is made clear.

Earlier in the book, Andrew and Christine buy second-hand furniture from a Jewish dealer who tries to cheat them. While we are not told directly that he is Jewish, there can be no doubt. His name—Isaacs—is repeated many times, and Cronin draws a caricatured figure for ridicule

4.   R. Grunberger, *A Social History of the Third Reich* (London: Penguin Books, 1971), pp. 452-53.

5.   A.J. Cronin, *The Citadel* (London: Gollancz, 1937).

6.   Review cited on fly-leaf of the 1937 edition.

WISE *Images of Anti-Semitism*

and contempt. We are told: 'Mr. Isaacs caressed his nose. His eyes, liquid against his sallow skin, were sorrowful as he studied the order book' (p. 103). Later, the couple laugh hysterically as they recall the encounter, so much so that Christine has 'tears running down her cheeks' (p. 105).

Another reason why this book was so favoured by the Nazi regime is that the kindest, warmest person the couple meet in London is 'a fat little...German woman'. Frau Schmidt runs a delicatessen shop where they feel at home and where Christine always goes for comfort. There is a long description of all the marvellous German foods for sale in the shop: 'soused herrings, olives in jars, sauerkraut...pastries, salami'— all, we are told, 'very cheap' (p. 207). The description of Frau Schmidt herself is a sentimental stereotype that might have come from one of the Nazis' own books: 'Her larded, pastry-cook's face would wrinkle up, almost closing her eyes, beneath her high dome of blonde hair, as she smiled' (p. 207).

This novel is anti-Semitic because the Jewish characters are portrayed as rather unsavoury and unlikable, in complete contrast to, for example, the German woman and the devout, Christian wife. On the other hand, most members of the cast are stereotypes. However, the poor characterization has not diminished the British popularity of the author: Cronin is often included in recommended book-lists for young people, and a couple of years ago BBC Radio 4 dramatized an edited version of *The Citadel* in their 'Classic Serial' slot.[7] Despite the anti-Semitic undertones, Cronin maintains an exciting narrative, and in this book, he does make valid points about the need for health reforms.

E. Nesbit, the Edwardian classic children's author, is probably best known for her book *The Treasure Seekers*, first published at the turn of the century.[8] In this story, children from a poor family take a loan from a man whom they call, with true dramatic irony, the G.B.—Generous Benefactor. The G.B. is revealed to the reader as an avaricious money-lender—he charges 60 per cent interest (p. 98)—whose real name is Rosenbaum (p. 92). The G.B. is obsessed with money, which he is careful not to give away:

> Then he took out a sovereign, and held it in his hand while he talked to us... And all the time he was stroking the sovereign and looking at it as

---

7. BBC Radio 4, dramatized in four parts, 7 February 1997–28 February 1997.
8. E. Nesbit, *The Treasure Seekers* (London: Ernest Benn, 1958 [1899]), p. 98.

> if he thought it very beautiful… Then at last he held it out to Dicky, and
> when Dicky put out his hand for it the G.B. suddenly put the sovereign
> back in his pocket (p. 98).

This is a perennial stereotype: the image of Jews caressing money (or
their noses, as in Cronin's furniture dealer), and refusing to part with it.

In another book by Nesbit, *The Story of the Amulet*, the Queen of
Babylon makes a trip to the city where she comments on the men's
'beautiful long, curved noses'.[9] Notice the flattering adjective—
'beautiful'—when describing a supposed racial characteristic. The
Queen of Babylon works her magic to dress the men in Babylonian
clothes, which she declares suit them better than their black city coats.
Nesbit describes the members of the Stock Exchange as 'a noisy lot'. In
case we haven't gathered that they are Jewish, we are told that they are
called Lionel Cohen, Henry Hirsh, Rosenbaum and Levinstein. Having
humiliated the men enough, the Queen then gives the command to her
guards thus: 'Kill them!' she cries. 'Kill the dogs!', and the guards
obey—they go round chopping off the Jews' heads. It is, in fact, a
pogrom. Subsequently, this bloodthirsty scene is turned into a dream—
but nonetheless, it happens.

In later books, Nesbit tries to make amends. *Harding's Luck*
appeared in 1909: at the end of Chapter 3, Dickie, the boy hero, makes
'with triple lines of silvery seeds, a six-pointed star'.[10] Nesbit is apparently unaware of it being a Jewish star, a star of David. However, it
does precipitate magic. In *Harding's Luck*, we briefly meet a Mr
Rosenberg, who, we are told, is 'dark, handsome and big-nosed'
(p. 63). Mr Rosenberg has a lisp, a mannerism often attributed to Jewish characters in popular literature. Later, Nesbit introduces a philan-
thropic pawnbroker while making an extraordinary plea for the Jews.
The pawnbroker instinctively knows that the child Dickie is special,
because we are told:

> With the unerring instinct of his race…he [the pawnbroker] knew that
> this was…something real. The sense of romance, of great things all
> about them transcending the ordinary things of life—this in the Jews has
> survived centuries of torment, shame, cruelty and oppression… What I
> mean is that the Jews always see the big beautiful things; they don't just
> see that grey is made of black and white; they see how incredibly black

9. E. Nesbit, *The Story of the Amulet* (London: Ernest Benn, 1969 [1906]),
pp. 133-37.
10. E. Nesbit, *Harding's Luck* (London: Ernest Benn, 1961 [1909]), p. 73.

black can be, and that there may be a whiteness transcending all the whitest dreams in the world (p. 100).

Nesbit certainly seems to have had what her biographer, Julia Briggs, describes as a 'change of heart', but I think the lady doth protest too much. There are some inconsistencies in the character of the pawn-broker: Briggs maintains that, originally, the author did not mean him to be Jewish, as the character alters halfway through the book. In the first chapter, we are introduced to him merely as a 'stout gentleman' with no Jewish reference attributed to him. Briggs points out that Nesbit never would have described a Jew as 'a gentleman', no matter how sympathetic she was. Briggs also reminds us that, while Nesbit tends to reduce Jews to stereotypes, this is similar to her treatment of the servant classes, who are not allowed to be fully developed characters.[11] This seems paradoxical in light of Nesbit's socialist political views—for instance, she was in favour of easily available healthcare; but, as we have already seen in the case of Cronin, such political generosity is not necessarily extended to written characters.

Foreigners and the working classes are also thinly drawn by John Buchan, in *The Thirty-Nine Steps*.[12] This adventure story has a thrilling plot and pace that beg the reader to go on turning the pages, yet the xenophobia in Buchan's class-ridden novel reaches much further than Nesbit ever ventured. The opening chapter of *The Thirty-Nine Steps* has the character Scudder elaborating on a Jewish plot:

> The Jew is everywhere, but you have to go far down the backstairs to find him...ten to one you are brought up against a little white-faced Jew in a bath-chair with an eye like a rattlesnake. Yes, sir, he is the man who is ruling the world just now (p. 8).

By Chapter 4, Richard Hannay has decided that Scudder's 'yarns about the Balkans and the Jew anarchists and the Foreign Office conference were eyewash...' (p. 44). However, it is never made wholly clear that the conspiracy is not a Jewish one. Nor is this the last mention made of Jews—there is a strange aside in Chapter 6:

> My chief trouble was that I was desperately hungry. When a Jew shoots himself in the City and there is an inquest, the newspapers usually report

11. J. Briggs, *A Woman of Passion: The Life of E. Nesbit 1858–1924* (London: Hutchinson, 1987), p. 292.

12. J. Buchan, *The Thirty-Nine Steps* (London: J.M. Dent, 1964 [1915]).

> that the deceased was 'well nourished'. I remember thinking that they
> would not call me well nourished... (p. 73)

This is a brief reminder of the associations of Jews with corpulence and greed, in strong contrast to Hannay, our Anglo-Saxon hero.

The dénouement of *The Thirty-Nine Steps* does not reveal the scheming evil-doers to be Jewish: they are Germans, who have almost fooled the narrator into believing they are Englishmen. And why had this been possible? Because the narrator, while apparently at ease 'perfectly well with two classes, what you may call the upper and lower' (p. 136), is unfamiliar with the new middle classes. So deep is his uncertainty, that he is as wary of suburbanites as he is of a poisonous snake:

> But what a fellow like me doesn't understand is the great comfortable,
> satisfied middle-class world, the folk that live in villas and suburbs. He
> doesn't know how they look at things, he doesn't understand their con-
> ventions, and he is as shy of them as of a black mamba (p. 136).

Buchan, then, is uncomfortable with anybody out of his milieu. Despite his claim to understand the working classes, they are portrayed as no more than simple Cockneys. Buchan's mistrust of the rising middle class reflects attitudes prevalent among the Edwardian upper class; this unease had already been expressed by other British writers, such as Anthony Trollope, since the nineteenth century.

A few years earlier, while John Buchan was still working for Lord Milner in South Africa, a far more pernicious book became the best-selling English novel of 1903. *When it Was Dark*[13] was written by Guy Thorne, pen name of Ranger-Gull. The book is subtitled *The Story of a Great Conspiracy*—and that is exactly what it is.[14] In short, the book describes the attempt by a Jew to overthrow the whole of the Christian world, by fraudulently disproving the Resurrection. The malevolent Constantine Schaube prefigures any devilish Nazi invention. We first meet Schaube when he pays a visit to the vicar, who, appropriately enough, is discussing the anti-Christ with his curate. The melodrama unfolds, with huge, unsubtle clues: as soon as the Jew enters the vicarage, a china image of Christ falls to the floor and shatters (p. 23). In case we have not gathered the significance of this accident, it is

13. *When It Was Dark* (London: Greening, 1903). This book seems to have lost its popularity: the library copy I read had not been borrowed for 21 years.

14. The plot is analysed in depth by C. Cockburn, *Bestseller: The Books Every-one Read 1900–1939* (London: Penguin Books, 1975 [1972]), pp. 27-50.

mentioned again, by the curate, Basil Gortre, in Chapter 8 (p. 247).

We are constantly reminded that Schaube is Jewish: for example, he is called 'this Jew' (p. 21) and 'the Jew' (p. 273). We are told that a memory flashed through 'the Jew's mind' (p. 203) and 'relief crossed the Jew's face' (p. 345); Llwellyn, his co-conspirator, blackmailed into working with Schaube, labels him 'my Jewish partner' (p. 346); and, in case we forget: ' "Hush!" said the Jew, menacingly' (p. 348).

Schaube, a member of Parliament, is supposedly 'head of the anti-Christian Party' (p. 234). 'The man was an infidel, no doubt. His intellectual attacks upon the Christian faith were terribly damaging and subversive' (p. 29). In common with other Jewish men in the book, Schaube is very wealthy: in fact, 'a millionaire' (pp. 5, 26). We are told that, at barely 40, Schaube is the most powerful North-country millionaire (p .19), while

> his brilliancy, his tremendous intellectual powers, are equalled by few men in England. His career at Oxford was marvellous…the man [has] an ascetic temperament…he is one of the ten most striking looking men in England. His manners are fascinating (pp. 19-20).

The frequent allusion to Schaube's 'tremendous intellectual powers' is an ambivalent stereotype of Jewish cleverness. Schaube is, by all accounts, an extraordinary scholar:

> Schaube possessed a profound and masterly knowledge of the whole Jewish background to the Gospel picture, not merely of the archaeology, which in itself is a life study, but of the essential characteristics of Jewish thought and feeling, which is far more (p. 33).

Schaube's intellect and knowledge make him all the more dangerous. It is not clear how Schaube could possibly have managed to fit in more than a life-time's study, and still found the time to become a millionaire. Everything about Schaube, including his bank balance, is very large indeed:

> The man was tall, above the middle height, and the heavy coat of fur which he was wearing increased the impression of proportioned size, of massiveness, which was part of his personality. His hair was a very dark red, smooth and abundant, of that peculiar colour which is the last to show the greyness of advancing age. His features were Semitic, but without a trace of that fullness, and sometimes coarseness, which often marks the Jew who has come to the middle period of life. The eyes were large and black, but without animation, in ordinary use-and-wont. They did not light up as he spoke, but yet the expression was not veiled or

obscured. They were coldly, terribly *aware*, with something of the sinister and troubled regard one sees in a reptile's eyes... He was a strikingly
handsome man... Most people...called him merely indomitable, but
there were others who thought they read deeper and saw something evil
and monstrous about the man... (pp. 25-26).

Several lines of this very same description are repeated much further
on in the book, now concluding: 'A massive jaw completed an impression which was remarkable in its fineness and almost sinister beauty'
(p. 185). On one hand, Schaube is portrayed as super-human: his
wealth, his size, his intellect, his good looks and charm. Yet, at the
same time, he is shown as less than human: he has 'reptile's eyes',
while later he is accused of being 'as cold-blooded as a fish', a man
who enjoys his asceticism (p. 274). By the time of his demise, he has
been reduced to making a 'quick snake-like movement' (p. 344) and
'an animal moan' (p. 348). During this period, while he is apparently
becoming more bestial, simultaneously, it seems, 'His features grew
markedly Semitic' (p. 346). Schaube is also a supernatural figure, with
'the smile of a devil' (p. 47), 'evil and devilish egoism' (p. 210), who
stands 'like Lucifer' (p. 246); and he is actually called a devil (p. 286).
He is even called the Anti-Christ, one who knows 'that Christ is God'
yet is set to destroy him (p. 47).

Schaube's colouring (pp. 25, 185, 413, 425) was no coincidence: red
hair was traditionally associated with Judas and was a means of identifying Jewish characters on the stage (as was a big false nose).[15] Thus
when the curate's fiancée, Helena, innocently points to 'that red-headed
woman with the furs' (p. 91) the inference is that the lady is Jewish—
and actually probably rather vulgar. This would be in contrast to the
simply dressed Helena, whose 'style...with its slight hint of austerity,
accentuated a quiet and delicate charm' (p. 12). Helena outshines any
foreigner: 'Her beauty was Saxon, very English, and not of a type that
is always appreciated at its full value on the Continent, but it shone the
more from Latin contrasts...' (p. 92).

In *When it Was Dark*, appearance tells the reader exactly what to
expect of each person's character, so we know that Basil Gortre's
fiancée is surely as pure as her 'white arms and pale gold hair' (p. 30).
Indeed, she sees only the potential good in people—even in the evil

15. F. Felenstein, *Anti-Semitic Stereotypes: A Paradigm of Otherness in English
Popular Culture, 1660–1830* (Baltimore: Johns Hopkins University Press, 1995), p.
239.

Schaube: 'Yes, I should call him a good man. He will come to God some day' (p. 31). Helena's 'eyes were placid, intelligent, but without keenness' (p. 12): her naïvety is an intrinsic part of her femininity, while intellectual discernment may be left to her fiancé, the curate.

Jewish women, meanwhile, are not seen as truly feminine, in a desirable sense. For example, an older woman, Mrs Bardilly is portrayed as astute rather than womanly: '...a quiet, matronly woman, very Jewish in aspect, shrewd and placid in temper, an admirable *châtelaine*' (pp. 189-90). An attractive young woman, Gertrude Hunt, is seen as merely a temptress: 'a dark Jewish girl with eyes full of fixed fascination, a trained regard of allurement' (p. 63) with 'something sordidly shameless' about her room (p. 64). She is, nevertheless, 'insolently beautiful' (p. 129). Gertrude redeems herself by moving towards Christianity and helping to trap one of the conspirators: though, of course, as a fallen woman, she is inevitably doomed to die of an incurable disease. Mrs Herbert Armstrong, a novelist and intellectual woman, anti-Christian though not apparently Jewish, has 'a massive, manlike brow'. Her formidable appearance contrasts with that of the unhappy, long-suffering wife of Schaube's fellow conspirator, Robert Llwellyn, 'this gentle Christian lady' (p. 400). Her misery does not disguise 'white, even teeth' and 'large and blue, once beautiful' eyes (p. 59).

The book is full of stereotypes who are characterized by their physiognomy: thus Gortre has a 'strong and hearty face' (p. 32), which becomes a 'good and saintly face' (p. 244) through his struggles with evil. Father Ripon, the new vicar, is a man in control of his appetites: 'too active to be portly' and with 'a nobility and asceticism [that] conformed the face into something saintly' (p. 111). In Schaube, self-denial is suspect, a symptom of callousness, while in the vicar, it contributes to 'the underlying saintliness of his character' (p. 111). All practising Christians are depicted as pure, including Sir Michael Manichoe, Mrs Bardilly's brother, 'the stay and pillar of "Anglicanism" in the English Church' (p. 180), 'an early convert to Christianity, during his Oxford days' (p. 116), and now a Conservative MP leading 'the moderate "Catholic" party' (p. 116). Sir Michael's Jewish roots have mellowed: 'The oriental strain of cunning in his blood had sweetened to a wise diplomacy' (p. 181). We are told that his 'combination of a Jewish brain and a Christian heart was one which had already revolutionised Society nearly two thousand years ago in the persons of eleven distinguished instances' (p. 183). Sir Michael embodies the qualities of the disciples, while the origins of Christ's own Jewish family are not mentioned.

Anti-Semitism pervades the whole novel, and is reinforced even at unexpected moments: at one point, Spence, a journalist, visits a music hall, where: 'One elderly Jewish-looking person reminded him of a great grey slug' (p. 161). The only decent Jews in this book embrace Christianity; they do this with full feeling, not just 'in name', like 'the wealthy Jews' of Walktown (p. 7).

The epilogue to this book is one of the most unpleasant pieces that I have ever read. Three schoolgirls visit an asylum, where, together with the chaplain, they laugh at the inmates. The description of the reified patients is absolutely chilling, while the party thrill to view these 'things'. Did the Edwardian reader laugh with them? Did any find distasteful such callous mockery of the mentally ill? Schaube, now an 'idiot' inmate, has 'grown very fat... The features were all coarsened, but the hair retained its colour of dark red' (p. 425). Reduced to an 'ungainly' imbecile, Schaube nevertheless retains his colouring, the emblem of his Jewishness. The schoolgirls have enjoyed themselves: one declares 'That Schaube creature was the funniest of *all*!' (p. 425).

Thousands of people read *When it Was Dark*. The Bishop of London recommended it from the pulpit at Westminster Abbey, where he called it a 'remarkable work'.[16] The novel was declared by Field Marshal Lord Montgomery to be a major influence on his life.[17] (This may go some way to explain Monty's more extreme colonial views, just recently made public.)

Buchan's and Nesbit's literary treatment of Jews, foreigners and servants is symptomatic of class attitudes endemic in Britain at that time. Nesbit's intention was not the same as that of the Nazi propaganda machine. She may have wanted Jews and servants in their place, but there is no hint that she wanted them eradicated. Buchan's prejudice is more overt, yet he probably considered himself to be honourably writing for a universal audience. Guy Thorne's anti-Semitism is so extreme that his book has much more in common with Nazi propaganda. The popularity of his novel in its heyday forces one to the unhappy conclusion that he was reflecting popular Edwardian attitudes. In particular, Thorne's barbaric ridicule of the mentally ill is frighteningly close to the Nazi position.

16. Cockburn, *Bestseller* reproduces part of the Bishop's sermon (p. 27).
17. In a radio broadcast, December 1970, cited by Cockburn, *Bestseller*, p. 8.

Figure 2 shows an illustration taken from a Nazi publication (c. 1933) that depicts the life of *Der unverbesserliche Jude Kohn* (The Incorrigible Jew Kohn). Ten connected tales tell of how the eponymous anti-hero supposedly came into the country, traded and deceived farmers, changed his name and poisoned the wells—rehashing the mediaeval mythology that had blamed Jews for the Black Death. This image focuses on the head of a stereotypical Jew—big nose, top hat and thick glasses—superimposed onto a spider's body. The Jew has been turned into an arachnidan monster—half-man, half-spider. The inference is that the Jew is predatory, like a spider that entices flies into its web.

Figure 2. Illustration from Horand H. Schacht, *Der unverbesserliche Jude Kohn* (The Incorrigible Jew Kohn). Cited in *Antisemitismus und Holocaust: Ihre Darstellung und Verarbeitung in der deutschen Kinder- und Jugendliteratur* (Oldenburg: Bibliotheks- und Informationssystem der Universität Oldenburg, 1988), p. 84. Reproduced by permission of BIS Universität Oldenburg, Germany.

This spider image, however, was not new—it was in Britain decades before. Figure 3 shows an image taken from the novel *Trilby*, published in 1894. Written and illustrated by George du Maurier, *Trilby* is a deeply anti-Semitic book. Here is an extract from the blurb on the book-jacket:

For...years this famous story of the domination of the artist's model by the hypnotic evil genius Svengali has stirred readers of normally widely differing tastes. Yet...*Trilby* is also a novel of conspicuous charm. So powerful was the image of the saturnine Svengali that, to the generation of readers of the novel at the time—and it was immensely popular—his name was synonymous with villainy... Part of his fascination lies in the apparently contradictory elements in his character: musical, artistically gifted but crafty and malevolent.

All this is very disturbing, because we know that Svengali is a Jew from the minute we are introduced to him. We are told that he is 'of Jewish aspect, well-featured but sinister' and that 'His thick, heavy, languid lustreless black hair fell down behind his ears to his shoulders, in that musician-like way that is so offensive to the normal Englishman' (p. 8).

" AN INCUBUS "

Figure 3. George du Maurier, 'An Incubus', in *Trilby* (London: J.M. Dent, 1969 [1894], p. 106).

Throughout the book, we are reminded over and over again that Svengali is Jewish, and—even worse—he is foreign. Trilby is the innocent English woman whom he controls with his hypnotic powers. However, Trilby is not so pure that du Maurier lets her survive. We are informed that she has at one time—perish the thought!—posed naked as an artist's model. This flaw in her purity is surely provided so that the Victorian reader was able to accept her inevitable death. The spider image that is shown in Figure 3 is the last illustration of Svengali in the book. George du Maurier gives us a last glimpse of the evil foreigner as a 'powerful demon' (p. 106) trapped in its own web. The writer's daughter, the novelist Daphne du Maurier, wrote that her father 'was not ashamed to put his ideals upon paper'. She claimed that her father 'as a humorous draughtsman...was never malicious or unkind...never from him the sneer, the acid half-truth behind an innuendo, the damning Judas-thrust that passes for wit'.[18] Yet isn't anti-Semitism based on 'malicious half-truth'? Daphne's use of the word 'Judas' in itself has anti-Semitic connotations.

George du Maurier also worked as a cartoonist for *Punch*: in Figure 4, one of his cartoons from 1894, he ridicules a 'new woman'—the Victorian equivalent of today's feminist—who just happens to be called Miss Goldenberg. No prizes for guessing her religion. Nor is it a coincidence that she is talking to a vicar's wife. The contrast is made between Christian delicacy and apparent Jewish callousness.

Like George du Maurier, many children's book illustrators started their professional life working for *Punch* magazine. Figure 5 shows an 1851 *Punch* cartoon, drawn by John Leech, who also illustrated a children's volume of 'Jack the Giant Killer'. You can see the stereotype of the Jewish money lender, with his exaggerated nose and hunched shoulders, teaching a child to be dishonest. He is a sort of Fagin figure who might have come straight from the pages of *Oliver Twist*.[19] Throughout *Oliver Twist*, Dickens reminds us that Fagin is a Jew. Like Guy Thorne's evil Schaube, Fagin has red hair to signify his Jewishness. Dickens uses adjectives that consistently reduce Fagin to a beast: the imagery is both bestial and demonic.[20]

18. D. du Maurier (ed.), *The Young George du Maurier: A Selection of his Letters 1860–1867* (London: Peter Davis, 1951), p. ix.

19. In fact, John Leech did make some sketches for Dickens's writing, and was also famous for his drawings of London life.

20. For a detailed analysis of Dickens's description of Fagin, see Felenstein,

A "NEW WOMAN."

The Vicar's Wife. "AND HAVE YOU HAD GOOD SPORT, Miss GOLDENBERG!"
Miss G. "OH, RIPPIN'! I ONLY SHOT ONE RABBIT, BUT I MANAGED TO INJURE QUITE A
DOZEN MORE!"

Figure 4. The Vicar's Wife: 'And have you had good sport, Miss Goldenberg?'
Miss Goldenberg: 'Oh, rippin'! I only shot one rabbit, but I managed
to injure quite a dozen more!' George du Maurier, 'A New Woman',
Punch 107 (1894), p. 111.

Dickens presents a devilish description of a Jew; nevertheless, this
was mild compared with the vitriol printed in *Der Sturmer* (The
Stormer), the Nazi weekly newspaper published by the notorious anti-
Semite Julius Streicher. In *Der Sturmer*, Streicher incited hatred
through mendacious stories and nasty cartoons, such as Figure 6, which
shows Jews as vampires. The artist has signed his name in the left-hand

Anti-Semitic Stereotypes, pp. 238-43.

THE DEALER IN OLD CLOTHES

TEACHING THE YOUNG IDEA HOW TO STEAL.

Figure 5. John Leech, 'The Dealer in Old Clothes (Teaching the Young Idea
how to Steal)', *Punch* 20 (1851), p. 25.

bottom corner: Fips. He illustrated other publications for Streicher: see
below.

Trust no Fox on the Green Heath and No Jew upon his Oath[21] was
written and illustrated by Elvira Bauer, an 18-year-old girl. It wasn't

21. Elvira Bauer, *Trust No Fox on the Green Heath and no Jew upon his Oath*
(Nuremberg: Sturmer Verlag, 1936). My thanks to Ben Barkow at the Wiener Library, London, for showing me this and other publications.

her first book—she had tried another, called *Ten Little Negroes*,[22] which no doubt had a similarly crude content. *Trust no Fox* was rejected by many publishers before being accepted by Julius Streicher at Der Sturmer press.[23] There was a sort of reciprocal promotion: the book mentions *Der Sturmer*, and the paper carried advertisements for the book. There is no story-line to this work; it is simply a catalogue of anti-Semitism.

The preceding spread to that of Figure 7 shows Streicher in profile, a bull-necked man, surrounded by happy Aryan children—all part of the mutual self-promotion. Figure 7, the sixteenth illustration, tells us that *Der Sturmer* is known throughout the world. The samples of newspaper extracts reproduced in it give a fair idea of the repetitive anti-Semitic content of *Der Sturmer*. On the right of this picture are some wholesome-looking Aryan children. They are in extreme contrast to the caricatured group of elderly Jewish men, grotesquely mimicked by the three carrion crows in the centre foreground.

Towards the end of the book, we are told that schools 'will be nice' when there are no more Jews in them. The statement was prescient.

In the July 1938 issue, *Der Sturmer* recommended its readers to take a book on holiday with them: Ernst Hiemer's *The Poisonous Mushroom*. It was a sequel to *Trust No Fox* and called itself 'a *Sturmer* book for young and old': its aim was clearly to indoctrinate the whole family. The illustrations were drawn by 'Fips', who also drew Figure 6. Here there is another grotesque caricature, this time of Jews as toadstools.

The opening picture of the book is seductively pleasant: it shows two attractive children picking a toadstool in the woods. But the text instructs us that, in the same way that 'a single poisonous mushroom can kill a whole family, so a solitary Jew can destroy a whole village, a whole city, even an entire Volk'.

The second chapter is entitled 'How to Tell a Jew'. Here, there are instructions on how to recognize Jews from both their appearance and their smell. Each chapter closes with a little rhyme: this one finishes with the lines: 'Then must youth fight with us to get rid of the Jewish Devil'. There are 17 short chapters in this book, each one presenting evil deeds Jews are supposed to have committed. *The Poisonous Mushroom* crudely but persuasively repeats its message. Unlike the Edward-

---

22. A. Baumeister, 'Dreams, Hopes, and Realities', in S. Milton (ed), *The Art of Jewish Children: Germany 1936–1941* (New York: Allied Books, 1989), p. 73.

23. Baumeister, 'Dreams', p. 73.

ian reader, its young audience would have had no access to an alternative view. Nor did Nazi books seek to address an inclusive audience: Jews and other minorities were already being removed from the population. In 1938, the British peace group, the Friends of Europe, were so concerned about the distribution of *The Poisonous Mushroom* that they

Figure 6. Illustration by Fips from *Der Sturmer*, May 1934. Reproduced by permission of the Wiener Library, London.

issued a pamphlet of their own. Their leaflet had a foreword by the then Bishop of Durham, Reverend Herbert Hensley Henson (Revd Henson had publicly denounced Nazism and anti-Semitism since 1933). He wrote: 'Anti-Semitism, of which *The Poisonous Mushroom* is a disgusting but characteristic expression, is a danger to civilisation itself'.[24]

In November of that same year, 1938, in Paris, a young Jewish boy shot Ernst vom Rath, a German diplomat. He did this in protest against the way in which his parents had been treated by the regime.[25] In retaliation for this single assassination, the Nazis led a pogrom throughout Germany, beating up thousands of Jews and smashing their premises—hence the name *Kristallnacht*, the Night of Broken Glass.

Figure 7. Elvira Bauer, *Trust no Fox on the Green Heath and No Jew upon his Oath* (Nuremberg: Sturmer Verlag, 1936). Reproduced by permission of the Wiener Library, London.

Whatever the reaction of individuals, there can be no doubt that Kristallnacht was an orgy of violence perpetrated by ordinary citizens. Some might have felt ashamed afterwards. However, the testimonies of sur-

24. I am grateful to Ben Barkow for bringing this pamphlet to my attention.
25. Hershel Grynzpan was 17. His parents had lived in Hanover, Germany, since 1914. They were among the 18,000 Polish Jews forced out of Germany and into pigsties on the edge of Poland.

viving victims make depressing reading: they tell of the indifference of
their German neighbours, even when family members died in the attack.
How could this be? That is always the question we ask ourselves when
we look at the Holocaust—how could decent citizens have allowed it?

Figure 8. Title page illustrated by Fips, from Ernst Hiemer, *The Poisonous
Mushroom* (Nuremberg: Sturmer Verlag, 1938). Reproduced by
permission of the Wiener Library, London.

Daniel J. Goldhagen provides some insight with the reminisces of
Melita Maschmann, a loyal member of the Hitler Youth. Melita was
from a prosperous German family, both her parents were university

educated, yet they were virulently anti-Semitic and she imbibed from them a contradictory and abstract hatred for Jews. Of Kristallnacht, Melita Maschmann wrote:

> For the space of a second I was clearly aware that something terrible had happened there. Something frighteningly brutal. But almost at once I switched over to accepting what had happened as over and done with and avoiding critical reflection. I said to myself: The Jews are the enemies of the new Germany. Last night they had a taste of what this means.[26]

Anti-Semitism was present in Germany before the Nazis seized power; it was a phenomenon used and manipulated by them. Nazi propaganda infiltrated each aspect of everyday life so that even intelligent teenagers and their educated parents could believe in an 'hallucinatory image...of the Jew'[27] that bore no resemblance to any individuals whom they might have known personally. This abstract[28] belief of the Jew as 'bogey man'[29] paved the way for the annihilation of six million.

I began this essay referring to the film *Cabaret*. In the second act of the play, the landlady makes the decision not to marry her Jewish lodger. She confronts the central character and his girlfriend with her decision. The landlady faces the young couple, and asks: 'What would you do? What would you do, if you were me?' We have to ask ourselves the same question: What would I do? And what would I have done, as an ordinary citizen in Nazi Germany? The answer is: we do not know. None of us knows what courage we might have had then, we can only examine our behaviour now. That has to be a lesson of the Holocaust.

---

26. D.J. Goldhagen, *Hitler's Willing Executioners: Ordinary Germans and the Holocaust* (London: Abacus, 1997), p. 103.

27. Goldhagen, *Hitler's Willing Executioners*, p. 89.

28. Goldhagen argues that 'All antisemitism is fundamentally "abstract"...yet simultaneously real and concrete in its effects', *Hitler's Willing Executioners* (p. 34).

29. Goldhagen, *Hitler's Willing Executioners*, p. 89.

PHILOSOPHY OF PSYCHOTIC MODERNISM: WAGNER AND HITLER

Arthur Gibson

1. *Romanticism and Modernism*

a. *Nineteenth-Century Anti-Semitism*

A racist attitude towards Jews is of course only one example of anti-Semitism; other sorts of anti-Semitism deserve attention, such as antipathy towards Arabs by nineteenth-century imperialists attacking areas of the Middle East. Moreover, internecine war between Semitic groups is an internal example of anti-Semitism. So, anti-Semitism against Jews is a subset of a complex, ethnically plural Semitic problem. Discrimination against Semites is itself a component of the more general issue of disadvantaged ethnic minorities, and other economically disadvantaged majorities. Such evident global perspectives exemplify the point that the present topic should be placed in a generalized context of cultural and political forces. They impinge on topics which at first may seem only indirectly to bear on our subject. This also concerns the ways in which factors which are logically irrelevant to the status of a group are taken (falsely so) by external elements averse to the group to be evidence of the group's inferiority or guilt.

Nineteenth-century Europe, as with many other periods and places, seems to have had as part of its basic beliefs that the Jews should be isolated as instances of the foregoing depiction of them. That this is so may be less surprising in the perspective of two of that century's precursor influences: Martin Luther and Frederick the Great. These were two of Hitler's three heroes. The other was Richard Wagner. All four were significantly anti-Semitic. It is likely that the vehemence of Hitler's attack on Bonhoeffer had much to do with the latter's detestation of Luther's anti-Semitism, together with his rejection of the priesthood of that branch of Christianity. Whatever one's justified aversion to Hitler, the question of how one sorts out and assesses the causal relations between Hitler and Wagner is an unstable affair. It is important not to fall into a retrojective version of the genetic fallacy: that of confusing a chicken with an egg, of not conflating Hitler with Wagner. Conversely, since we are dealing with the dynamics of creative influence, together with the role of mental cause (Wagner) and its effect on a will (Hitler), both of which had responsibility to exercise discrimination over falsehood, we should be ready to infer conclusions about the nineteenth-century misuse of the influence which was later paraded as propagandized culture by Hitler.

There is, indeed, a lot of culture bound into this issue. Paulus von Eitzen's (1602) wandering Jew story came to breed influence, with eight printings in its first published year: allegedly the Jew Ahasuerus passes through Hamburg in 1542, having originally jeered at Christ on the cross in 33 CE. With the Enlightenment, the tide of such influence was temporarily pushed back and humanized, in some quarters. In French (for example, Edgar Quinet in the epic poem *Ahasverus* [1834], as well as the lengthy popularization of his ideas in Eugene Sue's *Le juif errant* [1845]) and English (Shelley, with *The Wandering Jew: A Poem* [1887]), the myth was romanticized by alignment with classical Greek troubled hero figures.

Conversely, German literature became possessed with negative and historicized versions of the myth. So here we have another genetic fallacy: myth became history. In the nineteenth century, the anti-Semitic theme became much more trenchant in its obsessive use of the notions of Jewish stubbornness and absence of love, which were supposed to be embodied Jewish identity in and as the wandering Jew. Tied into this focus was the rejection of Christ, and anti-Semitism began to be a thesis of the theology of nature pressed as political insight. For some German Hegelians,[1] the Jew was a fossil, a 'culture of the living dead' who ghosted and counterfeited the idea of immortal renewal—always there, but never other than a threatening unbelieving shade to Christianity.

We find nationalist analogues of this in Ludolf Holst's (1821) manic demolition of Jews and championing of 'pure' nationalism, and while the Jewish Börne's (1821) counter-attack was considered agreeable in some Germans' views, it was largely because he had become Protestant and thereby rejected elements of Jewishness which were under attack. Part of Holst's argument concerned psychology: the Jewish ego was

---

1.   Wagner mentions that he had some success in reading Hegel's *Philosophy of History* (see Wagner 1983: xx).

different from other humans'. He had a causal theory to argue that this unique and subhuman ego was accordingly a mentality which had an (im)morality distinct to other humans.

This had a pragmatic realization. It would be incorrect to think, for example, that the stamping of 'Jew' in a passport and banning of them from pavements, as well as the associated abuse, are of twentieth-century provenance; they were in place in the 1820s. Holst also maintained that the proper consequence of his insights was that the Jews should not be allowed public office or social space. These were practices established early in nineteenth-century German ports and cities. The ancestry of Nazi attitudes to Jews is therefore clear: it was in the heart of early nineteenth-century Germany.

The trend underlying such customs was finalized in Hitler's *Mein Kampf*[2] as a futurist nightmare, retailed as a central ingredient of a pragmatic plan for society. It was a typical psychosis: a possible world is asserted to be the actual world, and the boundaries between them are fiddled, so as to obscure the differences. Oddly, much of German literature's use of the wandering Jew motif was ambiguous over this sort of difference—the difference between myth in a mental state and actual history. To that degree, both Wagner and Hitler made explicit inner dynamical moods in some spheres to become explicit public culture. It is a significant instance of how indeterminacy functions to see that this biography of a purported single human—the wandering Jew—was used as a foil to mirror the actual migration and persecution of whole societies of Jews through various periods of history.

Recently, some Germans have made creative moves to account for such historical patterns. One could summarize one pattern which has a history turned into a dramatic tragedy in Hamlet: Hamlet ghosts history. The postmodern (East) German Heiner Müller maps this German (perennial?) loss of innocence in his *Hamletmachine* (1987). This play, as Müller states in his introduction to it, can be read as a pamphlet against the illusion that one can stay innocent in the world at large. In this vein, Müller quotes from Freiligrath, a close friend of Karl Marx: 'Germany is Hamlet, never quite knowing how to decide and because

---

2.   The publication of Hitler's *Mein Kampf* was initially in two volumes (1925 and 1926), later (1933) collected together in one. The citations of *Mein Kampf* in the present chapter are done in two different ways. Where a quotation is given, this is from the recent translation by Manheim (1992). Where there is no quotation, I refer to the 1933 German edition.

of that always making wrong decisions'. The situation produces blind dogmatism vaunting itself as supreme insight. For example, Heidegger, we now discover, sent a signed copy of one of Goebbel's books recommending persecution of the Jews as a gift to a colleague. Heidegger claimed to have made the correct decision, yet interviews with him by the postwar denazification committee were perplexed by the indeterminacy and amorality of his consciousness and conscience. Here we have a key to understanding features of the mentalities which function in anti-Semitic modes, though this is not Müller's significant point. Indeterminacy in consciousness parades unrecognized amid dogmatic forms of concepts.

b. *Modernisms*

A comment on the term 'modernism' (and its variants) is appropriate. All such designations have precise and disputed uses in research literature. Many thinkers who employ these words conclude, as do I, that there may be no such 'thing' as modernism. The term was not used, or not used in any of our contemporary ways, by, for example, Baudelaire, while he crafted a specific use for his *modernité* which is not synonymous with modernism. Such unease with definition, and resistance to the tendency to reduce a cluster of complex and often opaque relations to a 'name', should be taken as a presupposition of the present chapter. Given such qualifications, however, without spending a whole book on each term's purported or putative definition, we can move carefully and boldly in an attempt to understand further the intricate phenomena which are typically assumed in employing words such as modernism, neo-classicism, postmodernism, indeterminacy and psychosis. We must also be aware that other specialists may have a greater technical knowledge, while such competence can on occasions itself presuppose questionable definitions.

A consciousness may be in a state of never quite deciding on a matter, while at another level deciding that conclusions (indecent in the case of Heidegger) should be implemented. I suggest that this is a characteristic of internal properties of modernism, if they are relevantly functioning with other phenomena to be discussed below. We usually associate indeterminacy with twentieth-century properties, states and events. But wherever under-determined or over-determined functions operate or hold, there is indeterminacy of various sorts. This is because even where there are true or false states as represented with functional accuracy by propositions, the identities of contingency are unstable and prone to indeterminacy. So as to appreciate this state of affairs and its relation to Wagner, as well as the twentieth century, the following concentrates on the French poet and critic Charles Baudelaire, not least since he and Wagner reacted to each other's works, and have significant relations.

Baudelaire ironized the function of uncertainty, ambiguity and indeterminacy by developing a secular modernism, though he did not use that term and was unaware of how it would be used to package his ideas. In fact, we should be massively cautious here. There is a large problem of how—or if—we can retroject modernism into those who crafted its seeds. This is both the standard problem of the misleading function of purporting to 'name' a movement or influence; and it also has to do with the elusive indeterminacy of Baudelaire's sensibility, which is too easily distorted by later uses of his ideas by others. With regard to the period around 1846, he was concerned with utopian socialism—the idea of colour and nature matching art so as to produce a unity in the world of nature and aesthetics, as well as a political realization of this in a secular humanism (see Kelley 1964, 1975). Baudelaire was actually producing the conditions which would mould later modernism. Central to this impetus was his concern to conceive the relativity of value in terms of art.

This produced a certain tension in his aim to construct a universal art—a total art work, as Wagner phrased it. Later, however, and at the time when Wagner began to emerge as an influence, Baudelaire introduced some ideas of the absolute into poetry and aesthetics. Some of these elements mirrored, if not matched, Wagner's. Both were concerned with universal art, and elitism, as each variously embraced the need for relativity as sensitive to circumstance and individual experience. The conjunction of both these universalizing and relativizing roles in their arts amounts to an implicit function of indeterminacy, since in the final analysis, they are incompatible. Certainly, they can in principle be integrated; but since Baudelaire and Wagner resorted to equivocation and ambiguous nuance in their symbolic domains, indeterminacy had a free reign at points in their works, though disguised by explicit determinate tendencies.

Wagner was interested in the varying Romanticist ideas of *correspondence* between the various arts, the world, and concepts of god(s). This type of enterprise was also fundamental to, though realized differently in, Baudelaire. The latter's poem 'Correspondences' displays a forest that assumes partial identities of trees as pillars within the church and the domain of the familiar spirit. In this, there are all the materials for a strict mimetic correspondence between language and nature. Yet Baudelaire's aim is to destabilize realistic correspondence in literature, by posing indeterminacy (though he does not use the term). In Romanticism and even in early modernism, with Victor Hugo's *Les Misérables* (1860), realism had been held in position by a straightforward presupposition about mimesis—the imitation of the world was seemingly achieved by matching it with words and pictures, and the grotesque had been incorporated along with the sublime. For Baudelaire, this was insufficient. Even with Hugo's egoism, in which evil forces hung around the ego, and yet God was the absolute thing to copy as a means to secure correspondence with the world of unity, not so with Baudelaire and Wagner: uncertainty about a given belief—a weakness of will which has always troubled humanity—gave way to the generalization that mind and language themselves were by nature in a relation of misleading correspondence to the external world, to the absolute, to themselves.

The inner principle of the relevant Romanticism before Baudelaire was that realism presupposed the concept of true representation of the likeness of the world in language. The rubric which enabled this concept to be implemented by artists was that nature had to be a type of implicit dictionary. Rather like the mediaeval world's book of nature, creative compositions matched the implicit dictionary of the world. Hugo argued that infinity was in art and it came from God. Correspondence was the inner cement bonding such equations.

With *modernité* under Baudelaire, however, things became indeterminately related to correspondence. He still maintained that there was correspondence in nature with language, but this was unstable: mimesis was ambiguous, and there was inextirpable obscurity in our creative attempts. Furthermore, there was no convenient implicit dictionary in nature by which we might read off or check for the accuracy of our correspondences. Deism had taken over in Baudelaire's middle period. For him, there is no divine code in human language or the world, and his writings show that he believes this deeply as a truth about humanity. He even avoided allowing us evidence of the chronology of his poetry, so that we are barred from placing his poetic images in a developmental sequence. This was not carelessness, but an attempt to internalize the indeterminacy of a biographical life into the internal semantic relations of his narratives, by which to code in the ambiguity of consciousness.

This relates to a deep problem in the analysis of consciousness, which can only briefly detain us here. We need allow for the thesis that, as Penrose (1997) argues it, understanding itself, and even consciousness, can be, or are, non-algorithmic. You will recall that an algorithm is a theorem which encapsulates in its logical form the slogan that a given array of possible permutations only has a certain permissible and possible form of expression which one can in principle calculate by the algorithm. This has a predictive and retrojective value. If consciousness and understanding are computable and reflexive functions, then the rationality of which they themselves are functions can be said to be assessable by algorithmic computations. Negatively used, such legislation eliminates certain possibilities which violate or are not accounted for by the algorithmic function.

Stated plainly in psychological terms suitably interpreted for the present context, we may conclude that human consciousness shows in principle that it has one of two, or a mixture of two states. First, that it can know itself and can thereby recognize all its functions. Secondly, to the contrary, that human consciousness is irreflexive—that it cannot or does not habitually know itself. The two states seem to be mixed on the analogy of quantum states, in which indeterminacy and ambiguity function at the perceptual and recognitional level. This is partly why I have argued in other pieces of work (Gibson 1997, 1998) that having a concept is not necessarily a recognitional concept. This applies itself to the identity of inference, as Lewy (1976) proved. Consequently, we seem to have consciousnesses which are sometimes disposed to misconstrue and misinterpret phenomena, as well as our exhibiting capacities for recognition. We often mix these two disparate states. The result is indeterminacy of perception, and therefore indeterminacy in consciousness. Obviously, if having a concept is not itself in principle a recognitional capacity, part of the human problem is that we will not be aware, or not aware in a relevant descriptive accuracy, of just when or in precisely what ways this is happening.

Certainly, humans have strong abilities to perceive and recognize; that is not in dispute here. What is, is the proportionality ratio that exists between having data, having a concept which interprets them, and the degree to which humans might generalize over the data's relations and infect the results with obscurities and errors. That this operates seems evident. The problems of what its causes are gives rise to massive debate and disagreement: Is it a matter of mere incompleteness of information or experience? Is bias intrinsic to human perception? Do all of us or certain groups in particularly pressured or luxuriant contexts comply with factors which would alleviate difficulty? Is the influence of the possibility of power or national achievement a causal function that deforms our objectivity? Is it human nature?

Central to possible answers to these questions, and to a number of theories, are the roles of the will and the influence of ideas on states of human perception. It is worthwhile considering that these two functions are themselves subject to the argument just adduced. Namely, will and epistemological influence are susceptible of conceptual and perceptual indeterminacy. I suggest that some such blend of states is internal to human consciousness generally. In the perspective of this, we may view the nineteenth century as one not dissimilar in certain ways to any other century of human experience. That is to say, there is a tendency for indeterminacy of consciousness to operate.

On the basis of the foregoing analysis, it is plausible to presuppose that the functioning of such indeterminacy is variable in proportion to relevant phenomena and imagination which stimulate its performance, or pressures which produce deformation of otherwise generally accurate perception. This scenario is not a causal or deterministic one. It incorporates, as proposed above, the notion that contingent relations can themselves be indeterminate, including the situation when binary true/false propositions are functions. If this seems solely of academic import, we may remind ourselves of a problem mentioned above: how is it that ordinary German citizens, even in times of peace, deemed law-abiding cultured Jews to be subhuman? Either we draw a short, quick, savage conclusion about what the minds of such people are, and then have the problem of explaining why it is that a proportion of humanity tends to behave in this way—'but not us!' Or shall we generalize, and allow that humans have common mental properties which from time to time unleash themselves in such and such a way, due to external forces and internal lack of rectitude? If the latter, we need to do rather a lot of explaining.

So, applying the above arguments, a thesis internal to the present chapter's line of thinking is that the nineteenth century, as a precursor to Hitler, was similar to other centuries with respect to human mentality. But the foregoing analysis amounts to a new theory: in the nineteenth century, there is generalized indeterminacy of mental states in propositional states, with dispositions paraded as transparency and evident or self-evident propriety with causal influence. Yet the states of indeterminacy were for the first time in history the content of concepts which asserted a worldview with indeterminacy as one of its functions, and not merely an implicit dispositional slip of individuals.

When the 1860s witnessed Germans burning Jewish books in the market place, the writer Auerbach interrupted a concert of Wagner's to shout out that such Germans had done this because of reading Wagner's book *Judaism in Music*; he added that if they did this to Jewish books today, then they would do it to their bodies tomorrow. Wagner was genuinely shocked that someone could think that this sort of action could follow from reading his work, and shouted a denial that Germans could ever resort to such degradation of Jewish people. The Second World War proved how wrong Wagner was on the latter issue, and how prescient Auerbach had been; it remains to assess whether or not Wagner was wrong on the former topic of reading. Reading is a type of causal *and* indeterministic experience. The influence of an idea on the mind and emotions is itself causal, even by the indeterminate infiltration of dispositions into a reader.

The movements termed 'modernisms' (in the plural since they vary in form and date, and from country to country) are difficult to hold under that ragbag term. One reason is that they have problematic relations to the previous dominant, though somewhat short-lived, cultural paradigm, Romanticism. Romanticism can be summarized as that collection of influence and ideas which uses alienation, attenuation of emotions and their intensification, with an emphasis on the individual's role, in an attempt to enhance experience.

Similarly, yet differently, modernism employs alienation, attenuation and individuality. In the writings of Romantics such as Victor Hugo, Chateaubriand, Alexandre Soumet, Goethe, Schiller and Herder, usually God or gods have a function, whereas for the modernist realist such as Baudelaire, God is (becoming) absent. Thus, though this is the parting of the ways in contexts of the history of Christian belief, Romanticism not only is a parent of modernism, but it is also largely internal to modernism as a set of genetics of the latter's components.[3]

3.   Sartre, in his study entitled *Baudelaire* (1947), forces, I believe, a too sharp separation between the Romanticism and *modernité* of Baudelaire in his enthusiasm to enforce the 'committed writer' scenario.

For example, this is why one may, to some extent, identify Samuel Beckett's *Sans* (1969) as a Romantic work: alienation, individuality, intensity of emotion; and with Beckett, like so much twentieth-century modernism as well, the atheist appears to have an anxiety-complex about whether or not God is really absent, or the shadow of his past identity still casts a spell. Atheist modernism is still shaped in the perspective of a God who was there.

Therefore, there is in modernism a form of nostalgia which at first seems antithetical to the idea of modernism, yet modernisms contrast the unique present with the traditional institutional past, though this contrast is a recurrent historical feature. Stated another way, there is an indeterminacy of identity in modernism and its engagement with Romanticism. In short, the psychological indeterminacy which was adduced for mentality in the foregoing has an explicit analogue, perhaps for the first time in history, in a generalized collective state of public culture. This is just one reason why one can give privileged attention to the nineteenth century's culture, not least as relevant causal antecedent for the twentieth-century part of our subject. It is perhaps the first time that belief-conditions of groups of societies and civilizations came to manifest and propagate conceptual indeterminacy which matched levels of uncertainty not only in what it is to be *individual* human belief and will, but also in the identities of an individual human consciousness itself.

As early as 1846, *modernité* is employed by Charles Baudelaire (his *Salon de 1846*), though we should be wary of conflating this term with the technical expression 'modernism'. These two terms are related yet distinct, and, since a word is not a concept, we should note that the associations of the term 'modernism' contain senses which would have been unknown to Baudelaire, though he composed many of the creative and critical conditions whereby modernism came to be formed. The sense of relativity, utopian socialism, the possible unity of art and nature by use of extreme ambiguity in versions of correspondences with nature, are involved in *modernité*. The concept of a movement and of non-elitist looking forward as a rejection of the past are germane to modernism, though not Baudelaire. The egg produces a chicken, while the identities of their relations are asymmetrical and preserve differences; so it is with the future modernisms to whose birth, we now see retrospectively, Baudelaire made major contributions.

This sets the scene for the question of the roles of the indeterminate uses of 'Satan' in the opening of Baudelaire's later *Les fleurs du mal* (1861). It assists us to explain this diabolic issue in a motif. 'Satan' had a complex ancestry in addition to its use in Christian theology. During the only recently past French revolution, the terms together with expressions for 'demons', 'devils' and the like, were assigned by both sides of the revolution as labels for the enemy. This was not only a claim that the Devil had his angels who possessed the enemy: the range of semantic values included rich personificatory employment of the words in a thematic polemic, sometimes utilizing Revelation 16's use of some of the terms for Armageddon. The fact that frogs have a symbolic function in this apocalypse gave obvious uptake for application to a variety of French political powers.

So some few years later, we find Baudelaire composing a new tune on the indeterminacy of 'Satan' in his poetry. What does 'Satan' indicate in his poetry, and has the term contrary functions in different phases of Baudelaire's literary development? Eugene Holland (1994) has shown how fractures occur in Baudelaire's poetry, mirroring his biography. It seems also that on occasions, *Les fleurs du mal* ascribes ontological or mediated actual capabilities to Satan that cannot always be, but sometimes can be, reduced to personificatory roles, though one would not thereby be committed to consigning Baudelaire to a Catholic ontology. The matter is a complex one beyond the scope of the space available here; but a summary of the probable outline of Baudelaire's usage has to do with his thesis of the problematic identity of correspondence introduced above. The sense of Satan is itself indeterminate. Although it is difficult to demonstrate with certainty that Baudelaire offered a thesis of satanic indeterminacy about consciousness, it seems clear that this is how he sometimes uses it. That is to say, Satan maps Baudelaire's own mental states of indeterminacy. This seems to be a symbol for what human consciousness is or is prone to manifest.

In associating Beckett and Baudelaire over the poetics of death, Christopher Ricks (1993: 166-68) introduces T.S. Eliot's remark (1951: 421): 'Genuine blasphemy…is to the complete atheist as to the perfect Christian'. Eliot adds, 'It is a way of affirming belief'; and we may demur from this judgment, while accepting the relevance of the first part of the quotation. We discover, then, an ambivalence in the ideas central to modernism. There is an indeterminacy over a variety of central functions and values related to belief. In the paradigm example of the modernist poet, Baudelaire, we have specific terms such as

'Satan' whose semantic functioning in his poetry are indeterminist. In all probability he did not know himself what the precise indeterministic function of his use of 'Satan' was in a given context, save to explain that the range of senses corresponded to a history and his grasp of a problem with a varying range of alternatives whose sum is the set of nuances in the particular poem. Consequently, gathering the previous considerations, we may include a new ingredient in an attempted explanation of nineteenth-century modernism: indeterminacy. This is absent, in the relevant range of senses, from Romanticism, though it has covert functions and is not generalized nor fundamental in the way indeterminacy is in *modernité*.

2. *Wagner*

Richard Wagner was Baudelaire's hero. When the former came to Paris, Baudelaire was ecstatic. For Baudelaire, Wagner's 'total work of art' was perfection. When Wagner went to Paris,[4] there was mutual admiration between Wagner and Baudelaire. The former sought out the latter at his home on at least two occasions, we discover from Wagner's letter written at the time to Baudelaire (cf. Crepet 1906: 451-52). The reason was that, in Paris, Wagner had had a very bad reception, except for Baudelaire's championing of him in reviews and an article.

As modernists, we should note that the sometimes popular idea of a forward-looking figure for the future of art was not quite either Baudelaire's or Wagner's perception. Both in various ways looked to the past—as elitists—as a means to the future. In particular, Baudelaire is like someone hoping for a revival of a past renaissance, yet finds himself unexpectedly dragged by his creativity into the future, thinking all the while he was walking in the opposite direction. He contrasts with the sort of hero-poet Arthur Rimbauld was to become. We may paraphrase this ignorance on the part of Baudelaire of himself as a form of indeterminacy of consciousness and ignorance of its relations to his own concepts.

In a certain sense, Wagner was extremely Romantic, not only in his sexuality, but in his cultural ideas. He was an anachronism in dress—Baudelaire was a dandy, but Wagner's absorption with neo-Classical

---

4.   In a certain sense, Wagner escaped there subsequent to his part in the Dresden uprising, fighting alongside Bakunin who was later sentenced to death in his absence and fled to Russia.

royal matters was almost too primitive to be even Romantic, and he certainly was not a modernist in these respects. If we pitch Romanticism to start just before the end of the eighteenth century, and to end soon after its commencement, with Wagner coming into fashionably unfashionable vogue in the 1850s, we see that he was an anachronistic modernist who turned the mould inside out: he drew out of modernism the seeds of Romanticism and restated them so as to supersede modernism, with a prior form: nostalgic Romanticism. This is evident in his resort to his perceptions of Classical Greek tragedy as his model for future opera.

In sum: Wagner's position in relation to movements is that he was mentally indeterminate in a range of respects. Nor is this simply a matter of the usual issue with genius: greater than the sum of the parts of movements of which he was a product. Rather, Wagner's egotism was a vortex which pulped the identity of *modernité*, so as to revert to a mythical past. This pointedly supports Nietzsche's criticism: Wagner had betrayed his possible future by a retreat into egoistic self-glorification using a somewhat tardy Romantic version of Classical mythology retailed as the requisite German national cultural identity. Goethe would have been disappointed with Wagner, but Hitler was not.

This latter alternation advertises a dangerous judgment: was Hitler's attraction to Wagner a function of Wagner's *own* causal influence, and—therefore—were Hitler's tastes somehow foreshadowed or mapped by Wagner's creativity? Wagnerians withdraw in horror from such accusations; and, alternatively, those like Stravinsky, who hated Wagner's music, are too ready to reach such conclusions without appropriate complex assessment. The problem which this chapter has thus far attempted to isolate is this: indeterminacy is a function of the century, of modernisms, and covertly of Wagner's writing. How does one become committed to the inference that he should be blamed for Hitler's use of him, when the interface has indeterminacy in its identity?

There are two spheres in which this possible influence operates. First, Wagner's literary output, and secondly, his music. A feature of the second is that, unusually for a composer of opera, Wagner composed the dramatic dialogue, as well as the music. At his best, the literary merit of Wagner's dialogue is as good as some of Heine's average poetry compositions, and Wagner learned a good deal from this poet. We may sense a certain class-consciousness and victimization of minorities in Wagner's operatic dialogue, together with a disposition to fantasize; yet it is difficult to sustain an argument that Wagner has any *explicit* anti-Semitism *in* his operas, with a minor possible exception.

Conversely, this can not be said of his non-operatic literary and polemical compositions. Despite the foment of anti-Semitism in the Germany of the 1860s, and even with the opportunity to edit such racism out of the forthcoming second edition of his *Judaism in Music*, he retained its manic tone and specific insults. In parts of it, he had introduced the Lutheran translation's use of apocalyptic language from Revelation 17—the fall of Babylon engulfed in flames, in which the harlot has to go through her *Untergang*, her inferno. His employment of such terminology, however, is to depict the proposed future for the Jews, and, in his claim, the need for them to be expunged from the land of Germany to learn how properly to be human or German. The allusive semantic field of *Untergang*, even metaphorically, is extremely nasty, and at least presupposes the removal of what we would now call primary inalienable human rights. It is difficult to exclude some nuance of a use of fire or a destructive note to 'achieve' transformation of the Jews' rights and identity and probably their lives, in his polemical language.

The context of his initial writing of *Judaism in Music* in 1848–49 is of a piece with this framework, which he later refused to change. Wagner having failed at the corporate and commercial level in Paris, a certain Princess Wittgenstein offered him financial support to write a missive to articulate her own hatred of the Jews. He had recently asked for and received a loan from the Jewish poet Heine. It seems as some inducement or in appreciation of the transaction, that Wagner had announced to the world: Heine was the new Goethe. So he contradicted this stance quite quickly, in writing for the princess. Even this was insufficient for the internal dynamics of Wagner's racism with regard to Heine, who incidentally had been fairly restrained and proper in his request concerning another matter: that lawyers assess similarities between some of the text in Wagner's operas and Heine's own poetry, for alleged plagiarism by Wagner, in which the wandering Jew myth has some function. In Wagner's *My Life* (1983),[5] we find that, under the

---

5.   References to Wagner's autobiography are complicated by its odd history of publication. Originally available to only a limited group during his lifetime, it was only published for a wider (German-reading) audience in 1963. This version maintained the original headings from Wagner's journals, but suppressed some material dealing with Wagner's sex-life. In 1976, a corrected version was published which

encouragement of Lizst and his daughter Cosima, Wagner then announced to his new social world that Heine's poetry was the 'shit' that shores up the wall of an African mud hut. This sort of contrary tension in Wagner's mental space is not merely an opposition of false judgments. The textures of rhetoric and fabrication, as well as self-induced conviction of the rightness of his position, amount to a basis for obsessive disregard for realism and correspondence with the actual external world. If we add to this his involvement in living out indeterministic fantasies, we have the makings of an argument for his being episodically psychotic, or at least subject to multiple false consciousnesses induced by the contagion[6] of his egoism. It is significant to relate this to Robert Jacobs's observation that:

> After [Wagner's] long sojourn in Switzerland, where he had written megalomaniacal theoretical treatises... Wagner settled in Paris in the Autumn of 1859... A French friend had suggested that something should be done to dispel the impression, created by critics exasperated by [Wagner's] *The Artwork of the Future* and *Opera and Drama*, that Wagner was a phantasist endeavouring to foist on the world a crazy 'Music of the Future' (*Zukunftsmusik*) (1979: viii).

Significant though his theoretical works may be, the role of the ego stands out with his disposition to fantasy. It is quite similar to Hitler's, and is elsewhere, we see above, attached to his views of the Jews. Though he was capable of kindness to individual Jews, to one such recipient, Hermann Levi, he asserted, 'As a Jew all you need to learn to do is to die'. This did not seem a recommendation about the seeming merits of suicide. If we gather together such varieties of contrariety, ambivalence and ambiguity, we are confronted with an extraordinary mentality which could internalize extreme conflicting states and double standards. It is likely that, since it is probable that Wagner sincerely held such views, and we should allow some degree of disingenuousness and intense economic pressures, the morass which was his mental state in such contexts appears to display indeterminacies in the topics and contents which the foregoing briefly itemized. Wagner's contradictory behaviour is thus likely to be a manifestation not only of nineteenth-

included the supressed material, but which deleted the original headings. References in the present chapter are to the 1983 translation of the 1976 German edition.

6. I am here alluding to Ian Hacking's (1995) thesis that media can infiltrate consciousness as a sort of semantic virus.

century indigenous anti-Semitism, but also the indeterminacy which falsely accommodates such phenomena.

We are still ignorant of how music has causal influences on people. So we cannot now accurately generalize from the above to the influence of Wagner's music on morality, but it seems evident that music has causal effects on human consciousness. It is also clear that the figures and leitmotifs of Wagner's music depict possible worlds which are fantasies. If it is correct to identify these as operational causes which together influence humans of certain dispositions, then it is a short step to acknowledge that a human thus disposed, who has knowledge of Wagner's immoral prejudices, will readily take the influence of Wagner's music as a function of those prejudices. So we do not have to adduce the conclusion that Wagner's music is itself anti-Semitic to conclude that his music will contingently be in conjunction with the causal influence of his anti-Semitism.

Beyond this, there is a further quite difficult psychological problem for the philosophy of mental causality in relation to aesthetics, of which we as yet have no philosophical understanding. Is there a causal interface of a transitive sort between a composer's musicality and his or her literary epistemology? That is to say, could a composer such as Wagner have entirely intransitive relations between his various conceptual faculties, as well as the relations of these to his behaviour? Most unlikely, one would think. Of course, we should not infer from this that there is a generalized law of causal inference by which if a person is morally bad then his music will be similarly so. With the above sketch of Wagner we are tackling something quite distinct to this scenario, however. We are concerned with the existence of related fantasies in Wagner's musical drama, his theoretical explanation of them, his contradictory fantasizing about Jews in personal and political dealings with them, not as the sole basis for suggesting causal influence through his music, but as a multiple function of the ways in which observers— such as Hitler, and others—are willingly subject to causal influence of both music and ideas, because they have read Wagner's anti-Semitism.

Clearly this goes further. In depicting human mentality, we are not consigning the mind to being a passive function. Wagner knew that he had influence, that he could combine music and the politics of anti-Semitism. After all, it was he, not critics, who produced the literary conjunction: *Judaism in Music*. So we have here the issue of mental causality and the subject's own interference with his internal mental configurations to produce a transitive connection in the interface between music and words. It is not therefore convincing to dismiss the influence of Wagner's anti-Semitism contingent on his music's influence by distracting us to a different problem from which we are not attempting to infer the impropriety of Wagner's influence.

3. *Indeterminacy in the Early Twentieth Century*

We can appreciate one bridge from Wagner to Hitler by tuning in to a mood of poetic culture at the turn of the century with Mallarmé, who in no sense made a contribution to the later Nazi concepts, but whose enthusiasm for Wagner provoked him to link indeterminacy in his poetry with some of Wagner's creative elements. The expressions implementing conditional probabilities in Mallarmé's *Un coup de dés* (1914) are relevant to isolating an aspect of surprising expansion of sense. This work is almost a poetic paradigm of the counter-intuitive disguised as the self-evident—the use of standard types whose values seem to impart a new typology. Also, as Florence (1986: 42-45) notes, Mallarmé employed Wagnerian vocabulary at times, while stretching it into rapid shifts between different levels of (logical) generality. Christopher Wintle states, in relation to Beethoven's sonata Opus 10 No. 3, that

> The usefulness of formulating empirically-derived principles for music, in the harmonic, melodic, formal or whatever sphere is twofold: first (invoking the structuralists' *langue*), to propose models, which through development and variation may generate any number of utterances; secondly, and reciprocally (the structuralists' *parole*), to show how distinct musical events, within or between pieces, may be interrelated by reference to one or more governing principles, however irreducible the events themselves may seem at first sight (1985: 147).

The *Ring*'s sword-motif concerns Wotan's disposition, which emerges as the main thematic voice of the *Ring*, and is akin to use of an indeterminate cosmological constant (cf. Gibson 2000a). One chord can evoke a whole tonality, in a way which shows that creativity in content, orchestration and harmony constitutes the context of musical usage in this work. This involves the sword-motif contributing a criterion of thematic identity, parallel with the cosmological function as a chord which self-defines the context. In this way Gibson (2000a) argues, one can speak of a logical conclusion in a piece of music—its resolution, which has a live metaphor relation to the cosmological constant; the latter is similar, for example, to a logical conclusion—the endgame of the universe, concluding in a new beginning.

Lacoue-Labarthe (1994: 38-40) suggests that, in Wagner, music implements *types* which *personify meaning*; and this could apply generally to music, utilizing the notion to develop a live metaphor concept (see Gibson 1997, 2000b). Introducing the category of live metaphor to map these relations between cosmology and music, we can guard against absolute identification of the two subjects' syntaxes with each other, using a relative identity relation which preserves their own undoubted autonomy at many levels. In this manner, creativity is directly interrelated with the cosmological and other constants. This has some parallel with the fashion in which the theory of the leitmotif pertains to its origin and context. Such intricate and subordinate details should not be allowed to suggest a too close alignment between cosmology and music, and the use of live metaphor notions should guard against too strong an identification of the two. Kant's *Critique of Judgement* posits the 'invention' of a rule as a function of genius. The ontology of the universe mirrors, as live metaphor, the 'rule' which is its counter-intuitive cause, that is, aesthetic.

We might readily re-run and transform the above relations with cosmology and music employing Mozart instead. Bowie (1993: 103-104) anchors his comparison in the arts, developing a psycho-analytical model, citing Barth, who believed that Mozart's 'music is…demanding, disturbing, almost provocative'. I suggest that a carefully qualified link of some aesthetic music values with cosmology exposes fresh counter-intuitive possibilities for ontology and epistemology. It is precisely in the marginal and the unstable, momentary, counter-intuitive states in which cosmology has its origin and generality, amid arrays of other permanent levels of transcendental reality, that the texture of creativity is apprehended. This instability threatens the possibility of adequate analysis, but also it invites contrasting quests and questionings.

4. Hitler

a. Modernisms and Hitler

Indeterminacy is not necessarily absent from those who show signs of embracing opposite properties. This is particularly the case when an individual has an eclectic desire to absorb disparate elements. There seems to be a psychological principle by which, if a person is internally fragmented, yet proclaims a profile of seamless integration, then we can expect to discover contrary blends of opposed features. If we add to this the variety of stages through which people go when moving from childhood through adulthood, together with the ebb and flow of these at later stages of reminiscent, false recollection, and dislocation, then we have a complex concept.

Hitler was an extreme realization of such dynamics. There are grounds to recognize this in him: his aversion to modernism, and his glorification of his interpretation of a stiff neo-classical monumentalism. But he also attempted to train as an artist with modernist expressionists. He was totalitarian; yet the inner functions of his political theory are anarchical to the point of displaying some characteristics of chaos theory. The allusion to 'chaos' here is neither lightly intended, nor is it a programme for something such as anomalous monism, in which the psychological indeterminism and brain science are bases for suggesting a philosophy of mental states. Peter Smith (1998) has warned against such equations, in that the move from one macro-dynamical state to another can be deterministic, and he has much to recommend about the virtue of a general preformal notion of chaos, because of the present limits to mathematical enquiry into chaos. The present thesis rests on a view about consciousness and its relation to perception, in which more extreme states are a condensation of usual mental states in humans, and that chaos proportionately increases with the enlargement of the function of indeterminacy.

As a child, Hitler was obsessed with Wagner's operas. As a teenager he dressed as a dandy, replete with kid white evening gloves; later, the carefully crafted white uniforms, shoes and gloves of the Nazi High Command echo not only a feminine tonal play, quite unacknowledged by the consciousness of those who castigated someone who was not the full military man, but also the ambiguity of the nineteenth century's modernist gender identities. As a teenager, Hitler's hope to become an artist and join the expressionists momentarily opened up possible psychological spaces for healthy exploration which he soon closed off, when he was rejected during an interview at an expressionist art college (which had been built by Ludwig Wittgenstein's father).

Uses of 'new' in avant gardes and modernisms are often simple, philosophically primitive assumptions; they associate with fantasies about a new realm for which there is supposedly no antecedent sense.

Some literary futurisms embody these naive oppositions. This is illustrated, for example, by Central European Futurism in the form of the German Sturmkreis poets, part of the first avant garde of the twentieth century. They argued that there was a necessity to create a new language, by virtue of destroying an old one (cf. White 1990). Such a stance may be read metaphorically as a form of alienation which obscures the complicated mixture of functions fictionally forced into the single term 'new'.

The avant garde presents the new moment as singular and without antecedents. Actually 'the new moment' is complexly multiple, and it is a result of a metaphoric use of its environment and the latter's pasts. Significant avant garde is thereby characteristically a counter-intuitive mimesis of its surrounding typologies. The manifesto logic of some avant gardes might be viewed as follows: literary sense is rather like a line drawn through time, as strings of sentences. This naive form, I suggest, corresponds to the inaccurate simplicity of some such ideas of 'the new'. The past is a line up to, for example, 1908—brought to an end with the futurist Filippo Tomasso Marinetti publishing his 'Manifeste du Futurisme' in *Le Figaro* in 1909. Before 1909, we have the old; after, there is the new: a total dislocation, a fracture, a discontinuity, a new thing in the earth.

In unexpected ways, Hitler was a counterfeit of the expressionism which at a point he yearned to join, and was a deviant form of an old avant garde—a term which, of course, has a military origin. In positioning fragments of his mentality in such ways, we get a purchase on both his abnormality, and on his normativity.

b. *Hitler's Sanity*

It is a worn but important debate that asks the question of whether Hitler was a unique case or typical of any of those unemployed workers who had been soldiers in the First World War. If we add the concept of indeterminacy developed above, we may counter-intuitively conclude that he was both. He was an uneven blend of the nineteenth-century's identities: a new sense of human individuality, and the neglect of the individual by states, bound together into mental indeterminacy with a psychotic unpredictable dynamic.

Remarkably sane people seem insane. Criminal biography can be so enlarged in scope that the author, as psychotic, stands as proxy for a nation or the world. Rarely can such an author attempt to place the external world in symmetry with his own literariness, yet this was so in *Mein Kampf*. Such an abnormal case is worth reflection, because its very extremity highlights subversive functions which in isolation are easily tolerated as mere inconveniences or 'necessary evils'. Although ethics and literariness are separable elements, they are contingently merged; and definition of literature should thus incorporate ethics. Yet institutional readings can bolster and obscure the recognition of a major corrupt figure. In a restricted sense, Hitler's *Mein Kampf* is a condensation and distortion of many contemporary tendencies. Contradictions are confidently explained away.

There is a logic which we may redeploy to this sort of polemic: paraconsistent logic. This is the doctrine that a particular proposition can be both true *and* false in a specific single context, and all others. If we add to this the foregoing proposal of mental indeterminacy in the ways its believers articulate the logic, then we have a logic model for *Mein Kampf*. Treatments of paraconsistent logic (for example, Epstein and D'Ottaviano 1995: 349) are fond of citing Walt Whitman's

> Do I contradict myself?
> Very well then... I contradict myself.
> I am large... I contain multitudes.

The similarity of this prose to the mad Legion's speech in Luke 5 is evident. This precedent serves to introduce my suggestion that paraconsistent logic is a model which fits the phenomena of multiple personality, especially as explained by Ian Hacking (1995), though he does not draw attention to this connection. Hacking describes the functioning of multiple personalities as a 'semantic contagion', often under duress from and coerced by media influence. I think that these can be modelled by paraconsistent logic, and be employed to map psychosis and some states of schizophrenia. A key feature is that a weak (some might argue a homonymic) sense of 'negation' is used to relate a collection of propositions which are true (and false) to a model of the world, but not consistently extensionally to the world, as with Epstein and D'Ottaviano (1995: 360). This is like a psychotic's conflation of an imagined world with the actual world, with recipes to avoid recognizing and equivocate over the differences. Epstein and D'Ottaviano (1995: 361) actually state that, 'From their own semantic point of view such theories are consistent, corresponding to a possible description of the world'. But many people will believe that the use of 'possible' here is itself paraconsistent, that is, only if we are confused about what is true and false is it possible to accept paraconsistent logic as a possible description of the world. Epstein and D'Ottaviano plausibly note that, only when the classical true or false logic is applied to the para-consistent theory, is inconsistency detectable. So this really is parallel with a psychiatrist convincing a psychotic that the latter's world really is not the actual world. This state will thus have mirrored an element in and of ancient consciousness, which may be not unlike Hitler's use of Wagner at Bayreuth and his policy at Auschwitz.

c. *Twentieth-Century Anti-Semitism*

Some of the prejudices concerning Jews in European society obviously recur in occult political form in Hitler's writing. Bryan Cheyette (1993) has portrayed how some English and Irish writers participate in absorb-ing anti-Semitic and related assumptions. He highlights the assumption, epitomized by Shaw, of the superman whose ideals are partly embraced by Hitler (Cheyette 1993: 116-20), illustrating how social mythology in mainstream literature facilitated the partial 'civilizing' perception of Hitler's views.

Influential writers can be victims of such institutional bias. Ludwig Wittgenstein (1889–1951) went to the same school in Linz as Hitler, and for one year (1904–1905) they were taught by the same history teacher, Leopold Potsch. In some sense they were products of the same anti-Semitic teacher, both partly Jewish, both anxious to hide their Jewish identity, but with Hitler as high priest, and Wittgenstein as par-tially believing sacrifice. Ray Monk (1990: 279-80) explains that in the period 1929–31 Wittgenstein used Nazi slogans, which might have come out of *Mein Kampf*, to express his anxieties. Quoting from a dream of his own, Wittgenstein stated guiltily, 'I think: must there be a Jew behind every indecency?' Two biographical subjects tangentially intertwine, overlap, part and thus show that there is no causal law influencing their ethical identities, while both are disparately hyp-notized by at times common influences.

It is a reactionary version of and reversion to an extreme nineteenth-century German imperialism, accidentally married to a naive philo-sophy of pseudo-working-class realism, cemented together into a uni-verse of futurist animistic nineteenth-century Romanticism. As such, *Mein Kampf* is in collision with modernism, and competes with the various forms of futurism contemporary with Hitler. Rejected by the German expressionist artists, when he approached them early in his painterly career, Hitler retreated to an autistic form of realism, while evolving his ethics into a psychotic surrealism. The poet Andre Breton (1896–1966), one of the founders of surrealism, contemporary with Hitler, and for a time a collaborator with Trotsky (1879–1940), was forging an artistic vision which shows how the world might be seen from a largely other-worldly viewpoint. The *Manifeste du surréalisme* (1924) stated that surrealism is 'Thought dictated in the absence of all control exerted by reason, and outside all aesthetic or moral pre-occupations'. This is an idealized manifesto style, with other elsewhere matched by the 'pure thought' associated with the 'rhetoric of the irrational', especially as promulgated by those absorbing Italian futurism. Although surrealism is fundamentally different from the world of Hitler, his pulse of disorder accesses surrealistic types of formalized chaos, particularly through German expressionism. Although Hitler was later averse to the movement because of his teenage rejection at its hands, he seems to have internalized and inverted some of its rationality. He was like a living fantasy, turning nightmares into devices to seduce the unwary. The definition of literature here has to account for the conversion of literature into history and the reversion of history into narrative, from child to adult, from adult to child.

Mein Kampf could be thought to be parodied in this stolid artifice by the rhinoceros army in Jean de Brunhoff's *Babar* (1934). The composer Poulenc set *Babar* to music, and he thus constructed a development for melodrama. In sung melodrama, there is the use of the midpoint between spoken drama and operatic or Leider performance of words to music, with instrumental accompaniment. Long before, Rousseau had written the libretto and composed music for a naturalist melodrama; and we can see in his philosophy a similarity to motifs in *Babar*. Rousseau's natural world was that of the noble savage conceiving a perfect order untainted by false civilization. Hitler's philosophy was a counterfeit and inversion of such naturalism, with his imaginings fantasizing elements that his autobiography enfolded into the re-ordered world of his psychosis.

d. *Hitler's Psychotic Modernism*
The route I have taken is to propose that relevant modernisms are in some respects (and only in some) subsets of, as well as departures from, varieties of Romanticisms. This relational property enables one to explain how Wagner's and Hitler's differing, yet overlapping, frequently reactionary approaches to the Romantic ingredients of modernisms

can facilitate psychotic attenuation of the mythologies and realisms associated with modernisms. I have argued that indeterminacy is already a central feature underlying, or implicit in, nineteenth-century modernisms. If this indeterminacy is married with such attenuation, unpredicted effects can emerge. Crudely expressed, such considerations lead to the strange situation that someone whom most regard as a madman took over most of Europe, with the support and popular adulation of much of his chosen native nation—Germany.

In relation to this, Rosenbaum (1998) has drawn attention to the presuppositional focus of works which attempt to assess Hitler's psychology, for example, by plausibly criticizing Bromberg's and Small's (1983) study which claims to explain Hitler's anti-Semitism by reference to his sexual problems. The present chapter aims to side-step some such clinical claims, while not necessarily disputing them. It seeks to do this by examining some of Hitler's statements and the events themselves.

There are notorious problems internal to attempts to retroject from empirical events in the external world a version of an individual's mentality. Nevertheless, it seems rather obvious that these problems are largely irrelevant as objections to the demonstrable causal connections between the external world ruled, and influenced, by Hitler. I argue that we can enter this domain of psychohistory without assuming a particular theory about the origins of Hitler's functioning identities. So the present chapter has avoided a review and introduction of psychiatric or psychoanalytical terminology applied to Hitler, leaving such scrutiny to others. Nevertheless, this chapter deploys the premise that philosophy can contribute to interpretation of Hitler's identity and the history of which he is part. In certain senses, this priority includes a conjunction of philosophical psychology with political philosophy. Both of these specialties can benefit from engagement with the historical data and theories. The central issue here is that, central to Hitler's biography is a function of German society's collective nazification, not least in the relation of each to the influence of *Mein Kampf.*

Nor was Hitler's sadistic attitude to the Jews only a product of his later aggression. Early on in *Mein Kampf* (Hitler 1992: 48, 53), using language which is traceable to him at the age of 15, before the First World War, he states:

> There were few Jews in Linz…their outward appearance had become
> Europeanized and had taken on a human look; in fact, I even took them

for Germans. The absurdity of this idea did not dawn on me because I saw no distinguishing feature but the strange religion...

Was there any form of filth or profligacy, particularly in cultural life, without at least one Jew involved in it? If you cut even cautiously into such an abscess, you found, like a maggot in a rotting body, often dazzled by a sudden light—a kike![7]

In a context which is difficult not to interpret as the desire to achieve extermination of the Jews, Hitler (1933: 60) concludes with a form of paranoid narcissism (in what seems a psychotic perversion of Romantic nineteenth-century narcissistic decadence), and, perhaps unconsciously, resorts to hebraism ('peoples'), by stating:

If with the help of his Marxist creed, the Jew is victorious over the other peoples of the world, his crown will be the funereal wreath of humanity and this planet will, as it did thousands[8] of years ago, move through the ether devoid of men.

Eternal Nature inexorably avenges the infringement of her commands.

Hence today I believe that I am acting in accordance with the will of the Almighty Creator: *by defending myself against the Jew, I am fighting for the work of the Lord.*

The reductionism of Hitler's first person pronoun, and the presupposed singularity of and for the 'Jew', betray a psychotic possible world launched by his false Romantic narcissism. If we adopt Freud even as a provisional and approximate sketch of some relevant distinctions, for example as delineated by Wollheim's (1971: 179-86) account of Freud's use of 'narcissism', we will be sensitive to Freud's location of the notion between the functions of the erotic and the death instinct. Without going any further here into these complex and partially unresolved areas, we nevertheless can locate sadism as an internal property of the relation of this dualism attached to the erotic. Within this focus, Hitler's egoism takes on the proportions of paranoia. Where the theory is over- or under-determined for the evidence, we should not only consider the prospect of the cause being in the limitations of psychological theory, but also that we have entered a chaotic conceptual space. This is the exceptional class into which Hitler falls, as a

---

7. The English translation masks the strength of the German original: 'Sowie man nur vorsichtig in eine solche Geschwulst hineinschnitt, fand man, wie die Made im faulenden Leibe, oft ganz geblendet vom plötzlichen Lichte, ein Judlein.'

8. 'Thousands' was changed to 'millions' in the second edition.

conjunction of individuality and the displacement of human rights, embroiled with the puzzling way in which this conjunction led to his own violation of his own 'right' to live: suicide. To what extent this masochistic ending was originally mapped into the sadism of Hitler's narcissistic responses to his origins is a vexed question. The answer surely not only pertains to his response to nineteenth-century Europe's culture and his childhood, but also to his contemporary society.

A problem within the perspective of Hitler's autobiography as propaganda, in connection with anti-Semitism in the German people, is the question of, to what extent did Germany's people's individual exercise of choice to oppose Hitler become compromised by threats against the individual? Clearly, beyond this there is the issue of whether or not such a threat is a justifiable ground for consent to Hitler's policy, even where death for the dissenter is the outcome. Certainly, most people will understandably conclude that it is not rational to expect individuals under such duress to act in a way which goes beyond their own survival interest. And the typical sort of response to criticism of the German people in this very disturbed historical context is to consider it a sufficient ground, for compliance with Hitler's public policies, that they were scared and life was at risk. When this is the case, it is evident that one is not in a position to criticize.

The reason for mentioning this scenario, however, is not only to acknowledge its historical accuracy for a range of situations, but also to point up the circumstance where this was not a true account of the pressure on the individual. Rather, for much of the time there was unpressured initiative on the part of many Germans to associate with the Hitler phenomenon and enhance its glorification. An upshot of this state of affairs is that Hitler's autobiography and biography are not properly conceivable solely as the function of his individuality, but also of society's responses. Hitler's individuality and control are important; yet they should also be apprehended as functions of a collective context: the nazification of a society of individuals.

Accordingly, with regard to the relationship between Hitler and his influence, such states of affairs cannot be reduced to the explanation that the German people were always misled by deception or were unwilling partners, as Ian Kershaw (1998: 482-84) demonstrates in his biography of Hitler. In view of the importance of his research, it is worth quoting him at some length; he states, in a summary of more detailed analyses, that:

Many of the neo-conservative intellectuals whose ideas had helped pave the way for the Third Reich were soon to be massively disillusioned. Hitler turned out for them not to be the mystic leader they had longed for in their dreams. But they had helped prepare the ground for the Führer cult that was taken up in its myriad forms by so many others. And their way of thinking—rejection of 'ideas of 1789' [the French Revolution] and the rationality and relativism of modern thought in favour of a deliberate plunge into conscious irrationalism, the search for meaning not in individuality but in the 'national community', the sense of liberation through a 'national awakening'—was the platform on which so much of the German intellectual elite bound itself to the anti-intellectualism and primitive populism of Hitler's Third Reich.

Hardly a protest was raised at the purges of university professors under the new civil service law in April 1933 as many of Germany's most distinguished academics were dismissed and forced into exile...

The symbolic moment of capitulation of German intellectuals came with the burning on 10 May of the books of authors unacceptable to the regime. 'Here sinks the intellectual basis of the November revolution to the ground,' proclaimed Goebbels at the spectacular scene at the Opernplatz in Berlin, as 20,000 books of poets and philosophers, writers and scholars were cast into the flames. But [this] had not been initiated by Goebbels. It had been prompted by the leadership of the German Students' Association... Not just Nazi organizations had taken part. Others on the nationalist Right had also been involved. Local authorities and police had voluntarily assisted in clearing out the books to be burned from public libraries. University faculties and senates had hardly raised a protest of note at the 'Action'. Their members, with few exceptions, attended the bonfires...

Scarcely any of the transformation of Germany during the spring and summer of 1933 had followed direct orders from the Reich Chancellery... But [Hitler] was the main beneficiary... [T]he Führer cult was established...throughout state and society, as the very basis of the new Germany... Already in Spring 1933, the personality cult surrounding Hitler was burgeoning, and developing extraordinary manifestations... 'Hitler-Oaks'..., trees whose ancient pagan symbolism gave them special significance to *volkisch* nationalists and Nordic cultists, were planted in towns and villages all over Germany. Towns and cities rushed to confer honorary citizenship on the new Chancellor.

The neo-conservatives' rejection of the French revolutionary ideas of 1789 was itself an attempt to reverse aspects of modernism, deform a Romanticism, and restore in their places the earlier eighteenth-century neo-Classicism. In certain respects, neo-Classicism is a subspecies of Romanticism, though quite different from post-revolutionary

Romanticism. By unifying approaches developed variously by Stendahl and Baudelaire, we may conclude that an epicentre of such contrasts is that, for the neo-Classicist, the *past* is the baseline of sensibility, while for the post-revolutionary Romantic, the *present* is, though clearly Baudelaire was attracted to past elitisms, while later writers were impelled to democratize the present.

Neo-conservatives of 1933 paraded, what Kershaw accurately terms, their 'conscious irrationalism' as a self-conceived form of Classical rationalism. This blend is indicative of what I have earlier spoken of as a type of modernist indeterminacy. It can be isolated as the concept of a counterfeit—here of modernism, and as a generalizable concept. Against this counterfeit one can contrast, for example, Baudelaire's implicit and positive use of the genuine thing—modernist indeterminacy. Although, in the earlier part of this chapter we have found that Baudelaire precisely locates some pulses of significant insight in the past, so as to produce new insights, yet German neo-conservatives failed to isolate actual history; and they imposed on it a counterfeit.

Since Kershaw's analysis here concerns 1933, it is hardly justified to talk of coercion that would have prevented free choice in such a Germany; and he identifies voluntary responses to have participated in such extremism. This at least shows that humans engage in the implementation of concepts of which they may only have a counterfeit. Or that the identity of human consciousness is susceptible of voluntary indoctrination of which the agent has no decision-procedure for identifying error. Or, that humans disengage from applying ethical criteria when contrary social circumstance attracts them through opportunist Romanticism. No doubt, each of these, and others, intermingle in an unholy hybrid. Moreover, these options and judgments need to be qualified by the function of complacency stimulated, or created by, a population's growing economic satisfaction subsequent to the dire economic conditions to which Germany had been subject since the First World War. Nevertheless, it appears to be untenable to employ such a consideration, though substantial, to deflect the above conclusions, that the German nation was largely composed of willing adulants of a Führer cult which amounted to a barely disguised form of madness. Certainly we must accord the indigenous function of anti-Semitism in a number of European countries including Germany, disgusting though it is, as an unquestioned element in a partially uninterrogated worldview which, we have seen from the earlier part of this chapter, stems from at least a previous century's indoctrination. Yet even this is not sufficient to allow that the German population was anaesthetized from ethical reflection enough to be blind to the programme for extermination of the Jews, so publicly stated, for example, in *Mein Kampf* from the mid-1920s.

Obviously, blindness of this type, if sometimes not degree, extends outside of Germany to other apparently tolerant countries such as England. It was Harold Nicholson who reported of his London Club members for 1939, that a sample of English aristocrat members, given the choice, would have explicitly selected Hitler as ruler in England rather than allow an English socialist into power. France, though many opposed anti-Semitism, found itself with a Vichy Government (partly due to a power-base which had Romantic hopes for a monarchist revival) which, later in 2 June 1942, went to considerable lengths to implement with extreme severity the harsh racist law *Statut des juifs*, and the transportation to concentration camps, not content to leave it to the Germans (Kedward 1978: 164-67). Nor is such influence to be regarded as a temporal island untouched by our presents: the year is 1987, the place is The Johns Hopkins University, and a Belgian doctor in his early thirties, arriving as guest at a private dinner, confidently announces to fellow diners that there is a smell of Jews here, though the Jewish friends present were not encouraged to leave.

In a world in which such psychotic fantasy becomes pragmatic success, the notion of ethical human sensibility is inverted to a counterfeit subverting, yet proclaiming, it. In Germany, the neo-conservatives' counterfeit Romanticism, tied to a misappropriation of neo-Classicism—and perception of its ancient antecedents—had had shocking consequences. Fundamental to this is the blindness of (im)moral agents to the significance of their/our own concepts, and the counter-intuitive identities of their own contingencies.

It seems that the causal dynamics of such patterns, when associated with indeterminacy, have a habit of imitating their opposites. Kershaw is certainly correct to note the conscious irrationalism of such German people for the period circa 1933. But if one reads such writers, they believe themselves to be models of rationality. So we humans can ape the opposite of that which we conceive as what we are. That is to say, we should construct a concept of a counterfeit as true belief. This itself requires prior attention to what it is to be falsehood.[9] If we apply such a

---

9.　For an in investigation of falsehood which could be presupposed here, see Denyer 1991.

scenario to the Third Reich, all hell lets loose; and did.

Kershaw's subtle analysis proves that, regarding extorting individual's obedience from the mass of German citizens, in 1933 Hitler was largely in a stand-off state. With psychiatric relevance, it is worth noting that he was already extraordinarily unpredictable and inaccessible, to all but three of his colleagues, and even at this stage he was not usually available until after lunchtime, not because of affairs of state, but with his being obsessed with fantasy films in his private cinema. Kershaw shows that, at this time, a great part of the German people were possessed with devotion to him to the point of violating some human rights of noncompliant people.

e. *Chaos in Psychotic Modernism*

Kershaw's (1998) monumental biography of Hitler is conceived as a structuralist analysis. Although this approach has important merits, it is worthwhile probing further to combine other elements with this framework. In a previous section (Modernisms and Hitler), I introduced a notion of chaos, and elsewhere (Gibson 2000a). I propose that it is a feature of cultural indeterminacy—the sort of indeterminacy which the foregoing locates in some nineteenth-century culture.

I should like to add to this sketch by making the proposal, outlined only impressionistically here, that chaos subsumes institutional order, as an internal property of that order. This is both a generalized thesis, and it disposes a peculiar twist in relation to Hitler. But first, we should note that, for some people, it is paradoxical to associate order with chaos in certain ways. Perhaps this relation can be convincingly explained, to such a puzzled response, by presenting a facet of a theoretical explanation, though the present context permits only a little space to develop it. Does not chaos exhibit ordered principles? Are there not laws of chance? Are there not chaotic systems? Do we not find that coin-tossing series produce virtual symmetry over long sequences? Consequently, internal to chaos there are forms of order. Just as there are law-like principles internal to chaos (such as topological entropy), much of such mathematics comes from areas outside of it.

Perhaps we may take the following either as an analogy, live metaphor, or the basis of a structural relation between order and chaos. Just as there are law-like principles of chaos—order matched to map disorder—so I propose that political systems of a given range are associated in relevant ways with chaos. As with chaos and order in which it is perplexing to observe what it is for a chaos to have a systematic representation, so with particular social systems which appear to be highly ordered, they are actually chaotic (either instead of or as well as). No doubt the relations between order and chaos vary in different functions and contexts, so the foregoing is a conceptual policy with varying realizations and scopes. Clearly there are many distinctions between formal mathematical order, social regimentation and deviant nazified forms of the latter; yet there are sufficiently well-attested trans-contextual principles of chaotic systems applicable to organic, social situations to warrant appropriate degrees of generalization over distinct domains, though chaos theory is at an early stage of development.

With these provisos, a scenario can be lifted out from the foregoing. It is a paradox of social and institutional order that chaos is associated with it at junctures where it is deemed absent. Enthusiasts of order will demur from the claim that chaos is internal to order, and maintain that such disorder is a product of external imposition on a closed felicitous system. This does not at all explain nor allow for the foregoing state of affairs in which chaos and chance have law-like properties at least reminiscent of, and in particular contexts internally manifest, order. We can infer from accurate depiction of these states that it is not tenable to conclude from the presence of order that it implies the absence of chaos.

I should like, then, to apply these considerations to Hitler's own biography and the nazification of Germany. A full treatment would require a separate book, but a few remarks in closing are in order. The phenomena and interpretation which comprise the subject of this chapter have already given a firm place for indeterminacy in modernism *as* a subspecies of Romanticism. It was noticed that the neo-conservatives who were one of the principle causes of Hitler's succession to a supreme position of power in Germany themselves displayed features of irrationality while intending to acclaim the opposite. Hitler's own speeches and writings are a baffling mixture of order and chaos. The implementation of his policies was a disguised form of chaos paraded as the retrieval of ancient order. The point to make in this familiar territory is that this is not merely a consequence of things going wrong at the hands of Hitler, though they did. Rather, we should initially attend to the internal potential of any ordered (or over-ordered) system: it has within it the properties of chaos as a function of that order. That is to say, within almost all ordered systems there is an inbuilt property of chaos, and not only potential for instability, disorder and its misuse.

Politicians view their pragmatisms as the art of the possible. Politics is also the practice of implementing order to regulate a perceived chaos. If a politician such as Hitler envisages that the elimination of chaos will be achieved by the imposition of total order, his politics will eventually fail. A reason for this is the principle that, in the relevant sense, chaos itself is an internal property of order. Evidently, this principle satisfies social conditions which are a complex requisite whereby order itself can be used to facilitate freedom. This is tantamount to the notion that the social and empirical states which instantiate chaos are themselves the conditions according to which freedom is operable. Hitler's attempts to close off freedom, therefore, were based on misconceptions of what order is. Of course, the imposition of militarized order will achieve much to eliminate, for a time, physical freedom, and to some degree by indoctrination, the freedom of people. But the present line of argument suggests that there is an internal fatigue function in such order. For example, we could scan catastrophe mathematics into Nazi order, and note how the negation of a system can be achieved by its internal properties.

In a certain sense, Hitler's suicide was a sort of counter-intuitive function of the order that led to it. And it is a deep matter to integrate this biographical function with the various attempts, some successful, and perhaps at least the last imposed, of his various women partners to commit suicide.

It is by now trite to align the end of Wagner's *Ring* with Hitler's demise, but the narcissism of both, the inferential contingent instabilities and indeterminacies within the *Ring*'s plot, together with Wagner's (other literary) and Hitler's varying anti-Semitic appropriation of order misleadingly to depict, obscure or advertise the chaos within mind and life, enabled the nineteenth-century birth of modernism to be terminated in a chaotic counterfeit of order. Neither was content merely conceptually to disallow a Romantic myth of the wandering Jew. The indigenous anti-Semitism in their Europe may be comparable with, for example, the classical and mediaeval worlds' attitude to women, and thus taken as a piece of worldview to whose obscenity they were partially blind. However, Wagner's lack of self-criticism regarding such a perverse view, and not least his uncritical Romanticized reflections on

Schopenhauer's 'world as will' philosophy, amount to a warning to us all, to interrogate our assumptions with the perceptions of a cultural context other than our own. The vacuous mythology which presupposes that there is an autonomous nationalist identity with its own aesthetic and ethical identities may have been a misappropriation by Hitler of Wagner's music. But such false reductionism is aided by Wagner's autobiography *My Life* and his *Judaism in Music*, to the detriment of the Jews.

Hitler was explicitly concerned to impose on freewill in such matters. As Hitler (1933: 430-31) remarked in *Mein Kampf*, immediately after contrasting his speeches with the alleged Jewish 'lying dialectical skills and suppleness' of 'the Marxist movement', in which he compared the effects of a speech of his with a performance of Wagner's *Parsifal*, and the importance of this opera being enacted in Bayreuth, as opposed to anywhere else in the world:

> In all these cases we have to do with an encroachment upon man's free-dom of will... In this wrestling bout of the speaker with the adversaries he wants to convert, he will gradually achieve that wonderful sensitivity to the psychological requirements of propaganda.

BIBLIOGRAPHY

Baudelaire, C.
    1975   *Salon de 1846* (ed. D. Kelley; Oxford: Clarendon Press).
    1996   *Les fleurs du mal* (C. Pichois; Collection Poesie, 85; Paris; Gallimard, 2nd edn [1861]).

Beckett, S.
    1969   *Sans* (Paris: Les Editions de Minuit [*Lessness*; London: Calder & Boyars, 1970]).

Börne, L.
    1821   *Die Wage: Eine Zeitschrift für Burgerleben, Wissenschaft und Kunst* (2 vols.; Frankfurt am Main: In der Hermannschen Buchhandlung, 1818–21; Tübingen: Bei Heinrich Laupp, 1821).

Bowie, M.
    1993   *Psychoanalysis and the Future of Theory* (The Bucknell Lectures in Literary Theory, 9; Oxford: Basil Blackwell).

Breton, A.
    1924   *Manifeste du surréalisme: Poisson soluble* (Paris: Sagittaire).

Bromberg, N., and V.V. Small
    1983   *Hitler's Psychopathology* (New York: Random House).

Brunhoff, J. de
    1934   *Babar* (Paris: Hachette).

Cheyette, B.
1993   *Constructions of the Jew in English Literature and Society* (Cambridge: Cambridge University Press).

Crepet, E.
1906   *Charles Baudelaire: Etude biographique d'Eugène Crepet, revue et mise à jour par Jacques Crepet, suivie des Baudelairiana d'Asselineau, recueil d'anecdotes publie pour la première fois in-extenso, et de nombreuses lettres adressées à Ch. Baudelaire* (Paris: Leon Vanier).

Denyer, N.C.
1991   *Language, Thought and Falsehood in Ancient Greek Philosophy* (London: Routledge).

Eitzen, P. von
1602   *Brief Description and Account of a Jew Named Ahasuerus* (Leiden).

Eliot, T.S.
1951   'Baudelaire', in *idem*, *Selected Essays* (London: Faber & Faber): 419-30.

Epstein, R.L., and I.M.L. D'Ottaviano
1995   'A Paraconsistent logic: J_3', in R.L. Epstein (ed.), *The Semantic Fondations of Propositional Logics*; New York: Oxford University Press, 2nd edn): 349-73.

Florence, J.
1986   *Mallarmé, Manet and Redon* (Cambridge: Cambridge University Press).

Gibson, A.
1997   'God's Semantic Logic: Some Functions in the Dead Sea Scrolls', in S.E. Porter and C.A. Evans (eds.), *The Scrolls and the Scriptures: Qumran Fifty Years After* (RILP, 3; JSPSup, 26; Sheffield: Sheffield Academic Press): 68-106.

1998   'Modern Philosophy and Ancient Consciousness: I Think, therefore I Am Gendered?', in M.A. Hayes, W.J. Porter and D. Tombs (eds.), *Religion and Sexuality* (Studies in Theology and Sexuality, 2; RILP, 4; Sheffield: Sheffield Academic Press): 22-48.

2000a   *God and the Universe* (London: Routledge).
2000b   *Text and Tablet* (Aldershot: Ashgate).

Hacking, I.
1995   *Rewriting the Soul* (Princeton, NJ: Princeton University Press).

Heine, H.
1982   *The Complete Poems of Heinrich Heine* (trans. H. Draper; Oxford: Oxford University Press).

Hitler, A.
1992   *Mein Kampf* (trans. R. Manheim; intro. D.C. Watt; London: Pimlico) originally 2 vols.; *Mein Kampf: Eine Abrechnung Amman* (1925) and *Mein Kampf: Die Nationalsozialistische Bewegung* (1926) later in 1 vol. (1930).

Holland, E.
1994   *Baudelaire and Schizoanalysis* (Cambridge: Cambridge University Press).

Holst, L.
1821   *Judenthum in allen dessen Theilen* (Mainz: n.p.).

Jacobs, R.L.
    1979   'Introduction', in R. Wagner, *Three Wagner Essays* (London: Eulenburg Books).
Kedward, H.R.
    1978   *Resistance In Vichy France* (Oxford: Oxford University Press).
Keitel, E.
    1986   *Reading Psychosis* (Oxford: Oxford University Press).
Kelley, D.J.
    1964   'Charles Baudelaire's Salon de 1846' (2 vols.; PhD Thesis, University of Cambridge).
    1975   *Baudelaire: Salon de 1846* (ed. D. Kelley; Oxford: Clarendon Press).
Kershaw, I.
    1998   *Hitler 1889–1936: Hubris* (London: Allen Lane).
Lacoue-Labarthe, P.
    1994   *Musica Ficta: Figures on Wagner* (Stanford: Stanford University Press).
Lewy, C.
    1976   *Meaning and Modality* (Cambridge: Cambridge University Press).
Mallarmé, S.
    1914   *Un coup de dés jamais n'abolira le hasard* (Paris: Editions Gallimard).
Marinetti, F.T.
    1909   'Manifeste du Futurisme', *Le Figaro* 20 February. Reprinted New Haven, CT: Yale Library Associates, 1983.
Monk, R.
    1990   *Ludwig Wittgenstein: The Duty of Genius* (London: Cape).
Müller, H.
    1987   *Hamletmachine* (trans. C. Weber; London: Almeida Theatre Company).
Penrose, R.
    1997   *The Large, the Small and the Human Mind* (with A. Shimony, N. Cartwright and S. Hawking; ed. M. Longair; Cambridge: Cambridge University Press).
Quinet, E.
    1834   *Ahasvérus* (Paris: A. Guyot; London: Bailliere).
Ricks, C.
    1993   *Beckett's Dying Word* (Oxford: Oxford University Press).
Rosenbaum, R.
    1998   *Explaining Hitler* (London: Macmillan).
Sartre, J.-P.
    1947   *Baudelaire* (Paris: Editions Gallimard).
Shelley, P.B.
    1887   *The Wandering Jew: A Poem* (ed. B. Dobell; The Shelley Society's Publications, Second Series, 12; London: Reeves & Turner).
Smith, P.
    1998   *Explaining Chaos* (Cambridge: Cambridge University Press).
Sue, E.
    1845   *Le juif errant* (4 vols. in 2; Paris: Paulin).
Tanner, M.
    1979   'The Total Work of Art', in P. Burbidge and R.S. Sutton (eds.), *The Wagner Companion* (London: Faber & Faber): 140-224.

Wagner, R.
 1983   *My Life* (trans. A. Gray; ed. M. Whittall; Cambridge: Cambridge University Press) = *Mein Leben* (Munich: Paul List, corr. edn, 1976 [1963]).
 1910   *Judaism in Music: Being the Original Essay Together with the Later Supplement* (trans. E. Evans; London: Reeves [1848–49]).
White, J.
 1990   *Literary Futurism* (Oxford: Oxford University Press).
Wintle, C.
 1985   'Kontra Schenker: *Largo e mesto* from Beethoven's op. 10 No. 3', *Music Analysis* 4.1-2: 145-82.
Wollheim, R.
 1971   *Freud* (London: Collins).

METAPHYSICS AND THE HOLOCAUST

Louis P. Blond

An incongruous declaration appears as the title for this essay. One could legitimately question the connection between metaphysics and the Holocaust as an empirical event. The aim of this essay is to understand metaphysics as conceptual thought in relation to the identity and judgment of the object that it is describing. My intention is to comprehend the Holocaust, as object, through the fixing of its meaning within a metaphysical analysis. I am, therefore, suggesting that the Holocaust exists independently of a fixed conceptual meaning, as the event is known as object, in a general sense, without having acquired an adequate description. In the absence of an adequate description, meaning is capable of existing deprived of its object and it is for this reason that I describe the Holocaust as existing out of context with itself. Consequently, the Holocaust persists as an indeterminate object and remains as such 'unfinished'. As Friedrick Shlegel expressed the idea through the German nation: 'Germany is probably such a favourite subject for the essayist because the less finished a nation is, the more it is a subject for criticism and not for history'.[1] History concludes conceptualization by placing concepts and events in context, whereas 'unfinished' elements require further analysis to achieve their description.

Part of the Holocaust's resistance to conceptualization is due to the terms and disciplines involved. The 'Holocaust' appears to degrade metaphysical analysis, as the empirical event exceeds the movement of conceptual thought. Metaphysics, which has traditionally aligned itself with the good and the truth, subsequently risks debasement if it allocates a metaphysical meaning to horror. What shape would a metaphysics of horror take? Is a metaphysics of horror as valid as a metaphysics of the good? These question are beyond the scope of the

---

1. F. Shlegel, *Philosophical Fragments* (trans P. Firchow; Athenaeum Fragments, 26; Minneapolis: University of Minnesota Press, 1991), p. 21.

present paper; nevertheless, they exist as the uninvited guests of post-Holocaust thought which call into question the very validity of our unexamined metaphysical precepts.

One of the major fatalities of post-Holocaust metaphysics has been the philosophical system itself which, after a reading of Hegel, assumes a distorted form that incorporates 'all' into its geographical limit to the extent that 'nothing' exists external to itself. To exist is to be 'systematized', and in the modern philosophical idiom, 'system' and its associated descriptive terms ('totality' and the 'absolute') conjure up political nuances of totalitarianism which occur within our condensed conceptual framework. The association is made between philosophical thought and political action which, distilled as ideology, affects metaphysical totalities within the empirical world of politics. As Emil Fackenheim states, after the Holocaust 'Systems are gone':[2]

> The system, the form of presenting a totality to which nothing remains extraneous, absolutizes the thought against each of its contents and evaporates the content in thought. It proceeds idealistically before advancing any arguments for idealism.[3]

The terms 'system', 'absolute' and 'totality' acquire the same perfume. In presenting the 'system' as systematized thought, Adorno then nominates the system's interior as a 'totality'. However, if all is included within this interior (as nothing remains external), how then can we *see* or *think* an interior? The 'system' as totality assumes the air of uniformity and not heterogeneity. Adorno names this process as 'absolutization', a homogenous agency that aims at uniformity through the obliteration of the content of the world; the source of its heterogeneity.

If the essence of the totalizing system is integration, at the expense of content, Adorno is equally guilty of duplicating this action when subsuming the Holocaust under universal terms in order to fix its metaphysical meaning. Adorno describes the Holocaust as 'absolute integration',[4] which can be understood as the negation of individual experience for the good of the metaphysical absolute—the system. Individual

2. E.L. Fackenheim, *To Mend the World: Foundations of Future Jewish Thought* (New York: Schocken Books, 1982), p. 5, states after the Holocaust: 'Systems are gone. What remains…is the systematic labor of thought.'

3. Theodor W. Adorno, *Negative Dialectics* (trans. E.B. Ashton; New York: Seabury, 1973), p. 24.

4. Adorno, *Negative Dialectics*, p. 24.

phenomenon is thus absorbed into the 'all'. The Holocaust is seam-
lessly integrated into a fatality of absolute systems. Through defining
the Holocaust, philosophy once more expunges the event of its content.
Meaning is re-routed into a critique of a metaphysical absolute which
strangely circumvents the empirical object of the Holocaust in history.
It is necessary to reject this interpretation of the Holocaust and those
interpretations that depict the Holocaust as a rational process informed
by reason.[5] This can be accomplished using Adorno's own description
of the twofold character of the system that contracts the totalizing
superstructure which is offered to us as a depiction of absolute systems.

The system, whose most complete expression is found in Hegel,
allows for, even necessitates, internal microanalytics which require
objects to formulate themselves as self-reflective phenomena that offer
their own descriptions. Hegel's philosophical system requires objects to
present themselves and their own relations *to* the absolute. A political
reading of this absolute system would have us believe that the superstructure imposes itself upon the individual phenomena. A thinker such
as Rowan Williams would argue that Hegel's framework describes the
relation between phenomena and the absolute as one of relatedness.
Identity is produced through the interaction of the two elements.[6] A
thinker must remain aware of this pattern of thought and equate such a
configuration to the definition of 'system' that is upheld when discussing Nazism. A philosophical definition of 'system' includes space
for complex relations that do not necessarily imply absolute negation of
objective phenomena. In keeping with this, I wish to advance the possibility of a deeper understanding of the systematics of Nazism and its
relationship with genocide.

I describe the Nazi 'system' as a 'systematics', which is an order that
has the appearance of a system, yet contains unexamined or even irrational precepts. A systematics is not a philosophical system. Systematics correspond to process, classification and order which, as Adorno
points out, never profess the inner unity of their categorization. For this
reason, systematics are expelled from the philosophical definition of
system. Furthermore, Fackenheim's description of the character of the
'Nazi system' is one that identifies a systematics, not a wholly inte-

5.   A specific example of this interpretation would be Z. Bauman, *Modernity
and the Holocaust* (Cambridge, MA: Polity Press, 1991).
6.   R. Williams, 'Logic and Spirit in Hegel', in Phillip Blond (ed.), *Post-Secu-
lar Philosophy* (London: Routledge, 1998), pp. 116-30 (117).

grated, coherent system but an order containing internal paradoxes and elements of chaos that seek to paralyse life and thought within systems 'systematically calculated to deceive'.[7] If a system aims at deceit, then a schism has already been exposed and it seems reasonable to assume that the metaphysical meaning of Nazism remains undisclosed.

Cultured Nazism

Nazism aimed at the reawakening of German cultural values in the face of cultural decadence which, prior to the radicalization of German nationalism, stands as a coherent project within a wider analysis of German Romanticism. From Goethe to Nietzsche and beyond, various German thinkers and poets have rejected their decadent cultural epoch and sought to resurrect a true and natural German spirit. The strength and form of German Romanticism varies greatly, and I include Goethe here as an untypical and decidedly non-radical romantic who mediated his desires through the power of an ultimately benevolent God. However, the call for authenticity that Goethe utters is an emblematic war-cry. It is the cry for a devaluation of knowledge and the reawakening of a more primordial figure of man as deed:

> If we could only alter the Germans after a model of the English, if we could only have less philosophy and more power of action, less theory and more practice…let us remain in a state of hopeful expectation as to the condition of us Germans a century hence, and whether we shall then have advanced so far as to be no longer savants and philosophers but men.[8]

The early Nietzsche corroborates this aspiration with his comprehension of German culture in aesthetic terms. He reconfigures culture within the artistic sphere of men and is opposed to cultural definitions that correlate the German spirit with national or state interests. In reference to the Franco-Prussian war of 1870–71, Nietzsche criticizes a decadent cultural description which is precisely linked to national conquest:

7.   E.L. Fackenheim, *The Jewish Return into History* (New York: Schocken Books, 1978), p. 58.

8.   Johann Wolfgang Goethe, *Conversations of Goethe with Johann Peter Eckermann* (trans. J. Oxenford; New York: Da Capo Press, 1998), pp. 256-57; cf. p. 291, letter written 12 March 1828. This is the book of which Nietzsche exclaimed 'The best German book there is'.

> In the present case there can be no question of a victory of German cul-
> ture, for the simple reason that French culture continues to exist... Our
> culture played no part even in our success in arms. Stern discipline, natu-
> ral bravery and endurance, superior generalship, unity and obedience in
> the ranks...have nothing to do with culture. [9]

What this passage immediately reveals is the opposition which
Nietzsche, as Goethe before him, had to cultural definitions dependent
upon onto-political structures such as the state: in short what could be
defined as imperial culture.[10] Nietzsche also divulges the ultimate consequences of a cultural victory: for a culture to be victorious it must
supersede or destroy the conquered culture, at the very least, it must be
independent of it. Nietzsche, subsequently, offers his definition of true
culture: one that would contain a 'unity of artistic style in all the
expressions of the life of a people.'[11] It is, at this point, unclear as to
what 'artistic style' means, however, it is Nietzsche's insistence upon
unity that defines his opposition to a more contemptible modern culture.
Nietzsche resists the residue of styles which signify a culture in decay,
suggesting that German culture exists as the accretion of all the forms
and curiosities of all ages and climes—a uniformity of cultural sedi-
ment is not necessarily cultural unity. This Nietzsche names as cultural
philistinism:[12]

---

9. F. Nietzsche, *Untimely Meditations* (Cambridge: Cambridge University
Press, 1997), pp. 3-4.

10. It is worth noting that this definition is almost a mirror image of British cultural definitions at the time when Britain defined itself precisely in terms of natural
discipline, order and state destiny and justice.

11. Nietzsche, *Untimely Meditations*, p. 5. To enter into the Nietzsche debate is
not my present aim. Nevertheless, I do not take Nietzsche to be a proto-Nazi, for his
opposition to biological racism and anti-Semitism is present in his work. His use of
'race' is metaphysical. However, one can cite Derrida's question of him: 'A metaphysics of race—is this more or less grave than a naturalism or biologism of race?'
(Jacques Derrida, *De l'esprit, Heidegger et la question* [Paris: Galilée, 1987] pp.
118-19, as quoted in Martin Heidegger, *Nietzsche* [2 vols.; trans David Farrell
Krell; New York: HarperCollins, 1991], p. xxii).

12. *Bildungsphilister*. Nietzsche brags that this word 'has survived in the German language' since his essay. However, *Bildung* is a problematic word to render
into English: *Bild* has the meaning of 'picture' or 'image'; *bilden*, to shape, to form
and to educate; whereas *ungebildet* means 'uneducated' or 'uncultured'. F. Nietzsche, *On the Genealogy of Morals and Ecce Homo* (trans. W. Kaufman and R.J.
Hollingdale; New York: Vintage Books, 1969), pp. 276-77.

> [A] systematic and oppressive philistinism does not constitute a culture (*Bildung*), even an inferior culture, merely because it possesses system: it must always be the antithesis of a culture namely a permanently established barbarity. For that uniformity which is so striking in the cultivated people of Germany today is a unity only through the conscious or unconscious exclusion and negation of every artistically productive form and the demand of a true style. An unhappy contortion must have taken place in the brain of the cultural philistine: he regards as culture precisely that which negates culture, and since he is accustomed to proceed with consistency he finally acquires a coherent collection of such negations, a system of un-culture… If he is allowed to choose between a stylistically agreeable action and one of the opposite kind, he invariably elects the later, and because he always does so all his actions bear the same negative stamp. It is precisely this negative stamp that enables him to recognise the nature of the 'German culture' he has patented: whatever does not correspond to it he adjudges hostile and inimical to him.[13]

It thus becomes apparent that a system that does not aim at unity but aims at uniformity, is not a system at all but what I describe as 'systematics'. A systematic uniformity can only decipher itself as unity through a methodology of negation where non-uniform, extraneous elements experience negation. That this uniformity now renames itself as 'unity' and 'system', exposes the possession of the original term by reference to an inferior concept. The lower is superpositioned upon the higher. As Nietzsche expresses it, a 'system of un-culture' is proliferated.

What Nietzsche provides for us is a definition of negative cultural assertion—a proto-Nazi 'metaphysics', the higher moment here being the complicity with which a cultural definition can acquire an absolutist character:

> Much knowledge and learning is neither an essential means to culture nor a sign of it, and if needs be can get along very well with the opposite of culture, barbarism, which is lack of style or a chaotic jumble of all styles.[14]

Within this definition of systematic cultural barbarity parading as system lurks the embryonic essence of Nazism. 'Culture' and 'barbarity' become homogeneous terms, not because of the inherent weakness of German cultural achievements (let us not forget Goethe, Kant and Hegel, to name but a few), but due to the association of their achieve-

---

13. Nietzsche, *Untimely Meditations*, p. 8.
14. Nietzsche, *Untimely Meditations*, p. 8.

ment with barbaric ends. To align one's culture with state or national aims (alongside merely bad aesthetic references) is, for Nietzsche, to dedicate one's culture to illegitimate ends. Culture within the limits of a uniformity which expels difference through systematic negation is a dilution of the high with the poisonous waters of barbarism. As Nietzsche expresses, the high 'can get along very well' with what it is not—the barbaric.

The affirmation of this barbaric culture implies the assertion of contradictory values. Once this is understood, the contradictions between previously paradoxical concepts such as Nazi brutality and a Nazi cultural renaissance fall: the assertion of German culture requires the negation of other cultures which challenge its hegemony. The term 'cultured Nazi' contains no contradiction; in listening to Beethoven or Mozart and exterminating Jews, the 'cultural Nazi' can contribute to the one ideal—the extension of German culture.

Nietzsche saw this phenomenon present in German society in 1873. However, the metaphysical move involved in a systematics of negation is the leitmotif of both decadence and Nazism. The paradoxical moment occurs with the integration of Nietzsche's thought into Nazi ideology which gives birth to a new systematics of un-culture—but *un-culture* it is:

> All the great civilisations of the past became decadent because the originally creative race died out, as a result of contamination of the blood... The most profound cause of such a decline is to be found in the fact that the people ignored the principle that all culture depends on men, and not the reverse. In other words, in order to preserve a certain culture, the type of manhood that creates such a culture must be preserved... He who would live must fight. He who does not wish to fight in this world, where permanent struggle is the law of life, has not the right to exist.[15]

Hitler, quite in keeping with Romanticism, relocates culture in man. A decadent culture would separate man from his object, thus falsifying itself through a dualistic detachment from its source. To reposition culture, and hence Germany, correctly, one must resurrect the cult of man and preserve him as the site of culture and the nation. The antithesis of this formula is all too evident in Nazi horror where the preservation of the one necessitates the elimination of the other—systematic negation.

---

15. A. Hitler, *Mein Kampf* (Bombay: Jaicao Publishing House, 1988), p. 242.

This systematics can be clearly seen in the First Racial Definitions issued on 11 April 1933, where we can see the political consummation of this negative 'metaphysics':

> On the basis of paragraph 17 of the Law Regarding the Restoration of Professional Service of April 7, 1933, the following decree is issued:
>
> Addendum paragraph 3. (1) A person is to be regarded as non-Aryan, who is descended from non-Aryan, especially Jewish parents or grandparents. This holds true even if only one parent or grandparent is of non-Aryan descent. This premise especially obtains if one parent or grandparent was of Jewish faith. (2) If a civil servant was not already a civil servant on August 1, 1914, he must prove that he is of Aryan descent, or that he fought at the front, or that he is the son or the father of a man killed during the World War. Proof must be given by submitting documents (birth certificate and marriage certificate of the parents, military papers). (3) If Aryan descent is doubtful, an opinion must be obtained from the expert on racial research commissioned by the Reich Minister of the Interior.[16]

It is apparent that the definition is primarily a negative exclusive one, requiring proof for admittance into the bracketed category of 'Aryan', those remaining outside the bracket being 'non-Aryan'. Judgment is derived from the race of parents and grandparents and not the individual. The criminal judgment precedes definition as parent and grandparent are excluded from the definition which is aimed at offspring, yet the inherent tautology in the statements utilizes the forerunners of offspring to condemn their children to criminal activity.

A criminal definition of race is tautologically definable and inescapable; via being, one enters a racial category, and via a process of exclusion, all enter the category of non-Aryan. One has to prove oneself into Aryan existence.

Racial categorization is a tautology whose prerequisite for inclusion is existence. It becomes starkly clear that this carefully prepared definition has been constructed to provide no escape from cognomenation.

This is an explicitly example of the 'system of un-culture'. It proceeds negatively as an exposition of perfect form—just as a sculptor reduces stone to unveil an inherent beauty of structure, so Hitler is sculptor of the *Volk,* removing the heterogeneous elements that mask the strength of unity (or, rather, uniformity) of the nation. The homogeneous nature of Nazism can be seen only a year after this decree, at

16. P.R. Mendez-Flohr and J. Reinharz (eds.), *The Jew in the Modern World* (Oxford: Oxford University Press, 1980), p. 490.

the Nuremberg Party Convention of 1934 filmed by Leni Riefenstahl, where Hitler repeatedly makes reference to the gathering irrespective of class or caste or background, united only through the hearts of the people. The contrast of the language of inclusion with the faces of the pure German *Volk*, is a powerful reminder of the uniformity of the project.[17]

The above racial decree is a wholly more thorough process than a positive definition of 'Jewishness', requiring positive proof before inclusion into the targeted bracket. The decree provided a precedent in ontological definition, and one that could always be revisited in its vital structure of the 'non-defining' of criminals through the indirect routing of definition through parents whom, *a priori*, exist.

This dichotomy of Aryan/non-Aryan survived until 1935 as a highly effective definition aimed at the exclusion of Jews from public life, while not being unduly volatile in the eyes of the German populace.

'Metaphysical' Nazism

Nietzsche describes, and struggles with, a spiritual problem as it presented itself in his contemporary experience. As with all the thinkers of his tradition there remained a fundamental void in human life and worth, a problem that extended itself to all aspects of German and European life. If Germany was not well, then nor was Europe. One cannot ignore the angst of the times. Nietzsche located this problem in metaphysics and the corrosive affects of 'poor theology' which divides and internalizes the subject. A 'poor theology' would generate a fundamental dualism within the subject, one that separates man from his object—the world—and that which is most vital within the world—man. This condition of division and dissatisfaction is named as bad conscience.

There are two powers that preclude man from migrating toward a natural condition of vitality: the 'God of morality' and the 'God of metaphysics'. In *Thus Spoke Zarathustra*, Nietzsche defines the 'God of morality' as the God of conscience. This God subjects the conscience to its historic dilemma, forcing it to chose between good and evil. Nietzsche portrays morality as a process of internalization, whereby the conscience limits man's naturally aggressive vitality and turns it inward.

---

17. L. Riefenstahl (director), *Der Triumph des Willen* (1934).

The 'God of metaphysics' is a rationalized principle—the 'Author of the world'—a principle aligned to absolutes which claim an external viewpoint on the world. This is the God of other worlds, duality, which acts as a destructive power as the subject looses its will in the face of metaphysics. Before an active absolute the subject is but a passive participant.

For Nietzsche, it is due to the appearance of these two Gods that bad conscience results, causing the world to lapse into decadence, sickness and nihilism. Bad conscience is the morbid state caused by the internalization of man's aggressive subjectivity. Yet for Nietzsche these two Gods are not absolutes—they are false Gods that subjugate man's natural spirit to the prevailing power, or 'social conditions'. Bad conscience predominates when the social order is built upon the ancient theologies of worship that revealed these two Gods, and it is precisely these orders against which man must react.

Nietzsche, however he prepares the ground, locates the spiritual degradation he experienced within dualism. His solution is to reconnect the severed provinces of man, subject and world through recourse to unity. How the unity is achieved and what it would entail is not my immediate concern: at present I would like to focus on 'unity' as opposed to uniformity and a culture of systematic negation. Within unity there is a space for heterogeneity and difference. Nietzsche's aim would be to devalue the moral conscience (and the God thereof) and transfigure man into a vital subjectivity in full affirmation of the world that is.

If Nazism draws upon Nietzsche's philosophy, it does so with this aim in mind. Nazism grasps the problem as one of social order. A simple solution would be to reformulate the social order, accordingly, to liberate the aggressive subject. However, in order to achieve this aim Nazism maintains a connection with the metaphysical God in the form of the German ideal. Nietzsche devalues metaphysics and places spirituality firmly within the subject, a situation that does not occur in Nazism.

Nazism flounders upon the retention of the 'God of metaphysics'. Consequently, when morality is expelled the desired flight to primordial essence is burdened by 'metaphysical' ends. Nazism is a future philosophy that reduces all means to a future ideal:

> The man [the guiding star] who lays down the programme of a movement must consider only the goal. It is for the political leader to point out

the way in which that goal may be reached. The thought of the former will, therefore, be determined by those truths everlasting, whereas the activity of the latter must always be guided by taking practical account of the circumstances under which those truths have to be carried into effect.[18]

Such is the belief in his own ideals that Hitler stipulated that one has to 'renounce contemporary fame', as only 'posterity will grant them its acknowledgement'. Hitler considered his destiny to encompass the role both of political philosopher and of practical politician, he embodied idealistic greatness that must be carried through by the will and guile of the politician.

Hitler proposes an 'ethical' teleology that defines its ethics in terms of its end; the end is the Reich and the moral principle is the Reich. What occurs, as a result, is the eradication of ethics *per se*. To live a good life one devalues one's own life and the life of others, and lives for the future Germany. One collapses ethos and telos into the one principle. Morality, or the 'God of conscience' vanishes in the maintenance of His doppelganger, the 'metaphysical' ideal.

> We can not be disloyal to what has given us sense and purpose. Nothing will come from nothing if the development is not based on a greater order. This order was not given to us by an earthly superior, it was given to us by God who created our people.
> This is our vow tonight. Every hour, every day, think only of Germany, the people, the Reich, the German nation and the German people.[19]

This vision is achieved with reflective thought, the idea in the abstract. As Hitler repeats, there is only one thought—the German people. This thought has its empirical point of departure but its aim is an unqualified definition of the German people as pure form. What is strangely missing in this formula is 'reality' as a communication with the empirical world. To remove the division between dualities is a familiar project of German philosophy. However, in collapsing the abstract and empirical worlds into only an abstraction that, by definition, refuses completion, the abstract form is divorced from its source— the world. One becomes a mystic. This phenomenon is viewed through out the Nazi period in its romantic pageantry and epic sense of fantasy.

18. Hitler, *Mein Kampf,* pp 181-82.
19. Riefenstahl, *Der Triumph des Willen.*

The God of the German people lurks beneath the horizon. The over-coming of internalization and division that social realignment hoped to achieve cannot be realized. Any succession is undermined by a ground-less God that is detached from the social condition He hopes to affect. The formula is unstable and masks a fundamental dualism. To achieve the ideal, the subject has to submit to a new social order that demands configuration to the ideal. The subject is dissolved into the national destiny, the greater will of the *Volk*. For the individual, the triumph of the will proceeds with the surrendering of the will to the 'metaphysical' ideal. The 'metaphysical' ideal internalizes every subject. The new social order encompasses the people *en masse*, and guides them toward the ideal of the perfect German form. Bad conscience occurs at every step along the way as the populace are alienated by the metaphysical God they hoped to emulate—Germany.

In order to realize this ideal, one has to violate any relationship that remains with reality. For, as perfection is approached, any form that contradicts the perfect form suffers negation. An increasingly radical political extremism and fanaticism can never bridge the gap between empirical and ideal man. The nation can never liberate itself from bad conscience and from nihilism's vital structure of un-culture.

This form of negation, or 'absolute integration' as Adorno would phrase it, does not resemble integration into an absolute as mediated by truth. Negation of this degree corresponds to an ordered nihilism whereby the end to this 'metaphysical' prescription is the extermination of all extraneous elements which contravene the ideal form. Further-more, there is nothing in this formula to prevent the eradication of the German people themselves, a thought which remains coherent within Nazism's 'philosophy':

> The greatness of the one [political philosopher] will depend on the abso-lute truth of his idea, considered in the abstract... The significance of a political philosopher does not depend on the practical success of the plans he lays down but rather on their absolute truth and the influence they exert on the progress of mankind.[20]

One of the more abiding characteristics of the Holocaust is its affect upon language and various forms of thought which continue to inhabit our conceptual apparatus. To associate the Hitler's thought and the Holocaust with the language of philosophy and metaphysics is to asso-

20. Hitler, *Mein Kampf*, pp. 181-82.

ciate reason with irrational and emotive ends, and ultimately to give reason a nihilistic appellation. The use of reason that occurs within the modern idiom is one that associates reason within the subjective consciousness. Reason, as I have argued can be used to support 'system', 'process', 'order' and 'classification' without recourse to truth. Reason becomes a appliance to be used to achieve one's aims. It is this account of reason that allows Bauman to state:

> At no point of its long and tortuous execution did the Holocaust come into conflict with the principles of rationality. The 'Final Solution' did not clash at any stage with the rational pursuit of efficient, optimal goal-implementation. On the contrary, *it arose out of a genuinely rational concern, and was generated by bureaucracy true to its form and purpose.*[21]

To accept Nazism as a rational process informed by reason (and therefore metaphysics) one would have to accept certain premises within the Nazi agenda: that the Jews are not fit to live in Europe:

> Anti-Semitism based upon purely emotional grounds will find its expression in the form of pogroms [which are capricious and thus not truly effective]. Rational anti-Semitism, however, must pursue a systematic, legal campaign against the Jews, by the revocation of the special privileges they enjoy in contrast to the other foreigners living among us. But the final objective must be the complete removal of the Jews (*die Entfernung der Juden ueberhaupt*).[22]

If we further excavate this premise we discover the commonly held Nazi assertion that Jews are sub-human and, therefore, not fit to live among human beings. Irrationality lies at the base of all of Nazism's racial categories and to accept these assertions is to accept their irrational premise.

There is another account of reason mediated by truth which would provide a critique of this mode of thinking. An irrational premise does not become rational through the use of systematics and process. Nazism is the assertion of negative systematics that refuses unity and accepts only uniformity as integration. The eradication of the extraneous elements is merely consistent.

---

21. Bauman, *Modernity and the Holocaust*, p. 17.
22. Adolph Hitler to Adolph Gemlich, 'A Letter on the Jewish Question', 16 September 1919, cited in Mendez-Flohr and Reinharz (eds.), *The Jew in the Modern World*, p. 484.

THE NATURE AND SIGNIFICANCE OF RELATIONS BETWEEN THE HISTORIC PEACE CHURCHES AND JEWS DURING AND AFTER THE *SHOAH*

Melanie J. Wright

1. *Introduction*

As we enter the twenty-first century, Jewish–Christian relations, in terms of both the participation in dialogue between members of the traditions at popular, scholarly and institutional levels, and the study of Jewish–Christian encounter in specific historic and contemporary contexts, is broadening. There nevertheless remains in academic writing on the subject an almost exclusive concentration on relations between Jews and members of the three main subdivisions within Christianity—Catholicism, Orthodoxy and Protestantism. In this essay, I want to offer something of a supplement by focusing on relations between Jews and western Christians who regard themselves as 'neither Protestant nor Catholic';[1] members of the Historic Peace Churches (HPCs)—those Churches that identify themselves as Anabaptist[2] (such as the Men-

---

1.   W.A. Cooper, *A Living Faith: An Historical Study of Quaker Beliefs* (Richmond: Friends United Press, 1997), p. 71.

2.   Anabaptist means literally 're-baptizer' and was applied to the sixteenth-century radical reformers who argued that child baptism was insufficient and advocated voluntary adult baptism only. Anabaptist emphasis on voluntaryism and the radical separation of Church from State ensured the opposition of both Catholic and Protestant wings of Christianity, and for many years 'Anabaptist' was used widely and loosely as a term of abuse in both popular and academic discourse. F.H. Littell, *The Origins of Sectarian Protestantism: A Study of the Anabaptist View of the Church* (New York: Macmillan, 1964) notes that most writers have handled Anabaptism in one of two ways, either dismissing it as peripheral or basing their treatment upon hostile polemics (p. 139). (In its identification of Anabaptism with Protestantism, Littell's own work reflects a now dated trend in Anabaptist historiography.)

nonite[3] and Hutterite[4] Churches), or Quaker.[5] These groups are numerically insignificant perhaps, but the stories of their encounter with Jews are striking to anyone who knows about Jewish–Christian relations generally in the modern era.

2. *Historic Peace Churches*

Church historians and other scholars have variously labelled the phenomena I am styling Historic Peace Churches. Sociologist Max Weber designated them 'believers churches',[6] because of their traditional emphasis on a community of believers and no others. Adherents have themselves sometimes used this label,[7] but it can be problematic in dialogue contexts because it may be perceived as presumptuous (as is also the case with other ecclesiastical names like 'orthodox' or 'catholic'). In contrast, 'HPC' is a relatively neutral, descriptive epithet. It also has

3.   Anabaptist historiography is a focus of much debate (theories of polygenesis versus monogenesis), but the Mennonite churches traditionally trace their origins to the Dutch radical reformer, Menno Simons (1496–1561), who emerged as a leader of Anabaptist groups in the 1530s. Anabaptism's emphasis on the division of Church from State implied a denial of national boundaries in Church organization, and the Mennonite Church grew to have Swiss, Russian, Dutch and German branches.

4.   Jakob Hutter, executed in 1536, taught his persecuted followers, the 'Hutterites', to live in communities characterized by common ownership, drawing on Acts 2.4-5. In the 1920s the Hutterites were refounded in Europe (most early groups had migrated to North America to escape persecution) by Eberhard Arnold who founded what became known as the Rhön *Bruderhof* (literally, 'a place where brothers live') in Germany, 1927. See M. Baum, *Against the Wind: Eberhard Arnold and the Bruderhof* (Robertsbridge: Plough Publishing, 1998).

5.   The Religious Society of Friends grew out of groups of Seekers and radical reformers that proliferated during the era of the English Civil War. One early leader, George Fox (1624–91), stood trial for blasphemy in 1650 and told the judge to 'tremble at the word of the Lord'. The judge then denounced Fox and his associates as 'Quakers'. The title stuck, but members of the Society prefer the appellation 'Friends' (H. Gillman, *A Light That is Shining: An Introduction to the Quakers* [London: Quaker Home Service, 1988], p. 7).

6.   M. Weber, *The Protestant Ethic and the Spirit of Capitalism* (trans. T. Parsons; London: George Allen & Unwin, 1930), pp. 144-45.

7.   Note, e.g., D.F. Durnbaugh, *The Believers' Church: The History and Character of Radical Protestantism* (Scottdale, PA: Herald Press, 1985) and the recent Anabaptist and Brethren Churches sponsored series, the *Believers Church Bible Commentary* (also published by Herald Press in Scottdale, PA, and Waterloo, ON).

the advantage of being an expression that Anabaptists and Quakers have used to refer to themselves collectively since the 1930s, which is the period currently being considered.[8]

Despite their diverse cultural, geographical and theological origins, the HPCs share a number of common emphases that define them as a particular grouping within Christianity. The part these emphases have played in HPC relations with Jews, and the impact that relations with Jews have in turn had upon these features, is interesting and distinctive, so at the risk of labouring points, it seems useful to outline them briefly before going further.

a. *Radical Church–State Separation*

The HPC model of Church is of a voluntary, free association of believers.[9] In the sixteenth and seventeenth centuries, this view, combined with an emphasis on biblical texts characterizing the faithful as in the world but not of it,[10] brought members into conflict with the dominant concept of the state Church.[11] Anabaptists in particular still often speak of Christianity as 'fallen', the fall having occurred in the fourth century, when Emperor Constantine established Christianity as the supreme religion of the Mediterranean and western Roman world, persecuted dissenters, and 'endowed the Church with the powers of the sword'.[12] In the modern era, this central belief that Church and State should be separate is manifest in a range of behaviours. These include a reluctance to

8.   The title 'Historic Peace Churches' can be traced to the 'Conference of Historic Peace Churches' held in Kansas in 1935. Quakers, Mennonites and Brethren came together to discuss means of furthering common principles and formulating joint strategies for gaining legal exemption from military service in the event of a second world war. See H.S. Bender, 'Society of Friends', in H.S. Bender *et al.* (ed.), *The Mennonite Encyclopedia* (5 vols.; vols. I–IV, Hillsboro, KS: Mennonite Brethren Publishing House; vol. V, Scottdale, PA: Herald Press, 1955–90), IV, pp. 561-65.

9.   Claus Felbinger, writing in 1560, asserted that 'God wants no compulsory service', quoted in W.R. Estep, *The Anabaptist Story* (Nashville: Broadman Press, 1963), p. 143.

10.   E.g. Jn 15.18-19.

11.   In this respect, it is clearly inaccurate to regard Anabaptists and Quakers as mainline Protestants—both Martin Luther and Jean Calvin envisaged a form of government which embraced Church and Nation.

12.   V. Green, *A New History of Christianity* (Stroud: Sutton Publishing, 1998), p. 24.

use secular legal systems, abstention from the swearing of oaths,[13] voting in elections or paying taxes (e.g. church tithes), and a refusal to serve as a magistrate or similar civic officer.

b. *Commitment to Non-Resistance/Pacifism*

Non-resistance or pacifism is another consequence of the conviction that true Christians are not owned by the world. For early Anabaptist leader Conrad Grebel (1524), Christians 'must reach the fatherland of eternal rest, not by overcoming bodily enemies with the sword, but by overcoming spiritual foes'. They 'use neither the worldly sword nor engage in wars...among them taking human life has ceased entirely'.[14] Similarly, the Society of Friends' first corporate statement was pacifist: 'We do testify to the world that the Spirit of Christ...will never move us to fight and war against any man with outward weapons, neither for the Kingdom of God nor for the kingdoms of this world'.[15] Practically, this has led to a refusal or reluctance on the part of HPC members to serve in the armed forces during both war- and peace-time. It can also be taken to imply an avoidance of any activity which might sustain war (such as working in munitions-related industries or providing medical aid on the battlefield) and an obligation to undertake mediation work in order to avert conflict.

c. *Implicit Theology*

For HPC members, faith is not verbalized, but lived: 'Just as the body without the spirit is dead, so faith without works is also dead'.[16] Not only is systematic theology less important than action, it may be regarded as positively dangerous—a challenge to the necessity for the individual Christian to apprehend directly and respond to G-d's will. In the context of a study like this one, the emphasis on *living faith* (*lebendiger Glaube* in Anabaptist texts) means that we cannot expect to find

13. 'It was Christ's command that we should not swear', explained G. Fox (*Quaker Faith and Practice: The Book of Christian Discipline of the Yearly Meeting of the Religious Society of Friends [Quakers] in Britain* (London: Britain Yearly Meeting, 1995], § 20.49). This principle derives from Mt. 5.37; Jas 5.12.

14. Quoted in Durnbaugh, *The Believers' Church*, p. 256.

15. Quoted in Cooper, *A Living Faith*, p. 107.

16. Jas 2.26. The HPCs' emphasis on being 'doers of the word' (Jas 1. 22) distinguishes them clearly from Lutheran Protestantism with its appeal to justification by faith.

much in the way of formal treatises outlining HPC theologies of Judaism and the Jewish people. Sources equivalent to those found in mainstream Christian groupings simply do not exist. However, this does not necessarily mean that Anabaptists and Quakers do not wrestle with issues in Jewish–Christian relations. Instead of searching in vain for documents produced by doctrinal committees, we must look for the implicit theology embedded in personal writings such as journals, diaries, and memoirs. Moreover, since for the HPCs faith is lived, and people's life-stories are often conceived of as being religious teachings or signs,[17] it will also be appropriate to attend to the actions of Anabaptists and Quakers during our chosen period: What attitudes or theologies are attested by behaviour (individual and group) in relation to Jews?

d. *Egalitarian Ecclesiology*
Like the common emphasis on implicit theology, the HPCs' egalitarian ecclesiologies impact on attempts to investigate relations with Jews. Anabaptists and Quakers radicalized the widespread Reformation notion of the 'priesthood of all believers'. In simple terms, they share a rejection of both sacerdotalism and clericalism (the latter sometimes more theoretical than actual). So, Anabaptist groups have ministers and some have bishops (but select them by lot and for temporary periods only); the Society of Friends goes further and many Friends' churches do not have any ordained ministers or formally recognized, trained leaders.[18]

To a certain extent, the Society of Friends and Anabaptist churches we see today arose from attempts to form a degree of coherence from diversity. However, their retention of loose, fluid authority structures, coupled with an extremely 'low church' approach to ministry and leadership roles, means that, unlike most denominations, HPCs do not

---

17. See section on 'suffering', below, and for a modern example of the narrative approach in a Hutterite work, M. Burn (ed.), *Outcast But Not Forsaken: True Stories from a Paraguayan Leper Colony* (Rifton, NY: Plough Publishing, 1986).

18. See *Faith and Practice*, §27.35–27.36. Some North American meetings (called 'pastoral meetings') do have ministers and programmed worship, but this is a relatively late, nineteenth-century development. There was no formalized ministerial preparation until the establishment of the Earlham School of Religion in 1960 (Cooper, *A Living Faith*, p. 81.)

have any mechanisms for the imposition of unified teachings on relations with Jews—or any other issues.

e. *Suffering*

Finally, all HPCs to some extent define themselves in relation to historical experiences of persecution. In the Society of Friends, this is illustrated by the very name of the Britain Yearly Meeting's[19] standing executive committee which is known as 'Meeting for Sufferings', a designation stemming from the recording by this committee of the sufferings and persecutions of seventeenth- and eighteenth-century Quakers. The current version of the book of discipline of British Friends, *Faith and Practice*, includes records of early tribulations and martyrdoms, most famously that of Mary Dyer.[20] *Faith and Practice* is by far the most widely known and used Quaker text, found in all meeting houses and a majority of Quaker homes. Individuals receive a copy when entering into membership of the Society. Friends are formally advised to read it[21]—and those who do will develop a sense of belonging to a community that has suffered.

If nearly all Quakers possess a copy of *Faith and Practice* (or its equivalent), Hutterites have carried with them across the world the *Chronicle of the Hutterian Brethren* (*Grosse Geschichtbuch*) and Mennonites and Amish, the *Martyrs' Mirror* (*Martelaersspiegel*).[22] The Hutterian *Chronicle* recounts some 2175 sixteenth-century martyrdoms. Likewise, the *Mirror*, compiled in 1660 by Tieleman Jansz van Braght,

---

19. Britain Yearly Meeting in session is the final constitutional authority of The Religious Society of Friends in Great Britain, the Channel Islands and the Isle of Man.

20. *Faith and Practice*, §19.18. Mary Dyer was twice sentenced to death and brought to the scaffold in Boston. She was finally executed in 1660 for her refusal to obey laws banning Quakers from entering Massachusetts. On the history of Meeting for Sufferings in securing relief from the obligation to swear oaths, pay tithes to support the established Church, etc., see §7.01.

21. *Faith and Practice*, §1.02.

22. The English-language versions of these texts are: *The Chronicle of the Hutterian Brethren [Grosse Geschichtbuch]* (trans. and ed. The Hutterian Brethren; Rifton: Plough Publishing, 1987), and T.J. van Braght and J.F. Sohn (trans.), *The Bloody Theater or Martyrs Mirror of the Defenseless Christians who Baptised Only upon Confession of Faith, and who Suffered and Died for the Testimony of Jesus, their Saviour, from the Time of Christ to the Year A.D. 1660* (Scottdale, PA: Herald Press, 5th edn, 1950).

contains over 1000 pages detailing the death and torture of martyrs including around 800 Anabaptists.

Persecution and suffering are themes that have shaped the Peace Churches' discourses and self-definitions down to the present day. Thus one typical contemporary guide written for a general Mennonite readership asks, 'Will you leave the past behind to discover a living faith to join others who choose to follow Christ regardless of the cost? Is your life a witness to the Spirit, water and *blood*?'[23]

3. *Peace Churches and Jews during the* Shoah

Like that of the majority Churches in continental Europe, the record of HPCs during the *Shoah* is riven by inconsistencies and confusions, and for some groups is also a source of great shame. In the context of a short essay I can hope only to be suggestive and impressionistic. (In particular I do not devote much attention to Jewish attitudes towards the HPCs.) Because HPCs place emphasis on doing Christianity, and tend to offer comparatively little in terms of textual evidence, I shall map the contours of HPC behaviour during the time of Hitler, pointing out along the way where the distinctive features outlined in section 2 above do (or do not) appear to have been significant or determinative factors.

a. *Quakers*
The foci of Quaker–Jewish relations prior to and during the *Shoah* were the Friends' International Centres located in Vienna and Berlin.[24] The Centres were venues of multi-lateral dialogue where people of differing nationalities and religions met to discuss issues of mutual concern. Those with contacts at the Berlin Centre included some notable thinkers from both Jewish and Christian traditions—Emil Brunner, Martin Buber, Rudolf Bultmann, and Rudolf Otto. In exchange, Friends held events in the Central Office for Jewish Adult Education (*Mittelstelle für jüdische Erwachsenenbildung*) run by Buber and Franz Rosenzweig.

---

23. H. Loewen, S. Nolt, C. Duerksen and E. Yoder, *Through Fire and Water: An Overview of Mennonite History* (Scottdale, PA: Herald Press, 1996), p. 142.

24. The Quaker International Centres, dependent upon the resources of British and American Friends, and publication sales for their survival, were conceived as places of 'mission, service, study and interchange…setting forth anew the way of reconciliation' (J.R. Carter, 'The Quaker International Centre in Berlin, 1920–1942', *The Journal of the Friends' Historical Society* 56 [1990], pp. 15-31 [15]).

Quaker readiness to work with or learn from Jews in this way, while not seeking to convert them, reflected the Christian Universalism of their belief that there was 'that of G-d in everyone', that is, that regardless of outward affiliation anyone might possess—and heed—the divine 'inner light'.[25] Conversely, the willingness of Jews (and non-HPC Christians) to participate in joint events reflects the perception of Quakerism in 1930s Germany. Because Friends' 'action' was far more visible than 'theology', the Society was often perceived more as an ethical or charitable movement of interest to people from a range of faith traditions, than as a religious tradition in its own right. (For this reason also membership remained comparatively low. The German Yearly Meeting of 1935 records just 230 members of the Society, although thousands counted themselves 'friends of the Friends'.)[26]

These pre-*Shoah* relations between Jews and Quakers continued during the early years of the Nazi regime. At odds with the Nazi ideological account of Jews as sub-human and Judaism as a corrupt, inherently evil system, Quakers continued to offer a forum in which Jewish voices could be heard publicly. When in February 1935 Buber was no longer permitted to speak to the general public or at Jewish meetings, Friends invited him to address events in Frankfurt and Berlin.[27] At the same time, a Berlin youth group was started for children from socially isolated backgrounds, including the children of Friends and the 'racially persecuted', among them some Orthodox Jews.[28] In later years, of course, even these projects would become impossible. In lieu of events-based opportunities for Jewish–Christian encounter, Friends began printing Hasidic stories to illustrate moral and ethical topics.[29] This move was far from being a neutral dissemination of folk tales. In finding spiritual values (and Quaker-like implicit theology) in these sources, the products of an increasingly publicly demonized Jewish religion and culture, Friends were making a defiant, quasi-political statement. The activity was particularly risky in view of the fact that,

25. On this issue, see Cooper, *A Living Faith*, pp. 12-17.

26. Carter, 'Quaker International', p. 17; A.S. Halle, 'The German Quakers and the Third Reich', *German History* 11 (1993), pp. 222-36 (222).

27. P. Vermes, *Buber* (New York: Grove Press, 1988), p. 67; M. Friedman, 'Martin Buber', *EncJud*, IV, col. 1431.

28. H.A. Schmitt, *Quakers and Nazis: Inner Light in Outer Darkness* (Columbia, MI: University of Missouri Press, 1997), p. 51.

29. Halle, 'German Quakers', p. 233.

like many other religious minorities in the Third Reich (for example, Hutterites, Latter Day Saints, and Jehovah's Witnesses), Quakers were highly dependent on income generated by publication sales for their survival.

If certain aspects of the pre-Nazi relationship were perpetuated into the late 1930s, Hitler's harsh policies on Jews and other 'subversives' meant that Quaker–Jewish relations became increasingly linked to those between Quakers and the state. Friends became involved in assisting Jews who sought to emigrate, and interceding (with some limited success) for the growing number of people in camps. For example, the Friends' Vienna office recorded 2408 cases of individuals and families, as well as 882 unaccompanied children who were assisted to leave in 1938 and 1939.[30] There was a special concern for the so-called *konfessionlosen Juden*—Jews who were non-observant and so fell outside the remit of existing Jewish (and Christian) community organizations.

All this work (but not the activities of 'almost all Friends' in Germany who were involved in hiding Jews in later years)[31] required of Quakers a degree of cooperative contact with the Nazi regime. If they were to succeed as they wished, they inevitably had to recognize and work with authoritarian, secular structures. Without such a 'corruption' of HPC principles regarding the radical separation of Church from State, the achievement of immediate humanitarian goals would not have been possible.[32] However, in the postwar era, this pragmatism and the deceit that was entailed in non-violent resistance to the Nazi programme caused Friends much pain. Margarethe Lachmund, a member of a documented network of Friends willing to help Jews in different areas of Germany, summed up the sense of failure experienced by many after the war:

---

30. Schmitt, *Quakers and Nazis*, p. 187.

31. Schmitt, *Quakers and Nazis*, p. 187. Approximately one in every eight German Quakers went to prison or concentration camp, or was interrogated by the Gestapo as a result of his or her anti-Nazi activities (pp. 190, 195-96).

32. There were, however, other factors that made some petty officials of the Nazi party willing in the pre-war years at least to work constructively with Jews. Most significantly, as children and students some of them had been beneficiaries of the *Quäkerspeisungen* (Quaker feedings), which provided meals for over one million of the poorest in the shattered Germany of the late teens and early 1920s.

During the Hitler years, Quakers in Germany, even in our own homes, frequently laid aside our cherished witness to the truth. So often we were afraid, lacked courage, and even shut our eyes to terrible occurrences... Afterwards we often felt that this hypocritical way of living had poisoned the whole of our lives.[33]

Lachmund's view is typically Quaker. Although she was involved in personally assisting Jews, the knowledge that in doing so she did not live consistently according to her faith's principles, because she had to lie and defraud others, means that she can only regard her actions during the Nazi era as failed.[34]

Moreover, the fact that figures like Lachmund[35] did much to aid and maintain contact with Jews during the *Shoah* should not be allowed to obscure the problematic larger picture of Quaker–Jewish relations. Friends' reputation for pacifism and charitable actions undoubtedly led them to enjoy and 'exploit' a greater measure of freedom than was experienced by many other groups within the Third Reich. But collectively Quakers did not differ from most Churches, in that they were not willing to take any stand against Nazism that might jeopardize the survival of the Society in continental Europe. Indeed, in 1933 the Executive Committee of the Yearly Meeting explicitly asked Friends 'to act with careful restraint and on their own responsibility and not to assume that they must act as Quakers, or could achieve more by acting in the name of Friends than on their own'.[36] Such statements make it hard to avoid the conclusion that survivalism circumscribed collective action,

---

33. Cited in B. Bailey, *A Quaker Couple in Nazi Germany* (York: William Sessions, 1994), pp. 94-95, 262.

34. Friends' sense of failure was not confined to the postwar era. As early as 1931, a German meeting had written to the Jewish community of Berlin expressing 'pain and shame' at the actions of a Nazi gang who harangued Jews on *Rosh ha-Shanah* and stating that 'we, too, feel responsible and guilty, because we have not done enough to decontaminate a hate-filled atmosphere. We therefore ask your forgiveness.' Although not actively participating in the anti-Semitism, Quakers regarded themselves as culpable because they were members of a society in which it took root (Schmitt, *Quakers and Nazis*, p. 21).

35. Bailey, *A Quaker Couple*, pp. 97-100, 102-103 describes the actions on behalf of Jews of a number of Quaker individuals, including her mother, Mary Friedrich.

36. Reproduced in Carter, 'Quaker International', p. 27.

and the preservation of the Religious Society of Friends, rather than of European Jewry, was the paramount concern.[37]

b. *German Mennonites*

The story of Mennonite–Jewish relations during the *Shoah* is more complicated than that between Jews and Quakers, largely because the Mennonite Church was marked by longstanding divisions along national-ethnic boundaries (including distinctive Swiss, Russian and German traditions). Each Mennonite church behaved differently during the *Shoah*. In particular, the ignorance of many North American Mennonites concerning the plight of Jews,[38] and the very mixed behaviour of Dutch Mennonites—some of whom approved of the Nuremberg Laws, while others risked all to aid Jews and Jewish Christians[39]—has been well documented elsewhere. One important study just published has even examined the pro-Nazi sentiments of Mennonite emigrants in Latin America who confused support for Hitler with their strong emotional attachment to German culture.[40] In this essay I do not want to replicate this work. For reasons of contrast and cohesion, I shall look mainly at the behaviours of Mennonites in Germany during the *Shoah*.

The dominant continental reputation of the Society of Friends as a social welfare agency meant that Quaker individuals were able to maintain some positive relations with Jews. German Mennonites, how-

37. C.E. King ('Strategies for Survival: An Examination of the History of Five Christian Sects in Germany 1933–1945', *Journal of Contemporary History* 14 [1979], pp. 211-34) argues that religious minorities' responses to the Nazi regime were essentially survival strategies.

38. See A. Davies and M.F. Nefsky, *How Silent Were the Churches? Canadian Protestantism and the Jewish Plight during the Nazi Era* (Waterloo, ON: Wilfred Laurier University Press, 1997), Ch. 7.

39. G.D. Homan, '"We must...and can stand firmly": Dutch Mennonites in World War II', *The Mennonite Quarterly Review* 69 (1995), pp. 7-36, provides a succinct account of the behaviour of individual Dutch Mennonites and congregations, finding that the war period has left the community with parallel legacies of 'faithful discipleship' and 'collaboration'. Picking up where Homan leaves off, P.J. Dyck and E. Dyck, *Up from the Rubble* (Scottdale, PA: Herald Press, 1991), describe the impact of the war upon Mennonites (primarily Russian Mennonites and Russian Mennonites of Dutch descent), many of whom eventually left continental Europe for the Americas.

40. J.D. Thiesen, *Mennonite and Nazi? Attitudes among Mennonite Colonists in Latin America, 1933–1945* (Kitchener, ON: Pandora Press, 1999).

ever, felt themselves to be in a far more vulnerable position. During the Third Reich, they managed to safeguard the existence of their denomination, yet in that process according to general HPC opinion, 'they defended neither the gospel nor the Anabaptist heritage'.[41]

When Hitler achieved power, German Mennonites joined many other churches in congratulating him on his victory.[42] However, their communications made it clear that unlike some Christian groups whose support for Hitler was *because* of their explicit theologies (for example, of Jews and Judaism, or of Church obedience to the state), the Mennonites were willing to jettison some of their key principles in order to be able to 'join' the National Socialists. Prominent leader Benjamin Unruh reassured the Nazi leadership that historic Mennonite opposition to military and other state service had grown out of the group's persecution by regimes of the past. Now, the Third Reich promised much for all Germans, and so Mennonites would willingly abandon their pacifism and join the Aryan struggle.[43] (In fact, HPC history suggests that Unruh's claims are unconvincing. Anabaptists were largely persecuted *because* of their unwillingness to acknowledge various forms of state authority over believers.)

As a result of this seeming *volte-face*, there were no German Mennonites among those conscientious objectors who were executed during the Second World War.[44] Mennonites were party to the Nazi enterprise and all that it meant for European Jewry. Moreover, records suggest that, in the early 1930s, the German Foreign Office and Propaganda Ministry even contemplated using Unruh as a pro-Hitler 'envoy' to other peace churches. On more than one occasion, he offered the Friends state money to be used in, for example, the feeding of poor Nazi families in Austria.[45] The resources would have provided Quakers with an opportunity to carry out effective relief work. However, taking

---

41. D.G. Lichdi, 'National Socialism [Nazism] (Germany)', in *Mennonite Encyclopedia*, V, p. 617.

42. On 10 September 1939, the *Konferenz der ost- und westpreussischen Mennoniten* sent Hitler the message, 'it is with profound thankfulness that our Conference senses the vast ascendancy which G-d has granted our Volk through your endeavours; for our part, we pledge our joyful collaboration in the reconstruction of our fatherland from the power of the Gospel' (Lichdi, 'National Socialism', p. 617).

43. Schmitt, *Quakers and Nazis*, pp. 133-34.

44. E. Horsch Bender (ed.), 'Germany', in *Mennonite Encyclopedia*, II, p. 497.

45. Schmitt, *Quakers and Nazis*, p. 87.

the money would also have neutralized Friends by leaving them beholden to the Reich. In particular, aid programmes for the 'racially persecuted' would have become untenable.

Why, then, did the German Mennonites act in a way that seems so alien to their Peace Church heritage? Which factors led them to override HPC principles? As has already been indicated, German Mennonites felt themselves to be in a precarious position in the pre-war era. The victims of more than a century of what would today be termed 'ethnic politics', they were desperately keen to prove their credentials as real Germans. Many were fairly recent returnees from the new Soviet Union. Their ancestors, facing persecution in Prussia, had originally been invited to settle in Russia by Catherine the Great, but late nineteenth-century Russification policy had seen them subjected to increasing pressures. (By the 1920s, the persecution had reached such proportions that it has become customary to rank the twentieth with the sixteenth century as a period of great trial for Anabaptists.) In the aftermath of the Russian Revolution, North American, Dutch, and the residual Mennonite population of Germany had coordinated the 'rescue' of ethnic Germans from the new Soviet state. Unruh himself coordinated the *Brüder in Not* (Brothers in Distress) agency for this purpose. However, once returned to Germany, the Mennonites found that, just as in Russia they had been distinguished as aliens, so now they were often regarded as not being true Germans. Seen against this context, the German Mennonite capitulation to Hitler's ideology becomes intelligible (he was, after all, seen as anti-Communist, and therefore against the Russian persecutors), if in no way justified.

c. *Hutterites*

If German Mennonites capitulated to Hitler and thereby jeopardized their identity as Anabaptists during the *Shoah*, the Hutterites consistently perceived themselves to be in absolute opposition to the Third Reich. In March 1933, leader Eberhard Arnold discerned that, 'it was evident in the last speech of the Chancellor of the Reich in which direction the swastika is moving. The course of the Cross is a completely different one.'[46] He spoke out against the race laws, and re-wrote his book *Inner Land* to 'claim the swastika for all peoples, regardless of

---

46. M. Hindley, ' "Unerwünscht": One of the Lesser Known Confrontations with the National Socialist State, 1933–37', *German History* 11 (1993), pp. 207-21.

race or colour, and quite specifically *for the Jews*'.[47]

When the Plebiscite was held to affirm Hitler's Reich chancellorship late in 1933, the Hutterites collectively rejected the regime, voting *en masse* and pasting to their ballot slips a statement that made their opposition clear. Privately, Arnold wrote to Hitler outlining the Bruderhof's classically Anabaptist claim that 'Jesus Christ...is the only Führer'.[48] More publicly, in a talk given in 1934, he asserted that 'Hitler is a... Lord of hell' and likened the situation in the new fascist state to that described in the biblical book of Revelation.[49] Thus began a period of Nazi raids on the *Bruderhof*, with German troops undertaking 'manoeuvres' and target practice there. Eventually, in April 1937, the *Bruderhof* was dissolved (ostensibly for financial irregularities) and the members given just a few hours to leave.[50]

Particularly after wrestling with the problems of Mennonite activity during the *Shoah*, it is easy for members of other Churches, shamed by their own denominations' records, to admire the Hutterites' record of opposition to Hitler's regime. They acted with an unrivalled unity of purpose to proclaim a clear message of opposition to National Socialism. No Hutterites collaborated with the Nazi plan for the dehumanization and destruction of Jews.

However, one unintended consequence of the Hutterian upholding of non-worldliness was a lack of effective action on behalf of Jews. The community might have been expected to undertake this kind of work, as, like other HPCs, their members included a few 'non-Aryans' and in some senses they owed their very existence to Jews. Originally an isolated group that found inspiration in historic Anabaptist teachings, Arnold and his followers had made connections with old order Hutterites in the United States through the Austrian historian Robert

47. Baum, *Against the Wind*, pp. 120-21, 182-83, 187; E. Arnold, *Inner Land: A Guide to the Heart and Soul of the Bible* (Rifton, NY: Plough Publishing, 1976), pp. 336-37.

48. E. Arnold, *Torches Together* (Rifton, NY: Plough Publishing, 1961), p. 185.

49. Talk given in 1934 and printed after E. Arnold's death under the title, 'Christians and the State: An Interpretation of Romans XIII in Conjunction with Revelation XIII', *The Plough* 3.1 (1940), pp. 1-7 (4).

50. Baum, *Against the Wind*, p. 219. After a brief period in Liechtenstein, the community moved to Britain, from where the majority of members were again obliged to emigrate in 1941 (this time to Paraguay) on account of their pacifism and German citizenship.

Friedmann.[51] Arnold's views on faithful life in community were also strongly influenced by Gustav Landauer, the Jewish social philosopher, and, like German Quakers, he had contacts with Martin Buber.[52]

In short, while the Hutterites provide the clearest example of a historic peace church retaining its integrity during the Hitler time, their commitment to non-worldliness meant that they engaged in relatively little positive action on behalf of Jews. Despite previous relations between Hutterite founders and Germany's Jewish community, there was no concerted effort to speak out collectively for Jews or to undertake any kind of public project with or for them during the Third Reich.[53]

In examining the behaviour of Historic Peace Churches in relation to Jews during the *Shoah*, it is clear that there is no simple correlation between those relations and the maintenance of Peace Church principles. German Mennonites jettisoned a commitment to pacifism and non-resistance and so allied themselves with Hitler's anti-Semitism. They were inevitably involved in perpetrating the *Shoah*. At the other end of the spectrum, the Hutterites declared Hitler demonic, but their sense of opposition to the Nazi state was so absolute that relatively little was achieved on behalf of Jews. Somewhere between these two positions stands the Religious Society of Friends. At times, Quakers were compromised in terms of their holding onto the distinctive HPC characteristics outlined above in section 2. They certainly could have been less ambiguous and far more unified in their opposition to Hitler. However, in larger numbers (as a proportion of membership) than other churches during the Third Reich they secured safety or relief for a

---

51. Friedmann later became a Mennonite, and wrote one of the few theologies of Anabaptism (R. Friedmann, *The Theology of Anabaptism: An Interpretation* [Scottdale, PA: Herald Press, 1973]).

52. M. Tyldesley, 'Martin Buber and the Bruderhof Communities', *JJS* 45 (1994), pp. 258-72, demonstrates relationships of personal contact, correspondence and intellectual influence between Buber and Hutterite leaders, springing from their shared attraction to Landauer's views.

53. This is not to say that there was a total lack of concern for Jews within the Hutterite community. A 1938 edition of *The Plough*, the *Bruderhof*'s periodical publication following the flight to England, printed a letter from a recent visitor to the Vienna Quaker Centre, John Sturge Stevens, urging government action to relieve the suffering of Austrian Jews and offer them sanctuary in Britain (1.2 [1938], p. 67).

number of Jews, and in the early years of the Hitler time at least, strove to maintain some form of meaningful Jewish–Christian relations.

4. Post-1945 Relations with Jews

a. *Church Statements on Relations with Jews*

One common device used in survey volumes that attempt to cover a range of Christian responses to Jews and Judaism is the collection of a series of examples of official Church statements on the topic. Hence Helga Croner's two edited collections, *Stepping Stones to Further Jewish–Christian Relations* and *More Stepping Stones to Jewish–Christian Relations*,[54] and *The Theology of the Churches and the Jewish People: Statements by the World Council of Churches and its Member Churches*[55] are standard works on many undergraduate and seminary reading lists. A booklet produced by the British Council of Christians and Jews, *Jews and Christians: What Do the Churches Say?*, similarly answers its title's question by reproducing thematically organized selections from statements agreed and issued by authoritative Church bodies.[56] These declarations are certainly important, heralding as they do serious attempts by Churches to correct harmful teachings and build future relationships of mutual respect. However, given the emphasis on implicit theology and egalitarian ecclesiology in the HPCs it comes as no surprise that a reliance on such sources as indices of relations with and attitudes towards Jews is inappropriate when considering these groups.

To date, the HPCs (specifically, European Mennonites) have produced only one such statement.[57] Entitled 'We, the Mennonites, and the

54. H. Croner (ed.), *Stepping Stones to Further Jewish–Christian Relations* (New York: Paulist Press, 1977), and *idem* (ed.), *More Stepping Stones to Jewish–Christian Relations: An Unabridged Collection of Documents 1975–1983* (New York: Paulist Press, 1985).

55. World Council of Churches, *The Theology of the Churches and the Jewish People: Statements by the World Council of Churches and Its Member Churches* (Geneva: WCC Publications, 1988).

56. M. Braybrooke, *Jews and Christians: What Do the Churches Say?* (London: The Council of Christians and Jews, 1992).

57. Of course, *some* Anabaptist and Quaker groups are members of the World Council of Churches and so are signatories to the declarations made by that ecumenical body. A full and up-to-date list of the WCC's member Churches can be found on the Council's internet WWW page at URL: http://www.wcc-coe.org (version current at publication of this volume).

Jewish People: A Call for Taking a Stand in our Days', it was distributed to the participants at the Mennonite Regional Conference,
Elspeet, The Netherlands, in May 1977. It regards the *Shoah* and the
founding of the State of Israel as demanding of Mennonites a frank
elucidation of their position in relation to Jews. Interestingly, it also
argues that as people who have rejected attempts to create a state
Church, Mennonites should have special understanding of 'the right of
the Jews to independent existence of their people'. However, they have
been silent during the momentous twentieth century and so 'must con-
fess before G-d', acknowledging guilt, and re-asserting that, 'In the
end, we know G-d—specifically in the Messiah—as No One other than
the G-d of Israel'.[58]

b. *Implicit Theology: Weakness or Strength?*
Setting aside the issue of whether the production of such a statement is
an authentically Anabaptist exercise (or whether it instead illustrates the
pressures faced by European Mennonites to re-cast themselves along
mainstream Protestant lines), the Elspeet document introduces a central
problem in HPC postwar relations with Jews. Indirectly and explicitly it
suggests that HPC reliance on implicit or embedded theology is inadequate in the light of the challenge posed to the Churches by the *Shoah*.
Is this the case? Does an examination of HPC–Jewish relations highlight a general systemic weakness that blights the Peace Churches,
impeding attempts to reassess positions on Jews and Judaism?

It is not hard to find evidence to support the suggestion that reluctance to theologize, coupled with extreme low-church approaches to
authority, makes it harder for Anabaptists and Friends to effect revolutionary advances in relations with the Jewish people. No HPCs have
structures in place that could disseminate authoritative guidelines such
as those issued by the Vatican, for example, the vital 'Notes on the Correct Way to Present the Jews and Judaism in Preaching and Catechesis
in the Roman Catholic Church (1985)'.[59] In consequence, complacent,
negative or supersessionist attitudes may go unchallenged, as can be

58. This paper is reproduced in full in Croner (ed.), *More Stepping Stones*,
pp. 205-206.

59. This and other similar documents are discussed in E.J. Fisher and
L. Klenicki (eds.), *In our Time: The Flowering of Jewish–Christian Dialogue* (New
York: Paulist Press, 1990). See also the contribution of Michael Hayes to this par-
ticular volume, pp. 426-45.

seen in a series of examples drawn from a range of traditions within the Religious Society of Friends. One major recent British Quaker theological work seems to imply that first-century Judaism was moribund: 'The Jewish Temple was built on rock, bedrock, very solid, stable, firm, unmoving, unchanging, dead. But the Christian church is built on the living rock of humanity, fallible, unreliable, turncoat, quarrelsome, misunderstanding, but capable of rising to great heights of insight, love and self-sacrifice.'[60] In a recent issue of *The Conservative Friend*, 'Judaism' is only used either in relation to Jewish practice in the first century or when other Christian groups are criticized as misguided and departing from Jesus' message, in which event they are likened to 'that same Jewish religion of outward "conservation" of traditions and rituals and dusty old buildings'.[61] Here, 'Judaism', 'Jew' and 'Jewish' are still essential components of the rhetoric of Friendly polemic—something that many majority Christian Church publications would no longer countenance. Finally, Lilamani Woolrych (Rowntree Fellow in 1992–93) reported that British Quakers exhibited somewhat contradictory attitudes on issues of inter-religious and inter-ethnic politics. Within the current British membership, it is possible to hear, 'I wouldn't want black neighbours', and 'I don't mind black people, it's Jews I don't like'.[62] Ironically, these problematic views may co-exist with a confidence that Friends are at an advantage when compared with other Christian groups approaching interfaith issues, because of 'their openness, freedom from Creeds, and their hospitable approach to, and acceptance of, members of other religious systems'.[63]

60. J. Scott, *What Canst Thou Say? Towards a Quaker Theology* (London: Quaker Home Service, 1980), p. 27. This brief work has been described as 'significant', and as epitomizing contemporary Quaker theology. See A. Heron, *Quakers in Britain 1895–1995: A Century of Change* (Kelso: Curlew Graphics, 1995), p. 96, and M. Davie, 'A Study of the Development of British Quaker Theology since 1965 with Special Reference to Janet Scott's 1980 Swarthmore Lecture' (DPhil thesis, University of Oxford, 1992). Elsewhere, Scott does speak against the persecution of the Other, including Jews (*What Canst Thou Say?*, pp. 39, 51).

61. C. Lindes, 'Friends of the Truth', *The Conservative Friend* 6 (November 1998), p. 8. *The Conservative Friend* is published by the conservative Ohio Yearly Meeting of Friends (OYM). Its readership consists principally of Meeting's members and attenders, and those from other Meetings who are in unity with OYM.

62. L. Woolrych, *Communicating across Cultures: A Report* (York: The Joseph Rowntree Charitable Trust, 1998), pp. 14, 16.

63. R.G. Meredith, *Learning of One Another: The Quaker Encounter with Other*

The same implicit approach to theology that makes it possible for Peace Church adherents to maintain discourse and attitudes that other church members may regard as, at best, old-fashioned, and at worst, dangerously anti-Semitic, has also provided grounds for new appreciations of what HPCs can learn from Jews. Significantly, a growing minority of Anabaptists and Quakers find inspiration in the Jewish model of 'lived faith', as they work out what it might mean to be a member of an HPC in the new millennium. This goes beyond a fascination with Hasidic tales, and is prepared to value the halakhic life. For example, Harvey Gillman suggests that Quakers can learn from Orthodox Jews about bringing the sacred into all of life: 'An Orthodox Jew has a blessing for all aspects of life. There is a blessing for when it thunders, for a glass of wine, for entering a new house, and so on. Life is a blessing.'[64] Christine Trevett writes that Judaism's 'mode of *wrestling* with God has spoken clearly to my condition at times' and models her attempts to work through the contemporary questions facing the British Society on aspects of the *Siddur*.[65] Mennonite Perry Yoder also suggests that Anabaptism can be modified usefully as a result of encounter with Judaism because 'If true belief is inseparable from its manifestations in life—that is, if faith is faithfulness—then the *Talmud* offers a heuristic model for constructing this type of theology'.[66]

Cultures and Religions (North Hobart: The Backhouse Lecture Committee, 1997), p. 5. Similar sentiments are expressed in another James Backhouse Lecture of several years earlier, see K.E. Boulding, *The Evolutionary Potential of Quakerism* (North Hobart: The Backhouse Lecture Committee, 1964), pp. 21-22. Cautions against this kind of Quaker complacency in interfaith matters are expressed by Rex Ambler in *The End of Words: Issues in Contemporary Quaker Thought* (London: Quaker Home Service, 1994), p. 30.

64. H. Gillman, *A Minority of One: A Journey with Friends* (London: Quaker Home Service, 1988), pp. 43 and 109. This work and that of Scott, quoted earlier, are printed versions of the annual Swarthmore Lecture, intended to interpret to Friends their message and mission, and to bring before the public the Quaker 'message'. As such, the lectures represent some of Friends' most public statements on issues. For another example of a Jewish Friend relating the *Shoah* experience to Friends generally, see, e.g., B. Gibson, 'From Auschwitz to Hiroshima', *The Friends' Quarterly* 29.8 (1995), pp. 337-41.

65. C. Trevett, *Previous Convictions and End-of-the-Millennium Quakerism* (London: Quaker Home Service, 1997). This is an extended printed version of Trevett's Swarthmore lecture.

66. P. Yoder, 'The Importance of Judaism for Contemporary Anabaptist Thought', *Mennonite Quarterly Review* 69 (1993), pp. 73-83.

If Gillman, Trevett and Perry Yoder look to Judaism as a guide for the future development of the Peace Churches, the late John Howard Yoder devoted himself to a more extensive, detailed consideration of various distinctive aspects of Anabaptist–Jewish relations and arrived at some striking, radical conclusions.[67] For Yoder, the painful horror of the *Shoah* and his own studies of the New Testament period[68] both point towards the need for a reconsideration of this relationship. Like others who argue that the *Shoah* highlights failings in Christian theology not just in relation to Jews, but more generally, Yoder sees twentieth-century events as evidence that 'Christendom'—the unholy alliance between faith and the political establishment—'should not be found wanting only from the perspective of the Jews whom it mistreated, but also for the sake of Jesus whom it claimed to serve and thereby defamed'.[69] Anabaptists can play a key role in finding a solution to this twofold problem, because they have a history of positive contacts with Jews and have much in common with them. For example, the radical Jewish philosopher Spinoza enjoyed Mennonite hospitality in the Netherlands; rabbis assisted the prominent Anabaptist intellectual Hans Denck[70] when he translated the prophetic literature of the Hebrew Bible into German. Both groups have also carried German 'dialects'[71]

---

67. For many years, much of Yoder's work on Judaism and Anabaptism was unpublished. It was, until recently, accessible on-line, but is now forthcoming as a publication (J.H. Yoder, 'The Jewish–Christian Schism Revisited'). The lack of earlier publication was in part due to Yoder's own awareness of the complexity of the issues involved, and at times perhaps also because of a reluctance on the part of other dialogue participants to tolerate certain kinds of diverse voices, as discussed elsewhere in this paper.

In addition to the work of John Howard Yoder, a longer piece than this would also need to cover the significant contribution made by another North American scholar, William Klassen. In *Love of Enemies: The Way to Peace* (Philadelphia: Fortress Press, 1984), Klassen decries and offers a useful corrective to ethical supersessionism, the popular but misguided tendency to draw a contrast between 'vengeful' Judaism and Jesus' 'love command' (see especially p. 43).

68. E.g., J.H. Yoder, *The Politics of Jesus* (Grand Rapids: Eerdmans, 1972).

69. J.H. Yoder, 'The Context of This Study: What Needs to Change in the Jewish–Christian Dialogue and Why'. Internet WWW page at URL: http://www.nd.edu/~theo/jhy/writings/j-cschism/preface.htm (version current at 6 September 1999).

70. Denck was a leader of sixteenth-century south German Anabaptism.

71. The Anabaptist 'equivalent' of Yiddish is Plattdeutsch, a form of low German preserved by old order Mennonites and the Amish.

with them around the world. Above all, both Anabaptists and Jews have been the victims of persecution and vilification—in part because they have had to demonstrate to the world what it means to combine a life of service to G-d with statelessness.[72]

In writings produced over a period of three decades, J.H. Yoder advocated a reconstruction of Christianity that expresses solidarity between Anabaptists and Jews. Most significantly, this entails a complete re-conceptualization of the central myth of Peace Church history. Anabaptism has traditionally contended that Christianity 'fell' (departed from Jesus' message and goal) with the conversion of Constantine and the creation of Christendom.[73] However, for Yoder, this is fallacious. Christians should accept that unfaithfulness occurred before then, with the renunciation of Judaism and the parting of the ways. To quote Yoder, in the period 'somewhere between the New Testament canon and the middle of the next century', Christian apologists tried to make their message intelligible to Gentile philosophers, explaining that they 'could have the God of the Jews without the Jews', and so Christianity adopted 'Greek or Roman provincialism instead of Hebrew universality'. In addition, Christianity lost with its Jewishness its sense of Scripture as a blessing, its capacity for decentralized and voluntary congregationalism and its valuing of life in *galut* and apart from state authority structures.[74] For Yoder, *these* were the precise features restored by the radical reformers of the sixteenth century, and which their modern descendants must also hold as normative.

c. *Practical Solidarity*

John Howard Yoder was the most famous Anabaptist scholar of the twentieth century, and his writings on relations with Jews arguably more extensive than those of any other single figure within the HPC

72. J.H. Yoder, 'Salvation is of the Jews', a paper condensed from a Sunday morning sermon at College Church, Bethel College, November 1992. Internet WWW page at URL: http://www.nd.edu/~theo/jhy/writings/j-cschism/salvation.htm (version current at 6 September 1999).

73. See section 2a of this paper.

74. J.H. Yoder, 'Tertium Datur: Refocusing the Jewish–Christian Schism', a paper originally presented 13 October 1977, in a campus lecture at the University of Notre Dame, sponsored by the Department of Theology and the Notre Dame Graduate Theological Union (forthcoming). See also *idem*, 'The Jewishness of the Free Church Vision', one of the Menno Simons lectures presented at Bethel College, Newton, Kansas in 1982 (forthcoming).

tradition. Yet even his writings do not carry any formal authority within the peace church family. Judged against the common emphases I outlined earlier, they are also 'incomplete' as distinctively HPC–Jewish relations. The primacy of living Christianity and the view that 'faith by itself, if it has no works, is dead' (Jas 2.17) means that for these to take full shape, some kind of practical action grounded in experience is also needed.

As during the *Shoah*, the Hutterites have maintained a commitment to holding all things in common, and in the postwar era their commitment to communal living or 'full community' has served as the basis for practical, lived solidarity with Jews, in the form of contacts and exchange visits with members of Israeli *kibbutzim*. For example, at the Urfeld conference in 1996, representatives of the *Bruderhof* met with Catholics living in community and Israeli 'kibbutzniks', both secular and religious. From the Hutterite perspective, the 'ultimate goal' of such contacts is 'the discovery of what it means to know that in G-d's plan, Jews and Christians belong together'. This quest is distinctively Hutterite, insofar as the starting point is 'to dialogue about the origins and essence of the spiritual impulses that drive them to seek a brotherly and sisterly way of life' (that is, to live communally).[75] But Hutterite–Jewish relations do not begin and end with the discussion of the pains and pleasures of *Bruderhof* and *kibbutz* life. Once brought together, the two parties have been able to address other concerns, including the events of the *Shoah* (the collective expulsion of Hutterites from Nazi Germany means that, like many religious Jews, they regard this period as a unique episode in the human–divine relationship), and the politics of the Middle East.[76]

d. *HPC–Jewish Relations Assessed by Other Dialogue Participants*
HPC–Jewish relations take place within a wider context of encounter between Jews and Christians, and, at times, Anabaptists and Quakers have been severely criticized by other more prominent Christian participants in the dialogue. Sometimes, this occurs within a context of a

75. S. Ehrlich and H. Ehrlich, 'A Meeting of Hearts: Conference at Urfeld', *The Plough* 47 (1996), pp. 18-21.

76. See, e.g., J. Dorkam and S. Ehrlich, 'Dialogue', *The Plough* 57 (1998), pp. 18-21. The two participants in this plain-spoken written exchange are friends from the American Hutterite centre at Rifton, New York, and Kibbutz Palmach Tsuba in Israel.

general critique of Christian attitudes towards and relations with Jews. For example, Franklin Littell cites a publication sponsored by the American Friends Service Committee, which makes the refugee problem into the biggest issue in a study of peace in the Middle East, as one among other examples of the problem of 'cultural and theological anti-semites who keep the fire smouldering under the surface'.[77] On other occasions, HPCs are seen as meriting particularly harsh judgment. In his famous study, *Jews and Christians: The Contemporary Meeting,* the late A. Roy Eckhardt (like Littell, a Methodist minister) presents an extensive critique of Quakers. Friends should, he argues, serve as a 'lesson...paradigmatic of all Christian hostility to Jews', and more specifically as an example of the dangers posed for Jews by what he terms the 'once heretical Protestantism' which is inextricably linked with 'Christian hypocrisy and Christian antisemitism'. Chiefly, Eckhardt suggests that Friends' contemporary funding of medical and educational programmes for Palestinians, and their calls in the 1980s for Israel to negotiate with the PLO are 'not separable from the phenomenon of antisemitism', and demand a perfectionism of Jews not demanded of others. Put simply, Quakers talk peace but are 'murderers' of Jews.[78]

This censure is not restricted to Quakers. J.H. Yoder reported similar 'conflicts' with Eckhardt at a 1984 conference in Bloomington, Indiana, when the latter apparently decried Yoder's views, especially his questioning of the view that 'Jews would not bring any discrimination upon themselves by their apartness or by their truth claims'.[79] In his writings, Yoder certainly does depart from this view, accepted as a norm in much contemporary Jewish–Christian dialogue. However, rather than being seen as examples of anti-Semitic projection of responsibility for Christian failings onto Jewish victims, in this case (and similar cases), these remarks arguably could (or must?) be reassessed as insights from someone who himself is a member of a group whose 'apartness' and 'truth claims' have been the cause of much *unjust suffering*. Given the

77. F.H. Littell, 'American Protestantism and Antisemitism', in N.W. Cohen (ed.), *Essential Papers on Jewish–Christian Relations in the United States: Imagery and Reality* (New York: New York University Press, 1990), pp. 171-87 (175).

78. A.R. Eckhardt, *Jews and Christians: The Contemporary Meeting* (Bloomington: Indiana University Press, 1986), pp. 108-10.

79. Notes appended to the paper, 'Earthly Jerusalem and Heavenly Jerusalem: A Mislocated Dualism' (forthcoming).

findings of this study, Eckhardt's statements on Quakers in particular seem unhelpfully simplistic, to say the least.[80] Without doubt, the historic peace churches, like the Catholic, Orthodox and Protestant families of churches, are culpable of having failed cither to act effectively on behalf of or with Jews during the *Shoah*, or yet to recognize what needs to be done in order to prevent its repetition. However, both occasional accusatorial, inequitable remarks and the widespread omission of Peace Church history from most discussions (popular and scholarly) of Jewish–Christian relations suggest a prevalent unwillingness to attend to peace church self-identification as 'neither Protestant nor Catholic', and a refusal to give space in dialogue contexts to distinctive HPC ideas. Jewish–Christian relations is broadening—but at the start of the third millennium of the two traditions' co-existence it is still not yet fully inclusive.

5. *Conclusions*

This brief investigation of HPC–Jewish relations during the *Shoah* and in its aftermath is at an end. As I stressed at the beginning, the essay has been limited in scope. I have not been able to speculate on the likely implications for HPC–Jewish relations of late twentieth- and early twenty-first century developments within Anabaptism and Quakerism.[81] Crucially, there has also been little opportunity to explore the per-

80. In places, Eckhardt's discussion almost appears to be distorted by a general antipathy towards the members of the Society of Friends. Among other remarks, he refers to 'the special problem of "the Friends" *as they like to call themselves*', says Quaker 'ideology' (not 'belief') is 'imperialistic', and that pacifism is an illusory 'spell' (Eckhardt, *Jews and Christians*, pp. 108-110, my italics).

81. Among these internal developments two seem to me to be most significant: (1) all the HPCs are progressively becoming non-European phenomena. Major areas of growth are Latin America and Africa. For many of these newer HPC adherents, relations with Jews are likely to be of less importance that those with, say, Islam and the African Traditional Religions; (2) in Europe and North America, the Society of Friends is likely to be subject to further division and fissure in the near- to mid-term future. This could result in a polarization of attitudes with some groups being effectively non-Christian universalists, and others maintaining (or adopting) a more non-worldly and conservative Christian position inspired by contacts with old order Anabaptists and early Quaker writings. As the material in section 4 suggests, neither stance will inevitably result in the formation of positive attitudes towards Jews or Judaism.

spective of Jewish participants in relations with HPCs.[82] I certainly do not wish to advocate a model of Jews as passive victims on whose behalf Christians do (or do not) act. To repeat myself again, Jewish–Christian relations continue to grow: this is an extension of existing studies and others will in turn want to supplement and correct me.

However, all this has not, I hope, precluded the essay from offering a modest contribution to the study of Jewish–Christian relations in the modern era. Taking a cue from the Anabaptist and Quaker emphasis on faith in action, it has provided a narrative sketching of the HPCs' at some times rather distinctive, at others surprisingly unremarkable, responses to Nazi anti-Jewish policy. It has also highlighted the tremendous diversity in postwar reappraisals of HPC relations with Jews. I have argued that, within some traditions, there have arisen reassessments that are at least as radical as those suggested within the major Christian Church families. Conversely, others have essentially failed to reflect anew and in depth on Jews and Judaism—perhaps (but not necessarily) in a way that highlights wider systemic problems within a particular variant of the HPC model.

Most importantly, I also hope that the project has made some suggestions as to both the areas of investigation and the more inclusive methods that might be employed in further studies of Jewish–Christian relations. I believe that scholars and practitioners of interfaith relations both may find much in a consideration of HPC behaviours during and after the *Shoah*. It is now recognized that these Churches exercise in certain areas an influence far out of proportion to their numbers.[83]

---

82. A few extant works hint at this aspect of the Jewish–HPC encounter. E. Wilcock, *Pacifism and the Jews* (Stroud: Hawthorn Press, 1994) looks at Jews whose pacifism brought them into contact with HPCs during the war, either in joint efforts to avert conflict, or as inmates in American camps for conscientious objectors (Chs. 6 and 7). Schmitt's already quoted work is in part a tribute to the Friends who assisted his flight from Germany in 1934 (*Quakers and Nazis*, preface). In the contemporary era, Christopher Rowland detects an implicit community of sympathy between Jewish writer Daniel Boyarin and the HPCs. See D. Boyarin, *A Radical Jew: Paul and the Politics of his Day* (Berkeley: University of California Press, 1994), particularly Ch. 10, 'Answering the Mail: Towards a Radical Jewishness', and C. Rowland's review of the work in *JJS* 47 (1996), pp. 372-74. Finally, the Kibbutz scholar Yaacov Oved has chronicled the relationship between *kibbutzim* and the Bruderhof (Y. Oved, *Distant Brothers* [Rifton, NY: Plough Publishing, 1993]).

83. See, e.g., the comments in Littell, 'American Protestantism', p. 174.

Pacifists within other Churches draw on their teachings on non-resistance, and as many previously 'established' or dominant Churches find themselves operating in an increasingly religiously plural age, where Faith and State are separated in law, they sometimes turn to the HPCs for models of how to live without power. Part of what is entailed in 'living without power' is a reassessment of the grounds for relations and solidarity with other religious adherents, and this in itself is a practical argument for attending to what minority Christian groups have said and done in the area.[84]

Finally, our concentration on the deeds committed for good or ill by those individuals who were and are far removed from the world of interfaith colloquia, or academic institutes, or ecclesiastical pronouncements, is a reminder of the vast areas still unexplored by students of Jewish–Christian relations. It is also a sobering (for ivory-towered academics!) intimation that Eliot was right in saying that, 'the growing good of the world is partly dependent on unhistoric acts' performed by those who live 'a hidden life, and rest in unvisited tombs'.[85]

84. See D.J. Hall, *The End of Christendom and the Future of Christianity* (Valley Forge, PA: Trinity Press International, 1997) in which the author argues that Christendom's account of the 'rise of the Church' goes hand in hand with anti-Judaism (pp. 10-11), and suggests that majority churches in North America can learn to respond to the post-Christendom situation by looking to the example of Anabaptist traditions (p. 33).

85. G. Eliot, *Middlemarch* (London: Penguin Books, 1985), p. 896. Thanks to Amy, Lydia, Naomi and Rebecca for helping me to rethink Eliot in 1998–99.

FROM *NOSTRA AETATE* TO 'WE REMEMBER:
A REFLECTION ON THE *SHOAH*'

Michael A. Hayes

1. *Introduction*

On 17 March 1962, Pope John XXIII passed the Great Synagogue in Rome and paused to bless the crowd outside. Twenty-four years later Pope John Paul II entered the building to address the Jewish community of Rome.[1] This short journey from the street outside into the building itself could be a metaphor for the movement of the Roman Catholic Church in its relations with the Jewish faith, from interested passer-by to partner in dialogue. John XXIII, in calling for a major self-evaluation by the Church expressed in the Second Vatican Council, began the movement, which continued under Paul VI and had developed to the extent that John Paul II could take Catholic–Jewish dialogue into the Synagogue itself. That dialogue, while marked by much goodwill, is also rooted in significant difficulties.

Jacques Dupuis,[2] an important Catholic theologian of interfaith dialogue, writing in the context of Christian encounter with other world

1.   Recounted by the Chief Rabbi, Professor Elio Toaff, and referred to by Pope John Paul II on the occasion of the Pope's visit to the Great Synagogue in Rome, 13 April 1986. The text of the Pope's address is in F. Gioia (ed.), *Interreligious Dialogue: The Official Teaching of the Catholic Church (1963–1995)* (Boston: Pauline Books and Media, 1997), pp. 332-37. The incident is also recounted by J. Beozzo, 'The External Climate', in G. Alberigo, *History of Vatican II* (5 vols.; trans. J. Komanchak; Maryknoll, NY: Orbis Books, 1995), I, pp. 357-404 (359), 'Driving along the Lungotevere John XXIII found himself in front of the Roman synagogue. The pope had the roof of the car removed and blessed a group of Jews who were leaving the temple. Rabbi Toaff, an eyewitness of the event, recalled that "after a moment of understandable bewilderment, the Jews surrounded him and applauded him enthusiastically. It was in fact the first real gesture of reconciliation." '

2.   J. Dupuis, *Jesus Christ at the Encounter of World Religions* (Maryknoll, NY: Orbis Books, 1993), pp. 230-42.

religions, distinguishes between the demands of dialogue with world religions that are 'indispensable psychological conditions' and the demands that are 'intrinsic to authentic dialogue'. The former include a positive attitude; an ability to rise above prejudices; an openness to the presence of the mystery in other traditions; a genuine desire to seek truth together. The latter presupposes a willingness to enter into the experience of the other. He notes also the difficulty in this demand when he asks, 'to what extent is it possible and legitimate for partners in dialogue to enter into each other's experience and share a faith different from their own?'[3] He says that 'one may not, on the pretext of honesty in the dialogue bracket one's faith (employ an *epoche*), even temporarily...'[4] Furthermore, the Christian 'may not dissimulate their own faith in Jesus Christ, the universal Saviour, and in his finality in the order of salvation'.[5] Can interfaith dialogue then ever take place? Can interfaith dialogue ever be more than mere politeness, a living in tolerance? This essay seeks to describe how the official Roman Catholic Church's relationship with the Jewish faith had developed in terms of interfaith dialogue over the last 35 years.

In the context of Catholic–Jewish dialogue, the 1974 Vatican Document 'Guidelines and Suggestions for the Implementing of the Conciliar Declaration *Nostra aetate* (par. 4)'[6] describes dialogue as presupposing

> that each side wishes to know the other, and wishes to increase and deepen its knowledge of the other. It constitutes a particularly suitable means of favouring a better mutual knowledge and, especially in the case of dialogue between Jews and Christians, of probing the riches of one's own tradition. Dialogue demands respect for the other as he[7] is; above all respect for his faith and his religious convictions.[8]

3. Dupuis, *Jesus Christ*, p. 232.

4. Dupuis, *Jesus Christ*, p. 232.

5. Dupuis, *Jesus Christ*, p. 232.

6. Vatican Commission for Religious Relations with the Jews, 1 December 1974.

7. As all Vatican documents are published in Latin, this paper retains an official English translation, in this case from A. Flannery (ed.), *Vatican Council II: The Conciliar and Post Conciliar Documents* (Dublin: Dominican Publications, study edn, 1992), p. 744. The paper presumes in every incidence an inclusive reading even when the language appears exclusive.

8. Vatican Commission for Religious Relations with the Jews, 1 December 1974, 'Guidelines and Suggestions for the Implementing of the Conciliar Declaration *Nostra aetate* (par. 4)', section 1.

The Vatican Secretariat for Non-Christians published in 1984 a document entitled, 'The Attitude of the Church towards Followers of Other Religions: Reflections on Dialogue and Mission'.[9] This document distinguishes four forms of inter-religious dialogue:

(1)   the dialogue of life, accessible to all;
(2)   the dialogue of a common commitment to the works of justice and human liberation;
(3)   the intellectual dialogue of the scholars;
(4)   and the dialogue of the sharing of religious experiences in a common quest for the Absolute.

This document stresses, therefore, that the starting point for interfaith dialogue is not dogma, but a dialogue for life that has at its heart 'concern, respect, and hospitality towards the other. It leaves room for the other person's identity, his modes of expression, and his values' (no. 29).

A corpus of Roman Catholic Church teaching on Catholic–Jewish relations can be found in five documents:

(1)   the Second Vatican Council's 'Declaration on the Relationship of the Church to Non-Christian Religions' (*Nostra aetate* par. 4), 28 October 1965;
(2)   'Guidelines and Suggestions for the Implementing the Conciliar Declaration *Nostra aetate* (par. 4)', 1 December 1974;
(3)   'Notes on the Correct Way to Present the Jews and Judaism in Preaching and Catechesis in the Roman Catholic Church', 24 June 1985;
(4)   discourse by John Paul II to representatives of the Jewish community at the Great Synagogue, Rome, 11 April 1986;
(5)   the Vatican Document 'We Remember: A Reflection on the *Shoah*', 16 March 1998.

---

9.   The Vatican Secretariat for Non-Christians was established by Pope Paul VI in 1964, but was renamed the Pontifical Council for Interreligious Dialogue (PCID) in 1988. It is also worth noting here that the PCID does not have responsibility for Christian–Jewish relations. These are assigned to the Commission for Religious Relations with Jews, which comes under the competence of the Pontifical Council for Promoting Christian Unity. This does not, however, preclude the inclusion here of this important 1984 statement.

While a first reading of these documents might suggest simple repetition, more careful analysis discloses important sequential developments. This essay suggests that much of the Church's teaching in this area takes the form of a spiral pedagogy, whereby the teaching is revisited at a higher level in the light of experience so that understanding of the essential truths continues to be developed.

2. The Second Vatican Council[10]

Rabbi A. James Rudin, writing about the impact of the Second Vatican Council's document *Nostra aetate* states that 'the post-1965 documents have broadened and strengthened Catholic–Jewish relations, but they were all set in motion by *Nostra Aetate*. Like the Magna Carta, the declaration of Independence, and the US Constitution, *Nostra Aetate* broke new ground and provided the mandate for constructive change.'[11] In Roman Catholic terms, the Second Vatican Council (1962–65)[12] is a

10. B. Huebsch, *Vatican II in Plain English: The Council* (Texas: Thomas More Publishers, 1996), pp. 64-65, highlights the major questions that would be discussed at the Council: the relationship of the Pope to bishops; the role of lay people; religious liberty; revelation; relationship with the Jewish faith; Christian unity; reform of the liturgy; the Church's relationship to the modern world.

The Council produced 16 documents over 4 sessions between 1962 and 1965, each session lasting about 8 weeks. The documents are: Constitution on the Sacred Liturgy (*Sacrosanctum concilium*), Decree on Mass Media (*Inter mirifica*)—4 December 1963; Dogmatic Constitution on the Church (*Lumen gentium*), Decree on Ecumenism (*Unitatis redintegratio*), Decree on Eastern Catholic Churches (*Orientalium ecclesiarum*)—21 November 1964; Decree on the Pastoral Office of Bishops in the Church (*Christus dominus*), Decree on Priestly Formation (*Optatam totius*), Decree on the Sensitive Renewal of Religious Life (*Perfectae caritatis*), Declaration on Christian Education (*Gravissimum educationis*), Declaration on the Relation of the Church to Non-Christians (*Nostra aetate*)—28 October 1965; Dogmatic Constitution on Divine Revelation (*Dei verbum*), Decree on the Apostolate of the Laity (*Apostolicam actuositatem*)—18 November 1965; Declaration on Religious Freedom (*Dignitatis humanae*), Declaration on the Missionary Activity of the Church (*Ad gentes*), Decree on the Ministry and Life of Priests (*Presbyterorum ordinis*), Pastoral Constitution on the Church in the Modern World (*Gaudium et spes*)—7 December 1965.

11. A.J. Rudin, 'The Dramatic Impact of Nostra Aetate', in E.J. Fisher, A.J. Rudin and M.H. Tanendaum (eds.), *Twenty Years of Jewish–Catholic Relations* (New York: Paulist Press, 1986), pp. 9-18 (15).

12. T. McCarthy, *The Catholic Tradition: The Church in the Twentieth Century*

pivotal formative experience of its ecclesiology, and of how it understands itself and its relationship to the world.[13] In the preface to the first volume of *History of Vatican II*, Giuseppe Alberigo writes that 'in the age-old course of Christian history the great conciliar assemblies constitute a spinal column. Knowledge of their unfolding offers the church an awareness of one of its basic choral dimensions and evidence of crucial instances of the Spirit's interventions in history.'[14] Developing that thought, Walter Kasper states 'the continuity of what is Catholic is understood by the last council as a unity between tradition and a living, relevant interpretation in the light of the current situation'.[15]

In attempting to create a historical assessment of the Second Vatican Council, John O'Malley in the 1980s wrote that 'we now must reckon with the inescapable obvious phenomenon of change in a Church that previously boasted that it did not change'.[16] He sees change in the Church as a necessary precondition for maintaining its identity. Moreover, he views change in the Church under three different guises: 'developments', 'reforms' and 'reformation'. 'Developments' he understands in terms of events that have an effect within the Church but without the Church having self-consciously initiated changes.[17] Relying heavily on the work of Thomas Kuhn,[18] O'Malley understands 'reform' as changes that occur in the Church within a framework of reference. These changes are more in the nature of adjustments rather than funda-

(Chicago: Loyola University Press, 1998), pp. 65-66, identifies the ten most important principles endorsed by Vatican II as: *aggiornamento*; religious freedom; ecumenism; interreligious dialogue; social mission; reform; laity; collegiality; and regional and local diversity.

13. The Church's ecclesiology is particularly articulated in *Lumen Gentium* and *Gaudium et Spes*.

14. Alberigo, *History of Vatican II*, I, p. xi.

15. Quoted by F. Sullivan in M.A Hayes and L. Gearon (eds.), *Contemporary Catholic Theology: A Reader* (Leominster: Gracewing, 1998), pp. 335-48 (346).

16. J. O'Malley, 'Developments, Reforms, and Two Great Reformations: Towards a Historical Assessment of Vatican II', *TS* 44 (1983), pp. 373-406 (374).

17. O'Malley gives examples such as the Hellenistic influence on the early Church; Constantine's edict of toleration; the developments of the Feudal Church; the establishment of universities in the thirteenth century; the development of the printing press and mass media; the role of women in society; the emergence of democracy.

18. T. Kuhn, *The Structure of Scientific Revolutions* (Chicago: University of Chicago Press, 2nd edn, 1970). O'Malley has a footnote stating 'the book has been the subject of an immense amount of discussion and controversy' (p. 374 n. 8).

mental changes.[19] 'Reformation', on the other hand, involves a para-digm shift,[20] it involves a change in world view, a radical change in any model of understanding.[21] In other words, changes occur in the Church as a result of external developments which are usually covert, from overt internal adjustments, or from a conscious shift in world-view. The Second Vatican Council according to O'Malley needs to be understood as falling between 'reform' and 'reformation'. However, in terms of assessing the effect of an event such as the Second Vatican Council, O'Malley is clear that 'the change was clearly identifiable as relating to the impulse that initiated it, that it clearly displaced or notably modified older institutions, that it created mechanisms and agents to perpetuate itself so that a reversal of course would for a long period of time be virtually impossible'.[22] It is certainly the case that the development of Roman Catholic–Jewish dialogue is a direct result of the Second Vatican Council and its desire to evaluate its relationship as 'the Church in the modern world'. To the extent that dialogue is still very much in process and deeply rooted in the work of the Council, we are still too close in time to judge this development as either 'reform' or 'reformation'.

3. *The Second Vatican Council's 'Declaration on the Relationship of the Church to Non-Christian Religions'* *(*Nostra aetate, *par. 4), 28 October 1965*

Of the 16 documents from the Second Vatican Council, the shortest, *Nostra aetate* ('In our Time', its full title being 'Declaration on the Relations of the Church to Non-Christian Religions'), was promulgated on 28 October 1965,[23] towards the end of the Council. Its small size is

19. Here O'Malley makes reference to changes such as the Fourth Lateran Council's (1215) decree *Omnis utiusque sexus* regarding annual confession and communion during the Easter season.

20. While he uses the term 'paradigm shift', O'Malley is conscious of the difficulty in applying such a construct to the history of Christianity since a total paradigm shift is by definition impossible for the Christian.

21. The Gregorian Reform of the eleventh century and the Lutheran Reformation of the sixteenth century fall under the category of 'reformation' for O'Malley.

22. O'Malley, 'Developments', p. 378.

23. For a full commentary on the origins of the declaration and a history of the text, see J. Oesterreicher (trans. S. Young, E. Young and H. Graef), 'Declaration on the Relationship of the Church to Non-Christian Religions', in H. Vorgrimler (ed.),

not congruent with its importance. From the early stages of the preparations for the Council, it had been the intention of Pope John XXIII that the Council would deal with the Church's relationship with the Jewish faith[24] and religious freedom. He was very conscious of the suffering of the Jewish people during the Second World War, and was anxious to condemn anti-Semitism. However, the preparatory schema on a document on the Jews was abandoned before the Council began 'not because of the ideas or doctrine expressed in the schema but only because of certain unhappy political considerations at the time'.[25] This was mainly due to Jewish–Arab hostility in the early 1960s and the presence of some anti-Semitic sentiment. By 1963, however, a chapter was included in the draft document on ecumenism entitled 'On the Relations of Catholics to Non-Christians, Especially Jews'. This chapter and a chapter on 'Religious Freedom' proved to be too controversial and were later considered as separate documents. In July 1964, another draft document was produced: 'Declaration on the Jews and Non-Christians'. This draft document was still opposed by Arab bishops and the Eastern Christians at the Council but rather than being dropped altogether, it was expanded to include other world faiths, including Islam, Buddhism and Hinduism. Its title was changed to 'Declaration on the Relation of the Church to Non-Christian Religions'. The section on the Jewish faith is the longest of the declaration, paragraph 4. It begins by remembering 'the bond that spiritually ties the people of the New Covenant to Abraham's stock...the Church of Christ acknowledges that, according to God's saving design, the beginning of her faith and her election are found already among the Patriarchs, Moses and the prophets'. Highlighting the significance for the Christian Church of the exodus and the 'Ancient Covenant', the Church cannot 'forget that she draws sustenance from the root of that well-cultivated olive tree onto

---

Commentary on the Documents of Vatican II (London: Burns & Oates; New York: Herder & Herder, 1969), pp. 1-136. Also A. Hastings, *A Concise Guide to the Documents of the Second Vatican Council* (2 vols.; London: Darton, Longman & Todd, 1968), I, pp. 195-203.

24. J. Beozzo, 'The Attitude of the Jewish World: Judaism, an Unexpected Theme' and 'John XXIII and the Jews' in Alberigo (ed.), *History of Vatican II*, I, pp. 357-404 (392-94).

25. Cardinal Bea, June 1962 quoted by D. Nicholl, 'Other Religions (*Nostra Aetate*)', in A. Hastings (ed.), *Modern Catholicism: Vatican II and After* (London: SPCK, 1991), pp. 126-34 (127).

which have been grafted the wild shoots, the Gentiles'. The declaration underlines very clearly the Church's special relationship with the Jewish faith in terms of a common inheritance. Furthermore, the declaration states that 'God holds the Jews most dear for the sake of their Fathers; He does not repent the gifts He makes or the calls He issues—such is the witness of the Apostles'. The declaration calls for 'mutual understanding and respect' and closer biblical and theological dialogue. The declaration is clear that the Passion of Jesus cannot be a charge against all Jews. It condemns any form of anti-Semitism, but, as Jamison, Lundy and Poole observe, it fails to deliver an overt condemnation of the holocaust.[26]

4. *Guidelines and Suggestions for Implementing the Conciliar Declaration* Nostra aetate *(par. 4) (1 December 1974)*

In calling itself *Guidelines and Suggestions*, the document emphasizes the restricted nature of its content. This is underlined in the introductory note. There are two main limitations in the document. First, it is above all a *pragmatic* document—it is concerned to recall the teaching of *Nostra aetate*, and then to offer practical, concrete suggestions dealing with dialogue, the liturgy, teaching and education, and common social action. The second limitation is in the nature of the documents of the universal Church, which cannot take account of all individual situations and so can only offer examples which it is hoped can be adopted in local churches in an appropriate manner. The introductory note recognizes that, while this work is but a first step in developing relations with Judaism, it is nonetheless an important one.

At the beginning of the preamble, the document refers to its genesis in the declaration *Nostra aetate*, and in the context of the 'memory of the persecution and massacre of Jews which took place in Europe, just before and during the Second World War'. The document also acknowledges that, while Christianity might have common roots in Judaism, over 2000 years there has been a deepening gap, marked by mutual ignorance and frequent confrontation. The document hopes to offer practical suggestions whereby the intention of the Declaration *Nostra aetate* can begin to be realized.

26. C. Jamison, D. Lundy and L. Poole, *'To Live Is to Change': A Way of Reading Vatican II* (Chelmsford, England: Rejoice Publications, 1995), p. 121.

The 'spiritual bonds and historical links' of the Church with Judaism, to say nothing of the dignity of the human person, would not only condemn all forms of anti-Semitism and discrimination, but also impose an obligation on Christians of acquiring a better knowledge of Judaism. In order to help relations between 'Catholics and their Jewish brothers', the document suggests four areas to be worked on.

a. *Dialogue*

In a very frank admission, the document acknowledges that in the past relations have 'scarcely risen above the level of monologue'. Dialogue requires not only a deeper knowledge of the other, but also a deep respect. While it is incumbent upon the Church to preach Jesus Christ, this should be done without infringing respect for religious liberty and with sensitivity to the Jewish difficulties with the mystery of the Incarnation. While history may have led to suspicion between the Church and Judaism, Christians must acknowledge and deal with their own responsibility. Apart from friendly talks, the document encourages study, prayer and social action as ways of deepening dialogue.

b. *Liturgy*

Christian liturgy owes a great deal to Jewish liturgy, particularly in their joint reverence of the Scriptures. As the Vatican II Constitution on Revelation *Dei verbum* states, the Old Testament is not replaced by the New, but both illumine and explain each other. This requires an emphasis on the *continuity* of faith between the New and Old Covenant. This is not to deny the original elements in Christianity, but to acknowledge that perfect fulfilment of both covenants awaits the glorious return of Christ at the end-time.

In terms of homilies on scriptural texts, there is a call for an authentic interpretation, and for care in not distorting the meaning of passages of Scripture which seem to show the whole Jewish people in unfavourable light. The document also encourages a careful translation of passages of particular sensitivity, notably some uses of 'the Jews' in John's Gospel, and the use of the words 'pharisee and pharisaism' when used in the liturgy.

c. *Teaching and Education*

In dealing with developments in Catholic understanding of Judaism, the document lists seven points:

(1) It is the same God who speaks in both Covenants;
(2) Judaism at the time of Christ and the apostles was a complex reality, with various trends and values;
(3) The Old Testament and the Judaism found there must not be characterized as a religion of fear and legalism;
(4) Jesus was a Jew and saw himself as a Jew. He taught in terms of the Law and saw his teaching in continuity with and as fulfilment of the Covenant;
(5) Jesus' death cannot be attributed to all the Jews of his time, nor to the Jews since;
(6) The fall of Jerusalem did not end the history of Judaism, which has developed its own traditions;
(7) The Church, like the prophets, awaits the final times when all will know God fully.

Such appropriate education is for widespread dissemination by all the usual means. There is also a need for deeper study of Jewish–Christian relations, a work for institutions of higher education. Specifically mentioned is the establishing of chairs of Jewish studies.

d. *Joint Social Action*
Jews and Christians share many basic principles of life and action in the world as a response to a loving God. This should enable them to work closely together for peace and social justice at international, national and local levels.

e. *Conclusion*
The document notes that there is a long road to travel, but it is a task for the whole Church, as it is in pondering her own mystery that the Church encounters the mystery of Israel. The task then is not just for specialists or for those in frequent contact with Jews, but for all Catholics. It is the responsibility of local bishops to ensure, through the appointment of individuals or the setting up of commissions, that this task is addressed at local level.

The Commission for Religious Relations with the Jews, which published this document, is to be at the service of this task, and significantly, it hopes that it will work together with other Christian bodies to carry this out. This too it does in the light of the Council which called for such ecumenical undertakings where possible.

5. *Notes on the Correct Way to Present the Jews and Judaism in Preaching and Catechesis in the Roman Catholic Church (24 June 1985)*

The purpose of this document is to make clear that there is an appropriate way to present the Jewish faith in preaching and teaching. As regards the latter, the document from the beginning focuses on 'children and young people'. The demand for this clear instruction comes from the remit of *Guidelines and Suggestions* (1974) dealing with paragraph 4 of *Nostra aetate* mentioned above. In essence, therefore, these *Notes* are a detailed exemplification of the theological principles of Catholic–Jewish relations inherent in *Nostra aetate*. The document is divided into six parts dealing with: religious teaching and Judaism; relations between the Old and New Testament; Jewish roots of Christianity; the Jews in the New Testament; the liturgy; Judaism and Christianity. The document consists of various points for attention when treating each of the specified areas.

a. *Religious Teaching and Judaism*

(1) The origin of the Church can be traced to the patriarchs and prophets.

(2) Because of the unique link between the Church and Judaism, Jewish studies should not be regarded as 'occasional and marginal' but as essential in catechesis.

(3) The link is not simply a historical link concerning the origins of the Church, but is a contemporary one. There are important contemporary faith links with Judaism.

(4) Dialogue should be seen to have three components:[27]

- (a)   respect for the other;
- (b)   knowledge of the basic components of Judaism; and
- (c)   an awareness of how 'the Jews define themselves in the light of their religious experience'.

(5) There is a tension in teaching about Judaism from a Catholic standpoint which requires the balancing of four sets of ideas:

---

27. These three principles for dialogue are taken from *Guidelines and Suggestions*, I (1974).

(a)   promise and fulfilment: where it is important to show that they throw light on each other;

(b)   continuity and newness: where it is important to reveal the metamorphosis from one to the other;

(c)   singularity and universality: where there is a need to show that the uniqueness of the experience of the people of the Old Testament is open to a wider extension; and

(d)   uniqueness and exemplary nature: where the uniqueness of the Jewish people is to have the force of example.

(6) Any study of poor quality reflects not only badly on Catholic–Jewish dialogue, but also serves Christian identity badly.

(7) Sensitivity and respect for other faiths does not mean that the Church ignores her mandate to preach the gospel. 'Church and Judaism cannot then be seen as two parallel ways of salvation, and the Church must witness to Christ as Redeemer for all.'

(8) The demands of *Nostra aetate* to counter any form of anti-Semitism should not be seen as simply combating an evil. The educational work should actually foster a love of Judaism which was chosen by God for communicating his revelation.

b. *Relations between the Old and New Testaments*
The document then spells out 11 principles for addressing the relationship between the Old and New Testaments.

(1) The use of the term 'Old' Testament as a traditional usage does not imply in any way that it is outworn. It stresses above all the need to recognize a continuity between the Testaments whereby the election of Israel receives its full meaning in the election of Jesus Christ.

(2) The events and people of the Old Testament are truly related to the Christian faith—Abraham is 'truly the father of our faith', and the events of the Old Testament take on an exemplary and universal significance.

(3) There is a tension between the continuity and discontinuity of the Old and New Testaments. Traditionally the Church dealt with this tension by employing the notion of 'typology'. This notion carries with it various difficulties, implying that the Old Testament needs to be interpreted by the New if it is to have any meaning.

(4) Where such typology implies simply a rupture between the Old

and New—as in the case of Marcion[28]—this tendency must be rejected.

(5) Typological interpretation suggests that the Old Testament is read as a preparation and in some degree a foreshadowing of the New.

(6) Christians then read the Old Testament in the light of the Christ event. This is authentic Christian interpretation, but does not coincide with Jewish reading of the text which also has value, and can be a valuable source of discernment for Christians too.

(7) Typological reading does not exhaust the Old Testament, but simply points to the 'unfathomable riches' it contains.

(8) Typology also reminds us that the Church too is part of God's plan on the way to fulfilment. Perfection is not yet achieved, and, until it is, all that has led to that fulfilment retains its own value, not losing its significance and becoming simply a stage on the way.

(9) The Exodus, for example, is a real event of salvation and liberation. That salvation and liberation had been accomplished by Christ and gradually are realized in the sacraments of the Church, but the *fullness* (my emphasis) of salvation and liberation awaits the coming of the kingdom.

(10) The eschatological hope of both Jews and Christians draws them together, even if from different starting points.

(11) As we await the coming of the kingdom of God as promised in the Old and New Testaments, Christians and Jews should work together for its advent. Catechesis can help young Christians to work with Jews for justice and peace in the world.

c. *Jewish Roots of Christianity*

The document continues with nine points concerning the Jewish roots of Christianity which can be addressed by catechesis.

(1) Jesus was truly a Jew of the first century, conscious of his Jewish tradition, which is an essential part of the doctrine of the Incarnation.

(2) While it is true that Jesus had a complex relationship with the traditional laws of Judaism, he also showed himself observant of the law of Moses.

(3) Jesus' ministry was associated with synagogue and Temple worship, with the feasts of Judaism and above all the Passover.

---

28. There is a footnote (n. 2) at this point in the text: 'A man of gnostic tendency who in the second century rejected the Old Testament and part of the New as the work of an evil god, a demiurge. The Church reacted strongly against this heresy (cf. Irenaeus).'

(4) There is a constant play in the Gospels of Jesus belonging to Israel and yet being open to the Gentiles.

(5) Jesus' relations with the Pharisees 'were not always or wholly polemical' (e.g. Lk. 7.36; 13.31; 14.1; Mk 12.34).

(6) Jesus shared some pharisaical doctrines, for example, resurrection of the body, prayer, fasting (cf. Mt. 6.1-18), almsgiving, and so forth. Similarly Paul always regarded Pharisee as a title of honour (cf. Acts 23.6; 26.5; Phil. 3.5).

(7) Both Jesus and Paul adopted pharisaical methods of teaching.

(8) It is important to note also that the Passion does not mention the Pharisees negatively. Indeed, it could be argued that 'if Jesus shows himself severe towards the Pharisees, it is because he is closer to them then to other contemporary Jewish groups'.

(9) All the above should help in understanding Paul's (Rom. 11.16-36) claim that the Church finds its origins in Judaism.

d. The Jews in the New Testament

The document then continues with an exploration of the Jews in the New Testament. The term the 'Jews' is often short-hand for Jesus' adversaries as the *Guidelines and Suggestions* (1974) notes. To be objective with regard to the Jews in the New Testament, certain principles need to be followed:

(1) As *Dei verbum* states, the compilation of the Gospels was a long and complex process. Therefore some of the hostility and confrontation depicted in the Gospels may relate to subsequent struggles between the early Church and the existing Jewish communities from which it had sprung. Care needs to be taken of the implications of this, especially when Christians are dealing with the events of the Passion of Christ.

(2) Nonetheless, there were clashes between Jesus and some Jews, for example, the Pharisees (cf. Mk 2.1-11, 24; 3.6, etc.).

(3) The claim of Jesus' followers that Jesus was the Messiah was rejected by the majority of Jews (Romans 9–11).

(4) The preaching of the early Church and its claims certainly led to the rupture with Judaism; this break cannot be played down.

(5) Despite this, Scripture reminds us that faith is a free gift (cf. Rom. 9.12), and we should not judge the consciences of others.

(6) The Church teaches that it is certainly wrong to attribute to subsequent generations the refusal of belief of those of the time of Jesus. Quoting from the Vatican II declaration on Religious Liberty

(*Dignitatis humanae*), coercion in such cases is quite unacceptable.

The question of the responsibility for Christ's death had been addressed by *Nostra aetate*: not all the Jews of Jesus' time nor the Jews of subsequent generations can be held responsible for the death of Jesus. This document draws attention rather to the responsibility of Christians for their own conscious sin for which Christ died. While the Church is the new people of God (*Nostra aetate*, par. 4), the Jews should not be regarded as repudiated by God 'as if such views followed from the holy scriptures'.

e. *The Liturgy*

Jews and Christians find a common heritage in the Scriptures for their liturgy. The Office of the Church relies heavily on the Old Testament and the eucharistic prayers reflect the Jewish tradition.

f. *Judaism and Christianity*

The document also notes areas of attention linking Judaism and Christianity in history. The history of Israel does not end in 70 CE, and Christians should be aware of the faith history of the Jews subsequently. The political state of Israel should not figure as religious but political history.[29] The long history of Israel is a sign of the people being a chosen people, 'we must rid ourselves of the traditional idea of a people *punished*'. Despite 2000 years of negative relations, we should be aware of the richness of Jewish faith history, including an awareness and understanding of 'the meaning for the Jews of the extermination during the years 1939–45, and its consequences'. Education and catechesis are important in helping to deal with racism and anti-Semitism which the document deplores in the words of *Nostra aetate*, and reinforced in *Guidelines and Suggestions* (1974). However, education and catechetical teaching should aim not just at eliminating discrimination and promoting tolerance, but at being an essential step towards true dialogue and understanding. This is to help overcome what the document acknowledges as a painful ignorance which leads to caricature of Judaism. The notes are there to help this process.[30]

29. See H.P. Fry (ed.), *Christian–Jewish Dialogue: A Reader* (Exeter: University of Exeter Press, 1996), pp. 126-28 on the 1993 Vatican's formal recognition of the State of Israel.

30. E. Fisher, 'Official Roman Catholic Teaching on Jews and Judaism: Commentary and Context', in E.J. Fisher and L. Klenicki (eds.), *In our Time: The*

6. *Discourse by Pope John Paul II to Representatives of the Jewish Community at the Great Synagogue, Rome, 11 April 1986*

The significance of this discourse is not so much in terms of what is new in the Church's teaching, but rather in the context of the place in which the Church's teaching is articulated as a 'contribution to the consolidation of the good relations between our two communities'. As alluded to in the introduction to this essay, the symbolism of the move from blessing the crowd outside the synagogue to addressing the community within is highly significant in terms of how far Catholic–Jewish dialogue had moved in 24 years. This was the first ever visit by a Pope to the Great Synagogue in Rome,[31] and he began his discourse by thanking the Chief Rabbi, Professor Elio Toaff, for his reception using words which recognize dialogue from a Jewish perspective. The Pope said this reception by the Jews of Rome was marked 'with great openness of heart and a profound sense of hospitality'. In spite of legitimate advances in terms of plurality in social, civil and religious levels, the Pope reiterated *Nostra aetate* in deploring any form of anti-Semitism. Furthermore, he spoke 'of abhorrence for the genocide decreed against the Jewish people during the last war'.

Recognizing that dialogue with the Jewish faith is a path which 'is still at the beginning', the Pope reminded his audience of *Nostra aetate* especially in terms of:

(1)   the bond that exists between Christianity and Judaism;
(2)   the fact that not all Jews either at the time or now can be blamed for the passion of Christ; and
(3)   the fact that it is not lawful to say, nor can it be deduced from the Scriptures, that the Jewish people are 'repudiated or cursed'.

He used the opportunity to remind his own Church of the importance of knowing and putting into practice the 1974 and 1985 documents mentioned above as part of the process in this dialogue for which his

Flowering of Jewish–Catholic Dialogue (New York: Paulist Press, 1990), pp. 19-24, offers a chart 'listing several areas in which the wording of the 1974 Vatican *Guidelines* and the...*Notes* have specifically clarified wording left "creatively vague" by the Second Vatican Council' (p. 19).

31.   See Fry (ed.), *Christian–Jewish Dialogue*, p. 100.

visit had a deep symbolic significance. Mutual collaboration in terms of the pursuit of human dignity and in the area of individual and social ethics were also highlighted. The Pope called for the particular Christian–Jewish relations in the city of Rome to 'be animated by fraternal love'.

The discourse concluded with the Pope reading a significant text from the psalms in its original Hebrew:

> *hodû la Adonai ki tob, ki le olam hasdô yomar-na Yisrael ki le olam hasdô yomerû-na yir'è Adonai, ki le olam hasdô* (Ps. 118.1-2, 4).

> O give thanks to the Lord for he is good, his steadfast love endures for ever! Let Israel say, 'His steadfast love endures for ever'. Let those who fear the Lord say, 'His steadfast love endures for ever'.

7. The Vatican Document 'We Remember: A Reflection on the Shoah' 16 March 1998

In his formal reception of this document prepared by the Vatican Commission for Religious Relations with the Jews, Pope John Paul II stated: 'On numerous occasions during my Pontificate I have recalled with a sense of deep sorrow the sufferings of the Jewish people during the Second World War. The crime which has become known as the *Shoah* remains an indelible stain on the history of the century that is now coming to a close.'[32] Noting that the joy of a Jubilee of the Third Millennium of Christianity is based on forgiveness and reconciliation with God and neighbour he calls the Church to 'repentance of past errors and infidelities'.

The document is addressed in the first instance to 'brothers and sisters of the Catholic Church' and then to 'our Jewish friends...to hear us with open hearts'. It is significant that it uses the term *Shoah*, meaning catastrophe, rather than holocaust, as the former is the preferred Jewish term. It describes the *Shoah* in this way:

> This century has witnessed an unspeakable tragedy, which can never be forgotten: the attempt by the Nazi regime to exterminate the Jewish people, with the consequent killing of millions of Jews. Women and men, old and young, children and infants, for the sole reason of their Jewish origin, were persecuted and deported. Some were killed immediately, while others were degraded, ill-treated, tortured and utterly

32. The Vatican, 12 March 1998.

robbed of their human dignity, and then murdered. Very few of those who entered the Camps survived, and those who did remained scarred for life. This was the *Shoah*. It is a major fact of the history of this century, a fact which still concerns us today.

Because of the closeness of Christians and Jews in terms of common 'bonds of spiritual kinship', there is a moral imperative to remember the *Shoah* in order that it will never happen again. This 'moral and religious memory' should lead to a serious reflection on the causes of the *Shoah*. The document traces the difficult and tormented history of relations between Jews and Christians. It recognizes that 'the balance of these relations over two thousand years has been quite negative'. These include:

erroneous and unjust interpretations of the New Testament;
anti-Judaism;
discrimination;
expulsions;
forced conversions;
until the end of the eighteenth century in the 'Christian' world not always enjoying a juridical status;
scapegoating;
with the rise of a 'false and exacerbated nationalism' in the nineteenth century accusing the Jews of having a disproportionate influence;
in the twentieth century the rise of National Socialism in Germany included making a distinction between 'so called Nordic-Aryan races and supposedly inferior races'.

The document outlines how the Church in Germany condemned racism. In 1931, various pastoral letters were written by German bishops 'condemning National Socialism, with its idolatry of race and State'. Pope Pius XI condemned Nazi racism in an encyclical letter read in German churches on Passion Sunday 1937, *Mit brennender Sorge* ('with ardent concern'). Pope Pius XII's first encyclical *Summi pontificatus* (20 October 1939) warned against theories that denied the unity of the human race and deified the State.

The extreme ideology which refused to acknowledge any transcendent reality and included anti-Semitism had, according to the document, its roots outside Christianity. However, the document asks whether this ideology which caused the *Shoah* 'was not made easier by the anti-

Jewish prejudices imbedded in some Christian minds and hearts. Did anti-Jewish sentiment among Christians make them less sensitive, or even indifferent, to the persecutions launched against the Jews by National Socialism when it came to power?' The document recognizes that there is no easy way to answer these questions, as they are 'subject to multiple influences'. It does highlight in particular, however, that the closing of borders including countries of 'Christian tradition' to Jewish emigrations during the early years of the Third Reich, 'whether due to anti-Jewish hostility or suspicion, political cowardice or short-sightedness, or national selfishness, lays a heavy burden of conscience on the authorities in question'. Moreover, in countries where mass deportation took place, it asks, 'Did Christians give every possible assistance to those being persecuted, and in particular to the persecuted Jews?' While many did help, others did not. In a contrite spirit, the document states, 'We deeply regret the errors and failures of those sons and daughters of the Church', and repeats the sentiment of *Nostra aetate* in condemning any form of anti-Semitism together with a condemnation of all forms of genocide.

In an optimistic conclusion, it calls on the Catholic Church to 'renew the awareness of the Hebrew roots of their faith'. It prays 'that sorrow for the tragedy which the Jewish people has suffered in our century will lead to a new relationship with the Jewish people'.

7. Conclusion

Nostra aetate is the foundation of current Roman Catholic–Jewish dialogue. Having this as a constant reference point means that each step in the process revisits and builds on this foundation. The subsequent four documents can be seen as articulations of and developments from that foundation rather than as new departures. While this essay offers in the main a descriptive account of the corpus of Roman Catholic teaching on this dialogue and has not attempted to offer a thorough analysis of these documents,[33] one can recognize a real development in Roman

---

33. Cf. on 'We Remember: A Reflection on the *Shoah*', R. Hill, 'Christians and Jews: Redeeming the Past', *The Tablet* (21 March 1998), pp. 372-73; Editorial, 'Holocaust Text Gets Cool Reception from Jewish Opinion', *The Tablet* (21 March 1998), pp. 390-91; J. McDade, 'Christian Repentance and the Shoah', *The Month* (April 1998), pp. 150-51. For analysis of other documents cf. R. Neudecker (trans. M. Costelloe), 'The Catholic Church and the Jewish People', in R. Latourelle (ed.),

Catholic reflection. Furthermore, it has been interesting to note over recent years the regular occurrence of issues that indicate a certain tension between the Roman Catholic Church and the Jewish faith, including the cause for the canonization of Isabella of Spain; the presence of the Carmelite community at Auschwitz; the role of Pope Pius XII during the Second World War; the beatification of Sr Teresa Benedicta (Edith Stein). The existence of difficult issues need not be an obstacle to dialogue, but can be seen as a sign of *real dialogue*. Real dialogue must contain issues of concern to both parties. Such controversies are an indication that Catholic–Jewish relations have moved from monologue to dialogue. The rise of historical consciousness has brought these and other issues to the fore. Dialogue is a means of enabling Roman Catholics, while witnessing to their own faith and way of life, to acknowledge, preserve and encourage the spiritual and moral truths found in Judaism, together with Jewish social life and culture (*Nostra aetate*, par. 2). It is dialogue such as this that Pope John Paul II sought to embody on his historic visit to the Great Synagogue in Rome in 1986, and it is to such dialogue that all members of the Church are called.[34]

Vatican II: Assessment and Perspectives, Twenty-five Years After (1962–1987) (3 vols.; Mahwah, NJ: Paulist Press, 1989), III, pp. 282-323; G. Wigoder, 'The Churches and the State of Israel', *The Month* (January 1999), pp. 3-10; E. Fisher, 'A New Maturity in Christian–Jewish Dialogue: An Annotated Bibliography 1975–1989', in Fisher and Klenicki (eds.), *In our Time*, pp. 106-17; Fisher, Rudin and Tanerbaum, *Twenty Years of Jewish–Catholic Relations*; E.J. Fisher, 'Jewish–Christian Relations 1989–1993: A Bibliographic Update', *CCAR Journal: A Reform Jewish Quarterly* (winter 1994). Beozzo, 'Attitude of the Jewish World', offers a footnote (n. 102) outlining a bibliographic survey of Jewish–Christian relations during the last 40 years.

34. The case for developing Catholic–Jewish dialogue has been further advanced by the visit by Pope John Paul II to Yad Vasham, Israel's principal Holocaust memorial on 23 March 2000. During this visit the Pope stated that the Catholic Church was deeply saddened by any acts of anti-Semitism by Christians. 'I have come to Yad Vasham to pay homage to the millions of Jewish people who, stripped of everything, especially of their human dignity, were murdered in the Holocaust... We wish to remember. But we wish to remember for a purpose, namely to ensure that never again will evil prevail, as it did of the millions of innocent victims of Nazism... Jews and Christians share an immense spiritual patrimony, flowing from God's self-revelation. Our religious teachings and our spiritual experience demand that we overcome evil with good.'

BACK TO THE FUTURE: A CENTURY OF JEWISH–CHRISTIAN RELATIONS IN POLAND

Sue Jackson

Introduction

In September 1998, I travelled to Poland on behalf of the Women's Studies Programme at the University of Surrey Roehampton, to develop work with the Center for Women's Studies at the University of Lodz. This visit was tied up with many issues for me: excitement at the opportunity offered, but a host of other feelings too. As a Jew, I knew that I would find it difficult and painful to be in Poland, a site of severe anti-Semitism in both the past and present; and site too of the mass extermination camps, including Auschwitz-Birkenau. In addition, Poland was home to two of my great-grandparents, before they escaped to England from the pogroms.

In this essay I shall explore a century of Jewish–Christian relations in Poland, concentrating on three periods: the early 1900s; the war years; and the present day. However, a fourth period will also be present: the future. Discussions of Jewish–Christian relations are not easy. There has been hurt, pain and mistrust, which cannot be forgotten nor easily forgiven in forward movement (see Maybaum 1979, for further discussion). Do journeys back leave us embedded in the past, or can they help to find a more hopeful future?

By the late 1800s, Jews had a long and varied history in Poland, where they had arrived in substantial numbers in the fourteenth and fifteenth centuries (see Bamberger 1957), with Poland being regarded 'as the safest country in Europe for Jews' (Johnson 1987: 231). In the larger towns in particular, Jewish communities lived and worked along-side their Christian neighbours: Catholic Poles and Lutheran Germans. However, these were also the pogrom years. Jews were chased out of smaller towns and villages by native Poles, and life could become difficult in the larger towns and cities. Many Jews, including my great-grandparents, made the brave and monumental decision to pack up and leave.

They were the lucky ones. Throughout the 1930s, anti-Semitism was rife in Poland, with a popular nationalist doctrine of 'Poland for the Poles' (see Wistrich 1991: 157). In 1939, Hitler invaded Poland and the unimaginable was to happen. While Christian neighbours looked on, Jews were murdered in their millions. From a pre-war total of three and a half million (Wistrich 1991: 157), today there are approximately 6000 Jews left in Poland (see Gilbert 1991: 123; Massil 1996: 169). The Carmelite Sisters of Auschwitz insist that the Jews have no special rights there, and continue to place crosses as symbols of suffering. Poland today has been described as a country of 'anti-semitism without Jews' (see Wistrich 1991). The Pope, himself a Pole, has started to speak out on such matters.

In tracing my journey back to the future, I shall draw on a range of sources, including my own experiences while in Lodz. Inspired by Martin Gilbert's moving book *Holocaust Journey* (1997), I kept a diary during my visit to Poland, and will weave my own autobiographical journeying into the text (for a discussion of autobiography in research see, e.g., Stanley 1990; Stanley 1992; Jouve 1992; Blair and Holland 1995). Remembering the past is not easy (see Gilbert 1997: 400-406), nor is re-membering: taking apart and putting back together again, sometimes forming different pictures. Martin Gilbert has subtitled his *Holocaust Journey* 'Travelling in search of the past'. However, I shall conclude my essay by asking how this journey back can also enable travelling in search of the future for Jewish–Christian relations in the century to come.

September 1998

I prepare for my trip to Lodz in Poland. I decide that, to go, to keep integrity with myself, this has to be a Jewish experience for me. I ask if it is possible from Lodz to visit Krakow, with its former Jewish quarter of Kazimierz; and also to visit Auschwitz. This seems to be a political decision. I think I am saying 'I'll come, but I don't forget'. Before I leave I am filled with foreboding. I have been devouring reading material before I go, and have been thinking too much of pogroms and anti-Semitism, of death and extermination. I start to feel I will die in Poland, murdered while walking along the street perhaps. I try to shake off the feeling, and prepare my academic papers.

14 September 1998

I am ready. I look at myself in the mirror before I go, in my new knee-length black jacket. I see the face of a yeshiva student looking back at me from a turn of the century shtetl. As the plane takes off, I start to say the shema to myself, the central daily prayer with which—blessing God's name—I ask for protection for my journey. It sounds hollow. How many of the six million said the same words, asked for the same protection, as choking, spluttering, terrified, unanswered, they died?

As I get off the plane a man greets me, shows me his identity card, and asks if he can help. I need the Polish Express autobus to Lodz and he explains that, as this is Sunday, the bus does not stop at the airport, but there is a service to take people into the city, where I can catch the bus. He takes my luggage and walks ahead. I follow. He loads my luggage into a car and tells me to get in. This seems wrong. Is this where I am to be murdered? So soon? We drive to the city where, in the pouring rain, he unloads my cases and asks for an exhorbitant sum of money. I question it, but end up paying. Here, after all, is the bus. I get in. Its first stop? The airport! So, I am being robbed and cheated as soon as I arrive in Poland. I expect my great-grandparents were, too.

Is this why they left? Between 1880 and 1900 around 150,000 Jews left Poland. Unemployment and poverty were high, and so were the pogroms. Young Poles would swarm into the Jewish quarters, including the Jewish quarter of Lodz, and beat up, and even kill, Jews (Raphael 1998).

15 September 1998

The next morning, my itinerary includes a sightseeing tour of Lodz. I am met in my hotel by a charming young woman, a student, who tells me she and her family have lived in Lodz for generations. I already know quite a lot about Lodz. I know that at the end of the nineteenth century, about the time when my great-grandparents left Poland, a third of Lodz's population were Jews. I know from my guide that Lodz was, until recently, at the centre of the textile industry in Poland, although many factories have now closed. She doesn't tell me (does she know?) that much of it was developed by Jews. During the first part of the twentieth century, one-third of the textile factories were owned by

*Jews, as were over a quarter of the small workshops. Jews formed a
third of the workforce, almost entirely employed in the textile industry. I
am shown the palace of the great industrialist Israel Poznanski, with no
mention made of his religion.*

This mix of different groups—Jews, Catholics and Lutheran Germans—was not unusual, both in larger towns such as Lodz, and in the
smaller shtetls. What was life like for these different groups co-existing
together in Lodz at the turn of the century? By the late nineteenth
century, Jews were no longer confined to a separate Jewish quarter—
although many indeed continued to live in it—but settled throughout
the city. Previously, there had been severe restrictions on where Jews
set up home, but by the turn of the century Jews were very active in the
textile industry, both as factory owners, like Israel Poznanski, and as
workers. In these factories, Jews, Catholics and Lutherans worked side
by side, with both Jews and non-Jews employing Jewish and non-
Jewish workers.

However, although they lived and worked in the same city, often in
close proximity, the groups in part lived separate lives. Jews had
restrictions on what they ate; dressed differently; often spoke a different
language (Yiddish). However, Eva Hoffman, in writing about the shtetl
of Bransk—somewhat smaller than the larger city of Lodz—says that
there is little evidence of hostilities or tensions between Jews and Poles
throughout the mid-nineteenth century. Jews had been a part of the
scene for a long time, and tended to be taken as a 'given': simply '"different" people whose existence does not impinge on one's own' (Hoffman 1998: 135). Nevertheless, each group—Jews and Poles—viewed
their neighbours as Other, as not the norm, different to themselves.
However, by the end of the century, with changing political ideologies,
life became harsher: anti-Semitism started to rise and emigration began
to look like an ever-growing option. Jews started to become equated
with that which was not Polish: as capitalists with no loyalties to the
nation.

In the larger cities, including Lodz, there was much public debate
about what constituted Polishness: 'To the nationalist thinkers, the
prospect of a Jewish sub-culture in Poland, pursuing its own beliefs,
education and civic institutions, was becoming unacceptable, even
intolerable' (Hoffman 1998: 144).

Jews as well as Poles fiercely debated these issues and there were certainly many secular Jews who were intent on entering Polish society. Nevertheless, in late nineteenth-century Lodz, there was much social and cultural activity which the Jews of Lodz instigated for themselves. There were numerous political associations and cultural institutions; charity and social work; growing educational organizations; and Zionist societies. Jewish drama companies and musical groups were formed, and Lodz was home to Jewish poets and authors. Jews formed an active part of Lodz society.

My guide takes me to see an exhibition of postcards of Lodz. There are only two postcards obviously of Jews—early twentieth-century per-haps—standing looking at the camera. With so many Jews living in Lodz, why only two postcards? The lack of postcards with images of Jews is as powerful to me as the numerous postcards of non-Jews that adorn the exhibition.

This is not the fist time that there has been a lack of postcards of or from Jews. Martin Gilbert describes the excitement of Jews in the Lodz ghetto in 1942 when they received a postcard from a Jewish family who had been deported. This event merited an entry in the Lodz ghetto *Chronicle*, although 'no mention was made of the lack of postcards from any of the 44,000 Lodz deportees' (Gilbert 1997: 369). Despite so many deportees, over 115,000 Jews remained in Lodz. A further 74,000 had already left in 1939, many fatally taking refuge in Warsaw, but no less fatally than had they remained. By 1944, almost the whole of the remaining Jewish population had been deported, including over 76,000 to Auschwitz. When the Soviet Army arrived in January 1945, of the 233,000 Jews in Lodz before 1939, only 870 Jews were left in the city. Today there are about 100 Jews left in Lodz. I could find out nothing about them.

I ask my guide if she could take me to the only remaining synagogue in Lodz. On the way, scrawled in various places along our route, we pass what I take to be anti-Semitic grafitti: Stars of David, with Polish words I can't understand. I don't like to ask my guide to translate, but I walk on feeling defiant.
    We have trouble finding the synagogue. Through a street of flaking buildings, we enter a courtyard and through that into another one. We find it, brave and lonely, bars at windows, padlock on doors. My guide

*takes my photograph, standing outside. I automatically smile for the
camera, but feel sorrow and despair. My guide chooses that moment to
ask me if I would also like to see Lodz's cathedral. I say yes, as I don't
know how to say no. With no apparent irony, she tells me that over 95
per cent of Lodz's population are Catholic. We walk around inside the
cathedral, and I'm screaming silently to the probably now dead population, where were you? What did you do?*

The answer, of course, is not so easy. Within the very first days of the
German invasion, Jews were pulled from their houses, herded together
and shot in front of their Christian neighbours. Throughout the German
occupation there could be no possible doubt as to what the Germans
were doing to the Jews. So what did Polish Catholics do?

Some did everything, risked their lives and sometimes gave their
lives to help Jews. In her book *Shtetl*, Eva Hoffman recounts several
such stories. A woman hid a Jewish family because 'when a person
needs help you have to help them…that's our faith…that you help those
in need' (Hoffman 1998: 208). The woman had heard her priest give a
sermon on helping other people. He too helped to find a hiding place
for the family in question. The Home Army, a resistance force, helped
some Jews escape the ghettos. There is evidence of Polish prisoners
helping a few Jews to escape the camps (Gilbert 1997: 161), and there
are no doubt many heroes whose stories go untold. The Poles suffered
enormous, indescribable tragedies of their own in the war, with three
million dead and their country destroyed, and yet some still acted so
courageously towards the Jews.

And some did nothing. Why? Because they were frightened, certainly. The Germans left them in no doubt that to help a Jew was pun-
ishable by death and indeed they would have seen Catholic neighbours
murdered—at times whole families brutally killed—for even small acts
of human kindness. Others did nothing because it was easier; or
because they were anti-Semitic; or because they harboured old grudges;
or because they were thankful that it was not, for the moment, them.

And some did worse than nothing. Some Polish citizens, seeing Jews
confirmed as the Other they always suspected, allowed their prejudices
to be fed, and joined in beating, even murdering, their Jewish neighbours. There is evidence that some members of the Home Army murdered Jews while their colleagues were trying to rescue them (Hoffman
1998: 238). Some were informers for a variety of motives:

> Under Nazi stimulation, brutality was becoming normalised... As Jewish
> lives were further devalued, as Jewish men and women were reduced to
> hunted animals, it became easier for some Poles to identify with the
> aggressor...and give away Jewish lives as casually as one might
> slaughter a non-human creature (Hoffman 1998: 227).

And would Jews have helped their Christian neighbours in similar
circumstances? What would I have done, in that time, in that place, and
in the shoes of a Polish Catholic? Who knows?

But that is us as individuals, with our bravery and our cowardice; our
strength and our frailty; our love and our hate. What about the Church
as an institution? Could it have done more? Through the late 1930s,
through political upheaval and economic disasters, there was a steep
rise in both nationalism and anti-Semitism in Poland. The Church cannot hold itself outside of politics. It has to take responsibility, both for
actions and for silences. While some priests clearly tried to fight the
growing tide of prejudice, others used their pulpits to feed the myths
and prejudices of their people, particularly in the villages among peas-
ant communities. In such a climate, Robert Wistrich argues that the
Catholic Church was an 'active promoter of pre-war anti-semitism',
encouraging the peasantry in an 'instinctive' anti-Semitism, encouraged
by the priests (Wistrich 1991: 158). Throughout the 1930s: 'the
Catholic Church contributed to the reactionary climate by tolerating
anti-Jewish sermons. Anti-Semitic literature, produced within the
Church...began to proliferate' (Hoffman 1998: 191).

Throughout the war years, throughout the indescribable atrocities,
throughout the massacre of six million Jews, the Pope, Pius XII, said
nothing to condemn the terrible situation, stating that his 'condemnation would not only fail to help the Jews, it might worsen the situation' (Davis 1998). It is hard to imagine how the situation could have
possibly been worsened.

16 September 1998

*I spend the morning at the Center for Women's Studies. Here it is hard
at first not to think about difference and Otherness, but I soon become
more passionate about my work, my research, and start to think about
all that women share together.*

*I have lunch with a woman whom I warm to immediately. As we get
to know each other a little over lunch, I slowly start to talk about my*

*Polish roots, my Polish Jewish roots. She is very interested, and we dis-
cuss religion for a while. She knows from my programme that I will be
visiting Auschwitz. She has, she tells me, visited several times. She talks
in a quiet voice of horror, and of shame, and of the crosses that have
been, and continue to be, erected. She talks a little about the history of
the Jews in Poland, and asks if I have visited the synagogue. She tells
me that it is still in weekly use for services: her friend prays there. She
also asks me if I have visited the Jewish cemetery. She starts to give me
directions, then offers to take me that afternoon. It has grown cold, and
she insists on driving me back to my hotel first, for a jumper. We drive
into the cemetery together.*

*I am filled with emotion as we reach the walls and enter. We pass the
prayer hall and move towards the monument to the six million. We
stand quietly as I search for a stone to place in remembrance. We move
into the cemetery. I have read that there are 180,000 surviving tombstones here, although there doesn't seem to be that number. It is a quiet
place, much of it overgrown, but the autumn colours add to the feeling
of peace. Many of the stones are very old: some are inscribed in
Hebrew, others in Polish I guess, although the names do not seem to me
to be Polish names at all, but ones with which I am familiar.*

*We stroll quietly together through the pathways. If I was alone, I'd
like to spend longer, reading the inscriptions. Perhaps my relatives are
here, but it no longer seems to matter. I feel a connection with these
Jews of Lodz, family or not.*

*We pass the mausoleum of Israel Poznanski, whose palace I saw
yesterday, and the silence is broken for a moment as we smile together
at his grand marble tomb and elaborate mosaics. We walk on, and
come to the 'ghetto fields'. Neither of us is sure what they are, these
large bleak areas of concrete blocks marking unnamed tombs. Perhaps
there are 180,000 graves here after all? They are bleak and grim, with
no overgrown greenery—no plants or greenery at all—to soften the
impact. We return to the car in silence.*

As war broke out, the Jews of Lodz were herded into a small ghetto
area. On 1 March 1940, on a day known as 'Bloody Thursday', many
Jews were murdered during an organized pogrom. Shocked and dazed,
thousands of Jews found themselves inside the ghetto without having
been allowed to take any property with them. On 1 May 1940, with
180,000 Jews inside, it was sealed off (Bayfield 1981: 94). Inside, peo-

ple soon began to starve. This, together with overwork, lack of hygiene and overcrowding, all led to epidemics quickly spreading through the ghetto, with tuberculosis killing many of the inhabitants. 'The sick, lying on their mattresses, became skinny and emaciated, thin as rails, leaving only marrowless, parched bones, with dead skin drawn tightly over them and limbs running with pus. They lay thus awaiting the approach of their redeemer, death' (eyewitness account, cited in Bayfield 1981: 95). It was to the ghetto field of Lodz Jewish cemetery, nameless, buried under slabs of concrete, that their remains were consigned, their bodies carted there by Poles on German orders.

17 September 1998

After another day at the Center for Women's Studies, tonight I'm taken out to visit the pubs of Lodz, whose fame, I'm told, is spread throughout Poland. Over a drink, my companions ask about my trip to Auschwitz, which they have noted from my itinerary. They try to come up with 'better' suggestions for 'sightseeing', and suggest I spend time in Krakow. I say that I do plan to visit the former Jewish quarter of Krakow, Kazimierz, although they think I will enjoy the old city and the castle more. Later, when I say that my great-grandparents lived in Poland, we discuss the problems of tracing ancestors. My hosts suggest that the best way I can do this is through church records: it has not occurred to them that I could be Jewish, nor that the records have long since been destroyed.

18 September 1998

This afternoon I return to the Jewish cemetery in Lodz. My lunch companion today says she wants to show me something different in Lodz, something which I will not yet have seen. Poland, she says, is said to be an anti-Semitic country without Jews. She tells me something of the history of the Jews in Lodz, the vast numbers living here until 1939. She does not seem to know that I'm Jewish.

She drives me to the Jewish cemetery. I do not say that I have already been here: indeed, I'm pleased to be able to visit again. She clearly knows this cemetery well. She points out names to me, tells me individual stories. She shows me the horror of the plaques on the wall: testimonies to complete families wiped out in the camps; to people

*murdered in the Lodz ghetto. She tells me of a saint's day in Lodz,
where people light candles to commemorate the dead. At that time, she
says, she and a group of Catholic friends come to the cemetery to light
a candle for the Jews. We walk slowly among the graves, some damaged, she tells me, not by time and the elements, but by vandalism.
When will it stop?*

*It is a strange day. We walk in sunshine and showers, and she gives
human faces to the people lying there. This is, she tells me, the biggest
Jewish cemetery in Europe. There* are *180,000 graves here. Still we
walk and walk—I barely touched on it earlier in the week. I wonder
from time to time if I will come across a Coffer: my great-grandparents' name. Is that the name they had in Poland, or was it anglicized
on their arrival, with no English at their disposal? They must have felt
lonely and afraid, arriving on England's shores. Or did they feel alive
and full of hope?*

19 September 1998

*I'm on the train about half-way between Lodz and Krakow. I'm sud-
denly, unexpectedly, overcome with pain. My eyes fill with tears. I can
no longer read, but look out of the window at the passing scenes that
the Jews of Lodz, herded into their cattle trucks, would not have been
able to see. Will I be able to cope with the journey from Krakow to
Auschwitz? Will the visit first to Kazimierz give me courage or leave me
in more despair? I need human comfort to help me through: a hand
held in mine; arms to shoulder each other. But I need, too, to be alone.
I will not be able to speak as I journey on.*

*The train grinds to a halt in the middle of nowhere. I can sense the
fear, the relief, in the trucks. Is their journey ended? What will be here?
The conductor walks up and down. Three men stand outside, working
on the line, looking at the train. Did they stand there and look, then?
What did they think, as the trucks kept coming? The train groans a
little, and moves on.*

*And so, to the hotel, and a taxi to Kazimierz, the former Jewish
quarter of Krakow. I am dropped off in Szeroka Street. How to describe
my feelings? Disbelief? Wonder? I walk slowly up and down, incredu-
lous. Here are synagogues, Jewish restaurants, signs in Hebrew. That
the buildings survived the war is ironic, both tragedy and blessing. The
Nazis intended Kazimierz to become a museum of vanished races.*

But before the Jews all but 'vanished' from Poland, what was life like for them then? In the late 1930s, there were almost three and a half million Jews in Poland, the largest Jewish community in Europe (Wistrich 1991: 157). People lived and worked in close proximity together: Catholics, Jews, and other minority groups. Nevertheless, many Jews—most perhaps—remained distinctive in terms of religion, culture, speech, dress and customs, continuing in the Otherness to which they had been assigned for so long. Dangerous times were growing, and Poland was ripe for them to reach their culmination:

> Before the war Jews had already suffered from an increasingly hysterical and nationalistic Polish antisemitism which led to the deaths of hundreds of Jews in the late 1930s, to economic boycotts, government discrimination and open calls from most Polish political parties for the mass emigration of Jews (Wistrich 1991: 157).

In 1939, there were 64,000 Jews in Krakow. By 1943, the Baedeker Guide described Kazimierz as a 'former place of residence of the Jewish population of Cracow, now free of Jews' (Gilbert 1997: 180). That any Jews of Kazimierz survived is partly due to the now Hollywood-famous Oskar Schindler. A man of many imperfections, acting through a mixture of motives (as most of us do for most of the time), Schindler saved many hundreds of Jews from certain death in Auschwitz and other notorious concentration camps (see Keneally 1982). A tree in his honour still stands in the Avenue of the Righteous in Israel's Yad Vashem museum, and Schindler himself lies buried in a Catholic cemetery in Jerusalem.

I decline the offer of a 'Schindler tour' of Kazimierz, and instead make my way alone to the Remuh Synagogue. This is the only one of the many synagogues and prayer houses still in use, with a community of just 100 Jews, mostly, the attendant tells me, old. He is an elderly Jew himself. Everyone else is gone, he says, and points upwards. I walk in and see this living building: the ark, the bimah, siddurim and tallitim on pews. I stand there and weep. I go into the adjoining cemetery, dating from 1533, one of only two remaining Renaissance Jewish cemeteries in Europe. The walls of the courtyard leading into the cemetery are now made of shattered tombstones, once—like the Jews of Krakow—whole and strong, but used by the Nazis for target practice.

I go into the bookshop and talk to another Jew behind the desk. We talk of Auschwitz. He tells me not to go on any organized tour, which, he says bitterly, concentrates on Auschwitz I. Make time, he advises, for Auschwitz II—Birkenau. It was here that the plans for the mass exter-mination of the Jews were formed and put into force. We talk for a while, quietly, sadly, and I move on.

The Old Synagogue, dating from the fifteeenth century and now a museum, is closed. Other synagogues and prayer houses are now pri-vate residences or businesses. But I find and enter the seventeenth-cen-tury Isaac Synagogue. This building has had a chequered relationship with the Christian community. Protests from the church delayed its inauguration. When, a few years later, Swedes destroyed one of the churches, the king decided to present the synagogue to the church. Eventually persuaded to change his mind, he ordered the Jews to pay for the reconstruction of the church instead. The synagogue's changing fortunes hit its lowest point during the Second World War when, bereft of its community, it fell into neglect and decay. The building was restored to the now tiny Jewish community in the early 1990s, and is being reconstructed as another museum.

I return to Szeroka Street for lunch. This is the most unreal—sur-real—moment of my trip. I sit at a table in the square in the weak mid-day sun and eat borscht and cholent at the Ariel restaurant, and think of my great-grandparents.

And, in the afternoon, Auschwitz. I have been told the wrong station to catch the train. A mad taxi-dash through Krakow, and I reach the station at 2.57 pm, with the train leaving at 3.00 pm. I see it as I run into the station, and just manage to jump on. I'm not sure if I wish I'd missed it. And so, the slow, slow journey onwards: only 50 km, but one and a half hours on the train. This is a small branch line, filled with local people presumably travelling home, many with heavy shopping bags. The ordinariness seems bizarre. A man opposite me strikes up conversation. He speaks little English, but wants to know why I am going to Osweicim—Auschwitz—when there is nothing there but the camp. Lacking courage, I just say I am interested. He gets off at one of the stations and a student moves across to take his place. Do I mind if he speaks to me, he asks, as he wants to practise his English. Resigned to not being left alone with my thoughts, I agree. He tells me he lives at Osweicim. I feel shocked. I hadn't thought of it as a town, with people living their lives. I ask him whether he has visited the camps, and he tells me no, he hasn't.

At the station we part company, and here is Osweicim town before me. It looks like any other small town. A town surely as full of people then, going about their daily lives, as now. How could they have not known? A sign indicates that buses leave outside the station for Auschwitz musuem. Is that what it is? A museum? I'm short of time, and jump in a taxi, asking the driver to go straight to Birkenau, where over a million Jews were murdered.

The camp is virtually deserted, and I move past the main watchtower, past the barbed wire fences and perimeter watchtowers.

For Rudolf Vrba, arriving in Birkenau in 1943, the camp was

> an incredible sight, an enormous rectangular yard with a watchtower at each corner and surrounded by barbed wire... Yet what first struck me was a mountain of trucks, cases, rucksacks, kitbags and parcels stacked in the middle of the yard. Nearby was another mountain, of blankets this time, fifty thousand of them, maybe a hundred thousand. I was so staggered by the sight of these twin peaks of personal possessions that I never thought at that moment where their owners might be (Gilbert 1997: 157).

To the side of me is the railway track which brought so many, so many, to their deaths.

Primo Levi recalls how that dreadful journey, which many did not survive, came abruptly to an end:

> The door opened with a crash... A vast platform appeared before us... We were afraid... [The] method was often adopted of merely opening both the doors of the wagon without warning or instructions to the new arrivals. Those who by chance climbed down on one side of the convoy entered the camp: the others went to the gas chamber... Thus, in an instant, our women, our parents, our children disappeared. We saw them for a while as an obscure mass at the other end of the platform; then we saw nothing more (Levi, cited in Gilbert 1997: 148).

I enter the camp and walk seemingly alone in the grounds, slowly, painfully. Occasionally I pass other visitors, pain as clear on their faces as it must be on mine.

There are directional arrows from time to time, and notes describing the sectors. Here, I read, is the hut where children were kept, on whom the Nazis performed their experiments. I cannot enter. Here are wooden huts originally designed as stables to accommodate 55 horses, and used for 1000 prisoners at a time. I walk into one of the brick

*barracks. I am overcome with the horror of it. 'Oh God', I hear myself
saying out loud, 'Oh God, Oh God'. After some minutes—how many? I
don't know—I go back into the light and, standing on my own at the
end of the twentieth century in Birkenau, Poland, I say kaddish, the
memorial prayer for the dead.*

*I walk slowly on. The sun is shining. I hear birdsong. Somewhere a
dog starts barking. I reach the site of the crematoria, blown up by the
Nazis as they made their escape. My guidebook tells me that in the
ruins it is still possible to discern the underground changing room,
where the victims were made to undress before being gassed. I don't
wish to 'discern' them. I pass the ponds filled with human ashes, and
stop at the monument to the victims of Auschwitz and say a silent
prayer. I walk slowly back through the camp, and to the exit, my heart
heavy for the million who couldn't do the same.*

What I have not seen are the crosses that I know have been erected just
outside Birkenau, but Gilbert describes seeing some of them:

> Continuing along the perimeter road at Birkenau, we reach the former SS
> headquarters, a substantial pre-1914 brick building with a three-storey
> tower. It is now a Catholic convent. The two crosses which adorn the
> building, the one on top of the tower being visible from afar, seem extra-
> ordinarily out of place (Gillbert 1997: 168-69).

The crosses that Gilbert saw have now multiplied into a field. The
first, centre of much controversy, was erected in 1988 by Carmelite
nuns as a symbol of suffering. These crosses were the tip of the iceberg.
Catholic activists have now erected 200 crosses near the site at
Birkenau (Paul 1998). Many were planted to commemorate the Christian dead of Auschwitz I, originally designed to imprison and even
murder Polish political prisoners. Most of these were Catholic: some
were people who challenged the Nazi regime, and paid for it; some
tried to save Jewish lives, and also paid with their lives. It is right that
these people be remembered. However, many more crosses were
planted to show that the Jews have no special case at Auschwitz. Adam
Raphael describes watching two of these crosses being erected: 'This
week, five grunting, struggling men erected two 13-ft wooden crosses,
complaining, as they worked, that Jews controlled the government and
the church' (Raphael 1998). Although Cardinal Glemp, head of the
Roman Catholic church in Poland, has said that the crosses should not
have been planted at Auschwitz—the grave of one and a half million

Jewish women, men and children—it is Jews, he has suggested, and not Catholics, who need to search for 'understanding and compromise' (Raphael 1998). Sister Margaret Shepherd, speaking on behalf of the Council of Christians and Jews, while recognizing the depth of suffering of Catholic Poles at the hands of the Nazis, has said:

> The erecting of dozens of crosses (at Auschwitz) rocks once more the fragile boat of restored relations between Christians and Jews, especially in Poland. That the symbol of the cross should be used in such a way— indeed, as a weapon—is reprehensible, and is more than a disturbing reminder of the troubled history between Jews and Christians (Shepherd 1998).

I climb into a waiting taxi, and ask the driver to stop at Auschwitz I on the way to the station. I have been warned of the commercialization, but I'm not quite prepared for it. There is a hotdog stand in the car park; souvenir kiosks (God knows what they sell); and cafeterias. There are coaches and cars; and lots of people milling around; and bustle and busy; and groups of schoolchildren: nothing of the quiet and desolate solitude of Birkenau. A plan points to places of special interest: a gas chamber and crematoria I; the 'wall of death' where prisoners were shot; and the collective gallows. I don't need to see these; nor the cloths of human hair; nor the suitcases of the departees. I don't go through the gates proclaiming 'Arbeit macht frei' ('work brings freedom'). Instead, I return to the taxi and back to the train. Thankfully this time no one speaks to me. Tomorrow I fly home.

Today, Jewish–Christian relations are as delicate and as fragile as they have been in the past, and as they will no doubt continue to be in the future. Issues continue to be problematic, with different readings of events, and misunderstandings and mistrust. There has been much discussion of late, for instance, in the Jewish press, regarding the decision in 1997 to canonize Teresa Benedicta of the Cross following her beatification in 1987. Teresa Benedicta was born a Polish Jew, Edith Stein, in 1891 and died in Auschwitz in 1942 (Cowan 1997). Who was she? Edith Stein took on her new name in 1922, when she became a Carmelite nun (the order who have since erected the crosses at Auschwitz). The church claim her as Teresa Benedicta, one of their newest saints: Jews insist she is still Edith Stein, a woman who died in Auschwitz not because she was a Catholic martyr, but because she was a Jew. How, then, do I address this woman here, in this essay, trying to recognize that Edith Stein is *also* Teresa Benedicta, except by giving her the dual personality under which she died?

The canonization has evoked much criticism from the Jewish community. Sir Sigmund Sternberg, for instance, a leading interfaith activist recently retired as chairman of the International Council of Christians and Jews, described his work for Jewish–Christian dialogue as 'placed under heavy shadow' by this decision (Rocker 1998). The church, says Sir Sigmund, is sending out mixed messages. There were many Christian martyrs from the holocaust period. It is disturbing that the church chooses to honour one who rejected her people. In a letter to the Papal envoy to Britain, Archbishop Pablo Puente, Sir Sigmund stated: 'Edith Stein died at Auschwitz not because she was a Catholic but because she was a Jew… In proclaiming Edith Stein a Christian martyr, many Jews suspect an attempt to bleach out the fact that the mass slaughter of their people took place in the midst of Christian Europe' (Rocker 1998). But is this the case? The Pope has declared that Teresa Benedicta's saint's day will be celebrated as a Holocaust memorial, to remind the world of 'that bestial plan to eliminate a people, which cost millions of Jewish brothers and sisters their lives' (Gruber and Cowan 1998).

In the last 35 years, the Vatican has made four significant statements to help to build Jewish–Christian relations, starting with the *Nostra aetate* issued in 1965, which aimed to refute the long-made accusation that the Jews were responsible for the death of Christ. The Vatican *Guidelines* and *Notes*, of 1974 and 1985 respectively, also moved relations forward. The *Notes* speak of the Jewish people as 'the people of God and the Old Testament' (Winter 1998). But it is to the most recent Vatican document that I now turn. In March 1998, after working on it for 10 years, the Vatican released a document of the Pontifical Commission for Religious Relations with the Jews, entitled 'We Remember: A Reflection on the *Shoah*'. This appears to offer hope and a way forward to the future. It chooses, for instance, to use the Hebrew word Shoah, emphasizing the uniqueness of the Holocaust to Jews, and expresses 'deep regret for the "errors and failures" of Roman Catholics during the holocaust' (Winter 1998). Nevertheless, this document has been described as adding the least of these four documents 'to the reconciliation between the two faiths' (Winter 1998). There is, states Rabbi Mark Winter, 'too much effort to exonerate Pope Pius XII; and too great an attempt to balance out those brave and heroic Catholics who worked to save Jews where they could with the much larger numbers of Catholic perpetrators' (Winter 1998).

Nevertheless, attempts to move forward have to be made. Indeed, despite his reservations, Rabbi Winter describes this latest Vatican document as constructing 'a new floor under Catholic–Jewish reconciliation', showing the 'exceptional personal commitment of Pope John Paul II to the Jewish people'. He concludes that 'this reconciliation has witnessed the transformation of profound enmity into deep friendship' (Winter 1998). This seems to me to be a little too optimistic. When does enmity turn to friendship? And, maybe more importantly, how? There are many, many stories of Catholics risking their lives to save Jews. Of the many instances, Gilbert tells a wartime story of a devout Catholic woman who, risking her own life and that of her family, hid and protected a young Jewish boy, treating him as her own (Gilbert 1997: 142). Neither of the boys' parents survived the war, and the woman, anxious to adopt the boy she had come to love, asked her local priest if he would baptize the boy. The priest, hearing that this would have been against the parents' wishes, refused. This priest was destined later to become the present Pope.

Of course, such stories do not 'balance out' the perpetration of evil. But 'balance' is too simplistic a calculation. How can we start to count the lives saved, the lives lost; those who helped, those who betrayed? And indeed, what is the use in counting? Polish Jewry—once alive, thriving, vibrant, teeming with life—is no more. The horror of this overwhelms, can drown out any attempt to move into the future. Indeed, for Polish Jewry there *is* no future. Questions remain. Was it an accident of fate that the Germans hatched their plans for the mass extermination of the Jews in Poland? Was it that so many of the world's Jews lived in Poland, that it made this a more efficient task? Or was it that they knew that—unlike some other states in Europe—the Polish people themselves would offer little resistance to this plan? To remember is to enter a sort of madness, from which there is no escape. How, then, to re-member: to take apart and reconstruct, to find some answers, to journey from this hell back to the future? I do not have the answers but can at least, like the children at the Seder table, ask the questions. If the past that is the century now closed is a foreign country, then the future is a foreign country too. It is territory waiting to be explored, with borders waiting to be crossed. Jews and Christians alike need to explore how we can search for ways to build the bridges which will enable us to cross those borders together.

BIBLIOGRAPHY

Bayfield, T.
        1981   *Churban: The Murder of the Jews of Europe* (London: Michael Goulston
                    Educational Foundation).
Bamberger, B.
        1957   *The Story of Judaism* (New York: The Union of American Hebrew Con-
                    gregations).
Blair, M., and J. Holland
        1995   *Identity and Diversity* (Clevedon: Multilingual Matters).
Cowan, S.
        1997   'Pope gives $50,000 to Jewish Relief Agency', *Jewish Chronicle* (18
                    April).
Davis, J.
        1998   'Vatican Document on the Holocaust', *Jewish Chronicle* (24 April).
Gilbert, M.
        1991   *Jewish History Atlas* (London: Weidenfeld & Nicholson).
        1997   *Holocaust Journey: Travelling in Search of the Past* (London: Weiden-
                    feld & Nicholson).
Gruber, R., and S. Cowan
        1998   'Vatican "unwise" Says Sacks', *Jewish Chronicle* (16 October).
Hoffman, E.
        1998   *Shtetl* (London: Secker & Warburg).
Johnson, P.
        1987   *A History of the Jews* (London: Weidenfeld & Nicholson).
Jouve, N.W.
        1992   'Criticism as autobiography', in F. Bonner *et al.*, *Imagining Women*
                    (Cambridge, MA: Polity Press): 113-15.
Keneally, T.
        1982   *Schindler's Ark* (London: Hodder & Stoughton).
Massil, S. (ed.)
        1996   *The Jewish Year Book* (London: Vallentine Mitchell).
Maybaum, I.
        1979   'Jewish Understanding of the Christian: Christian Understanding of the
                    Jew', in D. Marmur (ed.), *A Genuine Search* (London: Reform Syna-
                    gogues of Great Britain): 221-25.
Paul, G.
        1998   'Priest Barred from Holocaust Conference', *Jewish Chronicle* (25
                    September).
Raphael, A.
        1998   'Too Many Crosses to Bear', *Jewish Chronicle* (4 September).
Rocker, S.
        1998   'Top Inter-Faith Activist Joins Attack on Stein Canonisation', *Jewish
                    Chronicle* (23 October).

Shepherd, Sister M.
    1998   'The Pain of the Auschwitz Crosses', *Jewish Chronicle* (11 September).
Stanley, L.
    1992   *The Auto/biographical I* (Manchester: Manchester University Press).
Stanley, L. (ed.)
    1990   *Feminist Praxis* (London: Routledge).
Winter, Rabbi M.
    1998   'Vatican Shoah Paper "is a result of political compromise within
                Church"', *Jewish Chronicle* (20 March).
Wistrich, R.
    1991   *Anti-Semitism: The Longest Hatred* (London: Methuen).

THE SENSE OF MISSION IN JUDAISM AND CHRISTIANITY

Armida Veglio

The understanding of 'mission' in Judaism and Christianity is an area where there has been some progress in Christian–Jewish relations, and a profound change in our own time in the Christian approach. However, it is still an area where there is tension between Jews and Christians. It is a very sensitive area for non-Christians, since the past Christian approach conjures up memories of forthright proclamation, crusades, a lack of understanding of another's culture, and so on. In this essay, I will look first at Jewish ideas of mission; secondly at Christian ideas of mission with respect to religions other than Judaism and the changes which have taken place in this thinking; and thirdly at changes in the Christian approach to Judaism.

For Jews, 'mission' is essentially their role of being witness to their relationship to God by faithfully living out their response to God's gift to them of Torah. This is not in the Christian sense of bearing witness, but rather by carrying out the *mitzvot*, a Jew witnesses to God's providence by what he or she does. For example, in the Talmud we find the following discussion on keeping the Sabbath: 'Why does this man refrain from work on the Sabbath? Why does he close his business on the seventh day? He does so in order to bear witness to the fact of God's creation of the world, and to his providence over it' (*b. Mek.* 104a). The doing of the *mitzvot* is important.

The Torah is described as 'the book of the covenant' (Exod. 24.7). God promises to be faithful to his people if they keep his *mitzvot*: 'Know therefore that the Lord your God is God, the faithful God who keeps covenant and steadfast love with those who love him and keep his commandments, to a thousand generations' (Deut. 7.9). In return, the people accept the covenant and agree to obey the *mitzvot* as a sign of their commitment to God's will: 'All that the Lord has spoken we will do, and we will be obedient' (Exod. 24.7). Note that 'we will do' comes first before 'we will be obedient'.

Isaiah 42.6, 7 sums up the witnessing as their role as the people of the covenant:

> I am the Lord, I have called you in righteousness,
> I have taken you by the hand and kept you;
> I have given you as a covenant to the people, a light to the nations,
> to open the eyes that are blind,
> to bring out the prisoners from the dungeon,
> from the prison those who sit in darkness.

The idea of the light of the nations does not in any way have a corollary of proclamation or conversion of others. Rather the people are called to witness to the covenant by their very existence. Pinchas Peli explains from an Orthodox point of view the reason why the first verse of the *Shema* is written on the Torah scroll with the ayin of *Shema* and the daleth of *ehad* larger than the other letters: 'The last letter of the first word and the last letter of the last word make up, according to the rabbis, one Hebrew word, *ed. Ed* means a witness. Israel, by its very being, is a witness.'[1]

However, some Jewish thinkers, for example, Leo Baeck in the Reform and Progressive tradition, have derived even from this idea of witness a clear notion of mission, a sense of a task to bring all people to God. He writes: 'Only in Israel did an ethical monotheism exist, and wherever else it is found later, it has been derived directly or indirectly from Israel. The nature of this religion was conditioned by the existence of the people of Israel, and so it became one of the nations that have a mission to fulfil.'[2]

Israel's mission, then, is to lead other peoples to monotheism; not to lead them to become Jews. Baeck continues:

> The idea of election is therefore nothing but the vibrant realisation by the religious community that it possesses the knowledge of the truth, the divine revelation. In the consciousness of this unique vital possession of the covenant with God, the community gained the capacity to act with freedom and to remain different to numbers and success.[3]

The emphasis is on the possession of truth, rather than a concern to convert or to expand. Baeck writes: 'Religious universalism is thus a

---

1.   P. Peli, 'Hear, O Israel: Witness to the One God', *SIDIC* 16.2 (1983), p. 7.
2.   L. Baeck, *The Essence of Judaism* (New York: Schocken Books, 1961), p. 61.
3.   Baeck, *The Essence of Judaism*, p. 63.

fundamental part of the Jewish religion; it becomes the principle of an historical religious task. Israel is a world religion in that it sees the future of mankind as a goal of its pilgrimage...the One God can have only one religion to which all are called and which cannot therefore find its historical fulfilment until all men are united in it.'[4] The fulfilment of the one religion to which all humanity is called is eschatological and dependent on the fulfilment of God's will. It is not about conversion of others to Judaism here and now.

In the Sabbath Morning Service, there is a prayer which reads:

> Then all who inhabit this world shall meet in understanding, and shall know that to you alone each one shall submit, and pledge himself in every tongue. In your presence, Lord our God, they shall bow down and be humble, honouring the glory of your being. All shall accept the duty of building your kingdom, so that your reign of goodness shall come soon and last forever. For yours alone is the true kingdom, and only the glory of your rule endures forever.

So it is written in the Torah:

> The Lord shall rule forever and ever.
> So it is prophesied:
> The Lord shall be as a King over all the earth.
> On that day the Lord shall be One, and known as One.[5]

The task or mission of Jews is to prepare the way for all peoples to share in the truth which they possess. However, God's intention, while it is for all people to come into his kingdom, is not that all people should become Jews—Jonah was called to preach to the Ninevites, not to convert them to Judaism, but to lead them to mend their ways (Jon. 3.10). In Judaism, then, there are differences of emphasis, but however the understanding of mission is explored or extended, there is very much a sense of God bringing the nations into the kingdom, rather than the aggressive sense of mission which has at certain times been associated with Christianity.

In Judaism, there is not an expectation that everyone must become Jewish to be part of God's kingdom. All people must live their lives according to God's covenant with Noah, which entails six laws: not to

4. Baeck, *The Essence of Judaism*, p. 68.

5. *Forms of Prayer for Jewish Worship* (ed. the Assembly of Rabbis of the Reform Synagogues of Great Britain; London: Reform Synagogues of Great Britain, 1977), p. 169.

profane God's name, not to commit murder, not to steal, not to commit adultery, not to be unjust, not to cut limbs from living animals (Genesis 9). Gentiles do not need to become Jews, but only to keep these laws to be acceptable in the sight of God whose Kingdom extends to the whole world.

Christianity, on the other hand, has been associated with the idea of mission as sending out to proclaim and convert; to convert, not in the sense of bringing about a change of heart, or renewal, but to bring about a conversion to Christianity. The first followers of Jesus were Jews and addressed their message to fellow Jews: Peter addressed 'Men of Judaea and all who dwell in Jerusalem', and later, 'Men of Israel, hear these words...' (Acts 2.14, 22). It was Paul who asked the question whether this message was addressed to the Gentiles too. By the time the Gospel of Matthew was written the answer was a definite yes; Christians ought to reach out to Gentiles: 'All authority in heaven and on earth has been given to me. Go, therefore, make disciples of all the nations, baptizing them in the name of the Father and of the Son and of the Holy Spirit, and teaching them to observe all that I have commanded you' (Mt. 28.19, 20).

Throughout the history of Christianity there has been a tension with regard to mission. There is the element Baeck describes in Judaism of a conviction of possession of the truth and the desire to make that known, but there is also the conviction that there is the absolute necessity of conversion to Christ to be saved. Pagans were thought to be completely in the dark, or at best enlightened to a limited extent, while awaiting the good news of the gospel, and Christian missionary activity often went alongside an expansionist vision which has been tainted by triumphalism. This began with the conversion of Constantine and the establishment of Christianity as the state religion of the Roman Empire, but in different guises it persisted after the collapse of the Empire into the period of the expansion of the mediaeval kingdoms and on into the age of exploration and colonization when the opening up of new parts of the world to Europeans gave more scope for missionary and imperialist expansion. Contact with other cultures did, however, widen the vision of the Church, and sowed the seeds of an appreciation of cultures other than that of European Christendom.

For Christianity, any real development or change in its sense of mission took place in the twentieth century. Anti-colonialism has led Christians to question how Western culture has been made integral to the presentation of the gospel. Christianity is beginning in this century to realize that it can learn from other religions. For the Catholic Church, the beginning of a change in approach is exemplified in the documents of the Second Vatican Council and later.

In *Ad gentes*, the Decree on the Missionary Activity of the Church, there is a traditional approach. It opens:

> The Church has been divinely sent to all nations that she might be 'the universal sacrament of salvation'.
>
> The pilgrim Church is missionary by her very nature.
>
> The specific purpose of this missionary activity is evangelisation and the planting of the Church among those peoples and groups where she has not yet taken root.[6]

Other documents take a different approach. *Dignitatis humanae*, the Decree on Religious Freedom, declares the right of every human being to seek the truth without coercion or pressure, and upholds both the individual and the communal right to religious freedom.[7]

Nostra aetate, the Decree on the Relationship of the Church to non-Christian Religions, calls for real dialogue and *Gaudium et Spes,* the Decree on the Church in the Modern World, describes the Church's mission as one of service in preparation for God's kingdom. It also asks the question whether attempts to convert others to Christianity will aid harmony or lead to more tension which will harm the Church's mission to promote God's kingdom of justice and of peace.

Pope Paul VI's encyclical, *Evangelii nuntiandi*, makes it clear that evangelization is first carried out by the witness of Christians' lives: 'Above all the Gospel must be proclaimed by witness...all Christians are called to this witness'.[8] However, he goes on to say that although all must witness by their lives, some must be trained to proclaim. 'Nevertheless this [witness] always remains insufficient, because even the finest witness will prove ineffective in the long run if it is not explained, justified...and made explicit by a clear and unequivocal proclamation of the Lord Jesus.'[9]

---

6. *Ad gentes*, 7 December 1965, nn.1, 2, 6.
7. *Dignitatis humanae*, 7 December 1965, p. 681 n. 4.
8. *Evangelii nuntiandi*, 8 December 1975, p. 30 n. 21.
9. *Evangelii nuntiandi*, p. 30 n. 22.

A further document from the Pontifical Council for Inter-Religious Dialogue and the Congregation for the Evangelization of Peoples in 1991, *Dialogue and Proclamation*, quotes Pope John Paul II: 'Just as inter-religious dialogue is one element in the mission of the Church, the proclamation of God's saving work in Our Lord Jesus Christ is another... There can be no question of choosing one and ignoring or rejecting the other.'[10] While this document takes the trouble to spell out what it means by dialogue at different levels the openness to other traditions which is required and the importance of dialogue which leads people to deepen their religious commitment and recognize with respect the free decisions of persons taken according to the dictates of their own conscience, it insists that the proclamation of Christ is essential.

We are left with enormous questions, but before exploring them further I will turn to specifically Christian–Jewish relations which have always been in a different category and are quite unique. From New Testament times onwards there has been an attitude of contempt apparent in Christianity, as well as an interpretation of Christianity as fulfilling Judaism and making Judaism no longer necessary. Both of these approaches have led to opposition and persecution, but there has also been a lingering respect for Judaism and a suspicion that Judaism should survive as a separate faith as part of God's plan.

Nostra aetate, as well as the subsequent documents, *Guidelines and Suggestions for Implementing the Conciliar Document* and *Notes on the Correct Way to Present the Jews and Judaism in Preaching and Catechesis*, speak forthrightly against any such opposition or supersessionist view. They show a concern to redress the balance in the distortion Judaism has often suffered in Christian thinking. In particular there must be a recognition of Judaism as a religion valid today, not just a religion of the past which finished in 70 CE and which was superseded by Christianity. The promises of God have not been withdrawn.

Christians are called therefore to appreciate as well the validity of the Hebrew Bible as it stands, and not just as the Old Testament in preparation for the New. In reading the New Testament, Christians should try to understand the background against which it was written; to appreciate the fact that Jesus was truly a Jew; to realize that much of the conflict portrayed in the Gospels is a reflection of the situation of the early Church.

---

10. *Dialogue and Proclamation*, n. 6.

Up until Vatican II there was no serious official questioning of the negative portrait of the Jews painted by Christians nor of the consequences of anti-Judaism for the development of anti-Semitism in Western culture.[11] Now there are official statements from the Vatican on what the Catholic approach to Judaism should be. In *Nostra aetate* a much greater appreciation of Judaism is given. It is pointed out that the Christian Church is indebted to Judaism and does not replace or supersede it.[12] The *Guidelines for Implementing the Conciliar Document* (1974) is a practical document rather than a theology,[13] but some of *Nostra aetate*'s points are made more explicitly. True dialogue is called for. Christians should be ready to listen to the Jewish experience, especially in the light of the appalling suffering of the *Shoah* in this century. Attempts to convert Jews must be rejected by Catholics. Although Christians believe God's promises are fulfilled in Christ, they also recognize that the messianic age is not yet complete. We await, with the Jews, the complete reign of God witnessing together to the 'not yet'. It is not a case of Christians saying 'yes' and Jews 'no' to God's reign[14]— we are *joint* witnesses.

In summary, Jewish approach to mission is to be a witness by the covenant. God will bring all peoples into his kingdom at the end of time. The Christian approach values witness, but sees proclamation of Christ as essential. Progress in the coming together of different faiths has certainly been made in recent decades, but questions remain, particularly for Christians. It is difficult for Christians with a history of missionary activity which sets out to proclaim Christ as the universal Saviour and which sees the church as the universal sacrament of salvation to be able to enter into real dialogue with either Jews or members of other faiths. A Christian believes in Christ as Saviour, but if this means that all people must become Christians to be saved or even that all other faiths are seen as preparation for the gospel and adherents of those faiths as anonymous Christians, the Christian is not going to be in a position to enter into real dialogue.

11. E.J. Fisher, 'Official Roman Catholic Teaching on Jews and Judaism: Commentary and Context', in E.J. Fisher and L. Klenicki (eds.), *In our Time* (New York: Paulist Press, 1986), p. 4.

12. Fisher, 'Official Roman Catholic Teaching', p. 5.

13. *Guidelines*, preamble.

14. Fisher, 'Official Roman Catholic Teaching', p. 11.

We have not yet reached the stage of a complete answer to this problem, but perhaps there are some ways forward. Christians can learn from the Jewish approach of seeing all fulfilled in God's kingdom at the end of time. Christians do recognize that the fulfilment of the kingdom is not yet. Perhaps more emphasis could be placed on this aspect. After all, all peoples recognize that we are still in a process of struggle in human development. Christians could trust more in God's working in a variety of ways in the world, trust that God can bring all things together at the end of time, and place more emphasis on the 'not yet' of the Kingdom.

Proclamation of Christ is regarded as essential in all the Catholic documents mentioned above. If proclamation is essential, it can only be done in certain circumstances. The 1991 document parallels 'to proclaim the name of Jesus' and 'to invite people to become his disciples in the Church'. This has to be done in the setting of dialogue and learning from each other and only to those who would welcome such an invitation, as the document says, 'when the time is right'.[15] If for Christians the proclamation of Christ means the proclamation of Christ to all as universal Saviour, how can they genuinely enter into dialogue with others? If proclamation of Christ means proclamation by Christians of their own faith alongside a trust in God to bring all to completion at the end of time, then there is the possibility of a true and genuine dialogue.

15. *Dialogue and Proclamation*, n. 76.

WHY TEACH JUDAISM?

Anne Clark

1. *The Nature of Society*

In drawing up the terms of reference for the 1985 report of the Committee of Inquiry into the education of children from ethnic minority groups (the Swann Report), the government of the time characterized British society as 'both multi-racial and culturally diverse'.[1] The opening sentence of Chapter 8 of the report, which is concerned with religious education, describes 'the wide range of religious beliefs which now form part of the overall diversity of religious experience in Britain today [as] one of the most vivid manifestations of the diversity of our society'.[2]

The chapter goes on to cite the contribution of religious education to intercultural and international understanding as one of the central reasons for its inclusion as a crucial element in the education process:

> ...an understanding and appreciation of religious diversity contributes to, and is indeed vital to, the development of a young person's understanding of the motivations, values and outlook of people from a range of religious backgrounds, both within this society and in other societies.[3]

The Swann Report stresses the role of multi-faith education in challenging and overcoming racism, and asserts that, in addition, it makes a significant contribution to the personal development of the individual child:

> In order for [young people] to be considered fully educated, they must have some understanding of the nature of belief and of different belief systems and of how these have and are still influencing human

---

1. Committee of Inquiry into the Education of Children from Ethnic Minority Groups, *Education for All* (London: HMSO, 1985), p. 3.
2. Committee of Inquiry, *Education for All*, p. 465.
3. Committee of Inquiry, *Education for All*, p. 469.

experience. Such knowledge can by extension help in the formation of pupils' own personal beliefs and values, whether religious or non-religious. [4]

2. *The Legal Requirement*

The Education Reform Act 1988 required that religious education should be taught to all pupils in full-time education (except for those withdrawn at the wish of their parents).[5] Religious education in county-maintained, voluntary controlled and most grant-maintained schools should be taught in accordance with a locally agreed syllabus.[6] Such a syllabus should 'reflect the fact that the religious traditions in Great Britain are in the main Christian, whilst taking account of the teaching and practices of the other principal religions represented in Great Britain'.[7]

In its 'Guidance to Agreed Syllabus Conferences', the School Curriculum and Assessment Authority recommended that *all* the other five principal religions should be included in the syllabus as a whole.[8] As Judaism is one of these principal religions, it follows that Judaism must be included in all syllabuses. There are, however, a number of sound educational reasons for teaching Judaism, aside from the legal imperative.

3. *Educational Reasons for Teaching Judaism*

Understanding the Jewish Roots of Western Society
Although the pluralist nature of contemporary British society at the beginning of the twenty-first century is undeniable, Christianity is still the religion that has, up to now, most deeply and extensively conditioned the country's culture. This is the reason given by the government for its insistence that, 'as a whole and at each key stage the

4. Committee of Inquiry, *Education for All*, p. 468.
5. See Education Reform Act 1988 (London: HMSO, 1988), §§2.1a and 9.3.
6. See Education Act 1944 (London: HMSO, 1944), §§6–29, as amended by the Education Reform Act 1988 and Education Act 1993 (London: HMSO, 1993), §§138-40 and 142.
7. Education Reform Act 1988, §8.3.
8. See *Model Syllabuses for Religious Education* (London: School Curriculum and Assessment Authority, 1994), model 1, p. 5; model 2, p. 4.

relative content devoted to Christianity in the syllabus should predominatc'.[9]

Christianity did, however, develop from Judaism. The teachings of the New Testament grew out of the teachings of the Pentateuch. In order to understand the roots and development of Christianity, it is necessary to study Jewish history and the Hebrew Bible. This is, of course, an approach fraught with pitfalls as, in unskilled or unscrupulous hands, it can lead to a study of Judaism solely as the precursor of Christianity, rather than the presentation of the Jewish religion as a vibrant, living tradition in its own right. Given the underlying relationship between so many Christian and Jewish ideas and practices, Judaism is probably the most accessible non-Christian religion represented in this country. Teaching Judaism in the classroom will allow children to experience a non-Christian faith that is not so distant from their own experience. This can provide an excellent bridge to the study of those religions that are much further removed from the Christian norm of thought.

It is not just Christianity that has been shaped by the teachings of the Hebrew Scriptures, but the very fabric and aspirations of Western society. I will cite just a few examples: the Torah is the source of the ten commandments, which are acknowledged as a foundation of religious and moral conduct for all humanity. Though we may debate the way in which some of the rules included in 'God's top ten' are observed in our time (such as the injunctions to honour parents and keep Shabbat), the negative commandments (e.g. the prohibitions against murder, theft and committing perjury) have been embodied in the legal systems of many modern societies.

The account of the Exodus from Egypt, of God's intervention in history to rescue the Israelite slaves, has proved an inspiration to many oppressed minorities through the centuries. The basic human entitlement that 'no one shall be held in slavery or servitude' was set down in the Universal Declaration of Human Rights,[10] the fiftieth anniversary of which was celebrated in 1998.

---

9. *Circular 1/94: Religious Education and Collective Worship* (London: Department for Education, 1994), Paragraph 35.

10. *The Universal Declaration of Human Rights* (New York: United Nations General Assembly, 1948), Article 4.

Finally, there is the notion of environmental responsibility, postulated in the opening chapters of Genesis and expanded upon most memorably in *Eccl. R.* 7.28:

> In the hour when the Holy One created the first human being, God took the person before all the trees of the Garden of Eden, and said to the person: 'See My works, how fine and excellent they are! Now all that I have created, for you have I created. Think upon this, and do not corrupt and desolate My world; for if you corrupt it, there is no one to set it right after you.'

Of course, it is not just Jewish texts which have had an impact on the world in which we live. Jewish men and women have made an important contribution to the evolution of Western Society. Examples of this are Jewish influences on Western philosophy, art, music, literature and language, the significant Jewish presence in the American film industry, and the achievements of individual Jewish doctors, scientists, politicians, novelists, dramatists, poets, painters, sculptors, composers, performers, and so on.

An understanding of Judaism is essential for an appreciation of this contribution. In her article, 'Judaism in the Home, Synagogue and Classroom', Angela Wood asserts that people cannot be 'considered educated unless they are aware of Jewish thought and culture as a dynamic, living presence in today's world'.[11]

A heightened understanding of the Jewish experience will also give pupils insight into contemporary events, such as the significance for the Jew of Zionism and the modern State of Israel, and the effect of the Holocaust on the Jewish people. As well as being important understandings in themselves, such insights can help pupils develop sensitivity to the struggles for self-determination of minority groups all over the world.

A knowledge of the painful history of Christian–Jewish relations, and of the persecution suffered by the Jews at Gentile hands over the centuries, will help young people understand the ambivalence felt by many Jews towards the current millennium celebrations. It could, moreover, give rise to much fruitful discussion about the appropriateness of such

---

11. A. Wood, 'Judaism in the Home, Synagogue and Classroom', in A. Wood (ed.), *Religions and Education, Shap Working Party 1969–89* (Isleworth, England: BFSS National RE Centre, 1989), pp. 111-13 (111).

extravagant public celebration of 2000 years of Christian culture and civilization within the context of a pluralist society.

Understanding Judaism in the Context of Religious Studies
There is still a tendency among teachers to misappropriate or misrepresent Jewish teachings. Thus, another reason to teach Judaism, when working with older children or adults, is to address theological misconceptions. A good example of this is the notion that the God of the Hebrew Bible is the God of justice, whereas the New Testament God is the God of love. Genesis 2.4 speaks of the time 'when the Lord God [*Adonai Elohim*] made earth and heaven':

> Jewish tradition interprets the names Elohim and Adonai as explanations of the two sides of the nature of God, the former representing the quality of justice, the latter reflecting the quality of mercy. The Midrash says that the world was originally created by God as Elohim (Gen. 1), but that afterward He is called Adonai Elohim (Gen. 2) because He saw that without the added quality of mercy creation could not have endured.[12]

The fact that love and justice do not stand in opposition to each other is emphasized by the proclamation at Sinai of what Jewish tradition has identified as the thirteen attributes of God: 'The Lord! the Lord! a God compassionate and gracious, slow to anger, abounding in kindness and faithfulness, extending kindness to the thousandth generation, forgiving iniquity, transgression and sin; yet He does not remit all punishment' (Exod. 34.6-7). Another popular misconception is the notion that Jesus coined the phrase 'love your neighbour as yourself'. He was, in fact, quoting from Lev. 19.18, where it forms part of what is known as 'The Holiness Code'. By virtue of its content, as well as its central position in Leviticus, and therefore in the Pentateuch, this chapter was regarded by the Rabbis as the kernel of God's teaching.

Clive Lawton points out that the religious experience of most of the children in Britain has been conditioned by their encounter with Christianity. This has led them to compartmentalize religion separately from the rest of their existence. He asserts that a study of Judaism will help young people to expand their perception of religion. Thus it is eye-opening for them to discover that a religion such as Judaism can embrace every dimension of a person's life: 'In Judaism it is overt, and

12. W.G. Plaut (ed.), *The Torah: A Modern Commentary* (New York: Union of American Hebrew Congregations, 1981), p. 31.

often expressed by very practical and concrete traditions. The Jew whose days, weeks, months, years, food, dress, ethical standards and family life are defined by his religious commitment is an example of the extent to which religion can become an all-embracing framework for living.'[13] Moreover, an exploration of Jewish life will lead both student and teacher to question the usual definition of religion: 'Judaism is the most accessible culture for exploring the phenomenon that most religions of the world do not appear to define themselves purely spiritually. To be a Jew is to be part of a family, a culture, a history, a spiritual system and much more.'[14]

The fact that Judaism is a very practical religion, concerned with deed rather than creed, makes it ideal for experiential learning in the classroom. Children can cook and taste Shabbat and festival foods. They can handle Jewish religious articles—and experience, for example, how it feels to put on a kippah (skullcap) and wrap oneself in a tallit (prayer shawl). There are many artefacts that can easily be made in the classroom: a flag for Simchat Torah, a dreidel (spinning top) for Hanukkah, and so on. Children can also experiment with carrying out ethical practices, such as visiting a sick person or delivering food or clothing to the homeless, and then share the experience in the classroom afterwards.

Lawton points out that one of Judaism's major concerns is how it transmits its traditions and framework of identity from one generation to another. 'Therefore, within Jewish tradition itself, the framework exists for teaching children about Jewish traditions.'[15] The Passover seder was designed as a learning experience for children. Similarly, the Hanukkah candles, increasing in number from one to eight during the eight days of the festival, and the many special seasonal foods, all generate interest, knowledge and awareness on the part of the Jewish child. The imaginative teacher in the county school can use this same framework to generate interest, knowledge and awareness on the part of all the children in the class.

Angela Wood urges schools to teach Judaism in a Jewish way. She points out that there is no actual Hebrew word for religion, and recommends the use of 'songs, blessings, discussion, ritual actions, stories,

---

13. C.A. Lawton, 'What Can Pupils in County Schools Learn from Judaism?', *British Journal of Religious Education* 3.4 (1981), pp. 123-30 (123).

14. Lawton, 'Pupils', p. 124.

15. Lawton, 'Pupils', p. 123.

food and lots of humour because these are how Jews communicate'.[16] She encourages the teacher to turn the classroom into a Jewish community for at least some of the lessons and suggests a variety of possible settings:

> ...home on Shabbat or Yom Tov (festivals); a yeshiva debating vociferously in pairs or small groups some burning issue of the day; an immigrant absorption centre in Israel; ...a bet din (rabbinical court) considering a candidate for conversion, adoption, divorce; a synagogue/kibbutz activities committee; ...a short service; ...or...an imaginary huddle of Jews in, say, Somerset who want to meet for prayer, study and society and are considering their priorities.[17]

However, as Wood herself admits, some of these activities may seem daunting to the teacher, demanding a high level of knowledge, skills, confidence and sensitivity. On the other hand, celebrating Shabbat or festivals is an accessible and rewarding avenue into the teaching of Judaism. 'Because there are no Jewish sacraments, this has the added advantage of not treading on anyone's doctrinal or ritual toes.'[18]

Rabbi Jacqueline Tabick points out that 'even within the Jewish community, the festivals constitute one of the main vehicles for educating Jews on our people's faith, history and ethical ideals. As such, they provide a useful means of imparting some of the major teachings of Judaism to pupils in secular schools'.[19] On an experiential level, celebrating festivals in the classroom through story, song, food, symbols, ceremonies, role play, arts and crafts and so on, can help a child understand what it feels like to be a practising member of a faith community. Moreover, for both teacher and pupils, festivals and celebration provide a relatively non-threatening route into the study of world faiths.

Wood describes the impact of celebrating a Friday evening meal in the classroom: lighting candles, saying Jewish prayers, singing Jewish songs, and eating Jewish food. 'For 40 minutes we are as Jewish as is humanly possible. And we remember it for always.'[20]

In my own work, I have been involved with a number of schools in the preparation and enactment of a Passover seder, using the 'Passover

16. Wood, 'Judaism in the Home, Synagogue and Classroom', p. 112.

17. Wood, 'Judaism in the Home, Synagogue and Classroom', p. 112.

18. Wood, 'Judaism in the Home, Synagogue and Classroom', p. 112.

19. J. Tabick, 'Teaching Judaism through its Festivals', *British Journal of Religious Education* 3.4 (1981), pp. 147-50 (147).

20. Wood, 'Judaism in the Home, Synagogue and Classroom', p. 112.

Seder for Primary Schools',[21] which I co-authored. Over a period of days or even weeks, children have studied the biblical account of the Exodus, designed and made seder plates, matzah covers and hagadot, learnt Passover songs and prepared the special foods for the seder. The culmination is when we all sit down together round a beautifully laid table and celebrate a seder, with food and drink, song, story and discussion.

Another aspect of Judaism that is very suitable for exploration in the classroom is the life-cycle from birth through puberty, marriage and child-rearing to death. Each one of these events has its own rituals and structures, and it provides a framework for the teacher and pupil to explore subjects of intense and universal concern, perhaps at one remove. Once again the Jewish approach is intensely practical and it allows a certain freedom of theology and philosophy while legislating the practices.[22] Lawton singles out two rites of passage for particular consideration. Studying the Jewish approach to death and mourning can help a student face the issue of death. Learning about Bar and Bat Mitzvah as a formalized system of marking a young person's transition into adult responsibilities within the Jewish community can be very helpful to lower secondary pupils grappling with their own transition into adulthood.

4. *The Role of the Jewish Community*

Another asset for the teacher is the willingness of the Jewish community to explain itself. Lawton points out that this is partly to avoid misunderstandings, 'but also a product of the fact that the Jewish community has been settled in Britain for a few more generations than the newer minority religions and therefore has been able to deal with the initial settling problems that preoccupy a new community and can afford a little more time to develop relations with the world outside'.[23] The Jewish community has set up specific organizations concerned with the presentation of Judaism to non-Jews. The two best known of these are the Jewish Education Bureau in Leeds which operates a mail order service for a wide range of Jewish books, teaching resources and reli-

---

21. A. Clark and S. Malyan, *Passover Seder for Primary Schools* (London: Wandsworth Borough Council, 1992).

22. See Lawton, 'Pupils', p. 124.

23. Lawton, 'Pupils', p. 125.

gious articles, and the Education Department of the Board of Deputies of British Jews which has produced a number of publications written specifically for non Jews, and is also able to arrange Jewish London tours and provide speakers on a range of topics within Judaism. Most synagogues are happy to open their doors to school visits on weekdays. Teachers may even be able to bring small groups of secondary pupils to attend Shabbat or festival services. In addition, pressures of communal work permitting, there are a number of rabbis and other senior Jewish educators who are willing to go into local schools to present Judaism to non-Jewish children. Such contact allows Jews to explain their religion in their own terms and enables the non-Jewish student to encounter Judaism as a living tradition, rather than solely from the pages of a textbook. Another advantage for the classroom is what Lawton describes as 'the Jewish determination not to convert or persuade',[24] which is helpful in allaying parental anxiety about the exposure of their children to committed Jews.

For non-Jewish children, an encounter with a sensitive, articulate adult Jew, maybe a parent or teacher from within the school community, or a visitor from outside, can be a powerful vehicle for combatting prejudice and stereotypes. This is another benefit of the involvement of practising Jews in religious education and is, in itself, a very important reason for teaching Judaism. The Jewish people have suffered centuries of persecution, the flames of which have been fanned by misinformation and fear. Knowledge and understanding of Jewish beliefs and practices coupled with opportunities for young people to meet with committed Jews are effective weapons in combatting anti-Semitism in British society. Clearly this benefits the Jewish community, but also the wider community, which can only be divided and diminished by racial or religious discord.

Another less obvious way in which the Jewish community benefits from the teaching of Judaism in school is in terms of the Jewish education delivered to the *Jewish* children in the classroom. The majority of Jewish children in this country do not attend Jewish schools, and there are many unaffiliated young Jews in county schools for whom the Judaism taught at school is the only Jewish education they receive. At the other end of the spectrum, there are Jewish children from committed backgrounds who attend non-denominational schools. For these young

24. Lawton, 'Pupils', p. 125.

people, the sensitive teaching of Judaism in the classroom serves to encourage confident and positive identification with their faith, to validate their religious experience and to lessen the disjunction many of them feel between their home lives and their secular schooling.

The sympathetic treatment of Judaism or indeed of any of the non-Christian faiths, in schools, will benefit children from all faith communities. As Lawton points out in the final sentence of his article, 'it will encourage members of other minority groups in the school to feel that even if their own religion is not specifically dealt with, the school is not entirely blind to the possibility of a variety of lifestyles and the richness of differing approaches to religious experiences and identity'.[25]

25. Lawton, 'Pupils', p. 130.

INDEXES

INDEX OF REFERENCES

OLD TESTAMENT

NEW TESTAMENT

INDEX OF AUTHORS